The Pursuit of Happyness

中英对照

当幸福来敲门（双语版）

〔美〕克里斯·加德纳 著　米拉 译

A poignant journey was from homeless single fatherhood to the pinnacle of Wall Street

清华大学出版社

北　京

Chris Gardner

The Pursuit of Happyness

EISBN: 978-0-06-074486-1

Copyright © 2006 by Chris Gardner. All rights reserved.

Published by arrangement with HarperCollins Publishers, USA.

English language and Chinese language bilingual edition copyright © 2012 by Tsinghua University Press.

北京市版权局著作权合同登记号　图字：01-2012-2025

本书封面贴有清华大学出版社防伪标签，无标签者不得销售。
版权所有，侵权必究。举报：010-62782989，beiqinquan@tup.tsinghua.edu.cn。

图书在版编目(CIP)数据

当幸福来敲门(双语版)/(美)加德纳(Gardner, C.) 著；米拉 译. —北京：清华大学出版社，2012.4
（2022.11重印）
书名原文：The Pursuit of Happyness
ISBN 978-7-302-28066-8

Ⅰ. ①当… Ⅱ. ①加… ②米… Ⅲ. ①英语—汉语—对照读物 ②加德纳，C. —自传
Ⅳ. ①H319.4：K

中国版本图书馆 CIP 数据核字(2012)第 025340 号

责任编辑：陈　莉　王佳佳
封面设计：周周设计局
版式设计：牛艳敏
责任校对：成凤进
责任印制：宋　林

出版发行：清华大学出版社
网　　址：http://www.tup.com.cn, http://www.wqbook.com
地　　址：北京清华大学学研大厦A座　　邮　编：100084
社　总　机：010-83470000　　邮　购：010-62786544
投稿与读者服务：010-62776969, c-service@tup.tsinghua.edu.cn
质　量　反　馈：010-62772015, zhiliang@tup.tsinghua.edu.cn

印 装 者：三河市铭诚印务有限公司
经　　销：全国新华书店
开　　本：185mm×260mm　　印　张：26.25　　字　数：689千字
版　　次：2012年4月第1版　　印　次：2022年11月第19次印刷
定　　价：88.00元

产品编号：043777-02

Prologue
Go Forward

Whenever I'm asked what exactly it was that helped guide me through my darkest days not only to survive but to move past those circumstances and to ultimately attain a level of success and fulfillment that once sounded impossible, what comes to mind are two events.

One of them took place in the early 1980s, when I was twenty-seven years old, on an unusually hot, sunny day in the Bay Area. In the terminally overcrowded parking lot outside of San Francisco General Hospital, just as I exited the building, a flash of the sun's glare temporarily blocked my vision. As I refocused, what I saw changed the world as I knew it. At any other point in my life it wouldn't have struck me so powerfully, but there was something about that moment in time and the gorgeous, red convertible Ferrari 308 that I saw slowly circling the lot—driven by a guy obviously in search of a parking spot—that compelled me to go and have a life-changing conversation with him.

序言
奋力前行

是什么指引着我走出生命中那段最为黑暗的日子,最后不仅侥幸得以生存,而且终获成功,实现自我?每当人们问及我这个问题时,我脑海里就会浮现出两幅场景。

其一是在20世纪80年代初,当时我大概是27岁的样子,那天天气奇热,明晃晃的太阳悬在湾区上空,在旧金山总医院门口,黑压压停了一片车子。我刚走出大楼,迎面而来的耀眼阳光刺得我睁不开眼睛。定睛一看,眼前的一切让我从此改变了对世界的认识。若是换个时间地点,这件事对我的影响也许不至于此,但此时此刻它的发生,使我的生活截然两样。一辆火红惹眼的法拉利308敞篷车在前面的停车场缓缓驶过,显然是在找停车位,我鬼使神差地上前和车主攀谈起来,而那番话却就此改变了我的一生。

The PURSUIT of HAPPYNESS

Some years before, fresh out of the Navy, I had first arrived in San Francisco—lured to the West Coast by a prestigious research job and the opportunity to work for one of the top young heart surgeons in the country. For a kid like me who'd barely stepped foot outside the six-block square of the 'hood in Milwaukee—not counting my three-year stint as a Navy medic in North Carolina—San Francisco was the be-all and end-all. The city was the Land of Milk and Honey and the Emerald City of Oz rolled into one. Rising up out of the bay into golden glowing mists of possibility, she seduced me from the start, showing off her studded hills and plunging valleys as she laid herself out with arms open. At night the town was an aphrodisiac—with city lights like rare jewels sparkling down from Nob Hill and Pacific Heights, through the better neighborhoods and along the rougher streets of the Mission and the Tenderloin (my new 'hood), spilling out of the towers of the Financial District and reflecting into the bay by Fisherman's Wharf and the Marina.

In the early days, no matter how many times I drove west over the Bay Bridge from Oakland, or north from Daly City heading toward the Golden Gate Bridge, which stretches right up to the horizon before dropping down into Marin County, those views of San Francisco were like falling in love all over again. Even as time went by and I got hip to the weather—the periods of gray foggy skies alternating with days of bone-chilling rain—I'd wake up to one of those glorious, perfect San Francisco days and the beauty wiped away all memory of the gloom. San Francisco remains in my mind to this day the Paris of the Pacific.

Of course, back then, it didn't take long to discover that she was also deceptive, not necessarily easy, sometimes coldhearted, and definitely not cheap. Between steep rents and the chronic car repairs caused by the toll the hills took on transmissions and brakes— not to mention that pile of unpaid parking tickets all too familiar to most San Franciscans—staying afloat could be a challenge. But that wasn't going to mar my belief that I'd make it. Besides, I knew enough about challenge. I knew how to work hard, and in fact, over the next years, challenges helped me to reshape my dreams, to reach further, and to pursue goals with an increased sense of urgency.

In early 1981, when I became a first-time father, overjoyed as I was, that sense of urgency kicked up another notch. As the first months of my son's life flew by, I not only tried to move ahead faster but also began to question the path that I'd chosen, wondering if somehow in all my efforts I wasn't trying to run up the down escalator. Or at least that was my state of mind on that day in the parking lot outside San Francisco General Hospital as I approached the driver of the red Ferrari.

几年前，我刚从海军退役下来，就来到了旧金山。深深吸引我的是在西海岸的那份优厚的研究工作，同时也因此有机会为当时美国一位顶级年轻心脏外科医师效力。那时我是个懵懵懂懂的毛头小伙，刚刚从威斯康星密尔沃基这种小地方走出来，全部资历不过是在北卡罗来纳州做过三年的海军军医而已。旧金山对我来说几乎是一辈子的终极梦想，因为这里可以说是应有尽有，充满冒险刺激。而对我这种毫无背景的普通百姓来说，这遍地黄金的大都市，从一开始就充满了诱惑，这里的山川幽谷，这里的每寸土地都让我无法抗拒。入夜，整个城市更是风情万种，从诺布山到太平洋高地，城市灯火宛如宝石般晶莹璀璨，从高档住宅区到贫困的教会区和田德隆区(也就是我在这里的栖身之地)都是如此，灯光从金融区的大厦流泻而下，从渔人码头到玛利那区无不在闪烁着温柔的光。

早些时候，不管我驾车从加州奥克兰朝着海湾大桥西行，还是从加州达利城到金门桥一路北上，每当看到金门桥拔地而起，与海峡那边的马林县玉带相连，无论多少次经过这里，旧金山的此情此景都会让我动容动情。即便是日子久了，有时赶上天公不作美，或是大雾弥漫，或是阴雨连绵，都不会影响我欣赏旧金山的曼妙之美，大自然的妙笔自会抹去心中的阴霾。时至今日，旧金山在我心中都永远可与名城巴黎齐名媲美。

当然，即便在那时，我也很快发现这座城市有它冷漠的一面，而且，想在这里生存下来实属不易。高昂的房租、修车费用以及在山间穿行停停走走一路交的过路费，更别提所有旧金山人都司空见惯的成堆的停车罚单，想在这里落脚绝非易事。但是，所有这些都无法动摇我在这里活下去的决心。再说，困难对我而言并不新鲜，我知道自己该怎么去努力，实际上，在接下来的几年间，正是因为困难和挑战，我才在梦想的道路上走得更远，更具紧迫感，积极实现个人的目标。

1981年初，我初为人父，在乐不可支的同时，我更觉得要加紧努力。儿子来到世上的头几个月很快就过去了，我自己也奋力向前，拼命工作，但不免也开始心存疑虑，自己选择的这条路是否正确？所付出的一切会不会灰飞烟灭？至少，当我在旧金山总医院门口，上前去和法拉利车主搭讪的时候，我就是这么想的。

This encounter would crystallize in my memory—almost into a mythological moment that I could return to and visit in the present tense whenever I wanted or needed its message. I see the sports car in front of me just as if it's today, circling in slow motion, with the whirring sound of that unbelievably powerful engine as it idles, waiting and purring like a lion about to pounce. In my mind's ear, I'm hearing the cool calling of a horn blown by Miles Davis, my musical hero—who, back in the day, I was positive I was going to be when I grew up. It's one of those imagined senses in the sound track of our lives that tells us to pay attention.

With the top down and the light glinting fire-engine-metallic-red off the hood, the guy at the wheel is every bit as cool as the jazz musicians I used to idolize. A white guy, dark-haired, clean-shaven, of average height and slight build, he's wearing the sharpest suit, possibly custom-made, out of a beautiful piece of cloth. It's more than just a wonderful garment, it's the whole look—the tasteful tie, the muted shirt, the pocket square, the understated cuff links and watch. Nothing obnoxious, just well put together. No flash, no bullshit. Just sharp.

"Hey, man," I say, approaching the Ferrari and waving at him as I point out where my car is parked, nodding to let him know that I'm coming out. Am I seduced by the Ferrari itself? Yes. I am a red-blooded American male. But it's more than that. In that instant, the car symbolizes all that I lacked while growing up—freedom, escape, options. "You can have my spot," I offer, "but I gotta ask you a couple of questions."

He gets that I'm offering a trade here—my parking place for his information. In my twenty-seven years of life so far, I have learned a little already about the power of information and about the kind of currency that information can become. Now I see an opportunity to get some inside information, I think, and so I draw out my trusty sword—a compulsion for question-asking that has been in my survival kit since childhood.

Seeing that it's not a bad deal for either of us, he shrugs and says, "Fine."

My questions are very simple: "What do you do?" and "How do you do it?"

With a laugh, he answers the first question just as simply, saying, "I'm a stockbroker," but to answer the second question we extend the conversation to a meeting a few weeks later and then a subsequent introduction to the ABCs, of Wall Street, an entirely foreign but mesmerizing venue where I am just crazy enough to think I could do what he and others like him do, if only I can find an opening.

Despite the fact that I had absolutely no experience and no contacts whatsoever, looking to get my big break into the stock market became a major focus over the next several months, but so did other urgent concerns, especially when I suddenly became a single parent amid a series of other unforeseen, tumultuous events.

这次邂逅在我脑海中仿佛生了根，每当我回顾那一刻，当时的场景就会历历在目。我甚至可以看到那辆跑车就在自己面前，仿佛就是在此时此刻，车子缓缓地兜着圈子，我可以清楚听到法拉利强劲有力的马达怠速时的嗡嗡声，那种感觉就像是狮子准备扑向猎物前的喉鸣。我似乎还能听到偶像迈尔·戴维斯的爵士小号在耳畔响起（小时候，我还一度梦想长大后成为戴维斯那样的人物）。其实我们有时确实会有这样的感觉，让我们预感到一些重要事情即将发生。

法拉利通体火红，红得耀眼，红得闪亮，开车的家伙酷味儿十足，完全可以与我曾崇拜的爵士音乐家一争高下。他皮肤白净，暗色的头发，胡子刮得干干净净，中等身材，体态匀称，衣着相当考究，很可能是为他度身定制，用料更是上乘。其实他不仅仅是衣着考究这么简单，从着装搭配来看，此人就绝非等闲之辈，领带相当有品位，条纹衬衫，装饰方巾，低调的袖扣和腕表，华丽自在而绝无张扬之感。

"你好啊！"我边打招呼，边凑上前去，挥着手，指向我停车的地方，示意他我要离开了。我这么做是因为法拉利的诱惑难以抗拒？确实，我也是血性男儿，有着七情六欲，但问题似乎并非如此简单。此时此刻，法拉利代表的正是我所一直或缺的东西——自由自在、浪迹天涯和无尽选择。我接着说道："你可以停在我的位置上，不过我想请教你两个问题。"

他意识到我是有条件的，用停车位来换问题的答案。在我活在世上的这 27 年间，我对知识的魔力还是略知一二的，也知道知识有时就能变成亮闪闪的真金白银。现在机会来了，很有可能我会问出一些绝对内幕消息，所以我亮出自己的绝密武器——打破沙锅问到底，这是我自孩提起就屡试不爽的独门秘笈。

也许觉得这个提议对两人都算不错，他耸耸肩，应了下来。

我的问题很简单："你是以什么为业的？"再有就是，"怎么才能做到如此成功？"

他不禁乐出了声，第一个问题他答得十分干脆、简单："股票经纪人"。但要说清楚第二个问题还真费了番工夫，以至于几周后，我们又见了面，接下来他还给我介绍了华尔街的一些基本情况，这地方对我而言绝对陌生却充满神奇，我当时竟然不知天高地厚地想，自己和他们这些专业人士一样也能在华尔街干出点名堂来，只要能给我个机会。

虽然我在证券方面没有丝毫经验可谈，而且从未接触过这个行当，但我在接下来的几个月中，梦寐以求的就是挤入证券市场，而这期间，需要应对的还有更多棘手的问题，特别是突然间自己成了单身父亲，还有很多当时无法预见的生活动荡。

By this time period, San Francisco's conflicting attitudes toward a growing homeless population were already well known. What officials declared was a new epidemic in homelessness had actually been developing for more than a decade as the result of several factors—including drastic cutbacks to state funding for mental health facilities, limited treatment options for the large number of Vietnam vets suffering from post-traumatic stress syndrome and alcohol and drug addiction, along with the same urban ills plaguing the rest of the country. During the long, cold winter of 1982, as government programs to help the poor were being eliminated, the economy in the Bay Area, as in the rest of the country, was in a downturn. At a time when jobs and affordable housing were becoming harder to find, access to cheap street drugs like angel dust and PCP was starting to get easier.

Though some business leaders complained that the homeless would scare tourists away, if you happened to visit San Francisco in the early 1980s, you were probably unaware of the deepening crisis. You might have heard about what neighborhoods to avoid—areas where you were warned about the winos, junkies, bag ladies, transients, and others who, as they used to say in my part of Milwaukee, "just went crazy." Or maybe you did notice some of the signs—the long food lines, multiplying numbers of panhandlers, the mothers and children on the steps of overcapacity shelters, runaway teenagers, or those sleeping human forms that sometimes looked more like mounds of discarded clothing left in alleys, on park benches, at transit stations, and under the eaves and in the doorways of buildings. Maybe your visit to San Francisco reminded you of similar problems in your hometown, or maybe even alerted you to the increasing percentage of the working poor who'd entered the ranks of the homeless—gainfully employed but overburdened individuals and families forced to choose between paying rent and buying food, medicine, clothing, or other basic necessities. You may have paused to wonder what kinds of lives and dreams and stories had been lived before, and perhaps to consider how easy it would be for anyone to fall through the cracks of whatever support had once existed, or to face a sudden crisis of any proportion and simply stumble into the hole of homelessness.

此时的旧金山对待无家可归的人群存在着相当矛盾的态度，这已是人所共知。政府称无家可归问题是新出现的城市顽疾。其实不然，这一问题存在已有十年之久，主要是由于精神疾患治疗设施的州拨款大幅缩水，战后大量越南老兵的创伤后压力心理障碍症导致酗酒吸毒，却未得到有效救治，其实这并不仅只限于老兵，酗酒吸毒在全国各个城市屡见不鲜。1982年那个漫长的寒冬，当政府宣布取消其贫民救助计划时，与国内其他地区一样，湾区的经济形势一路走低。这时，找份活干，找间房住，已经日益艰难，倒是要搞到天使粉、普斯普剂这类便宜的街边毒品要容易得多。

虽然有些商业人士认为无家可归者有碍市容，影响旅游业，遂对此颇有怨言，但如果你有幸在20世纪80年代初去过旧金山，可能还不会感受到那里有着如此深层次的危机。可能会有人告诫你有些地方不要去，说是醉汉、地痞、流浪女、流浪汉，还有些疯疯癫癫的人在那经常出没，在老家明尼苏达密尔沃基把这些人叫做"神经病"。或许你会注意到一些迹象，领取救济食品的人排起了长队，街头行乞的人数多了很多，母亲带着大大小小的孩子挤在窝棚里艰难度日，十几岁的孩子离家出走，露宿在街边的人蜷缩着身体更像是一堆被随意丢弃的垃圾，公园长椅上，车辆换乘站里，楼房的门廊下，都可以成为这些人暂时的栖身之地。也许，在你自己的城市里也存在类似于旧金山的这类问题，也许你意识到有更多的工作族正步入无家可归者的行列，他们确实有所收入，但不堪重负，在支付房租和购买食品、药品、衣物等生活所需之间艰难做出选择。也许你会思忖，他们曾是怎样的生活和度日，他们曾怀揣着怎样的梦想，也许你会想到如果生活的支撑一旦化为乌有，任何人都会垮掉；一场飞来横祸足以使人陷入困境，从此过上入不敷出、朝不保夕的生活。

The PURSUIT of HAPPYNESS

Chances are, however, no matter how observant you might have been, you wouldn't have noticed me. Or if you did happen to spot me, usually moving at a fast clip as I pushed a lightweight, rickety blue stroller that had become my only wheels and that carried my most precious cargo in the universe—my nineteen-month-old son, Chris Jr., a beautiful, growing, active, alert, talkative, hungry toddler—it's unlikely you would have suspected that my baby and I were homeless. Dressed in one of my two business suits, the other in the garment bag that was slung over my shoulder, along with the duffel bag that was filled with all our other earthly possessions (including various articles of clothing, toiletries, and the few books I couldn't live without), as I tried to hold an umbrella in one hand, a briefcase in another, and balance the world's largest box of Pampers under my armpit, still while maneuvering the stroller, we probably looked more like we were going off on a long weekend somewhere. Some of the places where we slept suggested as much—on the Bay Area Rapid Transit subway trains, or in waiting areas at either the Oakland or San Francisco airport. Then again, the more hidden places where we stayed could have given away my situation—at the office, where I'd work late so we could stretch out on the floor under my desk after hours; or, as on occasion we found ourselves, in the public bathroom of an Oakland BART station.

That small, cell-like, windowless tiled box—big enough for us, our stuff, and a toilet and a sink where I could get us washed as best I could—represented both my worst nightmare of being confined, locked up, and excluded and, at the same time, a true godsend of protection where I could lock the door and keep the wolves out. It was what it was—a way station between where I'd come from and where I was going, my version of a pit stop on the underground railroad, '80s style.

As long as I kept my mental focus on destinations that were ahead, destinations that I had the audacity to dream might hold a red Ferrari of my own, I protected myself from despair. The future was uncertain, absolutely, and there were many hurdles, twists, and turns to come, but as long as I kept moving forward, one foot in front of the other, the voices of fear and shame, the messages from those who wanted me to believe that I wasn't good enough, would be stilled.

Go forward. That became my mantra, inspired by the Reverend Cecil Williams, one of the most enlightened men to ever walk this earth, a friend and mentor whose goodness blessed me in ways I can never sufficiently recount. At Glide Memorial Methodist Church in the Tenderloin—where the Reverend Williams fed, housed, and repaired souls (eventually accommodating thousands of homeless in what became the first homeless hotel in the country)—he was already an icon. Then and later, you couldn't live in the Bay Area without knowing Cecil Williams and getting a sense of his message. Walk that walk, he preached. On any Sunday, his sermon might address a number of subjects, but that theme was always in there, in addition to the rest. Walk that walk and go forward all the time. Don't just talk that talk, walk it and go forward. Also, the walk didn't have to be long strides; baby steps counted too. Go forward.

无论你对生活的观察多么细致入微，你也许都不会注意到我的存在。也许会碰巧瞟上一眼，看到我步履匆匆，手推一辆轻便的破烂蓝色儿童推车，这在当时是我唯一的运输工具，装着我世间最珍贵的宝贝——一岁半的俊俏儿子小克里斯多夫，他活蹦乱跳，机灵淘气，还在牙牙学语就已喋喋不休，时不时向我索取食物。你可能做梦也想不到我们爷儿俩已经无家可归。我身着职业装，这行头我总共不过才有两套，另一套就塞在我肩扛的衣物袋里面，还有个袋子里面装着我们的值钱家当（杂七杂八几件衣物、卫生用具，还有几本书，没有这些书我就没法活下去）。我一手提了把伞，另一只手还要拎着公文包，腋下还要夹上硕大的一包帮宝适纸尿裤，同时还要控制婴儿推车，看上去我们俩就像是去什么地方度周末长假一般。我和儿子经常过夜的地方就是在湾区地铁换乘站，再有就是奥克兰或旧金山机场的候机大厅，还有个更为隐蔽的藏身之处就是我的办公室，我经常刻意加班，下班后就可以在办公桌下的地板上舒展腿脚，当然有时候也要躲进奥克兰捷运车站的公共卫生间暂避风雨。

那个小小的卫生间，虽说没有窗户，但是大小还算合适，放下我们两个还有这些行李都不成问题，再加上马桶和洗手池，足够我们梳洗之用。那里虽然让我感觉到压抑束缚，但是锁上门，与外界隔绝，至少不会有什么猛兽闯进来，也算是上苍赐予的安全所在。这就是我在20世纪80年代的生活写照，那时我也处于生活的中转站，连接我的过去和未来，仿佛就是在人生的地铁站。

只要我还坚持朝着前方的梦想前进，梦想自己有朝一日也能开上红色法拉利，我就不能让自己倒下。未来会怎样，谁都不知道，纵然会有诸多坎坷和羁绊，但只要我是一直在一步一个脚印奋力向前，所有那些恐惧和羞耻，所有那些对我能力的质疑，都会烟消云散，不复存在。

奋力向前，就是一直激励我的信条，这是世上最伟大的威廉姆斯教士对我的告诫，他是我的挚友和恩师，他对我善意的帮助不一而足。在旧金山田德隆区的格莱德教堂，就是威廉姆斯教士生活和居住的寓所，他在那里尽心尽责地帮助穷人，并为成千上万无家可归的人提供衣食住所，这里也成为美国第一家穷人旅馆，他已成为众人心中的偶像。在那之后，在湾区无人不知威廉姆斯教士，大家都不同程度受到他思想的鼓舞。他告诉我们要奋力向前，永不放弃。在礼拜日，他的讲道可能会涉及诸多话题，但却有着亘古不变的主题——永不言弃，奋斗不息，这不只是言谈，而是要身体力行，抑或，不一定总要大踏步前进，积跬步同样也能至千里，只要一直向前。

序言

The phrases repeated in my brain until they were a wordless skat, like the three-beat staccato sound as we rode the train over the BART rails, or like the *clack-clack-clack* syncopation of the stroller wheels with percussion added from the occasional *creak*s and *squeal*s and *groan*s they made going over curbs, up and down San Francisco's famed steep hills, and around corners.

In years to come, baby carriages would go way high-tech with double and triple wheels on each side and all aerodynamic, streamlined, and leather-cushioned, plus extra compartments for storing stuff and roofs to add on to make them like little inhabitable igloos. But the rickety blue stroller I had, as we forged into the winter of 1982, had none of that. What it did have—during what I'm sure had to be the wettest, coldest winter on record in San Francisco—was a sort of pup tent over Chris Jr. that I made of free plastic sheeting from the dry cleaners.

As much as I kept going forward because I believed a better future lay ahead, and as much as I was sure that the encounter outside San Francisco General Hospital had steered me to that future, the real driving force came from that other pivotal event in my life—which had taken place back in Milwaukee in March 1970, on a day not long after my sixteenth birthday.

Unlike many experiences in childhood that tended to blur in my memory into a series of images that flickered dimly like grainy, old-fashioned moving pictures, this event—which must have taken up little more than a split second of time—became a vivid reality that I could conjure in my senses whenever I wanted, in perfectly preserved detail.

This period was one of the most volatile of my youth, beyond the public turbulence of the era—the Vietnam War, the civil rights movement, echoes of assassinations and riots, and the cultural influences of music, hippies, black power, and political activism, all of which helped to shape my view of myself, my country, and the world.

During my childhood and adolescence, my family—consisting of my three sisters and me, our mother, who was present in my early life only sporadically, and our stepfather— had lived in a series of houses, walk-ups, and flats, punctuated by intermittent separations and stays with a series of relatives, all within a four-block area. Finally, we had moved into a small house in a neighborhood considered to be somewhat upwardly mobile. It may have only been so in comparison to where we'd been living before, but this house was nonetheless "movin' on up"—à la the Jefferson family, who still had another five years to go to get their own TV show.

The TV on this particular day was, in fact, the focus of my attention, and key to my mood of happy expectation, not only because I was getting ready to watch the last of the two games played in the NCAA's Final Four, but because I had the living room all to myself. This meant that I could hoot and holler all I wanted, and that I could talk out loud to myself if I so pleased, and answer myself right back. (My mother had this habit too. When others asked what she was doing, she'd always say, "Talking to someone with good sense.")

这些话一次次在我的脑海中浮现，一下下敲入我的内心深处，仿佛列车行进时候的滚滚车轮声，又像旧金山街头孩子们玩的轮滑鞋，在街头巷陌间躲闪腾挪时发出的声响，显得铿锵有力，掷地有声。

这些年来，婴儿车的种类也在不断翻新，融入了很多高科技成分，每侧双轮甚至三轮的都有，还有气动式、流线型，加入皮垫、配上遮阳篷不一而足，再加上储物空间，看上去活像个爱斯基摩小屋。但是我在1982年冬天用的那个破烂不堪的蓝色婴儿推车却没有这些新鲜玩艺儿，然而它却经历了旧金山有史以来最为寒冷的冬天，小克里斯头顶上只有个简易帐篷为他遮风挡雨，那还是我从干洗店要了块塑料布给他做的。

我步履维艰，尽力前行，因为相信更美好的明天在前方等着我们，而且我还坚信，旧金山总医院门前的那次邂逅就是在为我指明前行的方向。此外，还有件事给我留下了难以磨灭的印象，那是在1970年3月，我刚过完16岁生日不久，那时我还在威斯康星的密尔沃基。

与许多童年时的残破记忆不同，那些记忆由于时间久远，已经变得模糊不清，仿佛老式电影一般，图像不再清晰可见。而这件事却大不相同，仿佛是用胶片高速录制而成，每当我想起来，那每个细节都是真真切切，栩栩如生地浮现在眼前。

这是我年轻时经历的非常动荡的一段时期，恰逢乱世，越战、民权运动、刺杀暴乱频频，文化方面，音乐、嬉皮士、黑人运动、政治行动主义等大行其道，所有这些都促成我对自身、对国家和世界形成自己的观点和看法。

在我孩提时代和青少年时代，家里有三个姐妹、我，还有母亲，母亲在我幼时的记忆里时断时续，再有就是继父，我们搬过很多次家，地下室、公寓，有时一家人还不得不分开，临时寄宿到亲戚家里，但都不过是在四个街区的范围内活动。最终，我们有幸搬到附近的一所小房子里，境遇算是有所改善。但所谓改善也仅仅是和我们以前的居住条件相比而言，在这里过了5年后，我们才有了自家的电视机。

在这个特殊的时期，我在电视上倾注了自己全部精力，电视是我快乐的源泉，不仅是要眼巴巴盼着美国NCAA大学篮球四强赛，更重要的是整个客厅都是我的天下，挑台选台随心所欲，如果我愿意，都可以大声自言自语，自问自答（妈妈也有这个习惯，当别人问起她时，她总是说自己是在自得其乐）。

Another cause for feeling good that day was that my mother happened to be the only other person at home. Even if she wasn't sitting down beside me to watch the game but was somewhere nearby—busy ironing clothes in the adjacent dining room, as it so happened—it was as if the house was breathing a sigh of relief for just the two of us to be there, something that almost never occurred, especially without my stepfather's menacing presence.

March Madness, which came every year at the end of the college basketball season, was always thrilling for me, and an excellent distraction from heavier thoughts I was having about the tightrope I was walking from the end of adolescence into manhood. The tournament was always full of surprises, Cinderella stories, and human drama, starting with the nation's sixty-four top teams in thirty-two matchups as they rapidly whittled down to the Sweet Sixteen, then the Elite Eight, and ended up with the two games of the Final Four before the winners played for the championship title. All eyes this year were on how UCLA would fare in its first season without seven-footer Lew Alcindor (soon to become Kareem Abdul-Jabbar) after he had led them to three consecutive titles. The team that seemed destined to make sure UCLA didn't go home with the championship this year was Jacksonville University, a heretofore unknown college program that boasted not one but two stars, Artis Gilmore and Pembrook Burrows III, both over seven feet tall. It was unusual enough at this time for players to hit the seven-foot mark, let alone to have two of them on the same team.

Known as the original Twin Towers, or sometimes the Towers of Power, Gilmore and Burrows had helped Jacksonville obliterate their opposition and had brought them to the Final Four to face St. Bonaventure. As time for the tip-off neared, the excitement was only heightened by the announcers' predictions about the careers and riches awaiting the two giants in the NBA or the ABA.

As it happened, Jacksonville would win the game and then lose the championship to UCLA after all. And Artis Gilmore would go on to success in the NBA while Pembrook Burrows would be drafted by Seattle before turning to a career as a Florida Highway Patrol officer.

None of that is of any consequence as I'm sitting there, so engrossed in anticipation of the tip-off and so very caught up in the announcers' hype of both the athletic ability and fortune awaiting Gilmore and Burrows that I say out loud to no one, "Wow, one day those guys are gonna make a million dollars!"

Moms, standing at the ironing board just behind me in the next room, says very clearly, as though she has been sitting next to me the whole time, "Son, if you want to, one day *you* could make a million dollars."

那天感觉良好的另一个原因是恰好只有妈妈和我在家，即便是她没有坐在我身边陪我看比赛，但她就在屋里屋外忙忙碌碌，比如在一旁的厨房熨衣服之类，现在她正忙乎这些事情，家里只有我们俩让人感到无比轻松惬意，这种时候很少有过，特别是凶巴巴的继父在家时，更不可能。

每到"三月疯狂"，也就是每年大学篮球赛季的尾声，都让我兴奋不已，也只有这时我才能从沉重的思想包袱下分神出来，得以片刻喘息，此时的我正处于青少年到成年的转型期，如履薄冰。联赛自然异彩纷呈，惊喜不断，灰姑娘一夜成名这类人间悲喜剧竞相上映。从全国64支顶级球队中选出32强，继而产生16强，然后进军8强，最终4强赛打响，胜出的两支球队争夺最后的冠军称号。那年所有人都在关注加州大学洛杉矶分校，想知道在卢·阿尔辛多（也就是后来在NBA征战20载的阿卜杜勒·贾巴尔）缺席的情况下，该队如何拿下第一赛季，要知道阿尔辛多带领校队已连续三个赛季捧得总冠军的殊荣。 杰克森维尔大学的出现似乎让加州大学洛杉矶分校该年度注定与冠军无缘，前者本来名不见经传，结果却出了两名球星：阿提斯·葛尔莫和彭鲁克·巴罗斯三世，两人都有7英尺高，那年月有一名7英尺的队员应属不易，更不敢想能有两名这样的队员同时为同一球队效力。

葛尔莫和巴罗斯被誉为"双子塔"，也有人称之为"大力双塔"，两人联手，为杰克森维尔大学重写历史屡建奇功，让该队破天荒的首次闯入四强赛，与圣文德大学狭路相逢，一决高下。开赛之前，解说员预言"双子塔"会在NBA或ABA职业篮球联盟大展宏图，这更让赛场一片沸腾。

后来，杰克森维尔大学果真赢得比赛，但是在接下来的总决赛中不敌加州大学洛杉矶分校，从而与冠军无缘。葛尔莫果然如愿进入NBA续写他的辉煌，而巴罗斯却去了西雅图，后来成了佛罗里达的一名高速公路巡警。

但当我在电视机前聚精会神看比赛时，所有这些后来发生的事情自然不得而知，只是听了解说员在开赛前的煽情预言，想到"双子塔"的惊人天赋和等待他们的大笔财富就让我兴奋不已，忘乎所以地大喊："这俩家伙迟早要拿到100万！"

妈妈在我身后的另一间屋子里，正站在熨衣板前面，她异常肯定地告诉我，那口气仿佛是她就一直坐在我身边没离开过半步："儿子，如果你愿意，有朝一日你也能挣到100百万。"

序言

Stunned, I allow her pronouncement to seep in, without responding. No response is necessary, as Bettye Jean Triplett née Gardner has gone on record with a statement of fact, not to be questioned, or responded to. It is as factual as if one would say on Friday that "tomorrow is Saturday."

It was biblical, one of the ten commandments handed down from God to Momma: "If you want to, one day you could make a million dollars."

All in an instant my world turned inside out. In 1970 the only way a kid from the ghetto like me had a chance to go make a million dollars was if he could sing, dance, run, jump, catch balls, or deal drugs. I could not sing. I am still the only black man in America that cannot dance or play ball. And it was my Momma who'd set me straight about becoming Miles Davis.

"Chris," she had said after hearing me say how I was going to be him one too many times, "you can't be Miles Davis because he already got that job." I had understood from then on that my job was to be Chris Gardner—whatever that was going to entail.

Now she had told me, and I was sixteen years old and I believed her, that my job could be to make a million dollars—*if* I wanted to. The amount of the money wasn't what mattered when Moms said it; the operative part of her message was that if I wanted to do something, whatever it was, I could.

I not only believed her then, at age sixteen, but I continued to believe that statement in all the days that followed, including that fateful day in San Francisco when I got the first inkling of a future in Wall Street, and in those moments pushing up the hills in the downpour with my son looking up at me from his stroller through rain-splattered dry-cleaning plastic, and in the desolate hours when the only place of refuge was in a BART station bathroom.

It was only later in my adulthood, after those days of wandering in the desert of homelessness, believing in the promised land my mother had told me about and then finding it, and only after generating many millions of dollars, that I understood why these two events were both so essential to my eventual success. The encounter with the driver of the red Ferrari showed me the way to discovering *what* the arena was in which I could apply myself and also to learning *how* to do that. But it was my mother's earlier pronouncement that had planted the belief in me that I *could* attain whatever goals I set for myself.

Only after looking as deeply as I could into my mother's life was I able to fully understand why she said those words to me at the time that she did. By recognizing the disappointments that happened in her life before and after I came along, I was able to see that, though too many of her dreams had been crushed, by daring me to dream she was being given another chance.

我一时语塞，怔怔地听她说完每个字，其实当时我没有回过神也是正常的，因为母亲贝蒂·让·崔普雷特曾这样说过，事实就是事实，无需质疑和回应。这就是个简单的事实，就像今天是周五，没人会去证明明天会是周六一样。

这句话本身宛若《圣经》一般，就像十诫从上帝传至母亲之手，"如果你愿意，有朝一日你也能挣到一百万。"

也就在那一瞬间，我的世界发生了天翻地覆的变化。1970年，像我这样生活在贫民区的孩子若想挣到一百万，那就得能歌善舞，要么能跑会跳，再么球艺高超，实在不行就只能贩卖毒品。我一没有天生的好嗓子，估计也是全美国唯一不会跳舞不善踢球的黑人，也就是因为妈妈，我痛下决心，一心想成为迈尔·戴维斯那样的爵士大师。

当她无数次地听我说要当迈尔·戴维斯爵士大师之后，她说："克里斯，你不可能成为戴维斯，因为他自己已经成功做到了。"之后，我终于明白，我只能做好克里斯·加纳，具体怎样只能靠自己了。

而在我满16岁的时候，在我对她笃信无疑时，她告诉我，我也能挣到一百万，前提是只要我自己愿意。倒不是这笔钱对我有多么重要，重要的是她说我只要想做什么，我就能做得到。

我不仅在16岁的时候对妈妈的话深信不疑，在之后的日子里也同样如此，包括在旧金山那次命中注定的邂逅让我对华尔街产生非分之想时；在大雨滂沱中，我推着婴儿车艰难前行，儿子透过我用塑料布自制的简易遮雨篷眼巴巴地望着我时；当我孤立无援，只能在捷运车站的卫生间勉强过夜时，我都没有对母亲说过的话产生丝毫怀疑。

也就在我成年后，才意识到经过那些无家可归的日日夜夜，而始终坚信母亲对我当初的承诺，以及后来我努力兑现这种承诺，这一切才更具意义，也只有在自己真的有数百万美金进账时，我方才明白这两件事其实对于我之后的成功意义非凡。邂逅法拉利车主让我明白该在哪个领域去实现个人的发展，以及如何去发展，但是更早些时候，母亲对我的断言，让我根深蒂固地相信，只要我努力，自己设定的目标终将会实现。

只有尽可能深入地了解了母亲这一生，我才可能完全理解她当时为何会对我说出这番话来。通过了解她前前后后所经历的失意和痛苦，我才意识到她自己的梦想曾一次次的破灭。而让我敢于梦想，才又给了她重温旧梦的机会。

To fully answer the question of what it was that guided me through and became the secret to the success that followed, I had to go back to my own childhood and take the journey back to where my mother came from—in order to understand at last how that fire to dream got lit in me.

My story is hers.

究竟是什么指引我走出生命中的低谷,而且终获成功,要回答这个问题,就要从我孩提时候说起,还要谈及母亲出生的地方,因为只有这样才能真正了解是什么最后点燃我的梦想,并指引我一直前行。

我们的命运紧密相连,我的故事也就是她的故事。

Contents

Part One

Chapter 1   Candy 3
Chapter 2   The No-Daddy Blues 23
Chapter 3   Where's Momma 63
Chapter 4   Bitches Brew(side a) 85
Chapter 5   Bitches Brew(side b) 117

Part Two

Chapter 6   The World Beyond 155
Chapter 7   Pictures of a Life 181
Chapter 8   Turned Out(an intro) 217
Chapter 9   Turned Out(advanced) ... 243
Chapter 10   California Dreamin' ... 273

Part Three

Chapter 11   Roses in the Ghetto ... 327
Chapter 12   Sphere of Influence ... 349
Epilogue 483

目　录

第一部

第一章　糖果 3
第二章　渴望父爱 23
第三章　妈妈在哪里 63
第四章　即兴精酿(上) 85
第五章　即兴精酿(下) 117

第二部

第六章　外面的世界 155
第七章　生活的影像 181
第八章　人生的抉择(上) 217
第九章　人生的抉择(下) 243
第十章　加州的梦想 273

第三部

第十一章　贫民区的玫瑰 327
第十二章　圈子 349
尾　声　祝福永存 383

Part One

第一部

Chapter 1
Candy

In my memory's sketch of early childhood, drawn by an artist of the impressionist school, there is one image that stands out above the rest—which when called forth is preceded by the mouth-watering aroma of pancake syrup warming in a skillet and the crackling, bubbling sounds of the syrup transforming magically into homemade pull candy. Then *she* comes into view, the real, real pretty woman who stands at the stove, making this magic just for me.

Or at least, that's how it feels to a boy of three years old. There is another wonderful smell that accompanies her presence as she turns, smiling right in my direction, as she steps closer to where I stand in the middle of the kitchen—waiting eagerly next to my sister, seven-year-old Ophelia, and two of the other children, Rufus and Pookie, who live in this house. As she slips the cooling candy off the wooden spoon, pulling and breaking it into pieces that she brings and places in my outstretched hand, as she watches me happily gobbling up the tasty sweetness, her wonderful fragrance is there again. Not perfume or anything floral or spicy—it's just a clean, warm, *good* smell that wraps around me like a Superman cape, making me feel strong, special, and loved—even if I don't have words for those concepts yet.

第一章
糖　果

在我的记忆当中，幼年的岁月只剩下一个大概的轮廓，就像印象派的画作一般，留下的只是一些模糊的影像，但是有幅场景却让我难以忘怀——在铁锅中加热的薄糖浆饼散发出的诱人香味，随后只见糖浆饼噼啪一阵作响，神奇地变成了一个个的糖块。接下来，一个漂亮女人的身影出现了，她就站在炉子前，魔术般地为我变出这些糖块来。

至少对于 3 岁的我来说，这就是我当时的感受。她转身冲我甜甜一笑，似乎都会散发出一种奇妙的香味，我就傻傻地站在厨房的中间，眼巴巴地坐在 7 岁的姐姐奥菲丽娅身边，旁边还有两个孩子，鲁法斯和普齐，他俩也住在这里。她把冷却的糖块从木勺上取下来，然后掰成小块，放到我伸出的小手中，看着我开心地大吃特吃，享受着糖果的美味。然后她身上特有的甜美香味再次出现了，那绝不是香水、花香或是香料的味道，那种味道清香四溢、温馨亲切，在我周身上下围绕，仿佛用超人的神奇斗篷将我紧紧包裹住一样，让我感受到一种深切的关爱，而在当时所有这些我根本无法用语言表述出来。

The PURSUIT of HAPPYNESS

Though I don't know who she is, I sense a familiarity about her, not only because she has come before and made candy in this same fashion, but also because of how she looks at me—like she's talking to me from her eyes, saying, *You remember me, don't you?*

At this point in childhood, and for most of the first five years of my life, the map of my world was broken strictly into two territories—the familiar and the unknown. The happy, safe zone of the familiar was very small, often a shifting dot on the map, while the unknown was vast, terrifying, and constant.

What I did know by the age of three or four was that Ophelia was my older sister and best friend, and also that we were treated with kindness by Mr. and Mrs. Robinson, the adults whose house we lived in. What I didn't know was that the Robinsons' house was a foster home, or what that meant. Our situation—where our real parents were and why we didn't live with them, or why we sometimes did live with uncles and aunts and cousins—was as mysterious as the situations of the other foster children living at the Robinsons'.

What mattered most was that I had a sister who looked out for me, and I had Rufus and Pookie and the other boys to follow outside for fun and mischief. All that was familiar, the backyard and the rest of the block, was safe turf where we could run and play games like tag, kick-the-can, and hide-and-seek, even after dark. That is, except, for the house two doors down from the Robinsons.

Every time we passed it I had to almost look the other way, just knowing the old white woman who lived there might suddenly appear and put an evil curse on me—because, according to Ophelia and everyone else in the neighborhood, the old woman was a witch.

When Ophelia and I passed by the house together once and I confessed that I was scared of the witch, my sister said, "I ain't scared," and to prove it she walked right into the front yard and grabbed a handful of cherries off the woman's cherry tree.

Ophelia ate those cherries with a smile. But within the week I was in the Robinsons' house when here came Ophelia, racing up the steps and stumbling inside, panting and holding her seven-year-old chest, describing how the witch had caught her stealing cherries and grabbed her arm, cackling, "I'm gonna get you!"

Scared to death as she was now, Ophelia soon decided that since she had escaped an untimely death once, she might as well go back to stealing cherries. Even so, she made me promise to avoid the strange woman's house. "Now, remember," Ophelia warned, "when you walk by, if you see her on the porch, don't you look at her and never say nuthin' to her, even if she calls you by name."

虽然我不知道她究竟是何人，但我却莫名其妙地感受到一种从未有过的熟悉与亲切，这倒不是因为她以前来过，也是这样给我做糖吃，而是因为她看我的目光，用那双仿佛会说话的眼睛，似乎在说，你认识我的，对吧？

在我童年的这段时日，就是我5岁前的大部分时间里，我的世界一分为二，一部分是我熟悉的，另一部分是不为我所知的。让我感觉熟悉、安全的东西其实屈指可数，甚至少得可以忽略不计，而更多的却是我无法理解的令人生畏的世界。

在我三四岁的时候只知道姐姐奥菲丽娅是我最要好的朋友，罗宾森夫妇对我们也非常好，我们住在他们家。只是我不知道罗宾森家其实是个福利院，或是这类机构，我们的具体身世，包括亲生父母在哪里，为什么不和自己的父母生活在一起，怎么有时得和舅舅、舅母及他们的子女住在一起，这些我们都一无所知，与福利院其他孩子的身世一样，都是一个又一个的谜。

最重要的是姐姐会照顾我，而我和鲁法斯、普齐以及其他男孩子可以在外面一起玩耍胡闹。后院以及周围的街区，这些地方都是我非常熟悉也是很安全的，在这里我们玩各种游戏，踢盒子、捉迷藏，甚至能一直玩到天黑。但罗宾森家隔门的邻居是绝不能靠近的。

每次路过那家时我都尽量小心翼翼地绕道而行，知道住在那儿的白人老太太可能会突然出现，对我恶言恶语，因为姐姐奥菲丽娅和周围的人都说那老太太是个巫婆。

当我和姐姐经过那所房子时，一想到那个老太太，我就吓得要死。姐姐却说："我不怕。"为证实她的胆量，她径直走进那家的前院，从老太太的樱桃树上，旁若无人地摘了一把樱桃。

姐姐得意地笑着，嚼着樱桃，但几天后，当我在罗宾森家待着的时候，只见姐姐三步并作两步冲上台阶，磕磕绊绊得几乎摔倒，上气不接下气地说那个巫婆因为她偷了樱桃要抓她，还扯着她的胳膊说："看我怎么收拾你！"

她几乎吓得半死，刚缓过神来，她就决定既然已经死里逃生，何不干脆一不做二不休呢，再去偷些樱桃回来。即便如此，她一再告诫我，要我发誓以后一定要离老太太家远点，"记住了，千万别去她那，就是偶尔路过，看到她在凳子上坐着，也不要搭理她，她就是叫你的名字，也不能吭声。"

I didn't have to promise because I knew that nothing and no one could ever make me do that. But I was still haunted by nightmares so real that I could have sworn I actually snuck into her house and found myself in the middle of a dark, creepy room where I was surrounded by an army of cats, rearing up on their back legs, baring their claws and fangs. The nightmares were so intense that for the longest time I had an irrational fear and dislike of cats. At the same time, I was not entirely convinced that this old woman was in fact a witch. Maybe she was just different. Since I'd never seen any white people other than her, I figured they might all be like that.

Then again, because my big sister was my only resource for explaining all that was unknown, I believed her and accepted her explanations. But as I pieced together fragments of information about our family over the years, mainly from Ophelia and also from some of our uncles and aunts, I found the answers much harder to grasp.

How the real pretty woman who came to make the candy fit into the puzzle, I was never told, but something old and wise inside me knew that she was important. Maybe it was how she seemed to pay special attention to me, even though she was just as nice to Ophelia and the other kids, or maybe it was how she and I seemed to have a secret way of talking without words. In our unspoken conversation, I understood her to be saying that seeing me happy made her even happier, and so somewhere in my cells, that became my first job in life—to make her feel as good as she made me feel. Intuitively, I also understood who she was, in spite of never being told, and there is a moment of recognition that comes during one of her visits—as I watch her at the stove and make observations that will be reinforced in years to come.

More than pretty, she is beautiful, a stop-you-in-your-tracks-turn-around-and-look-twice beautiful. Not tall at five-four, but with a stature of nobility that makes her appear much taller, she is light brown–skinned but not too light—almost the color of the rich maple syrup she stirs and heats into candy. She has supernaturally strong fingernails—capable of breaking an apple in half, bare-handed, something that few women or men can do and something that impresses me for life. She has a stylish way of dressing—the color burgundy and paisley print dresses stand out—with a scarf or shawl thrown over her shoulder to give her a feminine, flowing look. The brightness of color and the flowing layers of fabric give her an appearance I would later describe as Afro-centric.

But the features that most capture her beauty are her expressive eyes and her amazing smile. Then and later, I liken that smile to opening a refrigerator at night. You open up that door—smile— and the light fills up the room. Even on those nights ahead when the refrigerator contains nothing but a lightbulb and ice water, her smile and the memory of her smile are all the comforts I need.

其实根本用不着什么承诺，因为我知道自己说什么都不会这么做的。但我还是吓得夜里老做噩梦，梦里的一切真真切切，好像自己真进了老太太家，屋里黑幽幽的，四周都是凶狠的猫，龇牙咧嘴，弓着背，随时准备向我扑过来，我总是做这个噩梦，以至于很长一段时间，我都被一种无言的恐惧所笼罩，甚至对猫这种动物也一直心存厌恶。与此同时，我也拿不准那个老太太是不是真的是巫婆，也许她就是行为举止和别人不大一样而已。但我除了她之外就没见过什么白人，所以就自以为白人大概都是这副样子。

再说，姐姐是为我解释未知世界的唯一渠道，我对她言听计从、深信不疑，全盘接受她的说法。但是我那几年东拼西凑出来的对自己身世的那点了解却总是让自己感到愈发的迷惑不解，当然这些主要是姐姐告诉我的，不过姑姑舅舅他们也透露过一些。

那个会做糖果的漂亮女子，也是个谜，但不知怎么，我打心眼里认为她是个关键人物。也许就是因为她好像对我格外在意，虽然她对姐姐和其他孩子也不错，但感觉不一样，要么就是我俩之间可以不用通过语言就能交流，在我们无言的沟通过程中，我终于明白她只要见到我快乐的样子，她会更快乐。因此，从骨子里面我认定自己一定要让她开心，就像她让我开心一样，这似乎成了我份内的事。我好像已经模模糊糊地意识到她是谁，虽然没人告诉过我她的真实身份，从她来看我的那一刻起，我好像就意识到什么似的，我仔细端详着她在炉边忙碌的样子，她那身影和神态我后来也曾多次见到。

她不是一般的漂亮，可以说是楚楚动人，美得让人不由得驻足凝望，她并不高，但却透着一种高贵的气质，显得个头比她实际还要高几分。她肤色浅棕，颜色有点像她用枫糖熬制的糖果。还有她的手劲大得惊人，不用任何工具就能把苹果掰成两半，这可不是一般人能做得到的，这本事也让我佩服得五体投地。她衣着打扮也别有味道，紫色的印花连衣裙使她更显得亭亭玉立，就连她肩头的披肩或头巾都在她的十足女人味上又添了一抹飘逸。明亮的色彩，衣着的层次感，卓显了一种别样之美。

但是最打动人的还是她那双传神的眸子和极富魅力的微笑，那种微笑甚至让我想起夜里打开的冰箱，里面温暖的灯光照亮我的面庞，让我满心欢喜。即便更多时候，冰箱里除了冰水，再无其他，但是想起她微笑的感觉，刻在我记忆深处的微笑，足以让我备感温暖，让我心满意足。

第一章 糖果

The PURSUIT of HAPPYNESS

When the recognition occurs exactly, I don't recall, except that it takes place somewhere in my fourth year, maybe after she hands me a piece of candy, in an instant when at last I can respond to that look she has been giving me and reassure her with my own look— *Of course I remember you, you're my momma!*

* * *

Ours was a family of secrets. Over the years, I heard only parts of my mother's saga, told to me by a variety of sources, so that the understanding that eventually emerged was of a kind of Cinderella story—without the fairy godmother and the part at the end where she marries the prince and they all live happily ever after. The oldest and only daughter of the four surviving children born to parents Archie and Ophelia Gardner, Bettye Jean came into this world in 1928, in Little Rock, Arkansas, but was raised in Depression-era, dirt-poor, rural Louisiana—somewhere near the town of Rayville, population five hundred. With the trials of poverty and racism, life wasn't easy for the Gardners. Bettye and her brother Archie— who cried grown-man tears when he recalled what it was like walking the long, dusty country roads to school in the thirties and forties in Rayville—had to keep their heads up as white children rode by in horse-drawn wagons or on horseback, looking down at the two of them, pointing, calling them "niggers," and spitting on them.

Yet, in spite of hard times and hateful ignorance, Bettye's childhood was relatively stable and very loving. Adored by her three younger brothers—Archie Jr., Willie, and Henry—she was, in fact, a golden girl of promise, a star student who finished third in her class when she graduated from Rayville Colored High School in 1946. But her dreams quickly unraveled the moment it was time to go off to college and pursue her calling as an educator, starting with the devastating sudden death of her mother. Like Cinderella, while she was still in mourning, almost overnight her father remarried, leaving Bettye to cope with a domineering stepmother—who went by the ironic nickname of Little Mama—and a new set of competitive stepsiblings. Just at a time when Bettye Jean was depending on the financial support from her father to go to college, Little Mama saw to it that the money went to her own daughter, Eddie Lee—who had graduated in the same class as Bettye but wasn't among the top students.

Rather than giving up, even though her heart was broken by her father's refusal to help, Bettye found work as a substitute teacher while she put herself through beauty school. But once again, when she needed financial assistance from her father to pay for her state licensing fees, he said no.

Chapter 1 Candy

自从见到她油然而生的那种熟悉感觉出现后，我并未更多地回忆那一瞬间。但在我四岁的一天，可能是她在什么地方又递给我糖果的时候，用她那温柔的目光询问地看着我的时候，我终于意识到了那种熟悉的感觉究竟意味着什么，我也同样深情地回望着她，当然记得，你就是妈妈!

* * *

我家有很多秘密，许多年来，关于妈妈的事情我只知道一星半点，这还是从不同人那里听来的。最后拼凑出的结论是，妈妈就是个灰姑娘，只是她没有善良的教母，最后也没有遇到英俊的王子，更不用说幸福地生活到老。妈妈名叫贝蒂·让，1928年生于阿肯萨州的小石城，父母是阿奇和奥菲丽娅·加德纳，四个孩子中只有母亲这么一个女孩，她正好赶上经济大萧条的年月，在路易斯安那州的一个贫困乡村长大成人，那里离雷维尔镇不远，小镇不大，只有500多人。生活贫困加之种族主义作祟，加德纳一家的日子过得很是艰难。当时，也就是20世纪三四十年代的时候，母亲贝蒂和舅舅阿奇沿着雷维尔镇尘土飞扬的乡间小路步行去上学，旁边常有驾着马车或骑着高头大马的白人孩子耀武扬威，冲着他们吐口水，骂他们是"黑鬼"。后来舅舅阿奇一想起这段日子就忍不住心酸落泪。

虽然生活艰辛，加之种族歧视，但是母亲的童年过得还算太平。三个哥哥小阿奇、威利、亨利都护着她这个妹妹，她其实相当出色，是一个品学兼优的好学生，1946年从雷维尔镇有色人种高中毕业时，她的成绩在班上名列第三，马上就面临着考大学，她一心想着大学毕业后能成为教育工作者，也就在这时，宛若晴天霹雳，外婆突然过世。和灰姑娘一样的是，当她还沉浸在丧母之痛中的时候，才几天工夫，她父亲就闪电般地再婚了。从此母亲贝蒂就不得不小心应对着自己恶毒的继母，随即，继母也得了个"小妈"的"雅号"，而且继母自己还有好几个孩子各个都不好对付。当贝蒂指望父亲资助自己上大学的时候，小妈却将这笔钱据为己有，作为自己的亲生女儿艾迪·李的上学费用，艾迪和贝蒂本是同班，而且成绩平平。

父亲拒绝伸出援助之手，这让贝蒂心痛欲碎，但她还是没有放弃，通过美容学校的培训，她找了份代理教师的工作。但注册州立教师资格还是需要费用的，她向父亲求援，可得到的是又一次的断然拒绝。

第一章 糖果

The PURSUIT of HAPPYNESS

With all the talent, brilliance, and beauty that had been naturally bestowed on Bettye Jean Gardner, she had apparently drawn an unlucky card when it came to men—most of whom seemed destined to disappoint her, starting with her own daddy. There was Samuel Salter, a married schoolteacher who professed his love for her and his plan to leave his wife, but who must have changed his mind when she became pregnant. True to form, her daddy and Little Mama were no help. They let it be known that she had embarrassed them enough by being single at age twenty-two, but for her to be an old maid *and* an unwed mother was too much shame for them to bear. On these grounds, they put her out.

Thus began my mother's four-year trek to Milwaukee, where all three of her brothers had settled. Along the way she gave birth to my sister—named Ophelia for her beloved mother—before crossing paths with a tall, dark, handsome stranger during a trip back to Louisiana. His name was Thomas Turner, a married man who swept Bettye Jean off her feet either romantically or by force. The result was me, Christopher Paul Gardner, born in Milwaukee, Wisconsin, on February 9, 1954—the same year, auspiciously, that school segregation was ruled in violation of the Fourteenth Amendment by the U.S. Supreme Court.

In keeping with other family mysteries, my father was a figment of the vast unknown throughout my childhood. His name was mentioned only once or twice. It probably would have bothered me much more if I weren't so occupied trying to get to the bottom of other more pressing questions, especially the how-when-where-why my smart, strong, beautiful mother ever became entangled with Freddie Triplett.

Tall and dark, but not exactly handsome—at times he bore a strong resemblance to Sonny Liston—Freddie had the demeanor of some ill-begotten cross between a pit bull and Godzilla. At six-two, 280 pounds, he did have a stature and brawn that some women found attractive. Whatever it was that first caught her attention must have been a redeeming side of him that later vanished. Or maybe, as I'd wonder in my youthful imagination, my mother was tricked by a magic spell into thinking that he was one of those frog princes. After all, the other men who looked good had not turned out to be dependable; maybe she thought Freddie was the opposite—a man who looked dangerous but was kind and tender underneath his disguise. If that was the case, and she believed in the fairy tale that her kiss would turn the frog into a prince, she was sadly mistaken. In fact, he turned out to be many times more dangerous than he looked, especially after that first kiss, and after he decided she was his.

Chapter 1 Candy

虽然，贝蒂·让·加德纳拥有与生俱来的出众才华和姣好容貌，但她与异性交往时却屡遭不幸。其实从她自己的父亲开始，似乎男人就是注定要让她吃尽苦头。萨缪尔·梭特是个已婚的学校老师，对贝蒂表白真情，并信誓旦旦要离开自己的妻子，与贝蒂重建家庭，可当贝蒂身怀有孕之后，他却改变了初衷。果不出所料，父亲和继母根本不愿与这事有任何瓜葛，相反觉得贝蒂22岁还没嫁人已经足以让他们抬不起头来，现在她不仅是个老姑娘而且还成了未婚妈妈，这让他们更是接受不了，索性将她逐出家门。

从此母亲开始了前往威斯康星密尔沃基长达四年的跋涉，因为她三个哥哥就居住在那里。就在路上，姐姐降生了，母亲为纪念她深爱的妈妈，就给姐姐取名叫奥菲丽娅，在回路易斯安那的途中，她又邂逅了一个高个子的英俊黑人，他就是托马斯·特纳，一个已婚男人，不知是情之所至还是他强迫使然，他俩上了床，结果就有了我，克里斯多夫·保罗·加德纳，1954年2月9日，出生在威斯康星的密尔沃基，幸运的是，也就在同一年，美国最高法院裁定学校种族隔离制违反了第十四条修正案。

为保守我身世的秘密，童年的我对父亲几乎一无所知，他的名字也就提过那么一两次，可要是不让我一门心思去发现其他问题的答案，我可能会更痛苦难熬，特别是我那么漂亮的妈妈怎么会和弗莱迪·崔普雷特交往，是什么时候的事情，他们在哪里遇上的，等等。

有些时候，弗莱迪和拳王桑尼·里斯顿颇为相似，性情暴烈、攻击性极强。他是个大块头，身高1.88米，体重250斤，皮肤深棕，这可能会讨一些女人的喜欢。开始让母亲注意上他的估计是他的悔过之心，不过这一点后来就消失得无影无踪了。或是按照我当时的猜测，母亲一定是中了邪，把他当做被施了魔法的青蛙王子，以后能浪子回头。再有就是，她的那些俊俏男友，最后没一个能靠得住。或许她指望弗莱迪是个例外——虽然外表虽然凶狠，但却心地善良。若真是这样，而且她真的相信所谓青蛙变王子的故事，她可真就大错特错了。实际上，弗莱迪远比他的相貌更加凶狠，特别是当她一吻定情，决定以身相许之后，他就更加变本加厉了。

第一章 糖果

The PURSUIT of HAPPYNESS

No one ever laid out the sequence of events that led to my mother being prosecuted and imprisoned for alleged welfare fraud. It started out with an anonymous tip, apparently, that somehow she was a danger to society because she was earning money at a job—to feed and care for her two children (Ophelia and me) and a third on the way (my sister Sharon)—and was receiving assistance at the same time. That anonymous tip had come from Freddie, a man willing to do or say anything to have her locked up for three years because she had committed the crime of trying to leave his sorry ass.

It was because of Freddie's actions in having her sent away that Ophelia and I spent those three years either in foster care or with extended family members. Yet we never knew why or when changes in our living situation would take place.

Just as no one told me that it was my mother who came to make candy and visit us at the foster home under special, supervised leave from prison, no explanation accompanied our move when Ophelia and I went to stay with my Uncle Archie and his wife Clara, or TT as we all called her. Way back in Louisiana, the entire Gardner family must have signed an oath of secrecy because serious questions about the past were almost always shrugged off, a policy my mother may have instituted out of her dislike for discussing anything unpleasant.

Later on in my adolescence there was one occasion when I pressed her about just who my father was and why he wasn't in my life. Moms gave me one of her searing looks, the kind that got me to be quiet real fast.

"But . . ." I tried to protest.

She shook her head no, unwilling to open up.

"Why?"

"Well, because the past is the past," Moms said firmly. Seeing my frustration, she sighed but still insisted, "Ain't nothing you can do about it." She put a stop to my questions, wistfully remarking, "Things happen." And that was all there was to it.

Even as my questions continued, while waiting for clarification to arrive of its own accord, I went back to my job of trying to be as happy as possible—not a difficult assignment at first.

* * *

The land of the familiar where I grew up in one of the poorer areas of the north side of Milwaukee was a world that I eventually viewed as a black *Happy Days.* Just like on that TV show that was set in the 1950s—in the same time period in which my neighborhood seemed to be frozen even in later decades—there were local hangouts, places where different age groups gathered to socialize, well-known quirky merchants, and an abundance of great characters. While on the TV show the only black color you ever saw was Fonzie's leather jacket, in my neighborhood, for nearly the first dozen years of my life, the only white people I ever saw were on television and in police cars.

Chapter 1 Candy

没人知道是怎么回事，母亲被指控福利欺诈，并锒铛入狱。开始是一封匿名信，指控母亲对社会构成威胁，因为她要挣钱养家，照顾两个孩子（姐姐和我），而且她又怀上了第三个孩子（妹妹沙仑），同时还在接受社会救济。那封匿名信就是出自弗莱迪之手，他就是要想尽一切办法把她关上三年，给她个教训，因为母亲有离开他的想法。

正是由于弗莱迪的这种行径，母亲被带走了，姐姐和我不得不在福利院度日，或者寄宿在亲戚家中。而我们对背后的这些变故一无所知。

正像没人告诉过我那个来福利院给我做糖果的女子就是母亲一样，当时她还受到监狱的特殊监护，也没人给我们解释过为什么姐姐和我要搬到舅舅阿奇家，舅母叫做克拉拉，我们都叫她缇缇。整个加德纳家族似乎发誓要严守秘密，每当问及过去，人们都对此避而不谈，可能是母亲有约在先，不愿再提那些不愉快的往事。

我十几岁的时候，有一次我死磨硬泡，一定要她告诉我生父究竟是谁，为什么他不在我身边，母亲悲伤地望着我一言不发，我就不敢再吭声了。

"但是……"我还想坚持一下。

她摇摇头，不愿吐露一个字。

"为什么呢？"

"因为过去的事情就让它过去好了。"妈妈坚定地告诉我。看我一脸沮丧，她轻叹一声，但仍不肯改口，"无论怎样，过去都无法再改变了。"接下来，她的一句睿智的结语为我的问题画上了句号，"生活就是这样。"这事后来就再没提起过。

虽然我还是那么好问这问那，期待着有朝一日这些问题都能得到圆满的答案，但我还是很快又回到自己快乐的生活中来，开始时这倒是没什么难度。

* * *

我长大成人的地方是威斯康星密尔沃基北部最为贫困的地区，我熟悉这里的每寸土地，而且这里也成就了我孩提时一段还算幸福的时光。当时的左邻右舍正如电视里演的20世纪50年代的美国一样，以至于后来的几十年似乎也定格在这段时期里，没有太多变化——这里不乏经常一起玩的伙伴们，还有不同年龄层的人聚会热闹的场所，再有就是各种稀奇古怪的小商贩，最不缺的是形形色色的各色人等。当时唯一能在电视上见到的黑色就是名牌黑皮衣，而在我住的地方，至少在来到世上的头12年间，我只在电视和警车里见过白人。

第一章 糖果

The PURSUIT of HAPPYNESS

Some of the greatest characters in our *Happy Days* version were my own family members, starting with my three stubborn uncles. After both Willie and Henry got out of the Army, having traveled to many distant shores, the two returned to Louisiana long enough to join with Uncle Archie as each came to the simultaneous decision to get as far away from southern bigotry as he possibly could.

Their plan was to go to Canada, but when their car broke down in Milwaukee, so the story goes, they laid anchor and went no farther. The hardworking Gardner brothers didn't have too much trouble making Milwaukee home. To them, the fertile, versatile city that had been plunked down at the meeting place of the Milwaukee River and Lake Michigan— which provided rich soil for farming and ample waterways for trade and industry—was their land of milk and honey, of golden opportunity. To put up with the extremes in the seasons, the brutal winters and scorching summers, you had to have an innate toughness and the kind of deeply practical, hustling ability that my relatives and many of the other minorities and immigrants brought with them to Wisconsin from other places. Those traits must have existed as well as in the descendents of the true Milwaukeeans—members of tribes like the Winnebago and Potawatomi. There was another local personality trait not exclusive to the new arrivals of blacks, Jews, Italians, and eastern Europeans or the families of the first wave of settlers from Germany, Ireland, and Scandinavia, or the area's Native Americans, and that was an almost crazy optimism.

All that ambitious, pragmatic dreaming sometimes resulted in overachievement. It wasn't enough to just have one brand of beer, Milwaukee had to have several. The region couldn't just be famous for its dairies, it had to have the best cheese in the world. There wasn't just one major industry but several—from the brickyards, tanneries, breweries, shipyards, and meatpacking businesses to the dominating steel factories like Inland Steel and A. O. Smith and the automotive giant American Motors (deceased as of the late 1980s).

It was mainly the steel mills and foundries and carmakers that brought so many blacks from states like Louisiana, Alabama, Mississippi, Georgia, and all points south of the Mason-Dixon north to Milwaukee, Detroit, Chicago, and Cleveland. These blue-collar jobs were far and away preferable to a life sharecropping in the sweltering heat way down south in Dixie, in places where less than a century earlier many of our people had been enslaved. Seemed like almost everyone had family members that brought with them their country ways and who tended to stick together. Sam Salter— Ophelia's father—ended up with his family in Milwaukee, as well as other friends from Louisiana. The Tripletts, some of the nicest, kindest folks you could meet—with the exception of Freddie, the bad seed—had come from Mississippi.

我那些幸福时光的主角都是自己的家人，首先要提的就是我那三个倔脾气舅舅。威利和亨利舅舅双双退伍之后，去过遥远的海岸，后来两人回到路易斯安那呆了好一阵子，才不约而同地决定要尽可能远离南方，两人计划去加拿大，可车子在威斯康星密尔沃基抛了锚，于是索性就地留下来，没再继续他们的旅程。

勤勤恳恳的加德纳兄弟在威斯康星密尔沃基很容易就落下脚来，他们就选在密尔沃基与密歇根湖交汇的地方安顿下来，这里土地肥沃，适合耕作，水路四通八达，适合工业和贸易，绝对是他们的理想生存之地，为适应酷暑严寒，在这里生存需要内心的坚韧和顽强，以及脚踏实地的务实精神，而所有这些以及其他优良品质都是从不同地方移民到威斯康星的人们身上并不缺少的品质。相信在密尔沃基土生土长的当地人身上，也不乏同样的优点，如温尼巴哥和伯塔瓦托米部族就是这样的实例。还有些当地的特性也感染了这些外来移民，无论是黑人、犹太人、意大利人、东欧人，还是来自德国、爱尔兰、斯堪的纳维亚的第一拨移民潮以及当地的原住民，都受到这里极度乐观精神的鼓舞和感召。

所有这些雄心勃勃又不失实用性的梦想有时竟能催生一些超级成就。比如，仅有一个啤酒品牌大卖是远远不够的，密尔沃基响当当的啤酒品牌可以有若干。这里不仅奶制品闻名于世，它的奶酪产品甚至在世界上都数一数二。可圈可点的支柱行业不是一个两个，而是有十个八个，造砖、制皮、酿酒、造船、肉食品加工、钢铁（这里有美国的内陆钢铁公司、艾欧史密斯），以及诸多汽车巨头（20 世纪 80 年代后期才逐渐衰落）。

其实主要是钢铁厂和汽车厂使得很多黑人从路易斯安那、阿拉巴马、密西西比、佐治亚等南部诸州纷纷移至密尔沃基、底特律、芝加哥、克里夫兰这些北方城市，这些体力工作比起南方农场里挥汗如雨的田间耕作相对要好上很多，当时南方的农场主要采用分成制，而不到一百年前，干脆就是奴隶制。很多这样的移民以及他们的家人都沿袭各自家乡的习惯和做法，似乎这些东西已经和他们密不可分。姐姐奥菲丽娅生父的一家就是这样，他们来自路易斯安那，最后也在密尔沃基定居，崔普雷特一家人来自密西西比，很难找到像他们家那么好的人了，但弗莱迪绝对是家中的败类。

第一章 糖果

The PURSUIT of HAPPYNESS

As hard as everyone worked all week, at least in my neighborhood, over the weekend they played and prayed even harder. No such thing as casual drinking in our part of Milwaukee. From Friday evening when the whistle blew at Inland Steel—where all three of my uncles worked, Archie and Willie until they retired from there and Henry until his dying day, which came much too early—the party began and lasted until Sunday morning, when it was time to go to church and pray for forgiveness.

Between the ages of four and five, at which point I was living with Uncle Archie and Aunt TT, I'd come to appreciate the familiar rhythm of the working week. My uncle and his wife maintained an easygoing, peaceful atmosphere without too many rules. A devout Christian, TT made sure we got that old-time religion in us. Every Sunday, all day, we spent at the Tabernacle Baptist Church, and in summers we attended Bible school daily, plus we accompanied her to any and all special midweek meetings and were present for the funerals of every member of the church who ever died, whether we knew them or not. Most of this I didn't mind so much, considering all the entertainment value as I watched the various characters from the neighborhood I'd seen sinning all week now change their clothes and themselves. I loved the singing and shouting, the feeling of heat and passion, and especially the connection to community that I experienced at a time when I didn't know exactly who or where my mother was.

TT never tried to be a substitute for Momma, but she provided love and comfort all the same. Nobody could cook like Bettye Jean, but my aunt did make an unforgettable hot-water cornbread that a growing kid like me couldn't devour fast enough. Nor could I devour fast enough the books that TT seemed to have limitless funds to buy for me. My mother later reinforced the importance of reading, raising me with her own credo to spend as much time at our public library as possible. What she'd say to show me how powerful a building full of books could be was, "The most dangerous place in the world is a public library." That was, of course, only if you could read, because, Momma explained, if you could read, that meant you could go in there and figure anything out. But if you couldn't read, well...

It was TT, however, who first instilled in me the love of reading books and storytelling. Though I didn't read yet, after TT read books to me, by looking at the illustrations afterward, I could partly remember the words and stories, and I felt as if I was reading already. There were books of Greek and Roman mythology, children's classic fairy tales, adventure stories, and my early favorite genre—tales of King Arthur and the Knights of the Round Table. The story of the Sword in the Stone made a lasting impression on me, setting up the idea that someday, somehow, I would find the destiny that awaited me.

Chapter 1 Candy

日复一日，大家都在努力地工作，但在周末，大家则尽情嬉戏，还专心祷告，至少我家的这些邻里是这样的。我们这附近绝对没有酗酒这种事情发生。每到周五傍晚，美国内陆钢铁公司下班的哨音一响，派对聚会就开始了，而且会一直持续到周日的早上，然后人们就纷纷赶到教堂做礼拜，祈求主的宽恕。我的三个舅舅都在内陆钢铁公司上班，阿奇和威利舅舅一直干到退休，亨利舅舅则干到自己生命最后一刻，不过那一刻来得太早了些。

我四五岁的时候，和阿奇舅舅和缇缇舅母一起生活。我逐渐喜欢上了家里人每天上班的这种日子。舅舅和舅母没有那么多的清规戒律，家里总是洋溢着其乐融融、祥和的气氛。舅母缇缇是个虔诚的基督徒，而且要我们也完全信奉她的信仰。每个礼拜日，我们一整天都呆在会幕浸礼会，夏天的时候，我们白天参加圣经学习班，平时一旦有什么特殊集会，我们都会陪着她一同参加，同一教堂的教友若有故去，无论熟识与否我们都去参加葬礼。大多数情况下，我都是欣然前往，看到这些形形色色的街坊邻里，现在都换了庄重的衣服，与平日判若两人，这本身就非常有趣。我也喜欢大声唱歌，这让我感到兴奋和激动，特别是当我不大确定自己的母亲是谁，身在何处的时候，和大家在一起会让我产生一种归属感。

缇缇舅母从未想过要代替妈妈的角色，但她同样能给予我爱与关怀，妈妈的厨艺无人能及，但舅母的热玉米面包同样让人难忘，特别是像我这样正在长身体的男孩，更是吃都吃不够的。舅母还总能给我买来好多书，我也同样是看也看不够。后来，母亲也一再强调看书的重要，尽量找时间带我去公共图书馆，为了说明有万卷书的图书馆到底有多么重要，她会说："公共图书馆是世上最了不得的地方。"想想也的确如此，因为母亲告诉我，如果识文断字，你就会所向披靡，无人能挡，但如果大字不识一个，那就是另一回事了……

但是舅母缇缇却是第一个教会我热爱书、爱上讲故事的人。虽然当时我还不会认字，但舅母可以读书给我听，之后我自己看插图，也能大体记起故事的内容，我自认为这就是在读书了。我有罗马希腊的神话故事、儿童经典童话故事、历险故事，还有我儿时的最爱《亚瑟王和圆桌骑士》。《石中剑》的故事给我的印象最深，那时我就暗下决心，有朝一日，也要找到属于自己的天命。

The PURSUIT of HAPPYNESS

Books allowed me not only to travel in my imagination but to look through windows into the world of the unknown and not feel afraid. That was until TT brought me a book I had been dying to have, *The Boys' Book of Snakes*. A big light green book, the color of a garden snake, it captivated me for days on end as I studied every minute detail of the snake world—from the friendly-sounding milk snakes and coral snakes to the deadly rattlers, cobras, and pythons. During waking hours I was fascinated, but at night, especially during one particular snake-infested nightmare in which my bed was full of writhing, hissing poisonous snakes, I regretted ever seeing those pictures.

Apparently so did TT and Uncle Archie, who woke up in the middle of the night to find me wedged in between them in the bed. "What in the . . ." Uncle Archie started up, but no amount of placating or chiding could get me to my own bed. In the end, they both went back to sleep, letting me feel safe and not making me feel too embarrassed—until later when I was a big, strong guy and they teased me about it mercilessly.

The other window into the world of the unknown was the black-and-white TV set, and the finest vision I ever saw on it was of Sugar Ray Robinson standing next to a Cadillac.

"Now I seen all," Uncle Archie exclaimed, his hand on my shoulder, pointing at the TV screen. "Sugar Ray Robinson got himself a *pink* Cadillac!"

With black-and-white TV, we wouldn't have known it was pink if the announcer hadn't said so, but it was no less amazing.

Friday fight nights sponsored by Gillette Blue Blades was our time, me and Uncle Archie, to sit down together—without TT and Ophelia—and enjoy every minute, from our conversations beforehand where he'd tell me everything he knew about boxing history, and the moment we'd hear that suspenseful intro music leading into the announcer's booming "Gillette presents!" to the match itself.

Uncle Archie had a contagious aura of calm that he maintained even during the excitement of the fights or when crises came up. A man in his late twenties at the time, he never had a son, and I didn't have a father, so that drew us closer. Besides his hardworking ethic on the job, Archie used his quiet, strong intelligence to rise up through the ranks of his union at Inland Steel, setting an example for me about tenacity and focus. A very handsome guy who was the male version of Moms in looks—nut brown in color, slender, and on the short side but appearing taller than he was—Archie was an incredibly sharp dresser, something that influenced my later sense of style and the clothes habit I acquired long before I could afford it. Never overdressed, he was immaculate in his grooming, with his short haircut and neat trim mustache and clothes that weren't showy but always impeccable. Always.

书籍不仅让我张开想象的翅膀,而且也为我了解未知世界打开了一扇窗,使我不再感觉无助与害怕。一次,舅母给我买回来一本我朝思暮想的《蛇类百科》,那是本浅绿色的大开本书,就是花园蛇的颜色,我一头扎进书里,仔细研究着各类蛇的每个细节。从无害的奶蛇到致命的响尾蛇、眼镜蛇、巨蟒。白天我看得津津有味,可到了夜里做噩梦的时候,尤其是梦里到处爬满了咝咝作响的毒蛇的时候,我后悔得肠子都青了,悔不该白天看了这些东西。

显然,舅舅、舅母也是这么想的,因为半夜里他们发现我缩在他俩中间,就是说尽好话,我也死活不会到自己床上去。最后他们把我留下,就这么入睡了,我倒是感到分外安全踏实,他们也没有让我太难为情。不过等我长大成人之后,他们倒会抖落出这件事来,让我分外脸红,羞愧难当。

我的另一个了解世界的窗口就是那台黑白电视机。让我记忆最深的是看到次中量级拳手雷·罗宾森站在一辆卡迪拉克旁。

"这我都看见过的,"阿奇舅舅把手搭在我肩膀上,指着屏幕说:"罗宾森得到一部粉红色的卡迪拉克!"

在黑白电视上是看不出车的颜色的,除非是解说员在一旁讲解,但那阵势确实不一般。

周五晚上的拳击赛是蓝吉列刀片赞助的,我和舅舅阿奇一起看得不亦乐乎,分分秒秒都不错过,当然缇缇舅母和姐姐奥菲丽娅不愿凑这份热闹。拳击赛之前,舅舅还会告诉我有关拳击的方方面面。我俩全神贯注盯着屏幕,从悬念叠生的前奏,到主持人宣布"吉列倾情巨献",再到比赛本身,我们分秒不差,全程跟下。

阿奇舅舅冷静沉着、富有感染力,无论是拳击赛高潮迭起,还是险象环生,他都不动声色。那时他将近而立之年,但还没有儿子,而我又没有父亲,所以我俩非常亲近。他对待工作一丝不苟,尽职尽责,而且凭借自己内敛的性格和聪明睿智在内陆钢铁公司逐级而上,步步高升,为我们树立了耐性和专注的楷模。他和母亲相貌非常相似,肤色是栗色,身材匀称,个头不高,但是不显得矮。阿奇舅舅穿着非常得体,甚至影响到我后来的着装习惯和品位,当然这在当时我是可望不可及的。他仪容整洁,一丝不苟,精干短发,胡须整齐挺括,衣着并不张扬,但一尘不染,而且素来如此。

The PURSUIT of HAPPYNESS

In Uncle Archie's lore, no one could touch Joe Louis, the Brown Bomber, the fighter he grew up following on the radio—hearing, feeling, smelling, and seeing every move, jab, swing, punch, and step, all on a nonvisual medium. As a result, Uncle Archie could narrate those fights for me as well as any announcer of his time. Now we were watching history unfold together, with Sugar Ray Robinson still going strong, including his fight with Jake LaMotta, which I'd never forget. Sugar Ray and the other boxers were larger than life, superheroes who could do and have it all, including a pink Cadillac. What that said to a poor kid from the ghetto like me was everything, a very early precursor to the red Ferrari. But Sugar Ray Robinson and his Caddy were on television. I had something closer at hand to show me the beautiful world beyond the ghetto: the Spiegel catalog.

Through those dream pages, Ophelia and I lived vicarious lives as we played a game we made up with the household's catalog. We called it " this-page-that-page," and it was played simply by flipping randomly to a page and then claiming all the treasures pictured on it as mine or hers. "Look at all my stuff," I'd say after flipping to my page. "Look at my furniture—all these clothes are mine!" and Ophelia would follow, flipping to her page, singing, "Look at my stuff, my nice stove and my jewelry!" The Spiegel catalog must have been three hundred pages or more, so we never tired of this-page-that-page.

In the dead of winter one year, we changed the game in recognition of Christmas. When it was Ophelia's turn, she flipped to a page and smiled her big-sister smile, announcing that this page was for me, pointing to all the stuff she was giving me for Christmas. "I'm giving you this page. All this is yours."

Then it was my turn. I flipped to a page and exclaimed, "I'm giving you this page for Christmas. This is all yours!" I wasn't sure what made me happier, getting a page all for me or having one to give.

In those hours spent playing this-page-that-page, there was no discussion about who Momma was, where she went, or when she was coming back. But there was a feeling of anticipation I recognized. We were biding time, waiting for something or someone to come for us. For that reason, it wasn't a shock or even a memorable instance when, at last, I learned that Momma was leaving wherever she'd been—prison, I now know—and that she was coming to get me and Ophelia and our baby sister Sharon, who suddenly appeared on the scene.

在阿奇舅舅看来，重量级拳击手乔·路易斯是任何人都望尘莫及的，更得到"褐色轰炸机"的美誉。舅舅的成长过程中一直没少过收音机里路易斯的比赛转播，躲闪腾挪、左击右打，都是通过收音机的声音来判别的。因此，阿奇舅舅根本不用听解说员的讲解，就能给我生动地讲评每场比赛，而且水平绝对上乘。如今，我们一同看着这些拳击手们创造奇迹，此时的拳手雷·罗宾森正逐渐步入辉煌，他与杰克·拉莫塔的一场鏖战让我永远难以忘怀。雷和其他拳手都具备非凡的品质，简直就是超级英雄，他们无所不能，随心所欲，甚至可以拥有一辆粉红色的卡迪拉克，那就相当于现在的红色法拉利。对于住在贫民区的穷孩子而言，这绝对是至神至圣，匪夷所思。但是雷和他的座驾只是在电视上才有的，我手边也有件宝贝，能让我看到贫民区以外的精彩世界，这就是斯皮格商品名录。

这本册子里花花绿绿琳琅满目的商品，让我们的生活变得多姿多彩，我们就用家用商品名录来玩翻页游戏，游戏很简单，就是随意翻到一页，然后就称其中的宝贝玩艺儿都归自己所有。我先翻到一页，"这些是我的"，然后姐姐奥菲丽娅翻到一页，"这些家具和衣服都是我的"，"还有炉子和珠宝也是"。这本名录足有三百多页，所以我们的翻页游戏总是玩都玩不够。

有一年的深冬时节，因为圣诞将至，我们把游戏稍作改动。先是轮到姐姐，她随手翻到一页，她脸上露出那种姐姐式的大度微笑，说那一页的好东西都送我了，就作为圣诞礼物。"这页是你的了，都归你了。"

然后轮到我，我也如法炮制，翻到一页，"圣诞节了，这些归你了。"我也搞不清自己为什么那么高兴，是自己得到一页礼物，还是自己送出一页礼物。

这种翻页游戏我们可以一连玩上几个小时，期间谁也不会提妈妈是谁，妈妈去哪了，或是妈妈什么时候回来这类问题，但我们不约而同地有着这样的期待。我们在等，在等着什么事情，或是什么人来到我们身边。因此，当得知妈妈真的要离开她在的地方（后来我才知道那地方叫监狱），回到姐姐和我的身边，还有个忽然冒出来的妹妹沙仑，我们甚至都很平静。

第一章 糖果

Though Momma's Cinderella story hadn't worked out like in the storybook, I had the briefly held idea that a fairy tale was about to happen in being reunited with my mother. All the happy memories of the beautiful woman who made me candy filled me with wondrous expectation, and for one brilliant flash of time the reality of our being together made me happier than anything I could have dreamt. But those feelings were rapidly overshadowed from almost the first moment that Freddie Triplett bulldozed his way into my life. You would think that I would have had a honeymoon phase with the man who had become Momma's husband and our stepfather, but he was my enemy from the second I laid eyes on him.

While I had no inkling of the violence he was going to cause in our lives, I must have sensed that he was mean and seemed to take pleasure in hurting my feelings. My hunch was confirmed when he launched the line he loved to throw at me every chance he got, which killed me every time he said it, stirring up the sediment of anger and resentment that would later erupt. Unprovoked, out of nowhere, he turned to me that first time I can recall seeing him and proclaimed in no uncertain terms, eyes blazing and voice blasting, "I ain't your goddamn daddy!"

虽然妈妈版的灰姑娘故事和书上写的不一样，但我觉得和母亲团聚就会有童话般的奇迹发生，但这种想法并没维持多久。所有关于那个给我做糖果的美丽女子的美好记忆都一起涌上心头，我们相聚的那一刻简直让我忘乎所以，那种幸福超乎了我的所有想象。但是这一切很快就化为乌有，因为继父弗莱迪·崔普雷特闯入了我的生活。也许，你会以为我和这个作为母亲现任丈夫和我继父的男人之间会有段所谓的蜜月时光，其实不然，从他看到我的那一刻起，他就决定要和我作对到底。

我那时对于他的危害和暴力程度还一无所知，但我还是感觉到他的暴戾和凶狠，他似乎觉得伤害我的情感就能给他带来无尽快乐。我的直觉很快得到证实，只要有可能，他就会训斥我，让愤怒和怨恨在我心头一天天地积累，而这些终有一天会爆发出来。头一次见到他时，他就无缘无故地大发雷霆，怒目圆睁，大声呵斥："我才不是你那见鬼的老爸！"

Chapter 2
The No-Daddy Blues

Chris! Chris, wake up!" lisps the three-year-old voice of my sister Sharon, her little hand tugging on my shoulder.

Without opening my eyes, I force myself to remember where I am. It's very late on Halloween night, and I'm in my bed that occupies most of the small room in the back house where we're living now—behind the "Big House" on Eighth and Wright that is owned by Freddie's sister Bessie. As soon as these facts register, I ease back down into sleep, wanting to rest just a little longer. The irony is that while sleep sometimes brings nightmares, it's the reality of my waking hours that can cause me the greater fear.

From the time that Momma came to get us, first taking me, Ophelia, and Sharon—who had been born in the women's correctional facility during that time my mother was away—to live with her and Freddie, life had changed drastically and mostly for the worse. The world of the unknown that overwhelmed me when we stayed with Uncle Archie and TT seemed wonderful by comparison to everything that took place in the territory of the familiar over which Freddie Triplett ruled. Moms gave us all the love, protection, and approval that she could, but often that seemed to make him more brutal than he already was.

第二章
渴望父爱

"哥哥,哥哥,快醒醒!" 3岁大的妹妹沙仑奶声奶气地喊,边喊还边扯着我的衣服。

我迷迷糊糊睁不开眼,努力想记起我这是在哪里。今天是万圣节,夜已经很深了。我躺在自己的小床上,这张床几乎占满了整间屋子。这间小屋在我们住的房子靠里的位置,在"大屋"的后面,而第八大道右街上的这座"大屋"是弗莱迪的姐姐贝希的财产。一想起这些,我就准备转身继续睡觉,想尽量多休息一会儿。虽然,睡觉有时也会做噩梦,但白天现实的生活还是让我更加恐惧。

从妈妈回来接我们团聚开始,我、奥菲利亚和母亲离开我们接受改造时生下的妹妹沙仑,我们几个就要直接面对继父弗莱迪了,生活的平静从此被打破,而且每况愈下。回想和阿奇舅舅、缇缇舅母一起的那段日子简直是天堂般的幸福生活,而与之相比,在继父弗莱迪这里我们简直不堪忍受。妈妈付出了她全部的爱,试图保护我们,并说可以让继父对我们好点,但实际效果却适得其反。

My instincts told me that the logical thing to do was to find some kind of way to get Freddie to like me. But no matter what I did, his response was to beat me down, often literally. Ophelia and I almost never got whippings when we lived with Uncle Archie and TT, but with Freddie we all got whupped all the time, usually for no good reason other than he was an illiterate, belligerent, abusive, and complete drunk.

Initially, I thought Freddie might be proud of my academic success. At five, six, and seven years old, school was a haven for me, a place where I seemed to thrive at learning and in social interactions. My early exposure to books paid off, and with Momma's continuing encouragement, I quickly mastered reading. One of my favorite teachers, Mrs. Broderick, reinforced my love of books by frequently asking me to read aloud—longer than any of my classmates. Since we didn't have a television at this time, reading became all the more meaningful at home, especially because Momma loved to sit down after her long day of working as a domestic to hear what I had read or learned that day.

My mother still clung to the hope that she would one day obtain the necessary schooling and licensing to teach in the state of Wisconsin. Until that time, she devoted herself to doing what she had to do to take care of her four children—Ophelia, myself, Sharon, and the youngest, my baby sister Kim, who arrived in this time period. While Momma didn't complain about her days spent cleaning rich (white) people's houses, she didn't talk about her work either, instead living vicariously through reports of what my teachers had taught that day or by looking with me at some of the picture storybooks that I brought home. *The Red Balloon* was one book that I could read over and over, sitting next to Momma and showing her the photographic illustrations of a magical city where a little boy and his red balloon went flying, exploring the rooftops. Momma's eyes lit up with a beautiful serenity, as if she was somewhere up in the clouds, maybe dreaming of being that balloon and flying up, up, and away. I never knew that the magical city in the story was a place called Paris in a country called France. And I certainly had no idea that I would visit Paris on several occasions.

My accomplishments as an elementary school student obviously made Moms proud. But if I ever fooled myself into thinking this was going to win me points with Freddie, I was sadly mistaken. In fact, Freddie Triplett—who could not read or write to save his life—spent every minute waging a one-man antiliteracy campaign. In his early thirties at this time, Freddie had stopped his schooling in the third grade back in Mississippi and couldn't even dial a telephone until later in his life, and he could barely do it then. This undoubtedly fed a deep-seated insecurity in him that he covered up by declaring that anybody who could read or write was a "slick motherfucker."

我本能地认为，得想办法让继父喜欢上我，但不管我怎么努力，他都会把我的希望摔得粉碎，而且拳脚相加。在舅舅那里，我们几乎从未挨过打，但继父打我们那就是家常便饭，而这通常根本不需要任何理由，只要他喝得醉醺醺，四处撒酒疯时，我们就成了出气筒。

开始，我还以为如果自己学习成绩好，会讨得继父的欢心。在我六、七岁左右的时候，学校几乎成了我的避难所，我拼命学习，在学校的氛围中找到慰藉。从幼年开始接触书本确实让我受益匪浅，加之母亲的不断鼓励，我很快就能读书认字了。我最喜欢的女老师布罗德里克太太进一步帮我增强了对书本的兴趣，她常常要我在同学面前朗读课文，而别的同学就没这么幸运。因为当时家里没有电视，所以阅读就显得愈发的重要，特别是妈妈喜欢在忙完一天繁重的家务活后，坐下来听我讲述当天具体学了些什么内容。

母亲还一直觉得自己有一天能接受学校教育，获得在威斯康星州的教学资质。那时，母亲把心思都放在照料四个孩子身上，姐姐奥菲利亚、我、妹妹沙仑，还有刚出生的小妹金牡。妈妈任劳任怨，白天要去帮助有钱人（白人）打扫房间，晚上如饥似渴地听我讲述当天学的功课，或是和我一起看我带回家的故事画册。《红气球》这本书我百读不厌，坐在妈妈身边，给她看故事的插图，书里讲的是在一座魔法城市里，有个小男孩和他的红气球一起飞上了天，在屋顶探险的故事。妈妈的眼睛闪着美丽而宁静的光芒，仿佛她自己也飞上了云端，也乘着红气球一起飞，飞得越来越远。我当时根本不知道故事发生的这座魔法城市就是巴黎，是在一个叫法国的地方。更想不到，后来我会不止一次地去过巴黎。

我在小学取得的成绩着实让妈妈感到自豪，但我若是还认为自己能靠成绩讨得继父的欢心，那就大错特错了。实际上继父弗莱迪大字不识一个，他一生孜孜不倦地独自高举反扫盲大旗，决心要把反对识字的斗争进行到底。继父当时已经三十出头，可是在密西西比他上到小学三年级就放弃了学业。打电话这种事他还是很久以后才学会的，当时他连这都不会。所有这些自然让他没有安全感，为试图掩饰这一点，他称所有能读会写的人都是"狗娘养的"。

第二章　渴望父爱

Of course, in his logic, this would have included Momma, me, my sisters, or anybody he thought knew something that he didn't, which meant they could take advantage of him. You could see it in the crazed flare of his eyes that he lived in a world full of slick motherfuckers out to get him. Mix that attitude with alcohol and the result was big-time paranoia.

Though I started to figure out some of these dynamics early on, for a while I was actually willing to see past them and to be on my best behavior in the hopes that he'd somehow find a fatherly side of himself with me. That hope was shattered one afternoon during a visit from Sam Salter, Ophelia's daddy.

In an odd matchup, Salter and Freddie turned out to be great friends and drinking buddies. This made no sense, not only because both had kids by Moms, but also because they were so different. Just as he did every time he visited, Salter entered a room with warmth and a southern gentleman's charm. A nicely dressed, articulate high school teacher—who could read and write and talk trash so good everybody thought he was a lawyer, although Freddie never once accused him of being a slick motherfucker—Samuel Salter had nothing in common with Freddie Triplett, who took over any space he entered by siege. Sometimes Freddie cleared a room at gunpoint, waving his shotgun, hollering, "Get the fuck outta my goddamn house!" Other times Freddie cleared the room with a rant, gesticulating angrily with a lit Pall Mall in one hand and his ever-present half-pint of whiskey in the other.

Old Taylor was Freddie's brand of choice, but he also drank Old Granddad and Old Crow, or basically any half-pint of whiskey he could wrap his hands around. He didn't have a hip flask for his whiskey, like some of the more sophisticated black men I saw. Dressed in his workingman's uniform that consisted of jeans or khakis, a wool shirt, a T-shirt underneath, always, and work shoes, Freddie just carried his little half-pint bottle. Everywhere. It was an appendage. How he managed to keep his job at A. O. Smith— eventually retiring from there, pension and all—was another mystery to me. Granted, as a steel man, he was a hard worker. But he was an even harder drinker.

That afternoon when Salter arrived, Ophelia and I ran to greet him, followed immediately by Freddie's arrival in the living room. Whenever he came by, Salter brought a little something for us— usually two dollars for Ophelia, his real blood daughter, and one dollar for me, because he treated me as a pretend son. This day we went through the routine, with Ophelia getting a hug and a kiss and her two dollars before skipping off, waving, "Bye, Daddy!" and then it was my turn.

Salter grinned at my open hand and didn't make me wait, commending me first on my good work at school and then handing me the crisp single dollar bill. Happy feelings swirled up inside, and I couldn't help it as I asked, "Ain't you my daddy too?"

当然，若是按照他的逻辑，这其中也应该包括妈妈、姐姐和我在内，或是任何学问比他多的人，因为他们很可能会占他的便宜。从仇视的目光中，其实不难看出他每天就生活在这些"狗娘养的"人们中间，他们似乎时刻都在惦记着要揩他的油水。这种情绪再与酒精相混合就产生了严重的偏执与妄想。

虽然我逐渐开始意识到这其中的玄机，但是在一段时间内，我还是努力表现出自己最好的一面，希望以此感化继父，能唤醒他身上哪怕是一丁点儿的父爱。但一天下午，这个希望也破灭了，因为家里来了位客人，萨缪尔·梭特先生，也就是姐姐奥菲丽娅的亲生父亲。

机缘巧合，梭特和继父居然成了好友，酒桌上的兄弟。这实在是匪夷所思，不仅是因为他们和妈妈都有过孩子，而且两人差距实在太大。每次梭特来家里的时候，整个屋子都会充满一种特别的温暖，他周身都散发着那种南方绅士特有的魅力。他衣着得体，吐字清晰，是个典型的高中教师，他不仅识文断字，而且口才极好，说起话来滔滔不绝，甚至会让人误以为他是个律师。虽然继父弗莱迪从来没说梭特也是"狗娘养的"，但他们俩实在是相差太远，因为继父总是习惯用武力解决问题。有时继父会端着枪在屋子里开道，挥舞着他的猎枪，大喊大叫："让这些该死的东西给老子滚出去！"有时他会一手拿着半瓶威士忌，一手拿着点着的宝马烟，大声咆哮，手里还比比划划，在屋里横冲直撞。

老泰勒威士忌是弗莱迪的最爱，不过他也喝老祖父威士忌、老乌鸦威士忌或是顺手抄起的半品脱威士忌也完全可以。和那些讲究的黑人不同，他自己没有专用的威士忌小酒壶。他总穿一身工作服，牛仔布或卡其布，羊毛衬衫，穿件T恤衫当内衣，再加一双工作鞋，还有就是寸步不离身的小酒瓶子。就这样他居然能在艾欧史密斯公司一直干到退休，养老金什么的一分不少，这对我而言又是个不解之谜。的确，他是个尽职尽责的钢铁工人，但是喝起酒来，他更是尽力又尽心。

下午当梭特来的时候，奥菲丽娅和我跑上去迎他，很快继父弗莱迪也进了客厅。梭特每次来都会带点小东西，通常是给自己亲生的女儿两美元，给我一美元，因为他把我也看作是他的养子。今天也毫不例外，梭特先是抱了抱姐姐，亲亲她的脸颊，把两美元放在她手心，然后姐姐挥挥手，蹦蹦跳跳地跑开了，"爸爸，再见！"然后就该轮到我了。

梭特看着我张开的手心，倒也没让我久等，先是夸我学校功课不错，然后就给了我张崭新的一美元钞票。我心里乐开了花，周身洋溢着幸福的感觉，忍不住问了一句："你不就是我的爸爸吗？"

第二章 渴望父爱

"Yeah," said Salter, nodding his head thoughtfully, "I'm your daddy too. Here—" and he took out another dollar bill that he handed to me, saying, "Now you go and put that in your bank, son."

With a big smile on my face, even though I had no bank, I started to turn and strut off, one dollar richer, with Ophelia's daddy agreeing to be my daddy too, when I was met by Freddie's scowl as he bellowed, out of nowhere, "Well, I ain't your goddamned daddy, and you ain't getting shit from me!"

Talk about bursting my balloon. For a moment I glanced back at Salter, who shot Freddie a strange look that went right over my head and Freddie's as well. Probably Salter meant something along the lines of what I was feeling—that Freddie had no call to say anything, number one 'cause I was talking to Salter at the time, and number two 'cause it was cruel and unusual punishment. Freddie had just made his point one too many times, on top of his incessant commentary about the size of my ears.

Even when I was standing nearby, whenever anybody asked about where I was, he answered with a roar, "I don't know where that big-eared motherfucker is."

Then, as if he did not care, he'd turn and look at me with a grin—like it made him a bigger man for stomping on me and my self-esteem—while I stood there and felt my naturally dark shade of skin burn red with hurt and embarrassment.

Another time I was in the bathroom when I heard someone asking for me and had to hear Freddie snarl, "I don't know where that big-eared motherfucker is," behind my back. It was bad enough when he said it in front of me, especially since he enjoyed watching me try to mask my seven-year-old pain, but it was almost worse hearing him say it when he really didn't know where I was. Besides, when I looked at my ears in the bathroom mirror to see how big they were, I realized they were sort of big, which made his comments sting all the more. It didn't matter that I would grow into them one day.

Between Freddie's remarks and some of the kids in the neighborhood and at school calling me "Dumbo"—the flying elephant from the Disney cartoon movie—a toll was being taken on my self-esteem, compounded by the gaping hole left by having no daddy. Everybody else knew who their daddy was. Ophelia's daddy was Salter, Sharon and Kim had Freddie, my friends all had daddies. That needless comment from Freddie that afternoon when Salter gave me the one dollar made it clear to my young sensibilities, finally, that he was never going to warm to me. The question for me then became—what could I do about it?

"对呀，"梭特若有所思地点点头，"我就是你爸爸，来，拿着……"接着又掏出一美元递给我说："儿子，去把钱存到你的银行户头上吧。"

我乐得合不拢嘴，虽然我没有银行户头，但是突然多出的一美元，加上奥菲丽娅的爸爸同意做我的爸爸，让我兴奋不已。我正要转身，却听到继父弗莱迪狮子般的怒吼从天而降："好啊，我不是你这兔崽子的爹，给我滚得远远的！"

也就在那一刻，我瞟了身后的梭特一眼，看到他用一种奇怪的眼神看着弗莱迪，也许梭特心里想的和我不谋而合，就是弗莱迪说这些毫无道理，首先，我是在和梭特说话，其次，他的话实在过于伤人、过于蛮横无理。弗莱迪其实已无数次地重复过他的这些观点，此外还不断地挖苦我的大耳朵。

即便我就站在一旁，人们问起我是谁的孩子的时候，他也会咆哮道："鬼才知道这个大耳朵狗娘养的东西是谁的。"

然后他仿佛毫不在意似的，转过身来咧着嘴看着我，仿佛把我踩在他的脚下，碾碎我的自尊心，就能给他带来极大快感。受到这种侮辱，我即便是黑皮肤，此时也感觉脸已经窘得红到耳根。

还有一次，我在洗手间，听到外面有人找我，接着传来弗莱迪的咆哮："我怎么知道这个大耳朵狗娘养的东西在哪儿？！"他在人前这么说我已经让我忍无可忍，特别是看到我极力掩饰这话给我七岁的幼小心灵所带来的痛楚时，他是相当的满足，但听到他在不知道我在附近的情况下，还这么说，我几乎痛不欲生。我站在浴室的镜子前仔细端详自己的耳朵，想看看到底我的耳朵有多大，结果发现确实不小，这使得他的话显得愈发刺耳，即便是我长大后，这种感觉还让我心有余悸。

除了弗莱迪的恶言恶语不说，学校和邻居的孩子们也戏称我为小飞象"邓波"，就是迪士尼卡通片里的那只小飞象。所有这些仿佛是悬在我头上的利剑，时刻准备把我的自尊自信劈个粉碎，加上没有个名正言顺的父亲，对我而言这更是雪上加霜的事情。别人都知道自己的父亲是谁，姐姐奥菲丽娅知道梭特是她的父亲，弗莱迪是沙仑和金牡的父亲。再说，我那些朋友个个都有自己的父亲。那天下午，当梭特给我一块钱的时候，在我敏感的幼小心灵深处，已经清楚地意识到，我从继父那里是得不到丝毫温暖的。现在的问题是我该怎么办。

第二章 渴望父爱

My long-term plan had already been formulated, starting with the solemn promise I made to myself that when I grew up and had a son of my own, he would always know who I was and I would never disappear from his life. But the short-term plan was much harder to figure out. How could I fend off the powerlessness not only of having no daddy and of being labeled "you big-eared motherfucker" but, much more damaging to my psyche, the powerlessness that came from the fear that never seemed to let up at home.

It was fear of what Freddie might do and what he'd already done. Big-time fear. Fear that I'd come home to find my mother murdered. Fear that my sisters and I would be murdered. Fear that the next time Freddie came home drunk, pulled out his shotgun, and woke all of us at the end of the barrel, shouting, "Everybody get the fuck outta my goddamned house!" he'd make good on his promise to kill us all. It had gotten to the point by this time that Moms slept on the living room couch with her shoes on—in case she had to run, carrying the baby and dragging the rest of us out of the house fast. Fear that the next time Freddie beat Momma up within an inch of her life he would go that inch too far. Fear that I'd have to watch that beating or watch Freddie beat Ophelia or take the beating myself and not be able to do anything to stop it. What could I do that the police couldn't or wouldn't, as many times as they'd show up and either do nothing or take Freddie away and send him home after he sobered up?

The questions of what was I going to do and how was I going to do it loomed large. They followed me at school, snuck into my waking and sleeping thoughts, and stirred up the nightmares that had troubled me most of my young life, nightmares that went back to foster care when there was a supposed witch down the street. Some of the dreams I was having were so terrifying, I was too paralyzed to wake, believing in my sleep that if I could knock something over, a bedside lamp, for example, it would rouse someone in the house to come to my rescue and help me escape whatever terror was in that dream at the time.

"Chris!" Sharon's voice pierces my semiconscious state once more.

Now I open my eyes, sitting bolt upright, taking a fast inventory. Before I went to sleep, nothing eventful had happened, other than some Halloween trick-or-treating, after which Ophelia went to a party with her friends—where she is, apparently, at the present. Otherwise, it had been a fairly quiet night in the back house that we rent from my entrepreneurial aunt, Miss Bessie, the first in our extended family to own a home—which houses her beauty salon business, Bessie's Hair Factory, in the basement.

Crying, Sharon pulls at my sleeve, telling me, "Momma's on the floor."

我已经制定了长远的打算，我暗下决心，等我长大后，有了自己的儿子，一定要让他明明白白地知道自己的父亲是谁，而且我永远不会弃他而去，丢下他不管。但我一时间还想不出什么好的短期计划，怎么才能把"没爹的孩子"、"大耳朵狗娘养的东西"这种无形的标签拽下来，它不仅压得我喘不过气来，也在无情地撕扯着我的自尊，让我坠入一种深刻的恐惧和无尽的黑暗之中，无法自拔。

这种恐惧来自继父弗莱迪在家的所作所为，来自他可能会愈发的变本加厉。我害怕自己一回家发现妈妈已经性命不保；担心姐姐妹妹以及自己都随时可能一命呜呼；担心继父弗莱迪再喝得烂醉，回家把睡梦中的我们打醒，用枪口对着我们，"狗娘养的，都给我滚出去！"他不止一次声称要把我们全都干掉。现在妈妈每天都是穿着鞋睡在客厅的长椅上，就是为了一旦有意外，可以迅速抱上孩子，拽上我们去逃命。我还怕下次他再对妈妈动粗，要是妈妈躲闪不及怎么办，而我在一旁束手无策，只能眼睁睁地看着。要是他对姐姐奥菲丽娅大打出手，那我也根本没有任何办法，或者干脆就是对我拳脚相加，而我也只能就这么忍着，我到底该怎么办，警察来了也帮不上忙，因为以前他们来了也根本无济于事，或最多是把继父带走，等他酒醒了再放回来，仅此而已。

我该做什么？究竟该怎么做？这个问题压得我喘不过气来，就连在学校也会时不时受到这个问题的困扰，我为此寝食难安，坐卧不宁，甚至让我想起那些在福利院做过的噩梦，那是因为大家都以为街上住的那个老太太是个巫婆，小时候最恐怖的时候也就莫过于此。有些梦实在可怕，吓得我醒都醒不过来，在梦里我觉得若能碰倒床头灯之类的东西，屋里的人听到就来救我，让我离开梦中的是非之地。

"哥哥！"我在半梦半醒间，又听到小妹沙仑的声音。

我睁开眼睛，坐起身来，回想了一下都发生了些什么事。睡前，除了万圣节的"不给糖就捣蛋"游戏，家里什么事都没发生，之后，姐姐奥菲丽娅去参加了派对，看来她到现在还没回来。今天晚上后屋相当的安静，这里是我们从贝希姑姑那租来的，她自己做生意，而且在我们亲友当中只有她有房产，这房子的地下室就是她的美容沙龙——贝希美发屋。

沙仑带着哭腔，拽着我的袖子，说："妈妈在地上。"

Not knowing what I'm going to find, I throw off the covers, grab my robe, and hurry down the hall into the front room. There, lying face down on the floor, is Momma, unconscious, a two-by-four stuck in the back of her head and a pool of blood spreading underneath and around her. Sharon's cries begin to escalate as she stares down at our mother alongside me. "Wake up, wake up!" she screams. "Wake up!"

Fighting the paralysis of shock, I feel some other mechanism take over, and my immediate reaction is to assess what has taken place, like a crime-scene analyst.

First I observe that Momma was trying to get out of the house and move toward the door when Freddie attacked her with the two-by-four, bashing it into the back of her skull with such a force that the wood splintered into her skin, sticking into her, spewing blood not just underneath her but everywhere in the room.

Next, feeling the waves of terror that Momma is dead or about to die, I turn to see Baby on the telephone calling the ambulance. Freddie's baby sister, affectionately known as Baby, reassures me that the paramedics are on their way and goes to calm Sharon.

Amid all my senses trying to compute the mess of blood, fear, my sister's sobbing, and Baby's insistence that Momma is going to the hospital and she is going to be all right, and more blood, the volcanic question of *What can I do?* erupts in me. The answer: clean the stove! I have to do something, anything. I need a job, a duty to perform. So I race to the kitchen and begin to scrub our old-fashioned cookstove that seems like it's been used since the time of the Pilgrims and is caked with a grime of an unknown lineage. Using a scrap of a dishrag, Brillo, and soap and water, I commence to clean and scour with all my being, at the same time that I commence to pray. My prayer is even more elaborate than *Oh, God, please don't let Momma die*. It's that, but it's also *God, please don't let anyone come in here and see this place all dirty like this*.

The idea that the white paramedics and policemen will see the blood everywhere and then the dirty stove as well is too shameful to bear. So my job is to clean it up, to prove that decent people live here, not savages, with the exception of Freddie, who has drawn blood, once again, from a woman.

When the ambulance came, the attendants moved in quickly, spoke to Baby and Bessie, not to me of course, put Momma on a stretcher, with the two-by-four removed, took her out to the ambulance, and drove off.

Even then I continued to clean, the only task I could find to create order in the chaos. The world became very small for me that night. A part of me shut down in a way that froze me emotionally but was also necessary for my survival.

不知道到底出了什么事，我把被子扔到一边，抓起睡袍，匆匆跑去厅房，来到前屋。妈妈躺在地上一动不动，全无知觉，有个木板嵌在脑后，她身下和四周流了一摊血。看到妈妈不省人事，沙仑的哭声越来越高，"醒醒，醒醒！"她尖声喊着，"妈妈醒醒。"

我惊得目瞪口呆，慢慢才缓过神来，我的第一反应就是学着警察做犯罪现场分析，判断到底出了什么事。

首先我注意到，当继父用木板袭击妈妈时，她是想逃出家门去的，木板直接打到她的后脑勺上，用力太大导致木头直接打进皮肉之中，不只她身下有一摊血，血渍溅得到处都是。

接下来，让我惊恐万分的是妈妈是不是还活着，是不是危在旦夕。一旁的保姆贝碧（她主要负责照看妹妹）正在忙着打电话叫救护车，想到医护人员已经朝这里赶来，我才稍稍松了口气，转身安慰沙仑。

血渍、恐惧，妹妹在抽泣，贝碧一直在念叨，只要到了医院妈妈就没事了，屋里到处是血迹，我努力想从这一切中理出个头绪来。"我该做点什么"，这个问题一下子跳了出来，答案是收拾厨灶！我总得让自己手里忙些什么事情，做什么都行。我需要让自己做点事，所以我飞快地跑到厨房，开始擦洗家里的老式厨灶，这厨灶似乎从清教徒时期起就开始用了，但已经满是煤烟。拿了块抹布、肥皂，还有水，我开始全力清洗这个大家伙，同时我不停地祈祷，祈祷的内容五花八门什么都有，比如："主啊，别让妈妈死"，然后还有"主啊，别让人们进来，看到这里这么乱糟糟的"。

一想到那些白人医护人员，还有警察看到屋子里到处是血，再有这个脏兮兮的炉灶，实在是太难为情了。所以我要把这里收拾干净，让人觉得住在这儿的这家人是很讲究的，不是邋邋遢遢的。继父是个例外，他又一次让家里的女人受皮肉之苦，还流了血。

救护车到了，救护人员马上进屋来，和保姆贝碧和贝希了解了情况，当然没人顾及我，他们取下妈妈头上的木板，把她抬上担架，上了救护车，急驰而去。

即便在这时，我还在努力收拾着，想从混乱中找出条理来，这是我能想出的唯一法子。那天夜里，我的世界一下子变得那么小，我把自己完全封闭起来，让自己的情感冰封雪藏，也只有这样我才能熬过来。

My efforts didn't save Momma. Apparently what saved her was her thickheadedness. Literally. Thanks to the strength and resilience of her skull, Freddie's attempt to kill her had failed. She returned the next day, bandaged, battered, but conscious enough to promise he was never going to be allowed to return. With a resolve I hadn't heard before, she looked us all in the eyes and swore, "Well, he ain't coming back in here no more."

We might have gone an entire week without him, but before I could relax he had returned after all. I knew this roller coaster. We'd been on it since I could remember. Every time he came back, apologetic, contrite, he'd start off being real nice. But he was as predictable as rain. Nobody knew when he'd go off, but at some point everybody knew he would. Again, and again, and again.

Why Moms fell for it each time was confusing, without question. By the same token, I understood that we were sometimes in the most dangerous straits when we were trying to get away.

While I had no control over the short term, I expanded my long-term plan. Not only was I going to make sure my children had a daddy, I was never going to be Freddie Triplett. I was never going to terrorize, threaten, harm, or abuse a woman or a child, and I was never going to drink so hard that I couldn't account for my actions. This plan evolved over time as I studied at the virtual college of how to grow up and not be Freddie. For now, I could only hate him. It was an emotional truth that lived under my skin, close to the bone.

Small flickers of rebellion had begun to flare. As an antidote to my feeling of powerlessness, I did little things just to see if I could mess with Freddie. For instance, I knew that he couldn't read and was threatened by anyone who could—which gave me an opening.

Sometimes I'd start reading aloud, for no reason other than sending him a message—*I may have big ears, but I can read. Real good. You can beat us down, but you can't read.* Other times I was even more calculating, holding my book and pointing to a word as I asked Momma, very loud to make sure Freddie heard, "What does this word mean?" Or another variation: "What does this spell?" Or, at my most devilish, I might, out of the blue, ask her how to spell a particular word.

Momma had only to give me a gentle look, telling me just with the expression in her eyes—*Son, you know very well what the answer is*. It was our unspoken conspiracy, our private agreement that he wasn't going to break us. Then, out loud, she'd say, "I don't know," and the two of us would smile at each other with our eyes.

我所有这些努力没能帮上妈妈什么忙，倒是多亏她自己的头骨结实才让她捡回一条命来。第二天，她满头绷带，颤颤巍巍，但神志还算清楚，说绝对不许继父再回到这个家来。她能如此痛下这种决心，我还是头一次听到，她对我们大家，郑重发誓："他再也不可以回到这里了。"

接下来的整整一周，我们都没见到继父的影子，正当我刚要舒一口气时，他却回来了。这种反复我并不陌生。从我记事起，就是这样了。每次他回来都会信誓旦旦，要痛改前非。但是他的反复无常我们早已见怪不怪。谁也不知道他什么时候又会故伎重演，但是大家知道这是迟早的事，周而复始，没完没了。

我搞不清为什么妈妈每次都会心软，我也没问过。基于同样的理由，我知道每当我们想逃离这里时，往往会使我们处于更加危险的境地。

虽然短时期内，对于现状，我无计可施。但我进一步丰富了自己的长期计划。不但以后我的孩子要知道自己的父亲是谁，而且我也绝不会成为继父那样的人，不会威胁、恐吓、伤害女人和孩子，更不会使用暴力。我也绝对不会过度饮酒，让自己行为失控。这个计划不断地发展完善，仿佛弗莱迪是在给我上课，教会我怎样成长，怎样不去变成像他那样的人。而在当时我对他有的只是仇恨，那种渗透在我的血液里和骨子里的仇恨。

些许报复的小火苗在悄悄燃烧，对于一直困扰我的无能为力而言，这似乎是一剂解药。我就做点小小的尝试，看看自己到底能把继父怎么样。比如，我知道他自己不认字，因此感觉受到所有识文断字人的威胁，从这里我想出了点门道。

有时，我故意大声朗读，其实没什么理由，就是想让他知道：也许我耳朵确实比别人大，但我会读书，而且还成绩优异，你可以对我们大打出手，但你就是不认字。有时候，我还更过分，捧着书，故意问妈妈，声音大到继父肯定能听得到，"这是什么啊？"或是换个说法："这个字该怎么写呢？"有时我甚至就干脆问他本人，某个字该怎么写。

妈妈总是温柔地看着我，用她会说话的眼睛告诉我：儿子，答案你自己清楚的啊。这是我俩的秘密，知道他也奈何不了我们，所以她就大着嗓门回答："我不会，不知道。"然后我们两个相视一笑，开心之极。

Finally, in the dead of night that same winter after the two-by-four incident, Moms enlisted me and the rest of us in a full-scale rebellion. After Freddie unleashed on her, for the umpteenth time, and left the house to go drink in one of several local watering holes in the neighborhood, Momma got up from the floor, put ice on her swelling face, and began packing, urging us to help.

"We have to move," she said simply as Ophelia and I helped pack, throwing our clothes and stuff into bags, gathering up whatever we could because we knew, without being told, that time was of the essence. Instead of going to stay with relatives, we were moving to a place that Momma had rented on Sixth Street, just two blocks over from the back house on Eighth and Wright. After we piled everything into a shopping cart that we wheeled together over to the new place, all four of us in tow, I watched her face fall as she frantically rummaged in her pockets and purse. Looking up at the second-floor apartment, she shook her head mournfully, saying, "The key . . . I don't have the key." She looked shell-shocked, completely defeated.

Studying the building, I pointed to a pole, telling Momma, "I can climb up there, jump down on the porch, come through the window, and then open the door from inside." Being a scrappy, skinny kid at the time—used to climbing up tall trees for the fun of it—I not only thought I could do it, it was imperative that I succeed at opening up that door to our new life, free of Freddie. It was having a job to do, something concrete, and it was also a battle between him and me. I had to win. As proposed, I executed my plan—scaling the pole to the roof, jumping down from the roof to the porch, thankfully raising the window on the porch level, and sliding inside. From there, I opened the apartment door and flew downstairs, where the relieved look on my mother's face was all I needed to see. As we all settled in that night, I couldn't have felt more proud of myself.

Over the next few days Moms caught me looking worried and knew that I was scared Freddie would show up and try to conquer our new land.

"He ain't coming back," she reassured me in words. "No more. He ain't never coming back."

One evening I was summoned to the living room in the new place by the sound of a man's voice that seemed to be threatening. The conversation was about money or rent. Instead of belonging to Freddie, the voice turned out to be that of a white man I'd never seen before. A nondescript fellow in layers of winter clothes appropriate for the season, he was speaking in a disrespectful way that caused my mother to tremble.

Almost by reflex, I ran to the kitchen and returned with a butcher knife, pointing it at the white man. "You can't talk to my momma like that," I interrupted.

最后，就是发生木板事件的同一年冬天，深夜，妈妈和我以及其他孩子一道准备真正意义上的反抗了。弗莱迪用皮带抽打妈妈，这已经不知是多少次了，然后他扬长而去，到附近的酒馆喝个烂醉。妈妈从地上爬起来，用冰块敷在自己红肿的脸上，寻求我们的帮助。

"我们必须离开这里"，她没再多说什么，姐姐奥菲丽娅和我就开始收拾行李，把衣服和杂物收在袋子里，没等她发话，就很快干完，因为大家都知道此时此刻时间就是一切。我们没再和什么亲戚住在一起，母亲在第六街租了个住处，离第八大道右街的后屋只有两个街区的距离，我们把所有的家当都堆在一个购物车上，四个人站成一排就准备上路了。这时，我看到她神色慌乱，在口袋和钱包中翻来找去。抬头看着二楼的房门，她悲伤地摇了摇头："钥匙……我没有钥匙。"说完，她整个人几乎都要垮了。

仔细看了看建筑的构造，我指着一个杆子说，我可以爬上去，跳到走廊上，爬进窗子，从里面把门打开。我当时瘦瘦小小的，爬树对我而言不在话下。我不仅相信自己一定能做得到，更重要的是此举绝非寻常，这扇门是要通往新的生活，从此我们就不再受弗莱迪的骚扰。现在我知道自己要做什么了，要做些实实在在的事情，此时的我要和弗莱迪开战。我别无选择，只能赢。就按我说的，我逐步实施着自己的计划，顺着杆子爬上屋顶，从屋顶跳到走廊，幸好，窗户正好开着，我就势溜了进去，从里面把门打开，我飞奔到楼下，母亲的脸上满是自豪与欣慰，这对我来说比什么都重要。我们当晚就安顿下来，我从未感受过如此的心满意足。

接下来的几天，母亲看到我忧心忡忡，知道我是担心弗莱迪会再找上门来，把我们再次控制在他的魔爪之下。

"他不会来的，"母亲安慰我说，"他再也不会来打扰我们了。"

一天晚上，我正在新家的客厅，听到有个男人大嗓门说话的声音，似乎在威胁着什么，好像是在说钱或是房租的事情。但那人不是弗莱迪，而是个我以前从没见过的白人。那家伙穿着厚厚的冬衣，说话毫不客气，母亲在一旁吓得瑟瑟发抖。

几乎条件反射一般，我冲进厨房，拿了把切肉刀就转身回来，用刀指着那个白人，怒吼道："不许你这么和妈妈说话。"

第二章 渴望父爱

My mother threw me a look that spoke volumes, warning me to amend my tone and my words, to be polite.

I sent her a look right back, telling her that I would obey her. Turning back to the man, knife still in hand, I spoke again, this time saying, "You can't talk to my momma like that, *Mister*."

He backed down, soon leaving us alone. It was, unfortunately, not the last time I heard that dismissive, superior tone being used toward my mother, my siblings, and myself. Throughout my life I would battle that same reflex to want to strike back when certain individuals of a different race or class spoke to me in that way.

The more immediate consequence was that Freddie came back. The roller coaster crested the top and plunged down again. Each time I hated him that much more. Barely gone more than a week, we packed up and returned to the back house, with Freddie giving us a respite of no less than a week without violence. Disappointment, and not understanding why, ate at me. Because I didn't know that Momma had been in prison before, I couldn't yet grasp that she was mostly afraid that Freddie would send her back again. Only later would I fully understand that she had little financial independence, certainly not enough to raise four kids, and no means of escape, but I could already sense that she was stuck between the proverbial rock and a hard place.

This made my need to find that remedy to fix our situation that much more urgent. The answer came one Sunday afternoon, while watching Freddie eat a plate of Momma's cooking—in this case, her unrivaled neck bones. As a rule, watching Freddie eat was as close as a city boy like me ever got to a pig trough. But on this occasion it only took this once to watch him suck, break, and knock neck bones on the kitchen table to experience permanent revulsion. Lacking any sense of embarrassment, Freddie not only embraced the porcine essence of himself while eating but combined that with the apparent ability to fart, belch, and sneeze all at once. Who was this Sonny Liston–looking and –acting, Pall Mall–smoking, whiskey-drinking, gun-crazed giant pig man? Where was the humanity in a man who didn't seem to give a damn what anyone else thought of him and never missed an opportunity to batter, insult, embarrass, or humiliate any of us, especially me? Was it because I was the only male in the house, because I could read, because I was my mother's only son, or a combination of all of those things and others known only to himself?

The answers to those questions were long in coming, if ever. But finally, I had an answer to what my short-term plan of action should be. I wasn't even eight years old when it hit me like a strike of lightning, that Sunday afternoon, watching him suck on those bones as I thought to myself: *I'm gonna kill this motherfucker.*

* * *

母亲瞅了我一眼,让我注意措辞和语气,要礼貌些。

我们对视一下,我用眼神示意自己会听妈妈的话。我转身面对那个男人,手里依旧拎着刀,又说了一遍,但是口气缓和了些:"先生,请不要这么和我妈妈说话。"

他转身走了,屋里只留下我和妈妈。不过遗憾的是,这不是最后一次别人用这种趾高气扬、居高临下的语气对妈妈、对我以及姐姐妹妹发号施令。在以后的日子里,当那些白人或有钱人这么和我说话时,我一直都在咬牙克制着自己反击的冲动。

需要我们马上面对的事情就是弗莱迪又回来了。他周而复始的性格反复又要开始了。每经历这么一次反复,我对他的仇恨则会再添几分。刚刚一个多星期,我们又要收拾行李,回到那间后屋,而太平的日子弗莱迪最多能坚持个把星期。失望和不解啃噬着我的心。因为我当时不知道,妈妈曾经入狱,她最怕弗莱迪会再把她弄到监狱里去。再往后,我才完全明白,妈妈经济上无法独立,更无法养活四个孩子,所以就根本谈不上能逃脱了,但在当时我能理解的是妈妈确实有难处,她进退维谷。

我现在当务之急是必须马上想出应对之策。一个周日的下午,我突然有了个主意。当时我正看着弗莱迪在吃妈妈做的饭菜,是美味至极的炖猪颈骨。看弗莱迪进食就像城里的小孩看肥猪在猪食盆狼吞虎咽一般,我的内心总是充满了厌恶。但这次不一样,看着他敲骨吸髓,吧嗒着嘴,在餐桌上磕打着骨头,我对他的厌恶已经达到了极点。弗莱迪根本不知羞耻,因为他自己不仅吃相猪样十足,而且打嗝、放屁、打喷嚏从不掩饰,样样精通。就是这样一个粗鄙男人,不仅长相,甚至暴烈的性情和极强的攻击性和拳王桑尼·里斯顿颇有相似,而且天天叼着宝马烟,再加上嗜酒如命,还有威士忌不离手,此外还动辄就举枪对准自己的家人。他从不放过任何机会去嘲笑、侮辱、斥责、辱骂我们,特别是我,丝毫不会顾及别人对他的看法,这样一个人身上怎么会有人性可言。是因为我是家里除他以外唯一的男性?还是因为我能读书认字?抑或我是妈妈唯一的儿子?要么这其中有着很多只有他自己才知道的隐情?就不得而知了。

不知要过多久我才能真正找出这些问题的答案。但最终,我还是先明确了自己的短期行动计划究竟该如何实施。在那个周日的下午,看他啃着肉骨头时,突然一个闪念划过我的脑海,那时的我应该不再是个不谙世事的 8 岁男孩。我心中暗想:我一定要宰了这个狗娘养的。

* * *

The PURSUIT of HAPPYNESS

In contrast to the danger that lurked at home, outside on the streets of Milwaukee's north side—with all the fun and drama of our black *Happy Days* setting—I got to experience elements of a relatively safe and normal childhood. Safety came in part from knowing the lay of the land and also from having a sense of its boundaries. On the north border, running east-west, was W. Capitol Drive, above which the upwardly mobile bourgeois Negroes lived—where kids' daddies worked as professionals, some of them doctors and lawyers, others teachers, insurance men, or government workers. There in the center of the north side was our lower-income yet still industrious community—mostly working-class steel and automotive workers stuck in between the land of movin' on up (where we all secretly aspired to live one day, though we pretended we didn't want to be with all the nose-in-the-air folks) and the bridge to the white world at the south side, which was never to be crossed, went the unwritten law of the racial divide. One of the main arteries, running north-south, was Third Street, which was lined with some of the nicer stores like Gimbels, the Boston Store, and Brill's, as well as the Discount Center, right at Third and North, my favorite spot for buying clothes on a budget.

A couple blocks away from where we lived at Eighth and Wright was the lively intersection of Ninth and Meineke, near where I attended Lee Street Elementary School—coincidentally a school attended by Oprah Winfrey's sister Pat when they lived in Wisconsin—across from which was Sy's store. A big, balding Jewish guy, Sy was one of those few splashes of white in our community—even though I didn't know until later that being Jewish was different from being White Anglo-Saxon Protestant—and he was well liked for extending short lines of credit to regular customers like us. We also felt comfortable with the two black men who helped run the business for Sy and later bought the store from him. Henry and his son—aptly nicknamed Bulldog on account of that's what he looked like—were great characters and contributed to the inviting atmosphere.

Sy made and sold an array of incredible-tasting food, including the best sausage I ever ate in my life, and also offered an eclectic selection of home and personal items. Whenever Momma called for "Chrissy Paul . . ." it was her vocal signal that she was going to ask me to run an errand for her to pick something up at Sy's, anything from a can of Sweet Garrett, the snuff she loved to dip, or Day's Work, a popular brand of chewing tobacco, to some obscure personal item that I'd never heard of before. Whatever Kotex were, I had no idea. Much as I wanted to please my mother and return with what she needed, I almost always came back with the wrong item, especially when she asked, "Chrissy Paul, go run down to Sy's and get me some taupe stockings." I came back with any color but taupe. Eventually she started writing notes to Sy rather than have me try to figure it out.

与潜伏在家中的危险形成对比，密尔沃基城市的北部充满了我那些幸福时光里的欢乐和情趣，在那里我度过了自己相对安全和正常的孩提时光。安全感从某种程度上是来自对自己脚下这片土地和它的边界的了解。这里最北到东西走向的 W.卡皮托尔大街，再往北住的就是那些处于上升阶段的中产阶级有色人种，那些孩子们的父亲都是职业人士：医生、律师、教师、保险公司职员、政府职员，等等。他们与城市南部的白人富人区仅一桥之隔，但由于种族隔离的不成文法律，这座桥无法逾越。住在城市北部中心地带的就是我们这些低收入人群，但各个勤勤恳恳、老实巴交，大多是钢铁工人和汽车工人，这些人几乎永无出头之日。(当然，我们在内心深处无不盼望着有朝一日也能过上街那边那样的富足生活，但表面上对那些眼睛长在头顶上的傲慢家伙还是表现出不屑一顾。)南北走向的第三大道是个主要的商业区，街两侧商铺林立，其中不乏高档商厦，如金贝尔百货、波士顿店、布瑞尔商店，等等，在第三大道北街上还有我最常光顾的价廉物美的折扣店。

离我们住的第八大道右街不远，就是第九大道万利捷大街的路口，我就在那附近的里氏大道小学读书，凑巧的是美国著名的脱口秀主持人奥普拉·温弗瑞的妹妹帕特也曾就读于那里，她俩也一度在威斯康星州生活。小学对面就是著名的沙伊犹太商店，店主是个高个子的秃顶犹太人，是在我们这一带屈指可数的几个白人之一，不过后来我才知道犹太人肤色虽白，但与白人盎格鲁·撒克逊新教徒相比还是有区别的。店主他人很不错，还让我们这些老主顾时不时地从他那里赊点东西。他雇了两个不错的黑人伙计帮他打理生意，后来两个伙计还从他手里把店面买了下来。这两个伙计亨利和他的儿子(绰号斗牛犬，他和斗牛犬还真有几分神似)都颇有人缘，也都热情好客。

沙伊的厨艺相当不错，他自制自销的美味不可胜数，有我这辈子吃过的最棒的香肠，其中还有很多口味可供选择。每当妈妈喊："克里斯……"我就知道这是让我跑腿帮她去沙伊店买东西，要么是一罐加里特糖浆，这是她最喜欢作为蘸料的糖浆，或是一种流行的日日香嚼烟，要么是些稀奇古怪的个人用品，也不知道是做什么用的，比如高洁丝之类，可不管我是多么想让妈妈高兴，结果总是出些差错，特别是她说："克里斯，去沙伊店帮妈妈买双紫棕色的长袜。"我可能就会拿错了颜色。最后，她只好把要买的东西写成纸条，而不再口头告诉我要买这买那了。

第二章　渴望父爱

The **PURSUIT** of **HAPP**_y_**NESS**

Two blocks north from there, at Ninth and Clarke, was another landmark of the neighborhood that we familiarly referred to as the "nigga store"—not in any pejorative sense but because the owners, unlike most of the white-owned businesses, were black. Any money in my pocket, I was out the door to Ninth and Clarke to pick up a dollar's worth of candy and a bag or two of Okey Doke cheese popcorn.

The challenge for me, starting at the age of seven or earlier, was figuring out how to get that money in my pocket. Most of the older kids and all the adults I saw seemed to have similar concerns. Everybody, on some level, was looking for their particular hustle, their angle to get over. My cousin Terry, Bessie's thirteen-year-old son, was a ringleader of a group of cats I followed around some-times—they provided me with the fundamentals of being an entrepreneur, 1960s ghetto style.

Opportunity came knocking when the City of Milwaukee began building a stretch of Interstate 43 right down the middle of our neighborhood between Seventh and Eighth Streets. Since all the residential and business properties on Seventh Street were being evacuated and prepared for demolition, Terry and his cohorts figured they'd try their hands at junking.

Eager to join in, even though I had no idea what junking was, I tagged along and helped the older boys literally tear apart places that had been condemned, looking for materials—fixtures, lead, copper wire, window weights, old clothes, rags, even paper. This wasn't stealing—or so Terry would have argued—because we were really just helping the city to tear down condemned houses. And instead of the demo guys having to cart the stuff off, we helped by piling up shopping carts and rolling them all the way to the east side of Milwaukee, just short of where you crossed the river before hitting the lake. This was where Mr. Katz, a Jewish entrepreneur who bought this stuff by the pound, ran his junking business.

Wanting to increase our profit margin, we tried to be slick a few times, but we were no match for Mr. Katz—he had invented this game. Our silly ploy was to try to weight down our load—before he put our junk up on his scales—by wetting the rags and hiding them under milk cartons buried at the bottom of our heaps.

Mr. Katz knew all the tricks, backward and forward. He knew, almost instinctually, when the weight was too heavy for what he was seeing, as he immediately began to yell in Yiddish and start digging for the wet rags. It never worked. Nonetheless, we didn't fare too badly in the junking business with Mr. Katz as our regular buyer. That is to say, Terry and his friends didn't do too badly. My take of five or ten dollars was much less than each of their shares. Still, I was more than happy to spend my money on a few little things I wanted, without having to ask Momma for money for the movies or candy. It also introduced me to the main operating principle of any marketplace: supply and demand. The demand was obviously somebody out there who paid Mr. Katz for the junk we supplied. Not such a shabby deal.

从沙伊店往北两个街区就是第九大道克拉克大街，这一带最出名的就是"黑人店"，倒不是有什么歧视，只是这里的店主都是黑人，而其他地方的则多为白人。只要我兜里有点钱，就愿意去那条街上，买上一美元的糖果，或是一两包奶酪玉米花。

在我 7 岁以前，最大的问题就是怎么能让自己的兜里有点钱。可是比我大的孩子甚至所有的大人都在为同样的问题犯愁。但每个人都在想法子，用自己的方式来解决这个问题。我的堂兄泰瑞，也就是贝希 13 岁的儿子，是个孩子王。我也曾跟他们这帮孩子玩过几次，是他们给了我一些做生意的基本概念，当然那是 20 世纪 60 年代贫民区的做生意方式。

当密尔沃基开始修建 43 号州际公路路段时，机会来了，这段路正好经过我家，也就是第七大道和第八大道中间的区域。由于第七大道所有的商家店铺和居民都必须搬走，为拆迁做准备。泰瑞和他的伙伴们就琢磨着要收废品挣钱了。

我也摩拳擦掌，跃跃欲试，虽然不大清楚，收废品能怎么挣钱，我还是尽力帮些忙，帮那些大孩子们在废墟中刨来刨去，想找些废品，比如夹具、铅块、铜线、窗户配件、旧衣服、破布头之类，甚至连废纸也不放过。泰瑞讲这不算是偷，因为我们是帮市里清理这些废弃的房屋。大家还得把这些废品用车子推走，我们先是把购物车分门别类码满废品，然后把车一直推到密尔沃基的城东区，也就是河流与湖泊交接的地方。这里有个犹太废品商凯茨先生，他要把废品过秤后再付我们钱。

为了多挣点钱，我们还想过一些花招，但都被凯茨先生一一识破，因为这些把戏他以前也干过，自然什么门道都非常清楚。我们的把戏包括让废品增重，比如上秤前把破布浇湿，再把它塞到废品堆最下面的牛奶桶里之类。

凯茨先生一眼就能识破这些鬼把戏。当他感觉废品有些太重，就能立即猜到是怎么回事。他马上就大声叫骂，然后就在废品中翻找加湿的破布。我们这招根本没法蒙混过关。不管怎样，和凯茨先生做生意还是让我们的废品卖了不错的价格，也就是泰瑞和他的伙伴们挣了不少的钱。给我的远比他们自己拿到的要少得多，但也有 5 到 10 美元的收入。即便如此，我也高兴得不得了，因为不用再向妈妈要钱，就可以买些自己喜欢的小玩意，还可以看看电影、买点糖果之类。此外，这种经历还教会了我最基本的市场供求规律。所谓需求就是别人会从凯茨先生那里买走废品，而这些废品正是我们提供的。这生意是光明磊落的。

The PURSUIT of HAPPYNESS

Some of cousin Terry's other hustles weren't necessarily on the up and up, like the time he showed up in our backyard with cases of cigarette cartons and all of a sudden all the kids from the neighborhood, myself included, were back there smoking, with a vaguely suspicious-sounding story about these cases having fallen off a truck or some such thing. They were actually somehow stolen from a local tavern by Terry. It didn't matter to me. We were so cool, I thought. Even better, we didn't get caught.

But we usually did. In fact, part of the reason that we were given a lot of free rein to come and go as we pleased was that our friends' parents were keeping an eye out on all of us. This was made quite plain to me once when I went over to see the Ball brothers, Arthur and Willie. With this group of friends, football later became our thing, and once I started to get bigger and taller, I assumed the role of quarterback. Our games were all about passing, running, and scoring, which resulted in so many touchdowns that final scores would end up being something like 114 to 98, more like basketball scores. The Ball brothers were the best blockers any after-school team could want, on their way to becoming the biggest cats you ever saw in your life. Two of the nicest, most gentle guys I knew, they were the size of professional football linemen by the time they hit adolescence. Early on, one of the first times I went to their house happened to be a particularly hot summer day, and when I arrived it was apparent that the screen in the door to the Ball house had been knocked out and the door was just a wooden frame. So, rather than mentioning the obvious, I just walked right through the wood frame and into the house.

All at once, Mrs. Ball, their mother, came into view and shook her finger at me. "Boy, you better get back outta here and open that door! Where's yo' manners?!"

I stood there for a second, not understanding. The screen was knocked out, so the door was already open, wasn't it?

Mrs. Ball didn't see it that way. As I pivoted around to obey her, she added, "You weren't raised like that! I know your mother. Now, open that door like you got some sense. G'on back out there and open the door, you hear me?"

A heavyset woman, a little older than Moms, Mrs. Ball made it clear that this was her house and she was in charge.

Still saying nothing, I didn't know how I was supposed to go back out through a door that was already opened. Did I exit by stepping out as I had entered, or did I push open the frame of the door? With her standing there, hands on hips, eagle-eyed watching me, I opened the wood frame of the door, went back out, and closed it.

Now she said, "Come on in."

The moment I did, Mrs. Ball smiled and added, "How you doing, Chrissy?"

泰瑞忙活的另一些事情就不那么光明正大了。有时他会跑到我家后院，怀里还揣着几包香烟，然后附近的孩子们，包括我在内，就都会纷纷跑到后院一起分掉这些香烟。据他说这些烟是从卡车上掉下来的，或是怎样怎样，这种故事的可信度实在有待商榷。实际上，这些都是泰瑞从当地的饭馆里偷出来的，但此事和我无关。叼上烟卷显得我们很酷，很有派头。再说，我们也从未被抓住过。

但是事实并非如此。实际上，我们可以随处乱跑，想怎么玩就怎么玩，是因为朋友们的家长都在一旁留意着我们的表现呢。在我们去看保尔兄弟阿瑟和威力的时候，这一点就表现得越发明显了。跟着这帮朋友，我们开始把大量时间花在橄榄球上，等我长高长壮些后，我就开始打四分卫的位置。我们玩的比赛大多都是传球、奔跑、评分这类，最后有很多触底得分的机会，最终得分可以高达114比98的样子，简直像篮球赛一般。保尔兄弟是不可多得的阻卫，多少业余队都想要他们，他们完全有可能成为大球星，他俩不但人非常好，个人素质也相当不错，十多岁的时候就是职业橄榄球内锋的身材了。我最早去他们家是在一个特别酷热的夏天，我到他家的时候，看到门上的纱窗都拿掉了，只剩了一个门框子，其实我就是直接迈过门框进他们家的。

立刻，兄弟俩的妈妈保尔太太就出现了，她冲我摆摆手说："孩子，不能这么进来，你得退出去从门进来，太没样子了！"

我愣了片刻，不明白是怎么回事。明明纱窗已经拿掉了啊，所以门是开着的，不对么？

可保尔太太不这么看，看我没动地方，她又加了一句："你家里不是这么教育你的吧！我可认识你妈妈。出去，从门走进来，懂事点。转身出去，从门进来，听见了么？"

保尔太太是个大块头，比妈妈稍微年长一些，她说得很清楚了，这里是她家，她说了算。

我还是没说话，不知道自己该怎么办，该怎么退出去，重新走进一扇原本打开的门。是和自己进门一样再退身出去？还是先把门框推开再走出去？她双手叉腰，两眼盯着我，我还是先推开了门框，从屋子里退了出去，又把门框关上了。

接着她说道："进来吧。"

看到我重新进来，保尔太太高兴地说："克里斯，你好啊！"

Not everybody's family enforced the importance of manners in this way, but there were unwritten community rules for keeping kids out of trouble. In many households at the time, there was a distinction between abuse and being punished forcefully for something you did wrong. Rods were definitely not spared. Since everybody's mommas and daddies all knew each other, it was perfectly acceptable for somebody else's parent to give you a whuppin' if you stepped out of line. Then they'd call your momma and you'd get it from her when you got home. Then you'd have to wait for your old man to come home, and he would just mop up the floor with you again, giving you a whuppin' worse than any of the others.

Our household was slightly different. Freddie was excessive enough with beating us on a regular basis, whether we were being punished or not, so Momma chose not to whip us. As a true teacher, she was able to give us the real lessons we needed to learn without force; instead, her well-chosen words, the sharp tone of her voice, and the look in her eyes said all we needed to hear.

There were very occasional exceptions, like the one time I got it for stealing a nickel bag of Okey Doke cheese popcorn from the "nigga store." The African American woman who owned the store not only knew my momma, she announced—when she caught me trying to be slick and walk out the door all seven-year-old innocent and grabbed me by the collar—but also knew where Momma was employed. For my trying to shoplift a nickel bag of popcorn, both the police and Momma received phone calls. And after my mother had to come and collect me at the store before escorting me home, I got my butt whipped with all the ferocity of a woman hell-bent on making sure I would never steal again.

Being creative about it, Momma whipped me with the coiled-up, thick, old-fashioned telephone cord that caused the bell on the phone to ring each time she struck me. *Bing! Bing! Bing!* Besides the physical agony of it—harsh enough to make me wonder if she was going to kill me—the psychological piece of it was the fact that for weeks after that, every time the phone rang, I had flashbacks. As the last beating she ever gave me, it certainly prevented me from even thinking about stealing anything for a very long time—at least until I was a teenager.

Maybe part of my mother's fury was making sure that while I might enjoy tagging along with my cousin Terry, she didn't want me following in his footsteps. The reality was that we all sensed Terry was on his way to trouble, one of those kids born to be a hoodlum.

倒不是各家各户都这么严格要求规矩和礼仪,但是街坊四邻都有对管教孩子的不成文规定。当时对于很多家庭而言,娇惯放纵和严加管教是分得很清楚的,必要的时候棍棒肯定必不可少。因为家长们彼此都认识,若是谁家的孩子太过分,别人家的大人用鞭子教训孩子一顿也并不为过。然后他们还要告诉孩子的母亲,结果回家后还有一顿惩罚等着他。接着孩子还得等着老爸回来,等着又一顿的收拾,这顿打可比别人打得更狠、更凶。

我家的情况稍有不同。弗莱迪动辄就对我们拳打脚踢,这已成为我们的家常便饭,不管我们做错与否,都是如此,所以妈妈根本不会动我们一个指头。她就像老师一样,耐心地给我们讲道理,让我们真正能从中有所收获。而且,她用词也恰到好处,声音的高低、眼神的严厉,足以让我们知错改错。

但也偶有例外情况发生,一次,我从一家卖奶酪爆米花的黑人店里顺手牵羊,拿了一袋爆米花。店主人是个黑人老大妈,那天我正准备混在其他小孩子中间溜出去的时候,她一把抓住我的衣领,她不仅知道我妈妈是谁,而且还知道她在哪里上班。就因为我想拿一袋爆米花解馋,结果警察和妈妈都被惊动了。妈妈来把我从店里领走,带我回家后,把我一顿狠抽,让我牢牢记住这个教训,不可再犯。

而且极富创意的是,妈妈找来老式的电话缆线缠在一起,每抽打我一次,电话铃就响一声。那次打得实在是太狠了,我被打得皮开肉绽都有些怀疑她是不是想要了我的命。在那以后的好几个星期之内,我都心有余悸,甚至听到电话铃一响,就不由得哆嗦一下。这也是她最后一次对我动手,当然也让我在相当长的时间内没有动过偷东西的心思,直到我十多岁以后。

也许妈妈发怒也有泰瑞表哥的原因,虽然我喜欢和表哥他们一起玩,但妈妈不希望我步表哥的后尘。因为我们都觉得泰瑞表哥这么下去会出事的,甚至有朝一日会落到无法收拾的田地。

The PURSUIT of HAPPYNESS

"Hey, Chrissy," Terry was always calling across our backyard, inviting me up to the Big House, as he did one morning when a bunch of us—his sisters and mine—followed his lead by turning the large staircase into a Disneyland ride. This was a change of pace from the competition to see who could claim to be the most interesting character from different movies. My pick from *The Magnificent Seven* was the character Chris, played by Yul Brynner, a really cool-looking cat in that movie. Even though my name was a match, I'd been overruled by the older guys who got first picks. Movies had a powerful influence on me, like books, letting me look through windows into other worlds. Nothing shaped my view of life more than *The Wizard of Oz*, my favorite movie from childhood. One day I planned on living in Kansas where nothing bad ever happened except for a very occasional tornado.

In the meantime, I got to have some good old-fashioned playtime at Terry's instigation. We spent most of that day while the adults were out by sliding down the stairs in cardboard boxes that went zooming down the steps and colliding into bumpers we made from the couch cushions. When we exhausted the fun from that, Terry proposed, "Hey, Chrissy, let's do a pillow fight. Boys against girls!"

"Yeah!" I was all for it. It was him and me versus two of my sisters and three of my girl cousins.

Before long the pillow fight got out of hand, mainly because Terry decided to put a sizable piece of lead in his pillowcase. The next thing we knew he had smacked his sister Elaine in the head with his lead pillow, followed by shrieks, screams, and blood everywhere.

Everyone scattered as one of the older girls went to find Paul Crawford. This was Terry's father, a man who was always referred to by both names. Although he wasn't married to Ms. Bessie, Paul Crawford—a carpenter, handyman, and hustler—was very much present in the Big House, not only as our resident sheriff but as the provider of limitless supplies of one-hundred-pound bags of potatoes. We might have been money-poor but we weren't ever going to starve.

Paul Crawford was somebody else's daddy that I would have been proud to call my father, if that had been the case. He had a style, a hustling, tough guy, workingman's pizzazz, just in the way he was never seen without his fully loaded tool belt slung low, his workman's cap with an authoritative tilt, and, never without an unlit cigar hanging from his lower lip. The only time I ever saw Paul Crawford light it was the day he confronted his son about the serious injury inflicted on Elaine.

"克里斯，"泰瑞总是在后院喊我，让我去大屋玩。一天早上又是如此，他领着一群小孩，他的几个妹妹和我，把楼梯彻底变成了迪士尼乐园。开始是大家比赛谁模仿的电影角色更有意思，我开始选的是《七侠荡寇志》里面那个克里斯，是光头偶像尤伯连纳扮演的，他实在是太酷了。虽然我的名字也叫克里斯，但是开始选角色的那几个大孩子，还是没让我演这个角色。电影和书籍一样，对我产生了深远的影响，让我有机会接触和了解另外的世界。比如我小时候最喜欢看的《绿野仙踪》就整个影响了我对生活的看法。一天我甚至考虑去故事的发生地点堪萨斯居住和生活，因为那里除了偶尔有点龙卷风之外，没什么不好的。

同时，在泰瑞的教唆下，我玩得很是开心。趁大人不在家的时候，我们藏在硬纸箱子里，顺楼梯滑下去，撞在楼梯下面用沙发垫堆出的缓冲物上，等我们玩累了之后，泰瑞又说："克里斯，我们打枕头仗好不好，男孩女孩对攻。"

"好啊"，我举双手赞成，我和泰瑞一组，两个妹妹和三个堂姐分为一组，我们就开始了。

没多久，枕头仗就出事了，主要是因为泰瑞在自己的枕套上拴了一大块铅块，接下来，他就把妹妹忆莲伤着了，铅枕头把忆莲的头打破了，然后是尖叫、哭声，并且鲜血直流。

有个大点的女孩子跑去找保罗·克劳福德，其他人都散开了。保罗是泰瑞的父亲，但人们都习惯称呼他全名。虽然，他没和贝希结婚，但他常来大屋，他是个木匠、装修工人，能四处挣点小钱。住户有事尽可以找他，而且，他总是拿着一口袋一口袋的土豆过来，这样我们虽然手头不宽裕，但是却不至于饿死。

保罗确实很有做父亲的样子，虽然他是别人的父亲，我甚至希望自己能是他的儿子。他很有型，长得很结实，有那种体力工作型的派头，每天都斜挎着他那满当当的工具腰带，总是叼着没点着的雪茄。也只有在儿子泰瑞把妹妹的头弄伤的那天，我才见到他把雪茄点燃。

第二章 渴望父爱

Once she was bandaged and taken to the emergency room, Paul Crawford summoned all of us to the living room in the Big House, where the furniture had been pushed to one side. In an eerily close reenactment of *High Plains Drifter*, a film I saw many years later, Paul Crawford slowly took off his tool belt, pacing the floor and looking into our eyes, waiting for one of us to spill the beans on Terry. We all claimed not to know who was responsible, including Terry.

"Well," said Paul Crawford, striking terror in our souls, "somebody g'on tell me something," and he now pulled out his pants belt, pausing dramatically to light his cigar.

The only difference between this cigar lighting and Clint Eastwood's version was that in the movie he wore a cowboy hat; in Paul Crawford's version he wore his worker's hat. Instead of being a gunslinger, he was a belt slinger as it came alive in his hands, like an angry, out-of-control snake. Though his main focus was Terry, we all caught ricochet blows as Paul Crawford taught each of us the meaning of "putting the fear o' God in yo' black ass."

That was the end of our indoor ghetto Disneyland, cigarettes, and pillow fights.

Looking for less controversial pursuits sometime later when the weather had turned beautiful and sunny, Terry and I thought no one would mind if we built ourselves a little clubhouse in the yard out back with some of the loose lumber lying around.

Unbeknownst to us, Freddie did mind and had supposedly been hollering, "Stop making all that goddamned noise!" because he was trying to sleep. With Terry hammering on the outside and me inside the clubhouse hammering, we couldn't hear anything. Then I became aware that Terry had stopped hammering. Suddenly, the clubhouse begins to disintegrate around me with a giant reverberating sound going *Whop! Whop! Whop!* and the sun reflecting off the shiny metal blade of Freddie's long-handled ax.

All I know is that the clubhouse is being chopped down with me in it, and Terry has split. Not only does Freddie not give a damn that I'm inside, he seems uninterested in the fact that splintering wood has slashed into one of my legs, which is now bleeding a small river onto our structure-turned-woodpile as I shriek from pain. Freddie is impervious, like a human buzz saw, demonically possessed with turning our annoying noisy project and me into mulch.

Amid the *whop!*s and my shrieks and blood and wood splinters flying everywhere, Momma's voice enters the cacophony as she screams at Freddie, "Stop! Stop it!"

With a grunt, he brings his destruction to a grinding halt, defending himself by declaring, "I told him to stop making all that goddamn noise."

把忆莲包扎好送到急诊室后,保罗把我们都叫到大屋的客厅,家居都推到一侧了。那场景和我若干年后看的电影《荒野浪子》出奇的相似。保罗慢慢地摘下他的工具腰带,在地上踱步,看着我们的眼睛,等着我们谁先承认错误。大家都说不是自己的错,包括泰瑞也是这么说。

"好吧,"保罗开口了,我们一个个胆战心惊,"总得有人告诉我是怎么回事。"然后他就把皮带解下来,戏剧性地停顿了一下,点着了雪茄。

这点雪茄的动作和《荒野浪子》的主演克林特·伊斯特伍德如出一辙,只是在电影里,克林特戴了顶牛仔帽,而保罗戴的是工作帽。克林特拎着枪,而保罗拿着的是皮带,那根皮带在他手里仿佛是条怒不可遏随时准备出击的毒蛇。虽然他主要揍的是泰瑞,但我们也没有幸免,因为他要我们都长点记性。

这也就是我们室内贫民区迪士尼、香烟和枕头仗的大结局。

后来,等到风和日丽的时候,我们琢磨着看能不能找点不大会捅出娄子的事情来,所以觉得在院子里给自己盖一个小木屋,后院有的是没用的木板。

但没想到的是,却惹着了弗莱迪,他本来打算睡觉的,"烦死了,别他妈给我吵了!"泰瑞在外面叮叮咚咚,我在小屋里敲敲打打,我们根本就没听见。然后,我忽然发现泰瑞不敲了,小木屋四分五裂,然后听到嗖嗖的风声,一抬头,看到弗莱迪手持着长把的斧头,斧头刃在阳光下闪着寒光。

我所知道的就是我人还在里面,弗莱迪就抡着斧头把小屋给劈了,根本不顾我的死活,而且,有一块劈开的木头就扎进我的小腿,血流成河,我尖声大叫,血滴在搭屋子的木头上到处都是,即便这样,弗莱迪也根本不为所动,仿佛他就是把大电锯,要生生把我们的这个发出噪音的小木屋连同我一起消灭殆尽。

一边是弗莱迪的斧头虎虎生风,一边是我尖声呼救、鲜血四溅、木片横飞,这时传来妈妈迫切的声音,她在冲着弗莱迪大喊:"住手!住手!"

弗莱迪咕噜了一声,手中的大斧停顿了片刻,还在为自己的行为辩护着:"我告诉过他别弄出那该死的声音。"

第二章 渴望父爱

Leave it to Freddie to destroy anybody else's good time. Momma comforted me, making sure to clean out the gash on my leg and put a bandage on it. When it started to scab over, the irritation was so bad that I picked at it and the scab was soon infected. Momma applied another bandage that happened to fall off one day when she was at work.

After washing it off again, I looked for a big bandage to put over it and found what looked like a soft, fluffy, clean white bandage in that package from Sy's store. I placed it carefully over the scabbing area by tying it around my leg. Then, pretty proud of my precocious medical abilities, I thought I'd take a stroll through the neighborhood and show off my cool-looking bandage.

Who should I run into on the street but my cousin Terry? I strutted up, only to watch his horrified face looking me up and down.

"What is that on your leg, Chrissy?" he exclaimed. Before I could answer, he went on, "What you doing wearing a Kotex? You crazy?"

For the life of me, I didn't know why he was so angry and embarrassed.

Terry wagged his finger at me. "Don't you ever let me catch you wearing a woman's Kotex! Take it off! Right now! And don't you ever let me see you wearing those things again!"

Although the scar caused by the ax incident never went away, I did outgrow the delayed humiliation that hit me when I found out why Kotex weren't supposed to be used as bandages.

It was yet one more reminder of how much I hated Freddie, how badly I wanted him gone from our lives. But coming up with a way to get rid of him felt like one of those impossible quests given to young inexperienced knights to go off and slay unslayable, fire-breathing dragons.

How could I do it? With a gun? The prospect was terrifying. For Freddie, with his hunting and fishing country upbringing, gunplay was a natural prevalent thing, something he'd been doing all his life. It was also a form of addiction, like drinking, the only way he knew how to express himself when things didn't go his way, to placate that inner rage, to settle differences when kicking somebody's ass didn't do the job.

At age eight, my track record with a loaded weapon was dismal. A couple of years before, one of my friends and I had been playing in an alley near the Thunderbird Inn and found a .22 in an abandoned stove. Without knowing if it was real, we decided to test it out by aiming at somebody—a true nightmare scenario. We missed, miraculously, but the girl we aimed the gun toward could have been killed. When Freddie got that phone call, which may have come from Momma for all I know, he barreled for me. I knew what I'd done was terrible, stupid, and wrong, but I didn't want to get whupped, so I raced into my bedroom, slid under the bed, and held my breath. Before I had a moment to exhale, Freddie had lifted up the entire bed, exposing me there, shaking like prey. The belt lashing was bad, but the sense that he was omnipotent was worse.

妈妈不再理睬弗莱迪歇斯底里的破坏活动，安慰着我，为我清理腿伤，缠上绷带。本来伤口快要结疤，我却性急地把硬皮掀起，结果伤口很快感染化脓，妈妈又给我换了条绷带，结果有一天，她忙着干活的时候，绷带掉了。

我认真清洗了伤口，想找块大点的绷带盖上伤口，结果从沙伊店的商品口袋里找到一个又大、又柔软的清洁白绷带，我仔细地把绷带敷在伤口上，系在腿上。我对自己的包扎手艺相当满意，决定到附近走走，炫耀一下自己的超酷绷带。

结果在街上我碰到了表哥泰瑞，我挺胸抬头，非常骄傲，结果却看到他一脸惊愕，上上下下不停地打量着我。

"你腿上那是什么东西？"他问道。还没等我回答，他接着说："没事你带个高洁丝干什么，你疯了么？"

我一头雾水，搞不明白他为什么会这么恼火。

泰瑞用手指戳着我："别让我再抓到你带着女人的高洁丝到处乱跑！拿下来！现在就拿下来！别再让我看到你带着这东西，听到没有！"

虽然斧子的砍伤留下了永远的疤痕，但是后来当我知道高洁丝为什么绝不能用来当绷带之后，我花了不少时间才从那种羞愧和自责中走了出来。

这只是让我对弗莱迪的仇恨又多了一分，愈发希望他能从我们的生活中彻底消失。但一想到要除掉他，那种感觉就像是让几个毫无经验的年轻骑士去杀死一头刀枪不入的喷火恶龙，任务的艰巨和难度可想而知。

我该怎么办呢？用枪么？这事情一想起来就分外可怕。对弗莱迪而言，他从小就是看着大人靠打猎和捕鱼为生，舞刀弄枪他早已习以为常，这辈子都不会对枪支感到陌生和恐惧。甚至和酗酒一样，玩枪也让他上瘾，仿佛当事情一不如他的意，就只知道拿枪来摆平。只有这样，他内心的愤怒才能平息，这远比不痛不痒地踢别人几脚来得过瘾。

在我 8 岁的时候，枪械给我带来的感觉只有灰心丧气。几年前，我和一个朋友在雷鸟酒店外面的巷子里玩耍，在一个废弃的炉子里找到一枚 0.22 口径的手枪。不知这东西是真是假，我们决定拿个什么人试试——现在回想起来都有些后怕。多亏我们打偏了，否则我们瞄准的那姑娘就完了。当弗莱迪接到告状的电话，我猜可能是妈妈打来的，弗莱迪开始破口大骂。我知道自己做了件蠢事，也是件错事，但我不想为此挨打，所以我飞奔到自己的卧室，钻到床下，屏住呼吸，不敢出来。还没等我缓过神来，弗莱迪就过来把整个床都掀了起来，我暴露无遗，像个受惊的小兽哆嗦个不停。挨皮带抽的滋味是不好受，但是感觉他无处不在、无所不在那才更为可怕。

Besides, even if I'd had a gun and could use it, that wouldn't necessarily do the job. In fact, there was one night when news arrived that he'd been in a drunken bar fight and his best friend, Simon Grant, had shot Freddie in the stomach. *Glory Hallelujah, praise the Lord!* But Freddie's huge belly acted like a bulletproof vest. He bled profusely, but after they removed the bullet and kept him in the hospital overnight for observation, he went right on in to work the next day.

Not knowing what tactic would serve me in the quest I had absolutely resigned myself to undertaking, every violent episode was further proof that I had no choice but to do away with him. That was very much in my mind one night when he was obviously preparing to beat Momma again and I ran to call the cops.

Right near Sy's at the intersection of Ninth and Meineke was a bar called the Casbah. Sure that somebody would loan me ten cents to make a call on the pay phone outside the bar, I approached the first guy I saw—a cat who looked like a postcard version of a 1962 north-side Milwaukee player, with a snap brim hat, sharkskin suit, and pin knot tie.

"Mister, look," I say, dashing toward him, out of breath, "can you please give me a dime? I gotta call the police, 'cause my stepfather's about to beat up my mother."

This cat, he doesn't blink an eye, saying only, "You can't hustle me, nigger."

Now I want to kill this motherfucker in addition to Freddie.

After I find someone willing to trust me that my mother's life really is in danger, I get through to the police, and two police officers, both white, are sent to the house.

When they arrive, Freddie is sitting on the couch, and they're obviously surprised to see a man of his size. After they exchange nervous glances at each other, one of them clears his throat, asking, "Mr. Triplett, can we use your phone? We need to call the wagon."

One of the few times Freddie exhibits anything close to a sense of humor he leans in to them and replies, "Hell, naw, you can't use my goddamn phone to call the police to bring a wagon to take me to jail. Fuck you!"

It was ludicrous. They eventually coaxed him to go with them down to the station. Once he was gone, I asked Momma why they had tried to use our phone to call the police if they *were* the police and *were* already at our house. She said, "Well, maybe they thought they needed a couple of *big* police officers to get him out of here."

This was as maddening as the day that Momma ran to hide at Odom's corner store on Tenth and Wright. The owner, Mr. Odom, was the daddy of a school friend of mine, and he didn't try to stop my mother from lying down behind the counter.

而且，即便此时此刻我有一支枪，我也会用，也无济于事。实际上，一天晚上突然传来消息，他喝多了，在酒吧和人家打了起来，他最好的朋友西蒙·格兰特一枪打中了他的肚子，赞美主啊，感谢神！但是弗莱迪的大肚子似乎是有防弹功能，他是流了不少血，可是当取出子弹，在医院观察了一晚之后，他第二天就直接上班去了。

因为不知道自己到底该怎么做，所以每当有这样那样的意外出现，就愈发证明了我别无选择，只能干掉这个家伙。一天晚上，当他又准备对妈妈无礼的时候，我跑去叫了警察，那一刻我真的起了杀心。

离沙伊店不远的第九大道万利捷大街的路口，有个酒吧叫做卡西巴。希望能找个人借给我 10 美分，在酒吧外面的收费电话上报警，看到旁边有个人，我去碰碰运气。他头戴窄边帽，身穿鲨皮套装，戴着粉色圆点领带，活像个 1962 年密尔沃基北部区的球员从明信片上走了下来。

"先生，打扰一下，"我跑了上去，上气不接下气，"能给我 10 美分打个电话报警吗？我继父正在使劲儿打我妈妈。"

这家伙眼睛都没眨一眨，就说了句："小黑鬼，别挡路。"

我当时真想杀了这狗娘养的，当然要先干掉弗莱迪再说。

终于我找到一个人愿意相信妈妈真的性命难保，我终于借到了钱，叫了两个警察过来，两人都是白人。

等他们到了家，弗莱迪正坐在沙发上，而两个警察显然没想到他是这么个大块头。两人紧张地对视了一下，其中一人清了清喉咙，说道："崔普雷特先生，我们可以用下电话吗，得叫辆警车过来。"

弗莱迪当时的表现居然有些幽默的味道，他前倾了一下身体，答道："见鬼，你们甭想用我的电话叫警车来，把老子送到监狱，去你的吧！"

太滑稽了，两个警察最后连哄带骗地把他送到警局。弗莱迪一走，我就问妈妈，为什么警察人都来了，还要打电话叫警车来？妈妈答道："也许他们觉得应该叫上几个大个儿警官，才能把他弄出去。"

有一天更恐怖，为躲避弗莱迪的暴力，妈妈居然逃到第十大道右街的奥多姆街角店。店主奥多姆是我校友的父亲，看到妈妈躺到柜台后面，他也没说什么。

The PURSUIT of HAPPYNESS

Waving his shotgun, Freddie stalked her into the store, demanding that Mr. Odom tell him, "Where is that bitch?" Mr. Odom shrugged. "Well, she's not in here, Freddie, and you got to get out of my store with that shotgun. You hear me?"

Mr. Odom suffered no fools. Knowing this, Freddie, like all bullies, was actually a coward when confronted by someone who refused to be bullied. Without so much as an argument, Freddie turned around and left, continuing up the block, holding his shotgun in broad daylight, looking for Momma.

She was able to lay low until later that evening, when he apparently cooled down. For the next two days or so, Freddie's internal barometric pressure seemed to indicate that storms weren't imminent, as if the valve had temporarily released some steam. But the signs were sometimes misleading, so we all walked on eggshells, all of us—me, Momma, twelve-year-old Ophelia, four-year-old Sharon, and two-year-old Kim—all the time.

While I knew that we all feared and pretty much loathed Freddie, the question of how my mother really felt about our increasingly intolerable situation was left as unanswered as the question about who and where my real daddy was. That is, until I happened to stumble over one of the only clues to her inner world that I would ever have.

Around this time, Moms actually made one of the only references to the man who fathered me. Freddie had, once again, reminded me that he wasn't my goddamn daddy. Trying to console me, she mentioned offhandedly that I did have a daddy down in Louisiana, who had once sent me a letter with five dollars or so enclosed. I had never seen the letter, the money, or his name. Momma pointed out that she was always giving me money, as much as she could, which was true. But that didn't explain why she thought my seeing my real father's letter would cause me more heartache than not knowing anything about him.

That may have been on my mind when I was surprised to find myself home alone in the back house one late afternoon and decided to go rummaging in drawers, looking for that letter perhaps, and others. What I found instead was a letter written in Momma's careful, simple script, which had no salutation, even though it was obviously being sent to a trusted friend. It seemed to slip right into my hands when I reached into her bedside drawer to pick up Momma's little worn Bible she kept in there.

It was evident to me that even though Freddie couldn't read any of it, Momma was aware that if he just saw the letter, he would view it as an act of treason. For that reason, she probably had to write it in stealth and then keep it tucked secretly into her Bible, where he wasn't likely to find it.

弗莱迪手里挥着猎枪横着走进了商店，问奥多姆先生："那婊子在哪儿呢？"奥多姆先生耸耸肩："弗莱迪，她没来过，但别在我的店里摆弄你的猎枪，听到了吗？"

奥多姆先生可不是吃素的，弗莱迪也知道这点，他这种人其实是吃软怕硬，当遇到比自己还厉害的人时，他立刻就服软了。也没再多说什么，弗莱迪转身走了，在光天化日之下，拎着枪，招摇过市，找寻妈妈。

妈妈一直在柜台下躲到傍晚时分，后来弗莱迪好像终于冷静点了。在接下来的几天，弗莱迪体内的"气压阀"似乎放了些气，"气压计"显示暴风雨一时半会儿还不会爆发。但我和妈妈、12岁的奥菲丽娅、4岁的沙仑以及两岁的金牡，我们几个都如履薄冰，胆战心惊，因为"气压计"这种东西有时也没准儿。

我知道大家对弗莱迪又恨又怕，但母亲对于我们这种人间地狱般难以忍受的境地作何考虑，我却不得而知，这个问题就像我生父是谁，人在哪里一样，我无法知晓。直到有一天，我偶然了解到有关她内心世界的些许线索，我才有一点概念。

就在这次，妈妈才真正提及了那个让我来到人世的男人。之前，弗莱迪刚刚再次提醒了我，他不是我那该死的老爸。为了安慰我，她提到我的生父是在路易斯安那，有一次还给我寄来一封信，里面夹着5美元。我从没见过这封信，也没见过这些钱，更不知道他的姓名。妈妈说，她总在尽量给我钱花，这倒是没错。但这也没法解释，为什么她会以为我见到生父的信会心如刀割，比对他一无所知还要更加痛苦。

我的脑子里一直在想着这些事情，一天下午，我突然发现屋里除了自己就再没别人，我决定要翻一翻抽屉，找找有没有这么一封信，或是其他什么东西。可我找到的却是妈妈写的一张纸片，字迹很小心，用词很简单，也没有什么抬头落款，仿佛就是写给自己一个非常信赖的朋友的。我打开她床头的抽屉拿起她那本已经翻阅得很旧的小本《圣经》时，这张纸片就顺势滑落到我的手里。

我当时就意识到，即便弗莱迪不认字，妈妈也知道他要是看到这么一封信，也会认为这是在背叛。所以，她只能偷偷摸摸地写完这张纸片，并秘密地将它藏在自己的《圣经》里，弗莱迪基本是不会去碰这本书的。

第二章 渴望父爱

The **PURSUIT** of **HAPP**$\mathcal{Y}$**NESS**

There was much in the letter about things that were going on between her and the old man that I knew nothing about, and didn't understand, including a business proposition he had going in Detroit that never got off the ground. The contents were overwhelming, staggering, especially the sheer panic in the words at the very start of the letter: *Help, I fear for my life.*

Of course, I knew that snooping around wasn't right. But still, it took my reading of that letter to know the truth about what she was feeling and to know that she was trying to get help. For the next few days I watched her, making sure she didn't suspect that I'd found that letter. Without realizing it, I had already developed the family skill of being able to keep a few secrets myself.

As a result, when at long last I came up with a viable method of killing Freddie and began to concoct the lethal potion that he was going to mistake for alcohol, nobody had a clue about what I was doing. My first feat was to slip off with *his* cup, his stainless steel drinking cup, the only one he drank from and treated as lovingly as a silver goblet embedded with jewels. Next, without any watchful eyes, I poured a little liquid bleach in, some rubbing alcohol, with healthy doses of all the cleaning agents and medicines that had poison warnings on them, and finally mixed it all together by adding near-boiling water. All bubbling and foaming, it was better than anything any Dr. Frankenstein could cook up in a movie, but the horrific stench was a problem. How was I going to get Freddie to drink it now?

One possibility was to leave it in the bathroom and just hope that he would take a sip out of curiosity. Great idea. Except, when I got in there and heard voices coming near, I got nervous that he'd make me drink it out of curiosity. My next thought was to try to trick him that it was one of those fancy flaming drinks. Ridiculous as that was, I lit a match and tossed it in. *Poof!* A towering blue and orange flame shot up in Freddie's big steel cup! Besides my death potion being a bust, I was now going to burn myself up. The only option I could see was to empty the burning, foaming mess down the toilet. Throwing the top down, I figured that it was over but smoke and flames began to issue forth from under the lid.

"What's that goddamn smell?" came Freddie's voice.

Flushing the toilet—which miraculously made the smell disappear and didn't cause an explosion that burned up me or the house—I stepped out of the bathroom, returned Freddie's cup to where I'd found it, and answered, "What smell?"

Depressed that my effort had come to naught, I tried to comfort myself that it was a trial run and my next attempt would be successful. My latest plan was to try to do it in his sleep. Little did I know that my mother, with her gift for secrecy, was being pushed to a similar extreme. One night, after another brutal beating, she said out loud, to no one in particular, "He ain't never coming back." She added that if he did, she would kill him before he could hurt her or us again, stating matter-of-factly, "I'll do it when he's asleep."

信里写的很多内容是关于妈妈和一个老人之间的事情，这人我不认识，他们说的是什么我也不大明白。其中还提到他在底特律想做生意，但一直也没能落实。信里的内容很多，写的很费劲，字里行间透着惊慌和失措，特别是开头这样的一句话： 帮帮我，我对生活充满恐惧。

的确，偷看别人的信是不对的，但我还是把信从头看到尾，希望了解她心里的真实所想，想知道她到底需要怎样的帮助。接下来的几天内，我都小心观察母亲的反应，确认她并未察觉我动过这封信。连我自己都没有注意，我已经继承了家族保守秘密的这种能力。

最后，我终于找到一种更为可行的杀死弗莱迪的办法，我开始配制致命的药水，让他误以为是酒喝下去，没人知道会是我干的。首先，我成功地拿到了他的杯子，那是个不锈钢的饮水杯，他喝水就用它，而且爱不释手，仿佛这是个嵌满钻石的银杯。接下来，看到左右无人，我把各种液体倒入其中，有外用酒精、清洁剂、还有那些标有毒副作用的药品，我把这些充分混合后又加入了滚烫的开水。这东西像开了锅一样不停地冒着泡泡，远比电影《科学怪人》里弗兰肯斯坦博士配制怪物药水还要精彩，还要够劲儿。但问题是这味道实在难闻，我怎么才能让弗莱迪把这东西喝下去呢？

一个办法是把这东西留在洗手间，希望他能出于好奇尝上一口。这办法好是好，我刚进了洗手间，就听到外面有动静。我担心他会出于好奇，让我把这东西喝下去，这又让我心头一紧。我转念一想，觉得可以骗他这是好喝的烈性饮料。这主意实在荒谬，我随手点燃了一根火柴，扔了进去。"嘭"的一声，弗莱迪的宝贝杯子里窜出了长长的蓝色和橙色火舌，我配制的毒药转瞬化为乌有，连我自己也要被一同点着了。情急之下，我只能把这团火苗和泡沫倒入马桶。杯子底朝上扣在马桶里，总算是化险为夷，但问题是杯子里还冒着烟和火苗子。

"什么狗屎味道？"传来了弗莱迪的声音。

我慌忙冲水，居然怪味也一同消失了，而且没有引发爆炸，我和这所房子都幸免于难。我从洗手间溜了出来，把弗莱迪的水杯放回原处，一边若无其事的答道，"哪有什么味道？"

看到自己所有努力终以失败告终，我还自我宽慰，这不过是练练手，下次一定能成功。我的最新方案是趁他睡着不备，再下手，结果没有想到，妈妈与我不谋而合，而且还有过之而无不及，但她的保密工作实在过于出色。一天晚上，他再次对妈妈大打出手。之后，她大声说道："他不会再回来了。"但这话似乎不是具体说给谁听的。接着她又说，他若是再这样伤害她或是我们，她就会要了他的命，而且似乎是信誓旦旦："我会在他睡着的时候要了他的命。"

If she kept the details of her own fantasies of revenge a secret, there was one thing Bettye Jean Gardner Triplett couldn't keep from me. Toward the end of these three and a half years that had followed since she came to get us from Uncle Archie's house and just before she vanished again—without warning or explanation from others—I discovered that she had the astonishing ability to become almost supernaturally still. Shortly after finding her letter, I was in the living room watching TV in the evening, and she was at the dining table reading the newspaper when Freddie performed his one-man stampede to her side, ranting and raving, trying to agitate and engage her, outdoing all former tirades with language more foul and abusive than I'd ever heard.

On one level this was the most surreal atmosphere of denial, with Freddie acting the part of the ax murderer in the horror movie while Moms and I pretended to play the part of the kid watching TV and the mother reading the newspaper, a normal family at home. The more sound and fury that came from Freddie's raging storm, the more still my mother grew.

I'd never witnessed anything like this in my life before—or since. Her stillness was fueled by a million times the energy that thundered in Freddie. That was the most still I've ever seen anything or anybody be in my life. A table moves more. Momma sat there motionless, eyes on her newspaper, frozen, not even turning a page, as if she had vanished deep within herself to prevent herself from responding—because she knew that if she said anything, if she turned a page, flicked an eyelash, breathed, he would hit her. Her stillness defeated his storm. To my shock, he gave up, blew his wad of rage, and turned to her like he just changed the channel on a TV set and said, "C'mon, let's get it on!"

The ability to become still was born in me that night from watching Moms. It exists in the realm of instinct, when the choice is flight or fight. Stillness was my mother's only defense against a predator, the way prey can avoid the attack of a killer cobra or a shark by being so still as to be invisible. And it may have been in that moment of stillness that she decided the time had come for the prey to find another way to get rid of the predator, to enact her own plan to make sure Freddie wouldn't be coming back. It may have been then that she decided to take the necessary precautions to make sure that she had all of her children out of the house, me included, one night after Freddie had returned home drunk and passed out.

With her children out of harm's way, she followed through on her plan to burn the house down while Freddie slept. Or that was the story I would eventually hear. How he woke up and stopped the fire, I never did learn. But I do know Freddie used her attempt to kill him to support his claim that she had violated her parole from her earlier imprisonment—which he had also instigated. And once again, his actions caused her to be sent back to prison.

如果说妈妈要把自己复仇计划的具体细节严格保密的话，她有件事却没能瞒过我的眼睛。在她从阿奇舅舅那里把我们接回来三年半之后，她又一次消失得无影无踪，没有任何解释和说法。就在她销声匿迹之前，我发现她可以变得超级静止，那是在我发现她写的信后不久，我在客厅里看电视，她在餐桌前读报纸，弗莱迪在一旁仿佛是个要拼命激怒公牛的斗牛士一般，让母亲做出反应，他又喊又叫，大声咆哮，用最恶毒的语言攻击、羞辱她。

某种程度上，屋里的氛围有些超现实的感觉，弗莱迪仿佛是恐怖片里的斧头杀手，妈妈和我便是寻常百姓过着寻常的生活，我看电视，妈妈读报，弗莱迪的暴风雨愈发的猛烈，妈妈就愈发处乱不惊。

我以前从未经历过这种阵势，以后也再没机会见过。弗莱迪狂轰滥炸的能量却千万倍地转化为妈妈纹丝不动的定性。这是我这辈子所见过的最坚如磐石的人或事。也许桌椅都无法保持这种静止状态。妈妈坐在那里，就是一尊雕塑。眼睛盯着报纸，也似凝固了一般，不会翻动任何一页，仿佛她完全躲到自己的身体里，不愿对外界作出任何反应，因为她知道，只要她说一个字，翻一页纸，或是眨一下眼睛，甚至一个轻轻的呼吸，弗莱迪的拳头就会雨点般落在她身上。她的沉静居然战胜了暴风骤雨。我万万没想到，他最终选择了放弃，不再怒不可遏，而是突然间换了个人似的，"好了，就这样吧。"

那一夜之后，这种处乱不惊的能力在我身上也扎下了根。似乎它就存在于本能之中，当需要作出斗争与否的选择的时候，它就有可能被激活。面对凶狠的猛兽，妈妈唯一的反抗就是纹丝不动，当猎物面对眼镜蛇或是鲨鱼的攻击时，保持静止仿佛就是就此隐身不见。似乎，在那一刻，她决定作为猎物，保持冷静可以让她有机会实现除掉猛兽的办法，兑现她所说的弗莱迪不会再回来的承诺。似乎从那以后，她就一直小心行事，确保弗莱迪喝醉回家时，包括我在内的所有孩子都不在家中。

既然了解到孩子都不会受到伤害，她就开始着手实施自己的计划，在弗莱迪睡熟的时候把房子点着。这只是我后来听到的版本，至于他怎么会中途醒来，扑灭了大火，就不得而知了。但我知道弗莱迪还是利用母亲企图谋杀他，来支持他的指控，认为母亲已经违背了假释条例，而母亲上次入狱本身就是被弗莱迪阴谋陷害所致。最后，他的所作所为导致母亲再次锒铛入狱。

The full details were never revealed to me or my sisters. All I got from this time was a mechanism for becoming still when scary forces preyed on me. Fear of losing my life, losing the life of a loved one, or the fear of losing everything I have—those fears followed me for years. Stillness has been my refuge and my defense. Even later, as an adult, I would cope by being still. Very still. It's not something I would always feel good about, but it's where I go whenever there's too much chaos around me, when the world seems like it's crumbling, when I suddenly fear that everything or everyone I cherish is going to be taken from me in the blink of the eye.

I get still.

我和姐妹们最终都不知道具体发生了些什么。我所能做的就是当猛兽扑将过来的时候，保持静止，一动不动。因为我害怕会失去我所拥有的一切，这种恐惧跟随我好多年，挥之不去。纹丝不动是我的防御手段，也是我的避难方式。即便我后来长大成人，我还保留着这种能力。丝毫不动，宛若磐石。我并不会因此而感到骄傲，但是当我周遭有着太多的喧嚣，当世界就要分崩离析，当我害怕我所珍爱的人或事将离我远去，当我担心哪怕是眼睛一眨都会让一切飘然逝去的时候，我依然一动不动。

Chapter 3
Where's Momma

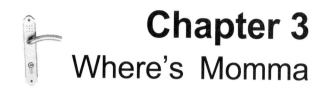

In the blink of an eye, one of my greatest fears came to pass.

After a return of only a few years, my mother disappeared almost as suddenly as she had reappeared. Everything in my world suddenly went to white noise—an infinite grainy uncertainty. When I blinked again, I found myself twelve blocks west at my Uncle Willie's house on Nineteenth and Meineke—where I would live for most of the next three years. It was as though the script I was living one day got switched and I had to just jump in the next day with a new script and a whole new cast of characters, without asking any questions.

Unlike the evasive reactions I'd gotten to questions at Uncle Archie's house when I was much younger, or the way that my mother would answer a question generally or partially, whenever I asked questions at Uncle Willie's house, he or his wife Ella Mae gave no response at all, like I was talking a foreign language.

第三章
妈妈在哪里

转眼间,我心中最大的恐惧还是过去了。

可母亲刚回来才几年光景,却再次消失了,与她当初回到我们身边一样的突然。我身边的一切乱成一团,充满了无数的未知和不确定。没等我回过神来,我已经在十二个街区以外的第九大道万利捷大街的威利舅舅家了,我在这里又住了将近三年的时间。仿佛我生活中那个早已熟悉的剧本突然被换掉了,我不得不马上另找一个剧本,要和一套全新的角色配戏,而我不可以问任何问题。

当初我在阿奇舅舅家的时候,我问的问题往往得到的只是些含混的答复,在家里,妈妈对我那些问题的回答也多为笼统或不全面,而在威利舅舅家,他和妻子艾拉梅则不做任何答复,仿佛我说的是外语,没人能懂一样。

Almost ten months went by—a lifetime to an eight-year-old— before I had even a clue about what had happened to Momma and where she was. Then, on one of the saddest occasions of my childhood —at a funeral, as it happened—I caught sight of her standing at a distance with a prison guard at her side. Until that piece of stark evidence showed up—a major puzzle piece that was only further explained decades later—I didn't know for those months whether or not she was even alive.

To make matters more confusing, it was about this time that Ophelia was sent away. Now the second most important person in my life was missing. Explanations, as always, were vague; but many, many years later I learned that Uncle Willie and Aunt Ella Mae had decided that my twelve-year-old sister would be better off living in a kind of detention home and school for girls who had trouble conforming to rules.

With a full house, counting me and their own three kids, it was understandable that my uncle and, in particular, my aunt saw fit to establish a fairly strict code of conduct. But compared to the easygoing atmosphere that Uncle Archie and TT had maintained, and in contrast to the chaotic drama under Freddie's drunken reign— where us kids could do what we wanted if we stayed out of his way—the new rules presented big-time culture shock. While Ophelia initially did her best to adapt to the rules, I initially rebelled, hating that I suddenly had a bedtime and had to do chores and that there was one way to do them.

Dishes? I had to do them if it was so ordered by Aunt Ella Mae—dark, tall, and big-boned, built like one of the last Amazons —who watched over us hawkishly in her cat-eye glasses. But dishes? This went against my rules. Actually, it was the subject of one of the few arguments I ever had with Ophelia when Momma had left her in charge and my sister had tried to force me to clean the kitchen—including the dishes. The one time in my life that I ever invoked a philosophy of Freddie Triplett, I refused, insisting, "Freddie says that washing dishes is for girls." Ophelia was ready to kick my ass, but I ran away laughing.

There was no running from Aunt Ella Mae. At one point she made me do the dishes for a month because she claimed to have spotted some grease on a glass—after I'd sworn to having washed it. She smirked, saying, "I can see grease, and I don't even have my glasses on." That was only the beginning.

A woman who stood at least six inches taller than Uncle Willie—who was preoccupied with much more pressing worries than the execution of household chores—Aunt Ella Mae, in my estimation, had simply figured out how to give us more work so she could do less. Plus she really took the adage "waste not, want not" to heart. To conserve milk, for example, she had all of us kids take turns eating cereal out of the same bowl, with a fork, one by one. Once I got wise to her system, I volunteered to go last, knowing that when my cereal was eaten I could turn up the bowl and drink the lion's share of the milk.

大概十个月就这么过去了，这对于一个 8 岁男孩儿几乎是一辈子的时间，这时我才依稀知道了一点有关妈妈的事情。之后，我参加了一次葬礼，那是我孩提时最为悲伤的经历，我看到妈妈站在离我不远的地方，旁边还有个狱警。不过我悬着的心终于放下了，毕竟她还活着，但具体发生了什么事情，我还是等了几十年之后才得以知晓。

让我更加费解的是，就在这时，姐姐奥菲丽娅被送走了。她对我的意义仅次于妈妈，但也从我的生活中消失了。有关于此的任何解释和说辞都含混不清，真正的原因我也是在很多年之后才知道，威利舅舅和舅母觉得应该把 12 岁的姐姐送到少年管教所，那里收的都是些不服管教的女孩子。

威利舅舅家很拥挤，我加上他们自己的三个孩子确实让人够受，所以舅舅，特别是舅母，觉得必须制定一整套严格的规矩要我们遵守，这也可以理解。但在阿奇舅舅缇缇舅母家是那种其乐融融的氛围，在弗莱迪那儿，他虽然每天酗酒闹事，但是只要我们躲得远远的，孩子们还是有相当的自由空间的，威利舅舅家的这些清规戒律确实让我非常吃惊，感觉到文化上的差异。一开始，姐姐奥菲丽娅还努力去适应这些规矩，而我干脆就是反抗到底，我没法忍受突然有了固定的起床时间，必须做家务，而且只能用固定的方式完成每件家务。

只要艾拉梅舅母吩咐了，洗盘子这类活也得我来做，她黑黑的，人高马大，是那种骨架很粗大的女人，像是亚马逊人的样子。她总是透过眼镜片，盯着我们的一举一动。但我怎么可能洗盘子呢？以前在家时，这种问题我已经和奥菲丽娅争吵过无数次了。以前妈妈曾让姐姐奥菲丽娅负责家里的事情，她也想让我打扫厨房，包括洗碗。为了反抗，我居然生平头一次引用了弗莱迪的观点，拒绝服从，"弗莱迪说过，洗碗这种事是女孩子干的。"奥菲丽娅气得要踢我的屁股，但是我笑着跑开了。

但在艾拉梅这里我无处可逃，首先，她让我洗了一个月的盘子，因为她看到玻璃杯上有油渍，我说肯定洗干净了，她嘲笑我说："这么脏，我不用戴眼镜都看得清楚。"这还仅仅是刚刚开始。

舅母比威利舅舅整整要高 15 公分，舅舅每天自己的事情都忙不过来，更无暇顾及家里这些琐事，据我估计，舅母艾拉梅就每天琢磨着让我们多干些，这样自己就可以少干些。而且她信奉勤俭持家，为了节省牛奶，甚至让孩子们用同一只碗喝麦片粥，一个吃完另一个吃，用同一套餐具进食，而只加一次牛奶。我了解到她的心思之后，就主动要求最后一个吃早点，这样就可以在吃完碗里的麦片后，再把牛奶一扫而光。

Maybe Ophelia was already at a breaking point from residual anger over our situation, or from an accumulation of the fear and hurt we all had experienced. Or maybe, because she was strong-minded in her own right, she expressed her defiance by acting out. A good, smart, loving person always, Ophelia didn't do anything specific—to my knowledge—to be sent away, but she must have at least talked back or disobeyed a rule or come home late one too many times. In any case, to blink my eyes yet again and find not just my momma gone but Ophelia too felt like too much heartbreak to bear. Adding insult to injury, Sharon and Kim were staying with family members on Freddie's side, so I was a stranger in a strange land—even if Uncle Willie and Aunt Ella Mae were family.

It was only after Ophelia was no longer in the household that I really appreciated how she had always been there for me, how we were there for each other. We hardly had ever fought, except for maybe once when I performed surgery on her Barbie doll and sort of decapitated it. Maybe this was about jealousy over her having more Christmas presents than me—some years my take was just socks. Or it could have been my displaced anger over Freddie telling me, "You the only one who ain't got no daddy," or it could have been an early exploration of my latent surgical skills. Of course Ophelia was mad at me for destroying her toy. But she soon forgave me. Then there was the time that I spied on her and her friends during a girls' club meeting. When I was detected looking through the peephole, one of her friends took a squeegee doused in soapy water and splashed it right into my eye! That burned like hell, but what really injured my eye was when I ran home and tried to wash the soap out with a rag that had cosmetics in it already. I was mad at Ophelia for not being more concerned—and it did cause permanent trouble for my eye.

For the rest, we had been almost inseparable, best friends. The previous July 4 stood out in my memory. Bessie's kids and some of our older relatives and friends had money to go to Muskogee Beach, the place to go. Because we didn't have that money, our option was to go to Lake Michigan to see the fireworks. To get there, we had to depend on Freddie to drive us there, drop us off, and come back to pick us up.

We arrived in time and enjoyed watching the fireworks with a large, local crowd. That was, until, as though choreographed, the last rocket burst into a thousand glittering chards in the sky and there was a sudden roll of thunder as the rain began to pour down. There was no shelter, and before long we realized that there was no Freddie to pick us up.

After it became really late, the only thing we knew to do was to walk home—like Hansel and Gretel trying to retrace and reverse our footsteps the opposite way he'd driven us. Combating the wet, cold, and hunger and our fear of getting lost, as we walked and walked we talked and talked. Still my main source of information about everything I knew nothing about, Ophelia decided to explain to me why the mail never came on time in our neighborhood.

也许，姐姐奥菲丽娅是对我们的处境充满愤怒，无法接受，也许是由于我们所经历的痛苦和伤害积得太深，忍无可忍终于爆发。也许她一心要捍卫自己的权利，用行为来表示她的愤慨和反抗。据我所知，奥菲丽娅素来可爱善良、聪明可人，其实没有做什么太出格的事情，但她还是被送走了，因为她至少顶过嘴、不听话、多次晚上回家太晚。不管怎样，也就是眨眼的工夫，妈妈离开了我们，而且奥菲丽娅也伤心欲绝。不仅如此，更让人不堪忍受的是两个妹妹沙仑和金牡还要住在弗莱迪家人那里，所以我彻底成了孤身一人，独自在一个完全陌生的环境中度日，虽然威利舅舅和艾拉梅舅母是我的家人。

当奥菲丽娅离开之后，我才意识到自己多么感激身边曾一直有她相伴，我们彼此对于对方而言是多么重要。我们几乎从不打架，只有一次，我给她的芭比娃娃做手术，结果把娃娃弄坏了，她才和我急了。也许我那么做，是因为她拿到的圣诞礼物比我多，好些年来，我只是得到了一双双的袜子，这难免让我心里不平衡。或许是弗莱迪说"家里只有你是个没爹的孩子"刺激了我，让我迁怒于这个布娃娃；或许也是我外科手术天赋最早的一次显露。当然，奥菲丽亚看我这么糟践娃娃怒不可遏，但还是很快就原谅了我。还有一次，我偷看她和她的朋友聚会，正当我从门上的小洞往里瞅的时候，被里面的人发现了。她的一个朋友顺手抄起一个沾满肥皂水的橡皮擦，直接就射中我的眼睛，当时就痛得火烧火燎一般，但真正让我的眼睛落下毛病的是我回家想用块布擦洗眼睛，结果布上已经粘上了化妆品，为此我和奥菲丽娅大发雷霆，但是我也落下了永久的眼疾。

而在其他时候，我们俩就是亲密无间的好朋友。早些年的一个7月4日（美国独立日），那天的事情我还历历在目。贝希的孩子们和一些年纪大点的亲戚朋友准备那天去穆斯科基海滩玩，可我们没钱去那种地方，所以就准备去密歇根湖看焰火。这还得靠弗莱迪开车顺路把我们放到湖边，等晚些时候，再来接我们回去。

我们到的正是时候，一大群当地人也正看得兴高采烈，焰火腾空而起，在天空中已是花海沸腾，华美壮丽。突然，空中响起一声炸雷，瓢泼大雨直泻而下。四周无处可藏，而且我们也意识到弗莱迪也不会来接我们了。

天色已经很晚了，我们知道只能步行回家，仿佛电影《奇幻森林历险记》里的男女主角一样，只能顺着弗莱迪送我们来的路，一直往回走。天气阴冷，大雨滂沱，道路泥泞，又冷又饿，再加上担心走丢，我们一路上只能边走边聊。此时我主要的信息渠道还是奥菲丽娅，她总是知道很多我不知道的东西，这次奥菲丽娅决定告诉我，为什么我们这一带的邮件总是延误。

"Why?" The rain was coming down so hard we had to raise our voices to be heard over it.

" 'Cause," she said, "our mailman's over at Luke's with Freddie." Luke's House of Joy, one of Freddie's favorite watering holes, was right across the street from the Big House at Eighth and Wright. We were pretty sure that's where he was this night, too drunk to remember or care to come pick us up. Ophelia reported that the adults in the neighborhood said that if you wanted to get your mail on time, you'd have to go to Luke's and find the mailman at his regular bar stool, sort through his bag, and take out what belonged to you. If you wanted to get your welfare check, said Ophelia, you'd have to go to Luke's and tell the mailman, "Nigger, you give me my check!"

The rain didn't let up for the whole hour and a half it took to walk home from the lake, but her stories and commentary made the ordeal much more bearable. When we arrived at home, nobody was there, so I managed to break in by squeezing through the milk chute.

That, in a nutshell, was how we survived as a team, cheering each other up, complaining to each other, distracting ourselves from thinking about the troublesome stuff that was too painful to discuss. With Momma gone and without Ophelia close at hand to be my ally, I couldn't imagine anyone filling the void.

But apparently, as the saying goes, nature abhors a vacuum, and by the time I blinked once more, my mother's three brothers had stepped in to occupy that empty place and make sure I wasn't left entirely unattended. They were father figures, teachers, entertainers, and preachers, each in his own way. The perfect antidote to the no-daddy, no-momma, no-sister blues, they collectively helped me to realize, just when I had started to feel sorry for myself, how lucky I was to be a Gardner.

Whenever I went to visit or stay with Uncle Archie, I took away lasting lessons about the value of hard work, goal setting, focus, and self-education. A union man in his blood, Uncle Archie eventually ascended the ladder to become president of his union, all the while reading, studying, and familiarizing himself with issues of concern to the community.

Then there was Uncle Willie, a character of the highest order who could turn a humdrum afternoon into an adventure full of international intrigue and espionage. Ever since he had come back from the Korean War, so I heard, Uncle Willie hadn't been quite right in the head. That was one of the euphemisms used for mental illness, which ran strong in different branches of our extended family, it turned out, as well as in the rest of the 'hood—where, besides not being able to afford help, most folks would go to a snake charmer before they'd seek out psychotherapy.

"是啊，为什么呢？"雨下得太大，我们不得不提高嗓门，才能听得到彼此说话。

"因为邮差总是和弗莱迪在鲁克的快乐屋酒吧喝酒，"她告诉我，这个酒吧弗莱迪常常光顾，离我们在第八大道右街的大屋只隔了一条马路。这天晚上弗莱迪肯定又是在那家酒吧，喝得烂醉，把要来接我们的事情早忘到脑后。奥菲丽娅又说，据附近的大人们讲，要想及时收到信件，就去酒吧找邮差本人，他在那里有自己的固定位置，你就直接翻看他的邮包，自己找自己的东西。若是你要自己的福利支票，就直接到酒吧找邮差，说："黑鬼，把我的支票给我！"

从湖边到家我们整整走了一个半小时，但是雨在半路就停了。一路上听姐姐讲故事，说这说那，让这段路好走了很多。我们到家的时候，家里空无一人，我还是从送牛奶的小门那里使劲钻进屋的。

就是在如此艰难的环境中，我和姐姐两人相依为命，彼此给对方打气，彼此抱怨，不管怎样，这都可以让我们分散注意力，不去想那些困扰我们的麻烦，因为这些事情太痛苦，我们根本不愿去提及。现在妈妈走了，姐姐也不在我的左右，我无法想象还有谁能填补这样的空白。

但是正如俗语所讲的那样，上天不会扔下任何一个人不管的。也就是眨眼的工夫，母亲的三兄弟相继出现，轮番填补着我身边的空白，他们充当着父亲的角色，同时也是师长、玩伴、传道士，他们风格各异，方法不同，但对我这个没爹没妈也没有姐姐陪伴的小孩而言，这已经是无尽的解脱。特别是当我开始为自己难过的时候，有他们就会让我深深感到作为加德纳家的一员，我是多么的幸运。

每当我去看望阿奇舅舅，或是就住在那儿的时候，我就又一次意识到勤奋工作、目标明确、专注和自学的重要意义。阿奇舅舅本来是工会的普通一员，后来他一直晋升为工会主席，这与他的博览群书、努力学习，以及熟悉社区工作等是分不开的。

然后就是威利舅舅，他是个很有意思的人，本是个平淡无奇的下午，可是有了他就完全不一样了，他能想出很多好玩的事情，比如国际间谍和充满阴谋诡计的大冒险。听威利舅舅说，自从从朝鲜战场回来以后，他的精神状态就不乐观。这不过是种委婉说法，意思是说他患上了精神疾病，我们这个大家族里是有些人在受着这种疾病的困扰的。结果，大多数人因为无法承受高昂的医疗费用，他们往往会去找舞蛇者，而不是去找精神病医师。这在当时并不鲜见。

第三章 妈妈在哪里

Calling someone crazy—an equal opportunity euphemism that could have applied to someone like Freddie, who was probably bipolar or borderline schizophrenic, made worse by alcohol—was really another form of denying how troubled someone was, which made the problem, if not okay, then at least typical. No matter how bad it was, you'd hear people say, "Well, the nigger crazy, you know. He just crazy." And no one contemplated therapy. That solution was crazy itself to a lot of people. "Oh, no," they'd say about Freddie. "He'll be all right. He just drunk. Probably he should eat something to coat his stomach against the liquor."

In point of fact, Uncle Willie had been diagnosed with some form of battle fatigue or shell shock that had become progressively worse, though he was harmless. Although I wasn't told about his condition during the time I was living in his home, it seemed he was convinced that he was in the FBI—of which he is still convinced to this day, and no one at the mental health facility where he lives has tried to correct him on that. Neither did I the first time I had direct experience working with him on "assignment," a little later in this era. On that occasion we were driving to do an errand one day in his unassuming green Rambler—one of the classic midsixties models made right there in Milwaukee—I couldn't help observing his cool outfit: a jacket and white shirt, tie with a stickpin in it, and little snap brim straw hat and shades. That became his undercover disguise; it helped him blend in, so he said. Without any reference to his "work," all of a sudden he pulled over, looked straight ahead, and spoke through clenched teeth, like a ventriloquist, so as not to appear to be talking to me.

"Yeah, they're over there checking me out right now," Uncle Willie said. "They're checking me out."

"They are?" I asked excitedly, thinking of Bill Cosby's *I Spy* series and all the latest James Bond stories I'd seen or read. Wow, this was cool!

Just as I turned my head to look over and see who was tailing us, Uncle Willie grabbed the steering wheel, whispering hoarsely, "Don't look! Don't look! They'll know we're on to them!"

Unfortunately, I had already turned and looked, only to discover that nobody was there. In one fell swoop, I realized that this meant many of the grandiose claims he'd made over the years, or that others had heard from him, weren't true. One of those claims that I heard from others, for instance, was that he had some original Picasso paintings stashed in an undisclosed location and that he had willed them to Ophelia. These were glamorous, bold visions, the kind of daydreams that I loved to think about and that I hated to learn were only true in his fantasy world.

称某人是个疯子，也是一种委婉说法，这实际是在否认这人存在严重的问题，从而使得这种情况不能得到有效控制。比如弗莱迪就是这样，他很可能患上了躁郁症或边缘型人格障碍症，酗酒让病情愈发恶化。可不管他怎么闹，人们总会说："那黑鬼就是个疯子，他就是疯了。"没人想过他是不是需要接受治疗。对于很多人而言，说这人疯了本身就已经是解决办法。提到弗莱迪，人们总是说："没事，他就是喝多了，酒醒了就好了。吃点什么东西，别让酒精太刺激胃就没事了。"

实际上，威利舅舅被诊断为战争疲劳症或炮弹震惊，后来病情继续恶化，但他不会伤及别人。虽然我住在他家的时候，就已知道他的病情，但我觉得没什么不对劲，舅舅只是说自己是联邦调查局的人，直到今天他也还是这么说，但他所在的精神病疗养院里没有人试图更正他的说法。后来，在我头一次和他一起玩"完成任务"时，我自己也根本没想过要更正他的说法。那一次，我们头一次一起开车去完成任务，他开着自己货真价实的绿色漫步者，那车是20世纪60年代的款式，就在密尔沃基本地产的。我不由得仔细端详了舅舅威利酷酷的行头：夹克衫、白衬衫、领带、领带夹针，还有一顶带边草帽。据他说，这套行头能帮他乔装改扮，便于打入敌人内部。但他只字不提这次到底是什么任务，突然他挺直了腰杆，只是说话却没有动嘴巴，仿佛是一个腹语者，这样就看不出来他是在冲我说话。

"他们一会儿就要检查我的身份了，"威利舅舅说，"马上就要查我了。"

"他们？"我兴奋至极，满脑子都是比尔·考斯贝主演的《我是间谍》系列里面的情节，还有就是007詹姆斯·邦德的故事情节，这实在太酷了。

正当我转身想看看后面有没有跟梢时，威利舅舅手握方向盘，压低声音警告我："别看，千万别看，否则他们就知道被我们发现了。"

不幸的是，我已经转过了身，结果发现后面什么人都没有。突然间我意识到，舅舅这些年来讲给我的他那些惊心动魄、光灿炫目的事情，当然也包括他讲给别人的那些事情，都不是真的。这其中还有这样的一个说法，是我从别人那里听来的，就是舅舅说他自己有些毕加索的画作，都是珍品，藏在一个秘密的地方，他已经立下遗嘱，要把这些画留给奥菲丽娅。还有很多这样很炫目的大胆说法，都曾让我陷入无尽的遐想，但如今我真不愿意得知这些不过是舅舅的想象而已。

第三章 妈妈在哪里

Still, he could be very convincing. Not long after I went on assignment with him, one of the Gardner relatives received a call from the Palmer House Hotel—one of Chicago's most luxurious, illustrious hotels, along the lines of the Waldorf Astoria in New York. It seemed that Uncle Willie—who frequented the racetrack—had checked in at the front desk by showing them his winning stubs from the track. With the explanation that he'd pay them the next day once he had time to cash them in, he charmed himself right into the presidential penthouse suite. Once the hotel management figured out that the stubs were worthless—just discarded stubs, not even somebody else's winning tickets—they called the family to come get Uncle Willie rather than have the negative publicity from police involvement.

As one of the family members along for the ride to coax Uncle Willie out of the penthouse, I had the fortune to catch a glimpse of the stuff of which dreams were made. The luxurious lobby of the Palmer House made the pages of the Spiegel catalog seem almost ordinary. And that penthouse suite—with multiple bedrooms, a bathroom that could house two families, a sitting room here, a living room there, and furnishings made of gold, silk, satin, velvet—was like nothing I'd ever dreamt of, let alone seen. To think that I'd ever stay in such a place was too much to dream, too crazy to want. But as I cajoled Uncle Willie into going home with us, I planted that fantasy inside myself just the same.

Many lifetimes later, after I'd found myself staying in the suites of a few extraordinary hotels, I was invited to the Palmer House Hotel to attend a reception hosted by the president of the National Education Association, one of my largest institutional investment clients. It didn't occur to me until I arrived at the reception, which happened to be in that very same presidential penthouse suite, why it was that I began to have such a powerful déjà vu. At first, I thought better than to confess the reason I was able to direct anyone who asked to the bathroom, the wet bar, or the exit to the patio, but then I did mention it to a couple of older women, who laughed right along with me.

One of them said, "We all have an Uncle Willie in our family." The other woman added, "And some of us have an Aunt Willamena too."

At the age of eight I obviously had few insights into the causes of mental illness. So when I started picking up on my family members not being quite right, it gave me something new to fear. If this crazy thing ran in the family, what did that say about me? What if I had it or was going to get it? The fear may have also been why I stayed away from becoming much of a drinker. I didn't want to lose the little control of my world I had, that modest feeling of being able to respond to rapidly changing surroundings, situations, and circumstances over which I otherwise had no control.

但他还是相当有说服力的。我们一起执行任务之后不久，加德纳家的一个亲戚就接到了帕玛屋酒店的一个电话，这是芝加哥最豪华最辉煌的酒店，与纽约的总统御用的沃多芙酒店齐名。经常光顾赛马场的威利舅舅住进了帕玛屋酒店，他在前台出示了他的赌马票根，称他赢了大钱，还说第二天只要抽空去把赌马赢的钱拿回来，他就立刻付账，而且他直接住进了总统套间。酒店方面很快发现，那些票根一文不值，不过是捡来的旧票根而已，连别人的中奖票根都算不上，所以马上联系家人把威利舅舅领走，但不愿惊动警方，以免让这件不光彩的事情进一步扩大影响。

当家里人开车把威利舅舅连哄带骗从总统套间弄出来的时候，我有幸看了一眼舅舅成真的梦想。帕玛屋酒店奢华的大堂让斯皮格商品名录里面花花绿绿的商品相形见绌。总统套房里面有好几个卧室，洗手间能放下两大家人，还有起居室和客厅，家具陈设都是金子、绸缎、天鹅绒的质地，这些东西我想都不敢想，更别提亲眼一见了。能住上这样的地方对我而言，简直是天方夜谭，白日做梦。但是当我哄着威利舅舅和我们回家的时候，在我的心里也埋下了这疯狂的种子，有朝一日，我也要住在这里。

很多年以后，我居然也真的出入于顶级奢华酒店的高级套房，一次，我应邀入住帕玛屋酒店，这次活动是美国国家教育协会总裁主办，他们是我最大的机构投资商。我到了会场之后，才发现居然是当年舅舅威利住过的总统套房，难怪有那种似曾相识的感觉。开始我没有道出实情，只是轻车熟路地告诉别人洗手间、酒水吧具体怎么走等，但后来我还是和几个年长的女宾提到这段经历，大家都笑得前仰后合。

其中一个说："其实我家也有威利舅舅这样的人物。"另一个也说："我家也有，不过是个女子。"

在我8岁的时候，对于精神疾病显然还知之甚少。所以当我发现家中有人患有这种疾病时，不由得忧心忡忡，担心自己会不会也被传染，人们会怎么议论我。若是自己也不能幸免，那该如何是好？这种忧虑也让我远离酒精，我不希望对自己所拥有的一切失去控制，我本可以对自己身边不断发生的变故迅速做出反应，而酒精会让我这种能力消失殆尽。

第三章 妈妈在哪里

At the same time, Uncle Willie's stories, delusional or not, gave me a worldview that I had never had before, replacing the old fear of the unknown with a desire to see some of the places he talked about. Besides the foreign ports of call he described from his time in the service—in Korea, the Philippines, Italy, and other stops along the way—he also talked about how beautiful and welcoming the women were over there, a subject that was to become an increasing source of fascination for me.

But the person who most opened the door to the world beyond our neighborhood and made me know that I had to go see it one day was my Uncle Henry—who came shining into my life in this era as if he had been sent just for me. We had seen Momma's baby brother only periodically in earlier years since he was stationed abroad at the time. Now that he was retired from the military and working as a steel man alongside my other uncles, he suddenly appeared on the scene—as suddenly as Momma had disappeared.

Whenever Uncle Henry came to look after us at Uncle Willie's house—or better yet, to take me somewhere on an excursion, just the two of us—it was Christmas, my birthday, and every other holiday rolled into one for me. He made me feel as special as Momma had when she visited at the foster home and made candy. Uncle Henry not only made me feel special but allowed me, for the first time ever, to feel love for a man—really to fall in love, in the way that boys fall in love with their fathers and yearn to be like them one day. I knew what that falling-in-love feeling was with the important women in my life, like Momma, with her spreading smile—always reminding me of an opening refrigerator door that the light of hope and comfort spilled from. I knew the love of my sister, how it was without condition or limitation. But until I was eight years old, when Uncle Henry took me under his wing of protection, love, and fun, the dominant messages from a male adult had mainly been "Get outta my goddamn house" and "I ain't your goddamn daddy," barked at me down the barrel of a shotgun.

Uncle Henry and I had an unspoken agreement whenever he came to stay with us—if Uncle Willie and Aunt Ella Mae happened to be going away for the weekend or out for the night—that I would go up to bed with the younger kids and sneak back down later. By the time I came tiptoeing downstairs, there was always a party going on, with Henry Gardner at the center. About five-ten—although, like Momma, he looked much taller—Uncle Henry was a pretty boy, single and loved by the ladies, with a lean physique and an athletic, tigerlike way of moving. In his hip goatee, he would scan a room, not missing a beat, knowing the ladies weren't missing him. Never once did I see him looking anything but perfectly attired, every crease, every cuff pressed to perfection.

与此同时，威利舅舅的故事，虽然有些疯狂，有悖常理，但还是影响到我看待这个世界的眼光。这是以前从未有过的，以往我那种对于未知世界的恐惧也不复存在，相反我渴望能去了解那些他谈及的地方。他讲起自己服役过的海外港口，比如朝鲜、菲律宾、意大利等以及他路上经停的地方，那里的女子如何美丽动人、热情好客，这都激起我对外部世界的极大兴趣。

但亨利舅舅才真正让我走出自己生活的这个小圈子，了解外面的世界，而且让我意识到有朝一日自己要出去闯荡，亲自领略这一切。他让我的生活充满阳光，仿佛是上天的安排，他在这个时候进入了我的生活。早些年，我们只是偶尔见过妈妈的这个小弟，那时他还在海外服役。现在他已经退役，与我其他的舅舅一起，成了一名钢铁工人，他突然出现在我的面前，就像妈妈的消失一样，事先没有任何迹象。

不管是亨利舅舅来威利舅舅家来看我们，还是把我带出去玩，那可是只有我们两个在一起，不管是圣诞、我的生日、还是碰巧赶上的什么节日，我都兴奋不已，乐不可支。那种感觉非同寻常，甚至可以与当年妈妈来福利院看我，给我做糖果相媲美。不仅如此，亨利舅舅还让我有生以来头一次对一个男人产生了如此强烈的情感，深深地爱上他，就像孩子深爱自己的父亲，并且渴望自己有朝一日也能成为像他那样的男人。我知道那种爱上生命中对自己十分重要的女人的那种感觉，比如妈妈就是如此，每当我看到她温暖的笑容，就像是打开了个特别的冰箱，里面希望的光芒倾泻而出，让我惬意，让我满心欢喜。我也了解那种姐弟情谊，无条件的奉献和给予。但直到我 8 岁，在亨利舅舅把我放在他的羽翼之下呵护起来之后，我才从男性家长那里第一次感到了爱与关怀，快乐幸福，而不再是被枪口对着，听到歇斯底里的咆哮，"从家里给我滚出去"以及"我才不是你这狗娘养的老爸"。

亨利舅舅和我有个不成文的约定，那就是赶上威利舅舅和艾拉梅舅母碰巧周末出门或整晚不回来，我和亨利舅舅就可以在一起。通常我是先和其他三个弟弟上床睡觉，等他们睡熟我就偷偷溜出来。等我蹑手蹑脚从楼梯上下来的时候，楼下多数是在开派对，亨利舅舅当然是里面最红的明星。亨利舅舅身高虽然不到 1.8 米，但是和妈妈一样，他显得比他实际身材要高，他仪表堂堂，身材健美，动作矫健，还是单身，所以深受女孩子们喜爱。他留着帅气的山羊胡，可以扫视整个房间，把每个人都照顾到。不管什么时候见到他，他总是衣着得体，一尘不染，衣领挺括，毫不含糊。

The PURSUIT of HAPPYNESS

At one of these parties, not long after I'd come back downstairs and was checking out Henry's different friends, watching the various guests—some playing cards, others in conversation, a few dancing—something remarkable happened. When I arrived, there was one distinct groove going on—with soul music, blues, and standards coming off the record player as singers like Sam Cooke, Jackie Wilson, and Sarah Vaughn stirred up the festive atmosphere. Between the music, laughter, chatter, and smoke, it was hot and happening, boisterous and loud. Then, all at once, the mood changed when a record was put on that I had never heard. Everything stopped: the laughter, the chatter, even the smoke. The record was Miles Davis playing "Round Midnight." Later I would appreciate the mastery of his trumpet playing, the haunting tone that crept under my skin, and the incredible complexities of tempo and melody. But what got me that night was the power of Miles Davis to alter the mood in the room like that. It was still a party, but much more intimate, more cool, more fluid. It even seemed that I moved differently with Miles on the record player. My decision to study trumpet didn't happen that night, but I did contemplate for the first time ever how powerful it would feel to be able to change the mood, to make strangers feel something transformational that way. The music bug done bit.

From then on, Uncle Henry and I had Miles Davis in common. The music and the time spent listening together formed a shelter in the storm so that all my angst was forgotten, if only for a while. On those many occasions when he let me stay up late and we'd listen to every Miles Davis recording he could get his hands on, he'd tell me about his overseas adventures in the Philippines, Korea, and Japan. "Come here," he beckoned to me in the middle of talking one night, and led me to the bookshelf, pulling out the encyclopedia Uncle Willie and Aunt Ella Mae had in their home.

He pointed out the facts and cultural descriptions of these different places, recommending that I always take advantage of resources like the encyclopedia. He made a point of emphasizing that the world was full of many different types of people with attitudes, customs, beliefs, and colors different from ours. Then there was the smile that lit up his face when he described the women over there. He might as well have been spinning the globe for me and egging me out the door, saying, "Here it is, Chris, the world is your oyster. It's up to you to find the pearls."

Nothing Uncle Henry said or did indicated that our time together would be limited for any reason, but looking back, I would later wonder if he knew on some level that he wasn't going to be around forever and was trying to pass on everything he had seen and learned in a short amount of time. In any case, his message wasn't explicit, but the theme was always clear: live large.

在一个派对上，我刚下楼不久，正打量着亨利舅舅这些形形色色的朋友，观察着这些客人的举动言谈，看到有人在打牌，有人在聊天，还有几个在跳舞，这时出了件很有意思的事情。我刚到，就听见音乐突然变得不同，传来了灵魂音乐和布鲁斯的曲调，只听唱片机上传来了标准曲目，山姆·库克、杰克·威尔森、莎拉·沃恩曼妙的歌声立刻在人群中点燃了一种节日般的气氛。在音乐声中，混杂着笑声、人们开心聊天的声音，还有烟草的味道，场面很是红火热闹，喧嚣鼎沸。突然间，一首从未听过的曲子响起，场上的气氛完全改变。一切都停了下来，那些笑声、谈天声，甚至吸烟的人都停了下来，仔细聆听。唱片里播的是爵士大师迈尔·戴维斯演奏的《午夜情深》。后来，我逐渐可以欣赏戴维斯高超纯熟的小号技巧，体会他音乐的沁人心脾，节奏和旋律的复杂更是超乎想象。但是那一夜，让我震撼的是，戴维斯可以如此轻而易举就让屋里的气氛完全改变。派对依旧在继续，但是人与人之间的关系更为密切，更酷更炫，更有一种流动的美感。我完全被戴维斯征服了。当然我并未当夜决定要学习小号，但是我生平第一次感受到人的思想和情绪可以瞬间发生如此巨大的变化，一群陌生人之间居然可以发生如此剧烈的化学反应。唯有音乐的魅力使然。

从此之后，亨利舅舅和我找到了一个共同的爱好，那就是爵士大师迈尔·戴维斯。我们一起享受音乐，同时音乐为我们构筑了一个避风港，让我可以忘却所有的害怕和伤心，哪怕只是暂时遗忘，也让我心满意足，更无奢望。很多时候，亨利舅舅都不会催我上床睡觉，我们一起欣赏他能找来的戴维斯的每首歌曲，他告诉我那些海外的历险，在菲律宾、朝鲜还有日本，所有那些他去过的地方。"来这里看看，"一天晚上正当我们聊得起劲，他领我来到书架边上，抽出威利舅舅和艾拉梅舅母家里的一本百科全书。

他指着书中这些异域奇邦，介绍相关的风土人情和地域文化，建议我要多看看百科全书这类东西，开阔眼界。他还强调世界之大，无奇不有，那里的人为人处世、风俗习惯、宗教信仰，甚至肤色都与我们有着不同。当谈到那里的女子时，他的脸上浮现了笑容。他甚至会转动地球仪，怂恿我大胆走出去，投身到广阔天地，"克里斯，这世界就是个大牡蛎，你要自己去找寻里面的珍珠。"

亨利舅舅的言行并没有特意在暗示，出于某种原因，我们在一起的时间可能会很有限。但是今天再回顾过去，我甚至怀疑他是否在某种程度上意识到我们不可能永远在一起，所以就努力在最短的时间内，把自己的所闻所见所学尽数教给我。不管怎样，也许他并没有直接讲出来，但是意思是十分明确的，做人要敢想敢干、敢做敢当。

That message wasn't meant in any kind of negative or selfish way. To me, it meant to dare to dream, to commit to living on my own terms, to pursue my vision—one that others didn't have to see, just me.

One of our earliest outings together had been to the Mississippi River, where Uncle Henry taught me to swim and where he'd take me boating whenever good weather came around. There was one day on the river that I remember as the essence of happiness, one of those perfect summer days that stretch on forever. Not a cloud in the sky, there was just the sound and smell of the gas engine, the two of us: Uncle Henry in the back gunning the Evinrude engine, steering us across the river, and me up front with my legs dangling over the side, kicking up the water and throwing spray back into my face. Sensations of well-being ran through my senses: the ups and downs of the small craft skimming over the mellow rolling of waves; the feel and sound of the waves slapping on the bottom of the boat; the spray of mist around me, lovingly touching my face and skin.

That was probably the most dangerous position possible in which to ride inside of a small boat, but that was part of what made it the most daring, spectacular fun I'd ever had. Decades hence I would recall that glorious day while watching *Titanic* and seeing Leonardo DiCaprio shout, "I'm king of the world!" That was the exact feeling that came over me on the Mississippi with Uncle Henry, a feeling of being completely alive. Uncle Henry had a look of satisfaction as he saw me happy, as if he had done well to set me on a path that he might not always be around to guide me along. Or so I later interpreted our most memorable time spent together.

One night at the end of that first summer I'd stayed with Uncle Willie and Aunt Ella Mae, I had gone to bed but was still awake when I heard my aunt cry out, "Oh, no!" followed by muffled crying from her and my uncle. I sat up in bed in a panic, not only because I had never heard grown-ups cry before, but also because I knew. It was Uncle Henry. No question. The pain was so pronounced it reverberated all the way up to the attic where I slept at the time. I prayed more genuinely than ever before: *Dear God, please don't let it be my Uncle Henry.* I didn't sleep, I prayed and prayed, feeling more powerless than ever to alter whatever it was.

The next morning, at breakfast, my Aunt Ella Mae, her eyes puffy under her cat-eye glasses, said in a somber, strained voice, "Henry had an accident. Yesterday. He drowned."

Reeling from the shock and sorrow that he was gone and the disbelief that he could have had an accident, because he knew everything and was careful and because he couldn't be gone, he couldn't, I barely pieced together the details. Aunt Ella Mae was really talking to me, since the younger kids wouldn't understand, but I was numb, devastated. In that place of stillness where I went to brace myself against hurt, I pushed away the haze and tried to understand the chronology of what happened. Uncle Henry apparently had gone out to fish from a small island, and the boat had come off its mooring and drifted away from shore. When he attempted to swim out to the boat and bring it back in to redock it, the undercurrent was too strong and took him down.

这其中并没有什么消极或自私的成分在内，对于我就意味着要敢于梦想，按照自己的方式去生活，追逐自己的梦想，这个梦想就扎根在我的脑海里，与别人无关。

我俩最早的一次出游是去了密西西比河，亨利舅舅还教会我游泳，天气好的话，他还会带我在河里一起划船。有一次，我们又去了河边，那天玩得最为开心，那还是在夏天，碧空万里如洗，只听到小船轻型发动机发出的声响，空气中弥漫着汽油的味道。当时只有我们俩，亨利舅舅在后面打开埃温鲁德发动机，我们在河面上飞速驶过，我就坐在船头，双腿搭在船的外侧，踢着水面，水花四溅，落在脸上。那种爽彻肺腑的感觉遍及全身。小船推开层层波浪，清澈的河水也被惊扰，一漾一漾地拍击着船底，激起细细的水雾轻柔地触碰着我的肌肤和面颊。

在小船上这么坐着，属于相当危险的姿势，但也给了我无尽的快乐和难以名状的美妙体验。数十年后，在电影院里，我看到《泰坦尼克号》的男主角莱昂纳多·迪卡普里奥说："我就是世界之王！"而当年在密西西比河上，我和亨利舅舅在一起荡舟的时候，那绝对就是这种感觉。看到我这么开心，亨利舅舅也露出了心满意足的神情，仿佛他已经完成使命，让我走上正确的道路，而他也许不能永远伴我左右。至少后来我就是这么解读我们那些最为珍贵的快乐时光的。

我和威利舅舅和艾拉梅舅母相处的第一个夏天就要过去了，一天晚上，我已经上床准备睡觉，突然听到舅母的惊呼："这怎么可能！"接着就是舅舅和舅母两人呜呜的哭声。我坐在床上，内心充满恐惧，不仅是我从小到大没见过大人这么痛苦失色，而且我知道是亨利舅舅出事了，一定是他出大事了。有种彻骨的痛在屋里肆无忌惮地蔓延着，连我睡的小阁楼上也没有幸免。我非常虔诚地祈祷，主啊，千万别是我的亨利舅舅。我无法入睡，一遍遍地祈祷，感觉到如此的无助，无力改变眼前发生的一切。

第二天早饭的时候，舅母艾拉梅镜片后的眼睛又红又肿，用悲伤痛楚的声音告诉我们："亨利舅舅出事了，昨天，他淹死了。"

震惊伤痛之余，我不敢相信他真的就这么走了，而且更不能接受他是溺水而亡，他谙熟水性，做事谨慎，这怎么可能呢？绝对不可能的事情。舅母还在说着事情的经过，我知道她是在讲给我听，因为三个弟弟太小，根本不懂，但是我似乎麻木了一般，整个人仿佛已被噩耗击碎。我又回到自我保护的静止不动状态了，我拼命回到现实中来，努力分辨着舅母的声音，试图了解到底发生了什么。亨利舅舅那天是去小岛上钓鱼，锚松动了，小船漂离了岸边，他想游过去把船拉回来重新泊靠，结果被一股强大的暗流带走，再也没能回来。

第三章 妈妈在哪里

How many times Uncle Henry had warned me about the undercurrent, how you could never tell just by looking at the surface, I couldn't count. It didn't make sense. Nothing made sense. My heart wanted to explode into a million pieces, but something inside wouldn't let me. It was that feeling of not allowing myself to cry, because I was sure that if I started I'd never stop. So I took all that emotion, that weight of the world hanging over me in the shape of a massive question mark, and dragged it deep down below, into a dangerous undercurrent of my own.

After attending so many funerals with TT, I thought that I'd know what to expect from Uncle Henry's funeral. But of course I was very young then, and we didn't really know any of the people from church who died. I was unprepared for the finality of his loss, as if I'd been waiting to hear that it was a mistake or even a trick so he could take off and have a foreign adventure without having to say goodbye. More than that, I was completely unprepared to see Momma there, the first time I'd seen her in almost a year.

Every time I tried to move toward her, various relatives blocked my path. We couldn't hug. She couldn't tell me where she was staying, what had happened, when and if she was coming back. The atmosphere was surreal enough with all the weeping and wailing, but to see Momma, real and in front of me, yet beyond my reach, was enough to put me in a grave next to Uncle Henry. Maybe because she knew it would have hurt too much, she didn't even make eye contact or try to speak to me. My only consoling thought was that she was glancing over when I wasn't looking. I wanted Momma to see that I was starting to get tall, that I was composed, strong, being a mostly good kid. Every time I looked over at her, hoping for some sign that she had seen me, all I saw was the pain of losing her baby brother and not being able to talk to her children. She kept her gaze down at the earth where they put Uncle Henry's casket.

When it hit me that the woman standing next to my mother was a female prison guard—the only white person at the funeral, dressed in a navy-colored uniform—it came down like a thunderbolt where she had gone. But as one monumental question was answered, a whole batch of confusing new ones were born. Why was she in prison? When was she coming back? Was she coming back?

Only much later would I piece together that this was her second imprisonment. But even that day my gut told me that Freddie was responsible. Though he was the one who should have done time for his abuse, Freddie told the authorities that she had attempted to burn the house down with him in it, thereby breaking her parole. Not surprisingly, he did it without an ounce of concern for what it would do to us kids.

亨利舅舅不止一次告诉我暗流的危险，从水面上根本看不出来，他这么告诉了我不知有多少遍。怎么可能他自己不知道呢？这怎么可能呢？我的心仿佛要碎成齑粉，但是有种力量拦着我，不允许我这么做。有种感觉告诉我不可以哭，因为我知道只要眼泪一流下来，就不可能停住。所以我就硬撑着，让那生命中难以承受的重量化为一个巨大的问号，然后使劲把它压下来，压到心底的最深处，压到我心中的暗流之中，将它吞噬。

我和缇缇舅母参加过许多葬礼，本以为我会从容面对亨利舅舅的葬礼。但是，当初我和缇缇舅母在一起的时候还太小，再说那些同一教区的死者我们其实并不怎么熟悉。但这次完全不同，对亨利舅舅的逝去我全无准备，我一直在等人说这一切是个误会，舅舅不过又是去国外冒险，没来得及和大家告别而已。不仅如此，我更没想到会在葬礼上见到妈妈，这是一年来我头一次见到她。

可每次我想靠近她，都被别人拦住。我们不可以拥抱。她也不可以告诉我她现在身处何处，究竟发生了什么，什么时候她会回来，以及她是否还会回来。所有人都痛哭失声，悲痛欲绝，让我感觉到有些恍惚，但我却可以真真切切地看到妈妈就站在前面，我却够不到她，这种痛苦让我有心和亨利舅舅一同而去。也许，她知道这种痛的深重，所以她根本不看我，也不和我说些什么。我唯一的希望就是在我不看她的时候，她哪怕是能瞥上我一眼。我希望妈妈知道，我已经长高了，也长壮了，而且基本上是个好孩子。每次我朝她的方向望去，都希望有些许迹象表明她已经看到了我，但我看到的不过是她伤心欲绝，因为痛失小弟，也因为不能和自己的孩子们说句话。她两眼紧紧盯着亨利舅舅的棺木，不肯抬头。

突然我看到母亲身边有个女狱警，那是葬礼上唯一的白人。她身穿蓝色制服，对我而言，她仿佛是晴天霹雳一般，我明白了这些时候妈妈是在哪里度过的，但是一个重大的问题终于有了答案之后，我头脑中却又生出更多的问题。她什么时候又入狱了？什么时候会出来？她还会出来吗？

过了很久之后，我才从不同的渠道打听到母亲第二次入狱的真实原因。但是就在葬礼的当天，我就感觉到弗莱迪与这有着不可推卸的责任。虽然是他在屡屡对妈妈施暴，但是弗莱迪告诉当局，是妈妈点着了房子，要把他和房子一同付之一炬，因此妈妈违反了假释条例，再次锒铛入狱。当然，他这么做的时候，丝毫没有想过孩子们该怎么办。

第三章 妈妈在哪里

The PURSUIT of HAPPYNESS

I was also reunited with Ophelia. Seeing her, Sharon, and Kim at the funeral was awkward, with our "don't ask, don't tell" family tradition. The warring configuration of emotions inside of me was so overwhelming that I reverted to the need for something to do, some plan of action to stick my focus on. For one thing, despite the fact that I hadn't seen much of Freddie since Momma had been gone, I resolved to resume the job of putting him out of our misery, a determination I'd only temporarily shelved when my poison potion exploded on me. And another thing, I decided, for however long my mother was going to be away, I was going to have as much of my childhood as I could muster. I was going to hang out with my group of friends, "my boys," get into a little trouble—instigate some of it too—go riding on our homemade skate trucks put together from wood and old skate wheels, and maybe figure out how to earn some chore money to buy myself a bike. Then me and my boys were going to cruise around town, out to the lake if we felt like it, or pedal all the way uphill to the highest point in our part of Milwaukee, near the water reservoir, and look out beyond, feeling like kings of the world. And then, living large, we were going to take that plunge down Snake Hill, the biggest rush of our lives, taking our feet off the pedals so we could go even faster, pushing the limits of danger and excitement and just letting it rip.

What I also decided at Uncle Henry's funeral was that I wouldn't cry. That was my signal to Momma that I was hanging tough and that she didn't need to worry about me.

For the next two years I did the best I could not to break down. My resolve was severely challenged one afternoon when I stopped by Baby's house, where my younger sisters were staying. One of the only redeeming aspects of having the scourge of Freddie in our lives was how good his sisters Baby and Bessie were to us. Baby saw how her brother rode me and tried to compensate, saying nice things whenever she could, and she would even kick a few dollars in my direction here and there.

"You hungry, Chris?" she greeted me that day, knowing the answer before I grinningly nodded yes and starting to take out some sandwich fixings. As she did, Baby remembered the laundry she was doing downstairs and asked if I'd go load the clothes in the dryer.

Without hesitation, I head down to the basement and begin to pull the wet clothes out of the washer when a smell surrounds me. It's the wonderful smell that first came into my senses when I lived in foster care. Not a specific perfume, nothing rich or heavy, just a clean, warm, *good* smell that wraps around me like a Superman cape, making me feel special, strong, safe, loved, and *her.*

我在葬礼上也见到了姐姐奥菲丽娅。在这里遇到姐姐，还有两个妹妹沙仑和金牡，会感觉有些古怪，再加上我家的传统"不打听，不多嘴"，更是让我十分难受。我心潮澎湃，又无法诉说和发泄，我只好下定决心，让自己能一门心思做点什么，我想到了一个行动计划。尽管妈妈走了之后，我就没怎么见过弗莱迪，我还是决定让他从我们的苦难生活中完全消失。这个想法一直都有，只是在我配置的毒药爆炸之后，才临时被搁置一旁。我还下定决心，不管妈妈离开多久，我都要尽量享受自己的童年时光。我要和朋友在一起，我们一起制造些小麻烦，也琢磨做些好玩的事情，用木头和轮子自制滑轮鞋，也许是想法子挣点零钱，给自己买辆自行车。然后我们就可以骑车在城里兜圈子，喜欢的话还可以去湖边玩耍，或是一直骑到水库附近的小山上，那是密尔沃基这一带最高的地方，在山顶举目四望，我感觉自己是世界之王。接下来，我就敢想敢干、敢作敢当，从山上一冲而下，双脚离开脚蹬，好让车速更快，更无遮拦，把危险撇到一旁，尽情享受速度的激情和快感。

在亨利舅舅的葬礼上，我还发誓自己不可以哭出来。这是我在向妈妈证明自己已经长大，她不必再为我操心了。

在接下来的两年间，我都没有掉过眼泪。但是一天下午，我的誓言经历了最为严峻的考验。那天我去了贝碧家，我那两个小妹妹和她呆在一起。弗莱迪给我们生活带来了如此之多的伤害，作为唯一的补偿，就是他那两个妹妹对我们非常之好。贝碧亲眼见过自己的哥哥曾如何待我，为了能有所表示，她总是对我问寒问暖，非常友好，甚至还时不时给我点钱之类的。

"克里斯，饿了么？"她迎了上来，没等我咧着嘴点头承认，她就拿出三明治的原料忙乎起来。突然，她想起来楼下还在洗着衣服，就问我能不能帮她把衣服放到甩干桶里。

当时我就应了下来，到了地下室，把湿漉漉的衣物从洗衣桶里拿出来，突然我闻到一种熟悉的味道。那是我还在福利院的时候，第一次接触到这种好闻的味道，不是香水，也不浓烈，那种味道清香四溢、温馨亲切，它在我周身上下围绕，仿佛用超人的神奇斗篷将我紧紧包裹住一样，让我感受到一种深切的关爱，是妈妈的味道。

第三章 妈妈在哪里

Standing there loading the dryer, not sure why my mother's presence is so vivid in my senses, I don't yet know that Baby happens to be storing some of Momma's clothes and things for her down here in the basement. I don't yet know that in a few weeks to come there will be one more blink, and that the channel will change, Momma will come home, and we'll all be reunited, living just as before.

Just like the scripts being switched back, we'll pick up where we left off—practically midsentence. Without explanation, and with Freddie.

All I know in the emptiness of Baby's basement is that I'm about to cry until I can't cry anymore, as the dam gets ready to bust from ten years' worth of pent-up question marks and a Mississippi River's worth of unshed tears.

But first, as her beautiful smell blankets me even more, just to be sure, I turn around and ask out loud, "Momma?"

我站在那里装着甩干桶，不明白为什么妈妈会如此清晰地出现在我的脑海。我不知道贝希碰巧保存了一些妈妈的衣物和物品，而且就放在了地下室。我更不会知道也就在几周后，一切又都变了，妈妈回来了，我们一家人又团聚了，和以前一样。

就像我们生活中的那个熟悉的剧本又突然被换回来一样，我们接着上次断开的部分继续生活。也是一样没有任何解释，而且一同回来的还有弗莱迪。

我在空无一人的地下室里，当时只知道一件事，就是我要哭，直到哭干自己最后一滴眼泪。因为大坝已经整整支撑了十年，实在无法扛住那些悬而未决的问题的重压，终于让密西西比河水一般的眼泪滂沱而下。

但在眼泪的闸门打开之前，我还是禁不住那美妙味道的诱惑，还想进一步确认，所以转过身来，大喊："妈妈，是你吗？"

Chapter 4
Bitches Brew(side a)

Chrissy Paul!" came to be a constant refrain, sung out in the Big House on Eighth and Wright, where we next lived temporarily with Bessie, not just by my mother, now free, to let me know she wanted me to run an errand, but by my sisters and girl cousins too.

Between the ages of ten and fourteen, without asking for it, I received intensive on-the-job training for a career as a professional gofer. But it was not what I had in mind in preparation for my illustrious future as Miles Davis, a goal I had obsessed over since hearing his music for the first time that evening with Uncle Henry.

Yet I was so grateful to Moms for listening to me go on and on about how desperate I was to learn to play, for finding and purchasing a secondhand trumpet for me, and for seeing that I had lessons too, that I couldn't say no to whatever it was she sent me out to get. Some of the errands I didn't mind at all, including the different stops I'd make on those days when we had to pay a few dollars on our grocery-store bills. A typical run might start with Moms saying, "Chrissy Paul, go on over to Baby's and pick up a package."

第四章
即兴精酿①（上）

"克里斯！"这声音仿佛是唱歌似的从第八大道右街的大房子里传来，我们和母亲就在这里和贝希阿姨临时凑合着住，倒是不用花钱，但我需要时不时地当差跑腿，连我那些姐姐妹妹、表姐表妹都可以支使我。

我在 10 岁到 14 岁的时候，连想都没想过，就接受了培养专业跑腿的在职培训。可这与我当时的远大理想相距甚远，我原本一门心思想成为迈尔·戴维斯这样的爵士大师，那天在亨利舅舅家头一次听到他曼妙的音乐，我就从此不能自拔，暗下决心，想一心向着这个伟大目标努力。

妈妈奈不住我一次次地央求，终于买来了一把二手小号，而且给我提了这样那样的要求，我也只好一切都照单全收，乖乖地让干什么就干什么。有些活我帮忙倒是没什么，比如到街边的杂货铺花几元钱买点这个那个之类。一般这类活计都是从妈妈这样张口喊我的名字开始的："克里斯，去贝碧家取个包包回来。"

---

① 编者注：Bitches Brew，爵士乐手迈尔·戴维斯(Miles Davis)作品，在 20 世纪 60 年代乐坛享有盛名。作者在此引为章标题以说明该作品对自己成长的重要影响。

I knew that meant we were getting a small loan to pay down another loan, even though the details were never discussed. It was all very discreet, as if to discuss how tight money was at home would be in poor taste. When I arrived at Baby's, she too didn't refer to the contents of the small folded package she handed to me, but of course I knew there were two or three dollar bills balled up inside. As the courier in these transactions, I may not have been privy to the exact numbers involved, but the process deepened my appreciation for my mother's ability to make ends meet—sometimes in order for us to eat that night.

This entire money thing was to become a subject of necessary interest, since I had no daddy to bankroll my wants and needs— like a certain style I wanted in my threads, which I learned to afford by economizing and stretching what cash I could earn doing odd extra jobs, and later, when having a car of my own would become a preoccupation. In the meantime, these money runs provided me with an introduction to a host of financial principles, like assets versus deficits, loans and interest, and how to get more value for less money.

Besides errands to Sy's and other local grocers, from time to time I'd stop to make payments at Uncle Ben's Store on Ninth and Meineke. A black-owned store, Uncle Ben's had a meat case where Moms occasionally had me get a dollar's worth of cold cuts—fifty cents' worth of salami and fifty cents' worth of cheese, dinner for a family of seven if you counted her, Freddie, me, Sharon, Kim, Ophelia, and our latest addition to the family, DeShanna, who was Ophelia's baby girl, born while my sister was in the detention home.

Unless I was literally starving to death, I refused to eat anything that came out of Uncle Ben's meat case. Nothing against Ben, but he had a cat he'd let snack on his deli meats. The sight of that cat sniffing and pawing the cold cuts horrified me from a scientific, medical standpoint. I might have only been twelve years old and was by no means an expert, but logic told me that a cat that just finished digging in kitty litter shouldn't be crawling over salami we were going to eat. But I kept my misgivings to myself.

One of the errands that I had least enjoyed was during the time when we were all getting settled back in together and DeShanna was still being kept in foster care, until Ophelia was able to get a job and bring her home to live with us. My assignment was to pick up DeShanna from the foster home, ten blocks away, and bring her to visit Ophelia at our house, and then return the toddler to the foster home.

虽然妈妈什么都没讲，但我明白我们这又是要拆东墙补西墙了。大家都心照不宣，仿佛说家里手头紧是见不得人的事情。等我到了贝碧家，她也是只字不提包里装的是什么，只是交给我一个折好的小纸包让我带走，当然我也清楚地知道里面包着的是两三个美元。做这种差事，我自然不会偷窥纸包里到底装了多少钱，不过这种事情让我对妈妈用心良苦维系一个家庭的生计而备受感动，有的时候我们几乎是靠这点钱才能解决当天的晚饭问题。

所有这些和钱相关的话题都让我颇费心思，因为没有父亲作为我的经济支柱，我不得不学会精打细算，省吃俭用，把自己打零工挣得的那点钱节省下来，甚至后来我曾一度以自力更生买辆自己的车子作为目标。与此同时，这些差事让我对一系列金融原则有了基本的认识，诸如资本和负债、借贷和利息，怎么通过更少的钱带来更大的价值之类，这些都离不开这时候的经历。

除了沙伊犹太店和其他一些小店，我还常光顾本叔叔的店，他家的店开在第九大道万利捷大街，本叔叔是黑人，他开的是肉铺，妈妈常让我从他那买一块钱的熟食回来，一半意大利香肠一半奶酪，这就是一家 7 口人的晚饭了，包括妈妈、弗莱迪、我、沙仑、金牡，还有姐姐奥菲丽娅的女儿德沙娜，那是她在少年管教所生的孩子。

虽然我饥肠辘辘，但还是不愿碰那些本叔叔肉铺里的食物。倒不是店主本人有什么问题，只是看到他家的猫总在店里吃肉让我接受不了，总是觉得从卫生角度这事情有点不可取。那时的我不过 12 岁，根本谈不上是什么专业人士，只是觉得猫咪刚在窝里刨来刨去，又过来动我们要吃的意大利香肠，实在有些说不过去。不过，这个秘密我没有说出去。

还有个差事让我头痛，就是需要大家都聚齐的时候，让我出马，把德沙娜接回家来。当时，德沙娜还寄养在福利院，只有姐姐奥菲丽娅找到工作后，才可以把她带回家来和大家生活在一起。我的工作就是把小家伙从 10 个街区以外的福利院带回家来，然后再把她送回去。

The PURSUIT of HAPPYNESS

Poor DeShanna didn't know me, and she barely knew Ophelia, so whenever she saw me coming, it was a gut-wrenching scene for all of us. The foster lady who was keeping DeShanna didn't make it any easier. As soon as the baby started to cry and throw a fit, screaming, falling on the floor, pounding her fists, and kicking her legs in the air, the foster mother started to cry too—giving me the evil eye, as if I had caused all this turmoil. Pretty soon I was ready to cry myself, because I had no say in the matter. She wasn't my baby, and I was just doing my job. The expression "Don't shoot the messenger" would resonate from this experience on.

When we finally got out the door, DeShanna cried all up and down the neighborhood as I tried to walk her to our place, causing me to have to pick her up and carry her. Every trip she seemed to scream louder, and she also got heavier. At that point, I'd have to put her down and coax her into walking. DeShanna made her displeasure known by screaming more and refusing to hold on to my fingers, like toddlers usually do. That meant I had to hold her hand, which gave her another reason to scream and try to pull away. People stopped and stared, saying nothing, but obviously thinking, *What is he doing to that child? What's wrong with that baby?*

The return trip after DeShanna visited Ophelia wasn't bad, especially as the two began to bond and the visit seemed to calm my niece down. But getting there the next time was just as horrific. We were all happy when social services finally allowed DeShanna to come live with Ophelia and the rest of us. Not surprisingly, the circumstances of how my sister had gotten pregnant weren't discussed. Didn't ask, and nobody told. But when I thought about DeShanna's situation, not having a daddy in her life, it was another reminder to myself that I wasn't going to bring sons and daughters into this world without having a presence in their lives.

* * *

"Chrissy Paul . . . !" rang through the house one day from three separate voices, almost like choir practice. Moms came first, continuing, "Go on down to the 'nigga' store and pick me up some Kotex."

Ophelia and my cousin Linda chimed in that they wanted Kotex too. This was the gofer job I most hated. Why couldn't they share the same package? Because Moms wanted the light red package, Ophelia the sky blue, and Linda the lavender. How could the same brand of sanitary napkin have so many variations? My cousin Terry had been through this plenty with his three sisters and walked by smirking. Whenever they asked him to go, he'd gleefully remark, "Send Chris!"

德沙娜不认识我，对自己的生母奥菲丽娅也不熟，一看到我来，就会又哭又闹，让大家谁都不好受。连福利院的阿姨都拿她毫无办法，小家伙又喊又叫，又哭又闹，在地上打滚，连踢带打，这阵势让福利院的阿姨都抹眼泪，对我怒目而视，仿佛这些都是我造成的。再下来，我自己都要掉眼泪了，我冤枉啊，这又不是我的孩子，我不过是履行职责罢了，不过是个跑腿的，这和我有何干系啊。

当我们终于能迈出大门，准备带她回家时，她就干脆躺在地上大哭大叫，我只好扶她起来，抱着她走。每次她号哭的动静似乎都更大几分，体重似乎也增重几分。后来，我只好放她下来，连哄带骗让她自己走。她心里不满，就继续大哭，不愿意拉我的手，这些都是小孩子惯用的一套。我只能去拉她的手，结果她就又哭，使劲要挣脱开来。路人都停下来，侧目观瞧，虽然嘴上没说什么，但分明是觉得：这人对孩子干了些什么？孩子有什么错？

回程似乎稍好些，德沙娜见过自己的妈妈，两人逐步建立感情，这个小外甥女好像情绪也平稳一些。可是下次再去接她，场面依旧混乱。当社会福利机构终于让她们母女团聚，可以把孩子接回家和我们生活时，大家终于皆大欢喜。不过，姐姐怎么会身怀有孕，家里人对此只字不提，也没有人问及，这是我们的传统。但一想到德沙娜的处境，想到她生命中不会有父亲的身影，又让我触动。我暗下决心，当自己的孩子来到世上后，我决不会离开他们。

* * *

"克里斯"，那天有三个人齐声喊着我的名字，就像唱诗班的排练一般。先是妈妈说："去帮我买些高洁丝回来。"

奥菲丽娅和表妹琳达也说要高洁丝，我最恼火的就是这种差事。她们就不能合用一包么？妈妈说要红色包装，奥菲丽娅要天蓝色，琳达要紫色。一个牌子的卫生巾怎么搞出这么多花样呢？泰瑞表哥见多识广，这种事情没少遇到过，可每当三个姐姐要他去买这些东西时，他就一脸坏笑地说："让克里斯去吧。"

Later, Ophelia at least felt sorry for me and started handing me a note and a brown paper bag for this errand, but it was too late. On my way home that particular day, I had my arms full with three different boxes of Kotex—which wouldn't fit in a store bag—when I heard a taunting voice behind me calling, "Hey, Pussy Man! Pussy Man!"

What was I going to do? Drop the sanitary napkins and go kick someone's ass? Or ignore them and suffer how fast this would get around school and the neighborhood? In my mind I could already see the mailman and Freddie—the Big Wheel was what everybody called him, fearing and almost admiring him—the two of them hanging on the bar at Luke's House of Joy telling everybody about the Pussy Man without no goddamn daddy. How was I going to live that down?

Still, I chose not to take the bait and kept on trudging back to all those waiting female family members who were having their cycles at the same time, not appreciating that my sensitivity to women could be an asset one day. Even though I was pissed off at whoever called me that, my MO with my peers by now was to take the path of least resistance whenever possible. It was bad enough to have to be in battle mode all the time at home, so at school and around the neighborhood I preferred using diplomacy.

Unfortunately, because I was on my way to being a big kid, always a head or more taller than anyone in my group of friends, whenever we went somewhere and got into an argument, it was inevitable that I was going to fight. That was street logic. Other kids would jump on me first to psyche out my friends, the tactic being that if you could beat me up, my buddies would fall in line. Tired of the routine, more than once I thought, *Man, I got to get me some big friends.* But before long I learned how to use my size and my intensity, with a look or a remark, to avoid a confrontation. There had to be serious provocation to make me hit someone.

One of my friends, Norman, discovered what serious provocation for me was when a group of us were walking back to Tenth and Wright one afternoon, informally playing "the dozens."

Norman had heard about what had happened a week earlier when Moms ran into a store to hide from Freddie—who'd chased her in there at gunpoint. This was not an incident that I'd witnessed, but I was still in a rage over accounts I'd heard about how Freddie had terrorized everyone in the store, pointing the shotgun at them and demanding to know, "Where is she?" and how when she snuck out and managed to get into a taxi, the cab driver wouldn't budge, even with my mother begging, "Take off, take off!"

至少奥菲丽娅还替我着想，把要买的东西写在纸上，还给我拿上个牛皮纸袋，但这已经无济于事。我怀里抱了三大包高洁丝，因为商店给的袋子里根本放不下，然后我听到自己身后有人冲我指指点点："瞧，这个娘娘腔！"

我该怎么办呢？把卫生巾往地上一扔，去踢那人的屁股，还是假装没听见，而放任这种事在学校和邻里间迅速传开？我眼前仿佛能看到邮差和弗莱迪两人泡在鲁克的快乐屋酒吧(人们都管邮差叫大轮儿先生，我对他还真有几分敬畏)，他们和周围人大肆宣扬"娘娘腔"就是那个没爹的野种，那我还怎么在这儿过下去？

最后，我还是忍着没发作，咬着牙回到家，谁让家里这些女性的生理周期都赶在了同一时间，我也一点没想过自己这种对于女性的敏感，有朝一日也许会成为一笔财富。虽然遭此奚落，但我和其他孩子相处的原则还是尽可能少发生冲突。因为家里已经充满火药味了，我希望在学校和街坊四邻还是尽量用外交手段解决问题。

但由于我的个子一天天长高，比周围的孩子高出一头甚至都不止，一旦发生争吵，动手可能就在所难免。因为街上就是这规矩。其他的孩子可能会先冲我动手，因为只要我这大个子被制服了，我那些朋友就自然不在话下。有时候我实在有些烦了，甚至觉得该换些大一点儿的朋友一起玩了。但不久之后，我就学会了要利用自己的身高和强势，用凌厉的眼神或是言语，来避免正面冲突的发生。只有真是迫不得已的情况下，我才会动手。

我有个朋友叫诺曼，见识了这种所谓迫不得已的正面冲突。那是在一天下午，当时，我们一群人正沿着第十大道右街往回走，边走边玩。

诺曼听说过一个星期之前，妈妈为躲避弗莱迪的毒打逃到一家商店，弗莱迪拎着枪在后面穷追不舍的事情。当时我倒是没有亲眼看见，但是也听人讲弗莱迪如何闯进商店，用枪口指着大家，问妈妈藏在哪里，把所有人都惊得面如死灰，魂飞魄散。妈妈偷偷溜出来，上了辆出租车想逃离这是非之地，可是听任妈妈怎么苦苦哀求，司机就是不为所动，车子压根就没动地方。听到这些让我火冒三丈。

I was sick when I heard how Freddie had run up, dragged Moms out of the taxi, and beat her bloody right there in the street with folks running out of shops and standing on stoops watching— doing nothing, saying nothing. Talk about insult to injury. No one could explain to me how the police and people of our neighborhood couldn't or wouldn't intervene. Even my uncles fell short in not standing up to Freddie. It wasn't fear, because any one of them could hold their own in a street fight; it was more about not getting in Momma's business. That didn't fly with me. Unbeknownst to me at the time, many communities were starting to break the silence about domestic violence, but whatever resources were available, we just didn't know about them. What I saw were too many people turning to look the other way, which I found—and still find—unconscionable.

Not that I needed any more incitement to kill Freddie Triplett, but when Norman decided to do his imitation of my mother running from my stepfather, it increased my sense of urgency tenfold.

"Hey, Chris!" Norman says, walking along, pretending to be Moms cowering. "Remember?" And then he does Freddie pointing his shotgun and says, " 'Where is she? Where is she?' Remember?"

Like a volcano, shocking even myself, I erupted on Norman, pummeling him with my fists and kicking him down the block, giving him the whipping I wish I could've put on Freddie.

From then on nobody ever had the nerve to bring up my momma, dozens or not. The exception to that was a relative of Freddie's, who was already in his twenties at this time and later started coming around too often for my liking, acting like he was entitled to boss Moms around and disrespect her any way he pleased. Once when I was in my teens, after she told him to lay off, he blasted her, saying, "You know you ain't talking to me because I'll knock your goddamn brains out."

As much as I wanted to do exactly to this creep what I had in mind for Freddie, I had to sit there and restrain myself. But I never forgot it. Though he didn't amount to much, I didn't become any more forgiving in the years that followed, and almost four decades later, when a family member invited him to a Thanksgiving dinner in Chicago—at my home, which I owned, to eat food that I bought—I couldn't eat. I couldn't sit in his presence because I didn't trust myself to not jump him and beat him within an inch of his miserable life. He was already missing a kidney, which meant that I could probably have killed him with one kidney punch. There was no forgetting what he had said to Momma and no forgiving. That was what being deeply provoked was to me.

更让我受不了的是，弗莱迪冲了出来，把妈妈从出租车里拽了出来，就在大街上大打出手，而周围都是跑出来看热闹的人群，大家却听之任之，一言不发。无论是这种肆意的伤害还是恶毒的侮辱，没有人出来主持公道。无论是警察还是街坊四邻，大家都是袖手旁观。甚至连我的舅舅们都没有插手管管这事情。倒不是因为什么害怕，其实弗莱迪根本不是我舅舅的对手，而是大家不愿意插手妈妈的家事。我也从没往这方面想过。在当时，很多社区已经不再对家庭暴力不闻不问了，但我对此却一无所知，即便是有这样那样的求助渠道，我们也根本没有听说过。我看到的只是人们的袖手旁观和若无其事。

我已经不需要更多的刺激就能坚定除掉弗莱迪的决心，但是当诺曼学妈妈在街上狼狈逃跑的样子时，我顿时就血往上涌，忍无可忍。

"克里斯，你看呀！"诺曼边走边说，学着妈妈躲躲藏藏的样子，"还记得吗？"接着他又模仿弗莱迪端着枪的样子，假模假式地说，"'她人藏在哪？在哪？'你还记得吗？"

我仿佛是火山一样，瞬间爆发了，连我自己都被吓了一跳，我一下子扑了过去，拳头雨点般地落在他身上，一脚接着一脚把他一路踢了回去，把所有对弗莱迪的积怨都发泄在诺曼的身上。

从那以后，没人再敢和我提妈妈的事情。但唯一的例外是弗莱迪的一个亲戚，他当时已经二十多岁了，而且还常来我家，对妈妈颐指气使，根本谈不上丝毫的尊敬。在我十几岁的时候，有一次，妈妈让他别闹腾了，他就破口大骂："你怎么敢这么和我说话，小心我把你的脑袋打烂。"

我当时恨得牙根痒痒，几乎就按耐不住又要大打出手，但我还是忍住了，咬牙坐在一旁，一声不吭。但我心里默默记住了这一切。虽然他并未屡屡如此，但我在很多年后仍无法释怀。大约40年后，有个亲戚邀请他来到我在芝加哥的家中参加感恩节晚宴，那是在我自己的家中，所有的食物都是我买来的，可我却根本吃不下。有他在场，我根本就没法坐下安心吃饭，因为我担心自己会忍不住对近在咫尺的他大打出手。他过得很惨，一个肾脏被摘除，已经是弱不禁风，只要我当腰给他一拳，他就可能命丧黄泉。他当年对待妈妈的方式根本让我无法忘却，更无法宽恕，他已经把我深深激怒。

But in other cases with my friends, when it came to someone having a laugh at my expense, I developed a fairly thick skin. Bottom line, I wanted to be liked, not so much to be popular with everyone—including my teachers and principals—but to be special, to have my own identity, to be cool.

To that end, the year before, I'd gotten it into my head that it would be the height of coolness to bring the glass eyeball belonging to one of Freddie's sisters to show-and-tell in my fifth-grade class. More and more, it seemed that whenever an idea got into my head, I had an ability to *focus* on it exclusively. This was the greatest double-edged sword I'd ever have to learn to wield. Whatever it was that drove me to pester Sis—as we called Freddie's sister—to let me take her glass eyeball to school, I couldn't say. But I was relentless.

In her early fifties, graying, Sis lived in her housecoat with her pint of whiskey in one of her housecoat pockets and a pack of Lucky Strikes in the other. Even outside the house, she rarely wore any other sort of attire, and never did I see her in dressy clothes. In 1965 in northeast Milwaukee, women did have a thing for housecoats: they'd put one over anything and wear it around town like it was a mink coat. Another member of the extended family, Miss Alberta, a great big, round, fat woman, had a habit of wearing five layers of clothes around underneath her housecoat, just another curious sight in our black *Happy Days* neighborhood. Sis wasn't far behind her.

Each time I went to beg, "Sis, can I take your glass eye to school for show-and-tell?" I got the same response.

Taking a swig of whiskey, each time her answer was, "No, motherfucker. Take my goddamn eye? No! Hell, no!"

Finally, I developed an alternative plan of action. Since I knew where she kept her glass eye—in a jar with some liquid to keep it wet at night when she slept—my plot was to stop by in the morning, borrow it while she was asleep, then return it at lunchtime just before her usual rising hour.

All went beautifully that morning, and when I arrived at school, I could hardly wait until my turn at show-and-tell. Nobody had ever brought in a glass eyeball. Sitting in my seat just before it was my turn, I couldn't mask the smile stretching across my face because this was going to be my day to shine.

All of a sudden, an ungodly screeching came ricocheting down the hallway, at first unintelligible but soon coherent enough for all of us to hear: "Chris! Chris! Give me back my eye. Give me my eye. I'm g'on whup your ass. Give me back my goddamn eye!"

In unison, every single classmate spun around and gawked at me.

但是在其他一些场合下，我那些朋友拿我开玩笑，我却可以一笑而过，毫不在乎。我的宗旨就是希望人们能喜欢我，不一定要包括老师校长在内的每个人都要喜欢我，但我至少要有自己的特点，有自己的身份。这才够酷。

为此，五年级的时候，我脑袋里突然蹦出一个想法，要是把弗莱迪姐姐的玻璃假眼拿到课堂上来做介绍与展示，那一定酷到极点。后来，一次次的实践证明，只要我有个什么想法出来，就一定会一心一意琢磨这事。这种能力是把双刃剑，让我以后受益无穷，也给我带来了不少麻烦。是什么让我缠着弗莱迪的姐姐希斯，借她的假眼拿到学校展示，我也说不大清楚，但我就是不达目的不罢休。

希斯姑妈 50 出头，头发花白，总穿一件家常外罩，一个兜里装一小瓶威士忌，另一个兜里揣一包好彩牌香烟。即便是在屋子外面，她也很少换件衣服，我更没见过她穿裙子的样子。在 1965 年的密尔沃基东北部，女人们都喜欢穿家常外罩，不管里面穿什么，外面都要套上这么件外罩，仿佛穿的是貂皮大衣一样，招摇过市。家里还有个远亲阿尔伯塔小姐，是个大个子的胖女人，她就习惯在这种外罩里穿上五层衣服，这就是我们当初幸福时光的一个有趣景观。希斯姑妈的穿着和这位远亲也有一比。

我每次央求姑妈的时候，得到的答复基本是一样的，"希斯姑妈，我把玻璃眼球带到课堂做展示行吗？"

每次她都是先一仰脖喝上一口威士忌，然后说："小混蛋，拿走我的假眼，你想都别想！不可能！"

最后我只好"曲线救国"，换了一套行动方案。我知道她夜里睡觉时，会把假眼放在一个盛着液体的小罐子里，保持假眼湿润。我计划在早上她没醒的时候，就把假眼拿走，然后中午时，再偷偷送回来，通常她要在中午过后才会起床。

那天早上一切进展顺利，我到了学校，几乎等不及一个个轮到自己再做展示了。之前，谁都没有把假眼带到学校过的。马上要轮到我了，我几乎抑制不住自己脸上漾起的得意微笑，马上就要到我大放异彩的时候了。

突然间，走廊里传来一阵阵尖声叫骂，开始还听不太真切，但很快大家都听得清清楚楚，是在喊我的名字，"克里斯！还我的眼睛，看我不打烂你的屁股。把眼睛给我还回来！"

班里的人齐刷刷地把目光投在我身上，都不明白出了什么事情。

Another torrent of screeching followed, clearly threatening: "Boy, give me my goddamn eye. I want my eye. I'm g'on whup your ass, you little thievin' motherfucker!"

With that, Sis threw open my classroom door and stood there out of breath, hair all scraggly and matted, in her slippers and raggedy housecoat, shaking with fury, glaring at everybody with her one good eye and her empty socket as she roared, "Give me back my goddamn eye!" Slack-jawed, the teacher and my classmates stared at me in bewilderment, not knowing who she was or anything about an eye. A complete fiasco.

Embarrassment weighed on me like cement shoes as I had to go up to Sis, in front of everyone, reach into my pocket, and pull out her eyeball. She squinted her good eye at what looked like a marble in my open palm and snatched it from me, plopped it right back into the socket in front of the class, turned around, and exited, cussing me out all the way back down the hall.

I thought my teacher was going to faint. One little girl did throw up. Apparently neither of them had ever seen the likes of Sis or the insertion of a glass eye.

The repercussions at home weren't terrible. Freddie was predictable, barking, "Chris, don't you be taking Sis's eye again, you hear me? 'Cause if you do, I'm g'on beat yo ass and you won't be able to sit down for a week!" That didn't bother me much because he'd use any excuse to beat my ass.

It was at school where I felt the pain. For a long while I was the laughingstock of Lee Elementary, and kids were talking about Sis and her glass eye for weeks. But of course, I lived to tell. Other than that debacle, I usually did well in school—as long as I was interested and challenged. Besides my increasingly voracious appetite for books, which now took me down the library aisles to find classics by the likes of Charles Dickens and Mark Twain, and a budding interest in history, I found math fun and kind of satisfying, with problems to be solved like games that yielded answers to questions that were either right or wrong, yes or no.

Not like the questions that dominated at home.

* * *

During the few years after Moms came back from prison, I tried to get a read on what they had done to her, how she had changed, or not, and what was in her heart. Freddie, the old man, was a prison for all of us, a ball and chain. He was an addiction, I supposed, the reason that no matter how many times she escaped or pushed him out the door, promising, "He ain't never coming back," he always did. After a while, I wondered if she was really *afraid* of Freddie anymore. I wondered if she stayed as a reminder to him that no matter what dreams he took away from her, he couldn't break her; even if he got her sent to prison twice, he couldn't defeat Bettye Jean. In fact, if she ever felt low, if she ever got down, Moms refused to reveal it.

又一轮叫骂开始了，比刚才更凶狠，"混蛋东西，把眼睛拿回来。给我眼睛。看我怎么收拾你，小贼娃子！"

接着，希斯姑妈一把推开教室的门，上气不接下气地站在门口，头发披散着，脚上只穿着拖鞋，随意披着家常外罩，气得浑身都在哆嗦，她用那只好眼扫视着大家，另一只眼框空空的，什么都没有，"把眼睛还我，混蛋东西！"她大声咆哮着，老师和同学们都惊呆了，大张着嘴巴，不明白这人是谁，为什么找自己的眼睛。教室里彻底乱作一团。

我尴尬万分，步履沉重地走上前去，在众目睽睽之下，从口袋里掏出了她的假眼。她用那只好眼瞅了瞅我手心的玻璃假眼，一把拿走，当着全班人的面，把假眼塞进了眼眶，转身走了，一路上还骂声不停。

我估计老师要晕过去了，有个小女生当时就吐了，显然谁都没见过这种阵势，也没见过有人这么当场装假眼。

家里的反应倒是没出我所料。弗莱迪当然又要大发雷霆，"克里斯，你要再敢动希斯姑妈的眼睛，看我怎么收拾你，我非打得你一个星期坐不下去。"他总是找各种理由来让我受皮肉之苦，我对此早已习以为常。

还是回到学校让我更难以忍受。很长时间之后，我都是学校里的笑柄，关于希斯姑妈和她的假眼的事，孩子们谈论了足足有几个星期不止。但我还是撑过来了。除了捅了这么个漏子之外，我在学校里过得还不错，那里有我喜欢的东西，也有我需要应对的挑战。而且，我如饥似渴地阅读，经常泡在图书馆，看那些狄更斯和马克·吐温的经典小说，我甚至对历史也萌生了兴趣，而且觉得数学也是趣味盎然，我喜欢解决那些是非对错的问题。

而我家里那些事情，很难讲清究竟孰是孰非。

* * *

在过去几年间，妈妈出狱后都和我们生活在一起。我总想理解她内心的真实想法，她是否不再像从前，还是从未改变，她真实的想法究竟是什么。老家伙弗莱迪是我们所有人的噩梦，他是镣铐，是锁链，让我们喘息不得，同时他挥之不去，因为无论母亲怎样逃离这个家，怎样把他关在门外，发誓不再让他回来，他还是出现在我们的生活中。有时候，我甚至想，妈妈究竟怕不怕弗莱迪，是不是只要她存在，就可以向弗莱迪证明，就是他夺走了妈妈所有的梦想，妈妈也打不垮，即便他让妈妈两次锒铛入狱，他也打不倒贝蒂·让·加德纳。而且，即便妈妈曾经心灰意冷，曾经痛不欲生，她也从未表示过。

第四章 即兴精酿（上）

The PURSUIT of HAPPYNESS

Rarely did she express impatience or frustration with me, even when I deserved it. But the couple of instances when she did, in her inimitable style of brutal understatement, she made her point better than with any ass whupping.

There was the time when she came home and presented me with a new pair of pants she'd bought from somewhere like Gimbels. When I looked at them and spotted the eight-dollar price tag, without thinking, and instead of being honored and grateful she'd spent that money on me, I said, almost as if to myself, "Man, for eight dollars, at the Discount Center, I could've got some shoes, pants, and a shirt *and* had money left over to go to the movies too."

Momma gave me a hard look that cut me to the quick, then snatched back the pants and said, "Boy, you too big a scrub to wear some eight-dollar pants!"

Too late for an apology, I felt as terrible as I should have, knowing that was the last I'd see of those pants. That day made me work even harder to watch my mouth. Not to excuse myself, but the tendency to use words in mean, hurtful ways, without thinking, was an ugly characteristic that I had picked up from Freddie. Actually, my three sisters and I all developed the ability to be verbally abusive in extreme situations. Even now I have to make a conscious effort, not always successfully, to keep my mouth in check.

In her way, Moms showed me how powerful both words and silence can be. After the telephone cord whuppin' she gave me for stealing a bag of popcorn much earlier, the next time I tried to be slick and steal something, she only needed to give me a disappointed look to invoke the pain of the cord.

At thirteen years old, hormones churning, big kid that I'm becoming, wanting to be cool and look good, I go out and decide to shoplift a pair of pants from the Discount Center, thinking I'm real slick. The stupidity of it is that getting caught never registers while my brain's concentrating only on the opportunity to slip on those pants underneath my own and fool myself that no one's going to suspect a schoolboy like me, my stack of books under my arms and all.

As I head out the door, reality sets in with a tap on my shoulder from a store manager. Now I am a criminal, schoolbooks and all. Bracing myself for a stern lecture and a warning, I get walloped by something much worse: the arrival of two white cops who push and shove me out to their patrol car and take me down to the station. Once more, I prepare for the painful phone call home and the subsequent arrival of my upset mother and crazy, drunk stepfather. Instead, I stand by as the desk officer makes the phone call and listen as he reaches the old man while, obviously, the plan changes. As he delivers the news to Freddie that I'm being held at the station until someone comes to get me, the cop starts laughing hilariously, then hangs up the phone and drags me off to a holding cell.

而且，在对我的态度上，无论我多么过分，她都很少丧失耐心和信心，但她少有的几次发火让我记忆犹新，她不会动粗，但是她言语中所透露的威严和力量绝对胜过皮肉之苦。

一次，她给我带回了一条八美元的裤子，一看就是从金倍尔百货这种地方淘回来的。我瞥见8美元的价签，非但没有感激她为我如此破费，反而不假思索，脱口而出："天，整整8块钱哟，要是我，足够从打折柜台买上鞋子、裤子、衬衫，再加上去看场电影了。"

妈妈狠狠地瞪了我一眼，让我不寒而栗，她拿起裤子，说了一句："这条8块钱的裤子，你实在不配穿。"

一切为时已晚，我惊惶失措，知道自己和这条裤子从此无缘。在那之后，我对自己的言行倍加小心。我不是为自己开脱什么，只是觉得弗莱迪用词刻薄恶毒、说话不假思索，这种恶习我已经有所沾染。实际上，我们兄妹几个都有这种倾向，在极端的情况下，会出言不逊，口无遮拦。时至今日，我还要对自己的言行多加小心，慎言慎行，即便如此，有时还会出言不逊。

妈妈用她自己的方式告诉我，语言和沉默都可以充满力量。小时候那次偷爆米花，她用电话线对我一顿狠抽，可在这之后，我又想有小动作的时候，她投来的失望眼神就足以让我心有余悸。

13岁时，青春期萌动，我长得又高又壮，也想摆酷，决定去打折店顺一条裤子，显摆一下自己，同时觉得自己身手敏捷，应该不成问题。这种掩耳盗铃的想法绝对愚蠢，我一心想着怎么样才能得手，把赃物藏在裤子里面溜走，就没有想过自己这种打扮的学生娃怎么会不引起店家的注意。

我刚迈出店门，店长就一把钳住了我的肩膀。我被抓了个正着，还夹着课本，人赃俱获。店长对我一顿数落，不仅如此，车上下来两个白人警察，把我直接带到警局。我如坐针毡，准备和家人通电话，接下来是妈妈焦虑不安地赶来接人，还有那个醉醺醺的继父一同赶到。可是当值班警员拨通电话，听到的是弗莱迪的声音，可这次好像情况有所不同。警察和弗莱迪说明情况，我被警局扣押，需要家人来接我回去，突然警察放声大笑，挂上电话，就把我关进了号子。

He explains that Freddie won't come get me. The quote from Freddie was: "Come get him? Naw, leave his ass in there. Fuck him!"

Muttering to myself under my breath, I take a book from the top of my stack and start to read, hoping that Melville and *Moby-Dick* and the escape through reading will calm me down.

This also causes the white cops to laugh their asses off. One of them asks, "You're not reading that shit, are you? 'Cause if you're so smart, what the fuck are you doing in jail?"

The other cop repeats Freddie's words, "His old man says, 'Leave his ass in there. Fuck him!'"

When Moms and Freddie do come to get me, neither one has to say a word, because they can see from my shame that I've gotten a crash course in what it feels like to be in a jam with the police, to be confined and locked up—none of which I've ever experienced. For a flash, the gloating look on Freddie's face makes me angry enough to forget I was the wrongdoer in this situation. Momma's disappointed expression corrects that misapprehension in a heartbeat.

Of course, there was nothing I wanted more in the universe than to make my mother proud of me. So naturally, on those few occasions when I let her down, it hurt me forever.

My trumpet playing, I hoped, could be something to make Moms proud. I practiced tenaciously, for both the youth concerts I was starting to do and Roosevelt Junior High School's band. One evening before dinner, instead of asking me to run over and pick up some essentials—my job, after all—Moms heard me practicing and decided she would go, as long as I'd keep an eye on the beans she had on the stove.

"Great!" I responded, glad that I didn't have to run out but could stay in my room and continue memorizing "Song for My Father" by Horace Silver—my solo at an upcoming concert. With my gift for extreme focus, I was so locked into practicing, I forgot all about the beans until a scorched smell came wafting into my room. When I ran to the kitchen and took a look, the beans were burned pretty badly.

Somehow I thought that it would make my mother less mad if I was practicing yet still aware there was a problem when she came home, as if I'd been checking on them all along. "Moms," I called from my bedroom when she came in the front door, "you better check the beans, I think they burned up."

The sound of the lid of the pot being removed and then replaced loudly echoed down the hallway. My stomach clenched. Momma worked her magic from day to day to stretch our resources and feed us all, and I had to let the beans burn up. Even though she probably wanted to kill me, Moms mustered the greatest control, walked slowly down the hall, and stood in the doorway of my room, saying quietly, "Chris, you know most of the arguments and fights Freddie and I get in are over you, and you can't even watch a pot of beans."

他说，弗莱迪拒绝来接我，原话是这么说的："什么？让这杂种就烂死在局子里吧，狗娘养的。"

我嘟囔了几句，从书包里拿出本书来，认真读了起来，希望梅尔维尔的《大白鲸》和自己的全神贯注，能让我平静下来。

结果这又成了这些白人警察的笑柄。一个人问："你小子还读这个，是不是觉得自己聪明绝顶啊，都这样了，还琢磨什么呢？"

另一个警察学着弗莱迪的腔调说："让这杂种就烂死在局子里吧，狗娘养的。"

当妈妈和弗莱迪真的来接我的时候，大家一句话都没说，因为我的悔改之意已经昭然若揭，这种关押的经历和如此的反省于我都是从未有过。余光中，我看到弗莱迪脸上的一丝得意，这让我怒火中烧，险些忘了自己的处境。可是妈妈的失望瞬间让我回归了理智。

当然，我最想做的事情莫过于让妈妈脸上有光，因此这种让妈妈伤心的事情，也会让我一辈子心怀愧疚。

我希望自己演奏小号能让妈妈引以为豪，于是刻苦训练，在青年音乐会上我有所表现，在罗斯福中学乐队里也积极表演。一天晚上，看到我在练习小号，妈妈本来想让我去买东西，结果转念自己动身去了，而只是让我帮着照看一眼锅里的豆子就好。

我满心欢喜，不用出去跑腿，只需要待在家里练习我的表演曲目——席佛的《父亲颂歌》。我那专心致志的特长此时得到了充分的发挥，彻底把锅里的豆子忘得一干二净。突然，一股刺鼻的焦煳味道弥漫在房间之中，我忙跑到厨房，豆子已经烧煳，无法挽回。

我觉得还是继续练习，等妈妈回来之后，报告出现了问题，好像自己一直都在照看豆子，这可能让她消消气。听到她回来，我说："妈妈，你看看吧，我觉得豆子可能烧煳了。"

只听锅盖咣当一声落在地上，走廊里都是回声，我心头一紧。妈妈每天挖空心思，给我们弄出这点食物实属不易，我却听任豆子烧煳都无动于衷。当时她一定想把我生吞活剥，但还是努力控制住了自己的情绪，缓缓走到客厅，站到我的屋门前，平静地说道："克里斯，我和弗莱迪的大部分争吵都是因你而起，我要护着你，可你却连一锅豆子都看不好。"

Her one statement spoke ten volumes, every inference cutting me to the bone. The harshest truth was that I had been selfish, caught up in myself and my trumpet practice. The other truth was that she would do anything for me, even incite his wrath if it meant taking my side. Was it true that I was the main reason they fought? If it was, that was crazy, as crazy as Freddie was. The thought just kicked up the flame underneath the burner of my hatred for him, scorching and burning me up like those beans.

Moms, having said her piece, let it go. She turned and went back to the kitchen, opened up a can of tomato sauce, and added some seasoning, salvaging the burned beans and turning them into a hearty pot of good beans that we had for dinner that night.

Yet for all that I knew about her, she was a mystery. Only a couple of times did I catch a glimmer of what she experienced in her inner world. One of those times was in passing, really, one night when Freddie was out and I'd finished my homework and the two of us saw that a Bette Davis movie was coming on television. Moms loved Bette Davis, I always assumed because of their names being almost identical. No, my mother said, all bluesy and philosophical, the reason she liked Bette Davis movies was because she was so strong and convincing. "And she plays them parts so good," Moms admitted, "you just have to get mad at her."

What else made my Momma happy? Probably it was when she felt that she was being who she was meant to be—a teacher. In her own way, to me and my sisters, she was our professor, our Socrates. It had to make her happy to see that she was getting through to us, seeing me respond to her repeated insistence that without the ability to read and write, I would be nothing more than a slave. When I left for the public library over on Seventh and North Avenue with only one book or question that I wanted to answer, but then got caught up exploring the card catalog and discovering book after book, reading all day long—that made Moms happy. Books made her happy. She loved reading, and she loved *Reader's Digest*. She got me hooked on it too. We both read it cover to cover and then discussed the issue together. Maybe the happiest I ever saw her was the day I found a poem in an old issue of *Reader's Digest* at the library and copied it down to read to her. Poetry hadn't done much for me, but there was something that grabbed me about the music and feelings in a poem by Elizabeth Barrett Browning. Momma listened quietly at first, becoming very still—as only she could do—when I read the first few lines: *How do I love thee? Let me count the ways. I love thee to the depth and breadth and height my soul can reach . . .*

By the time I finished reading "How Do I Love Thee," my mother had tears overflowing from her eyes. She said that was her favorite poem and my discovering it made her happy.

* * *

她话语不多，却字字珠玑，每个字都生生敲在我的脑海之中。我知道自己是自私的，一心只想着自己，自己的演奏，这毋庸置疑。再有就是，她为了我可以不顾一切，甚至为了我，不惜激起弗莱迪的一腔怒火和怨气。难道我是他们争吵的主要原因？若真是如此，简直太不可思议。但这个念头立刻又激发了我对他的仇恨，那仇恨的火苗足以将这些豆子烧成焦炭。

妈妈说完这些，就转身离去。回到厨房，打开一罐番茄酱，加了些调味料，那锅烧焦的豆子又神奇地变成一顿美味的晚餐，端上了饭桌。

就我对妈妈的了解而言，她还是一团谜。仅仅有过几次，她内心深处的真实想法有所表露，但转瞬即逝。一天夜里，弗莱迪出门了，我做完作业，电视上正在播放贝蒂·戴维丝的片子，妈妈喜欢贝蒂，我都怀疑这可能是与这个演员和妈妈同名有关。妈妈可不这么想，她觉得自己是喜欢贝蒂的伤感和哲理，情感真挚和强烈。妈妈说："她演得很入戏，没法不为她动容。"

还有什么能让妈妈开心的呢？估计就是能从事她心仪已久的教师职业。对她而言，就是教好我们兄妹几个，她就是我们的教授，我们的苏格拉底。我们终于能领悟她的意思，明白无法识文断字就只能做牛做马，一事无成。当我来到第七大道北街的公共图书馆，本想查一本书或是找个问题的答案，结果却在索引目录中流连忘返，一本接着一本，如饥似渴，在图书馆里泡上一天，没有比这更让妈妈开心的了。她也喜欢阅读，喜欢《读者文摘》，而且让我也欲罢不能。我们俩通常是一字不落地看完一本，并且一起讨论问题。一次，我在图书馆找到一本《读者文摘》的旧刊，把其中一首诗抄下来，读给她听，我从未见过她那么开心。以前，我对诗歌的感觉一般，但那首诗是出自英国女诗人伊丽莎白·巴雷特·勃朗宁笔下，其字里行间的乐感和真情让我动容。妈妈静静地听着，听到头几行的时候，她突然变得一动不动，她可以做到一动不动：让我怎样爱你？我来尽数告诉你。我可以爱你爱到地老天荒，爱到灵魂的深处……

我念到最后一句，"让我究竟怎样爱你"，我看到她眼中涌动着泪花。她告诉我喜欢这首诗，我的发现给她带来了快乐。

* * *

第四章 即兴精酿（上）

The PURSUIT of HAPPYNESS

Nineteen sixty-eight was the year of the Great Awakening for me. It set off a Big Bang in the universe of my being, exploding with the atomic energy of my own coming of age and the monumental changes taking place all around me. This period marked the dawning of my consciousness as a person of color, following on the heels of my discovery, lo and behold, that the world was not all black. Five years earlier, the adult reaction to the assassination of President Kennedy had been a hint about what it meant to be a minority and to lose a champion. But it was a year after that when I and some of my classmates were bused to a white school on the east side of Milwaukee that I saw with my own eyes what Moms experienced every day when she left the neighborhood to go to work. It wasn't just that with the few exceptions of janitors and a sprinkling of black kids, everyone was white, which was the polar opposite of the ghetto, where everyone was black except for a shopkeeper here and a policemen there. It was also feeling what it was to have my color as my identity, to be looked down on, to be regarded as less than, to feel shame, or to be invisible, a nonentity other than a dark-skinned black boy. But the real shock was when four little girls were bombed to death down in Birmingham, Alabama— because they were black.

Seeing Momma crying as she watched the TV coverage made the lightbulb go on. They could have been my sisters. And in fact, I now saw, in my connection to the black community at large, that they were indeed my sisters. With new outrage and fervor to protest all past, present, and future wrongs done to my people, I experienced a new sense of connection as I began to follow what was happening in the world outside Milwaukee. In 1965 the Watts riots in Los Angeles took place, the same year Dr. Martin Luther King led civil rights marches down in Selma, Alabama, and Malcolm X was killed in Harlem. The following year, when a coalition of Milwaukee minority groups and activists came together—organized by Father James Groppi, a Catholic priest—I took to the streets to march, along with two of my good friends, Garvin, a trumpet player in the school band with me, and Ken, or "Zulu," as we called him. A true character, Zulu was not a good-looking cat by any stroke, but he had brilliant acting talent and could have gone far putting it to use. Later on, he actually got on a kick that he was going to be in the movies and convinced me that I could be an actor too.

Testing out the possibility, I ran it by Moms over breakfast, stating matter-of-factly in between bites, "Yeah, I'm gonna be an actor when I finish school."

My mother nodded patiently and asked rhetorically, "Okay, Chris, go get the newspaper and you tell me—how many jobs they got in there for actors?"

But that wasn't enough to make me reject the idea, and I continued to drop comments about how I had the stature and voice and composure to be a fine actor.

That was until I asked Moms for five dollars for something— yet again.

1968年对我而言异乎寻常，仿佛我的宇宙发生了一次大爆炸，让我的原子能得以爆炸式地释放开来，我身边更是发生了很多巨大的变化。这段时期对我意味着生命开始重现色彩，随着我的发现，我的世界不再只有黑与白。5年前，大人们对肯尼迪遇刺所做的反应，或多或少预示着作为少数族裔，当竞争失利将意味着什么。但当一年之后，我和几个同学乘车来到密尔沃基东区的一所白人学校时，我终于亲眼目睹了妈妈年轻时离家工作时的情景，除了门房是黑人，除了零星的几个黑人孩子，到处都是白人，这与贫民区形成鲜明对比，那里只有个别店主和警察是白人，而余下尽数都是黑人。仿佛我的肤色就注定了我的身份，注定要被鄙视、低人一等，甚至让人视而不见。更令人发指的是有四个小女孩在阿拉巴马州伯明翰被炸身亡，仅仅因为她们的肤色是黑色。

妈妈看到电视里的报道黯然落泪，这些孩子年龄与妹妹相差无几，却遭此厄运。同时，我意识到自己与黑人社会的血脉相连，我们确实亲如手足。随着有色人种所有新仇旧恨的接连爆发，我开始意识到自己与黑人社会间的这种密切联系，开始理解和关注在密尔沃基以外的世界。1965年，洛杉矶爆发华特暴动，同年，马丁·路德·金在阿拉巴马的塞尔玛举行民权游行，著名黑人民权运动领袖马尔科姆·艾克斯在哈莱姆区遇刺。次年，密尔沃基少数族裔和激进分子联合行动，在天主教詹姆士·格罗皮牧师的带领下，进行游行，我也走上街头，参加了游行队伍，同行的还有两个好友，一个是小号手加文，他与我同在学校乐队效力，再有就是肯，绰号祖鲁。祖鲁名如其人，他人长得绝对谈不上英俊潇洒，但是演技超凡，而且绝对可以在这方面有所作为。后来，他果真准备在电影界发展，甚至还说服我，说我也完全可以干这个行当。

我还真动了这门心思，一天早饭时，我边吃面包边说："我毕业以后想当演员。"

妈妈耐心地点点头，委婉地问道："克里斯，你去拿份报纸，看看上面有多少份工作是招聘演员的？"

但我还是不死心，我继续念叨着自己的身体条件不错，声音也好听，举手投足都是做演员的好坯子。

然后我就张口向妈妈要5块钱，这已经不是第一次了。

The PURSUIT of HAPPYNESS

Eyes down on her newspaper, not even lifting them, instead of making a dig that maybe I could go out and hustle up more hours doing odd jobs after school, she said with trademark subtle sarcasm, "Well, why don't you just *act* like you got five dollars?"

How do you act like you've got five dollars? I got the point.

With that, I got over that fleeting ambition and rededicated myself to the trumpet. Zulu was the one who really should have stuck with it. He had a gift for marching and singing "We Shall Overcome" with the intensity and power of a movement leader, at the same time that he used every opportunity to pinch white women's booties. When they turned around to see who'd done it, Zulu plastered his face with the most noble of expressions and kept on singing.

Garvin and I were amazed. "If he did that to a black woman," said Garvin when we saw Zulu pinching several booties during a big march we did, "she'd turn around and slap his face."

"Yeah," I whispered back, "and tell his momma too."

St. Boniface Catholic Church, Father Groppi's home base, offered a haven away from the minefields in the Triplett household, and besides marching for important concerns like open housing and desegregation of clubs that still barred blacks, Jews, and Catholics, the organizers fed us—everything from doughnuts and sandwiches to a variety of homemade ethnic food. Fulfilling many needs, our young activism was often as fun as it was meaningful. To have such a powerful boost to my self-image—especially at a time when my preoccupation with the opposite sex was all-consuming— was a true blessing.

My self-esteem had suffered not only from Freddie's near-daily attacks but from the higher status my community seemed to give lighter-skinned blacks. For years I had hated Smokey Robinson for being the epitome of the kind of guy that every girl I knew wanted. Slender, light-skinned, green-eyed, with his wavy "good" hair and lilting voice, he had no idea how he ruined life for tall, muscular, dark-skinned, " nappy"-haired baritone guys like me. Even to this day, I swear, if he came in the room I'd have to challenge him to a damn duel for pain and suffering—including the time a girl I liked turned her nose up and told me, "You just a big black ugmo."

Mercifully, it soon turned out that Smokey wasn't the only singer happening. Yes, Smokey could sing, and he was an amazing songwriter and performer, but so were a lot of darker-skinned black guys. When James Brown, Godfather of Soul, came along and proclaimed, "Say it loud, I'm black and I'm proud," that was the Holy Grail for a kid as black as me.

她眼睛盯着报纸,头都没抬,她没有让我下课后多做点零活,却冷冷地用她标志性的口吻说:"你怎么不先表演一下自己挣到5块钱的样子出来呢?"

怎么才能扮出挣到5块钱的样子?我终于明白了妈妈的意思。

我终于收回了心思,专心致志地又回到小号的演奏上来。而祖鲁绝对是个演艺天才。他可以一边昂首阔步,高歌《胜券在握》,俨然一幅领导者的姿态,同时他又不失时机地对白人女子的美腿动手动脚。当人家转身察看时,他却一本正经,若无其事的样子,继续高歌前进。

加文和我非常纳闷,"要是他对黑人女子这么做,会怎么样呢?",一路上,我们看到祖鲁如此这般,屡试不爽,加文发话了:"那她一定会转身抽他耳光。"

我小声应答:"没错,而且还会找他的妈妈告状。"

詹姆士·格罗皮牧师所在的圣博尼费斯天主教堂和崔普雷特附近的人头攒动形成鲜明对比,外面是示威游行,反对黑人、犹太人、天主教等的居住和集会的种族隔离,牧师对我们盛情款待,多纳圈、三明治以及各式自制食品,应有尽有。参加这种活动能满足多种需求,当然受人欢迎。同时,还极大地提高了我的知名度,特别是在女孩子们面前,显得特别有身份。

平素里,我几乎每天都要面对弗莱迪对我自尊心的打击,同时周围人似乎对肤色浅的黑人更有好感。许多年来,我对史摩基·罗宾逊成为多少女孩子的梦中情人而耿耿于怀。身材修长、肤色浅咖、曲发碧眼、声音动听,对于我这样的人高马大、肤色黝黑的卷发男生来说,他简直就是我的"终结者"。时至今日,若是他走进屋来,我都会想和他痛痛快快地单打独斗一场,就是当时有自己心仪的姑娘不屑地说我是个丑八怪也在所不惜。

还好,会唱歌的不仅仅是史摩基一个,他确实在表演和创作上极具天赋,但这样的黑人还有很多,当灵歌之王詹姆斯·布朗大声宣称"我是黑人,我为我的肤色而骄傲"的时候,这对于我这样的黑小子而言简直是天籁之音。

The PURSUIT of HAPPYNESS

Before long, processes that never worked for me and hideous-smelling conks that only burned my scalp were out while Afros and naturals were in, along with dashikis and beads. Man, I took to that look so fast, I must have been the first and youngest black hippie in America. The dashiki thing didn't work in the 'hood in Milwaukee, but eventually I blended the Black & Proud look with hippie garb from secondhand garments bought at the Good Will and the Salvation Army to have the best beads, best bell-bottomed hip-pants, and best tie-dyes around, topped off by a big Afro. Smokey Robinson could kiss my ass.

James Brown was my man. When my boy Garvin and I started hanging out at St. Boniface and got into marching, we made it a policy to make sure everyone we knew shopped only where they accepted the Black & Brown Stamps that James Brown was promoting to help impoverished inner cities across the country. These were something like S&H Green Stamps. Our efforts seemed to go well until we filled up two shopping carts at the A&P in a white neighborhood and waited until we were in the checkout line before I asked the cashier, "Do you have Black & Brown Stamps? 'Cause if you ain't got no Black & Brown Stamps, we can't do no business here. We can't shop here." Black power, thirteen-year-old style.

So fast it made our heads spin, the police arrived on the scene and stood like backup singers behind the manager, who looked coldly into our faces and said, "You two put everything back, we'll just forget about it. But if you don't put it all back where it came from, you're both going to jail." As he turned to walk away and we sheepishly went to return each item to the shelves, most of the store personnel laughed themselves silly.

Nonetheless, we were proud of our efforts as we headed back to St. Boniface for a meeting and a march with the NAACP Youth Council, only to learn that the offices of the NAACP's Milwaukee chapter had been bombed. That instantly intensified the seriousness of what we were doing.

On July 30, 1967, on the heels of major riots in Detroit, Newark, Harlem, and D.C., a riot broke out in Milwaukee after word spread that police brutality had been used to stop a fight in a black nightspot. Though I was out there taking part in spirit, I was dismayed to see stores like Sy's looted. But that didn't stop me from rushing over to Third Street in the hopes of getting to the Discount Center before its contents were emptied. Unfortunately, by the time I got there nothing was left in my size and all I could grab were some clothes I could never wear. Fortunately, I wasn't dragged off to jail again with the almost two thousand other folks who were arrested—including my cousin Terry after he was caught actually trying on shoes and checking them out in front of a shoe mirror. The riot was significant enough that the National Guard was called in and a three-day curfew was imposed. Among the one hundred or so injuries, three people were killed that night.

不过，好景不长，不一会周围情景就乱糟糟令人发昏，忽然，一些非裔女子让我们眼前一亮，她们身着宽松上装，还缀满了珠子。我立刻兴致勃勃，当时我觉得自己应该算得上是美国最早的一批黑人嬉皮。她们这身打扮在密尔沃基一带并不多见，但我还是如法炮制，从善意救世军慈善机构弄了点上好的珠子回来，又搞了点二手的衣服，最棒的扎染牛仔裤，以及黑人爆炸头，再加上点那种"我为我的肤色而骄傲"的酷酷表情。这样的造型可以让史摩基·罗宾逊都自愧不如。

美国灵歌之王詹姆斯·布朗是我的偶像，当我和加文跑到圣博尼费斯教堂外面继续游行的时候，我们约法三章，决定让人们购物时认准黑褐标，这是詹姆斯力推的一个标志，旨在帮助美国老城区脱离贫困。这种标志就相当于一种返券，我们的计划似乎进行得不错，可是当我们来到白人区的A&P超市，在交款台前排队等待结账，我问收款员："这里有黑褐标吗，没有的话，我们就不买了。这地方没法买东西的。"13岁的我，俨然是一副初生牛犊不怕虎的样子。

一眨眼的工夫，警察就蹦了出来，站在超市经理的身后，经理冷冷地盯着我们，"你们俩把东西都给我放回去，这事儿就算了，否则的话，都给我进局子。"他转身走开，我们两个乖乖地把东西放回货架，超市的工作人员笑得前仰后合。

不过，我们回教堂参加美国有色人种民权促进会集会游行的路上，还是感觉得意洋洋，结果听到促进会密尔沃基分会被炸的消息，顿时我们觉得自己闯的祸有点大了。

1967年7月30日，就在底特律、纽华克、哈莱姆、华盛顿特区等地刚刚出现黑人抗暴行动之后，密尔沃基也出事了。据称，在一家黑人酒吧中有人打架，结果警察暴力执法。我虽然也精神上支持这种事，但是很遗憾的是像沙伊店这样的地方也被洗劫一空。不过，我自己也冲到第三大道的打折中心，在这里被清空之前，希望也能捞点什么。可惜等我去的时候，已经没什么我能穿的东西，只得随便抓了几件这辈子都用不上的衣服了事。幸运的是，我后来没被抓进监狱，要知道有近两千人锒铛入狱，其中还有我的表哥泰瑞，他刚好在店里买鞋，就在准备去结账的时候，被抓了起来。这次暴乱确实性质严重，都惊动了国民卫队，连续三天实施了宵禁，暴乱当夜，有100多人受伤，更有3人死于非命。

第四章　即兴精酿（上）

Amid this turmoil, Vietnam was raging, and young, poor Americans, black and white, were being sent off to fight and, in escalating numbers, coming home in coffins, addicted, or shell-shocked. Muhammad Ali had been my hero as a boxer even before he changed his name from Cassius Clay, back when he was a newcomer and turned the boxing world on its head by beating Sonny Liston. But when he refused to go fight in the war because, as he said, "I ain't got no quarrel with the Vietcong"—who had never, he went on, "called me 'nigger' or lynched me"—Ali became a different kind of lifelong hero to me, almost a symbolic father figure.

The defining moment in the evolution of my consciousness in this era—and for millions of Americans from all backgrounds— took place on the night of April 4, 1968. After returning to St. Boniface from an open housing march, I and my sidekicks Garvin and Zulu sit down hungrily in the meeting room to plates full of doughnuts, cold cuts, and chips when a suit-and-tie-type brother from the NAACP runs into our midst, wailing and choking, "Dr. King's been shot!"

Pandemonium ensues. Everyone's yelling, wanting to know what's happened. Someone's turning on a radio, another person runs to check the TV news, we're hearing snatches of reports about Memphis, Tennessee, the sanitation workers' strike Dr. King went to support, how he was shot on the balcony of his motel. Then suddenly a voice screams above the others: "He's dead! They murdered Dr. King!"

Now comes a silence. Shock. Disbelief. Lifetimes pass in these seconds. Then a wave of sorrow and rage explodes in the room, rocketing through me, carrying all of us outside into the street, as we begin to throw whatever we can get our hands on. Madness. Terror. Anger. The power underneath these emotions feels like the night of the riots multiplied to the nth degree, even though the fiery talk of storming into all-white neighborhoods to wreak havoc soon passes.

With the assassination of Robert Kennedy only a few months later, 1968 brought to a thunderous peak everything that had been happening in civil rights, protests over Vietnam, women's liberation, the sexual revolution, as well as what was going on in music and culture at large. Some of our idealism had been struck down at the same time that the momentum of power to the people was unstoppable. The promise of we shall overcome and we are going to the mountaintop hadn't been broken, but the struggle was going to be much longer and more arduous than we first believed.

Books, as always, fulfilled my need to find power through knowledge. Over the next few years I journeyed through black history by reading whatever I could get my hands on. Moms would never discourage me from reading any book, although she was slightly alarmed when I came home with *Die, Nigger, Die* by H. Rap Brown and *Soul on Ice* by Eldridge Cleaver.

在那期间，越南也不太平，很多美国的穷人，年纪轻轻，无论肤色如何，都被送上战场，而且数量与日俱增。走的时候，年轻力壮，而回来的时候，或者只剩一堆尸骸，或者成为瘾君子，或者精神出现问题。拳王阿里早在没改名之前，还是叫卡休斯·克莱的时候，就曾一度是我的偶像，后来他打败了桑尼·里斯顿，一举成名。但阿里拒绝参军入伍，因为他认为："我才不会和越共过不去，他们从来没叫我是什么'黑鬼'，也没侮辱过我什么。"阿里从此在我心目中无比高大，甚至可以取代父亲的形象。

我很多思想的转型也是在这一时期，数千万美国民众，无论背景出身如何，都在经历了1968年4月4日那一夜之后，思想发生了转变。从户外的游行队伍中回到圣博尼费斯教堂之后，我和两个铁哥儿们加文和祖鲁饥肠辘辘地坐在会议室中，正当我们大嚼特嚼多纳圈、冷切肉、薯条的时候，有色人种民促会中一个西装革履的家伙气喘吁吁地跑了进来，"路德·金中弹了！"

接下来就是一片混乱，大家吵吵嚷嚷，都想知道究竟发生了什么事情。有人打开收音机，有的看电视新闻，我们断断续续听到田纳西州孟菲斯清洁工罢工，路德·金前去支援，结果在入住的汽车旅馆的阳台遇刺。突然传来一个声音："他死了，他们要了他的命。"

突然人群一片寂静，鸦雀无声，震惊之余，无法相信。顷刻间，一个生命就此消逝。接下来是无比的悲痛和愤怒，充斥了整个房间，我也顿时受到感染，和大家一道涌上街头，把手里能够得到的东西，一通乱砸。到处是疯狂、愤怒和恐怖。仿佛那一夜骚乱积压下来的情绪顷刻间激增了无数倍，即便如此，从言辞激烈到白人区的天下大乱不久都销声匿迹了。

随着肯尼迪1968年的遇刺，不过几个月的光景，民权、反战、妇女解放、性解放，甚至在文化和音乐方面都发生了翻天覆地的变化。很多陈旧观念土崩瓦解，人民的力量势不可挡。我们相信最终会战胜困难，人民会取得最终胜利，但是斗争的过程却要非常漫长，远比预想的要艰辛得多。

书本总是我力量的源泉，在接下来的几年中，我如饥似渴地阅读手边能找到的黑人的历史，妈妈从来不会阻挠我读书，只是我把拉普·布朗的《黑鬼去死》和埃尔德里奇·克利弗《冰上灵魂》这种书带回家的时候，她会稍稍提醒我注意一下。

She was down with the antiwar movement and had no problem with the sweatshirts we wore and sold that had black-pride slogans on them like "Soul Brother" and "Black Power" and "Keep the Faith" and the generic "Sock It to Me." Moms even wore her "Soul Sister" sweatshirt while she was washing my clothes. But just to make sure I didn't get too radicalized or militant, periodically she would warn me, "Boy, if you gonna be another Rap Brown, you got to get out of here."

When I kept on reading, not because I was overly radical but because I wanted to know what something said before I rejected it, she'd ask, a little nervously, "You don't believe in all that stuff, do you?"

Of course, I reassured her, I didn't believe in it all and wasn't going to become militant.

Moms also knew that there were many other influences calling to me, none more powerfully than music. Only later did I truly appreciate how incredible it was to come of age in the heyday of every significant phenomenon that the late sixties produced, with everyone saying something that mattered: from James Brown and Bob Dylan to the Beatles, the Rolling Stones, Marvin Gaye, Stevie Wonder, the Temptations, Jimi Hendrix, Sly Stone, and, of course, Miles Davis—who capped off the 1960s with his groundbreaking *Bitches Brew*. Considered by some the greatest musical masterpiece of the twentieth century, it was almost as transformational as the invention of jazz itself. For me, it was as if Miles had poured everything that was happening historically, politically, socially, racially, and musically into a cauldron—mixing it all up with every emotional high and low, every hope and fear, every pleasure, sorrow, anger, and ecstasy—and created this big-time fusion.

That fusion also felt like a musical expression for what was going on in my personal life during my teen years—a simmering brew of new preoccupations and old ones. On the new frontier, right along with puberty, had come the most unbelievably constant interest in girls and sex. I loved everything about both. For several years now everything about the feminine species had turned me on. Everything, apparently, turned me on. All of a sudden, the wind would blow and my dick got hard. It had started earlier and without warning. Riding the bus, the jostling got my dick hard. Nobody explained to me that this was normal or that sometimes when your dick got so hard you thought it might break off or something, it was both normal to feel that way and not likely to happen.

On the one hand, having the ability to feel so potentially powerful was miraculous. Like you woke up one day and owned a high-powered expensive sports car you didn't even ask for. On the other hand, being a kid with churning hormones and limited opportunities to do anything about it was like owning a high-powered expensive sports car and not having your damn license yet! I had a couple of opportunities to go for a test drive, but until I had a regular girlfriend, I was left to do things like I did when I was a little kid staying at Uncle Willie's and I tried to get the attention of a neighbor girl by standing up on a milk crate under her bedroom window and breaking my kneecap in the process. So much for my attempts at serenading.

她也支持反战运动，甚至我们穿着印有标榜黑人身份和荣誉感的大背心，她也能接受，上面印着什么"灵歌老大"、"黑人力量"、"胜利在于坚持"，甚至再出格一点她也能接受，妈妈本人还穿着印有"灵歌大姐大"字样的大衫给我洗衣服。但原则是我不可以太过火或者出格，时不时她会警告我："孩子，若想变成拉普·布朗第二，你就别来见我。"

有时，我读书并非是自己过于激进，不过是出于了解的目的，想在了解之后再判断取舍，每当这时，她就会有点担心，"你才不会相信这些东西，对吧？"

当然，我会让她放宽心，自己不会相信这些，也不会变得动辄大打出手，用武力解决问题。

妈妈也知道有很多东西对我会产生影响，其中最大的就莫过于音乐。后来，我才意识到自己有多么幸运，居然和20世纪60年代这么多伟大的音乐巨擘经历了相同的时代，这些名字不胜枚举，詹姆斯·布朗、鲍勃·迪伦、披头士、滚石、马文盖、史提夫·汪达、诱惑乐队、吉米·亨德里克斯、斯莱·斯通，当然还有迈尔·戴维斯，一曲《即兴精酿》横扫20世纪60年代乐坛，时至今日，这首曲子仍是20世纪的经典名曲，其重要意义不亚于爵士乐本身。对于我而言，似乎是戴维斯把所有这些历史、政治、社会、种族、音乐等方面的东西一股脑儿地灌输给我，其中有夹杂着情绪的起伏、希望与失望、快乐和伤感、大喜和大悲，所有这些混合在一起，便是那个时代真实的情感记忆。

这种情感也仿佛音乐一般，索绕在我的经历之中。我十几岁时，就是在酝酿这种音乐般的意境，有的是基于即往，有的是来自当下。在接下来的时日，由于青春期的到来，我对女孩子和性产生了异乎寻常的兴趣，欲罢不能。一连几年，一切和异性甚至阴性有关的东西都会让我兴致勃勃，趣味盎然。甚至，突然一阵风起，都会让我起生理反应。所有这些出现的都毫无征兆，让我措手不及。甚至坐公车，马达启动都会让我出现反应。当时我觉得自己身体的某个部位就要炸开一样，可那时候没有人告诉我这都属于正常。

但从另一角度而言，能了解自己潜在的力量也是件妙不可言的事情。就像一觉醒来，忽然天上掉下一辆名牌跑车一样。但作为未成年的孩子，体内涌动着的荷尔蒙，却无法做任何事情，这本身就像空有跑车，却没有驾照一样让人难堪。我还真有一两次"试驾"的机会，可是在到我有了自己真正的女朋友之前，事情都难遂人愿，每次尝试的结局不过是与在威利舅舅家时的经历无二，那次我为了引起隔壁女孩的注意，特意爬上了她窗下的一个牛奶纸箱上，结果磕破了膝盖。

The most confusing thing to me was getting hard at inappropriate moments, like when the little old lady who paid me to shovel snow off her driveway and do odd jobs around her house needed me to help her get up from the couch. "Just help me, Chris," she asked. "Hold me until I get steady on my feet?"

"Yes, ma'am," I replied and carefully helped her up to a standing position, and as I leaned in to hold up a frail seventy-year-old spinster with failing eyesight, my dick got hard. That was more horrifying than any of the scary movies that my buddy Garvin and I spent all our money going to see up at the Oasis Theater on Twenty-seventh and Center. Knowing that it was nothing more than a ripple of human body heat and not anything about me being attracted to a senior citizen, I was still freaked out enough to curtail my part-time employment with her.

The only person in whom I might have confided these latest confusions was Ophelia, but she and DeShanna had since moved out of the house. That was rough on me as well as my younger sisters. Though we were half-siblings, none of us had been raised that way. They were my three sisters, and I was their only brother, plain and simple. That was in part because of how Moms insisted it was going to be, and also because we were all a team: us versus Freddie. Later, my baby sister Kim even used Gardner as her last name, putting it on every piece of identification she owned, even though she was born a Triplett. Kim and Sharon probably felt like me in wishing that Sam Salter could have been their daddy too. An equal opportunity abuser, Freddie didn't spare them much because he was their father.

What I did confide in Ophelia whenever I saw her was my ongoing preoccupation with putting an end to his brutality and him, even if it meant going to jail. Since Freddie was the reason she'd moved out—he'd actually campaigned to get her to do so— she understood my motivation. First of all, whenever she was going out on dates, Freddie showed up just in time to make sure the guy was disgusted—talking about the date's raggedy or uppity clothes, and farting, burping, slurping, scratching, whatever else he could do to make Ophelia want to slip through a hole in the floor. Anybody who came to pick her up, from then on, just honked, and she'd blow out of the house and keep on rolling.

Then he started going after her for not doing things right around the house. When one particular confrontation escalated and he warned her not to talk back or he'd kick her ass, Ophelia tried to walk away, but he blocked her path and bellowed, "Either I'm gonna kick your ass or you get your ass outta here. One of the two of them things gonna happen! You choose!"

The final straw came the next week when he began stalking into the bedroom that Ophelia and DeShanna shared with Sharon and Kim, my sisters sleeping three in the bed and the baby in a crib.

最让我难堪的莫过于这种反应来的太不是时候，比如，一个小个子老奶奶付费给我，让我帮她清扫车道上的积雪，再帮她干点家里的零活，顺便让我把她从沙发上扶起身来，"来，克里斯，帮把手，等我站稳了再松手。"

"好的，没问题，"我应答着，小心翼翼地帮她从沙发上起身，可当我俯下身，帮这个颤巍巍的70岁老太太站稳的时候，我又起反应了。这简直比我和加文两个倾其所有，去27大街的绿洲剧场看恐怖片还要吓人一万倍。我知道这不过是人体部位的接触使然，我绝不是对这位老太太有什么非分之想，但我还是战战兢兢，辞掉了这份兼职差事。

所有这些苦衷，我以往只能找姐姐奥菲丽娅倾诉，可她和孩子德沙娜刚从家里搬出去住，这对我们兄妹几个都不是件易事。虽然我们同母异父，可是相处的就像一家人。她们就是我的亲姐妹，我是她们的亲兄弟，就这么简单。一方面，是妈妈一直这么教育我们，另一方面是我们团结一心，一致对付弗莱迪。以至于后来，金牡改随母姓——加德纳，不再随自己的生父弗莱迪的崔普雷特，觉得只有这样才能说明自己的身份和所属。

妹妹金牡和沙仑大概也和我一样，希望萨缪尔·梭特也能成为她们的父亲，弗莱迪并不因为她俩是自己的骨肉，而对她们客气几分。我见到姐姐奥菲丽娅就会没完没了地诉说想让弗莱迪永远不再使用暴力，甚至想要了他的命，为此就是蹲大狱都在所不惜。既然是弗莱迪让她搬出的家，其实是逼她搬走的，那么她应该明白我说的意思。开始时，弗莱迪跟着她去赴约会，总是在关键的时候出现，让那男孩子难堪，对约会时的衣服指指点点，打嗝放屁、抓耳挠腮，极自己丢人现眼之能事，让奥菲丽娅无地自容，恨不得要钻到地缝里去。从此，无论谁带她出去都要被大骂一通，姐姐被连滚带爬踢出了家。

接着弗莱迪就开始在家里处处找茬。一次，当两人战争升级，弗莱迪称奥菲丽娅再要顶嘴就臭揍她，姐姐想走开，结果他挡在路上说："要么我揍你，要么你就老老实实挨揍！二选一，你看着办！"

最后一次爆发是他开始往三个姐妹的卧室里面闯的一周之后，奥菲丽娅、金牡和沙仑三个人挤在一个大床上，小宝贝睡在婴儿床上。

One night Ophelia felt so threatened by the volume of his voice and was so afraid that he'd hurt DeShanna, she picked up a large-sized protractor I usually used for my geometry homework and used the pointed end to let Freddie know, "You come in here and hit me, I'm gonna kill you."

Two days later my big sister and my niece left for good and went to live with our cousin Elaine over on Eighth Street—two houses away from Sam Salter. Ophelia saw her daddy every day, knew his wife and their kids, and whenever she needed anything and asked him for help, Salter gave it to her—though he did always say that it was his last two dollars.

Whenever possible I'd go visit Ophelia, sharing some of my concerns and secrets with her. But not all of them.

一天夜里，奥菲丽娅听着他嗓门太大，担心会伤到孩子，就顺手抄起我做作业用的大号量角器，指着弗莱迪说："你要是敢打我，我就要你的命。"

两天后，姐姐就和我的小外甥女搬走了，去和住在第八大街的表姐忆莲住在一起，那里离姐姐的生父萨缪尔只有两幢房子之隔。奥菲利娅从此可以天天见到自己的父亲，也认识了他的太太和孩子。每当需要帮助时，她就去找她的父亲，萨缪尔也每次都会慷慨解囊，只是会说这是他最后的 200 元钱。

每当我有机会去看望姐姐，都会对她吐露自己的秘密和心声，当然并不是毫无保留的。

Chapter 5
Bitches Brew(side b)

What you doin'? I ask Garvin on a Friday night as he and I, along with our friend Fat Sam, a guitar player, on our way downtown to the movies, pass by The Auditorium and Garun makes a beeline for the entrance door.

It's springtime, decent weather, not long after my thirteenth birthday as it happens, on one of the last days of the Home and Garden Show, a big annual convention, and he suggests we see if we can sneak in and check out the exhibits. As soon as we pull open the doors, a tide of people comes pouring out, allowing us to slip inside without paying.

Fat Sam says, "Let's just lay low for a minute," and I suggest we head up the stairs to the stands and lie down between the bleacher levels.

Before long the place has emptied, and we're in semidarkness, with exit signs providing a subtle glow, holding our breath as a guard with a flashlight makes his last rounds. Finally the coast is clear, and we hit our first stop: a bakery display, complete with wedding cakes, jelly rolls, pastries, and fresh breads, all tasting as fantastically delicious as the display we destroy looks. Stuffed to the gills, with our pockets filled for later, we start throwing powdered sugar doughnuts at each other and laugh uproariously with our faces covered in white sugary fluff.

第五章
即兴精酿（下）

一个周五的夜晚，我和加文还有吉他手胖萨姆在一起走着，打算抄近道，走综艺馆去市中心看电影，"你琢磨干点什么呢？"我问加文。

当时正是春暖花开，天气不错，我也刚过完13岁生日不久，恰逢一年一度的家居园艺展接近了尾声，加文就怂恿我们溜进展厅去玩。刚打开门，就有一大群人鱼贯而出，我们就趁机逃票，溜了进去。

胖萨姆说："我们都把头低下呆一阵子。"我则建议几个人沿着楼梯往上走，躺在看台的栏杆间隙。

不一会，场地里面就没人了，安全出口亮着昏黄的光，只见保安拿着手电，进行最后的清场巡视，我们躲在半明半暗的地方，屏住呼吸，一动不动。终于万事大吉，我们顺利躲过了巡视，我们首先跑到了糕饼展示区，到处是结婚蛋糕、果冻蛋卷、烤饼、新鲜面包，应有尽有，美味至极，在我们一通风卷残云之后，只见一片狼藉。我们各个口袋里都装得鼓鼓囊囊的，我们开始往彼此身上扔多纳圈玩，脸上都挂着白色的糖霜，大喊大叫个不停。

The PURSUIT of HAPP*y*NESS

At the next display, Garvin calls excitedly for us to come see what he's just found. Fat Sam and I join him and our jaws drop. In an ultracool display is everything that three budding musicians could want for making their own music and then some: amplifiers, stereos, transistor radios, microphones, reel-to-reel tape decks. To take anything is a crime, we know. But we're basically drunk on sugar, and our musical recording aspirations suddenly supersede our better judgment. Talk about kids in a candy store! After emptying our pockets of pastries to fit in radios and tape reels, we load up the larger items, stacking and rolling them any way we can. Sam goes for a set of Vox amplifiers on wheels while I claim a state-of-the-art reel-to-reel tape recorder, among other things. This is like playing a variation of this-page-that-page, only with real stuff.

Getting all this home is a major ordeal, less so for Fat Sam because he lives closest by in the projects, but no easy feat for me and Garvin. We weave through the alleys over to the north side, avoiding being spotted by the police. Every time I start to have second thoughts, Garvin urges me on, saying, "Man, we just made a good rip and we just got a little ways to go."

At the second-floor apartment where my family's living now, everybody's home, but I have no key. To sneak in, I have to use a ladder that I'd previously adapted from an iron fence in order to bring up the stolen goods and stash them in my small room in the back, where nobody ever comes in. Exhausted but triumphant, I relax, dreams billowing around me of recording my first jazz album and also making some money off the extra electronics that I don't need. Now my focus capabilities start to kick into overdrive. Who's going to buy the stolen merchandise?

The following afternoon, with everybody in my household out, I'm busy sweeping the stairs in the front hall of the building—one of the latest part-time gigs, that I did for five dollars, paid for by the super—and a group of neighbors who are new to the building return from their outing. For a flash, my instincts remind me that I don't know anything about these people. They're a very loud, argumentative household and appear not to be a family but just a group of adults sharing the rent maybe. Playing cool, watching them head up the stairs, I notice an additional threesome of guys with them who don't live in the building. They seem on the shady side, not the kind of cats to report a kid for selling hot electronics. Listening to my instincts, I lift my head up from my sweeping and say to the one who looks like the leader of the pack, "Hey, man, y'all want to buy some tape recorders? Want to buy some radios?"

Glancing at the other two, he shrugs. "Yeah, let's see what you got."

在下一个展区，加文大声嚷嚷着让我们看他的意外发现。胖萨姆和我凑上前去，结果眼睛都差点瞪了出来，展台上摆着足够我们三个毛头小子玩音乐的所有超级装备：功放、立体声、无线电、麦克风、磁带录音机等，不一而足。偷拿别人的东西是犯罪，这我们知道，不过当时我们已经吃了太多的甜食，头脑昏沉沉，加之，想做音乐的狂想瞬间盖过了理智，想想在糖果店的孩子就知道我们当时的样子了。我们把两把掏出了口袋里的饼干，装上收音机、磁带，接着又开始搬动那些大家伙，连推带滚，全力以赴。萨姆搞到一个带轮子的 Vox 功放，我拿的是个货真价实的磁带录音机，还有一些别的好东西。这可都是真家伙，毫不含糊啊！

把这些宝贝搬到家里可费了我们不少工夫，萨姆倒是轻松，他家就住在附近，我和加文可没这么轻松了。我们一路穿街绕巷，往北边走，生怕被警察看到。每当我思想有点动摇的时候，加文就说：“没事的，一会儿就到家了。”

我们现在住的地方是个两层的公寓，大家都住在一起，可我没有钥匙。为了不让别人发现，我只得爬梯子，这是我以前用铁栅栏改造的，这样就可以神不知鬼不觉地把赃物藏到我后面的小屋里去，那里没人会去的。我累得筋疲力尽，但是一想到马上就可以录制自己的首张爵士专辑，还能把其他的好东西卖个好价钱，我就心花怒放。接下来，我的脑子开始飞速地转动，该把这些东西卖给谁呢？

下午，家里人都出去了，我开始在前院打扫卫生，这是刚找的一份兼职差事，可以挣到 5 块钱，是刚从外面回来的几个邻居出钱让我干的。我忽然一闪念，这些人是干什么的，我都不知道。只知道他们一堆人嗓门很大，好像不是一家人，就是几个大人合住在一起，可能是分摊房租罢了。我瞥见他们上了楼，还有另外三个人也跟着上去了，但这几个人并不住在这里。他们行迹有点可疑，不太像那种找人买热门电子设备的样子，但我还是没有理会自己本能的判断。放下手中的扫把，抬起头来，和当中的那个好像是领头的人说："想买录音机么？还有收音机？"

瞅了瞅另外那两个人，他耸了耸肩："好啊，看看你有什么好东西。"

第五章　即兴精酿（下）

Cool. I'm Mr. Hustler now, a natural. The three follow me to our place and down the hall to my room, where I show them my stash. As they're picking up the stuff, looking it over, talking like it's not that interesting a deal, my instincts are starting to sound big-time alarms, telling me these dudes are bad news and that I've made a grave error in judgment. Edging into the hallway toward the closet where Freddie keeps his shotgun, I feel tremors of fear rippling through me as I try to keep my wits together. Just as I enter the closet and go to reach for the gun, the main guy grabs ahold of my arm, jerks me out of the closet, and the three jump on me, pushing me down, not hurting me but restraining me long enough to gather up all the stuff and get out—which does hurt.

Now furious at them as well as myself, I fret and fume, well aware that I can't call the police, and I certainly can't tell the old man. As if I've got any recourse, I sit and seethe, trying to do a crime sketch of each of them in my head. At least I'll tell Garvin and Fat Sam to keep an eye out for these motherfuckers, who are all in their late twenties and early thirties. The main guy is average size, nondescript, while the second is maybe tall and lanky, also leaving little impression. But the third man—who looked like he held back when the other two were jumping me—was distinctive in the way he walked with a pronounced limp, a cripple maybe, or gimpy, the result of a deformity rather than an accident.

Without any recourse, and with no sense of lessons learned, I feel like shit yet have no alternative but to return to sweeping the stairs. As is my habit, I shift focus and try to forget my failed stint as Mr. Hustler.

"Hey," a low voice calls to me after twenty minutes or so have passed. I look up and see the cat with the limp, standing there holding a grocery bag. He explains, "Listen, man, I brought you some of your stuff back. And I brought you some money."

Cool. That takes the edge off. We return to the apartment, and I do a quick inventory of what he's brought back. About a third of the goods are there, obviously his share, but the reel-to-reel tape deck is still gone. He hands me ten bucks, and as I go to put the money in my pocket, instead of moving toward the door to leave, he takes a step toward me and says, "I done you a favor, now I want you to do me a favor."

"Oh, yeah," I say, "what is it?"

"I want to play with your dick."

"Naw, man," I protest, thinking I still have the right to decline and a chance to maneuver him toward the door. Another error in judgment.

酷，我可以做生意了，我天生就是做生意的料。这三个家伙就跟着我穿过大厅到了我家，我给他们看了我的宝贝。他们挑挑拣拣，左看右看，说不喜欢，我的心怦怦跳，直觉告诉我这伙人不地道，我可能犯了个天大的错误。我小心地往走廊那边蹭，朝壁橱方向挪动，那就是弗莱迪放枪的地方，我觉得自己浑身都在哆嗦，同时努力在想着对策。我刚靠近壁橱，准备取枪，那个小头目样的人一把抓住了我的胳膊，把我从壁橱里拎了出来，三个人扑了上来，没伤到我，就是让我动弹不得，然后大摇大摆把我的东西都打包带走了，这才让我心痛不已。

我又悔又恨，恨他们，也恨自己，而且这种情况我没法报警，更没法子告诉弗莱迪。我坐下来，努力平静下来，脑子里想着这几个人的形象特征。至少可以和加文和胖萨姆说一声，让他们在街上注意一下这几个狗娘养的，都是二三十岁的样子。领头的那个家伙中等身材，没什么特征，第二个身材高挑，偏瘦，也没留下什么印象。第三个人好像就是那个从身后抓着我的人，另两个人从我身上跳过去，这人走起路来一瘸一拐，应该是天生的残疾，不像受了伤的样子。

结果没有任何办法，也没吸取经验教训，虽然非常懊恼，也只好回去继续扫地。这就是我做事的习惯，总是转移注意力，好忘掉自己不愉快的经商经历。

"嗨，"20多分钟后，有人低声地叫我。我往上一看，发现是那个跛脚的男子，站在那里，拎着一个购物袋。他接着说道："听着，我给你带了点东西回来，还给你带了点钱。"

太棒了，这就对了。我们转身回到家里，很快检查了一遍他带回来的东西，大概有三分之一的宝贝又回来了，显然，这是他自己的那一份，但是录音机不见了。他给了我十块钱，我把钱揣起来，他却没有离开的意思，他上前了一步："你看，我帮你一个忙，希望你也能帮我一个小忙。"

"好啊，说吧。"我答道。

"我想和你玩一玩。"

"想都别想。"我反抗着，以为自己确实能拒绝这无理要求，还想把他往门外拖，这是我又一个错误。

第五章 即兴精酿（下）

The PURSUIT of HAPPYNESS

The next slice of time, maybe ten, fifteen minutes, or shorter, do not take place in normal speed: parts of it stretch out in tortuously slow motion and other parts are heart-stoppingly fast. But even if I can't track time, I remember every detail of what happens, from the second he pulls a knife to my throat, forces me on my back, pulls down my pants, puts his dick between my legs, to registering the confused horror of my dick getting hard from the stimulation, to the true horror of him hoisting me into position so he can fuck me in the ass, right on the living room floor. Every grunt, every breath. His smell overwhelms. Funky. Rancid even, inhuman. White hot pain. Cold hard linoleum.

He finishes. Says, "Fine." Pulls me up by my shirt. Then pushes me into the hall, through the bathroom door, forces me face down onto the tile of the bathroom floor. Fucks me in the ass. Again. My brain understands he has raped me twice, but my emotions refuse to compute, all messed up over the fear that he's going to kill me after he's done. It's what he says next that starts my rage.

"Damn," he says, "I didn't even come."

In the terrible moment of fear in which I think he is going to make me do something else, he stands up, puts the knife away, as though he realizes other folks might show up soon, buttons up his pants, limps down the hall, and leaves. The smell lingers. Feeling sick, feeling dirty, permanently dirty, I start turning the analytical gears of my brain, trying to strategize what to do. What to do. No one can know. Not Freddie, the Big Wheel, who'll spread the story from Luke's bar across the city. Not Moms, who'll want to know how I got the stuff and how he got into the apartment in the first place. No police. No one. Instead, I'll take the mental record, spool it up on a tape reel, and stick it away, contained, not forgotten, but not to live in my consciousness every day.

A desolate quiet descends on the apartment as feelings of total powerlessness and hurt wash over me. The no-daddy blues plays in my imagination, taunting me that if I'd had a daddy, he wouldn't have left me unprotected—either from my own juvenile mistakes or from the street predators. To drown out those sounds, I walk into my room and take my trumpet out of its case and begin to practice, playing without passion, by rote, knowing as I do that now there are two motherfuckers in this world that I got to kill.

* * *

接下来的时间，可能是 10～15 分钟，也许没用这么久，时间似乎都发生了扭曲，有时我分分秒秒都特别难熬，有时我心跳加速，无法忍受。但是即便我无法看表，我还是可以清楚记得每一个细节，特别是当那家伙拿出了刀，抵着我的喉咙，逼我躺在地上，脱掉裤子，我惊恐万分，手足无措。所有这些都发生在我家的地板上，每一次呻吟，每一次喘息都是在这里。到处都是他的味道，恶臭难闻，令人发指。我痛苦不堪，难以言状。

他终于完事了，"起来吧。"抓着我的衬衫，把我从地上拉起来。推着我进了大厅，进了卫生间，这次他逼着我趴在瓷砖地上，又开始了第二轮。我的大脑告诉我他强奸了我两次，但我在情感上无法接受这一点。恐惧压倒了一切，我脑海一片混乱，只是担心接下来他会要了我的命。接下来他说的话，让我无比愤怒。

"他妈的，我还没玩够。"

最可怕的时刻到来了，我担心他要我做些别的什么。他站起身来，把刀子放到一边，可能也是担心会有人回来，他系上裤子，一瘸一拐地下楼走了。那难闻的味道久久不能散去，令人作呕，让人从心底觉得肮脏，挥之不去。我开始恢复思考的能力，考虑该怎么应对这件事情，该怎么办，谁都不能告诉，包括弗莱迪、"大轮"，他们会在快乐屋酒吧把这事情大肆宣扬，让全城的人都知道。也不能告诉妈妈，因为她会问我是从哪里搞来的这些东西，那人开始是怎么来家里的。也不能报警，谁都不能说。我自己仿佛是架录像机一样，把这一切默默地刻录在脑海里，小心地收藏起来，永远不会忘记，但也不会让它走入我的日常生活。

屋里一片凄清，我觉得自己如此的无助，痛苦一古脑儿地袭来，我无处藏身。没有父亲的保护，这种无助刺激着我的神经，若有父亲在身边，这一切就不会发生，我一开始就不会犯那种年幼无知的错误，也不会受到街上地痞的欺负。为了让自己能平静下来，我回到自己的房间，从箱子里取出小号，开始了练习，却没有丝毫激情可言，只是机械地吹奏，但我清楚地知道，这世上我需要干掉的是两个畜生。

* * *

The PURSUIT of HAPPYNESS

Was there anything positive that could be said about Freddie Triplett? He was, after all, my mother's husband, for better and for worse. What part of our day-to-day lives would count as better? Often I was hard-pressed to come up with anything, other than that the members of his immediate and extended family were wonderful. There was his sister Miss Bessie, always industrious, owner of the Big House and Bessie's Hair Factory, generous to relatives all up and down our various family trees. There was his sister Baby, always taking Momma's side over her own brother, even warning me to be careful when I started talking—probably too much—about how I was planning on killing Freddie.

Baby didn't try to talk me out of my plans, she just wanted me to do it right. She said, "Chris, if he find out that you trying to think of how to kill him, he g'on git that gun out and he g'on kill you first. You hear me? Believe me, so you remember that!"

She was right. The plan became not to plan but to seize a moment, as though by accident, so as not to give myself away to him or anyone else. My friends and I had been going downtown to watch the amateur wrestling matches, and even if a lot of that stuff was for show—as I'd learned, much to my disappointment—I had mentally practiced putting Freddie in any number of bone-crushing moves. It would have to happen fast, and I couldn't just maim him. Utter annihilation was the only way to go.

Shortly after Baby's warning, a golden opportunity for him to suffer a freak accidental death was given to me when Freddie and I went to move a refrigerator into her house. Barking orders, Freddie told me to go in front and pull the dolly up, while he took the position below, pushing the dolly and the refrigerator up the stairs. In perfect timing, I missed a step, on purpose, and let the refrigerator go. A priceless look of confusion and horror came over his face, and like a work of art, the next thing I knew Freddie had a refrigerator on his chest and they were both tumbling down the steps. All he said was, "Goddamn!" as it came down on him. "Accidentally." He slid down, veering backward, breathing his last breaths, and just before it crushed him to death, he braced himself, puffed out his chest, regained his footing, and bench-pressed all those hundreds of pounds of metal right back into place and up the steps.

He *was* Godzilla. Giving me the evil eye, he surely had no idea that accident had been deliberate. Otherwise, he would have crushed *me* with the refrigerator. Only Baby, seeing my disappointed face when we rolled the dolly inside, figured out what had really happened on the steps.

弗莱迪身上难道就真的一无是处吗？毕竟好歹他是我母亲的丈夫。关于他有没有一些值得称道的事情，我实在是想不出什么来，只是觉得他的那些亲戚人还不错。他的妹妹贝希就很好，她人很能干，大房子就是她家的，还开了一家理发店，她对我家的亲戚也都很慷慨和善。还有一个妹妹贝碧人也很好，每次都护着妈妈，我每次说要对弗莱迪怎样怎样的时候，可能是我实在说的次数太多了，她都会告诫我小心点。

贝碧并没有说让我别这么干，只是说要方法对路。她说："克里斯，要是他知道了你想干掉他，就一定会把枪拿出来，先要了你的命。明白吗？相信我，一定记住了。"

她说的没错，这个计划就不再是什么计划的问题了，而是该怎么抓住机会了。看似意外事故似的，这就不会给我和别人带来麻烦。我和朋友们一度喜欢去城里看业余摔跤比赛，当时这种比赛电视里也很多的，可是看这种东西，总让我觉得对手是弗莱迪，他应该被打得皮开肉绽才是。动作一定要快，不能打残废就算了，而是要他即刻毙命。

在贝碧提醒后不久，我终于等来一个千载难逢的机会，一次，弗莱迪让我帮着抬一个冰箱到贝碧的屋里。他大喊大叫地发号施令之后，让我到前面拉推车，他自己扶着底部，推着冰箱和推车上楼梯。这种机会太难得了，我故意踏空一级台阶，让冰箱滑落下去。看到他脸上的惶恐不安的表情，这实在是太美妙的事情了，宛若是观赏一件艺术品一般。冰箱应该会结结实实地砸在他的胸口，然后人和冰箱一起滚下楼梯，他叫骂了一声，就朝后倒去。结果他滑倒了，身体转了方向，冰箱没能要了他的命，他一骨碌又爬起来，他那几百斤的分量又上了台阶。

他简直就是头怪兽，恶毒地瞪着我，显然他没想到这次事故是我故意的，否则他会用冰箱把我砸死的。只有贝碧在看到我推推车时失望的表情时，猜出来刚才楼梯上究竟发生了什么。

Besides Baby and Freddie's other sisters, I was also fond of a friend of his who became my adopted uncle, a man everybody called Doodabug—a nickname that may have been some form of "Do the bug" or may not have been. Folks said he was so ugly, it looked like God just hit him in the face with a shovel. He was short, skinny, completely toothless, and drunk all day long, but everybody loved him just the same, even if he wasn't a blood relation to any of us. Once a player with the sharpest clothes, women, cars, and money, he fell into a hole of joblessness and alcohol and never got out. While he provided another lesson to me about the perils of being a drunk, he also became a living example of the old adage "where there's a will, there's a way." Don't ask me how he did it, but when Uncle Doodabug decided he was going to bestow on me a very special gift that nobody else had ever given me, he stayed true to his word and presented me with my first pair of silk drawers and a matching black silk T-shirt. I wore them until there wasn't anything left but the waistband.

Uncle Doodabug brought out the best in Freddie. In fact, at Luke's House of Joy, which Freddie ran like he owned it, because he was that mean, anybody who gave Uncle Doodabug a hard time would hear from Freddie: "You fuck with Doodabug and you'll have to deal with me."

But Freddie's protective nature wore off during one excursion when Uncle Doodabug fell asleep with a cigarette hanging out of his mouth in the backseat of Freddie's pride and joy—his 1964 powder blue Cadillac Coupe de Ville. With its darker blue vinyl top, dark blue interior, and fishtails, supposedly just like one that Elvis owned, that Caddy, the Elvis-mobile was the old man's sacred space, and nobody dared so much as drip sweat on the seats. Nobody except Uncle Doodabug, who fell asleep and didn't notice the smell of anything burning until Freddie—behind the driver's wheel—and I, in the front passenger seat, figured out that the burning smell was coming from the backseat floor upholstery. All of a sudden, Uncle Doodabug and the backseat were engulfed in flames. Freddie put the fire out with my orange soda, cussing at the top of his lungs, "Get outta my goddamn car, Doodabug, you drunken motherfucker! Get outta my goddamn car!"

No one was hurt luckily, although I couldn't help fantasizing about a scenario in which Uncle Doodabug and I survived the fiery inferno that took Freddie's life.

除了贝碧和弗莱迪的其他姐妹，我还对他的一个朋友颇有好感，绰号多达巴，我叫他叔叔。人们都说他长得实在太难看了，就像上帝用铲子拍过他的脸一样，他身材短小，骨瘦如柴，牙齿都脱落了，一天到晚醉醺醺的，但就是招人喜欢，虽然他和我们没有任何血缘关系，但都不影响我们对他的好感。他原本是穿着最体面的衣服，身边美女如云，票子车子根本不在话下，但如今却落得如此田地，终日靠酒精度日，没钱没工作。关于酗酒的危害，他本人就是活生生的例子，同时也成为那句老话"有志者事竟成"的经典范本，具体他怎么做到的，我也不清楚，但是当他许诺将送我一件非常特殊的礼物时，就真的做到了。我得到了有生以来头一条丝质内裤，还有一件配套的黑色丝绸体恤。这些东西我一直穿着，直到不能再穿为止。

多达巴叔叔能让弗莱迪表现出自己最好的一面。实际上，在快乐屋酒吧，弗莱迪就把那当成是自己的地方，因为他本人就不好对付。谁要是对多达巴叔叔无理，弗莱迪就说："你想要惹他，就首先来对付我。"

但是弗莱迪的好脾气有时也会用尽。一次外出的时候，多达巴叔叔抽着烟就在弗莱迪车子的后座睡着了，这车可是弗莱迪的宝贝，1964年的蓝色凯迪拉克威乐，深蓝色的乙烯基车顶，深蓝色的内饰，这估计和猫王的那款车一样，这辆车简直是老家伙的"圣地"，没有谁敢在这里横躺竖卧。也只有多达巴敢在这里睡觉，突然主驾上的弗莱迪闻到了一股烧焦的味道，我坐在副驾驶上，闻出来这味道是来自后座的装饰，突然间，多达巴和后座蹿出了火苗，弗莱迪用我的橙汁汽水浇灭了火，声嘶力竭地喊着："给我滚出去，你这醉鬼，离我的车远远的！"

幸运的是，谁都没有受伤，但我又情不自禁地想，若是多达巴叔叔和我都安然无恙，而弗莱迪却命丧火海，那该有多好啊！

Otherwise, Doodabug brought out Freddie's softer side. Whatever it was that had gone so vicious in Freddie, the only other time he seemed docile was when he was out in the middle of the river in any kind of boat with his best fishing gear and a half-pint of Old Taylor. In fact, if you could have kept Freddie out fishing or hunting, he might have been all right. A Mississippi country boy, he probably should've never come to the city. In the outdoors, the farther from the city the better, he was in his element. Sometimes I went out fishing with Freddie and other family members on both the Gardner and Triplett sides, and sometimes just with Freddie. In the groups, I was in heaven, listening to the men tell their fish tales up at the bait shop, seeing places way out in the boonies of Wisconsin and Minnesota, loving the summer days and nights, learning the art, science, and luck of success as a fisherman, wiping sweat off my forehead on a hot, hot day, and trying to find the sweet spot where a light breeze would cool me right off.

Alone with Freddie, I had to be more alert. It could have been that as I got bigger and posed more of a threat to him, he was trying a tactic of making me his underling, bringing me out on these fishing trips to possibly groom me to be a black Huckleberry Finn or something. Not that I trusted or liked him, but I actually enjoyed fishing and did feel somewhat safer when he didn't have any guns with him.

On the water, Freddie drank but didn't get crazy. There were even fleeting moments of camaraderie when we cooked up our catch in a skillet over a fire on the bank and ate it right there. And there were moments, out on the river in the boat, waiting for the fish to bite, just me and him, when the sky was clear and the sun not yet too high, that I could feel a sense of peace in him.

But by the time we returned home, he was back to his old self, beating Moms, me, and my sisters, going for his shotgun, waking us all up in the middle of the night to get out of his "goddamn house." Needless to say, I made sure to avoid hunting trips with him, though to his credit, he put a lot of food on the table. Freddie liked to call himself the "Great White Hunter of the Ghetto" because he could catch, trap, or kill anything he came across out in the woods. This was no exaggeration, except for the white part. He brought home all kinds of animals: raccoons, squirrels, rabbits, possums, turtles, geese, ducks, and a variety of winged creatures. Much to his regret, he never shot a deer, although he did bring one home strapped to the hood of his Elvis-mobile, like killing Bambi was something to show off. Not even local drunks asked, "Where did you shoot it?" because it was clear it hadn't been shot but run over.

Whether we fished together or he brought home a sack full of rabbits and squirrels or whatever, my primary job in our household was now no longer head gofer but Freddie's apprentice in gutting, scaling, skinning, declawing, cleaning, and deboning his kill. Not surprisingly, this involved knives. Sharp knives.

但很多情况下，多达巴叔叔还是让弗莱迪显示出自己温柔的一面，无论他平时怎样凶神恶煞，他也有自己柔和的时候，那就是他在河流中央，驾着小船，带着他最好的渔具，还有半瓶老泰勒酒时。实际上，只要能带他出去钓鱼或打猎，他就像个完全正常的人一样。他就是个密西西比的乡下人，没进过城。在户外的时候，离城市越远，他就会表现得越好，越会回归自然本真。有时候，我会和弗莱迪以及亲戚朋友一起去钓鱼，有时，我就单独和弗莱迪去钓鱼。和大家在一起的时候，就像天堂般的感觉。在鱼饵店听着大家讲述钓鱼的故事，看着外面的明尼苏达州和威斯康星州的美女，欣赏夏天那里的白昼和黑夜，学点艺术和科学，听听成功者的故事，天热的时候，像渔民那样，拭去额头的汗珠。找个舒服的地方，让微风扫去酷暑，带来舒爽和惬意。

和弗莱迪在一起的时候，就要多加小心了。可能是我个子一天天长高，对他构成了某种威胁，他开始改变策略，让我当他的下手，这种钓鱼的场合也带上我，让我觉得自己像《哈克历险记》里面的男主角。倒不是我有多么喜欢他，但我确实喜欢钓鱼，而且当他手里没拿着枪的时候，我或多或少会有些安全感。

在河面上，弗莱迪也喝酒，但是不会撒酒疯，当我们在河岸上埋锅做饭，就地解决温饱时，我们间甚至还有些类似亲情的成分产生，但这种时候转瞬即逝。还有些时候，当太阳还没升得太高，碧空如洗，只有我和他两个人，在船上垂钓，等待鱼儿咬钩的时候，我似乎可以感到他内心的平静。

但是当我们回到家中，他又固态复发，依然如故，对妈妈、我、还有妹妹大打出手，动辄举着枪对着我们，大半夜就把我们撵出屋子。毋庸置疑，我肯定会避免陪他去打猎，当然，他也会弄回一桌子好吃的。弗莱迪喜欢自称是贫民区的好猎手，因为他可以把在林子里碰到的一切动物抓回来。这绝对不夸张。他可以带回来各式各样的野味，包括獾熊、松鼠、野兔、负鼠、海龟、野鹅、野鸭，还有各种各样的飞禽。唯一可惜的是他从未打到过鹿，但有一次他用那辆宝贝凯迪拉克的车顶，放了一只鹿，仿佛这是件多么荣耀的事情。可是没人问他："这是在哪里打的啊？"因为显而易见，这是他碰巧撞死的，根本不是什么打的。

无论是我们一起垂钓，还是他带回来一袋子野兔、松鼠什么野味，我在家里的职责不再是当差跑腿，而是弗莱迪的学徒工，剥皮、去鳞、清洗、收拾这些猎物。当然这就少不了要用到刀子，锋利的刀子。

When it came to fish, I was amazed by the consistency in the anatomy: their bladder, stomach, heart, lungs, and gills. I didn't mind skinning, gutting, and cleaning the fish because the better I did my job, the more delicious it was going to taste when Moms battered and fried it all up and we ate her cooking with white bread and hot sauce. But I learned to hate gutting and cleaning the other animals. At first, it was interesting to be given on-the-job anatomy lessons. For someone who couldn't read or write, Freddie was a whiz at demonstrating how to identify the stomach, gall bladder, liver, and vital organs of several species. Even though Moms could cook anything that Freddie brought home—fried with rice and gravy, it was filet mignon to me, perfect with cornbread, greens, and maybe some yams on the side—cleaning and skinning anything with fur or feathers became a horrific undertaking after a while. Freddie's various hunting and fishing hauls were strewn throughout the little house at 3951 North Fourteenth Street, where we were living by the time I started high school. Our good fortune to have made it up to Capitol Drive to the better neighborhood, no longer in the ghetto, was due mainly to Uncle Archie, who owned the house we were renting. Fish showed up in the bathtub, possums in the freezer, and you never knew what else you were going to find.

That was the deal with the old man. You never knew if the outdoorsman or the psychopath was going to come to dinner. Every time I'd think he was mellowing, I'd come home and find a crime scene, police carting him away yet again. Everyone in the family was alarmed by Freddie's widening collection of handguns. Momma's stepsister Dicey Bell—who now lived in Chicago—was especially concerned. (Seemed like all those southern aunts and girl cousins had two names like Bettye Jean, Dicey Bell, Lillie Mae, and Eddie Lee.) The older relatives made sure their younger kids, particularly females, weren't left alone with Freddie.

On one occasion Moms and I were alone at home, and we knew we were in grave danger, with Freddie returning at any time. The moment he entered the house, without Moms saying a word, I knew by her look that she was telling me, *Go call the police.* That panic, that fear as I ran convinced me without a doubt that by the time I made it to the pay phone a block away she would already be dead. Racing back to the house, I imagined a bloody sight waiting for me, and my dread ballooned higher into a gigantic tower. It was a sensation that Spike Lee later captured in his film shots; moving the camera instead of the actor, he conveyed exactly how the wiring in our brains goes askew during a crisis. As the house came into sight that time, I saw that the police had just taken a loaded .38 pistol away from Freddie and were driving him away in their car. At least for a night.

当我收拾鱼的时候，发现鱼的内脏都出奇的一致，无外乎是鱼鳔、心肝肺肚，还有腮之类。做这些事我一点都不怵，因为收拾得越干净，妈妈烹饪的大餐就会越发美味，我们就会蘸着白面包和热酱汁享受美味。但是给其他动物开膛破肚实在是让我很为难。首先，能上一堂解剖课倒也不错，弗莱迪根本不识字，但是却能准确判断好几种动物的心肝肺等主要器官，确实不简单。而且妈妈可以把弗莱迪带回的所有东西都做成美味，加米饭炒，或浇上肉汁，做成嫩牛排，配上玉米面包或蔬菜，甚至加点山药，那就太美了。可是给这些野味开膛剥皮就是另外一回事了。弗莱迪在我们住在十四北街的时候就时不时去打猎钓鱼，我们在那里住到了我上高中的时候。后来这里修建工厂，我们就时来运转，可以搬到更好的街区，不用再住在贫民区了，这得感谢租给我们房子的阿奇舅舅，房子是他的。家里到处是弗莱迪的猎物，浴缸里装着鱼，冰箱里是负鼠，真不知道还有没有地方放得下别的东西。

这就是弗莱迪，你不知道他晚上会变成什么，是户外高手还是精神病人。每次我以为他会行为端正一些的时候，回到家中就会发现一片狼藉，警车把他带走。家里人都知道弗莱迪搜集了大量的手枪。妈妈有个妹妹叫戴希·贝尔，住在芝加哥，她就对此十分担心(好像南方的这些姑妈姨妈、表姐妹都喜欢叫这种名字，什么贝蒂·让、戴希·贝尔、埃迪·李之类的)。这些家人都特别嘱咐孩子们，特别是女孩子，不要单独和弗莱迪呆在一起。

一次，妈妈和我在家，我们知道要出事了，因为弗莱迪可能随时都会回来。他一进屋，妈妈都没说话，从她的眼神我就知道该马上报警。那种惊恐的表情让我觉得就是立刻跑到一条街以外的付费电话去报警，她恐怕都已经没命了。我发疯似地跑回来，脑子里全是血腥的场面，担心发生不测。我的恐惧几乎到了极点，那种感觉是导演史派克·李在他的电影中试图要表现的东西，只有镜头在移动，演员纹丝不动，那就是要表现我们身处危急时刻头脑中的真实反应。当回到家的时候，我看到警察刚把上了膛的三八式手枪从弗莱迪手中拿走，把他押上警车带走了，至少会把他关上一个晚上。

The PURSUIT of HAPP*y*NESS

By 1970, at age sixteen, a junior already, I honestly didn't think that I could survive the roller coaster anymore. Moms saw it happening and just urged me to hold on, pointing out that I had already skipped a grade and had only one more school year before graduating. By this point, playing music, having girlfriends, and hanging out with my buddies all provided outlets but school was no longer the haven it had once been. Besides the academics no longer being of interest, my antiestablishment attitude set me at great odds with the repressive, racially charged atmosphere.

A major confrontation arose in my sophomore year when the coach of the football team refused to play me as quarterback. An outrage. I had always played quarterback on every football team I'd been on, starting back when we were playing street football and going throughout my junior high seasons. Everybody knew Chris could throw the ball. That was my rep and my future, or so I imagined, since Moms had convinced me I wasn't going to be Miles Davis because he already had that job. After all, at sixteen, Miles had left home and was doing sessions with Charlie Parker and Dizzy Gillespie in New York City. I was in a hot band, but suddenly didn't see myself coming out anytime soon with my own *Bitches Brew*. Football might not have been a career, but I was damned good and the best candidate for quarterback.

The football coach of the recently integrated high school didn't share my vision. He took one look at me, saw a big black kid already six-one, not too far from my top height of six-three, and decided that I was an offensive tackle. Me block? Play on the line? Nothing against the offensive linemen, who are important to any quarterback, but that star role was the job I wanted. Besides the precision of my arm, I had the smarts, strategy, and leadership qualities to win football games and had been burning them up in practice. Sticking to principle, though I agreed to play on the line, I continued to raise the issue with the coach until our discussions became so testy, it was clear he wanted to throw me off the team. But unless he came up with a reason for doing so, he would look like a racist if he did.

The reason, announced to me in his office, was the discovery of contraband in my locker. With a shrug, he told me that I was being cut because, "you are a bad element for what we're trying to do here at this school."

The contraband? Books. To be more precise: *Die, Nigger, Die, Soul on Ice*, and *The Autobiography of Malcolm X.*

Thus ended any taste I had for athletics. That, combined with my continuing activism, my new observations about the gaps between the haves and the have-nots, black and white, and the stories I began to hear from the brothers returning from Vietnam fueled a desire to rebel against the status quo even more. Rather than becoming militant, I rebelled by making my own personal statement —my Afro, tie-dyes, and beads—and by putting my energies into the band that I was in.

1970 年，我已经 16 岁，基本是个小伙子了，真不知道自己能经得起多少次这样的折腾。妈妈看出了这一点，让我沉住气，说我已经跳了一年级，再有一年就可以毕业了。所以，玩音乐，交女友，和哥们儿弟兄一起玩，都让我分散了注意力。但是学校已经不再是曾经的净土，随着功课不再是我的主要兴趣点，我的反叛性格开始与周遭火药味十足的环境格格不入。

一次主要的对峙发生在二年级的时候，一次教练不让我打四分位。我顿时火就起来了，因为以往玩橄榄球，我都是打四分位的，从小在街上打球到高中一年级时，我都是如此。谁都知道克里斯投球不错。我的未来发展就指望四分位了，因为妈妈说，就别琢磨成为爵士大师迈尔·戴维斯第二了，因为第一已经无法超越了。但不管怎样，16 岁的时候，戴维斯已经离开家，和查理·帕克、迪吉·葛拉斯彼在纽约城演出了。我所在的乐队确实不错，但是我还没法很快奏出自己的即兴精酿。橄榄球没法成为我的事业，但是我四分位打得好啊，应该是最好的候选啊。

可是刚加入学校的橄榄球教练可不这么认为。他看了我一眼，看到一个1.85 米的黑孩子(后来我长到了 1.9 米)，觉得我应该是块进攻前锋的料。让我去绊倒对手，让我做前锋，倒不是对防守前锋有成见，这个位置对所有四分位都很关键，但是我要的是明星位置。再加上，我的投球准确度高，脑子活、有策略，这些都是赢球的关键啊，所以这些本领我在训练时都烂熟于胸。为了遵守规则，我同意打前锋，但是我不断和教练要求换位置，最后终于火药味渐浓，他准备把我弄出球队。但是如果他没有正当理由，这么做无异于把自己定位成种族主义分子。

终于，一天他在办公室里宣布了这么一条理由，在我的衣柜里，发现违禁品。他耸了耸肩，告诉我，我被开除了，"因为学校不能容忍像你这样的坏分子。"

什么违禁品，是书吗？就是《黑鬼去死》、《冰上灵魂》和《马尔科姆·艾克斯传》。

这件事让我对体育彻底倒了胃口。随着我对激进主义的进一步了解，我对于肤色和贫富差距的理解的加深以及越战归来的兄弟们的讲述，所有这些都让我对现状极为不满。我没有诉诸武力，而是以自身进行反抗，我的装束、非洲爆炸头、扎染、各种小串珠，我把所有的精力都投入到乐队当中。

The PURSUIT of HAPPYNESS

The Realistic Band happened to be a James Brown–style band, with strains of Sly Stone and Buddy Miles that I was pushing. Of course, I was totally down with Mr. Brown, and for years, whenever he was in town, I was there, taking in everything that he and his band did to create that unbelievable energy.

At each concert I'd start all the way back up in the bleachers of the Milwaukee County Stadium of sixteen thousand fans, and by the time James hit the stage I was in the front row. A mainly all-black audience, they went crazy, sheer pandemonium, before he even opened his mouth, and then every song he did was a showstopper, a religious experience. Something about how he did *Please, Please, Please*, just the guttural, pleading, soulful, slowed-down funk of it, was mind-blowing. That shit hit it, every time.

At one memorable concert a sister jumped onstage during that song and tore off the hot pink sequined cape he was wearing and threw it into the audience. The next thing we knew we had a feeding frenzy, everybody ripping and tearing up James Brown's cape. My piece, no bigger than a washcloth, became my most prized possession at the time. Moms, who loved her some James Brown too, was excited for me when I came home with my pink scrap of immortality.

To duplicate the James Brown sound—with its own rhythm and pulse that was off the charts—was an impossible goal. But we weren't bad. Our lead singer, Big Ed, a cat in his twenties and older than most of us, had started the band and then gone over to Nam while we kept the ball rolling. When he returned, he picked up the microphone where he had left off. For Milwaukee, he put on a good show, screaming and falling out, dressing up flashy, albeit somewhat strangely, in pants that were too short on his six-six frame and silk waistcoats that fit oddly. In my heart of hearts, I knew that music wasn't going to be my ticket to fame and fortune —one of several realizations that soon motivated me to find a job after school and on weekends.

The other concern was that, after he came home from Nam, Big Ed became increasingly volatile. Garvin and I stopped by to see him at his house one day to go over our playlist for that evening, with the TV showing news behind us, and as we made small talk, out of nowhere, Big Ed pulled out a .45, aimed it at the TV screen, right over my head, and pulled the trigger. *Ka-boom!* The TV just blew up! Just disintegrated! Not missing a beat, he put the gun away, some kind of sleight of hand, and kept on talking like nothing had happened. "Chris, what we playing tonight?"

Garvin and I got out of there as fast as we could. "Damn," I said, "all he had to do was change the channel!"

Turned out that he had shot up some other TVs, and his own mother had to hide her television set whenever he went to see her.

我们的乐队正好与詹姆斯·布朗一个风格，也受了些斯莱·斯通和巴迪·迈尔斯的影响，这两人是我力推的。当然我对布朗的崇拜是五体投地的，每当他来城里演出，我都会到场观看，认真品味他和乐队的每个细节，试图把他们所创造的那种音乐的魔力尽数掌握和吸收。

每次音乐会，我都会和密尔沃基体育场的1.6万名粉丝在站台上观看，每次詹姆斯登台的时候，我都会站到前排。观众都是以黑人为主，大家兴奋异常，全场沸腾，甚至没等他张口，人们已经近乎狂热，每首歌都会被大家的尖叫和喝彩所打断，人们仿佛都着了魔。他的唱腔圆润低沉、富有磁性，令人魂牵梦绕，触及心灵。每次都是如此，让人欲罢不能。

一次音乐会上，在他唱歌过程时，一个姑娘索性冲上舞台，一把扯下他那粉红色亮片斗篷，将之抛向观众。接下来是观众群中闻所未闻的冲动，所有人都冲将上来，争相撕扯着詹姆斯的斗篷。我抢到的那一片不过才巴掌大小，却令我如获至宝。妈妈也是詹姆斯的粉丝，看到我拿回家的那一小片斗篷，连她都感到兴奋至极。

效仿詹姆斯的声音，再现那种节奏和韵律，对于我们而言实在难以做到。但是我们的表现也不错，我们的主唱艾德二十出头，在我们几个中年纪最长，是他组建的乐队，后来去参加了越战。等他回来之后，他又重上舞台。在密尔沃基，他的演出也不同凡响，着装大胆出位，在台上高声尖声，动作夸张，虽然穿着的裤子和他近乎2米的身高相比有点短，丝质马甲也显得有些怪异，但都没有影响他的受欢迎程度。但在我的内心深处，我知道自己没办法靠音乐发家致富。也就是因为这样，我在放学后和周末的时候，又给自己找了份差事。

还有一点让我不安的是，艾德从越南回来之后，人就变得非常暴力。一天，我和加文路过他家，和他讨论晚上演出的曲目事宜，当时我们身后的电视里正在播放新闻。我们几个正在小声讨论着，突然艾德掏出一把45口径的手枪，瞄准电视就扣动了扳机，子弹就从我的头顶飞过。砰一声，电视顿时四分五裂。他手法灵活地把枪收了起来，若无其事地问我："克里斯，晚上咱们演什么呢？"

加文和我没多久就借机溜了出来，"我的天，他怎么这样，本来是换个频道就好了！"

艾德已经挥枪把几台电视都这么报废了，连他妈妈见到他来看望自己，都要把电视藏起来，生怕再发生不测。

Weed took his edge off. A few nights later Garvin and I were sitting in a parked car with Big Ed as he smoked a joint. When a police car pulled up behind us, Big Ed managed to throw out what was left of the joint before the two police officers approached.

We were ordered out of the car, and the two searched the smoky interior. Finding nothing, one of them said, "You must have been smoking marijuana in there because I smell it. I'm going to have to take you down and arrest you."

Big Ed said, "Take the smell to court, man. We ain't got nothing here."

For a tense moment, the cop looked shocked, like he couldn't believe what he had just heard. But it worked. He let us off with a warning.

My respect for Big Ed increased dramatically. For a cat who flipped out over the news and shot up TVs, he sure knew how to keep his cool in that situation.

The marijuana of the late sixties and seventies was nothing like the psycho-pot of later decades. For me, even though I had my fun drinking cheap wine in this era, smoking weed was preferable. Then again, I never wanted to get too high because I needed to be able to handle whatever insanity Freddie might pull at home.

Out with the boys after a gig in the same time period as our encounter with the cops, I smoked some crazy Thai-stick and went home paranoid as all hell, with a monster case of the munchies. Looking for something to eat, I tiptoed downstairs to the basement refrigerator and the moment I opened the door heard this *honk-honk-honk* poultry sound. Whirling around, I found myself face-to-face with a live goose. In our basement! Either I was way too stoned or Freddie had transformed the basement into an animal preserve.

In fact, Freddie had brought that live goose home for Sunday dinner the following night. This is his explanation when I wake up the next day. The three of us—Freddie, me, and the ill-fated goose—go together out into the backyard to the chopping block.

Freddie, whiskey thick on his breath at midday, hands me the ax. He smiles like the devil, as if to say that either I'm going to be initiated into chopping a live goose's head off, which I don't want to do, or, as the thought enters my head, I am going to be given my best shot to do what I've been trying to do for years.

When I hesitate at taking the ax, he says, "I'll do it then, goddamnit. You hold the goose."

Dizzy with opportunity, I realize that he is giving me this choice: to hold the goose while he chops its head off with the axe, or to chop off its head while he holds it. With the image of this drunken motherfucker chopping my fingers off, I opt for swinging the ax.

他还靠吸食大麻来给自己排忧解难。几天后的一个晚上，加文和我坐在路边的车里，艾德在一旁吸食大麻烟卷。忽然，一辆警车在我们身后停下来，两个警察朝我们走过来，艾德忙把手边的烟卷扔了出去。

警察让我们从车里出来，在烟雾缭绕的车里翻来找去，结果一无所获，一个警察说："你们肯定在抽大麻，我能闻得出来。走吧，跟我去警局一趟。"

艾德应道："好啊，你就在法庭上说你的鼻子可以作证，看看法官能拿我们怎么样？"

一时间，警察都没回过神来，似乎不敢相信自己的耳朵。但这话确实奏效了，他只是警告了我们几句，转身走了。

当下，我对艾德佩服得五体投地。这个因为新闻影响我们谈事就可以举枪击碎电视的家伙，他知道面对警察检查的时候，该怎么应对。

六七十年代的大麻比起后来的毒品还算不上什么。对于我而言，当时我也喜欢喝些廉价的酒精饮料，但也更喜欢抽点大麻。只是我不敢抽得太多，因为我需要保持头脑足够清醒，以便应对弗莱迪的疯狂之举。

在那次警察检查事件之后没多久，我和一些男孩子出去聚会，也抽了不少泰国棍儿，只是随便吃了点乱七八糟的东西，头重脚轻，昏昏沉沉。我想找点吃的，轻手轻脚地下了楼，打开冰箱，结果一开冰箱门就听到嘎嘎的叫声。面前居然出现了一头大白鹅，而且就在自家地下室里，这是我自己头脑发昏还是弗莱迪把家里变成了养殖场？

实际上，弗莱迪想把大活鹅作为第二天的周日大餐。所以第二天，我一觉醒来，弗莱迪就拽上我，在后院准备把这只倒霉的大鹅开膛破肚。

弗莱迪大白天就已经喝了不少的威士忌，浑身酒气十足，他递上来一把斧头，一脸的坏笑，让我亲手把鹅的脑袋砍下来，我当然不愿这么干，但转念一想，我是不是终于等到一个千载难逢的机会。

看到我犹犹豫豫地拾起了斧头，他说："算了，还是我来，你拿好了鹅头。"

我一时为这样的天赐良机而感到眩晕，这是他给的机会，让我二选一，要么他拿着鹅，我来砍，或者我抓住鹅，他来动手。一想到，这个醉汉可能会把我的手指头都一同剁掉，我决定还是我来动斧。

The PURSUIT of HAPPYNESS

Blade suspended in air, I look down at the goose and what comes to mind is an image of a cowering, vulnerable, powerless female, not unlike Moms when Freddie towers over her. I look over at him and see where on his anatomy to bring down the ax blade. My most prominent thought is a geometric calculation: do I have the absolute correct angle to enable me to generate sufficient force and velocity to kill Freddie with one stroke? There is to be no chop-chop-chop. I have *one shot, one swing.* I inhale, living a lifetime in my deliberation, thinking of the story I'll tell to explain the accident, reliving my previous failures, and not wanting to fail again. With a big inhale, I exhale and bring the ax down with all my might, decapitating mother goose.

Damn. After all that time, I finally had my real chance and couldn't do it. The only feeling I had in the aftermath was hard-core deprivation. As if a prize had just been dangled in front of me and I couldn't grasp it.

Freddie said, "Hey, good job. Now you just got to one, pluck him, two, boil him, and three, gut him."

Though it took me some years to realize how killing the old man would have ruined my life, I was deflated. Without anywhere to put my feelings of anger toward Freddie, I transferred them over to the savings account of the other guy I was still looking to kill— an opportunity that arrived shortly after the goose incident.

Sooner or later I had assumed that I'd cross his path. When I did, it was his limp and his smell that caught my attention, both unmistakable. The fear came back to me when I saw him. Not a fear he could do anything to me, but fear that maybe he might get away. Even more, with the rage bottled up for three years, it was fear about what I was going to do to him. After he passed me on the street, he turned and went into a tavern. I waited for over an hour, holding a cinder block.

Each time the tavern door opened, out would spill a mix of music, laughter, smoke, and the combination smells of beer and different kinds of booze, old tavern smells and human body smells. Each time, someone else came out. Maybe he had escaped. Maybe he had snuck out in the shadows. But then, at last, the door opened and the smells and sounds poured out one more time, and he came out alone, turning down toward where I was waiting. I needed him to see me; I needed to see the recognition in his eyes. When I came toward him, I saw not only recognition but fear, maybe the only time in my life that I caused fear to come into someone else's eyes.

"Oh, shit," he said, not even finishing the statement before I crowned him with the cinder block, bearing down with all my strength on the top of his head.

我把斧头高举过头，面前仿佛不再是一只鹅，而是一个手无缚鸡之力的女子，就仿佛是面对弗莱迪施虐时的母亲，我抬头看看弗莱迪，看看应该从哪里下斧头，我脑子里仿佛是在进行精密的几何计算，从什么角度下斧头，可以力道十足，同时能一斧解决问题，要了他的命。完全不可以失误，我只能一斧解决问题。只有一次机会。我深吸一口气，似乎那一瞬间无比漫长，想着以后该怎么解释这一切的发生，想起我以往的失误，决心这次绝不能再失手。我倾尽全力，手起斧落，那只母鹅即刻毙命。

天啊，我又生生错过了这次机会，我陷入深深的懊悔，久久不能自拔，仿佛煮熟的鸭子生生在眼前飞走了一般。

弗莱迪说："嗯，不错，接下来你就煺毛开膛，收拾干净就好了。"

尽管，我花了几年的时间才意识到，要是真的要了弗莱迪的命，我会搭上自己的一辈子，但这次失手还是让我沮丧了好久。我把对弗莱迪的满腔怒火都转到另一个人身上，我惦记着要他的命已经不是一朝一夕。杀鹅之后没多久，机会终于来了。

我觉得自己早晚会和他狭路相逢。有一天，这终于成为了现实，是他一瘸一拐走路的样子和身上的气味引起我的注意，没错，绝对是他。我不由得担心起来，不是担心别的，是怕他就此逃脱。甚至担心经过这三年的压抑和忍耐，我会对他做出些什么来。他从我身边走过，转身进了一个酒廊。我拎了块砖，等他出来，整整等了一个多小时。

每次酒廊的门打开，都会涌出一阵音乐和笑声，里面乌烟瘴气，混着啤酒和各类毒品的味道。每次，出来的都不是他。也许是他逃脱了，或者是他躲在什么阴暗的角落。最后，门又打开了，各种声音和味道又一次涌了出来，他一个人走了出来，朝着我等着的地方过来了。我需要他认出我来，等我迎着他走过去的时候，我看到他确确实实认出了我，而且还充满了恐惧。这恐怕是我有生以来头一次让人对我心生恐惧。

"见鬼。"他话音未落，我拎着砖就直接拍到他的脑门上，用尽全身的力气，直接拍了上去。

第五章　即兴精酿（下）

At first, he didn't fall, but he faltered. After more pounding, he finally crumpled to the sidewalk, and I threw the brick down, left it right there, and walked away. Didn't look back, didn't run. Right or wrong, I silently said the last words that I'd ever think about him—Got your motherfucking ass.

What became of him, I never knew. But I did know this: he had one gigantic headache and he would never forget me. For me, there was no need to keep the image in memory. I tossed it out that night on the street, like him, like the cinder block.

The score had been settled, the case was closed.

* * *

My destiny was probably carved on the Mississippi River when I was eight years old, riding in the motorboat with Uncle Henry, hearing stories about him going overseas and meeting women, seeing the world. Between him and Uncle Willie, it was only a matter of time before those stories caught up with me and sent me down to the recruiting offices.

There wasn't much holding me in Milwaukee. After that spring of 1970, while watching the March Madness NCAA finals when Moms gave me the greatest gift her wisdom could offer by saying, "Son, if you want to, one day you could make a million dollars," I knew that wherever my path lay, I was going to have to leave my home turf and go find it.

Sometimes in years to come I'd realize that I must have been born at the perfect time—to be able to witness everything that happened in every decade from the fifties on. Lucky for me that the mandatory draft was being phased out around the time I came of age. If I had been born a year or two earlier, I would've been drafted, and I probably would have been there in Vietnam too. It was also amazing to be growing up right in the middle of a sexual revolution at a time when the stereotypes of color were changing and black was especially beautiful. All of my early romantic relationships left me with positive feelings about what had gone on emotionally and physically.

My first serious girlfriend had been Jeanetta, the sweetest, prettiest girl in all of north Milwaukee. It didn't even occur to me how crazy I was about her until Momma said something to me after I came in late for the umpteenth time. "Boy, I used to be able to set my watch by you."

Jeanetta and I were unsophisticated in our lovemaking but no less passionate. Even after we broke up, every now and then we'd sneak down to her basement and go at it like bunnies.

一开始，他晃了几晃，但是没有摔倒。我又拍了几砖，他终于瘫软到路上。我把砖扔到一边，就扔在他身边，我没有回头，也没有跑开。无论是对是错，我对他说出了最后的几个字："去死吧。"

我不知道他后来怎么样了。但我知道如果他还活着，一定会头痛欲裂，这会让他永远都记着我的。而我则没有必要再记住这个人，我已经将这一夜，将这个人和那块砖，永远地抛在了路上。

这事就这么了结，结束了，全都结束了。

* * *

也许我的命运从 8 岁起就和密西西比河紧密相连在一起了。那时，亨利舅舅驾驶摩托艇带我一起出游，听他津津乐道地讲述那些外面世界的故事，还有各国各地的美女。他和威利舅舅两人对我的影响颇深，终究会有一天，因为他们讲过的故事，我会跑到征兵办公室去报名参军。

对于密尔沃基，我没什么可以留恋的。正像 1970 年的春天，正值每年大学篮球赛季决赛的"三月疯狂"，妈妈说出了她那经典的至理名言，"儿子，如果你愿意，有朝一日你也能挣到 100 万。"我知道，不管我设定怎样的方向，我都需要离开自己的故乡，去寻找、去发现。

多年以后，当我回顾从前，我意识到自己其实是生逢其时，可以亲眼目睹 50 年代以来，每个年代的真实发展变化。特别幸运的是，等我长大的时候，强制服兵役制度已经逐步取消。如果我再早生一两年，十有八九也就上了越南战场了。更奇妙的是，我经历了性解放的时期，人们对肤色的审美也发生了变化，特别是开始以黑肤色为美。我早期的浪漫史更让我觉得，所经历的一切在情感和身体上都是充满着愉悦的。

我第一个正式女友叫杰内塔，是密尔沃基北部最漂亮的姑娘，我都没有意识到自己对她是多么的疯狂着迷，直到一天，已经记不清是我第多少次的晚归，妈妈对我说："孩子，我以往是用你对表的啊。"

我们俩的床上功夫都不怎么老道，但是却从不缺少激情，并且乐此不疲。甚至等到我们分手之后，我们还时不时地钻到她家的地下室，云雨一番。

I next dated an uptown preacher's daughter who I found irresistible because she wore stockings. No other girl I dated had worn stockings, and she was also the first girl I'd ever dated who lived with both her mother and father. Most everyone I knew lived in a single-parent household. She was very reserved, quiet, and proper. She was a virgin who was willing to have sex—on condition that she have a baby right then. Not knowing much, I had plenty of life examples teaching me that high school parenting wasn't for me. We broke up before we got too serious.

My next girlfriend, Belinda, and I were soul mates, and we became serious fast. She was beautiful, black as me, gorgeous, with delicious, luscious lips, statuesque like an African queen. But what most attracted me to her was how smart she was. She read and made me read more, and she would ask questions. Belinda broadened my worldview beyond the African American experience, steering me toward books about South Africa and apartheid, the history of events like the Sharpsville Massacre, setting up an awareness of my connection to people of color around the globe. Belinda wore an Afro hairdo, was stacked, and had a big beautiful smile. I loved her, especially her body, which was unbelievable. Her behind was spectacular, shaped like a basketball. Swear to God, every time I saw her from the backside I wanted to start dribbling. Not only that, she was sexually uninhibited, doing things like jumping into my lap in the living room of her daddy's house as he slept in the next room. For me at that point, that was doing the wild thing.

Belinda and I had a date planned to go to the movies on the afternoon of Christmas Day, a welcome chance for me to skip out on the annual family holiday bash at the house of one of our relatives. Christmas, according to popular lore and actual accounts that I had heard from normal people, was supposed to be an occasion for family to gather to eat, drink, and be merry. Not in our family. The routine was that everyone got together to eat, drink, and then fight. Every holiday, religious, secular, patriotic, pagan, it didn't matter, by the third round of drinks the battles began. So as Moms, Sharon, and Kim followed Freddie out to his car, I just called after them, "Merry Christmas! Y'all go ahead to the party, I'm going to the movies with Belinda, so maybe I'll stop by later."

The house all to myself, a luxury, I go and put my clothes together for my date, then go into the bathroom and run a hot bath, the anticipation of a great long Christmas Day soak putting me in a serene, great mood. Moments after I lower myself into the water, close my eyes, and begin to enjoy a series of meditative images that take me out on the river on a hot day, relaxing without a care in the world, I suddenly hear, "Motherfucker!" this and "Bitch" that, coming from the front porch. Footsteps in the living room tell me that Moms and my sisters are home, with Freddie too. It's like a scene in that movie *Poltergeist* that came out some years afterward: "They're baaa-aaack."

我下一个女友是城里牧师的女儿，我无法抗拒的是她穿长筒袜的样子，而且她也是头一个和我交往的父母没有离异的女孩子。而我所认识的其他女孩大多是来自单亲家庭。她非常安静、矜持，举止得体，觉得发生关系就得要孩子。我虽然经历不多，但是身边有太多活生生的例子，还是高中生就怀孕生子明显不是我想要的。因此，我们没有太多接触，就决定分开了。

我下一个女友是碧琳达，很快我们就如胶似漆。她人长得非常漂亮，肤色和我一样，嘴唇长得非常性感，身材长得宛若非洲的女王。但是最吸引我的还是她的聪慧过人。她不但自己博览群书，也鼓励我多读多看，而且她还特别勤学好问。碧琳达让我的视野进一步开阔，不再局限于非裔美国人的范畴，而是放眼世界，广泛涉猎，比如南非的历史，或是一些不为人知的历史，如沙佩尔维惨案之类。这让我意识到自己和全世界的有色人种有着种种联系。碧琳达是非洲式的发型，很精干，而且笑起来很迷人。她的身体美轮美奂，让我着迷。她那浑圆的美臀，就像一个结实的篮球。每次我看到她的背影，都让我不由得兴奋异常。不仅如此，在床上她简直是百无禁忌。在她父亲的房子里，不顾老爸就在隔壁睡觉，她就敢扑到我身上，尽情狂欢，这简直让我心惊肉跳。

碧琳达和我准备圣诞节下午一起去看电影，这可以让我有理由从亲戚家的年度家庭聚会中抽身出来，按照当地人的说法，这种聚会就是一大家子人聚在一起，又吃又喝，开开心心的。但我家不是这样。一般情况是大家凑在一起，吃饭喝酒，接下来冲突打架必不可少。无论这些节日是宗教的、民间的、国家的还是其他什么的，一般酒过三巡，争吵就开始了。所以当妈妈、妹妹沙仑和金牡跟着弗莱迪出去时，我就冲他们喊上一声："圣诞快乐！你们都去聚会吧，我和碧琳达看电影去，可能回来晚一些。"

现在屋里就剩我一个了，简直是太奢侈的享受了。我去把赴约的衣服收拾出来，就去泡个热水澡。一想到今晚圣诞的快乐时光，我就不禁情绪高涨，忘乎所以。我刚泡在水里不久，就闭上了眼睛，开始想象着在炎热的天气里，自己驾船漂浮在河流之上，彻底放松，无牵无挂，尘世的烦扰尽数散去。突然，我听到一声大喊"去他妈的，狗娘养的你"从门口传来。接着传来母亲和妹妹的脚步声，当然还有弗莱迪紧随其后。这情形就像几年后的电影《鬼驱人》里的台词那样："他们又回来了。"

Lying in the tub, buck naked, I'm thinking, *Damn, I took too long.* But before I can swing into action, the door flies off its hinges and pointing dead in my direction is the barrel of Freddie's shotgun. Never before has he looked so much like the meanest, drunkest, craziest Sonny Liston as he does this day, raging at me with his deadliest "Get the fuck outta my goddamn house! Get out of my goddamn house!"

With no time to respond and ask what the hell I've done, and as everyone in the house literally scatters to run upstairs or down into the basement, I could kill myself for not bludgeoning him instead of that goose now that he's finally going to make good on his promise to blow me away. No choice now, I jump out of the tub, heart pounding through my chest, and race out the front door and onto the porch. Buck naked for all the world to see in Milwaukee, Wisconsin, on Christmas Day.

Before I can figure out my next move, I look down and see a cute little boy passing by, bundled up in his winter coat for the fifteen-degree weather. He looks something like I did at his age, with ears somewhat big for his head that he'll no doubt grow into. As he spots me, his smile widens straight across his face. Sincere as you please, he says: "Merry Christmas, mister."

Not answering him, I watch him walk on down the street, soon disappearing into the wintry Wisconsin mist.

Belinda didn't attempt to cheer me up when we did get to the movies later. There wasn't an ounce of merry left in me.

That day marked the last time I bothered to celebrate a holiday in the Freddie Triplett household, and unfortunately, it pretty much ruined Christmas. For many years I didn't bother buying a tree, and if I did mark the season, it was in the effort to do something that honored the spirit of Christ, in some spiritual context. It has taken me the balance of my life to truly enjoy Christmas. By the same token, Freddie's gift to me that year was to start my clock ticking for how soon I could get out of Dodge.

A short while later, Belinda and I broke up, not for lack of love but more because of timing and my immaturity at helping her deal with the death of a mutual friend. By that summer of 1971, I was seventeen years old and going into my senior year of high school. When I happened to be walking down Wisconsin Avenue, my stomping grounds of this era, I glanced up into the window of the army/navy surplus store and saw a girl through the glass holding a T-shirt up to her chest, as if she was debating whether or not to try it on. One look and I just fell in love. Shot through the heart.

我赤条条地躺在浴缸里，心想，坏了，我泡得时间太久，但还没等我起身，浴室的门就咣当被撞开，只见弗莱迪的枪口冷冰冰地对着我。那天他的作派简直可以与拳王索尼·利斯顿有一拼，那种冷漠刻薄、疯狂，还有酗酒无度，他冲我声嘶力竭地大喊大叫："给我从屋里滚出去，滚出去！"

当时根本不容我问他我做错了什么，屋里的人四散逃窜，或者躲到楼上，或是逃到地下室，我真后悔当初我砍下的是鹅的脑袋，而不是把他一斧子结果了。现在轮到他来要我的命了。我别无选择，只能蹦出浴缸，心怦怦直跳，直奔前门，跑到门廊，在圣诞节这天，在威斯康星密尔沃基的大街上，赤条条地暴露在众人面前。

还没等我反应过来下一步该干什么，一个可爱的孩子恰巧从门口路过，他穿着厚厚的棉服，来抵御户外零下十度的严寒。他和我小时候有几分神似，耳朵显得有点大，不过长大后一定会长匀称的。他一看到我就咧开嘴笑了，非常真诚地说了句："圣诞快乐！"

我没有答话，看着他沿着街走远，小小的身影很快消失在威斯康星的浓雾之中。

后来，我和碧琳达一起去看了电影，但并没有让我开心起来，那天我已毫无情趣可言。

那一天应该是我在弗莱迪家度过的最后一个节日，晦气的是，这让我对圣诞节从此没了兴趣。很多年之后，我都不愿去买圣诞树，即便我在日历上标出了圣诞节，至多不过是对耶稣表示敬意，这纯粹是精神层面的事情。又过了很久，我才能真正享受圣诞的快乐。而且，因为弗莱迪给我的这次圣诞大礼，我知道自己选择离开的时间已经为期不远了。

不久之后，我和碧琳达决定分手了，倒不是因为我们不再相爱，只是因为这种爱不合时宜，再有就是在帮她处理我们两个共同的朋友身故的问题上，我的方法不当。1971年夏天，我整整17岁了，已经读到高中三年级。一天，我走在威斯康星大街上，这是个改变命运的时刻，透过一家军需店的橱窗，我看到里面有个姑娘，她好像正在胸前比划着一件T恤衫，似乎想试一试这件衣服。也就是这一眼，让我顿时对她心生好感，一见钟情。

After I walked into the store and introduced myself, I learned that her name was Sherry Dyson and that she was from Virginia, a senior at Morgan State College, and in town with relatives. Light-skinned, with a full Afro and the most beautifully shaped breasts, just incomparable, she was not a movie magazine beauty, but in an understated, down-to-earth way a knockout. She was brilliant, kind, and had a sense of humor that put me at ease with her from our first conversation. After we met, we spent two days just talking.

At first, Sherry had no idea that I was four years younger than her, although after we went to see *Summer of '42*—a fittingly perfect romantic movie about an affair between an older woman and a teenage boy—I had to confess. For the rest of my life, every time I'd hear or even think of that theme song, I'd become seventeen years old again, crazy in love with Sherry Dyson, my dream woman from a well-to-do Richmond, Virginia, family. The daughter of a mortician father who owned the A. D. Price Funeral Home and a mother who was a high school teacher, Sherry had grown up all her life in one home, a gracious colonial house on Hanes Avenue, Richmond, Virginia—a street name I'd never forget, considering the deluge of letters and cards I addressed to her there.

At this stage of the game, having girlfriends had already provided me with some crash courses in basic economics. My last year of high school and the shocking discovery that I had amassed a nine-hundred-dollar phone bill calling Sherry long distance were all I needed to know that I had to do better than what I was earning as a dishwasher at Nino's Steakhouse, making at best a hundred a week.

After I hid the phone bill, Moms received a call from the phone company alerting her to the fact that our phone was going to be turned off for nonpayment. When she complained that she hadn't even seen a bill, Moms figured out fast what had happened. Staying extremely cool, she escorted me down to the offices of the phone company and made me confess why our phone bill was so high. A deal was struck to prevent the phone from being turned off that required me to turn over every cent I made for the rest of my teen years.

It was my own doing, but that didn't prevent me from throwing a fit at Nino's the next night when I reached a boiling point over being stiffed by the waiters, who were supposed to be sharing tips with me. This was from the same crew running back to the kitchen screaming for clean dishes. The manager shrugged and told me that I was lucky to have my job washing dishes as it was. Livid at everyone and delirious from the heat of "humping the hot Hobart," as we called running the dishwasher, I did the most disgusting thing that came into my head. I felt almost as bad afterward as the time I got into another financial rut from phone calls to Sherry and pawned Ophelia's television set. That night at Nino's I peed right onto the dishes coming out of the Hobart. Not once, but as many times as I could drink down enough liquid to make a statement of how I felt about my last hours on the job washing dishes at that steak house.

接着我就走进店里，自我介绍，她说自己是雪莉·迪森，来自弗吉尼亚，是摩根州立大学的高年级学生，这次是来看亲戚的。她肤色浅褐，也是非裔，美胸十分惹火，她不是那种杂志封面女郎，但她的美来自内在，一样摄人魂魄。她非常聪明，态度和善，而且谈吐幽默，头一次和她交谈就让我非常舒服，我们相遇之后，就喋喋不休整整聊了两天。

开始，雪莉不知道我比她小四岁，直到我们一同去看了电影《42年之夏》，那部片子讲的是一个成年女子和一个十几岁男生之间的浪漫故事，我不得不道出了自己的实际年龄。后来，耳边一旦响起那个电影的主题曲，我就马上会回到自己17岁的时候，回想起自己和雪莉疯狂相爱，她绝对就是我的梦中情人，来自弗吉尼亚里士满，家境殷实，她父亲从事殡仪行业，自己开了一家殡仪馆。母亲是高中教师。雪莉从小到大都和父母生活在一起，住在哈尼斯大道一所老式大房子里，这个地址我永生难忘，因为我曾往这里发过无数的卡片和书信。

在我这个年龄段，女友总让我的经济状况出现危机。在我高中的最后一年，我惊恐地发现电话费的金额居然高达900多美元，这都是给雪莉打长途的花费，而我在尼诺牛排馆洗盘子一周最多才挣100块。

我刚把电话单藏好，妈妈就收到电话公司的来电，说是家里的电话要欠费停机。妈妈奇怪自己根本没有收到任何账单，她立刻猜到了事情的原委。她对事情的处理非常冷静，带着我去了电话公司，让我自己解释为什么家里的电话费用总是居高不下。最后问题得以解决，家里的电话不会停机，但条件是我需要把未来几年挣到的每一分钱都用于交纳电话费。

我这是自作自受，需要专心挣钱，但我第二天还是在牛排馆和那里的伺应生大打出手，因为他们要分我的小费，而且还跑到厨房捣乱。经理表示对此无能为力，说我能找到这么一份洗盘子的工作实属不易，我被解雇了。当时我十分气恼，加之洗盘子机散发的热量让我昏头胀脑，我做了件非常过分的事情。因为工作丢得太不是时候，我刚刚因为和雪莉的长途电话欠债无数，还不得已把奥菲利娅的电视机当掉了。于是，为了报复，我开始在盘子上撒尿，不是一个两个盘子，而是不停地喝水，不停地往盘子上撒尿，让我在牛排馆的最后几小时，完全在泄愤中度过。

God must have had a laugh when the next job I obtained turned out to be handling bedpans and cleaning up pee and poop after old people. Even more important, I learned a new level of compassion that I had never known before, and I paid off the phone bill finally.

The person who helped get me the job as an orderly at the Heartside Nursing Home was Ophelia, now working there as a nurse's aide. For many reasons I wanted to do well, mainly because I was locking into a mindset that whatever I was going to do in life, I wanted to give it my all, to go beyond what was expected of me. My first step, which would come in handy in the next pivotal chapters of my life, was to learn as quickly as I could from whoever was the best at doing the tasks I'd need to master. With that thinking, I really got into doing this kind of work: serving the food, changing people's diapers, making up the beds, emptying bedpans.

Pretty soon, I was thinking, *Yeah, I can do this.* Soon after that, I could do it better than the top orderly there. In fact, management saw how good I was and gave me my own wing. Of the thirty-some-odd patients, all white, some were able to take care of themselves, while others needed a lot of help. The work was surprisingly rewarding. It felt good to help people, and even better when people acknowledged how well I treated them. Unlike some of the other orderlies and staff, I didn't ignore them when they rang my call button but would go and help immediately. Nobody else there was willing to give that kind of care. The truth was that I actually liked helping them, liked doing my job.

Mr. John McCarville, an old Navy guy, had lost the ability to speak. But he could salute. Every night when I put him in bed, or anytime I attended to something he needed, he gave me a strong salute. "Thank you," he was saying without words. "I appreciate your kindness." Gratitude shone bright in his eyes. Two patients whom we called the Flintstones—because one looked like Fred Flintstone and the other like Barney Rubble—were mentally retarded and middle-aged. The two had been on the wing so long that after they became a twosome as homosexual lovers, no one wanted to separate them. Fred was the aggressor and Barney was the submissive one. I was rather freaked out when I saw one of them eating his own feces.

"Is there any way to move them?" I asked my boss, thinking I wasn't equipped for that kind of behavior.

"No, they need to stay on this ward, so you gotta try to deal with it."

So I dealt with it.

Another patient was Ida, a tiny Italian lady with a gold tooth, never seen out of her hospital gown and tiny hospital shoes. Sweet as she could be, Ida was what we then called senile, probably suffering from Alzheimer's or some form of dementia.

我得到下一份工作时，上帝一定在偷笑，因为这次我要负责给老年人端屎倒尿。更重要的是，这份工作让我对同情和关爱又有了更深层次的了解，而且我终于付清了所欠的电话费。

是奥菲利娅帮我找到了这份工作，她也在哈特赛护理中心做护理助理。无论如何，我都想做好这份工作，因为我觉得无论要做什么，都要全身心投入，要做到最好。首先我需要问过来人虚心学习，这一点对我后来的生活都起到了关键的作用。出于这一点，我任劳任怨地做好每件工作，包括给患者送饭、换洗尿布、整理床铺和清理便盆。

很快我就可以得心应手，不久我甚至可以比最有资历的护理做得都好。实际上，管理层非常欣赏我的所作所为，决定让我负责完整的一片区域。那里包括三十多个白人需要照料，有些还可以自理，但有些需要精心的照料。这份工作让我获益匪浅。首先帮助别人本身十分快乐，加之患者对我非常认可，这更让我心花怒放。和别人不同的是，我任劳任怨，对于患者的召唤，从不怠慢，铃声一响，我就马上到位。别人很难做到这一点，我之所以如此，是因为我自己能乐在其中，并且觉得其乐无穷。

约翰·麦卡维尔是个老海军，已经丧失了语言能力，但他可以敬礼。每天晚上，当我把他扶上床，或是帮他做这做那，他就会认真地给我敬礼，那是无声的感谢，感谢我所做的一切。那种感激之情溢于言表。还有两个患者特别像《摩登原始人》里面的两个主角，他俩都是中年人，都有智障。他们俩在病房呆得太久，逐渐成了同性恋，彼此依恋，别人也不愿把他们分开。两人一个有攻击性，一个比较顺从。一次我甚至看到他们在吃自己的粪便，让我瞠目结舌。

"有没有办法把他们换个地方呢？"我问经理，因为没有设备能让我把他们搬动开来。

"他们只能呆在病房里，你自己想办法吧。"

我只好自己想办法了。

还有一个患者叫艾达，是个小个子意大利老太太，镶着金牙，总是穿着医院的病号服和一双小巧的鞋子，患有老年痴呆症。

The first time I saw her she padded up to me and asked, "Are you my little boy?" I was really concerned about how confused she was.

From then on, I answered, "Yes, Ida, I'm your little boy."

Serious as a heart attack, she then said, "Oh, that's funny. The last time I saw you, you weren't so tall. You weren't colored either."

Only once did I lose my temper and do something I instantly regretted. One of my patients, a wealthy woman from some blueblood family, constantly complained, becoming louder and more obnoxious by the day. She berated everyone, me included, and refused to eat. Then when she did want something, she wanted it *now!* If you didn't jump to it, she was going to call her lawyer. The ghetto in me just flew out one day when she started saying really nasty things, and instead of leaving her piece of lemon meringue pie on her plate, I picked it up and put it *splat* right in her face.

Instantly mortified, I said, "Oh, I'm so sorry," as I grabbed a towel and carefully started wiping the lemon meringue off her cheeks and nose.

She just needed the attention as it turned out. She looked up at me gratefully and said, "Thanks, son, that's the first time I had my face washed all day."

* * *

When my sisters preempted my announcement to Moms that I had gone down and enlisted in the Navy, almost a year after high school graduation, she may have expressed her disappointment. Maybe if my last years of high school hadn't been so unfulfilling— especially with the administration treating me like a dangerous Black Panther outlaw—I would have pursued the college education that Momma never had. But by the time I came to give her the news, Bettye Jean Gardner Triplett flashed me her signature smile that could launch a thousand ships and asked if there was time to throw a party.

For the last few months I'd been working at Inland Steel, thanks to Uncle Archie helping me get a job there. As much as I had learned working at the nursing home, the union wages were a significant improvement in my pocket. And yet, I discovered a cold economic principle: the more you make, the more you spend. That was obviously something that I didn't have to leave Milwaukee to learn. But there was so much more out there I didn't know, and the reality was that I did have to leave my hometown, land of the familiar.

我第一次见到她时，她拍拍我的肩，说道："你是我的小儿子吗？"我真不知她病得到底有多重。

后来我就顺着她回答："我是您的小儿子。"

她的表情非常严肃："噢，这就怪了，上次我见到你，你没有这么高，而且肤色也不一样啊。"

我只有一次向病人发了脾气，不过立刻就后悔了。有个患者有贵族血统，总是怨声载道，而且白天的时候，嗓门很大，非常烦人。她让所有的人都抓狂，而且还拒绝吃饭。可是她要是想拿到什么东西，必须马上就要得到。若没有立刻出现在她面前，她就要闹着找律师。有一天，她又闹事，我实在忍无可忍，把本来要放在她盘子里的柠檬派直接摔在她的脸上。

但我马上就后悔了，"实在对不起啊。"我抓起一条毛巾，小心地把食物从她的面颊和鼻子上擦去。

其实她只是想让人们注意到自己，她抬起头来，感激地说："谢谢你，孩子，这是这些天来头一次有人给我洗脸。"

* * *

1972年春，我高中毕业没多久，就报名参了军，当妹妹抢先告诉母亲这个消息时，她非常失望。我的高中其实没有完全读完，主要是校方认定我是个危险的黑豹党党徒，所以希望我能越早毕业越好，冬天时分就让我从学校毕业。我本应去完成妈妈未完的夙愿，去读大学。但当我亲自告诉她要去参军的消息时，她脸上绽开了贝蒂·让式的微笑，还问我有没有时间开个派对庆祝一下。

临走前的几个月，我一直是在A.O.内陆钢厂工作，这多亏了阿奇舅舅的帮忙，我才能得到这份工作。在护理中心我学到了很多，在钢厂工作让我的收入也丰厚了不少。但我发现了一条经济上的铁律，挣得越多，花得越多。我无须离开密尔沃基就可以明白这个道理。但是外面的世界有着太多的未知，所以我必须离开，离开这片生我养我的地方，去远方。

As to why I decided to join the Navy over the other branches of the service, it was possibly its superior marketing slogan, "Join the Navy, See the World," that did it. Or maybe it was all Jack Nicholson's fault, given the fact that I had just seen him in a role as a sailor in *The Last Detail* right before I went over to the recruiting center. Besides that, the Navy promised that I was really going to go see all the overseas places my uncles talked about. But the main motivation, even with Sherry not totally out of the picture, was getting to meet those women. I could hear Uncle Henry going on about the Italian women, and the Korean women who walked on your back to give you a massage that cured your spine of pain for the rest of your life. They had "feet like hands," I heard him say numerous times. I couldn't wait.

For the first eighteen years of my life, I'd guided myself without a father, believing that my fundamental responsibility was to protect my mother. Having failed to guarantee her protection by getting rid of Freddie, it was now time to put her lovingly and safely in God's hands and to go in pursuit of the happiness that was all my momma ever wanted for me.

我选择海军，选择到远方服役，很可能是因为当时的宣传口号："参加海军，了解世界。"也可能我去征兵处之前看了杰克·尼科尔森在电影《最后的细节》中出演的海员角色。不仅如此，海军使我还有机会去看异域风情，这些舅舅们都和我谈过。但是真正的动机不仅于此，尽管雪莉和我还有联系，可我就是想到不同的国家去结识各国美女。亨利舅舅讲过意大利女人的故事，还有韩国女人可以用脚踩背，帮你放松身体，消除疲乏。那脚上的功夫非常了得，就和手指一样灵巧。我已经听他讲过无数遍了。我实在迫不及待，也想亲自体验一番。

在我来到人世的这第一个18年间，我没有父亲的关照和保护，相信自己的最大职责就是让妈妈免受伤害。没有成功地除掉弗莱迪，我只有让慈爱的主保护着母亲，而自己去寻找幸福，这也是多年来妈妈希望我能得到的东西。

Part two

第二部

Chapter 6
The World Beyond

The USS Chris Gardner set sail—via airplane, the first time I'd ever flown—but instead of being sent to boot camp near a base like San Diego or in Hawaii, where all the recruiting photos were apparently shot, I was given a choice of going to nearby Great Lakes, Illinois, or Orlando, Florida. Opting for the farthest destination, imagining that would be a jumping-off place to all those foreign ports of call, I chose to go to Orlando. Land-locked Orlando. Hotter than hell with swamp-level humidity and steroid-fed insects.

第六章
外面的世界

克里斯·加德纳就要扬帆远航。还要坐飞机,这可是我有生以来第一次。但我没有去圣地亚哥或夏威夷的新兵训练营,征兵处的照片可都是在这些地方拍摄的,我只能在两个选择中间进行取舍,要么去离家不远的伊利诺伊州的大湖区,要么去佛罗里达的奥兰多。梦想着更远的征程,我选择了远离家乡的佛罗里达奥兰多。那里闷热潮湿,蚊虫肆虐。

Growing up on the roller-coaster ride engineered by Freddie Triplett, I was relieved by the institutional structure. Unlike an environment in which I could never do right, the Navy provided clear-cut guidelines for doing right or wrong and had a process for rewarding or punishing performance accordingly. There was definitely a part of me that resented authority and recoiled at the idea of having my individuality taken from me, but I understood the purpose and knew how to cope without losing a sense of who I was entirely. Of course, the transformation from being a nonconformist with my tie-dyes, beads, Afro, and light growth of facial hair to a clean-shaven, shorn, uniformed sailor was a shock and a half. The result was a terrible case of pseudo-folliculitis, for want of a better diagnosis, or big-ass bumps that a lot of cats, especially black guys, get from shaving for the first time. My hair was never the same after boot camp. As years passed I eventually gave up trying to grow it back right and was later grateful to Isaac Hayes for pioneering the shaved-head look.

The heat and humidity were rough from the start, but I didn't know what hot was until I had to stand at full attention in my dress uniform in the sun. My "training" in learning how to be still helped. I wasn't allowed to move or to react at all to the rivers of sweat running down my face and back, tickling my ass. Not a flinch.

In formation one afternoon I saw Senior Chief Petty Officer White, commander of Company 208, stride right up to me and braced myself for whatever he had to say.

"Son, you know what I know about you?" he asked, almost nose to nose with me as droplets of perspiration weren't just rolling down my face and body but touching me like long blazing fingers, like a parade of insects crawling and itching me. I didn't move. Officer White answered his own question: "What I know is that you've got a lot of self-discipline."

Not that I didn't make mistakes. Early on, in my enthusiasm, I saluted an officer indoors. Who knew you weren't ever supposed to do that? I didn't know. I was just saluting my ass off, chest puffed up, broadcasting—*Hey, I'm in the Navy, off to see the world!* As a consequence, I was sent to the deck—actually an expanse of lawn in front of the barracks—where I learned exactly how, where, and when to salute an officer. Surrounding this mock deck were statuesque palm trees inhabited by squirrels, a perfect setting for my superior officer to make me understand my station by ordering me to stand on deck and every time I saw a squirrel, run up to it, snap to attention, salute, and say, "Good afternoon, sir."

Please! Those squirrels must have had early vintage cell phones because the next thing I knew, squirrels seemed to just come out of nowhere, leaping from palm trees and scattering across the deck as I ran from one to the next, saluting and saying, "Good afternoon, sir." As intended, the humiliating part was the large audience of fellow recruits standing and watching from an upstairs barracks window while I dashed to and fro saluting a bunch of damned squirrels.

从小到大领教了弗莱迪的喜怒无常，军队里的令行禁止，赏罚分明，让我非常惬意。和家里永远分不清对错形成鲜明对比，军队里的一切都有明文规定，无论是赏是罚，一切都有章可循。我天性中确实有反叛的一面，这会让权威备感头痛，这是因为我不愿让自己的个性丧失殆尽。我也明白服从的重要性，但不会以迷失自我为代价。当然，我的变化是天翻地覆的，曾几何时，我是身着扎染，身上缀满小珠，毛绒绒的髯须，颓废浪荡，现在的我身着笔挺制服，脸和头发都刮得干干净净，一尘不染。结果就是我染上了须部假毛囊炎，这种病在头一次剃须的黑人中间很常见。我的发型自从进了新兵营就没再恢复过原样。几年过去了，我对于发型和留须方面做了彻底的放弃。这不得不感谢歌手艾沙克·海兹，给大家在剃头方面开了先河。

刚开始，酷热和潮湿确实让人难熬，但当我全副武装在烈日炎炎之下拔军姿时，我才了解到什么是真正的暑热难耐。我小时候对于一动不动的理解此时派上了用场。即便是大汗淋漓我都必须纹丝不动，任凭汗水沿着额头、脊背在身上流淌。全凭毅力，坚持下来。

一天下午，在练习拔军姿时，我看到208连的长官，二级军士长怀特直冲我就走了过来，我立刻挺直腰杆，等待训话。

"知道我注意到你什么了吗？"他问道，我们俩几乎只有寸把距离，大滴大滴的汗珠不仅是顺着脸颊和身体往下淌，而是像一把把利刃一样切割着我的肌肤，更像无数毛虫般让我痒痛难捱。但我纹丝未动，怀特长官自问自答："我觉得你的纪律性非常出色。"

我并非绝对不犯错误。刚入伍不久，我对什么都新鲜，一次，在屋里，我向一位长官敬礼。其实不应该这么做的。但我并不知道这一点。相反，我趾高气扬地敬着礼，还说："我是海军，来看世界。"于是我被带到了甲板上，这就相当于军营前面的草坪了。就在这里，我接受了教育，了解了究竟应该在什么时候，怎样对长官敬礼。在甲板周围，有很多棕榈树，上面还有小松鼠蹦来跳去，此情此景，让这位长官觉得这里非常适合我熟悉了解敬礼方面的规定和要求。所以他要求我站在甲板上，每看到一只松鼠，就要集中精力，上前敬礼，同时要说："长官，下午好。"

天啊，这些松鼠一定是有手机还是什么设备，因为接下来我就看到不知从哪里跑出来的那么多松鼠，在树上窜来窜去，或是干脆跑到甲板上来，而我只能一个接一个地蹦上去，敬礼，并说，"下午好，长官。"不过最过分的是，很多新兵都从楼上的军营，透过窗户观望，而我在一群松鼠中间蹦来跳去，一刻不停。

The **PURSUIT** of
HAPP_y_**NESS**

For the most part, however, I made it through boot camp with, as they say, flying colors. Graduates were given a choice of going either to a fleet or to an "A" school. Along with Jarvis Boykin, a fellow recruit I'd met at boot camp, I chose to go to an "A" school. This was a terrific opportunity, I thought, to build on the medical foundation that working at Heartside Nursing Home had given me. It was a stepping-stone to being a medic in the Navy's prestigious hospital corps, which I envisioned taking me to serve in the Philippines or Korea.

Boot camp had trained me well but had not gotten rid of my romantic streak. Not only was I ready to see the world beyond familiar shores, but I was beginning to think about the power of healing and helping the less fortunate, about changing and saving the world. Ironically, the school that I'd have to attend to set me on that path happened to be the U.S. Navy Hospital Corps School in Great Lakes, Illinois—not far from Milwaukee, Wisconsin.

There were more ironies to come. After doing that U-turn and ending up right back where I started up north, I faced the startling information that the U.S. Navy Hospital Corps provided medical backup and support for the U.S. Marine Corps. Actually, the Marine Corps was part of the Department of the U.S. Navy, something nobody had told me when I enlisted. My expectation was to be in an overseas medical naval facility, surrounded by slightly oversexed uniformed nurses like Hot Lips Houlihan from M★A★S★H. The last thing in the world I wanted to do was be in the Marine Corps. As I complained to Boykin and some of my other buddies I met in Great Lakes during the time we were being trained in the basics of first aid, "If I wanted to be in the Marine Corps, I could've joined the Marines. Man, please!" This was another reason I was increasingly concerned about where I was going to be stationed.

I started to get the sinking feeling that my vision of sailing off to sea was never going to happen. Hell, I began to worry, I might not even get out of the United States. That's why I was being careful to mind my p's and q's, just to be sure I was sent to one of the places I'd requested on my dream sheet and not shipped off with the Marines.

Fortunately, I had distinguished myself as a quick study when it came to the medical training we were being given. Everything looked promising on paper. As the twelve-week training period wound to a close, I had managed to stay out of the kind of trouble others had gotten into. I had already been discouraged from hardcore drinking by Freddie's example, in addition to the fact that I didn't really like the taste. But when the cats went out for beers off base, I went along and had a few. It practically went with the uniform. When my buddy Boykin and I headed off base to a bar called the Rathskeller one night, we had more than a few. We were drunk, sloppy drunk, which meant that we missed our ride and had to walk back to the base. Rather than walk the long way back through the main gate and be late, we decided to take a shortcut by jumping the fence.

但是在新兵营我最大的收获是知道了行行都可以出状元。新兵营毕业后，我可以选择参加舰队，或是去上军校学习。我和在新兵营遇到的另一个新兵贾维斯·博伊金斯一起选择了上学。我觉得这个机会相当难得，我在哈特赛护理中心就已接触了一些医学基础，现在可以借机继续深造，这样我就可能成为海军医院的医护人员，进而为我以后去菲律宾或韩国铺平道路。

新兵营确实让我得到很好的军事训练，但没有让我的浪漫倾向有丝毫减损。我不仅对异国他乡充满向往，而且开始憧憬用医术救死扶伤，甚至要改变并拯救世界。不过，可笑的是，我是在美国海军医学院继续深造，而学校就在伊利诺伊州的大湖区，离我威斯康星密尔沃基的家并不太远。

可笑的事情还有很多。当我几乎打道回府，北上到大湖区之后，我突然了解到美国海军医院为美国海军陆战队提供医护支持。实际上，海军陆战队是美国海军部的一部分，而我入伍时，没人告诉我这一点。我原本指望能被派往驻外的海军医疗机构，周围都是电影《陆军野战医院》里面的那种热辣女护士。我最不想去的地方就是海军陆战队。在我们进行紧急救助基础训练时，我和博伊金斯以及其在大湖区碰到的其他几个队友嘟囔着："要是想去海军陆战队，我早就去了。"我越来越担心自己会被派往驻军医院。

我担心自己扬帆远航的目标永远不会实现，甚至连迈出国门的机会都没有，倒不是我自己过于谨慎，只是我越来越觉得通过参加海军来实现个人梦想的机会日益渺茫了。

还好，我较强的学习能力在进行医学训练的时候得到充分展现。考试成绩非常理想。随着12周的训练课程接近尾声，那些令别人头痛的科目，我应对起来却不费吹灰之力。弗莱迪的酗酒无度让我对酒精无甚好感，加之我本身对酒的味道也不大感兴趣，可当大伙溜出基地喝啤酒时，我也愿意凑热闹一起去喝上几杯，而且我们就是穿着军服溜了出去。一天夜里，我们跑到一家德国啤酒馆，那天我们可真的喝多了，而且是酩酊大醉。错过了回去的车子，只能步行回基地。从正门回去要走很长一段路，我们肯定会迟到的，所以准备跳过栅栏抄近路。

第六章 外面的世界

It was pitch-black outside, moments before midnight, when we climbed the fence and looked down to see what appeared to be a solid landing spot, either the ground or a building top. Hitting down simultaneously on a heavy metal surface, we realized to our horror that we'd landed on a van. And not just any van. It was a van occupied by two brothers from the Shore Patrol. Judging from their groggy appearances, it was clear they'd both been taking a nap and we had awakened them. Now they were pissed.

"Goddamn!" said Boykin.

"Here we go," I said.

And so, the next morning, we had to go appear at Captain's Mass—where the captain would decide our fate. Boykin emerged from his hearing with the bad news that he was being shipped off to Southeast Asia. Even though the War in Vietnam was winding down, there was a great need for medics in bringing troops home. Not that I wanted to go there, but it would be overseas.

As I walked in and waited for the captain, I stood tall, hoping that he'd look at my file and the destinations that I'd requested and see it in himself to look past the previous night's misdeeds.

The captain strode in, took a seat, and looked me up and down. He thought for a second and then asked, "You play football?"

"Yes, sir, I play football."

"Fine," he said, making a note. "You're going to Camp Lejeune. They've got a good football team down there, and they need a big guy like you." He put my file away and called out, "Next!"

* * *

Bad news and good news. The bad news, as I had started to suspect before leaving Great Lakes and arriving in Camp Lejeune, was that I really wasn't going to get out of the United States. Seeing the world was going to mean exploring the backwoods of Jacksonville, North Carolina—where Jim Crow seemed like he was alive and well anytime we stepped foot outside the base. Not only that, but Camp Lejeune was the biggest Marine Corps base in the world, populated by sixty thousand marines and six hundred sailors. So now, true to my fears, I was in the Marines. The only positive glimmer on this bad news was that I was sent to the Navy Regional Medical Center, as opposed to the Fleet Marine Force—only because the captain who had sent me happened to be a close friend of the Navy hospital's football team, one of the better teams in the Navy.

当时已经接近午夜，外面一片漆黑。我们爬上栅栏，觉得下面好像是路面或是建筑物的顶端。我们纵身一跃，结果落在一个厚重的金属表面上，我们惊恐万状，这是个篷货车，而且是两个基地巡逻兵的车，从他们睡眼惺忪的样子看，一定是刚才正在睡觉，结果被我们吵醒了，一脸的懊恼。

"糟糕，"博伊金斯说道。

"我们栽了，"我应道。

第二天一早，我们就来到长官面前，等待发落。博伊金斯先出来了，带来的是坏消息，他要被派往东南亚。虽然越战已经接近尾声，但还需要大量的医护人员护送士兵回国。我其实也并不想去那里，但好歹这也算是出国了啊。

我进去了，等待上校进来，身体站得笔直，希望他能看过我的档案，真希望他看在我过去一贯表现出色的份上，能网开一面。

上校走了进来，拿了把椅子坐下，上下打量了我一番，沉思片刻，他问到："你打橄榄球吗？"

"是的，长官，我打橄榄球。"

"很好，"他在本子上记了些什么，"你就去北卡罗来纳州列尊营吧，他们那里有个很好的橄榄球队，需要你这样的大个子。"他把我的档案放到了一边，大声喊道："下一个。"

* * *

这真是喜忧参半，忧的是获悉自己要离开大湖区前往列尊营，我就怀疑自己够呛能离开美国了。到那里之后，能看看所谓大世面就是去北卡罗来纳的周围走一走，从基地出来透透气。不仅如此，列尊营号称是最大的海军陆战队基地，那里有着 6 万海军陆战队员，600 名水兵。正如我所担心的那样，我确实加入了海军陆战队。不过，好在我要去的地方是海军地方医疗中心，基本算是舰队陆战队，只是因为负责派遣我的这个上校恰好知道这家医院的橄榄球队，这支球队在海军里水平还算上乘。

The good news was that for the next couple of years I served, worked, learned, and lived in an environment that was not too different from a college setting. While the Navy took care of my basic costs of living, I played some football, received an on-the-job education to rival what most premed students at top universities receive, and had a great time too. When I arrived, a coordinator explained that the barracks were full and there was nowhere for me to bunk as of yet. Together with a group of three other guys who hadn't been assigned to barracks either, I was taken on a tour of the hospital.

When we came to a wing that hadn't been officially opened for patients, the coordinator announced, "This is it. You guys will be staying here."

In no time we turned that place into party central. It wasn't the penthouse suite at the Palmer House, but we took advantage of the space, converting the patient sun deck and TV lounge into our bachelor pad, hooking up our stereos into an impressive, multiphonic sound system. All of a sudden, everything was cool. What had seemed like a bad break turned out to be a blessing no longer in disguise.

The hospital was state-of-the-art, and the staff, both military and civilian, were some of the best and brightest in the nation. Again, when receiving my job assignment, which could have been anything from orthopedics, podiatry, or proctology to psychiatric, among others, I pulled a lucky card and was assigned to work in the General Surgical Ward with Lieutenant Commander Charlotte Gannon, an absolute jewel.

Dressed efficiently in her white uniform with her Navy cap and its emblem of three-and-a-half braids, Lieutenant Commander Gannon had come out of Massachusetts General Hospital and ran her ward with authority, excellence, and compassion. It was an ideal environment in which to learn, and I thrived under her supervision. Throwing myself into every aspect of my work, I couldn't do enough to help the patients—mainly Marines and their family members, as well as some locals who needed specialized surgery not available at other area hospitals. By this point, I had learned the power of asking questions and knew that the best doctors didn't mind being asked them.

Gannon appreciated my focus and my desire to know more and embraced my litany of questions: "What is that called?" "How do you do that?" "Why do you do that?" "Would you show me?" "Okay if I try?" She taught me so much that influenced me in making all kinds of life-and-death decisions. Thanks to my experience at Heartside and some good instruction at the Great Lakes Hospital Corps School, I was clearly superior to anyone working in my position. Very quickly I became one of her favorite people and was respected by several other doctors too, all of which came in handy whenever I got into jams or needed an advocate.

喜的是在未来的几年军队生活中，工作学习基本和在大学校园中相差无几。海军负责我基本的生活开销，我一部分时间花在打球上面，剩下就开始接受职业教育，其水准完全可以和那些顶级大学的佼佼者相媲美，而且我这段时光过得相当愉快。我到了驻地之后，协调员告知我军营已经满员，同行的还有另外三个人也无法安置，所以我们就直接开往医院。

在一个尚未对病人开放的病区，协调员宣布："你们几个就住这里。"

没多久，我们就把这里搞成一个聚会的地方。这里倒不是什么酒店的豪华套间，但我们的地方太宽敞了，把病人的阳台和电视间都统统改造成时尚单身公寓，挂上立体声音响系统，顿时这里变了个模样。刚才我们还为自己的运气不好而叹息，现在简直要欢呼雀跃了。

医院的设施条件一流，医护人员也分军人和地方两种，都是在军队系统中最棒的。给我分配工作的时候，本以为无外乎是整形外科、足科、直肠内科或是精神科这几种，可我又抽中一个"上上签"，和上尉夏洛蒂·甘农一起在普通外科病房工作，她是个地道的犹太人。

甘农医生穿着十分干练，白色制服，头戴海军帽，还有几条装饰带，她来自麻省总医院，做事风格果断威严，同时不失关爱。这里是学习的理想之地，我在她的调教下，茁壮成长。我全身心地投入到工作中来，乐于帮助患者，他们多为海军陆战队队员及其家属，也有地方医院没有条件医治的一些病人。这里，我知道了通过提问来学习知识，而且即便是最好的医生，也不会介意有人勤学好问的。

甘农医生非常欣赏我做事的专注，我积极好学，善于提问，她也非常赞许，"这种东西是什么？""这该怎么处理呢？""为什么要这样呢？""可以帮我演示一下吗？""能让我来试试吗？"她教会了我很多，甚至在很多生死攸关的时刻她都帮我拿了主意。多亏我在护理中心的从业经验，加之大湖区海军医学院的学习基础，我比同样职位其他人的表现要好得多。很快，人们都喜欢上了我，而且几名医生都对我刮目相看，所以我再有问题或什么事情，都有人乐于相助。

None of the other doctors seemed to mind my questions, mainly because they usually only had to explain something to me once and I got it. Though I didn't know it yet, many aspects of my medical work would translate to other areas, perhaps none more important than knowing how to organize my time. Plus I loved what I was doing, everything from changing patients' dressings and hooking up IVs to providing postsurgical wound care, examining tissues, and debriding wounds—often doing several procedures simultaneously. Besides being really good with these specific duties, I was mindful of how what I did played into patients' overall healing and well-being. To that end, I placed great importance on maintaining detailed chart notes that helped the surgeons and nurses follow a patient's care—what time a dressing was changed, what an injury looked like, what it smelled like, whether a wound seemed to be clearing up, improving, or the patient complained of this, the patient complained of that.

After a short period of time, all the cats—from every background—were asking for "Doc," as they called me. My reputation was such that anytime anyone got shot, they were advised before they got to the ward to make sure they asked for me, that when it came to gunshot wounds, nobody could fix them up like I could. Even if I was busy or wasn't there, whenever someone else was assigned to them, they'd say, "No, I'll just wait for Doc." The same went for anybody who wanted their dressings changed. Seemed like I'd come a long way since I tried to dress my own wound with a Kotex.

One of my toughest early assignments took me to a crash site where a van carrying a dozen or more Puerto Rican brothers, all Marines, had gotten into a terrible accident on their way up to New York City for the weekend. Aside from the blood and guts, I had to help pull twelve unconscious and/or drunken Puerto Rican Marines out of the van, with glass everywhere. One of the guys, Dominguez, had so much glass in his face that I had to use forceps to remove all the embedded shards. Otherwise, he would have been horribly scarred for life, like a human Frankenstein. That was my call, even though others in my position would have most likely just sewn him up with the glass in there. He never forgot that I fixed him up, and the two of us stayed tight for quite a while to come.

In addition to the fact that I loved what I did and loved that feeling of appreciation that I'd helped, it was inspiring to see patients who were seriously hurt overcome the conditions that had brought on their hospitalization. To see some of these real cracker hillbillies suddenly setting aside their prejudices was incredible. Several of the Marines, you knew, would for sure call you a nigger in a heartbeat, but lying prostrate in excruciating pain, unable to move, they were having personal transformations simply by saying, "No, I'll just wait for Doc. What time's he comin'?"

所有医生似乎都不介意我问问题，因为通常只要说上一遍，我就心领神会了。而且，虽然我没有意识到，但我在医护行业的学习也影响到我其他的方面，比如，最重要的莫过于我知道该怎么安排时间。此外，我自己也热爱这份工作，无论是帮助病人更换纱布、挂静脉输液吊瓶，还是术后伤口检查、检查器官、清创，很多时候，需要几项工作同时进行。在我认真做好本职工作的同时，我也会关注这会对患者的整体康复起到怎样的作用。为此，我做了详细的图表记录，帮助医生护士跟踪患者情况，几时更换的纱布，当时伤口情况如何，味道怎样，伤口是否有所好转，或是病人有怎样的反应。

没过多久，所有的病号都愿意找我，他们叫我小医生，我也在医院里出了名。受了枪伤的，都会主动来找我帮忙护理，没进病房之前，就先问清楚，是不是我来亲自处理伤口。因为这种事情，没人像我做得这么认真。若恰好赶上我忙不开，或是不在，换作别人去护理，他们就宁愿等着我回来再做处理。碰上要换纱布的，也是同样的情况。想当年，我自己却把高洁丝当作绷带闹过笑话。

我最艰巨的一次任务是去事故现场救助伤员，那次，一辆篷货车拉了十几个波多黎各弟兄，都是海军陆战队员，在去纽约城度周末的路上，车子出了严重事故。我从血泊中，把十几个不省人事的波多黎各弟兄拉了出来，到处是碎玻璃，有个叫多明格兹的，脸上都是玻璃碴子，我只好用镊子一块一块把玻璃清出来。否则，他一定会满脸疤痕，容貌全毁。而换作别人，很可能就是简单包扎了事，根本不会帮他清除嵌入皮肤的玻璃。他永远都不能忘记是我帮他处理了伤口，后来我们俩成了要好的朋友。

我除了喜欢我的职业之外，还喜欢帮助别人所带来的快感，同时因为很多病人痊愈后，心态会发生很大的改变。看到很多胸怀成见的人，突然不计前嫌，的确不可思议。有些陆战队员可能开始会叫我"老黑、黑鬼"之类，可是当他们躺在床上动弹不得，忍受着剧痛，他们就像完全变了个人似的，说："我还是等小医生来吧。他什么时候过来啊？"

第六章　外面的世界

They were waiting for a big black man like me to help them get through the crisis in which they found themselves. They seemed to be really changed, not because I changed them, but because they changed themselves by challenging their own beliefs. In turn, my own assumptions about folks who were different from me were challenged. For the first time since I had learned that the world wasn't all black, I really began to see people as people. Below the skin, I had learned, we're all pretty much the same.

Off the base, tolerance still had a long way to go. During an assignment answering the phone at the surgical clinic, I got a lot of calls similar to the one I received from a woman who barked, "My foot's broken. My foot's broken 'cause a two-hundred-fifty-pound nigger stepped on my foot."

"Okay, well, let me see if I got this right now? The foot is broken?"

"Yes!" she said.

"Now, did he break it because he was two hundred fifty pounds, or is it broken because he is a nigger?"

"Both!" she said.

Only every now and then did I meet people like that face-to-face. On a road trip out of town one weekend, my friend Pretty Willie and I—so much the opposite of pretty that he made my Uncle Doodabug look good—had to stop to fill up at a local gas station before we hit the road. Pretty Willie, who was from Aiken, South Carolina, warned that we might hit some unwelcoming spots farther away from base.

The local gas station didn't roll out the red carpet. In fact, no sooner had we pulled in than a skinny-ass old white woman came bearing down on us with a double-barreled shotgun, beady eyes blazing death as she announced, "I don't sell gas to no niggers! I sold gas to a nigger once, and he tried to burn my place down! So y'all just get out of here right now!" Nothing that overt had ever happened to me. Even Pretty Willie was as stunned as I was.

From my activism as a teenager, I knew that poverty and illiteracy made racism that much more pronounced. And there were a lot of poor folks, black and white, who lived in the vicinity of the base—even though I had little contact with them. Because I belonged to an institution now, I didn't have to suffer that poverty, something that made me want to help, even though I had no idea how.

他们需要我这样的大个子黑人帮他们渡过难关，这其中他们也在发现自己真切的改变。倒不是我刻意要改变他们，而是这让他们重新审视了自己的信仰。与此同时，我原本以为人和人之间存在着差异和区别，这一点也不再如此。我有生以来第一次觉得世界并非一片黑暗，我开始尊重每一个人。无论肤色如何，我意识到，原来大家都是一样的人。

在基地以外，有些时候还是需要忍辱负重。一次，在外科门诊，我负责接听电话，结果一连接了几个电话，都是一个女人尖声地叫嚷："我的脚折了，有个 200 多斤的黑鬼踩到我的脚上了。"

"好，来看看具体是什么情况。脚折了是吗？"

"对的，"她应道。

"那么，他踩折了你的脚，是因为他 200 多斤呢，还是因为他是个黑鬼。"

"都是，"她答道。

有时候，我还要亲自面对这样的人和事。一个周末，我和朋友帅哥威里出城，虽然叫帅哥，其实他和我那多达巴叔叔比起来，容貌不相上下。当我们正准备去当地加油站加点油，结果被路上的东西撞了一下。威里来自南卡罗莱纳州的艾肯，说我们可能撞坏了车子。

当地加油站并没有对我们热情相待。我们刚进去，就有一个瘦骨嶙峋的白人老太婆端着双筒猎枪走了出来，眼睛死死地盯着我们，"我才不给黑鬼加油呢。上次给那个黑鬼加油，他差点把我这都给点着了！给我滚！"以前从没经历过这种阵势，我和威里都吓傻了。

我在十几岁时，就对激进分子有所了解，知道贫困和无知使得种族主义愈发抬头。在基地附近，住着很多穷苦人家，有黑人，也有白人，但我和他们几乎素不往来。因为我现在的身份是军人。我本人无需经历那种贫困，但我希望对他们能有所帮助，却不知该如何行动。

第六章　外面的世界

The PURSUIT of HAPPYNESS

In the meantime, a picture was beginning to appear in my head about my future in the medical profession, beyond the Navy. Sherry Dyson was not so much in the forefront at that point, probably because our communication wasn't as hot and heavy as it had been, although we did still talk. Even so, she fit the picture of a doctor's wife, and every time I thought of the image of her holding that T-shirt up to her chest in the display window of the army-navy store, I actually couldn't envision my long-term future without her. But for the time being, since I had missed out on the chance to romance women in foreign lands, I gave myself license to sow big-time oats.

One of the highlights was a trip that I made with three of my buddies to Howard University in D.C. We had a fantasy-filled introduction to coed life at Candell Hall. On one floor young men were housed, and the next floor housed young women. Young beautiful early 1970s liberated women. When we got to this dorm and saw what was happening, we said, almost in four-part harmony, "We ain't going back to North Carolina!" We saw all those fine black girls and went AWOL. After spending all our money, we had no choice but to turn ourselves in to the Shore Patrol. We were issued orders, given fifty dollars to get back to Camp Lejeune, and promptly went AWOL again. Young and dumb, most of us nineteen years old, we couldn't stop ourselves.

With all those sisters at Howard, we thought we'd died and gone to heaven! Finally, we partied ourselves out and had to turn ourselves in to the Shore Patrol a second time. Instead of giving us money, this time they took us straight to the bus station and escorted us onto the bus. Everyone got home intact except for crazy Haze, who managed to get into a fight and go AWOL a third time. When he returned, he was put on KP, had his pay docked, and pretty much had the book thrown at him. The other two guys didn't fare as badly as Haze but definitely suffered some consequences.

Just as I was waiting for my fate to be determined, Lieutenant Commander Charlotte Gannon appeared, brushed by me with a serious look, and went to huddle with the officers in charge of discipline. She went straight to the point, explaining, "Look, that's my right-hand man. That's Gardner. Leave him alone."

That was it. Charlotte Gannon had my back and she had juice. As soon as we returned to the ward, of course, she warned me, "Gardner, look, don't do that anymore. Just do your job and I will forget about it!"

与此同时，我对于自己的未来开始有所构想，那应该是退役之后，在医学领域有所作为。雪莉·迪森和我现在也不那么热火朝天了，可能我们之间的交流沟通不再那么频繁，虽然我们还在保持联系。不过，她还是非常适合做个医生太太。每当我想起她在海军军需店试穿 T 恤衫的样子，就情不自禁地把她列入我远大的理想之中。鉴于我现在没办法远渡重洋，和异国女子言情浪漫，我就只好"因地制宜"了。

一次，我和三个霍华德大学的兄弟出去玩。在克莱姆登有了一个奇遇。那里的一楼住的都是青年男子，楼上的都是漂亮姑娘，而且都是 20 世纪 70 年代自由解放的年轻姑娘。我们来到这幢房子里，看到这里的一切，几乎异口同声地说："我们不回去了。"

我们和这些漂亮的黑美人夜夜笙歌，把身上的钱花了个精光之后，别无选择，只得找到基地巡逻兵，想办法让我们回去。他们给了我们 50 元钱作为回去的路费，结果我们转身就回到了克莱姆登。当年我们都不到 20 岁，莽莽撞撞，不懂得节制。碰上这些姑娘，我们简直欲仙欲死。最后，不得不再次去找巡逻兵，这回他们不给钱了，决定亲自送我们到车站，陪着我们上车。大家都回去了，但疯狂的海兹又第三次跑到姑娘们那里。等他回来之后，受了处分，还被冻结了账户，被罚了一大笔钱。另外两个人没这么惨，但也付出了代价。

正当我等待该被如何发落时，甘农医生出现了，她严厉地瞪了我一眼，就去和掌管纪律的军官交涉。她直入主题："这就是我的左膀右臂，克里斯·加德纳，这次就放他一马吧。"

就这么简单，甘农医生把我带出来了。我们一回到病房，她就警告我："不许这么胡闹了，好好工作，这事就算完了。"

第六章 外面的世界

From then on, I managed to keep on the straight and narrow. This was easier to do once I moved off base. After I met a sailor named Leon Webb—destined to be one of my best friends for life—we found an inexpensive trailer to rent and figured we could do our own thing and not get into trouble that way. Though I didn't have a car, I assumed that I could grab rides with Leon. It turned out to sometimes be more complicated than that, meaning I'd have to make sure I arranged rides from others when our schedules didn't coordinate. Although the Navy provided us with extra money for food and supplies, we lost the privilege of eating on base. We didn't quite understand that this was like real life—when the money ran out, we'd have nothing to eat. One memorably cold night—and it could get real cold out there in the sticks—our cupboard was completely bare except for a can of beans and an ostrich egg. Leon and I agreed that was the best ostrich egg we'd ever eaten in our lives.

Luckily, I was being fed and kept warm on some of those cold nights by a woman, ten years older than me, who lived off base not too far from where I was staying. Her cooking wasn't bad, she had a car, and she was fantastic in bed, a very kinky girl who introduced me to new things. It didn't bother me at all that there were other men in her life; to the contrary, that allowed me to play the role of a willing student without any relationship expectations.

One night in a moment of awkward timing, just as we start getting into it, I hear a knock on the door like a jackhammer—*boom, boom, boom, boom, boom!*—and a voice saying, "*Open the door, open the door!*"

She ignores it, trying to get back to where we were.

Boom, boom, boom, boom, boom! This cat's not going anywhere.

Aw, man. I stop and ask, "Who is that? He's not going away."

"Oh, that's Leon," she says.

I know my roommate's voice and that's not him. "Leon?" Whoever it is, I'm here and he isn't, he's stopping me from getting my groove on, so I say, "Open the door. I'm gonna kick this motherfucker's ass."

"No, no, that's *Leon*, and you don't want to do that. Trust me, he's a boxer and you don't want to do that."

"*Leon* who?"

"Leon Spinks!" She sees that I still don't get it and then reminds me, "Heavyweight champion of the base?"

"Oh," I say. *That* Leon.

从那以后，我谨小慎微。可一出了基地，就不是这么回事了。我碰到一个水兵，叫做里昂·韦伯，后来他成了我毕生的朋友。我们想法子租到一辆拖车，觉得这样想干什么都可以，同时还不会被抓到。我自己没有车，觉得可以蹭里昂的车，结果事情更为复杂，因为需要协调不同人的用车时间，等等。海军另外付我们费用，让我们购买食物和用品，不过我们就不能在基地进餐。当时，我们还没太明白这其中一个基本的道理，当钱花光了之后，我们就没吃的了。那天夜里十分寒冷，让我们刻骨铭心，橱柜里什么都没有了，只剩一小罐豆子和一个鸵鸟蛋。我们都觉得那是这辈子吃过的最美味的鸵鸟蛋。

不过幸运的是，这种寒冷的日子里，有时一位比我年长十岁的女子可以给我带来温暖。她住在基地外面，离我住的地方不远。厨艺不错，床上功夫十分了得，总喜欢玩点新鲜刺激的东西。我知道她生活里有别的男人，不过不妨事，我自己心甘情愿，也对这种关系不报任何期望。

不过，一天晚上出了乱子。房门敲的山响，有人在喊："开门，开门！"

她置之不理，希望继续我们的好事。

那人继续擂门，绝不善罢甘休。

我停了下来，"谁啊，他不会走的。"

"是里昂，"她说道。

我能听出来室友的声音，这人不是他。"里昂？"不管是谁，今晚我在这，别人就不能进来，不许坏我的好事。我说："开门，看我不踹他。"

"不是那个里昂，别惹事，相信我，他是个拳击手，不好对付。"

"他姓什么？"

"里昂·斯宾克！"她发现我还是不太明白，于是提醒了一句，"基地的拳击冠军，认识吗？"

"嗯，"我说道。原来就是那个里昂。

第六章 外面的世界

Leon Spinks!? Stationed at Camp Lejeune in the Marine Corps, he's already a boxing champ on the base, training for the next Olympics, and eventually will hold the title as heavyweight champion of the world.

Leon Spinks is outside drunk, cussing, wanting in because now it's his "turn." How'd I get into this predicament? How am I going to get out? No, I'm not getting into any duking match with Leon Spinks.

"I'm going to knock this door down!" he threatens, sounding like the Big Bad Wolf in the story of the Three Little Pigs. Next thing I know he's trying to huff and puff and blow down the trailer.

Because I'm a veritable walking encyclopedia of information, thanks to my long days spent in public libraries, I schematize the physics of this emergency and come up with a solution that maybe I've read somewhere or seen in a *Three Stooges* episode. So as he gets a running start to come batter the door down, my plan is that as soon as he hits the steps and puts his shoulder to the door, I'll open it and *bang,* he'll run into open space just as I fly out of there.

Just like clockwork, I time it right, opening the door as he runs in and collides with the table and then the wall, knocking himself out cold. Since he is so drunk already, it doesn't take much. Lying there on the floor, Leon Spinks has himself a good night's sleep, while my hostess shoos me out, not too pleased when I take her keys and her car but promise to leave it for her at the base.

The next time we're together, at my place this time, she convinces me to let her tie me up. Compared to all the missionary sex I've been having with other women, this is really forward. But since I've been tying her up, at her request, I agree. Using some intricate expert knots, she ties me to the bed, sprinkles baby powder all over me, and then tosses a big stuffed animal in the bed with me. "This is a little bit tight, okay?" she asks, but because we're just messing around and I'm thinking it's going to be quick, I don't complain.

There I am, spread-eagle, buck naked, covered head to toe in baby powder with a giant stuffed panda bear in the bed, and I close my eyes waiting for the seduction to continue. Nothing happens. I open my eyes and she has split. Gone. Just like that.

The only thing I can do is wait for my roommate to come home. Out in the country, who's going to hear me holler? Our landlady might, but I don't want her to see me this way. So I wait for literally hours, what feels like a day.

Finally, Leon's car pulls up. I have a fleeting panic that he's got Pretty Willie or Haze with him, or, God forbid, a woman. As still as I can be, I wait to see who comes in that door.

里昂·斯宾克！他在列尊营训练，已经是基地的拳击冠军了，准备备战奥运会，即将拿下世界重量级冠军称号。

他已经彻底喝醉了，死活要进来。这可如何是好，我怎么才能抽身出去？我绝对不是他的对手。

"看我不把门砸下来才怪！"他怒吼着，仿佛《三只小猪》里面的那只大灰狼。接下来，估计他要拿那辆拖车出气。

幸亏我有泡图书馆的习惯，博览群书，好像在《三个活宝》里面看过有关紧急状况下人的心理方面的介绍。我准备等他冲上台阶，肩膀撞到门上时，我就顺势把门打开，他冲将进来，我趁机逃脱。

一切都把握得分秒不差，我打开门，他一头撞进来，撞倒了桌子，接着撞到墙上，他终于清醒过来。不过他实在喝得太多了，没坚持多久，就趴在地上睡着了。里昂·斯宾克睡踏实了，女主人可把我赶出来了，还老大不情愿地让我把车钥匙带走，我一再保证一定会把车再还回来。

后来这次是在我这约会，她说服我要把我捆起来。比起以往的做法，这次实在是前卫得很。而且以前我曾捆过她，所以这次同意让她来捆。她用护士扣结结实实地把我捆在了床上，浑身上下洒满了婴儿粉，还在床上扔了一个大毛绒玩具。"是不是有点紧啊，宝贝？"以为没多久就会完事，我也没说什么。

然后，我就四仰八叉，赤身露体，全身上下都涂满婴儿粉，床头还放了一个巨大的熊猫玩具，等着她来爱抚我。结果，什么都没发生。我睁开眼睛，发现她已经开溜了。就这样把我扔下。

我只能等室友回来解救我。这么荒郊野外的地方，我就是喊，都没人能听得到。可能房东能听到，但我不想让她看到我这幅样子。所以我就等啊等，度日如年。

终于，里昂的车子停到屋外。我心头一紧，担心他会不会带着帅哥威里或海兹回来，甚至是带个女人回来，那就更糟了。我一动不能动，等着门开，有人进来。

第六章 外面的世界

From the bedroom, unfortunately, I can't see who it is. Seems like he's taking forever messing around with something in the living room. Now I can't take it anymore and call out, "Hey, man, look here, can you come here and give me a hand for a minute."

"All right, hold on for a minute."

Several minutes pass. "Naw, naw, man, you got to come on right now. I need you to hurry up and give me a hand."

"All right, man, hold on, I gotta go to the bathroom," he says and heads in but then starts to walk right past me. At last, he gets the full inglorious picture and begins to laugh uproariously, asking what the hell I'm doing with the bear and all the white shit all over me.

Now I'm laughing too.

After Leon mercifully untied me, the two of us commenced to laugh for three days. The joke was absolutely on me.

* * *

One of the hardest yet most powerful jobs for any medic in a hospital caring for hard-boiled Marines is definitely proctology. Certainly this job requires a unique skill-set and involves principles that could probably translate to other fields of endeavor. Who wouldn't benefit from experience working around a bunch of assholes?

And so, from the General Surgical Ward to the surgical clinic, I eventually became the base's foremost proctology expert. This meant that every Monday morning every asshole with a problem was at my front door. Whether that problem was hemorrhoids, thrombosed hemorrhoids, peri-rectal abscesses, pilonidal cysts, anything to do with the rectum, anus, and vicinity, they came by me en route to see the actual proctologist. After a while, however, the doctors just left me in charge and headed out to the golf course.

No sweat. It got to the point that I could drain an abscess and eat lunch at the same time. It didn't bother me. My expertise included any kind of dressing application or change, plus a variety of procedures to treat patients with pilonidal cysts—basically a cyst that develops in the crack of the ass and hair gets in it and it becomes infected. Very common, the cysts can just blow up and look like a third butt cheek. I lanced, drained, and packed it, making sure that the infection was out and that the gauze was packed properly to continue to draw the infection out.

Full bird colonels with chests full of ribbons came to me with a range of these problems. Rarely did I get any respect from the officers who were there to see the doctor and didn't feel they had to be gracious to the medic—even though I was the one responsible for setting them up in the upside-down dental chair used for exams.

在卧室里，我根本看不到是谁进来了。他好像在客厅要待一辈子似的，怎么都不进来。我只得喊出声来："你能过来帮我一下吗？"

"好的，稍等一会儿。"

又是好几分钟过去了，"能现在过来吗，赶紧的，来帮帮我。"

"好的，马上，我先去趟洗手间。"他边说边走进来，从我身边经过。终于，他看清了全部真相，笑得前仰后合，问我是怎么才把这些东西涂了一身，还放了个大熊猫在旁边。

这回，连我都忍不住哈哈大笑了。

当好心的里昂把我解救出来之后，我们一连笑了三天。这绝对是我闯的大娄子。

* * *

对医院护理的实习生而言，最难的一课就是肛肠科病人的护理，这一行需要特殊的技能，同时还需要其他方面的素质。每天冲着若干肛门进行工作，肯定会学到不少东西的。

从普通外科病房到外科门诊，我终于成为基地的肛肠专家。这就是说，每周一的清早，我门前就排好了一队各种肛肠患者，其中痔疮、血栓性外痔、骨盆直肠脓肿、肛门或周边的问题，应有尽有。他们来见识一下什么叫作真正的肛肠专家。没过一会儿，医生们都走了，出去打高尔夫球，剩下我一个人来控制局面。

毫不夸张地讲，我后来可以在处理脓肿的同时吃午饭，绝不会受影响。我的本事包括各种伤口包扎、换纱布，甚至处理藏毛囊肿(就是肛门附近的伤口因为毛发入内而发炎化脓)。很多情况下，囊肿就像个小酒窝，我把它切开，挤清脓液，包扎伤口，确保伤口清理干净，同时纱布包扎的方式正确，以便导出浓液。

胸前满是勋章绶带的上校都可能出现这一系列问题。这些前来就诊的军官很少能对我有几分尊敬，反而觉得这种病让他们脸上无光。不管怎样，我也要让他们曲身趴在治疗台上，仔细检查。

One colonel was in position, ass up in the air, when the doctor walked in and said, "Okay, I'm going to leave you here with Gardner, and he's going to set you up."

That was power. All of a sudden, the brass was completely vulnerable, his butt in the air, cheeks spread with tape, and I walked out, returning a moment later with the scope. The next thing I knew he was my best friend, saying, "Oh, Doc, oh, Doc, now, please, and, by the way, let me know if there's anything I can do for you?"

Sometimes, throwing in a little proctology humor, I'd claim to be out of lube.

Bad-ass Marines would turn into wimps: "Oh, Doc, oh . . ."

When the doctor wasn't in on one occasion, I prescribed suppositories for an officer, a full bird colonel. He was suspicious. "Don't worry," I told him, "I'm going to take care of you. Use these suppositories and we'll see you on Monday."

That Monday he and his wife marched into the ward, demanding to speak to my superior officer. Both looked at me with disdain, as if to say, *Who are you anyway? You're not a doctor and you're black!* Though I didn't know what I'd done wrong, I could see that he intended to write me up. Finally, he bellowed irately, "You don't know what the hell you're doing! You're dangerous! You shouldn't be here! And for all the good those pills did me, I may as well have been sticking them up my ass!"

It took all my self-control not to bust out laughing. He had taken the suppositories orally. This colonel was flying a $50 million jet, and he was taking rectal suppositories by mouth. Now his ass was still hurting and he was wondering why.

"Sir," I said calmly, "those pills that you took? You are *supposed* to be sticking those up your ass, that's the way they're going to relieve your pain and your swelling."

Sure enough, after I turned him upside down in my chair with his ass exposed, his whole attitude changed and he became a wimp just like all the rest of them. He also forgot about writing me up, and after his pain subsided, he was as grateful as the rest of my success stories.

一次，一位上校正摆着这么个姿势，医生突然进来说："就让克里斯来照顾你好了，就由他来处理。"

这意味着一种权力，突然间，他那所有的勋章都柔弱无力，臀部高高翘起，旁边都是些绷带，我起身出去，拿了个窥视镜回来。接下来，他成了我最好的朋友，"小医生，一定要帮忙啊，你觉得需要我帮你做点什么吗？"

有时，我会扔下一句肛肠科才会有的笑话："我是不是没有润滑剂了。"

长官就会满面愁容："可千万别啊。"

一次，当医生不在时，我就给一位上校开了一剂栓剂，他有些将信将疑。我安慰他："别担心，就用这药，看看周一效果怎么样？"

周一的时候，他和太太怒气冲冲地走进病房，要求见我的上司。夫妻俩对我怒目而视，仿佛在说，瞧你干的好事，你根本不是大夫，你这黑鬼。我虽然不知道自己做错了什么，但我知道他肯定要参我一本。后来，他实在压不住火，喊道："你根本不知道自己干了些什么，你这混蛋！你就不该呆在这，你给我的那些破药，那么难吃，一点都不管用。"

我强忍着不要笑出来，我给他开的痔疮栓剂，他居然都口服了，这个上校可是曾指挥过成千上万的飞机，却做出这样的事来。他现在痔疮依然如故，自己都不知道是怎么回事。

"长官，"我平静地告诉他，"那些药不是口服的，应该把它插入患处，这样就会消肿止痛了。"

当然，和别人一样，只要他曲体趴在治疗台上，他的态度就全变了，早就把要投诉我的事情忘到脑后。当伤口的疼痛减轻之后，他也是和其他患者一样，对我千恩万谢。

第六章 外面的世界

The **PURSUIT** of **HAPPYNESS**

In spite of an increasing level of self-confidence that my tour of duty at the Navy Regional Medical Center had given me, bouts of uncertainty arose from time to time, especially with the end of my term of enlistment just over six months away. Up until then, with an institutional structure providing me with four hundred dollars and change a month, free health care, and a sense of contribution, I had no worries. But suddenly, what to do beyond those six months had started to plague me with questions, conjuring up echoes of the no-daddy blues. Right or wrong, it seemed to me that if I'd had a father, he would have been able to give me concrete guidance. My uncles, my surrogate dads, had helped steer me into the service. Moms had told me that I could be successful at whatever I ultimately chose to do. What would my father, whoever this guy Thomas Turner was down in Louisiana—that name I had at some point gotten out of Momma—feel about the son he didn't know turning out to be a doctor? Wouldn't he want to claim me then?

Some of the enlisted guys I knew had decided to re-up, while others were heading home and getting set up in jobs, either engaged to be married and preparing to start families or returning to wives and kids already waiting for them. That was something I wanted one day, no question. But regardless of how worldly I thought I'd become, there was still a part of me that felt cheated about not getting to go off and see the world. Yet at this stage of my young adulthood, if I wanted to pursue a career in medicine, that would mean several years of schooling, which wouldn't exactly leave room for travel.

While stopping by the General Surgery Ward one afternoon, the answer to several of these questions arrived in the form of an offer from Dr. Robert Ellis. He was one of the doctors who had first heard good things about me from Charlotte Gannon and had then also taken me under his wing to train me. Truly brilliant, Dr. Ellis—or Buffalo Bob, as some of us sailors affectionately called him, on account of how intense he was and the fact that he was working in the Navy only under national duress—had received his training at Texas Children's Hospital in Houston with two of the world's most renowned heart and cardiovascular surgeons, Dr. Denton Cooley and Dr. Michael Debakey.

Now that Ellis was being discharged, he informed me, he was leaving for San Francisco to set up his own research lab at the University of California Medical Center and VA Hospital.

Knowing how well deserved and exciting this was, I shook his hand, congratulating him with all my heart—no pun intended.

"What about you?" he asked, aware that I had another six months to go.

I shrugged, letting him know that I was debating my options.

"Well," Dr. Ellis said, somewhat generally, "if you want to take a look at a career in medicine, I can help you with that."

在海军地区医疗中心，我对工作的自信日益增强，但还是有些不确定因素开始冒出来让我担忧，特别是再有 6 个月我就要退役了，这让我心事重重。在军队里，我现在每月都有 4 百多美元的补贴，免费医疗，同时给我一种成就感，工作生活无忧无虑。但突然间，6 个月后这一切就要改变，让我无法接受，这又让我想起没有父亲的痛苦。如果有父亲在身边，无论对错，此时此刻，他都会给我指明一个方向。我的舅舅们，告诉我应该参军。妈妈说过，不管我选择做什么，都会成功。我这个名叫托马斯·特纳的生父，远在路易斯安那，连这个名字都是从妈妈那里偶然得知的，他知道自己的亲生儿子想要成为一名医生吗？他知道有这么一个儿子吗？他愿意与我相认吗？

我认识的一些人还想继续留在部队，有些则准备回家，找份工作，或是想成家立业，要么就是回去和妻儿团聚。有朝一日，我也希望自己儿孙满堂。不管我自己有怎样世俗的想法，我一想到自己没有迈出国门，去看大千世界，就还是让我耿耿于怀。在我年纪轻轻的时候，若真想学医，就应该踏踏实实地在学校学习，而不是这么不远万里，抛家舍业地来到这里。

一天下午，我路过普通外科病房，困惑我的这些问题，终于尘埃落定了。罗伯特·艾里斯医生向我伸出了橄榄枝。他从甘农医生那里听到不少对我的褒奖之词，也曾让我到他的病房接受训练。他人相当聪明，水兵们都亲昵地叫他"水牛鲍勃"。他来服兵役实属无奈，之前，他曾在休斯敦的德州儿童医院从师于世界著名的心脏心血管外科大师，登顿·库利和迈克尔·狄贝基。

艾里斯医生准备退役了，他说准备去旧金山，在加州大学医疗中心建立个人实验室。

我知道他绝对实至名归，替他高兴万分，紧紧握着他的手，发自内心地祝贺他。

得知我还有 6 个月也将退役，他问我有什么打算。

我耸耸肩，说何去何从自己很难抉择。

艾里斯医生就像无所谓似的，提了一句，"要是你真想干医疗这一行，我倒可以帮帮你。"

第六章 外面的世界

My ears pricked up. I listened as he described the lab he was setting up and the research-assistant position he had to fill.

"You can come help me," he offered, letting me know the job was mine if I wanted it. "But it only pays seventy-five hundred dollars a year."

That was something of an improvement over my Navy pay. Not a dream salary. But a chance to be trained under one of the top doctors in the field, in San Francisco—about the farthest place I could go in the country and feel like I was visiting another part of the world.

"Think about it," he said. "Let me know."

I thought for two seconds and I let Bob Ellis know. "I'll take it," I told him. "I'll be there."

我的耳朵当时就竖了起来，听着他介绍着自己准备建立的实验室，还说需要一个助理的职位。

"你可以来帮我啊，"他说道，只要我想去，那这份工作就是我的了，"但是一年我只能付你7500美元。"

这已经比我在海军挣的多了很多，虽然不是特别理想，但是可以在业界知名的医生门下学习，而且还是在旧金山，这可是我所到过的最远的地方了，就像是来到异国他乡一样。

"好好想想吧，然后告诉我个结果，"他说道。

我考虑了两秒钟，就立刻告诉了他："我同意去，我会去的。"

Chapter 7
Pictures of a Life

You know, San Francisco must be the Paris of the Pacific," says the middle-aged, bespectacled, briefcase-carrying businessman standing next to me as I take in the sights at Union Square in the spring of 1976—a couple of years into my work with Dr. Robert Ellis at both the University of California and the Veterans' Administration Hospital.

"You know," I say, thinking back over the time since I'd been out in the Bay Area, "you are right."

Of course, at this point, not long after my twenty-second birthday, I've never been to Paris. But I am so impressed by this observation that I start describing my new home turf to others as the "Paris of the Pacific," a phrase I'll eventually make my own.

This happens to be a beautiful day. And a beautiful day in San Francisco is like a beautiful day nowhere else in the world. The blue of the sky—with not a cloud to be seen—represents the dictionary definition of "sky blue." A warm breeze is rustling the trees in the parks, and everyone, locals and tourists alike, is out on the streets, like me, with nothing better to do than to marvel at this beautiful city.

第七章
生活的影像

我正在欣赏着联合广场的春色,这时一个戴眼镜、手提公文包的中年男子凑到我旁边说:"旧金山简直就是太平洋上的巴黎。"时值 1976 年春天,在加州大学医疗中心和退伍军人管理署医院里,我已经与罗伯特·艾里斯医生共事了两年。

我的思绪一下回到自己初来旧金山湾区后的那段时光,我说:"没错,的确如此。"

当然,现在的我刚满 22 岁,虽然从未去过巴黎,但也被眼前的美景所陶醉,觉得这里真的就宛如"太平洋上的巴黎",很高兴用这种比喻来形容自己所在的城市,真是恰如其分。

今天碰巧天气不错,而且好到无以复加的地步。放眼望去,万里无云,碧空如洗,所谓"天蓝"应该就是取自这里。一阵暖风拂过,公园里树叶沙沙作响,无论是城里的居民还是观光客,每个人都像我一样,在街上怡然信步,尽享自然的恩赐。

The PURSUIT of HAPP*y*NESS

It was also thrilling to be in San Francisco at that cultural, historical time. Even though it was no longer the heyday of flower children and free love, in the 1970s the city was still Mecca for a guy like me who was once the first black hippie in America. With many of the tumultuous changes of the sixties behind us, with the achievements of the civil rights movement evident everywhere, with Nixon exposed and Vietnam over, the protest era had seemingly given way to party time. Nowhere did that seem more true than in San Francisco's freewheeling, anything-goes, experimental, tolerant atmosphere.

Part of my defense mechanism was the need I had for control that had been with me since childhood. This was also why I continued to resist the excesses of drugs and alcohol in these experimental years. Of course I tried stuff now and then, like the one time I smoked some angel dust and had to talk myself out of believing that I could fly. The moment the PCP reached my brain, I proceeded to do one hundred pull-ups on the heating pipe in my building—a supernatural feat when I stopped to think that in the Navy I could only do twenty-five pull-ups on a good day.

When I started looking out my window and trying to decide what landmark I should fly toward, something sober and wise inside me recommended: *Forget flying, how about a walk?*

From the Tenderloin, I walked and walked and walked, effortlessly, feeling that I was rising up with the angle of the hills, then coasting down them, being pulled toward one bridge and then toward another. Magically, I arrived in Chinatown, like I'd been sailing and had come ashore, coincidentally in the middle of a holiday marked by a lavish parade. Without being invited, I joined right in, dancing in the street with everyone in costumes and masks, many holding Chinese lanterns and papier-mâché creatures, many looking at me strangely, no doubt wondering, *Who is that happy man? He's not Chinese.*

By the time I started to come down, I was in a bar in North Beach, grooving to an eclectic band that comprised a snare drum and a harmonica. Man, I thought I had to be in Carnegie Hall. It was a good thing that I recognized how dangerous that high was. Music in itself can be a mind-altering experience, so to be on an even more altered level, the music was just mind-blowing. Out of control! When it came time to finally return to the Tenderloin, I trudged home not so effortlessly, sobering up fast and realizing that this wasn't a drug I needed to try again.

The reality was that for all my exploration during off hours, my major focus of experimentation was in the laboratory doing the work that Dr. Ellis had brought me out to do for him. My friend Bill who took me to the EST meeting had accused me of having bourgeois aspirations, and it was true—I was seduced by the idea of a potential career in medicine. If that was what I wanted, if I was passionate and dedicated, Bob Ellis was willing to place an incredible amount of trust in me, to teach me, and to open up an entirely new world in medical research, one that was different from the Navy world I'd worked in.

在这段时间来到旧金山，是件令人兴奋的事情。虽然那些充满爱、自由自在的花样年华已然不在，20世纪70年代，这个城市仍一度成为我这样的首批美国黑人嬉皮士的圣地。20世纪60年代的纷乱变迁已悄然逝去，民权运动的成果随处可见，尼克松继续执政，越南战争就此告结，充满抗议游行的时代让步于光鲜醉人的派对时代。没有哪个地方能像旧金山一样，生动地展现着随心所欲、自由自在的生存空间。退伍之后，我来到旧金山开始了新的生活。想想在军队里一切就是令行禁止、组织严明，而这里却崇尚个性和多元的文化，我仿佛来到异国他乡。

正是因为我从小就学会了要保护自己，我才能在那充满诱惑的年代里不断抵制滥用毒品和酒精的诱惑。当然偶尔我也会尝试一些新玩意儿，比如有一次我吸了些安琪儿粉，不自觉仿佛要飘飘欲仙。药性发作时，我甚至可以在楼里的暖气管上持续做100个引体向上，我停下来想到在海军服役期间，即使状态最好时也只能做25个，我这才意识到这是药力的神奇作用。

我向窗外望去，甚至觉得可以飞到外面任何一座建筑物上。内心残存的一点清醒神志告诫自己：还是不要飞了，还是走过去吧。

从田德隆区我优哉游哉地走啊走，感觉山丘天使指引我飞上天空，然后沿着山脉滑行，过了一座又一座桥。奇迹般地，到了唐人街，仿佛一艘航船终于可以靠岸。恰逢这里正在过节，人们身着盛装在街上欢庆。谁都没有主动邀请我，我就这样加入了游行的队伍，和那些穿着民族服装戴着面具的人在街上跳起舞来，许多人都手持中国灯笼和玩偶，他们奇怪地打量我，显然在纳闷：那个兴高采烈的家伙是谁啊？他可不是中国人哦。

兴奋劲儿过了之后，我到了北滩一家酒吧。酒吧有个电子乐队，有小鼓和口琴。我觉得自己到了卡耐基音乐厅。我终于意识到这么病态的兴奋非常危险，在我现在这种状态下，音乐可以改变思想，甚至实现极度快乐，完全丧失理智！当我最终返回田德隆区，朝着家的方向行进时，我终于不再轻飘飘的了，而是很快清醒起来，并意识到自己不能再磕药了。

事实上除了在我不大清醒的那几个小时，我主要的精力还是放在艾里斯医生交给我的实验室工作上。可我在潜意识里总是禁不住要想自己从事医疗事业的前景。如果那就是我的梦想所在，如果我就这样满怀激情，对此倾注心血，艾里斯肯定会对我备加信任，把技艺传授给我，并为我开启一片全新的医疗研究领域，这与我以前在军队服役时的情况完全不同。

The PURSUIT of HAPPYNESS

The project was being conducted in conjunction with the Veterans' Administration Hospital—located at the farthest beachhead of San Francisco at Fort Mylie, out by the Golden Gate Bridge—and the University of California San Francisco Hospital, near Golden Gate Park and Keysar Stadium. At the VA, where I spent most of my hours, the research aim was to create a laboratory—basically from an old operating room—that duplicated the environment in which the heart functions during open-heart surgery. Specifically, we were trying to determine what concentration of potassium best preserved the high-energy phosphates in the heart muscles. We would do a set of experiments with a high-potassium solution, a set with a low-potassium solution, and a set with a minimal-potassium solution, taking samples of heart tissue over time and using those results for our findings. Ultimately, it was the high-potassium solution that we found to be most conducive to preserving the high-energy phosphates—information that would transform how heart transplantation and surgery were done, as well as influence cardiovascular science. For an information sponge like me, this work put me right in my element.

"Gardner," said Dr. Ellis on one of my first days of work, "I want you to meet Rip Jackson."

I turned to take in the startling appearance of Rayburn "Rip" Jackson, imported to San Francisco by Ellis from back in Jacksonville, North Carolina. Just as Dr. Ellis looked the part of a young brilliant surgeon—average height and build, glasses, balding, with a nose like an eagle's beak, meticulously sniffing out details, passionate, and sometimes high-strung—Rip Jackson had the mega-wattage intensity of the medical scientist-technician genius that he was. Slim, short, and clean-shaven, with shocking white hair and small, piercing blue eyes, Rip extended his hand to shake mine and greeted me in an accent that was purebred country boy, straight out of the North Carolina backwoods. "Nice to meet ya'," he said, with barely a smile. "Heard a lot about ya', Gardner."

My instincts told me that Rip could have been a Ku Klux Klansman in his younger days. Something about him reminded me of that old woman at the gas station who threatened us with a shotgun. He wasn't so extreme, but as time went on certain comments he let slip confirmed that he was a bigot all right. Having worked for many Jewish doctors, he apparently was careful not to make anti-Semitic remarks. But perhaps because he'd had little exposure to black doctors, Rip didn't censor himself, for example, when it came to expressing how he felt about seeing an interracial couple at the hospital. He shook his head in disgust, commenting to me, "I think I'd rather see two men together than a black man and a white woman."

退伍军人管理署医院与加州大学部旧金山医院的合作项目正在实施中。退伍军人管理署医院位于旧金山最远的滩头梅里堡，就在金门大桥旁，加州大学部旧金山医院离金门公园和恺撒体育馆不远。我在退伍军人管理署医院里花了大量时间，研究目的是为建立实验室，实验室基本是在一个旧手术室基础上改造而成，模拟开胸腔手术时心脏活动的环境。具体说，就是要确定保存心肌中高能磷酸盐的最佳钾浓度。分别用高钾、低钾以及微量钾溶液进行实验，然后分别提取心脏组织的样本，并根据结果得出结论。最后，我们发现高钾溶液对维持高能磷酸盐最为有效，这一结果会对心脏移植手术产生影响，同时也对心血管系统科学的发展产生积极作用。我一直喜欢接受新事物，因此很适合这份工作。

我刚开始工作没几天，艾里斯医生来找我，说道："加德纳，来认识一下利普·杰克逊。"

我转过身来，却被利普的外表吓了一跳。利普是艾里斯从北卡罗来纳州杰克逊镇的穷乡僻壤带到旧金山来的，因为认准他是个可造之材。利普中等身材、戴着眼镜、秃头、鹰钩鼻，一丝不苟，满怀热情且有时容易激动。他极具医学天赋，小巧精干、没有胡须、一双蓝眼睛，不大但眼神非常清澈。利普和我握手，并用北卡罗来纳边远地区的纯乡下口音向我问候："很高兴认识你。"接着，他几近严肃地说："久仰大名。"

直觉告诉我利普年轻时可能是三K党的一员。他让我想起了那个在加油站曾拿着枪威胁我们的老妇人。不过他没那么极端，随着时间的推移，他的某些言论使我确认他有些固执。他曾为许多犹太医生工作过，所以说话时比较小心，不会随便说什么反种族主义的言词。但也许是他很少接触黑人医生的缘故，所以说话比较随意，比如，在医院里看到跨种族的夫妻时，他会不满地摇着头，表示："我宁愿看到两个男人在一起，也不愿看到黑人男子和白人女子在一起。"

Interestingly enough, it may have been a function of how well we got along that he made comments like that in my presence. In any event, from the beginning he saw not only that I wanted to learn from him but that I was quick to get IT, and he treated me with the utmost respect. The way we progressed was that he came out initially for a month, trained me to oversee everything that Dr. Ellis needed done for the next six months, and then came back at various intervals as needed.

His personal racist hang-ups aside, Rip Jackson was so great at the mechanics of building a laboratory and teaching me how to run it that he earned the utmost respect from me. Even though he wasn't a licensed medical doctor, his technical expertise equaled that of a top surgeon, and he trained me in this highly specialized area to do everything to support Dr. Ellis. Our responsibilities ranged from excision of hearts to catheterizing blood vessels and suturing, from ordering equipment and supplies to administering anesthesia, performing biopsies on heart tissues of patients, and analyzing the results.

Adding to the extraordinary education I was getting from Bob Ellis and Rip Jackson was a third exceptional rocket scientist in the medical laboratory—a guy by the name of Gary Campagna. Gary didn't have a medical degree either, but did for a vascular surgeon named Dr. Jerry Goldstein what Rip did for Dr. Ellis. A San Francisco native, Gary was witty and hip, an Italian American gentleman, and he took me under his wing, teaching me about technique and the importance of finesse. I now saw that it wasn't enough to know what you were doing; you had to have the hands, you had to have the right touch.

Gary had memorable sayings to emphasize certain techniques. In grafting veins, for example, precision was mandatory in first being able to control the blood flow—to shut it off, basically, like a spigot—in order to excise the portion where the graft needed to go, then to suture it all the way around without any blockages. In the clinical setting, I learned how to do that, to determine the kind of slice required for excising a portion of the artery, what type of sutures to use, what type of ties to make, what kind of graft ultimately would be needed depending on the condition of the vein. Gary warned me off making the common mistake of trying to handle the vein too abruptly, cautioning, "Stroke it, don't poke it."

These three—Gary, Rip, and Bob Ellis—were providing me with the equivalent of a medical school education, at least in this specialty. As the game plan now unfolded in my mind, I imagined that once our work was completed and I took the time to knock off a college education, I would be a prime candidate for any top Ivy League medical school in the nation. The prospect was thrilling. Could I really do that? Could I reach that far? My mother's words echoed—*If you want to, you can.*

有趣至极的是，我们却相处得很好，甚至他会当着我的面做出那样的评论。无论做什么，他从一开始就清楚我想向他取经，而且知道我悟性很好，对我也很尊重。为了相互促进，他起初会让我仔细观察，基本把艾里斯医生随后半年需要做的事情做到心里有数，然后在需要时会抽空来帮我。

暂且不去管他的种族主义倾向，利普在建立实验室方面还是相当擅长的，他还教我怎么运营实验室，从而使我对他倍加尊重。即便他并没有行医执照，但他的专业技术完全可以和高级外科医生相提并论，而且在这个高度专业化的领域里他还手把手地教我，全力支持艾里斯医生。我们的职责是从心脏切除到在血管中插入导管并缝合，再到订购医疗器械补给和进行麻醉，以及在病人的心脏细胞上进行活体组织切片检查并分析结果，所有这些都有涉猎。

除了从艾里斯医生和利普那里学习专业知识外，医疗实验室还有位高手——盖里·坎帕尼亚。盖里也没有医学学位，但曾为一个名叫杰里·高德斯特因的心血管外科医生工作，这就像利普和艾里斯医生之间的关系一样。盖里是旧金山当地人，机智诙谐，是个意大利裔美国人，他对我格外青睐，教我重要的技术和手法。我这才知道仅仅能明白自己在干什么并不够，还要具备正确的手法和手感才行。

为强调技术要点，盖里就总结出一些小窍门。比如嫁接静脉时，首先必须能够精确控制血流，就是要先切断血液供给，基本上就像关闭水龙头一样，然后切除嫁接需要接入的部分，然后严丝合缝地将边缘全部缝合。在临床实验中，我学习如何操作并确定切除部分动脉所需的切片种类，以及根据血脉状况确定最终所需的嫁接类型。盖里告诫我，不要操之过急，"要慢慢捋，不要使劲戳。"

盖里、利普和艾里斯医生三个人相当于对我进行了医学院的专科教育，至少就我们这块专业领域而言是这样的。随着对业务的逐渐了解，我设想着一旦工作完成我也就等于完成了大学教育，那时我就能去申请全国任何一家常春藤高级医科学院，前景令人兴奋。可这真是我的愿望吗？我可以走那么远吗？我又想起妈妈的话，*如果有梦想，你就能成功。*

The excitement didn't come just from the potential status and money that a career as a surgeon promised. To me, it was the challenge, the quest for information, the opportunity to apply my focus in a venue that required me to learn what amounted to a foreign language. It was starting to dawn on me that there was a language specific to all things and that the ability to learn another language in one arena—whether it was music, medicine, or finance—could be utilized to accelerate learning in other arenas too. Scientific language was fun to master—not only the medical words and meanings but also the prose, with its rhythm of urgency and its precise way of describing phenomena and processes. That understanding of process—how to get from here to there—was the real bait for me, what hooked me and made me want to learn more. Because I was so motivated and naturally curious, the learning felt easy.

Once I had learned the language, doors at the VA and the UCSF Hospital literally opened as Dr. Ellis brought me in to sit and talk with the top tier of his medical colleagues. In those settings few had any notion that I hadn't been to medical school and wasn't a doctor, let alone that I had never been to college and had barely finished high school. Sure, there were moments when I felt my lack of education, but I discovered that rather than pretending to know something I didn't, there was a way to ask, "Now, I'm not following you here, can you explain?" that most doctors were more than happy to answer.

In time, Bob Ellis developed so much faith in my mastery of our research that I went on to coauthor several papers with him on the preservation of myocardial high-energy phosphates—papers that were published in various medical journals and textbooks. Even some Harvard Medical School grads can't claim to being as widely published.

"Where did you go to med school?" was a question that inevitably came up, especially from the interns working under Dr. Ellis and Dr. Goldstein. It confounded Ellis that so many of the interns who were starting their residencies in surgery had so little practical awareness. They didn't have the hands, didn't have the eyes, didn't know the controls or the procedures. Some didn't know how to handle instruments. Instead of wasting his time on these basics, he started sending them upstairs for me to train. Suddenly, all those questions that I had been asking—"What are you doing?" "How do you do that?" "Why are you doing that?" "Can I try that?"— became questions that I was answering.

The interns were all bright and knew anatomy and physiology, biology and chemistry. But only a few had the hands. I frequently caught myself sounding just as intense as Dr. Ellis, Rip, and Gary combined. During tests that involved open-heart surgery on dogs, it was maddening to witness rough handling, as often was the case, of the canine patient's arteries and fragile organs. In my lab, as Dr. Ellis called it, I was free to say, "No, don't pull. You apply pressure gradually."

令我感到兴奋的不仅仅是可以拿到外科医生所意味的社会地位和不菲的经济收入。就我而言，那是挑战，是对知识的探索，是全心投身到某个领域的机会，这个领域仿佛有它自己专门的语言。我必须掌握。我逐渐明白所有事物都有其自己的语言，无论是音乐、医学或者金融，只要掌握了其中的精妙，其实在其他领域也能触类旁通。掌握不同学科的语言是充满乐趣的过程，在医学上就是如此，其行文的流畅、节奏的紧凑以及描述现象和过程的精准，都让我着迷。对我而言，如何触类旁通，这种过程才是真正的诱惑，让我心甘情愿想去了解更多。因为我强烈的求知欲，且天性好奇，所以学习起来备感轻松惬意。

毫不夸张地说，一旦我学会这门医学的专业语言，退伍军人管理署医院与加州大学旧金山医院的大门就会自然而然向我敞开。此时，艾里斯医生已经带我出席顶级的医学座谈会了。在那些场合里，我几乎忘记自己并没有上过医学院校而且也不是医生，何况自己其实从没有上过大学，甚至高中也仅仅是肄业而已。当然，也有感到知识匮乏的时候，但是与其不懂装懂，还不如直接发问，"这里我不明白，您能解释一下吗？"大部分医生都会欣然作答。

艾里斯医生很相信我对实验的掌握情况，和我合作了几篇关于维存高能心肌运动磷酸盐的文章——发表在各种医学期刊和教科书中，有些哈佛医学院的毕业生都没有发表过这么多的文章。

"你在哪儿上的医学校？"人们不免要问了，尤其艾里斯医生和盖里医生的实习医师都想知道这个问题的答案，这更让人难堪。不过让艾里斯感到懊恼的是很多实习医师在开始从事外科手术时，一点动手能力都没有。而且还没有基本的意识，什么都不懂，具体流程和操控都要从头学起，甚至有人连怎么操作设备都不知道。他把这些人送到楼上让我培训，不愿在这些基础问题上浪费自己的时间。结果，所有那些我曾问过的问题，"您在做什么？""该是怎么操作的？""为什么那样做？""我可以试试吗？"这些变成我每天需要面对和解答的问题。

这些实习医师都很聪明，他们都学过解剖生理学和生物化学，但只有少数人能够上手。我经常不由得言词很激烈，就像是艾里斯医生、利普和盖里三人合一。在给狗进行开胸腔手术的实验过程中，看到实习医师处理病犬的动脉和脆弱器官时毛手毛脚，我就几乎抓狂。正如艾里斯医生所言，这是我的实验室，我时不时要告诫他："不要拉，应该逐步加力。"

第七章 生活的影像

When an intern gave me that look that said, *Who are you to tell me what to do?* I was even more adamant, raising my voice and saying again, "No, you don't do it that way. You're not up under the hood of your car."

There may have been some bigotry involved, given the fact that the interns at the time were all white males from Ivy League medical schools and I was some black dude without a medical degree saying, "No! I don't want that. Give me the scissors!" But what really seemed to get on their last nerve was that they had to do what I said. Dr. Ellis made it clear to every intern he brought upstairs to me: "This is Gardner's world. Whatever he says goes. He's in charge."

My feeling was that if someone wanted to learn or was willing to try, I'd bend over backward to help. But some of the interns were so arrogant, they dismissed my input out of hand, as indicated less by what they said and more by their body language, which showed they didn't want to listen to me. In those situations, all I had to do was to tell Dr. Ellis, "You know what? This guy Steve—I can't help him." That was it. After that I'd never see the intern again. On occasion I was even more specific: "That guy Richard—he doesn't want to listen. You know what, don't waste my time, don't send him back to my lab." Dr. Ellis only nodded in agreement, respecting my opinion and appreciating that I was as passionate as he was.

Dr. Goldstein's interns in vascular surgery were some of my tougher challenges, giving me big-time attitude when I called their lack of finesse into question, reminding them of Gary Campagna's "stroke it, don't poke it."

"What exactly are your qualifications?" some of these interns were indignant enough to ask out loud.

My matter-of-fact response was: "I don't have a degree, but this is my room. You've been invited here. You're a visitor, and I'm doing my work. If I can help you, I will, but you have to listen."

In certain instances, I could see by the expressions of resentment on some of their faces that they had never had any black person in authority telling them what to do—they had never encountered a black person in control. Some were able to get past that hurdle; some weren't. For my part, I had to learn not to take some of their superior attitudes personally, in the same way that I couldn't take it personally when my mentors put me in that position of control. The powerful truth that emerged for me was something Moms had tried to tell me when I was younger—no one else can take away your legitimacy or give you your legitimacy if you don't claim it for yourself.

Before leaving for the Navy, I had apologized to her that I hadn't gone on to college, thinking how proud that would have made her. Momma surprised me by saying, "Boy, it's better to have a degree from God than from anywhere in this university system. If you got your degree from God, you don't need all this other stuff."

当有实习医师脸上露出不屑的表情，分明是在说，"你以为你是谁啊，在这里发号施令，"我的态度就会更加强硬，提高嗓门说道："不能这样，这不是在修汽车。"

也许他们会有些固执，毕竟当时那批实习生都是来自于常春藤医学校的白人，而我却是个没有文凭的老黑，还指指点点地说："你拿错了，我要的是剪刀！"之类的话。但真正令他们无法忍受的似乎是他们别无选择，只得照办。艾里斯医生把实习医师带到楼上见我，并对他们每一个人都讲清楚："这是加德纳的地盘。无论他说什么都要照办，这里由他全权负责。"

我想如果有人愿意学习、愿意动手，我会尽最大努力帮他。但一些实习生却非常傲慢，他们并不在意我在教他们知识。尽管他们嘴上没说，可从肢体语言中可以明显看出他们并不服管教。这样，我只能告诉艾里斯医生："这个叫斯蒂夫的家伙，我实在帮不了他。"就这样，以后我就再没见过这个实习医师。有时我会说得更具体："那个理查德根本不听话，不要浪费我的时间，别再把他送到实验室来了。"艾里斯医生只是点头应允，尊重我的意见，并赏识我身上那种和他一样的热情。

对我来说，盖里医生的血管外科实习生更难对付，当我说他们手法有问题的时候，也用了盖里医生的话，"注意要慢慢捋，不要使劲戳。"

"你到底有什么资格这么说？"实习生中有人大声反驳。

我实事求是地回应道："我没有文凭，但这是我的地盘，你是受邀到此的，你是客人，而我在干我的工作。如果我能帮到你，我会尽力而为，但你得听话才行。"

一时间，我可以通过他们脸上不满的表情看出，从来没有哪个黑人上司是这么和他们说话的，不过他们也从未碰到过上司是黑人的情况。有些人能过这个坎儿，有些人却不能。对我而言，我必须学会不把他们不可一世的态度当真，就像我的导师对我颐指气使的时候，我也不会当真一样。我想起一句妈妈说过的真理，她在我儿时就这么教育我，权利只能自己去争取，因为权利这东西别人夺不走，但也给不了你。

在离家去海军服役之前，我对自己没能上大学向妈妈表示歉意，心里想，如果我能上大学，她一定会非常骄傲。妈妈说的话却令我十分惊讶，"好孩子，从上帝那里拿到学位比在大学里获得的学位要强得多。如果你能从上帝那里毕业，那么你什么文凭都不需要。"

第七章 生活的影像

In my mother's language that didn't mean that an intricate knowledge of the Bible or religion was required. Rather, she was talking about self-knowledge, about an authentic belief system, an inner sense of oneself that can never be rocked. Others may question your credentials, your papers, your degrees. Others may look for all kinds of ways to diminish your worth. But what is inside you no one can take from you or tarnish. This is your worth, who you really are, your degree that can go with you wherever you go, that you bring with you the moment you come into a room, that can't be manipulated or shaken. Without that sense of self, no amount of paper, no pedigree, and no credentials can make you legit. No matter what, you have to feel legit inside first.

Momma's point of view certainly resonated during this period, not only when I was being questioned but when I questioned myself. There were times during meetings of more than one hundred doctors—some of the brightest minds in medicine—when I'd look around and notice that I was the only black man in the room. But if it wasn't an issue for me, it didn't have to be an issue for others. My blackness was a fact of who I was, yet the more comfortable and secure I became in my expertise, the less my color defined or distinguished me, and the more comfortable I became holding my own with white people further up the ladder than me or lower down. What distinguished me was my knowledge, my command of the information that was the focus of the research Robert Ellis was pursuing. This awareness gave me incredible confidence that I could succeed in this field of endeavor, and succeeding meant the world to me. That was why I was prepared to hang in for the long haul, even if it took me another fifteen years to attain the degrees necessary for me to practice medicine. Whatever it took, I was worth it, as was the effort to study and learn, day in and day out, repeating tests sometimes over and over again, like a blacksmith hitting an anvil every day.

There were only two clouds on the horizon—money and sex. Even though Dr. Ellis kept increasing my salary, up to around $13,000 a year by early '76, there was very little more he could squeeze out of his overall budget for the project. Even for someone who was willing to slum it, San Francisco was a costly place to live. Believe me, living in the Tenderloin—in the same neighborhood as the Y but in an apartment of my own at 381 Turk Street—I was definitely slumming it. My salary was stretched even without car payments or insurance. Since I couldn't afford a car, I hadn't even gone out to get my license yet, although I did know how to drive and sometimes ran errands for work in the hospital van. The necessity of getting a second job loomed. Then again, that would use up whatever free time I had for enjoying something of a social life.

母亲并不是让我去学习圣经或复杂的宗教知识，而是说，要具有自己真正的信仰，要孜孜以求，不轻易放弃的精神。一些人或许会对你的文凭、资质、学历提出质疑；还有些人可能会使出浑身解数毁誉你的价值。但你内在固有的东西是没人能夺去，无人能玷污的。这是你的价值所在，真正的自己，这个学位与你形影不离，你可以去任何地方，它都会不离你左右。如果没有这种对信仰的执著，那么文凭、出身和证书都不会使你感到自我价值的存在。无论做什么，首先必须意识到自己的内在价值。

这个时期，妈妈的观点在我内心产生了共鸣，无论是在我受到质疑还是我扪心自问时都是如此。在上百名医生参加的会议里，有些是医学界中的佼佼者，可环顾四周后，我才发现自己是这里唯一的黑人。但如果我自己不在乎的话，那么对其他人来说也没什么大不了的。肤色是我身份的一个不争事实，然而我的专业技术也日臻完善，我的肤色就不会给自己任何束缚，确立自己的价值和身份，与白人平起平坐，就越发令我无所畏惧。是我的专业知识，我对技术的掌握能力，让我鹤立鸡群，那也正是艾里斯医生所看中的。这让我对自己有了难以名状的自信，相信自己能通过努力取得成功，成功对我而言就意味着一切。这就是我坚持不懈的原因，即使再需要 15 年时间去拿个专业文凭，甚至无论付出怎样的代价，我都在所不惜。我不断地研究，孜孜以求，日以继夜，反复试验，乐此不疲。

不过也有两方面的问题没有解决，那就是金钱和性。即使艾里斯医生不断给我加薪，在 1976 年初，我的年薪才不过 1.3 万美金，这也是他能从整个项目预算中所能挤出来的极限了。因为在旧金山生活消费很高，为节省开支，人们甚至愿意住在贫民区。我住在田德隆区就是这个原因，就在特克街 381 号的公寓，显然这里快被我弄得乱七八糟了。即使不用支付车费或者保险费，我每个月的钱也并不宽裕。因为我买不起车，所以连驾照也没拿，而实际上我会开车，而且有时会开着医院的货车，去做些跑腿的工作。但看来还是有必要再找份工作，但这会占用我享受社交生活的一切闲暇时间。

第七章　生活的影像

The constant money crunch I could handle. But the sudden halt to my heretofore successful pursuit of the opposite sex was a shock to my system. What was going on? In a city like San Francisco, full of beautiful single women, I couldn't for the life of me figure out why nothing was clicking. Not that I wanted to fall in love, but what I really wanted, to get laid, wasn't looking good. There was a doctor I'd started seeing, one of the few African American women I'd met at the hospital. She was attractive in a smart, ambitious way, but she was uptight about sex. The chemistry never happened.

Then there was a pretty sister that everybody at the hospital was into. Sweet and curvaceous, with long wooly hair and a rich caramel complexion, she finally accepted my invitation to go to the movies, and we started hanging out. Seemed like it took forever to get an invitation back to her place, but when it happened at last, in a cruel twist of fate I was so tired from work that day I actually lay down on the bed to get comfortable with her and promptly fell asleep.

The next thing I knew this lovely woman scorned was shaking me by the shoulder and pointing to the door. Glumly, I scuffed on out of there, apologizing all the way. As I stepped outside a gust of wet wind smacked me in disdain. "Sure is cold out here," I said, hoping she'd change her mind.

"That's too bad," she replied, "because it's hot in here." Then she slammed the door in my face.

That was the sad state of my extracurricular life on that memorably beautiful spring day when I was out on my own at Union Square and the middle-aged guy with the briefcase struck up a conversation with me about San Francisco being the Paris of the Pacific.

As it's getting toward late afternoon, there is nothing out of the ordinary when he says, "Hey, I'm going around the corner to have a drink. Care to join me?"

Even though I don't drink much, I figure—*Why not?* I'm still getting to know the city and not sure where the women are hanging, so I tag along enthusiastically. The bar, a joint called Sutter's Mill, turns out not to be where the women are hanging. In fact, as we step inside the pitch-black interior of the place and I try to focus my eyes in the darkness, I don't see any women. What I do see are nothing but men, and two of them are in a corner kissing. Of course, I realize that this is a gay bar.

"You know what," I say to the guy, as if I just looked at my watch for the first time, "I got an early shift tomorrow, and, uh, great to meet you, but I gotta go."

Before he can say a word, I'm gone.

手头紧的问题我还可以勉强应对，但我的桃花运却戛然而止了，这对我确实是个打击。这究竟是怎么回事？旧金山到处都是漂亮的单身女子，可我就想不通生命中一直都没有出现真命天女。其实我并非想谈恋爱，而只是想找个人上床，可情况并不乐观。在医院里我见到几个非裔女医生，也注意上其中一个姑娘。她的聪慧进取很对我的胃口，但在个人问题上却很保守，我们之间从未发生过什么。

还有个美女，相貌可人，身材窈窕，长发披肩，肌肤浅咖，医院里的每个人都愿意和她打交道。最后她接受了我的邀请，同意一起去看电影，我们便开始拍拖逍遥了。可她一直都没让我去她家，但最终当我如愿以偿时，命运却和我开了个天大的玩笑。那天我实在工作太累，当我们一躺在床上时，我睡着了。

接下来，我记得这个美女不屑地把我摇醒，用手指着门口让我出去。我一边郁闷地拖着双腿往外走，一边赔礼道歉乞求原谅。一开门，外面一阵冷风袭来，"好冷啊，"我可怜巴巴地说着，希望她能改变主意。

"哦，是吗？"她回应道，"屋里太暖和了。"然后当面给我吃了一个闭门羹。

在这个难忘又美好的春天里，我独自一人消磨闲暇时光，在联合广场上备觉感伤，一个手拿公文包的中年人走过来，和我说"旧金山就是太平洋上的巴黎"。

已经接近傍晚，我也一直无所事事，这时他说："我要到街角那边去喝点东西，一起来吗？"

虽然我很少喝酒，但转念一想，为什么不呢？我并不完全了解这个城市，也不知道那些姑娘都躲在哪里休闲娱乐，于是我满心欢喜，紧随其后。当我们来到"萨特的磨坊"酒吧时，我却发现这里根本没有什么姑娘。屋子里的装饰都是暗色调的，我适应了一会，才看清屋里的一切，却没发现一个女人，看到的只有男人，还有两个男人在墙角接吻。我这才意识到这是"同志"酒吧。

我和那个人说，好像刚刚知道时间的样子："我明天很早就要换班，所以，很高兴遇见你，可是我得走了。"没等他张口我便转身离开了。

第七章　生活的影像

This isn't the first time I've been hit on by gay men in San Francisco. Usually, I have no problem explaining that I don't work that side of the street. Actually, compared to the attitudes in the Navy, I think of myself as extremely tolerant. Yet with my bad case of the no-woman blues, I'm not even in the mood to be polite.

Unable to establish a relationship here in San Francisco, I find myself picking up the phone more than usual to call my long-distance girlfriend, Sherry Dyson, who I have never quite gotten over since that first time I saw her with the T-shirt in the window of the army-navy surplus store. In this time period, she has returned to Virginia with her master's degree and is working as an educational expert in mathematics. Besides our regular phone contact, she has been out to visit a couple of times, although neither of us has made any moves to indicate that we should be getting more serious.

So we're talking one night and it hits me that there's no one who gets me like Sherry, no one who can just say, "Chris, you're full of shit," when I'm being too full of myself, and no one else that I've ever pictured with me in the life that I'm working toward. In a romantic rush, out of the blue, almost just to hear myself say the words, I change whatever subject we're on and ask, "All right, so when we gonna get married?"

Without skipping a beat, Sherry says, "Well, how about June 18?"

So much for sexual exploration and experimentation. Not sure what I had just gone and done, I said good-bye to the no-woman blues and prepared myself to enter into the institution of marriage.

* * *

For the next three years I lived what could have been called in some respects a storybook life. The wedding, held as planned on June 18, 1977, was picture-postcard perfect: beautiful, tasteful, and simply done in a park near Sherry's parents' home—a place that had become synonymous in my mind with stability and security.

Moms was there, glowing with pride. She and Sherry bonded immediately. My Navy buddy Leon Webb, soon to head out to San Francisco, flew in to be my best man, and he couldn't have been happier for me. We were all impressed with the Dysons' home. Nothing over the top, the house looked like something out of a magazine—exquisitely decorated with southern charm, rare artwork on the walls, chandeliers throughout the two-story space, gourmet food in abundance, and a bar stocked with wine and liquor imported from around the world.

这不是我第一次在旧金山碰上同性恋了。通常，我会称自己对这不感兴趣。实际上，跟在海军服役时的态度比起来，我觉得自己已经相当克制容忍了。然而，生活中没有女人，让我心情郁闷，无心过多注意礼貌细节。

看来在旧金山找到自己的另一半是不太可能了，我总是不自觉地给远方的雪莉打电话，自从透过军需店的窗子第一眼看到她穿 T 恤衫的样子以后，我就再也不能忘记她。现在，她已经硕士毕业，回到弗吉尼亚州，成为数学教育专家。除了经常电话联系外，她也来看过我几次，可我们俩都没有做出要继续深入的举动。

因此，一天晚上，我们在电话里聊着天，突然我意识到只有雪莉最理解自己，只有她在我狂妄自大时会说："克里斯，你其实什么都不是。"也只有她是我曾经想象中的生命伴侣。突然我不再苦闷，变得浪漫多情起来，话题一转，问道："说吧，我们什么时候结婚呢？"

雪莉毫不犹豫地说："好啊，6 月 22 号怎么样？"

对性的尝试和探索就此告终。我也不知道自己都说了什么或是做了什么，只知道已经告别了自己没有女人陪伴的痛苦，并即将准备走进婚姻世界。

* * *

接下来的三年时光就像故事书中那般完美。1976 年 6 月 22 日，我们的婚礼如期举行，格调高雅，美丽别致，地点就选在雪莉父母家附近的一个公园，那里已成为我心目中幸福平安的代名词。

妈妈来到我们的婚礼现场，露出骄傲的笑容。她和雪莉一见如故。我的海军战友里昂·韦伯，很快就从旧金山飞来为我当伴郎，他为我由衷地高兴。我们都被雪莉布置的房间深深吸引。房顶的线条非常简洁，就像杂志里的照片那样，装饰精致，带有南方气息，墙壁上挂着精美的艺术品，枝形吊灯从二楼房顶悬垂下来，屋里有丰盛的美食，吧台里存放着世界各地的葡萄酒和白酒。

The Dysons' way of life represented the ideal of home that had been in my dreams from the time I'd seen *The Wizard of Oz* as a kid. For a while, I'd even dreamed of moving to Kansas when I grew up because of that portrayal of safety and serenity. In Oz there were witches and maniacal flying monkeys and the same sense of imminent insanity that was in our household. Back in Kansas, folks were normal and kind, and there was no threat of not knowing what could happen next, how far it was to the pay phone, would the police come in time, would your mother and siblings be killed when you got back.

Part of the attraction, unquestionably, was my longing to belong to the world that Sherry came from—a world in which she had grown up adored as an only child, with the same mother and father together, the same house, with a sense of being anchored and with none of the chaos and violence that had afflicted my childhood. Her parents didn't seem to mind that I came from a different world and were as gracious as they could be in welcoming me to their family. Certainly, like Sherry, they saw that I had potential and was on a solid path to becoming a physician, even though I had a ways to go.

Still, I had begun to have misgivings about this marriage from the moment I spontaneously popped the question, much of which I passed off as typical prewedding jitters.

The first person I had told in San Francisco was Dr. Ellis. If I was looking for someone to beg me to reconsider, Robert Ellis wasn't that person. Genuinely pleased for me, he went on to loan me the hundred bucks I needed for a suit to get married in, and then he shocked me even more by suggesting, "Take an extra day off." For a guy who was as obsessed with work as Buffalo Bob, that was unheard of.

My next stop was the jewelry district on Market Street, where I miraculously found a diamond ring for nine hundred dollars that I bought on credit. It looked old-fashioned, with clusters of little diamonds in a flower shape and a band that turned out to be white gold. En route to Virginia on the airplane, I was so nervous carrying a diamond ring in my pocket that I had to check on it every five minutes to make sure it hadn't been mysteriously stolen during that time. It was the nicest thing I'd ever bought for anyone, and I was sure Sherry was going to like it.

My misgivings vanished the moment the two of us embraced upon my arrival. We had a deep connection, a comfort and fondness for each other that was really all that mattered. Watching Sherry take charge of the wedding made me admire her even more. She had planned everything, her Pops had written the check, and all I had to do was show up. I loved how she carried herself, her confidence, intelligence, and humor, her vivacious manner that attracted people to her in general. She was gorgeous in a wholesome, distinctive way, and her legs were great. I loved her strong personality and the fact that she had definite opinions about what she liked and didn't like. Therefore, it didn't bother me that she wasn't so crazy about the ring.

雪莉的生活方式代表了我对家的全部憧憬，我儿时看完《绿野仙踪》后所梦寐以求的就是这样的地方。我曾一度梦想着长大后能搬到堪萨斯州去，因为书里讲那是个安适静谧的地方。在奥兹国，有女巫和乱飞的猴子，一切和我儿时在家的情况非常相似，混乱而抓狂。在堪萨斯，那里的人都非常亲切和蔼，无忧无虑，无须担心距离电话亭还有多远，警察能否及时赶到，回到家里会不会发现妈妈和兄弟姐妹已死于非命，诸如此类的问题。

毫无疑问，我自己也一心想融入雪莉的世界。她是家中的独女，家人一直都对她宠爱有加，我想融入她所成长的环境中去，能和她父母一起住在老房子里，没有居无定所流离颠沛的痛苦，没有我小时候所经受的混乱和暴力的折磨。她的父母似乎并不在意我完全不同的生活背景，而是尽可能亲切热情地迎接我回家。当然，像雪莉一样，他们觉得我年轻有为，看重我为成为医生所付出的努力，以及具备的扎实基础，即使我还有很长的路要走，他们都不在乎。

然而，我还是从一开始就情不自禁对婚姻心存疑虑，但后来大多都烟消云散了，回想起来，其实那是典型的婚前神经过敏的表现。

在旧金山，我把结婚的消息首先告诉的就是艾里斯医生，因为他是不二人选。他由衷地为我感到高兴，还借给我几百美元，结婚时购置服装，更令我吃惊的是，他还建议我多休息一天，对于鲍勃这样的工作狂来说，那是闻所未闻的。

我接下来要去市场街的珠宝首饰区，在那里我惊喜地发现一枚 900 美元的钻戒，我刷信用卡把它买了下来。那是个老款钻戒，一颗颗小钻石排列成花冠的形状，箍圈是白金的。在去往弗吉尼亚的飞机上，我把钻戒揣在口袋里，紧张的每过五分钟就要检查一下看它是否安然无恙。那是我为别人买过的最贵重的东西，而且我肯定雪莉一定会喜欢。

下机后，我俩紧紧拥抱在一起，所有疑虑就烟消云散了。我们心心相印，彼此深爱对方，这才是最重要的。看着雪莉操办好婚礼的一切，令我对她更加欣赏。她订出周密的计划，她的父亲已经签好了支票，我需要做的就是出席婚礼。我欣赏她的风格，她的自信、智慧和幽默，她开朗活泼的样子，还有她的亲和力。她非常漂亮，身材出众。我爱她的坚强个性与爱憎分明。因此，她看到戒指后并没有表现出很痴狂的样子，我也没有因此感到不安。

The PURSUIT of HAPPYNESS

"Oh, it's beautiful," she reassured me. "Just not the cut I had in mind."

I had no idea what that even meant, but I wanted her to have what she wanted, so we agreed to exchange it when we went back to San Francisco. For all I knew, they might have been cubic zirconium, not even diamonds. That was something else I appreciated about Sherry, that she could educate me about the finer things in life. Caught up in the festivities, we both were in one major whirlwind, and it was only the next morning, after a farewell brunch, that the two of us had a chance to be alone as newlyweds. Neither of us said as much, but the reality had finally settled in. We were both probably wondering if we really had done the right thing.

Nonetheless, with our lives together ahead of us, we packed all of Sherry's earthly belongings into her blue Datsun B210 and hit the long road to San Francisco. Even though my mother-in-law had insisted that I get my driver's license while I was in Richmond, Sherry did most of the driving. In spite of the summer heat that hovered from start to finish across Interstate 80, the lack of air conditioning in the Datsun, and my frequent naps, we had enough to talk about and plan to make the trip at least a little less arduous.

Sherry had visited me before in the Tenderloin and was somewhat prepared for the seedy atmosphere that greeted us, although she was adamant that we move from 381 Turk as soon as possible. In no time, she got a job as an insurance claims adjuster, and shortly after that she greeted me with the breathless news, "I found a place on Hayes. I fell in love with it. It's a third-floor walk-up with hardwood floors, bay windows, and French doors!"

This was all foreign to me, but if it made Sherry happy, I was happy. Still in the 'hood, the area was known as Hayes Valley and had a lively black community feeling to it, not to mention that we were out of the 'Loin. Thus, we entered into a nesting phase as Sherry turned our new apartment into a warm, welcoming environment. She decorated amazingly on our budget—with potted plants like ficus Benjamins and wandering Jews adorning shelves and hanging from the ceiling, a nice brass bed, a wicker rocking chair, a stylish couch, new cookware and serving pieces. I was as into transforming our living space into a home together as she was.

In the kitchen, Sherry was a fantasy come true. Man, could she cook: soul food including the best fried chicken ever, pasta in every shape and form, and gourmet dishes to rival any of the great chefs of San Francisco. She was always coming out with new creations too. "Remember the way they made that dish at the Vietnamese restaurant?" she'd say. "I'm going to try doing something like that." And it would be even better.

We moved up in the world again after Sherry met me at the door one night and announced, "Wait until you see the place I found on Baker. It's in one of those Victorian buildings I've had my eye on. Chris, you'll love it! It's got five rooms, great sunlight."

"噢，真好看，"她的话再次证明了我的眼光，"只是和我想象中的加工不一样。"

我不知道那意味什么，但我想送给她她最想要的，所以我们同意返回旧金山后就去更换戒指，可能这并不是钻石而是块锆石。那是我欣赏雪莉的另一点，她可以教我欣赏生活中这些精美的事物。在婚宴上我们俩都忙得不可开交，就像刮了一场旋风，第二天早上告别午餐会结束后我们两个新人才有机会单独呆在一起。并没有多说什么，我们就这么结婚了。我俩也不知道这样做的是非对错。

然而，怀着对共同生活的美好憧憬，我们把雪莉的东西收拾打包放进她的达特桑轿车里，然后就踏上了去往旧金山的旅途。虽然在里士满时岳母坚持让我考驾证，但大多时间都是雪莉在开车。尽管在 80 号州际公路上夏天的热浪扑面而来，尽管达特桑车里没有空调而且我还经常打盹，一路上我们有聊不完的话题，也并不觉得旅程有多么艰辛。

雪莉以前到田德隆区看望过我，对眼前这里的条件简陋还是有所准备，但她决心要尽快从特克街 381 号搬走。很快，她找到了一份保险索赔调解员的工作，此后不久她又告诉我一个令人窒息的消息，"我在海斯找到住处了，我很喜欢那里。是个三层楼的公寓，硬木地板，有阳台，法式落地窗！"

我完全听不懂她在说什么，但如果雪莉高兴，我就高兴。那里离这不远，叫海斯谷，那里有个黑人聚居区，而且不用再住到田德隆区了。因此，我们又开始建造自己温馨的小巢，雪莉把新家变得温馨宜人。她充分利用有限的预算，对房间进行了漂亮的装饰，用本杰明榕和白花紫露草盆栽装饰橱柜，花草从橱柜顶部悬垂下来，还有张不错的铜床、一把柳条摇椅、一个时髦的长沙发、新厨具和餐具。我和她一样都很喜欢把我们新家变成温馨可人的样子。

在厨房里，雪莉厨艺高超，简直就是梦幻厨娘，花样翻新，层出不穷：我们的传统食物包括有史以来最好吃的炸鸡、各式面食，她的厨艺可以与旧金山大厨相提并论。她总能做出许多新花样来。"还记得越南饭馆里那道菜的味道吗？我要试着做一下。"结果她做出的效果甚至会更好。

一天晚上雪莉在门口对我说："等一下给你看看我在贝克大街的新发现，那有一片维多利亚式建筑，我一眼就看中了这栋房子。克里斯，你会爱死它的！共有五间屋子，采光很好。"之后我们又搬了一次家。

第七章 生活的影像

The **PURSUIT** of **HAPPYNESS**

I only laughed and went along with the plan, thinking not only how much she enjoyed recreating for us in San Francisco what she'd grown up with in Virginia, but also how lucky I was that she was educating me, elevating my sense of culture and style. She wasn't just giving me an awareness of what a Victorian-style building was, something I never knew, she was opening me up to a lifestyle that included theater, comedy, and social gatherings with fascinating, intellectual conversation. We filled my few nights off with trips to comedy clubs to see the likes of Richard Pryor or to dinner parties with a serious, creative crowd at the home of Sherry's cousin, Robert Alexander, a writer. Whenever we were there, I gravitated to the same group of three guys, very smart, hip, and active in the arts. One was a brother named Barry "Shabaka" Henley, and the other two were cats named Danny Glover and Samuel L. Jackson. Little did I know the three would later be in the top tier of actors on stage and screen.

But even while our portrait of a happily married life seemed to be what we both wanted, within a couple of years I began to confront a feeling deep down that something was missing. If I had been better at communicating my feelings or if I had taken the time to try to resolve what wasn't working, it would have been so much better than what I did by trying to ignore and run away from the problems.

Some of those problems had to do with basic differences in where we came from and in our likes and dislikes. Sherry liked the better restaurants on Fisherman's Wharf; I liked the countercultural vibe of the Haight. To me, the better restaurants were predictable; to Sherry, the anything-goes, hippie atmosphere of the Haight was too wild. Fairly conservative, she was a good churchgoing Episcopalian. That mentality was nothing like where I'd come from: straight-up Baptist, and that's all I knew. Episcopalians reminded me of Catholics in church, always doing calisthenics on cue— standing up, kneeling down, standing up again, kneeling back down again, reciting lines appropriately, in unison. Quiet, dignified, subdued. Being demonstrative with feelings seemed to be discouraged. Tears were dabbed away by handkerchiefs or simply held in. Not like in the Baptist church, where there was competitive shouting. No comparison. In the Baptist church where I grew up, when my big sister and I were taken there by Aunt TT, folks sang, danced, sobbed out loud, spoke in tongues, had dialogues with the preacher and God at the same time, and caught the Spirit in the most dramatic ways. Women threw up their arms, screamed, and fainted! Men jumped and shouted! Every Sunday somebody got carried out. As a kid, I didn't know intellectually what was going on, but it was exciting and real. Oh, man, it was hot too. Episcopalian churches were cool, hardly a drop of sweat to be seen. In the church where I grew up, you got high on the heat. Those fans everyone had didn't do a damn thing to cool us off.

我只是笑着按她的建议去执行，看她一心把我们在旧金山的家改造成她在弗吉尼亚时的样子，我觉得非常开心，同时还觉得能找到这样一个伴侣，帮我提升文化品位，确实是件幸事。她不仅让我了解了维多利亚风格的建筑，这都是我之前未曾接触过的，还让我接触了另一种生活方式，了解了戏剧、喜剧和那些不乏睿智交流的社交聚会。有几个晚上我们去喜剧俱乐部看了理查德·普莱尔的剧作，拜访了雪莉的堂兄罗伯特·亚历山大，在他家里与一些极有天赋的创造性人才共进晚宴。无论何时在他家里我总能碰到三个人，诙谐幽默，极具艺术天分。其中一位叫巴瑞"沙巴卡"亨利，还有两个是丹妮·格洛弗和塞缪尔·杰克逊。后来他们三个都成为舞台银幕上顶级的黑人演员。

幸福的婚姻生活似乎是我们俩的初衷，然而这些年来我内心深处总有一种失落感。如果我当初能更好地交流和表达自己的想法，或多花些时间解决这些矛盾，那结果可能比我试图忽视或逃避问题要好得多。

问题部分是因为我们的成长背景不同，个人喜好也有差异。雪莉喜欢渔夫码头的高档餐厅；而我喜欢海特那里反主流文化的品味。在我看来，高档餐厅索然无趣；而在雪莉眼里，海特那种容纳一切、嬉皮风格的氛围却过分狂野。她相当保守，是一个圣公会主教徒，经常去教堂做礼拜。这种观念信仰与我相去甚远，我是虔诚的浸礼会教徒。在我看来，圣公会主教徒就是教堂里本本分分的天主教徒，他们总是排队，动作整齐划一，起立、跪下、再起立、再跪下，庄重地一起小声背诵经文。似乎不会将感情外露，而只是用手帕默默拭去泪水或者含泪静默。而浸礼会教堂则不同，教徒可以肆意宣泄情感，二者不可同日而语。在我的成长阶段，缇缇舅母会带着我和姐姐去浸礼会教堂，那里人们唱歌跳舞，甚至抽泣，操着不同的口音，跟牧师和上帝一起对话，甚至还会戏剧性地表现出神灵的降临。妇女会张开手臂，尖叫着昏倒。男人们则会欢腾雀跃。每周日都会有些人去那里。我当时还小，并不知道究竟是怎么回事，但就是觉得非常兴奋，气氛热烈。而圣公会教堂总是阴凉冰冷，人们都不动声色。在我去的教堂里，那里的热浪足以激发起每个人的热情，手里不停地扇着扇子都让人无法冷静。

The **PURSUIT** of **HAPP**y**NESS**

Of course, I enjoyed going to church with Sherry, knowing it would open me up to new things. But there was a loudness, a wildness that was lacking. In my heart of hearts, I was slowly coming to face the truth that I didn't want to live a picture of a life—whether it was by having to live up to the role of doctor that I was striving for, or whether it was in my marriage. Sherry had to have been having similar concerns, especially when a parade of houseguests started descending on us.

When my best friend Leon Webb came out to get work in radiology, the path he'd begun in the Navy, that wasn't a problem, even though he stayed for three or four months. Sherry and Leon got along just fine. But when my childhood buddy Garvin came to stay for a while, she and he didn't mesh at all. This was her home, after all, so I was in the position of encouraging Garvin to find somewhere else to stay, soon, which unfortunately hurt our friendship. Of course, if things had been just peachy with Sherry in other respects, it wouldn't have been an issue at all.

The real problem that took me forever to admit had to do with what was or wasn't happening in the bedroom. We loved each other deeply, profoundly. We were presidents of each other's fan clubs, cheering each other on more than anyone else. But our sex life was nice, predictable, quiet. Not hot. I wanted to compensate for not getting to go around the world and meet all those foreign, exotic women. I'd had a taste or two of the X-rated versions, and I wanted more, what else could I say? But rather than say something or initiate what I wanted, I became aloof.

We might have been hamstrung from the start. After all, we had built our romantic relationship over telephone wires and on letter paper, always with that theme music of *Summer of '42* playing in the background. Early on, it had been a major turn-on to be the younger man with the more worldly, college-educated woman. Now I was looking to her to introduce more spice. But she didn't know that, and I didn't know how to shake up the routine.

Ironically, the safe, stable home that I'd wanted since childhood turned out to be too structured, too orderly, too rigid. Later I was able to take the long view and realize that I had gone from one institution, the Navy, to another, marriage, with barely a break in between. At the time, I didn't stop to think about it in those terms, except to realize perhaps that I'd learned the classic lesson: *Be careful what you wish for because you might just get it!*

Obviously, I had some serious inner conflicts about what really was the good life for me. Those qualms were put to the side when Sherry became pregnant, something that was as exciting and different as it was terrifying. Instead of questioning my marriage, I put those doubts on the back burner and suddenly began to question, for the first time, how married I was to the idea of becoming a doctor. Even though I was up at sixteen thousand dollars per year now, that wasn't going to support a family and pay for me to go to college and then med school. I went out and got a second job.

当然，我喜欢和雪莉一起去她的教堂，也想了解一下新鲜事物。可是这里缺少了一种喧嚣和狂野。我内心深处已慢慢接受了这种简单的生活，无论是为之努力奋斗的医生角色还是在婚姻生活之中，都是如此。雪莉可能也有类似的想法，尤其是当家里来人造访之后，更是如此。

我最好的朋友里昂·韦伯来旧金山准备找份放射科的工作，他在海军服役期间干过这个，所以对他来说不成问题，虽然他在我家待了三四个月，但雪莉和里昂相处得不错。可当我的好友加文在我家逗留时，雪莉却和他合不来。毕竟这也是她的家，所以不久我便劝加文另找地方。不幸的是，这伤害到了我们之间的友谊。当然，既然雪莉要这样，也就没什么好说的了。

我永远都得承认的真正问题其实和床上的事情有关。我们彼此相爱，情投意合，无人能敌。性生活很和谐，一切都在预料之中，但没有刺激。我一心想为自己没能周游列国，猎艳异域女子而获得补偿。我也曾出位过一两次，但是还渴望更多，我没有过多解释，却在性的问题上逐渐冷淡下来。

我们之间的关系逐渐开始降温。毕竟我们是伴随《42年之夏》的电影主题歌，电话诉衷肠，飞鸿传书，建立起这种浪漫关系的。一开始，一个不谙事故的年轻男子与受过学院教育的女子在一起的确令人兴奋。但现在我希望她能多点情趣，但是她并不知道我的想法，也不懂得打破常规。

讽刺的是，从儿时起我就期望拥有个安稳的家，可是到头来家对我来说却过于拘束、整洁、墨守成规。我回顾了自己这些年的经历，意识到自己已从海军的军队生活，毫无过渡地走向婚姻生活，那时，我会禁不住要想，对你的梦想要小心经营，因为你有可能就要美梦成真了，现在觉得这实在是太经典了。

显然，我对自己真正想要的美好生活是什么这个问题上是严重自相矛盾的。不过当雪莉怀孕后，我就什么都来不及想了，而是每天沉浸在兴奋和激动之中。我并没有再质疑自己的婚姻，而且把所有的疑虑都暂且搁置一边，并突然第一次扪心自问为何想成为医生。虽然我现在年薪已有1.6万美金，但还是不够养活一家人，再加上支付上学的费用和去医学院进修的费用，于是我去找了第二份工作。

The **PURSUIT** of
HAPP_y_**NESS**

Not out of her first trimester, Sherry miscarried, a disappointment to both of us, but one we took in stride. Now that I'd faced the need for more money, I kept up my second job working as a security guard at nights and on weekends, not doing too badly. That was, until I was sent to fill in on a graveyard shift at the pier as the guard of a creaky old unused ship. With nothing but a flashlight, I took up my post at a chair, freaked out by the horror movie sounds but too exhausted to stay awake, only to be nudged back into consciousness by something rubbing up against my leg. My first thought was of those cats in my nightmares about the witch woman's house back in Milwaukee. Instead, when I felt that same thing scratch me, I looked down and saw a rat the size of a large cat, its jaw unhinged and preparing to munch on me. As God was my witness, my time in the Navy notwithstanding, I had never been on a boat before and had no idea that there were rats on boats and had never dreamt that rats could be so goddamned huge. Screaming like a girl, I jumped straight up out of my chair. The rat screamed too and ran, and so did I, the two of us in separate directions. So much for my stint in security.

From then on, I managed to grab odd jobs here and there in my off hours, doing things like painting houses on the weekends and working for moving companies.

Though she said nothing, Sherry may have noticed that I was spending less time at home, not just because of these extra jobs, but because I was looking to break up the routine. Some nights I went by myself to hear music on Haight Street; other times I hung out with some characters I'd met in the neighborhood, watching football games, smoking some weed, passing time. Sherry wasn't overly fond of some of these cats, especially a couple of the guys who had moneymaking enterprises that weren't all on the up-and-up. In one of my covert acts of rebellion against too much structure, I actually went so far as to try to make extra dough dealing on the side. Besides the fact that I was a complete failure at it, I practically got myself killed when some big-time gangsters came waving guns to collect cash that I didn't have. Somehow I got hold of that cash real fast. It wasn't more than three hundred dollars, but to a ghetto boy like me, that hurt. When a couple of my friends next proposed that I go in with them on an insurance scam, I politely declined.

My short-lived life of crime had the fleeting effect of making me grateful for what I had at home and at work. It also taught me the major principle that there ain't no such thing as easy money. Banging on that anvil, that was the way. Even so, it was frustrating after five years that I hadn't been able to buy a car. Sherry's Datsun B210 still was our only means of shared transportation, though fortunately we could both take advantage of San Francisco's excellent public transit system. There were also morning rides to work that I hitched with my coworker and friend, Latrell Hammond.

雪莉怀孕三个月还不到就流产了，我们俩都很失望，但还是接受了这个事实，这事也就很快过去了。现在我们需要更多的钱来生活。我找了份夜勤保安的兼职工作，也还不错。但当我被派往码头的墓地，去看一艘破轮船时，情况就不太乐观了。拿着手电筒，坐在椅子上呆着，这就是我的工作，恐怖电影里的声音在我身边不时响起，但我太困了，昏昏欲睡。突然，恍惚中我感到有东西在蹭我的腿，我慢慢醒来，开始还以为是噩梦中密尔沃基市那个女巫养的猫，后来我感到是个东西在抓我，猛然向下一看，只见一只硕大的老鼠在用爪子抓我。上帝作证，在海军服役时我都没有上过甲板，根本不知道船上会有老鼠，更没想到还会有这么大个的老鼠。我像个姑娘一样尖叫着从椅子上跳了起来。那只老鼠也吱的一声跑掉了，我能做的就是本能地掉头朝反方向跑开了。

从那时起，闲暇时我就到处找零活干，比如在周末粉刷房屋或到搬家公司工作。

虽然雪莉什么也没有说，但她可能已经注意到我在家的时间越来越少了，并不是因为这些额外的工作，而是因为我开始不那么循规蹈矩。有时晚上我会独自一人去海特大街听音乐；有时我会和几个邻居一起消磨时间，看球赛、吸大麻。雪莉对这些人没什么好感，尤其其中有几个人是自己开公司，但生意并不乐观。有一次，为了在对井井有条的生活增添些叛逆的色彩，我甚至尝试从路人身上抢点钱回来，这确实有点过分了。我最后一分钱没得到，却招来一些无赖挥刀弄枪来向我勒索。当然我身上没多少钱，结果还差点把命搭上，周身上下，我一共才300块钱，也被尽数掠走。对于像我这样在贫民区长大的人来说，这简直就是要我的命。接下来，有朋友建议我和他们一起进行保险诈骗，但是我婉言谢绝了。

我生命中短暂的犯罪史使我对家和工作心存感激，并懂得世上没有不义之财，痛定思痛，那确实是板上钉钉的大道理。即使如此，五年之后我仍买不起车，这着实令人沮丧。雪莉的达特桑仍是我们唯一的交通工具，好在旧金山的公交系统非常发达，而且早上我还可以搭同事和朋友拉垂尔·哈蒙德的车去上班。

第七章 生活的影像

"Chris, listen to me," she'd begin every morning when I jumped into her much-abused, lime green 1961 Ford Falcon after she arrived to pick me up. Every morning she had some new advice she was selling, and it was usually good. A force of nature, Latrell had the gift of gab as one of the fastest-talking, most scandalous women I'd ever seen in my life, with the ability to sell you anything— including your own shoes that you had on your feet at the time.

Latrell and I were strictly platonic friends. She and Sherry were tight, so she had the best interests of my marriage in mind at all times. There were occasions, however, when I'd wonder if she had the best interests of me surviving her driving in mind. Latrell was outrageous. But because of her gift for gab, no matter how late we arrived at work—and she was chronically late—she could always pull it off. From the minute I hopped in the car, as I tried to follow her latest line of conversation, and as the two of us slid around on the Falcon's seatbeltless bench seats, Latrell gabbed away, putting on her makeup, drinking coffee, smoking and gunning for the green lights, all at the same time.

She acted completely unaware that I was praying aloud, "Oh, my God, don't let me die in this lime green Ford Falcon."

If we caught all the green lights, we could make it to work in fifteen, sixteen minutes. That's still not good if you're already late. But if one red light caught us, we were shit out of luck. Remarkably, while I didn't even bother trying to make excuses when a whole room full of interns were waiting for me to arrive, in her department Latrell had a new and exciting excuse every day— which her superiors never questioned.

Sherry was such a contrast. There was only one morning, to my knowledge, that she left the house without being organized and in control. That was revealed later that evening when she returned from work and confessed that something was wrong.

Was this the conversation that I had been hoping for and dreading at the same time? "What's wrong?" I asked.

"I think something's wrong with my ankles."

"Your ankles?"

"I've been walking funny all day," she explained. "I can't figure it out."

Being the investigative medical guy that I was, I suggested, "Let me take a look." When I did, at first I saw nothing. Then I realized, cracking up as I did, that she had become a fashion victim of what I called her shoe garden. Because she had amassed such a collection, she kept the shoes neatly arranged in a basket in our bedroom. But somehow in her haste to get to work on time, she'd grabbed two different shoes.

每天早上，当拉垂尔过来接我的时候，我钻进那辆灰绿色福特猎鹰，她便开始絮叨"克里斯，听着"。每天早上她都会给我出这样那样的主意，通常也还不错。她也确实不简单，应该算是我所见过的女人说话最快、最八卦的一个，并且能向你兜售任何东西，包括穿在自己脚上的鞋都在其中。

从严格意义上说，我和拉垂尔是柏拉图式的朋友。她和雪莉关系很好，所以她总是喜欢对我们婚姻生活问这问那。然而，有时候我也确实对她的驾驶技术颇感担心，每到这时她就会非常生气。不过她有饶舌瞎扯的天赋，虽然她经常迟到，而且无论迟到多晚，她都可以搞定一切。从我跳上她的车那一刻开始，我就跟不上她说话的节奏，当我在没有安全带的长椅上晃动的时候，拉垂尔就不再说话，化妆、喝咖啡、吸烟、瞄准绿灯，这些动作几乎同时进行。

她好像完全没意识到我在大声祷告："上帝，别让我就这么死在这辆福特猎鹰里。"

如果一路绿灯通行畅通无阻，那么我们就可以在15分钟左右赶到工作地点。不过如果已经迟到的话，那情况也似乎不妙。但如果遇到红灯，那我们就要走狗屎运了。当满屋子的实习生就等我一个人的时候，我也懒得给自己找借口；而拉垂尔和我却恰好相反，她每天都能找到新鲜理由，而且她的上司从未对此质疑过。

雪莉则完全是相反类型的人。据我所知，她只有一天早晨没有规整好，那还是晚上下班回到家后，我们才知道，她说感觉脚上不对劲儿。

难道这就是我一直期待却也惧怕的谈话吗？"怎么了？"我问。

"我感到脚有点毛病。"

"你的脚踝？"

"今天一天走起路来都不舒服，"她解释说，"也不知道怎么了。"

出于医生的职业本能，我说："让我看看。"可是开始我什么也没看出来。然后我突然大笑起来，原来是鞋子的问题。因为她已经买了很多鞋，都整齐地摆在卧室的整理箱里，但是那天急急忙忙赶去上班时，她不小心拿出两只不同的鞋子套在脚上。

第七章 生活的影像

She joined in laughing with me when she saw it for herself. That was so unlike her. But it was indicative of how together and consistent her routine normally was.

A short time after that incident, I had a reaction to a Richard Pryor line that was indicative of how much I was dying for a change in our sexual routine. Pryor was talking about some of the crazy things that doing blow could do to people. At the time, I had only tried it once and didn't get what all the hype was. Now Pryor was talking about how it affected your sex drive, and he was telling a story about how he'd be high and make up wild stuff to do, telling his lady, "Now, baby, I want you to go up on the roof. I'm going to run around the house three times, and on the third time I want you to jump off on my face."

Sherry didn't laugh. I didn't laugh either. Instead, I thought to myself, *Aw, yeah, that would be cool.*

That's where my mind was lurking. So when I meet this kind of cute, kind of plump, but fairly hip woman with a short tight natural who happens to have a nice little place and who happens to tell me, "I really want to give you a blow job," I do not say no. And when I say yes, and this kind of cute chick turns out to be a fellatio expert, I start to mess up bad. Really bad. It's stupid enough to be stepping out to get my dick sucked, but worse, I invite this woman to where I live when Sherry's at work one day and I have the afternoon off.

The whole time I'm doing it, I feel so good, but the minute I come sanity returns, and I know that this is one of the worst mistakes I've ever made in my life. Not just because it's wrong every which way, but because in the last few times we've gotten together, I've come to understand this woman is stone cold crazy. The next time I see her at her place, I let her know that while it's been swell, we shouldn't get together anymore.

"What are you trying to tell me?" she asks, fury in her eyes.

"Well, I don't want to see you anymore."

"Are you breaking up with me?"

Realizing that she's not getting it, I try to remind her that we weren't together that way to be a couple in the first place. "Look," I say, "you're the best, and I'll remember our time together, but nothing else is gonna happen between us. Let's just be friends."

Now, either she is not satisfied with how I've broken it off or she is really nuts, because a few mornings later I wake up in the morning to find that Sherry's car, the Datsun B210, has been brutally vandalized. A can of white paint has been dumped on top of the roof, spilling white stripes of paint right down the windows and the windshield wipers, everything. The tires are slashed, sugar's in the gas tank, and prominently etched by finger in the paint is a message that reads: *FUCK YOU!*

她也笑了起来，这太不像她的风格了，不过这也显示出平素里，她的生活是何等的严谨与协调。

那件事情之后不久，我想起了喜剧演员理查德·普莱尔的话，他一语道破我是多么渴望能改变一下床上生活的一成不变。普莱尔说的是他干过的那些出位的荒唐事情。我只尝试过一次，却并没觉得怎么快乐。现在普莱尔说的是这将如何影响你做爱的动力，还讲了他自己的亲身经历，他对自己的女人说："宝贝儿，现在到房顶上去，绕着房子跑三圈，到第三次时你就跳到我的脸上来。"

雪莉并没有笑，我也没有笑，心想：噢，那一定很酷！

那是我内心潜藏的想法，所以后来我遇见了一个可爱、身材丰满、穿着紧身裤的时髦女郎，当她对我做出种种暧昧举动时，我并没有回绝，结果发现原来这个可爱的小妞是个情场老手。我开始陷入困境，这太糟了，我竟然愚蠢到不忠于爱情。但更糟的是，一天在雪莉上班的时候，我把这个女人邀请到了自己家，并请了一下午假和她厮混在一起。

整个过程我都感觉极好，但当我恢复理智后便开始懊悔，这是我犯过的最低劣的错误，而且是大错特错。因为最后几次我和她混在一起的时候，我开始认识到这个女人如石头般冰冷疯狂。后来有一次在她的住处亲热时，我想就此罢手了。

"你想要说什么？"她问道，露出狂怒的眼神。

"好吧，我不想再见到你了。"

"你在和我谈分手吗？"

发现她并没有懂我的意思后，我解释道，首先我们不会因此就一直厮守下去。我说："你是最棒的，我会记住我们在一起的时光，但是我们之间什么也不会发生，就让我们当朋友吧。"

要么是她对我的分手方式不满意，要么是她真的发狂了，因为几天后的一个早上，当我醒来时发现雪莉的达特桑被糟蹋得不成样子。一罐白色的油漆从车顶泼下来，白色油漆顺着车窗和挡风玻璃流淌下来，流到了风挡雨雪刷，乃至整个车身到处都是。轮胎也瘪了，油箱里灌满了糖，车上还赫赫然写着：去死吧！

I know who's done it but I can't prove it. I can't let Sherry know. Standing there pissed off at myself more than anything, I decide that I've got to now lie big-time and say that I've got no idea who would have done something so violent. A random act, no doubt.

A brother from the neighborhood approaches as if to make conversation. "Hey, man," he says, "let me holler at you for a second."

Not wanting any chitchat, I turn away, letting him know, "Yeah, okay, talk to me later."

With a shrug, he insists, "I was just trying to tell you who did that to your car."

"Oh?" What else am I going to say?

"It was that little fat bitch with short hair," he says with a snicker. "Okay?"

Well, I know who did it, the street knows who did it, but thank God Sherry doesn't know, and the insurance agrees to cover it, only after they ask, "Mr. Gardner, what happened?"

"I don't know," I say in my most indignant voice. "I came out and found it like this. I must have made somebody angry, but I don't know who it was. Maybe whoever did this just made a mistake. I just don't know." The insurance claims person points out that a message like that is usually personal, not a random act or a mistake, but leaves it at that.

In the days that followed it was obvious from the whispers and looks that word had traveled through the grapevine. The incident soon passed but remained an ugly memory for me. Sherry never indicated that she knew anything about it, but she did seem to be picking up on my discontent, asking me more often than not where I was going or where I'd been out late the night before.

When we finally did have a talk, toward the end of 1979, with my twenty-sixth birthday not too far down the road, it was to confront a change of professional plans. I had decided that I wasn't going to be a doctor.

Baffled, Sherry groped for words. "Why? I mean . . ." She just looked at me. "Isn't that what you've been working toward?"

She knew that the challenge was gone. We had talked about that before. I was already the medical whiz kid. It was going to be ten years more of education before I could officially do what I already was doing. But it wasn't just that, as I explained to Sherry. My mentor, Dr. Ellis, had raised his concerns with me, opening my eyes to some of the trends that were about to radically alter the healthcare field. In plainer language, he had said, "Chris, you really need to reconsider being a doctor because it's going to become a vastly changed profession."

我知道是谁干的，但没法证明这一点。我还不能让雪莉知道，只能怒气冲天地站在那里。我决定要撒个弥天大谎，说自己也不知道是谁会做出这种事。肯定是有人恶作剧。

一个住在附近的老兄向我走过来，好像想要和我攀谈。"兄弟，我们聊聊。"

我并不想和他闲扯，于是想走开，只是说："好的，一会儿再说。"

他耸了耸肩，坚持说："我只是想告诉你是谁干的。"

"噢？"我还能说什么呢？

"是那个留着短发的小肥妞干的，"他偷偷地笑着说，"明白了吗？"

我知道是谁干的，整条街上的人都知道是谁干的，但是老天啊，雪莉并不知道，而且保险公司同意赔偿，他们就是问了问："克里斯·加德纳先生，出什么事了？"

"我不知道，"我做出一副怒不可遏的样子，"一出来，车就变成这个样子。我一定是得罪了什么人，但我也不知道是谁。也许是别人搞错了，真不知道是怎么回事。"保险索赔员指出这样的情况通常是由于个人恩怨，应该不是恶作剧或弄错了，不过就这样吧。

接下来的几天，从不断传来闲言碎语和异样的眼神中，我看出显然消息不胫而走。不过这事很快就过去了，但让我觉得十分恶心。雪莉从来没有表现出她知道此事，但似乎对我更加不满，更加挑剔，开始经常问我要去哪里，或头天晚上很晚的时候我在哪里。

当 1979 年底临近，快到我 26 岁生日的时候，我们终于谈起了我要改变职业计划的事情，我决定放弃医生的职业。

雪莉不知说什么好。"为什么？我的意思是……"她看着我说，"难道这不是你一直工作的目标吗？"

她清楚这一行已经对我没什么挑战了。我们之前也谈论过此事。其实在正式做医生这一行之前，我本应再上十多年的学，我能取得今天的成绩已经是奇迹了。但正如我向雪莉解释的一样，不仅如此，导师艾里斯医生也提出了一些忧虑，让我看清了这一行的发展变化趋势。用他的话简明地说就是："克里斯，你真的需要重新考虑一下是否要做医生，因为这个行当将发生翻天覆地的变化。"

What was coming down the pike at the time were versions of socialized or nationalized medicine, precursors to what became HMOs. As Dr. Ellis rightfully predicted, this meant that a top surgeon who might make several thousand dollars per surgery then could be looking at as little as a few hundred dollars for the same services in coming decades. Not only were the new insurance plans going to cover less, but they were also going to emphasize noninvasive procedures and create bureaucracies that set fee structures. Bob Ellis made it clear that he believed in me, that I had the talent and energy to succeed and, even more important, to make a contribution to others.

Except for the time that Moms had told me I couldn't be Miles Davis, no one else had ever put a hand on my shoulder to steer me in one direction or another. I had to listen. As I went on to explain to Sherry, there were plenty of options for me in the medical field, perhaps in administration, sales, pharmaceuticals, or the insurance business. I would start checking out some of those options as soon as I could.

There was even a sense of relief that flooded me. No longer did I have to play the part of a future doctor. But Sherry was anything but relieved. That future had been part of the package she married: Chris Gardner, college graduate, medical student, doctor. She had every reason to be disappointed, even though she expressed her support for whatever I decided to do.

After cheating on her already, I had made up my mind 100 percent never to repeat that mistake. Yet we were starting to drift further apart, our differences showing up in stark ways.

This comes crashing in on me on a Saturday after we head down to Fisherman's Wharf, just to do some sightseeing and some shopping, when I can't help but notice this fine woman out for a stroll. I don't want to ogle, but my penis stands up at attention to salute, rock hard. Everybody in the vicinity on Fisherman's Wharf gets a full view of me walking around with a major piece of wood bulging in my pants.

One brother walks by and comments, "Still strong, huh?"

What can I do? Kind of embarrassed, but not really, I glance over at Sherry and am shocked to see how livid she is. "That's disgusting," she says, mad as hell.

There's a part of me that wants to get mad too and tell her it's not disgusting, it's normal. There's another part that's regretting not having taken the time to be single and sow my wild oats a little more.

这时医疗行业出现了社会化或国有化的趋势,健康管理机构就是这方面的先河。艾里斯医生的判断没错,在未来的几十年里,一个高级外科医生原本每次做手术获取的几千美金,以后就变成几百美金。不仅新的保险计划的担保额度会减少,他们还将推广微创技术,重新确定收费机制。艾里斯医生表示,他相信我有取得成功的天赋和能力,更重要的是,我是块料。

除了妈妈告诫过我说我不会成为爵士大师迈尔·戴维斯第二,就再没有谁这么推心置腹地为我指过方向。我真的对艾里斯医生言听计从。我继续向雪莉解释,在医学领域我还有很多选择,也许在管理、销售、制药或者保险部门都有机会,我会尽快开始逐一尝试的。

突然我有一种如释重负的感觉,以后我不用再做医生了。但雪莉却并不感到轻松。她嫁给我一部分原因也有我要做医生在内:本以为克里斯·加德纳会顺顺当当大学毕业,再读医学院,最后成为医生。她完全有理由对我感到失望,虽然她嘴上说无论我决定做什么,她都会支持我。

我已经欺骗过她一次了,所以我下定决心不再重蹈覆辙。然而我们的关系却开始更加疏远,分歧日益加大。

周六我们前往渔夫码头休闲购物,我无意间注意到一个正在散步的美女,这彻底使我陷入尴尬的境地。我并不想调情,但小弟弟却变得非常坚硬,挺直立正敬礼。当我带着这个不听话的木棒四周闲逛时,渔夫码头附近的每个人都看到了眼里。

一个老兄走过来说:"不老实了吧?"

我该怎么办?有点尴尬,也其实不然,我瞥了雪莉一眼,却发现她脸色分外难看。"真够恶心的,"她非常生气地说。

我一方面想发火,告诉她这一点儿也不恶心,这是正常反应。另一方面,我却后悔没能多享受一下单身生活,没有继续放浪形骸。

It's funny how life can turn on such an unplanned minor event as a spontaneous boner or a thoughtless comment. In that moment the stage was set for my marriage to be over. I would always love Sherry Dyson to death. What she had given me was so much more than the picture of a life I was looking at, maybe more than any woman, other than Moms. Sherry gave me the gift of believing in me, of pushing me to set the bar high for myself, of sending me the message that I was worth it—sometimes when I had forgotten. Whether she was ready to admit it or not, back before we were married, she too had definitely felt some ambivalence about our longterm prospects, but her love was always unconditional. In years to come, she would become my best friend in the world, even though in the short term she would suffer terrible hurt for which I was sorely to blame.

The real turning point that changes everything in our marriage and our lives comes shortly after that day on the pier when we go out to a party together and my future—in the form of an exotic black goddess named Jackie—sees me checking her out and gives me a look. She is five-ten, statuesque, stacked, wearing a shimmering dress like she's poured into it, just oozing sexual energy. And without hesitation or premeditation whatsoever, I reach over, grin, and grab her ass. My favorite kind of ass, it feels just like a basketball. My hand lingers. She doesn't slap me, doesn't flinch. Just raises her eyebrow and smiles. As if to say, *What took you so long to find me?*

I hurried headlong as a door opened into a world that promised absolute sexual joys I couldn't even begin to imagine, a world that was also destined to turn into a horrendous nightmare, and that's putting it lightly.

搞笑的是，这个滑稽的生理错误，或欠考虑的话就成了生活中的一个意外，甚至在那一刻为我们婚姻的结束奠定了基础。我会爱雪莉一辈子。她所给予我的远远不止我所看到的生活影像，除了妈妈之外，她为我付出的相当多。雪莉信任我，鼓励我追求高目标，有时当我妄自菲薄时，她会让我重新认识自我。不管她是否愿意承认，在我们婚前，她对我们的未来也存在复杂矛盾的情感，但她对我的爱却是无条件的。以后她会成为我在这个世界上最要好的朋友，虽然在短期内她会因为我的所作所为遭受感情的痛苦折磨，但这一切的过错在我。

真正改变我们婚姻生活的一切转折点是那天我俩一起去码头参加一个派对时，我遇到一个叫杰姬的黑美人，她发现我在打量她并看了我一眼。她将近1米80，身材凹凸有致、妖艳照人，穿着一身金光闪闪的衣服，洒脱奔放，透出性感魅力。我想都没想，就毫不犹豫地凑了过去。她没有退缩。只是挑了一下眉毛笑了笑，好像是在说：你怎么这么久才找到我？

随着这扇门的开启，我便迫不及待地迈入了另一个世界，一个从未想象过的激情世界，但也是个注定要变成噩梦的世界，这么形容毫不为过。

Chapter 8
Turned Out(an intro)

For the second time in my adulthood, I was preparing to relearn that lesson about being careful what you wish for. Over the next thirty days, everything that I was and everything that I hoped to become flew out the window. I barely knew my name. After spending twenty-six years fighting powerlessness with a need for control, a need for clarity of vision, I eagerly tossed whatever control of my senses remained and took a flying leap off the plank into whatever unexplored depths lay below. Somewhere in the back of my mind I recalled tackling *The Iliad* and *The Odyssey*, thanks to a fondness for mythology that got me started reading early on. And even as I remembered the story of Ulysses—who tried to resist the call of the Sirens, those sea nymph creatures whose irresistible song destroyed the minds of sailors and sent them and their ships crashing on the rocky shores of the Aegean—the warning signals went right over my head.

    Within days of meeting Jackie—who lived within walking distance of me and Sherry, five blocks away around the corner—the ship that I'd been sailing turned into wreckage as I boarded a new vessel to destinations unknown. This was the beginning of the end of everything that had come before and the beginning of the beginning of everything that would happen from then on.

第八章
人生的抉择(上)

这是我长大成人以后，第二次重温那一课：小心自己的梦想。接下来的一个月里，我的一切和一切我所希望的都离我而去了。我几乎忘了自己是谁。26 年来，坚持着自我克制，怀着对梦想的追求，我一直在和命运抗争。现在我不顾一切地把所有残存的理智都抛之脑后，不顾世俗礼制，进入到一个从未接触过的世界。在记忆深处我回想起《伊丽亚特》和《奥德赛》，因为我喜欢神话故事，所以很早就开始读这些故事书了。直到现在，尤利赛斯的故事我都历历在目，他努力抵制海妖塞壬的呼唤，那些海洋女神丝丝缕缕诱惑的歌声充满了无法抗拒的魔力，摧毁了水手们的心智，让他们和船只在爱琴海上迷失方向并触礁沉没。而此刻警报就在我耳畔响起，但我却没有理睬。

在和杰姬相处的日子里——她住在五个街区以外的街角，离我和雪莉的寓所只有几步之遥，此时的我仿佛踏上一艘新船，前往遥远的未知世界，而从前我驾驶的船只已然不复存在。这是过往一切结束的起点，也是未来一切的开端。

Over at Jackie's apartment, on her Murphy bed with a brass headboard, on the floor, in the kitchen, against the wall, under the shower, sometimes all in the same night, we made love like there was no tomorrow. For thirty days in a row, after or before work, for hours at night or in the early morning, for whole days at a time when I skipped work, even as I tried to maintain the appearance of normalcy when Sherry and I crossed paths at our place or when I tried to recover my focus in the lab, my life became a blur. A sex-induced hypnotic haze. In my feverishly aroused state, I kept thinking that I'd get my fill, that I'd come down off this high, but Jackie kept on upping the stakes, taking me further to the outer limits. When her relatives came to visit and were in her apartment, she invited me up to the building's rooftop—where she opened her coat to reveal that she was wearing nothing but stiletto high heels, fishnets, and a garter belt. Dazed, mesmerized, in a trance, I could hardly wait to find out what was next. Everything that seemed missing before burst into being, like in *The Wizard of Oz* when the movie goes from black-and-white to Technicolor. The sex was so out of this world, so unbelievable, I had to tell myself, *Chris, man, you are not in Kansas anymore!*

Reason and rationality, my old friends, had split at some point in those thirty days. My moral compass, as they say, went on the blink too. Once we started to come back down to earth after that crazed month, Jackie began to press me about what my longterm intentions were. Probably I was hoping our adventure would run its course because I honestly didn't want to get divorced. But it was plain to me that I was nowhere near ready to break things off with Jackie.

At one point, she talked me into going back east to see relatives of hers. We had an enjoyable time meeting everyone and seeing a little bit of New York City—which towered in my senses like the Emerald City of Oz, magical and dangerous, as if you needed a special password to be allowed to enter—but staying with family members put a major damper on our sexual odyssey. After making love anytime and anyplace for thirty days and thirty nights, we had no privacy to do anything and I was in pain. When we finally headed to JFK to fly back to California, I was starting to count the minutes until we returned to her apartment.

A showdown was coming. In a perfect world, my wanderlust for the wild side would have run its course. But the reality was that the world wasn't so perfect, something I was beginning to realize big-time. Having my cake and eating it too wasn't going to happen. My hand was eventually forced, unfortunately, which added another layer of regret to the awful guilt I felt in the late spring of 1980 when I told Sherry I was leaving. What I did and said, how I did and said it, just destroyed her, and it will hurt me for the rest of my life how I bungled what would remain one of the most important relationships in my life. Sherry soon moved to Oakland, and though we had little contact, it took nine years to be legally divorced, partly because of how painful it was and partly because of the other drama that was going on.

在杰姬的公寓里，我们俩尽情云雨，仿若明天不复存在。连续一个月的时间，上下班前后，夜里的几个小时，一大清早睡眼惺忪时，在我逃逸工作的一整天里，甚至当我和雪莉不期而遇时，我试图保持清醒，或者努力把注意力集中到实验室的工作上时，我的生活还是变得迷茫了。我甚至有些精神恍惚。在我狂热的兴致下，我的理智不停地告诫自己该收手了，该让这种快感降降温了。但杰姬却一直在加码，一次次饶有兴致地将我推向极限。我开始眩晕起来，仿佛被催眠一样，忘乎所以，几乎迫不及待地要去发现接下来还有什么。似乎恍恍惚惚的东西突然变得清晰，就像《绿野仙踪》，电影从黑白画面瞬间换做彩色画面。男欢女爱，炽热升级，令人无法想象。我不得不告诉自己：克里斯，这再也不是在堪萨斯州了！

在之后的 30 天里，我的思想和理智，有时也会丧失殆尽，仿佛道德指南针失灵了一般。在那癫狂的一个月后，我们逐渐回到现实中来，杰姬开始向我施压，问我有何长久打算。可能我希望我们的冒险能得到继续，因为老实说我并不想离婚。但我也很清楚自己没有和杰姬分手的打算。

有一次，她说服我回到东海岸去看望她的亲戚。我们见了她家里的每个人，并在纽约城里游览观光，一起度过了美好的时光，这段经历令我极度兴奋，就像到了奥兹国里的翡翠城，既神奇而又危险，仿佛需要拿到特殊的密码才能通行似的，颇为有趣。但和她家人呆在一起却成了我们亲热的最大绊脚石。在过去的 30 个日日夜夜里，我们可以随时随地尽情享受男欢女爱，可现在我们却无法私会偷欢，实在令人扫兴，备感苦闷。当我们最终前往肯尼迪机场准备飞回加州时，我便开始盼着早点回到她的寓所。

摊牌的时刻悄然而至。在完美的理想世界里，我性格中追求狂野的流浪癖会继续发展下去。但事实是，这个世界并不完美，我开始越来越清醒地意识到鱼和熊掌不可兼得。不幸的是，我们终于要摊牌了，在 1980 年的晚春时节，我告诉雪莉要离开她，这在我已有的罪恶感中又增添了一丝悔意。我的所作所为，我向她坦白的方式，使她深受打击；我搞砸了生命中最重要的一段关系，也使自己在有生之年深感内疚伤怀。雪莉很快搬到了奥克兰，虽然我们中断了联系，但仍在九年以后才正式离婚，部分原因是事情本身令人痛苦，部分原因是其他戏剧性因素的出现。

Even if Jackie hadn't become pregnant within nineteen days of our meeting—a determining factor in my moving in with her because that's where I thought my responsibilities rested—I probably would have made the same decision. It was about sex. I had been turned out, and there was no going back in.

* * *

OJT— On-the-Job Training—was destined to be my watchword as I journeyed into fatherhood. The arrival of Christopher Jarrett Medina Gardner Jr. on January 28, 1981, at San Francisco General Hospital changed every focus, every priority of my existence. He had to be the most beautiful, the most brilliant, the most agile, the most intuitive, the most musical, the most soulful, the most athletic infant in the hospital ward. He had a wisdom and greatness about him from day one, no question. When I cradled him in my arms the first time, I had a strange feeling of familiarity, as if he and I knew each other from a previous lifetime. Without words, I swore on everything and everyone that I cherished in this world, reaffirming my lifelong promise that I would always care for him and that I would never be absent from his life.

Chris Jr. stared right up at me, knowingly, as if to say, *All right, Poppa, I'm counting on you.* Then he studied me, in a way that I never knew babies could do, as though he was seeing me when I was a little boy not knowing who my father was or where my mother was. It was my imagination of course, but he seemed to be saying, *And you can count on me too.* My son made me a better person, bringing purpose and meaning to my life, to an extent I'd never known before and would only fully appreciate later.

In the months leading up to Chris's birth, I got some OJT with Jackie, who revealed hitherto unknown aspects of her personality. When we met, she had been finishing up dental school at the University of California. Once she graduated, she expected to be able to take time off, chill for a minute, and then delay having to work so that she could study for her boards. Now that the smoke had cleared somewhat after our initial fireworks, it was apparent that she had a definite game plan, with quite an ambitious view of moving on up in life. At first she didn't pressure me so much as point out that it was time for me to cut the cord at the VA, something that I'd been delaying during the period that my personal life had been so turbulent. Since we were already rolling with an upwardly mobile circle of young black professionals—each of them some form of doctor, lawyer, or Indian chief—the fact that I was already in the medical field was cool with Jackie. Still, even though she acknowledged that I was doing significant work in research under Dr. Ellis, she didn't refrain from mentioning that the pay wasn't comparable to what her friends and their spouses were making.

然而在我们这共处的 19 天里，杰姬怀孕了，这是我与她同居的决定性因素，因为我觉得要对她负责任。但就是为了性爱，我也可能会做出相同的决定。既然我已然上路，就不准备回头。

* * *

随着我初为人父，边学边干，上岗培训注定成了我的口头禅。1981 年 1 月 28 日，小克里斯多夫·贾勒特·麦迪那·加德纳在旧金山总医院降生了。他的到来改变了一切注意力和我生命中的重心。在医院病房的监护室里，他就是那里最美丽、最聪颖、最敏捷、最有灵气、声音最悦耳、表情最动人、最活泼的一个。毫无疑问，从第一天起他就具备了智慧和伟大的意义。我第一次把他抱入怀中时，就有种奇怪的熟悉感，仿佛在前世我们已然相识。我默默地向这个世界上我所珍视的每个人发誓，对天发誓，并重申我一生的允诺：我会一直照顾他，永远不离不弃。

小克里斯多夫瞪着眼睛望着我，好像明白似的说：好吧，爸爸，就靠你咯。然后，他打量起我来，我以前从来不知道婴儿会这么做，好像他了解我小时候不知道自己的爸爸是谁或者妈妈在哪里一样。当然这只是我的想象，不过他看上去像在说：你也可以依靠我。儿子使我的生命更加完整，给我带来了生活的目标和意义。在某种程度上，我以前对此从未知晓，而且事后对此心存感激。

在儿子快出生的几个月里，我和杰姬手忙脚乱，一切都是现学现用。直至如今她才显露出个性中不为人知的某些方面。当我们相遇的时候，她即将结束在加州大学口腔学院的学业。一旦她毕业，就期待着能够抽出一部分时间冷静思考，推迟参加工作的时间，以便为取得资格认证而好好准备一番。我们之间最初迸发的激情火花现在已经逐渐降温。显然她有明确的职业目标，要好好生活，不断进取。起初她并没有给我施加很大压力，没有说要我离开退伍老兵管理署医院。其实在我个人生活动荡不安的那段时期，我延缓了离开那里的计划。自从我们接触了一群年轻有为的黑人专家圈子后，他们或是医生、律师，或是印度菜厨师，他们个个都事业有成。并且事业不断发展。我在医疗行业有所作为对杰姬来说的确很有吸引力，然而，虽然她承认在艾里斯医生的指导下我所从事的工作很有意义，但是她仍然不断地提醒我，现在这点薪水无法和她的朋友们相提并论。

Those comments didn't bother me because I already knew I wasn't earning enough to support a family. Publication in several prestigious medical journals may have been a thrill, but it didn't pay a bill, to borrow a line from the great Berry Gordy—one of my heroes and one of a very few black business entrepreneurs I knew about, who happened to have written the song "Money: That's What I Want." It wasn't the money conversation that bothered me. What did bother me was the question Jackie started asking with increased regularity about halfway through her pregnancy, a remark that seemed to come out of nowhere when she said it the first time one evening over dinner.

"You know, Chris," Jackie began, and I could tell from her tone of voice that I wasn't going to like what I was about to hear. She continued, "I have to ask you, how are you going to be a father when you never had one? How do you know what it means to be a father?"

Not saying a word, I sat and stared at her, my heart pounding. How could she ask me that? From the very beginning she knew one thing about me: that I had a real intense issue about not having a father. She knew I would do anything I could to be the father I never had. I was floored.

"Well?" she asked. I knew she was trying to push my buttons, but why I wasn't sure. Was it a test to make sure that I wouldn't leave her? If so, it was cruel because she knew from my history that I would never leave a child. Never.

We changed the subject and the tension passed. When she brought up the same question again, using exactly the same wording, "How are you going to be a father when you've never had one? How do you know what it means to be a father?" I caught on that this was another way to push me. Obviously, when it came to her pushing me sexually, I was a willing participant. But this line of questioning left me resentful, even though, in her defense, she was expressing practical concerns for the future.

The third or fourth time she brought up the issue, I barked back, "Don't you think it's a little late to ask me to fill out a father application?"

"What's that supposed to mean?"

"Maybe you should have asked about my résumé before you got pregnant. Because you knew I didn't have a father of my own!"

In a flash, Jackie turned silent and cold.

In spite of this unsettling dynamic, she did succeed in getting me to think about what it really meant to be a father—a theoretical part of the equation that was moot the moment Christopher was born. Now that we had a baby, the reality was that we were a family and I had to learn what it meant to be a good father OJT— on a practical, immediate basis. This was do or die. If I couldn't do or provide for him, it would be a betrayal of everything I had promised myself from as young as I could remember.

这么说倒是没什么，因为我自己心里很清楚这点钱是不够养活一个家的。在几本权威医学期刊上发表文章着实令人兴奋，但却不能支付账单，这是借用了贝里·高迪的一句歌词，他是我心目中的偶像，也是我所知道的为数不多的黑人成功人士，碰巧他写过一首歌，叫做《金钱：我的梦想》。真正让我困扰的并不是这些钱的问题，而是在杰姬怀孕期间，她开始越来越常提出一个问题，一天晚上进餐时她突然冒出一句话。

"克里斯，"杰姬开口说道，我从她说话的语气判断出这估计不会是什么好听的话，她继续说道，"我得问问你，如果你从来没有过父亲，那么你怎能当好父亲？你怎么知道作为父亲的意义？"

我一声不吭地坐在那里盯着她看，心怦怦直跳，她怎么能这么说话？从一开始她就知道这件事情：我没有父亲是残酷的现实，但她知道我会尽全力去做个称职的父亲，一个我不曾拥有的父亲。这个问题让我哑口无言。

"那好吧，"她说。我知道她这是激将法，但我不能确定为什么。她是要借此确保我不会离开她吗？如果是这样，那就太没必要了，因为她了解，我是不会离开孩子的，永远不会。

我们改变了话题，紧张的气氛消散了。当她再次提出同样的问题时，她还是用了同样的措辞，"如果你从来没有过父亲，那么你怎能当好父亲？你怎么知道作为父亲的意义？"我知道她就是想激我。显然，当她风骚撩人地和我调情时，我非常愿意和她共度春宵。但这样的问题使我非常恼火，虽然从她的角度考虑，她这么问实际上也是在为将来着想。

当她一而再、再而三地提出这类问题时，我受不了了，反驳道："让我现在再去重新考虑是不是该当孩子的父亲，你不觉得太晚了吗？"

"你是什么意思？"

"你在怀孕前就问了我的过去，你知道我没有父亲。"

杰姬立刻安静下来，冷冰冰地一句话都不说。

尽管这个矛盾仍未解决，但她却成功地让我开始思考为人父的真正含义，这个问题我从来都没有搞清楚过。随着儿子的到来。现在我们有了孩子，成了一家人，我不得不面对现实，快速学会当个好父亲。我别无选择！如果我当不好这个父亲，那就等于将背叛自己打小以来所做的一切承诺。

A major logistical problem was space, as our one-room studio was soon taken over by an oversized bassinet, changing table, and all the other infant-care items I never knew about until now. The next problem to solve was finding a day care situation for the baby while Jackie was at school and I was at work. The process opened my eyes big-time to the complex disparity of the child care pecking order—starting at the very top with the full-time live-in nannies, the part-time au pairs, and the live-out nannies to the on-call babysitters (with a wide range of hourly wages and various levels of qualifications), then the private, high-cost day care schools with waiting lists, to the less expensive but still credentialed city-funded child care programs, to probably the least costly: unlicensed care at the homes of women who took kids in for a daily fee. Fortunately, we were able to afford the next-to-the-last option by enrolling Christopher in day care at the Parent-Infant Neighborhood Center not too far from where we lived.

The quality of care was really great, even though I confessed to Jackie that I wanted something more upscale for our child.

"You know, Chris . . ." she began. I knew that tone. Her patience was wearing thin about when was I going to leave the VA. Before the baby arrived, she'd been subtle about it; now she was in full-court press. "What are you holding on to? You know you're not making any more money. Ellis told you he doesn't have any more to pay you." This was true. The National Institutes of Health, which funded our research, had turned down recent grant requests to raise my salary.

"I know," I said, trying to head her off at the pass.

"Stop saying you know and do something! You've got to accept it. You're not planning on a career in medicine, right? You've made up your mind you're not going to pursue this, right? You've got a baby to support and you need more money. So quit and get a better-paying job!"

She was right, though that didn't make it any easier to find a new position. It didn't make it any easier to give up my top-dog status in the laboratory and go to the back of the line at something new where I would have to work my way up again. But finally I began to look in earnest for whatever that next job was going to be. Jackie had every reason to be frustrated, after all. Now that she was studying for her boards to become a practicing dentist she obviously had her own issues with being thrust into motherhood. All her female friends from dental school had gotten board certification and were setting up their practices or marrying into situations with husbands in professional practices. I wasn't there yet, even if I had potential. Trying to understand her feelings, I also had to hold on to my confidence, to know that even if I was still on the come, my time would arrive sooner or later.

因为我们住的是一居室，若放上特大号的摇篮车、折叠餐桌，还有其他各式各样的我从未见过的育婴用品，我们就必须解决居住空间的问题。接下来就是当杰姬在学校上课而我在上班时，必须为孩子找个保姆。这个过程着实令我大开眼界，因为看孩子的方式多种多样，让人眼花缭乱。首先是住在雇主家里的专职保姆，其次是只需供食宿的互惠学生，再次是住在外面的阿姨，然后是随叫随到的保姆(根据小时工资和资质收费)，还有收费高的私立日托学校，再到收费较低但有资质的市立儿童看护机构，收费最低的要数没有营业执照的家庭主妇在家里看护小孩并按天计费。所幸，我们还能付得起倒数第二种的费用，于是便给儿子报了名，白天把他送到母婴邻家看护中心去，而且这离我们的住处也不太远。

那里看护孩子的质量真不错，即便如此，我还是向杰姬讲，希望有条件给孩子提供更好的成长环境。

"克里斯……"她又开始了，我一听到她说话的口气就猜出八九。她已经忍无可忍，希望我马上就离开退伍军人管理署医院。在孩子出世之前，她就已经流露出这个想法。现在她更像是全面逼近，"你还等什么呢？在那赚不到什么钱，艾里斯自己都说没法再给你涨工资了。"这是事实，美国国立卫生研究院负责为我们的项目提供资金，就连这里近期也拒绝了给我提薪的申请。

"我知道，"想让她别再这样针尖麦芒地怨声载道下去。

"不要说你知道，而要去做！你必须接受事实。你没准备在医学上有所作为吧？你已下决心不干这一行了吧？你得抚养孩子，需要更多的钱，所以干脆辞职，找份薪水更高的工作！"

虽然找份新工作绝非易事，但她是对的。放弃我实验室负责人的职位，然后回过头来重头打拼并不轻松。但我还是开始认真考虑下一份工作应该从哪里开始。毕竟杰姬这么说也有她的道理。为拿到专业认证，她正在努力学习，而突然之间要为人母，她也存在种种不适应。她那些大学的女友都已取得认证资格，要么已经在开诊所营业，要么丈夫就是这一行的职业人士。只有我，即便是很有潜力，但目前还一事无成。我试着设身处地为她着想，同时自己必须保持信心，虽然现在还在奋力拼搏，可是相信自己迟早会实现人生目标。

Two opposing drumbeats begin to sound. One of them is the steady, firm bongo beat of family and work, the familiar routine, putting the word out that I'm job hunting, hitting the pavements. The secondary beat is erratic, sometimes barely there, other times booming like a bass drum with the crash of cymbals, the ominous sound of domestic stress. Little arguments arise. Money, not enough of it, not fast enough. Sometimes it's me getting frustrated; sometimes it's her. Jackie runs hot and cold, giving and withholding. She works me; I call her on it. I shut down; she gets defensive. I yell; she punishes. Then it passes, we make love, we move on. Everything's okay again.

Then the arguing picks up, and the dynamic shifts radically one day when I arrive home and am greeted by her announcement: "Chris, this isn't working out, and I don't believe it's ever going to work and maybe you should just move."

Shocked into silence, I glare at her. *What the fuck?*

"You should just move. You shouldn't live here anymore."

That's not going to happen, I promise her. I need to be with my son. She knows that. Looking around, I don't see Christopher. "Where's the baby?" I panic.

"You can't see the baby now."

CAN'T SEE THE BABY? Those words strung together totally infuriate me. What has been a basic family movie with some conflict but mostly humor and love now turns into a horror flick. Dark, powerful feelings of fear and helplessness flood me. I'm standing there not knowing what to do, with anger I can't even quantify or verbalize, when the storm clouds break just as suddenly as they came over. No resolution. No apologies. Almost as if it was some kind of test.

The storm passes. Whatever provoked her ire subsides. We go back to normalcy. But I'm jumpy, not knowing if the next time she's going to threaten to take him and actually do it. All the old fears haunt me. Freddie's on the other side of the country, getting too old and sick to hurt Momma anymore, but I'm still caught up in the cycle of waiting for an ax to fall, not knowing what shock is around the corner. We're heading out to see some friends one day, arguing about whether we should go, and I'm outside on the sidewalk waiting for Jackie to bring six-month-old Christopher out in his baby carrier, and all of a sudden it looks like they're not coming. Oh no, we're not playing that, I roar to that effect, calling up at the apartment.

The minute she emerges from the house, I shock myself by marching over and grabbing the baby carrier with Christopher in it, instigating a tug-of-war between us, while I tell her, "You not gonna take my child from me!"

这时我的生活乐章仿佛有两种截然相反的节奏同时响起。一个是平稳坚定的邦戈鼓，也就是家庭工作这些日常的琐事，我在拼命找工作，孜孜不倦。另一个鼓点有些古怪，有时几乎毫无声响，有时突然迸发出尖利刺耳的声音，这就是家庭压力使然。争吵倒是不多了，但是钱永远不够用。有时我深受打击，灰心丧气；有时是她颓废不前。杰姬对我的态度时冷时热，反复无常，忽而主动爱抚，忽而冷言冷语，退避三舍。我闭口不言，她就喋喋不休。我大声反击，她反唇相讥。然后烟消云散，鱼水之欢，和好如初，继续生活，一切又恢复了往日的平静。

然后又开始争吵，我们之间的矛盾急剧升级。一天我刚进家门她就喊叫起来："克里斯，这不行。我不相信这能行得通，也许你应该搬走。"

我惊得说不出话来，眼睛瞪着她，心想，这又是怎么了？

"你必须搬走，别再住这儿了。"

我是绝对不会离开的，我承诺过，我要和儿子在一起。这她是知道的。我环顾了一下房间，没有看见小克里斯多夫，便惊慌地问："孩子在哪呢？"

"你现在不能见他。"

不能见孩子？这几个字彻底把我激怒了。家里原本上演着家庭轻喜剧，虽然冲突不断，但主色调还是幽默和关爱，可现在转瞬成了恐怖片。我顿时觉得黑暗袭来，一种恐惧和无助涌上心头，我站在那里，不知如何是好，气得一句话也说不出来。一切来得太过突然，仿佛忽然乌云密布，狂风暴雨马上就要来袭。没有任何预兆，也没有道歉，一切说变就变。

风暴过去了，不管是什么惹恼了她，现在她的愤怒平息了，我们又恢复了正常。但我却坐立不安，不知下次她是否真会把孩子带走。我心头又再隐隐作痛。弗莱迪住在西海岸，他现在老态龙钟，又疾病缠身，再也没法伤害妈妈了。但我仍忐忑不安，不知还会有什么意外发生。一天我们去见一些朋友，其实我们一直在为到底要不要去而争论不休。我先从家里出来，站在街边等着杰姬推婴儿车带六个月的儿子过来。刹那间，我似乎有种他们再也不会过来的感觉。不要开这样的玩笑，我一路跑上楼梯，叫喊着让杰姬下来。

她从房子里一出来，我都没想到自己竟会一把抓住婴儿车，要把孩子抢过来。我们之间仿佛展开了一场拉锯战，我冲着她大喊："你休想把孩子从我这里夺走！"

This may be the ugliest thing that I have ever done in my life, an act I will never forgive myself for. There aren't even words to explain to her, to my son, or to myself how wrong I am. But this is primal shit. That big banging drum of discord is all I hear as I finally wrest the baby carrier from her and carry him down the block and the next and the next until I spot a church and take a seat on the steps. I complain to my six-month-old son, "Man, this is fucked up! Is it gonna be like this forever?"

Christopher furrows his brow, as if trying to understand, gurgling unintelligibly.

I explain, "I can't let nobody take you from me."

He understands, I think, by the way he squints his eyes in recognition. Or maybe he's exhausted and needs to sleep.

In any case, there's only one truth that matters: he's my son and I love him, and I'm never going to leave him, no matter the cost.

Eventually I walk him back to the house, facing the fear thing, the weight of the unknown, that has come back with a vengeance, as I mentally square off with the problem, just as I did as a child, by giving myself something pragmatic to do. Money, that's the remedy, I realize.

In the months that followed, I supplemented what I was making at the VA with odd jobs, anything extra that came up, as I had in the past. To save on the cost of rent and give ourselves more floor space, we moved to Berkeley, where we were able to find a small house off an alley that had an unlikely patch of rosebushes in front. With the money situation eased, we were able to get an economy-sized sedan, nothing fancy, so we could commute to San Francisco for work and school.

Still looking for a position that would be a step up from research and keep me in medicine, I tried to cheer myself on, figuring that if I could just apply myself to the right thing, the money would be there and the pressure would ease up. Things weren't great with Jackie, but at this point the need for more money was coming from me, not her. As the sole breadwinner, not only was I responsible for the three of us, but I was paying much more attention to what was coming in and what was going out. In the past, when I basically only had me to think about—even when Sherry and I pooled our resources—it was a very different ball game. This was about putting food on the table for my growing child, Jackie, and me. More important, it was about creating a plan to provide for them in the future so we didn't have to live paycheck to paycheck.

I was hopeful, determined, focused. But something was holding me back, an old ball and chain that I had refused to recognize all this time—even with Jackie's doubts about how I couldn't know what it meant to be a father if I never had one. Had it not been for Christopher and a book I was reading to him out on the stoop one afternoon a short while after his first birthday, I might never have acknowledged how much the no-daddy blues was still plaguing me.

这也许是我做过的最不光彩的事情，这让我永远也无法原谅自己。我甚至都无法向她、向儿子甚至向自己解释这样做是多么的愚蠢。一阵肉搏之后，最后我从她手里抢过婴儿车，不知所措地带着儿子走过一个街区又一个街区，直到来到一个教堂门前，然后在台阶上坐了下来。这时我脑子里嗡嗡直响，只能向六个月大的儿子发着牢骚："老兄，实在太糟了！我们永远都会这样吗？"

小克里斯多夫皱着眉头，好像不大明白我在说些什么，嘴里发出咯咯的声音。

我又解释说："我不会让任何人把你带走的。"

我想他明白了，因为他歪着脑袋看着我，似懂非懂，或许是他累了想睡觉。

无论怎样，至关重要的是：他是我儿子，我爱他，我永远也不会离开他，不管抚养他要花多大代价，我都在所不惜。

面对着内心的恐惧，想到未来的不可预测，反而激起我的斗志，我准备要采取攻势。就像小时候那样，我此时需要考虑一些更实际的问题。钱，我要挣更多的钱。

接下来的几个月，我在医院工作之余，又找了些兼职工作。这种事情我以前也做过，我拼命挣钱。为节省租房的开销，住得更宽敞些，我们搬到了伯克利，在那找了所小路附近的小房子，屋外居然还长着蔷薇丛。随着经济状况的缓解，我们买了辆普通的经济型轿车，因此就能到旧金山去工作和学习。

我努力调整自己的情绪，仍希望能找到比实验室研究工作高级些的职务，而且还能继续留在医学行业里。如果能从事适合自己的工作，那么经济上就会好转，生活压力也会得到缓解。杰姬的状况也不大好，但此时需要我来赚更多的钱，而不是她。我是家里唯一养家糊口的人，不仅对我们三个人负有责任，而且也要操心每月收支平衡。过去，我基本上只为自己考虑，甚至我和雪莉一起生活时，都是如此。可现在情况完全不同了，家里有嗷嗷待哺的孩子，还要养活杰姬和自己。更重要的是，现在还要为将来制订计划，不能只靠这点微薄的工资过活。

我信心十足，全神贯注。但还有件事情让我耿耿于怀，也是我一直拒绝承认的一个问题，因为就连杰姬都觉得如果我从未有过父亲，怎能当好父亲。要不是因为克里斯多夫，要不是在他一岁生日后的一个下午，我俯下身子给他讲故事时用的那本书，我可能永远都无法知道没有父亲的痛苦仍在深深地折磨自己。

The PURSUIT of HAPPYNESS

Earlier we'd been sitting outside in the shade, playing with a ball, spending some time together, letting the California breeze cool us off, and I had an overwhelming feeling of joy as I paused just to look at Christopher. We hadn't cut his hair yet, and it was a long floppy 'fro that waved like a flag in the wind as he played without care or fear. The thought that flashed in my senses was, *God, this must be what heaven is like.* Nothing mattered except that I was here in this time and place, being with this beautiful little boy who was everything in the world to me. The idea occurred to me that this was something that was supposed to be passed down from generation to generation, fathers playing ball with their sons, sitting side by side to look at books together. It just hadn't happened when I was a son.

But now I had a son who loved to read and wanted to look at one of his favorite picture books.

In his slightly coherent babble, Christopher asked, "Who 'dat, Poppa?" or something along those lines as he pointed to an illustration of a colt standing with his family of horses.

To explain the concept of family to him, I pointed too, showing him the colt, the stallion, and the mare: "That's the little horse, and this is the horse's father, and the horse has a mother."

Christopher nodded, eyes bright, pointing with me as I repeated the identities of the horse family.

"Right! And, Christopher, you have a father and a mother. The little horse has a mother, and the little horse has a father. Just like you."

As if he understood exactly, he pointed and said, "Momma," and, "Poppa."

Well, this was amazing. So I went further, telling him that everyone in the world had a mother and father like that little horse. "Momma has a mother, and Momma has a father," I began, wondering how best to explain the concept of grandparents to a one-year-old.

Just then Christopher turned his face up to mine, and with a questioning look in his eyes, he pointed to me, as if waiting for me to say that I had a mother and a father too.

The way he looked just rocked me off my seat. The irony was that I had always imagined I would meet my father one day, even if it was just to confront him about where he'd been. But here I was, almost twenty-eight years old, and I had never met him. How could I meet him? I didn't know. Was he alive? Didn't know that either. Didn't know where he was or what he looked like. But the moment my son made his precocious comment, I knew it was time.

At work in my office at the lab the following day, I called directory information for Thomas Turner in Monroe, Louisiana. That was all I had finagled out of Moms all these years.

开始的时候，我们一直坐在外面的树阴下玩球，沐浴在加州怡然的和风里，一起度过美好时光。当我停下来看儿子的时候，我感到一种令人陶醉的莫名兴奋。我们还没给他理过发，当他无忧无虑玩耍时那头蓬松的头发在风中飘荡。我突然冒出个念头：天堂一定是这个样子的。除了此时此地和这个漂亮的小家伙在一起，再没有什么比这更重要的事情了，因为对我来说他就意味着整个世界。我感到这是一种世代相传的血脉联系，父子一起玩球，并排坐下一起看书。可我小时候却从未经历过这些。

然而，我儿子喜欢看书，拿着一本他最喜欢的图画书。儿子奶声奶气地问："那是谁，爸爸？"他指着看图识字中的小马一家问道。

为了向他解释家的概念，我也指着小马驹、公马和母马说："那是马儿子，这是马爸爸，还有马妈妈。"

克里斯多夫点点头，眨着眼睛，当我一遍遍念着小马驹一家三口时，他也跟着我一起用手指着那些插图。

"对！克里斯多夫，你也有爸爸妈妈。小马驹也有妈妈爸爸，就像你一样。"

他好像听懂了一样，指着图片说："妈妈，爸爸。"

这太神奇了，所以我进一步告诉他世上每个人都像小马驹一样有自己的妈妈爸爸。"妈妈有自己的妈妈和爸爸，"我说道，想着该如何向一岁大的孩子解释清楚外祖父母的概念。

就在那时，克里斯多夫昂起头看着我，流露出一种疑惑的眼神，他用手指着我，好像在等着我开口说我也有妈妈和爸爸。

他看着我的表情令我不安，我甚至从椅子上站了起来。要知道，我总想象着有一天会见到自己的父亲，要质问他这些年都去哪里了，让他正视这个问题。但如今我已经28岁了，却还从未见过他。我怎么才能见到他呢？我不知道。他还活着吗？我也不知道。不知道他在哪里，连长什么样子我都不清楚。不过当儿子像小大人一样提出这样的疑问时，我觉得是时候了。

第二天在实验室上班时，我拿起电话，直接打给了路易斯安那州门罗市，询问有关托马斯·特纳的信息。那是我这些年来从妈妈嘴里小心套出来的有关父亲的全部信息。

The operator had five listings. I asked for all five, deciding to just go down the list and take my chances.

When I made the first call, I asked the elderly person who answered, "Is Thomas Turner there?" "Thomas Turner is dead," said the elderly person, to whom I apologized.

Hoping that I hadn't missed the boat, I made the next call, explaining to the woman who answered that I was looking for a Thomas Turner who may have known Bettye Gardner.

The woman felt comfortable telling me, "You know what? I can think of two Thomas Turners. One drinks, and the other one used to drink, but he quit."

Going with my gut, I asked her how I'd get in touch with the sober Thomas Turner and found out where he lived. I gave the address to an information operator to make sure I had the right phone numbers.

Looking at it, I took a deep breath, not sure how to start if the real Thomas Turner answered the phone. Not knowing, I dialed the number and heard the sound of a phone being picked up and a deep male voice answering, "Hello?"

All I could think to say was: "Do you know Bettye Gardner? I'm her son Chris and I'm trying to find my father. Do . . ." Before I could finish, I was interrupted.

"Yeah," my father said. "I've been waiting for you to call a long time."

* * *

Just by virtue of having gotten to the bottom of a nearly twenty-eight-year-old mystery, a dramatic shift in energy took place in my life almost overnight. The man I'd met on the telephone wasn't much more than a voice, but he had encouraged me to come down to Louisiana to meet him in person, along with several siblings I never knew about.

While I promised to do that as soon as I could make the arrangements, what had been an insurmountable process of finding my new niche in the working world was all of a sudden a cakewalk. With my sights fixed on the possibilities of making my way in the business world, I quickly landed a job as a sales rep for a medical equipment and supply company called CMS. Based in San Bruno, in the heart of the then-developing Silicon Valley, CMS sold primarily to laboratories and hospitals. I was going to be starting out at just under $30,000 a year, nearly twice what I'd made in research, with the potential of making twice that—what the top earners were making.

话务员列出了五张单子，我问来了所有相关信息，准备挨个试，碰碰运气。

打通第一个电话时，我问接电话的老人："托马斯·特纳在吗？"

"托马斯·特纳已经去世了，"那个老人说，我忙向他道了歉。

希望自己没有永远地错失了良机，我于是打了第二个电话，向那个接电话的女人解释说要找一个名叫托马斯·特纳的人，他有可能认识贝蒂·加德纳。

对方告诉我，"我能想到的有两个托马斯·特纳。一个经常酗酒，另一个过去常喝，但现在已经戒掉了。"

我凭着直觉，问道怎么才能与这个清醒的托马斯·特纳取得联系，还问了他的住处。我把地址告诉了电话咨询台。

看着电话号码，我深呼一口气，不知道如果真的是这个托马斯·特纳接电话我该如何开口。我忐忑不安地拨通了电话，听到对方拿起话筒，一个男士深沉的声音传了过来，"喂？"

我所能想到的就是："您认识贝蒂·加德纳吗？我是她的儿子克里斯，正在找我的父亲，您……"话音未落，对方便打断了我。

"是的"，我父亲说，"我一直在等你的电话，已经等了很久了。"

* * *

这个埋藏了 28 年的秘密，在这一刻谜底终于揭开了。几乎一夜之间我的生命便发生了戏剧性的变化。电话那端的人并非只是说说而已，他还邀我亲自到路易斯安那去见他，那里还有几个我从未听说过的兄弟姐妹。

我答应他安排好之后就会尽快赶过去。然而，原以为重新找准工作定位难于上青天，可突然间一切变得如此轻松。我一心想转战商场，于是很快就找到一份销售代理的工作，为一家名叫 CMS 的医疗仪器供应公司效力。CMS 位于圣布诺，也就是当时正处于发展建设中的硅谷腹地，我主要是向实验室和医院销售设备。起步年薪就高达 3 万美元，几乎是我实验室工作的两倍，而且干得好，甚至还能翻一番。

Of course, those earners had been in the trenches for twenty years—building up their territories, books, and relationships—and I never thought of myself as a natural salesman. Then again, I'd been to college with every person I'd ever met, as Will Rogers said about myself, and had known some unbelievable characters who could sell you the raindrops falling on your head. I could learn to sell. Plus, I knew the power of information and knew how to spot the leaders and how to learn what they did and how they did it to be successful. Adding even more to my confidence was the fact that although I didn't know the business lingo, I was extremely proficient in medical language and understood the mindset of the buyers as well as the sales veterans at CMS.

So, goodbye to the future Dr. Chris Gardner, goodbye to wearing scrubs. My only lasting regret was the fact that I did have the hands. But looking at myself in the mirror in my business attire—a nice jacket, not a bad-looking tie—I was encouraged. This was a whole new venue, a challenge. The feeling of potential lit my fire again.

As a sales rookie, I had the triple whammy of being handed a brand-new territory in which to build relationships, representing a company not established in this territory, and being the only black person employed by CMS. By this point, I was a seasoned veteran at being the only African American in a cadre of white professionals, so that was a nonissue. The main issue was that I was starting from absolute scratch, which I discovered overnight by picking up some fundamentals about sales: (a) buyers like to buy from people they know, and (b) they like to buy established products.

Instead of being discouraged, I found the competition exciting. As far as I was concerned, I was really happy to have a shot, so rather than honing in on the challenges, my focus was fine-tuned to the questions: How do I get more business? What information do I need to expand my opportunities and build relationships? In the past I'd been able to find an expert and ask those questions, but at CMS that wasn't the case. As it turned out, the sales managers— who made a percentage of what the reps made—spent most of their time reinforcing their top producers. With rookies like me, the manager handed me my book, patted me on the shoulder, and said, "Go get 'em."

OJT once again, I dove in, clocking hundreds of miles a week on my sporty new maroon Nissan hatchback packed to the gills with brochures, supply samples, and equipment to show in demos, traveling daily from Berkeley to every far corner of Silicon Valley and back, unloading and loading sales materials countless times a day. Building on the philosophy of hitting that anvil, I agreed with the belief that sales success came down to a numbers game. What I also learned in making repeat calls was that the more down-to-earth and personable yet respectful I was, and the more I remembered names of secretaries and little details about buyers, the better my chances. My sales figures started to take off.

当然，那些干得好的顶级销售已经在这行打拼了 20 年了，都有了自己的地盘、客户群，建立起很好的人脉关系，而我却是初出茅庐。然后我又开始从头学起，向周围每个人学习，这其中还遇见一些神人，他们甚至有把稻草说成金条的本事。我在一点一滴地学习销售技巧。此外，我还了解知识和信息的力量，知道如何识别高手，去积极了解他们从事的工作以及取得成功的原因。让我备感自信的是，虽然我对经商一窍不通，但是我有医学背景，并懂得 CMS 这些医疗设备买卖双方的思维模式和心理需求。

所以，再见了，未来的克里斯·加德纳医生，再见了，低人一等的克里斯·加德纳。长久以来我唯一遗憾的就是没有一技之长。但看着镜子里身穿商界职业装的自己，夹克质量不错，领带也还看得过去，我就深受鼓舞。这是个全新的领域，全新的挑战，我内心再次燃起希望之火。

初入销售这一行，我需要面对重重考验，先要建立起人脉关系，公司的产品在当地没有什么知名度，而且还是 CMS 公司唯一的黑人员工，我几乎举步维艰。不过对于我的黑人身份而言，我已经习惯在一群白人中做事，所以这并不是太大问题。主要问题在于我需要从头开始，从学习销售的基本原则开始：一是买家愿意从熟人那里购买产品；二是他们喜欢购买知名的产品，而这两方面我都不具备。

我并没有灰心失意，相反备感欢欣鼓舞。就我而言，我真的很高兴能拥有这么一个前进的动力，所以与其被这些挑战吓倒，还不如将注意力集中到怎么拿到更多的生意上来。我需要怎样的信息来拓宽机会，建立人脉？过去我能向专家咨询，但这在 CMS 就行不通了。因为在这里，销售经理一方面可以在营销代表完成的业绩中占有一定的份额，而他们会花大力气巩固与大客户的关系。而对于像我这样的新手，经理则会递给我一本书，拍拍肩膀说："自己去看吧。"

我又要边学边干了，车里塞满产品图册、样品、演示设备之类的东西，开着我的新款运动系尼桑，每天都要跑上几百里的路程，从伯克利跑到硅谷里每个偏远的角落，然后再赶回来，每天把这些材料无数次地搬上搬下。本着持之以恒的理念，我也认准了销售业绩归根到底就是数字游戏。在和客户的反复电话沟通中，我还悟出了自己越求真务实、彬彬有礼，秘书的名字和买主的细节记住得越多，那么我的机会也就越多。我的销售额开始上升了。

On the downside, the competitive atmosphere extended to after hours, when managers and reps headed out to see who could drink the most. The schmoozing and drinking thing was part of the game, I understood, but it wasn't for me. Now that I was in business, I was serious about increasing my numbers, about making money. That didn't earn me any awards at CMS, but the guys in hiring at Van Waters and Rogers, a better-established competitor in the medical equipment and supply field, were impressed with my ambition and hired me on.

Not too long after starting the new job, I was able to purchase a plane ticket for me and Christopher to travel to Monroe, Louisiana. During a long, nerve-wracking flight from San Francisco to Memphis and then another puddle-jump to Monroe—with Christopher unusually calm, sitting on my lap the whole way—I reviewed the indignities of a childhood filled with being told by Freddie Triplett that I didn't have no "goddamn daddy." What was I going to say to my biological father? On the phone, I hadn't gotten around to asking why he never called or tried to meet me, even when he said that my brothers and sisters had heard so much about me. And what was I going to do if the scene got too heavy and I wanted to split? If Christopher got antsy?

Really clueless about what to expect, the moment of truth arrives as I lead my son down the rolling stairway of the prop plane and look over to see *him* standing there. Six-six, 280 pounds. Black as night. A country man who has been in Louisiana forever, he towers in front of me—nothing like I imagined.

The first thing that crosses my mind: well, I guess I won't punch him—which as a kid was always the first thing I envisioned doing to him.

His presence is huge, stunning. Beside him are two of his daughters, my half-sisters. Between me and Christopher and those three, we all look just like each other. Thomas Turner looks like he had just spit me out, there is no doubt.

As awkward as this encounter is, he seems fairly comfortable with it. That's because, I later learn, this scene has been repeated more than a few times before. The joke my sisters tell me later is that it's pretty much like the Olympic games: every four years somebody shows up. No need to ask questions, you just look at them, see the family resemblance, open the door, and let them on in.

Even with my scientific background now, I am still amazed by the miracle of genetics. My sisters Deborah and Janice and I really do look like identical triplets. When we get to Thomas Turner's house and sit down to talk, Deb says, "You know what? You look more like Pop than any of us. You even got hair on the back of your hands just like Pop."

当销售额出现下降趋势时，竞争就会愈发白热化，经理和销售代表就会加班加点，陪客户喝酒吃饭，以便拿到更多的份额。我明白饭桌上的沟通也是游戏的一部分，但这却不适合我。在商言商，我会努力提高业绩来赚钱。虽然我这番努力并没有为我在 CMS 赢得任何奖励回报，但同是医疗设备供应商的凡·沃特斯罗格斯公司的人力资源部却对我颇为赞赏，并雇佣了我，这可是 CMS 的一个强大竞争对手。

干上这份新工作不久，我终于可以买上机票，让自己和儿子前往路易斯安那州门罗寻找父亲了。从旧金山到孟菲斯的旅程非常漫长，接着我们又换乘飞机赶往门罗。一路上儿子异常平静，整个行程都坐在我的大腿上，而我脑子里一直想着弗莱迪在我小时候总是用我没有父亲这件事羞辱我，见到生父，我该说些什么呢？在电话里，甚至当他说我的兄弟姐妹听过很多关于我的事情时，我也没有转弯抹角地问他为什么没有来过电话，或者想法来找我。如果认亲场面过于沉重，或者我就此同他断绝关系，或者儿子对此难于接受，我该怎么办？

我对即将发生的事情忐忑不安，领着儿子顺着旋梯走下那架飞机的那一刻，我看到他站在那里，终于一切真相大白了。父亲他身高近两米，大概 250 斤这样的大块头，皮肤黝黑，是个从未离开过路易斯安那州的乡下人，他就在我面前站着，和我想象中的样子截然不同。

我想到的第一件事是：我不会揍他，儿时我总是想像着见到他的第一件事情就是要狠狠地揍他一顿，方解心头之恨。

一同来接机的一行人非常扎眼，他身边是我同父异母的两个姐姐，我和儿子与他们三个相貌出奇地相像，我们几个和托马斯·特纳几乎是一个模子里刻出来的似的。

虽然这种会面令人尴尬，可父亲却似乎相当坦然。后来我才知道，那是因为这种认亲的事情已不是第一次了。我的姐姐们戏谑地告诉我说这就跟举办奥运会似的：每四年就会有人现身，不用问任何问题，你只要看看他们的长相，就可以打开门，让他们进来就可以了。

即便我有着医学背景知识，可还是对这种遗传奇迹感到惊奇。姐姐黛博拉和贾尼斯与我看上去真的很像三胞胎。我们一起回到托马斯·特纳住的地方，坐下来攀谈起来，黛博拉说："你知道吗？比起我们你更像老爸。就连你手背上的汗毛和他都一样。"

Laughing, I can't believe they're checking me out to that degree, and I look at my hands and over at his. They're right!

Over the next four days of our visit I get to know the cast of characters who inhabit this very different version of an all-black *Happy Days* show, Louisiana style. With it hot and humid like nothing I've ever experienced, not even in the Navy in Orlando, our clothes could have just come out of the washing machine. Even our hair and fingernails are sweating.

As the days flew by, I couldn't help calling Moms to let her know that I'd made it over to Rayville, her old hometown, and was spending time with my father. Before coming, I had told her that I was going to Louisiana—not only to meet him for myself but so Christopher could meet his grandfather. Now that I was actually here, it was important to let her know that I'd put the pieces together. She was happy for me. But when I asked, "Momma, you want to say hello to him?" she didn't hesitate before answering, "No." Her unqualified response told me little more about their relationship, whether or not it was a relationship, and that was the full, final stop to the discussion. I would never know. The legacy of the family's "don't ask, don't tell" policy continued.

Getting to know the soil from which I had first sprung included a trip out to Delhi, where the absence of lights, neon, street signs, and cars turned the nighttime blacker than anything I'd ever seen; the stars looked like lightbulbs clearly outlining all the famous constellations. Blown away, I couldn't stop staring up, wondering what my life would have been like if I had been raised here. We met the family matriarch, my grandmother, a tiny, exquisite black woman named Ora Turner. Though she had never set eyes on me before, her greeting was to spread her arms wide and hug me to her. I was her grandchild.

"I use to ask yo' daddy where you was," my grandmomma said, stepping back to take me in, nodding in approval. "He didn't know nothin'. I use to always ask him where you at."

The next thing she needed to know was where I had been baptized. For a moment, I couldn't remember.

Alarmed, my grandmother, a fervent Christian woman, proposed, "Boy, I ought to take you out there right now, take you outside, back out to that creek, and baptize you myself. Lord, have mercy!"

That scared the shit out of me. A pitch-black night, nothing but the stars and the moon for light, and me getting dunked in a creek? That was all I needed to hear in order to remember being baptized at TT's church when I was six years old. Lord had mercy and my grandmother was satisfied.

我大笑着，真不敢相信他们打量我竟然到了这个程度，我看了看自己的手，又看了看他的，这确实太不可思议了！

在我们此行接下来的四天里，我认识了这一大家子人，他们仿佛是在上演一场完全不同的黑人版"快乐时光"秀，但呈现出路易斯安那的独特风情。我从未经历过如此炎热潮湿的气候，甚至在奥兰多海军服役期间也不曾有过，我们的衣服好像刚从洗衣机里捞出来一样，连头发和指甲都在往外冒汗。

随着一天天这样的过去，我忍不住给妈妈打电话，说我到了她的故乡雷维尔，并且和父亲呆在一起。此行之前我告诉过她将要去路易斯安那州，去见父亲，让儿子也可以见见爷爷。现在我已经到了，必须让她知道我们已经破镜重圆了。她为我感到高兴。但当我问道："妈妈，您想跟他打招呼吗？"她却断然拒绝了，这令我几乎无法理解他们之间的关系，或者是否还有任何关系，此次谈话就此结束。其中的奥秘，我永远也不会知道，家里"不要问，不要说"的传统仍在大行当道。

为了进一步了解我出生的故土，我还去了德尔希，那里没有路灯、霓虹灯、街道标记。没有车灯，夜里就是漆黑一片，比起我所见过的任何黑暗都有过之而无不及，星星却异常明亮，有名的星座都能清晰地识别出来。我忍不住惊奇地仰望天空，想象着如果自己在这里长大生活会是什么样。我们去看望了我的祖母，一个矮小精干的黑人妇女，名叫奥拉·特纳。虽然她以前从未见过我，但她还是张开手臂拥抱我以示欢迎，我可是她的孙子啊。

"我以前总是问你爸爸你在哪里，"奶奶说，退后一步点头示意我进去。"他什么也不知道，我也总是问起他你现在在哪里。"

接下来她就问我是在哪里受洗礼的，这我一时还想不起来了。

奶奶是个忠诚的基督徒，她提出来，"孩子，我现在应该带你出去，到小溪旁，亲自为你洗礼。上帝，宽恕他吧！"

这可把我吓坏了。一个漆黑的夜晚，伴着月色和星光，再把我泡在溪水中？我突然想起自己是在六岁那年，到缇缇舅妈教堂去接受的洗礼，仁慈的主，奶奶终于满意了。

Besides getting to know Deb and Jan, I met my other half-siblings—my brothers Junior and Dale and my sister Mary, who lived over in Shreveport. There were aunts and uncles and cousins too—one cousin so fine I regretted that we were related. Wherever we went, everyone was generous and hospitable, treating me like a celebrity. The social habits and pace of life seemed different from Milwaukee, but the more we hung out and talked, as the family stories and the jokes started to roll, the fewer differences I saw. As much as I considered myself a Gardner through and through, there were aspects of myself that I could now see had come from the Turner side of my family.

The most remarkable moment in the trip came one night close to the end when I decided to take Christopher with me on the train to Shreveport to meet my sister Mary, and my father went to the station with us. Not too late yet, it was already one of those tar-black country nights with only twinkling slivers of stars and moonglow to light our surroundings as we waited out by the tracks behind the station. Off to the side was a set of tracks heading off in another direction that Christopher found interesting. We were early, so I saw nothing wrong with my son going to check out the rails with his grandfather, especially since the two had gotten comfortable with each other right away.

The sight of the two of them walking along the railroad tracks made me catch my breath. There was my father, then in his midfifties, massive like a black oak tree, patriarch to more offspring than any of us may have known, walking with my son, a fourteen-month-old toddler, energetic and talkative. My father held Christopher's little fingers protectively, proudly.

As one of those memories that you capture and that remains unchanged through the years, the image of the two of them walking along in that night produced a surprising reaction in me that would come back every time I recalled it. What first flashed in my brain and my heart was—*How come that couldn't have been me? How come I never got a chance to do that?*

As time went on, I recognized that it wasn't anger of course. But I was jealous of my little boy, ridiculous as that was. Below that layer, in the core of my being, was simple hurt. The reservoir that stored all those years of abandonment had been stirred up by that sight and now hurt like hell.

At the airport, as the Louisiana contingency of my family came to see me off, with my sisters making me promise that we wouldn't lose contact, I looked down at Christopher and marveled at how our exchange about fathers and mothers had gotten me here. In that regard, I could take away with me a sense of completion. Even though I couldn't see it yet, a nearly twenty-eight-year-old load of resentment had been lifted. At long last, I let go of the no-daddy blues. I had a daddy, albeit one I didn't know well and never would, but I was no longer a fatherless child. That wasn't my song to sing anymore.

除了黛博拉和贾尼斯之外，我还见到了其他几个同父异母的兄妹，哥哥朱尼尔和戴尔以及我的妹妹玛丽，他们住在申里夫波特，还有婶婶、叔叔和堂兄弟姐妹们。有个堂妹人很好，很遗憾我们却是亲戚。无论我们去哪，人人都慷慨好客，仿佛我是个名人一样。这里的生活习俗和节奏与密尔沃基完全不同。但随着我对家族的了解越多，谈天的逐步深入，大家交往和交流的越多，我看到的差异就越少，我就越发觉得自己是加德纳一家的人，包括我身上的许多方面都继承了家族的特点。

一天晚上，我决定带儿子乘火车到申里夫波特去见我的妹妹玛丽，此次行程的幸福时光也接近尾声了。父亲陪着我们一起到车站。天色还不太晚，我们来到车站后面的铁轨旁候车。夜幕下只有星星闪闪发光，月色皎洁，照亮我们的四周。一旁是通往另一个方向的铁轨，儿子觉得很好玩。离列车到站的时间还早，所以儿子和父亲就一起过去看看铁轨，他俩从一开始就很融洽，非常默契。

他俩沿着铁道漫步的景象令我屏息凝神。那是我的父亲，50多岁的他犹如一棵橡树伟岸魁梧，他是许多我们仍未必知晓的兄弟姐妹的父亲。和他一起漫步的是我的儿子，一个14个月大，蹒跚学步的孩子，精力充沛，爱说爱笑。父亲疼爱地牵着克里斯多夫的小手，十分骄傲。

这幅场景一直留在我的脑海里，这么多年来从未改变过，他俩在那个夜晚一起漫步的情景令我异乎惊喜，每次回想起来都记忆犹新，历历在目。我心里闪现的第一个念头就是：为什么不是我？为什么我从来没有这样的机会？

随着时间的推移，我当然意识到那并非出于什么愤怒，但我却嫉妒自己的小儿子，这的确有些荒谬可笑。但我的内心确实很伤感。压抑了这些年来被抛弃的感觉瞬间都激荡起来，让我非常痛苦。

在路易斯安那机场，令我感到意外的是，一家人都来为我们送行。几个姐姐让我常与家人联系。低头看着儿子，我终于可以对有关父母的问题泰然处之。从这方面而言，我可以带着完整的自我离开了。即使我自己没有真正意识到，但近乎28年的怨恨就此烟消云散。经过这么多年的煎熬之后，我终于摆脱了没有父亲的苦闷。我有爸爸，尽管我还不了解他，而且永远也不会真正了解他，但我再也不是没有父亲的孩子了。没有父亲的烦恼永远不会再回来了。

Christopher and I flew back to California—a trip that seemed to take half the time it had taken to get to Louisiana. There was no denying that a circle had been closed. It was somewhat fractured, not a perfect circle, but gaps had been filled in my understanding of who I was and where I came from. Though many questions lingered about what might have been if things had happened differently in my upbringing, my preoccupation wasn't with that part of my past anymore. Yes, on that plane I was still hurting bad, thinking of my father and my son walking along those railroad tracks, hand in hand, as I turned and twisted that question in my mind like a Rubik's cube: *How come that couldn't have been me?*

But by the time the plane touched down, the hurt had begun to fade, and I felt renewed and revived—ready to take on the world, with a level of confidence and clarity of vision that I had never had before. Great things were right around the corner, I just knew it.

我和儿子飞回加州，这段行程似乎比来时缩短了很多。毋庸置疑，故事终于尘埃落定，虽有些裂痕，并非完美，但我知道了自己是谁，了解自己来自哪里，可以弥补这样的遗憾。虽然许多问题仍然挥之不去，比如如果在我成长过程中这一切未曾发生，那么我的生活又会怎样，我不会抓着自己的过去死死纠缠了。是的，在飞机上我仍痛心疾首，不停地想着父亲和儿子沿着铁道一起漫步，手牵手的画面，我脑子里就像魔方一样反复扭转出那个问题：为什么他牵着的不是我？

但是当飞机着陆，伤感便褪去了，我感到重获新生，带着自己从未有过的自信和视野，准备接纳这个世界。我知道，幸福美好就要到来了。

Chapter 9
Turned Out(advanced)

Bob Russell—the guy at the top of the heap at Van Waters and Rogers—walked around like he was the God almighty NBC peacock.

I didn't get what it was about him that made him such a fantastic producer, but when I found out that he was not only getting all the business but making $80,000 a year—compared to my $30,000 starting salary—I had to figure out what his secret was.

While I had thought that my trip to meet my father would give me and Jackie the break we needed to appreciate each other more and help put everything in perspective, the stress picked up exactly where it had been before—the same patterns, the same arguments. Her frustration with herself, with me, and with how her dreams weren't panning out always translated in my mind to the need for more money. So when I found out what Bob Russell was grossing, $80,000 became the magic number for me. *If I can ever get there, that's all I'll ever want,* I thought. At that time, I couldn't even dream any bigger. But if Bob Russell could do it, I could too.

第九章
人生的抉择（下）

鲍勃·罗素是凡·沃特斯罗格斯公司的高管，他走起路来就像是美国全国广播公司的那个孔雀标志一样，洋洋自得，自以为了不起。

我不清楚他到底有什么本事，能干出如此业绩，但我知道他不仅掌控着所有的商业运作，而且每年还能赚到8万美金，这让我3万美金的起始年薪相形见绌，所以我一定要探个究竟。

原以为我去探望自己的生父，能让我和杰姬有机会彼此冷静下来，能够珍惜对方，有助于从对方的角度考虑问题。结果问题又卷土重来，以同样的方式，同样的争吵再度爆发。在我看来，她所有对自己、对我的不满，对她未能实现的梦想的不满，最终都是因为对金钱无休止的渴求在作祟。所以当我知道鲍勃·罗素能挣8万美金，我简直都不敢相信。心想，有朝一日自己能挣这么多，也就别无所求了。在那一刻，那就是我的全部梦想。既然鲍勃·罗素能够做到，我也能够做到。

My confidence was apparently not shared by my sales manager Patrick, who had also apparently not been involved in the decision to hire me. It probably didn't help that I was a tall, black man and he was just a little bit taller than a midget.

A fussy Irish American, Patrick was what I called a "pen guy." He punctuated every sentence he uttered with a *click-CLICK* of his pen, emphasizing each and every point he made—and they were numerous since he knew everything and the new guys like me didn't know anything—with additional clicks.

What I learned wasn't so much how to be a better salesman as how not to be intimidated. So when Mr. Pen Guy started sending the message that he wasn't digging me, I found a way to let him know, *Hey, I'm not digging you either.* If he made a mildly snide remark, instead of really barking back, my reaction was to bend down, subtly reminding him that I was tall and he was short, and to say, in mock politeness, "I'm sorry. What was that?"

Patrick's face inevitably turned red. Of course, when he really pissed me off, I was less subtle as I cupped my hand to my ear, bent over, and said, "What? I can't hear you down there, all the way down there."

His only response in those instances was to *click-CLICK* away. Somehow my antagonizing him convinced him to teach me a thing or two about selling the Van Waters and Rogers line. During the middle of a sales call with a buyer, after I'd already started to take the order, he'd interrupt, reminding me, for example, that it was important to stress that even though competitors had the same products, Van Waters and Rogers had the superior products at a lower price. Then there was the time he stopped me and asked, "Gardner, where are the samples? You should have brought out the samples before writing the order."

In situations like that, I couldn't go off and ask why he didn't wait to tell me later but had to humiliate me in front of a buyer. Infuriating though it was, I learned by default that it was vital to distinguish the product I was selling from the competition as superior and less expensive. What was more, I learned that there were stages to selling. There were also numerous intangibles. Some of the skills could be learned and developed, but I soon saw the truth of the matter—that the best salespeople are born that way. Not everybody can do it, and not everybody should do it. Did I have what it took? I didn't know yet. But damn, $80,000? What did Bob Russell have that I needed to have?

销售经理帕特里克显然不会欣赏我的自信，很明显，当初不是他决定要雇佣我的。我是个高个子的黑人，可他却不比侏儒高多少，这个事实可对我没什么好处。

帕特里克是个爱挑剔的爱尔兰美国人，我背地里叫他"钢笔侠"，因为他总喜欢把钢笔掰得咔咔响，用咔咔声强调讲话中的每个重点，没完没了。因为他所知道的这些，对像我这样的新人来说，简直是闻所未闻，所以他更要多咔哒几声。

我虽然没从他那里领会什么销售之道，但也学会别被这些花哨东西吓倒。所以当钢笔侠表示他没想和我过不去的时候，我也会想办法让他知道："我也没想和你有过节。" 如果他出言不逊，我也不会直接反驳，而是会俯下身子，巧妙地提醒他我的身高优势，假装很有礼貌地回应："对不起，你说什么？"

帕特里克必然会面红耳赤。当然，如果他真把我惹怒了，我也会失去耐心，故意把手放到耳边，弯下腰来说："什么？我根本什么都听不清啊。"

每当这时，他唯一能做的就是把笔弄得咔咔响。在某种程度上，我越是这么和他对着干，他越要给我露几手，让我看看公司销售该怎么做。在给客户打电话销售的时候，正当我开始准备签订单的一刹那，他会打断我，提醒说，比如：即使竞争对手有着同样的产品，但我们公司的产品质量更胜一筹且价格更优，记住强调这点很重要。有时他会打断我和别人的谈话，故意问道："克里斯，样品在哪里？你在下单前就应该把样品准备好的。"

出现这种情况时，我绝对不能发火，还不能质问他为什么不等会儿告诉我，而非要在客户面前羞辱我。虽然这的确很令人气愤，但我也从中学到，要把公司产品质优价廉的特点凸现出来，才能和其他竞争产品一争高下，这是非常重要的一点。况且，我还了解到销售分不同的阶段。尽管仍有许多不甚明了的东西，我还需要继续努力并掌握一些技巧，不过我很快发现，最好的推销员其实是天生使然。并非人人都可以做这一行，也不是人人都该做这一行。可我自己具备这方面的潜质吗？我自己心里也没底，可是天啊，8万美金？鲍勃·罗素到底有什么本事，我怎么才能学会呢？

Whatever it was, I refused to be deterred, even with having to drive outrageous numbers of miles from Berkeley to every whistle stop in Silicon Valley, from San Mateo to San Jose, mostly down the road from the San Francisco airport. But the most important call I ever made was in the city proper at San Francisco General Hospital, where I went to deliver samples and a catalog to Lars Nielson, who ran a lab we should have been doing some business with. Even though the call went well and I expected to come back for the order, when I exited the building, the math I was doing in my head was telling me that I still had a long way to go to compete with Bob Russell. Yet what options did I have?

Just then, after being momentarily blinded by the sun's glare, I see the red Ferrari 308 circling the parking lot. The owner of the car, dressed in that perfectly tailored suit, who is the beneficiary of my parking spot after he answers my questions—"What do you do?" and "How do you do that?"—is a gentleman by the name of Bob Bridges, a stockbroker with Donaldson, Lufkin & Jenrette, who commands a salary of $80,000 a *month*!

Stop the presses. I don't have to be a math whiz to compare and contrast that with Bob Russell's $80,000 a year. Fuck Bob Russell!

At this stage of my life, I know as much about Wall Street, stocks and bonds, capital markets, and high finance as most people know about the preservation of myocardial high-energy phosphates. But even before I sit down to lunch with Bob Bridges in order to learn more about what exactly a stockbroker does and how to do it well, I'm already seeing myself in that arena. How can it be any different from everything I've ever done before? From working at Heartside Nursing Home and the Navy Hospital at Camp Lejeune in general surgery and the proctology clinic, to heading up a laboratory at the VA Hospital and the University of California Medical Center, to being the up-and-comer doing sales in the Silicon Valley, I've walked into jobs with no knowledge of the fields but have succeeded and done well in all of these areas. Not just done well. Done absolutely fucking fabulously well. No, my monetary success hasn't been overwhelming. But in growth and skill, I've excelled beyond my own expectations.

All that is enough for me to think I can do the same as a stockbroker. Despite the fact that this is the first time the notion has even come up on my radar screen, from here on out there is not one doubt that I have found my calling and that I'm going to be in hot, relentless pursuit of a career in that arena. For reasons I can't begin to explain, I know with every fiber of my being that this is IT.

To the average man or woman on the street, this certainty probably sounds crazy. Besides not having gone to college, I don't know anybody and have no connections or special privileges to help me even get a foot in the door. That is, except for Bob Bridges, who I don't know from Adam, other than the fact that I gave him my parking space.

不管怎样，我都不会气馁，哪怕是没完没了的赶路，从伯克利驱车到硅谷去，路上几乎每站必停，从圣马地奥市到圣何塞市，大多是要一路沿着旧金山机场往下走。但在我以往打过的所有电话中，最重要的就是在城乡交界处的旧金山总医院打的电话，我是去把样品和产品名册送交给拉斯·尼尔森，他开了家实验室，可能会有机会打交道。我去电话初次沟通就很顺利，而且还有望进一步洽谈订货。我走出医院大楼，头脑中飞快地计算出自己离鲍勃·罗素的水平还差很远，还需继续努力，可我别无选择。

就在此时，明晃晃的太阳光让我睁不开眼睛，片刻之后，我看到一辆火红惹眼的法拉利308敞篷车绕着停车场正在找车位。车子的主人，西装革履，穿着非常考究。他回答了我的两个问题："你以什么为业的？"，再有就是："怎么才能做到如此成功？"以此为交换条件，我就让他用了我的车位。这位绅士名叫鲍勃·布里奇斯，是唐纳森拉夫金和詹雷特公司的证券经纪人，一个月就能挣到8万美金。

我顿时轻松很多，鲍勃·罗素8万美金的年收入相形之下，已经不算什么。见鬼吧，鲍勃·罗素！

此时此刻，我对华尔街、股票债券、资本市场和巨额融资知之甚少，这和大多数人不了解如何保存高能心肌磷酸盐是一个道理。但为了解更多关于证券经纪人从业的技巧和经验，我还特意邀请鲍勃·布里奇斯一起共进午餐，可还没等坐下来，我就仿佛看到自己将在证券舞台上大显身手施展才华了。这个行当到底和我曾做过的工作有何差别？从哈特赛护理中心到列尊营海军医院的外科与肛肠科，到在退伍军人管理署医院和加州大学医疗中心建立实验室的工作，再到成为在硅谷做销售的积极进取的推销员，虽然我没有相关从业经验，但却成功进入所有这些领域，并且做得还不错。其实不只如此，我的表现是令人难以置信的出色。虽然我在金钱方面还没有彻底成功，但随着经验的积累和对技巧的掌握，其实我的表现已经超出了自己开始的预期。

想到这些，我信心百倍，自认为可以胜任证券经纪人的工作。尽管事实上我还是第一次听说这个行当，但已经被深深触动，准备就此启程。毫无疑问，我找到了自己的职业归宿，并将意气风发，满腔热情地在那片领域里扬帆远航，去追求自己的事业。虽然很难解释清楚，但我骨子里的每个细胞都知道，就是它了。

一般人如果听到我这种肯定的口气，可能会觉得我是个疯子。我没有上过大学，没什么背景，也没有任何关系能帮到自己，哪怕只是能让我入门都行，可这些都是奢望。幸亏遇见了鲍勃·布里奇斯，尽管当初我们并不相识，只不过把车位让给他而已。

Nonetheless, when we go to lunch and I ask, "What does a stockbroker do?" he patiently and generously describes his average day.

Basically, Bob says, every day he goes to his nice little office and he sits there, takes a couple of phone calls, and writes something down.

"Let me get this straight," I repeat. "You take a call and write something down. That's it?"

Bob goes on. "Well, yes. And I call people too, and we talk. I tell them stories about companies, and they send me money."

Another light flashes on in my head. This dude—wearing another custom-made, beautiful suit, at a cost of a couple thousand dollars easy—is selling, just like I'm doing. But instead of having to drive all around, up and down highways, to find obscure facilities and labs, carrying a small warehouse in the trunk of his car, he gets to go to one office, sits there, and talks on the phone. I want to say, *Damn, that's slick!* but only listen attentively as he conveys the secret to his success.

Bob is self-motivated, he says, setting his own goals. "Every day when I'm sitting there talking on the phone, I say to myself: *I'm not leaving until I make four or five thousand dollars today.*"

Again, the math is overwhelming. He sits there and talks to people until he makes four or five thousand dollars *that day*. I'm killing myself to gross four or five thousand *a month*! To be sure that I haven't misunderstood, I ask, "Bob, let me see if I got this right. You talk to people, some of whom you know, some of whom you don't know, some of whom you have to get to know, and you tell them stories about these companies and these investment ideas and opportunities, and they send you money?"

"That's what I do," he says, with total sincerity.

With total sincerity, I announce, "I can do that." Just for emphasis, I add, "Yep, I can do that. And you know what? I *want* to do that!"

Laughing, whether he believes I can or not, Bob offers to introduce me to some branch managers at the different brokerage firms in town. The fact that I haven't been to college is a liability, he admits. But he also tells me that there are training programs at these various companies for which I could qualify, even without a degree, and receive training in every aspect of the job—from the fundamentals of investment to financial planning and the full spectrum of economics and high finance—while I'm studying for the licensing exam. But in order to be hired on full-time—to do what he's doing—I have to be licensed.

开始进餐后我问道:"证券经纪人是做什么的?"他耐心细致地向我描述了自己一天的工作情况。

鲍勃说,他每天基本上就是走进他那间不大的办公室,然后坐下,接听电话,并记录一些信息。

"是不是这个意思,"我说,"就是接电话,再做记录,对吗?"

鲍勃继续说:"是的。我也会打给别人,聊一聊,我告诉他一些公司的故事,然后他们付给我钱。"

我眼前仿佛看到这么一幅场景,这位老兄又换上一套西装,笔直挺阔,英俊潇洒,虽然价值几千美金,对他来说也不在话下。他其实也是在做销售,这一点和我现在一样。但他不用像我这样在高速公路上一路狂奔、疲于奔命,寻找那些偏僻的医疗设施机构和实验室,后备箱里塞满各种货物,他只需到办公室,舒适地坐在那里拨打电话,就可以一切搞定。我心想:这简直太棒了!不过当他切入重点,传授自己的成功秘诀时,我可一直在全神贯注,洗耳恭听。

鲍勃是自我激励型的那种,他总会给自己设定目标。"每天当我坐在那里打电话的时候,就会暗下决心:如果今天不挣到四五千美元,我就不走。"

这个数字又让我深受打击。他坐在那里,就和别人谈话,一天就能赚到四五千美元!如果换了我,一个月能赚四五千美金,我都会兴高采烈,手舞足蹈。为了确保我没有搞错,我又接着问:"鲍勃,你看是不是这么回事,你和别人交谈,这其中有些和你很熟,有些你根本就不认识,还有一些是你需要去结识的,你会告诉他们关于一些公司的故事以及投资建议和机会,然后他们就会把钱给你?"

"对,就是这么回事,"他非常真诚地说。

我也非常真诚地应和道:"这我也能干得了。"然后又加了一句,表示加强语调,"我的确能干得了,我也想干这行!"

也不知他相信与否,鲍勃哈哈大笑。他主动提出可以把我引荐给城里证券公司的一些分公司经理。他也承认没有大学文凭可能会有些麻烦,不过他告诉我即使没有学位,这些公司的业务各有不同,其中可能有我能胜任的。我需要接受各个方面的培训,从投资的基础知识到理财策划以及经济学的方方面面,乃至巨额融资都有涉及,但要想胜任全职工作,也就是像他现在这样,我必须有从业资格。

Done, I thought. Chris Gardner, stockbroker. This was where I was supposed to be. Period. Despite the logistical nightmare that ensued, I knew from that lunch forward that it would be worth it. Geography became my first major obstacle. When Bob started setting meetings up for me, most of them were scattered across the financial district in downtown San Francisco, all of the meetings during the nine-to-five prime time of the working day. No early breakfasts and no meet-and-greets for drinks. Since my sales calls for Van Waters and Rogers were mostly all down in the Valley, also during the nine-to-five working day, that meant either being late or missing meetings that my pen-wielding boss Patrick was scheduling for me.

Most of my interviews were at the larger firms with training programs, like Merrill Lynch, Paine Webber, E. F. Hutton, Dean Witter, and Smith Barney, companies where Bob knew the branch managers. If there was any possibility that the hoops I had to jump through were going to discourage me, that was eliminated the moment I stepped foot in the first brokerage firm I visited. Talk about being turned out! One hit and I was hooked. It was something in the air that was instantly invigorating.

Sitting there waiting for my interview, I could feel my adrenaline pumping, like a contact high, just from watching all the activity that was happening simultaneously: phones ringing, ticker tape running, stockbrokers hollering out orders and transactions and stamping time clocks. It was all at once like visiting a foreign country and like coming home.

The impact was exactly what I felt the first time I heard Miles Davis and saw how his music could totally change the mood of everyone hearing it. The trading room had a similar kind of power. It was a nerve center, hooked into the doings and happenings of millions of other people all over the world. What a rush! Some rushes came and went; this didn't dissipate. This was sustained intensity.

Waiting for the appointment that day didn't bother me because the more I absorbed what was going on, the more certain I became that I could do this. There weren't any other black guys in the office, or at least not any that I could see. But that didn't alter my confidence. Not when there was a chance to make $80,000 a month!

Of course, I may have been naive about that being the going rate for most stockbrokers. Still, it was part of what had fired me up. Momma had told me that if I wanted to make a million dollars, I could. Eighty grand a month times twelve, with some overtime and bonuses thrown in—I figured it was only a matter of time and I'd be making that million in a year! Again, if Bob Bridges could do it, so could I.

没问题。克里斯·加德纳，证券经纪人，这正是我该去奋斗的职业生涯。尽管接下来这个月的日子我会不好过，但我清楚，那顿午饭是值得我为之节衣缩食的。需要跑来跑去四处面试，成了我的第一大问题。鲍勃开始逐步为我安排面试机会，但大部分都是在旧金山市区的金融商圈内，而且全部面试都集中在工作日早九晚五这段黄金时间。没有时间吃早餐，没有时间寒暄喝茶。因为我为凡·沃特斯罗格斯公司做销售的客户大都在硅谷腹地，并且预约都是要在早九晚五这个时间段会面，那么我要么上班就得迟到，要么就得把喜欢拿着钢笔指手画脚的老板富兰克给我安排的预约取消。

我的大多数求职面试都是在可以提供培训项目的大公司里进行的，像美林证券、潘恩·韦伯经纪公司、赫顿公司、添惠公司和史密斯·邦尼公司，等等，鲍勃认识这些公司的分公司经理。本以为会碰一鼻子灰，可随着我踏进第一家证券公司的大门，这点顾虑也就烟消云散了。我们谈到人生的抉择！我感同身受，势在必得。空气中仿佛都弥漫令人振奋的气息，我备受鼓舞。

我坐在外面等候面试的时候，心潮澎湃，仅仅在办公室里的所见所闻，就已经让我兴奋不已：电话声四起，自动收报机飞速运转，证券经纪人大声报单，确认时间点，等等。顷刻间，我仿佛来到异国他乡，但同时还有一种亲切感涌上心头。

这种感觉与我当初第一次听到迈尔·戴维斯的爵士乐时异曲同工，他的音乐能完全改变每位聆听者的心境。这个交易厅也有某种类似的力量，它仿佛就是神经中枢，连接着全世界数百万人的一举一动，甚至牵动着他们的命运。到处是争先恐后的繁忙场面！人们步履匆匆，往来穿梭，紧张的气氛始终不曾消散。

那天我并没有为等待面试而忐忑不安，因为我对这里了解得越多，就越加肯定自己可以胜任这个工作。在办公室里看不到什么黑人员工的身影，至少我没有看见，但我的自信根本不会动摇，月入 8 万美金的机会就在眼前向我招手。

当然，也许是我太过天真，明知可以从事证券经纪人这一行的人是凤毛麟角，却还一意孤行，其实，正是因为如此，才进一步激发了我的热情。妈妈曾说，如果我想挣到 100 万，那我就一定能行。每月 8 万美金，再加上加班费和额外的奖金，那么迟早我都会拥有百万年收入！那么，如果鲍勃·布里奇斯能做到，我也能做到。

Now that I had found the vehicle and venue to do what I believed I could do, it was only a matter of getting one person at one of the firms with a training program to agree with me. That wasn't so easy. Interview after interview, the answers varied, but they all translated to no. N.O. And with every no, as a parting gift, I invariably spotted the ubiquitous pee yellow parking ticket under the windshield wiper when I dashed out to my car. Another fifteen to twenty-five bucks that I didn't have, another reminder that I'd have to take time off from work one day and go to court to plead my case to have the tickets reduced or cleared. Still, I wasn't going to give up.

Racism wasn't the main issue, although it was a part of it. My understanding eventually about why I kept getting turned down was that it was " place-ism." The questions boiled down to connection, placement. What was my connection to the market? What was my connection to my peers, since I never went to college? My résumé showed lots of experience, but the objections piled up about what wasn't there. You're not from a politically connected family. You've got no money of your own. Who's going to do business with you? What's your connection to the money?

Place-ism. It made sense. But I just kept telling myself, *I know I can do this.*

At the San Francisco office of Dean Witter, a friendly broker named Marty made himself available to me. He was someone to whom I could turn for advice now and then, even if I didn't have an appointment. When he referred me to the Oakland office of Dean Witter, I assumed it was because I was black, even though when I got to that office, set in a mainly black section of town, there were no other employees of color to be seen. By that point, nothing mattered but getting in their training program. It had been a few months, and no one had given me any indication of interest, while I was starting to really jeopardize the job that I did have, with the Pen Guy on my back. The reality was that I was getting tight, and with that in mind I marched into the Oakland branch manager's office prepared to close the deal, not to pitch myself but to ask: "When can I start?"

Under the heading of the worst job interview ever, I sat there in this cat's office overlooking Lake Merritt, and as I was talking, he stared right over my shoulder, interrupting me to say, "Oh, that's so interesting, a horse has jumped into Lake Merritt."

I wanted to say, *Fuck that horse.* After all, Lake Merritt wasn't deep, so the horse wasn't in danger of drowning. But it was all too clear that he could have cared less about me. As professionally as I could, I stood and said, "Obviously, I've gotten you at a bad time, so why don't we try and do this again at a later date?"

既然前景一片光明，那么只剩下关键的一环，就是要看哪个提供培训项目的公司主管能赏识我，但这并不容易。面试一个接着一个，回复五花八门，但其实全都是回绝的意思。不仅如此，在我冲出公司大楼去取车时，还总能在车挡雨雪刷下面看到黄色违章停车罚单。又要交几十元的罚单，可我没那么多钱，这就意味着必须请一天假到法院去为自己辩护，以便减免不良记录。当然，我是不会轻易放弃的。

种族主义并不是主要问题，但我的肤色也是我屡屡被拒的部分原因，但我还是把真正的原因归结到"地位主义"，也就是所谓人际关系和身份定位。既然我从未上过大学，那么我与市场的关系是什么？我与周围人的关系是什么？在我的简历中工作经验确实很多，但人们更多质疑的是我所欠缺的东西，家族没有政治背景，没有个人资产，谁能和你做生意？你和钱的关系是什么？

"地位主义"听上去是个合理的解释。但我不停地对自己说，我知道自己能干这一行。

在添惠公司旧金山的办公室里，有个名叫马蒂的证券经纪人对我颇为友善。即便没有事先预约，我也可以不时地向他问这问那。当他推荐我去添惠公司奥克兰办公室去试试的时候，我想这可能和自己是黑人有关，因为那间办公室位于城里主要的黑人聚集区，可当我进来的时候，却并没看到其他有色人种的雇员。尽管如此，当务之急是接受他们的培训项目。几个月过去了，面试还是没有什么实质性的进展，可我手头的工作却要出乱子了，那个钢笔侠就要使坏了。而且我口袋里马上就没钱了，一考虑到这一点，我就马上冲到奥克兰分公司的经理办公室，准备和他摊牌，也没问能让自己干什么工作，便迫不及待地问："我什么时候可以开始上班？"

这是有史以来最糟糕透顶的工作面试，我坐在那家伙的办公室里，窗外就是美德湖。正当我开口和他说话的时候，他的目光从我肩上掠过，打断我说道："真有意思，那匹马跳进了湖里。"

我想说："这该死的马。"毕竟，美德湖并不深，所以那匹马没有生命危险。但显然他并没有在意我，我尽量表现出专业人士的样子，站起来说："显然，我的此次到访并不合时宜，那我们另行安排时间见面如何？"

The PURSUIT of HAPPYNESS

He agreed, and I excused myself, only to gallop horselike out to my car, pluck the parking violation ticket off the windshield, and haul ass down to the Valley, where I was supposed to be picking up Patrick to go call on an account. In my haste, I forgot to hide the pile of annual reports I'd been amassing from these stockbrokerages —Dean Witter, Paine Webber, EF Hutton—that was sitting on my front passenger seat.

It was in that split second when Patrick started to get in the car that I realized they were there. With veiled panic, I went to grab the papers just as he sternly asked, "Gardner?"

"Yes . . ." I began, sure that I was about to be busted.

Patrick peered at me with suspicion, asking, "Are you going to open a brokerage account?"

"Oh, yeah . . ." I answered, trying to look really cool, feeling relieved. "Yeah, I'm thinking about opening up an account."

But then, just to show he didn't quite buy it, he gave me a funny look and a click of his pen. In the days that followed, Patrick started to check up on me more closely. Though he didn't actually know that I was interviewing with other companies, he was obviously beginning to suspect something, especially when he found out that I'd been canceling appointments and showing up late for others.

To make matters more stressful, Jackie had been hinting that I was fooling myself into thinking I could make it on Wall Street. Her point of view, valid enough, was: "Well, most of the guys there in that business, don't they have MBAs?"

No matter how many times I explained about the training programs and that you didn't always have to have a master's degree, she had no evidence that was true. Her friend at this firm had his MBA, and her friend's husband at that firm had his MBA. "Chris, you don't even have a bachelor's. Don't you have to have some kind of degree to work in that industry?"

It was the credentials argument all over again: "You ain't got the papers." This from the woman with whom I was living, and the mother of my son.

You watch, I kept promising. I'm going to do this. I saw it, tasted it, smelled it. Even so, with money tighter than it had been in a long time, the Irish midget waiting to nail me, and Jackie worried, I knew something had to give.

Just when I thought I had exhausted all my options, I had a follow-up interview at E. F. Hutton: the culmination of several conversations was that the branch manager did not say no. He said, "We'll give you a shot." Walking me to the door, he shook my hand and told me that he'd see me two weeks later, at seven o'clock in the morning, to start the training program.

他同意了，我起身告退，飞奔出来，跑到车旁，从风挡雨刷上扯掉违章停车罚单，然后一股脑就开到硅谷，我本该到那里去接帕特里克去取些款项。忙乱之中竟然忘记把从添惠、潘恩·韦伯、赫顿这些证券公司收集到的年报藏起来了，就任它们赫赫然躺在车里副驾驶的座位上。

就在帕特里克上车的那一瞬间，我才意识到出问题了。内心极其惶恐，但又故作镇定，在我伸手准备把文件拿过来时，他厉声喝道："克里斯？"

"嗯……"我答应着，自己悔得肠子都青了。

帕特里克瞅着我，疑惑地问："你要开股票账户吗？"

"是的……"我回答，尽量做出一幅若无其事的样子，心里多少感到有了一丝挽回的余地，"是啊，我正在考虑开个户头。"

可是他却不买我的账，露出一幅古怪的神态，还咔哒了一下钢笔。接下来的几天里，富兰克开始对我严加看管。虽然他不可能知道我在其他公司里进行面试，但显然他已开始对我有所怀疑，尤其当他发现我一直在取消约会并为私事而屡屡迟到时，则更是如此。

不仅如此，杰姬还一直给我泼冷水，觉得我梦想在华尔街获得成功只是自己的一厢情愿罢了。但她的观点缺乏说服力："在那里做事的人，难道都和你一样没上过 MBA 吗？"

无论我怎么反反复复解释接受培训并不一定需要硕士学位，她都不愿相信这一点，反而说她在这个公司的朋友有 MBA 学位，她朋友的老公在那个公司也有 MBA 学位。"克里斯，你连学士学位都没有，难道为进那一行不考个什么学位吗？"

这又是关于文凭的争吵，"你没有毕业证。"这就是和我一起生活的女人，我儿子的母亲对我的看法。

等着瞧着吧，我不断地承诺。我会干上这一行的。我就是喜欢它，喜欢它的味道，还有它的气息。即便如此，但由于长时间以来我们手头一直很紧，那个爱尔兰小侏儒总是盯着我，还有杰姬每天忧心忡忡，所以我明白自己不得不做出些让步。退一步，海阔天空。

正当我一筹莫展的时候，赫顿公司的复试通知如雪中送炭般及时而至，和分公司经理聊了一会儿之后，他并未拒绝我，而是说："我们会给你一次试用的机会。"

他把我送到门口，握着我的手说，两周后，周一早上七点见，然后我就可以接受项目培训了。

I could have tap-danced out of his office, Gene Kelly style, into the San Francisco midsummer rain. Practically on wings, I kissed the parking ticket left on the car and called it lucky, promising myself to finally take a day off to go to court and take care of all the tickets. At long last, the validation that I wasn't crazy was here! My mental bank account started ringing up my stockbroker commissions.

Though I intended to close up some Van Waters and Rogers pending sales over the next two weeks, there was a slight wrinkle that turned up a few days later when Patrick announced, "Gardner, we don't think this is working out. You don't seem to be making any progress. We're trying to grow this territory, and you're just not cutting it."

Relieved, I admitted that the feeling was mutual and that I had other opportunities lining up that I wanted to pursue. *Big mistake.* The minute I said that, even before I could wrap up diplomatically, Patrick cut me off with a click and prepared to hurry me out. Just to clarify, I asked if this was a two weeks' notice, and Patrick explained that we were terminating our arrangement then and there. They would mail me the check.

Beautiful. A perfect plan: go home, wait the two weeks, start collecting unemployment, spend some time with the family, then head off to Wall Street, where I'm going to make more money than even Bob Russell, not to mention Patrick.

When what I thought was my severance check arrived but turned out to be a reduced amount for time I'd already worked, I learned that because I had "quit," there was no money for the two weeks that I would have worked and also no unemployment. That was a drag, but since I planned on conquering the stock market soon, I didn't sweat it.

In an experience to be filed under the heading of " best-laid plans of mice and men," after enjoying those two weeks—during which I don't get around to taking care of the parking tickets—to make a good impression I show up thirty minutes early on the appointed Monday morning and no one seems to know who I am.

Surprised at the lack of organization, I ask for my new boss, who is also the branch manager, the guy who hired me, the person who told me, "We'll give you a shot."

Oh, says one of the brokers, he was fired on Friday.

Standing there at the reception desk, for the first time as an adult I become conscious of the strength of my own sphincter muscle. To some, this could be a cause for irony, even humor. Not for me. There is not one iota of humor in me as I freak out, exiting the building to see that it's pouring rain but not bothering to use my umbrella. How could this have happened? The job that I left my other job for doesn't exist. I got no income. I'm having beefs with my woman. What the hell am I going to do? I don't know.

我本来可以跳着踢踏舞闪出他的办公室，冲进旧金山仲夏的雨幕下。实际上我却轻舞飞扬，从楼里飘然而出，亲吻着留在车上的违章停车罚单，看着它我心情如此舒畅，最后下定决心一定要请一天假去法院处理所有的罚单。终于，这一次我没有为罚单而恼羞成怒，因为我的脑子里已经在盘算着做证券经纪人能挣多少佣金了。

虽然在接下来的两周里，我本想把凡 沃特斯罗格斯公司尚未敲定的销售订单能有所入账，但几天后，出了些麻烦事，帕特里克称："克利斯，我们觉得有些问题，你似乎并没有做出任何业绩。我们正准备实现这块业务的增长，而你却一直停步不前。"

如释重负，我承认大家在这一点上是一致的，而且其他工作机会也在等着我。不过，大错特错的是，我本该事先就收拾好东西离开公司，万事大吉，但现在帕特里克咔哒一声就炒了我的鱿鱼，还准备催我快点离开。为确认一下细节，我问他是否我有两周的宽限，帕特里克解释说合同即时终止，支票会随后寄给我的。

棒极了，我当下制定出一个完美的计划：回家，等上两周，领取失业救济费，和家人多呆一阵子，然后直接到华尔街上班，在那里我要比鲍勃·罗素挣的还要多，帕特里克就更不足挂齿了。

最终我收到了那张所谓遣散费的支票，结果却发现数额少了很多，与我的工作时间根本不符。我这才知道这两周里我本该工作的，但由于"离职"，所以拿不到任何薪金和失业费。真是让人扫兴，不过既然我已准备驰骋证券市场，所以也就无所谓了。

不过却总是事与愿违。在享受了两周的美好时光后，这期间我甚至都没去处理罚单的事情，周一大早，我提前了半个小时就赶到了新的办公室，就为给对方留下个好印象，结果发现那里似乎没人认识我。

我一下子找不到了组织，就去问新老板的去向，他就是分公司经理，是他同意雇佣我，并且还说"我们会给你试用机会"的。

一个证券经纪人告诉我："他周五的时候被解雇了。"

站在前台旁，我气不打一处来。有些人可能会对我冷嘲热讽，甚至以此作为笑料。但作为当事人，我一点都乐不起来，连伞都没打，就跑出了大楼，任凭外面大雨倾盆。怎么会有这种事呢？我辞职就是为了一脚踏空？我没有了收入，我的女人满腹牢骚，抱怨不断。我到底该何去何从？我自己都不知道。

What I do know in the hours and days that follow is that nothing puts more stress on a relationship between a man and a woman than if the man has no job. At least, in the world I come from and inhabit, that's so. A man without a job, as far as my upbringing taught me, is no man at all. Any man that was a man had to take care of and provide for his family. Even old drunk-ass Freddie basically went to work every day. So it was unacceptable for me to wake up in the morning and not have anywhere to go to work— after being so sure that I was on the way to Wall Street and knowing that it was my responsibility because I made the decision to do what I did. I could only imagine how Jackie was going to take it.

Later I would refer to what happened next as a series of incidents and circumstances that taken all together might be seen as the perfect example of Murphy's Law. Complicating those principles was the crumbling foundation of my relationship with Jackie. When I first came home to tell her what had happened, she said absolutely nothing. What could she say? "Sorry, old chap, hang in there," but she didn't. We had no savings, no income, only bills. Not anything extravagant, just your normal run-of-the-mill living bills: food, rent, car note, day care, Pampers.

My first order of business was bringing in some bucks, immediately. Returning to some of the odd jobs I'd done when I was supplementing my salary at the VA, that same day I made fifty bucks painting houses all day for a friend in the contracting business. Fine. That meant we were going to eat that day and pay the gas bill. The next day my buddy hired me to work on a roofing job, and the next day I cleaned out a basement, and the day after that I did yard work. Whatever work I could scrounge up, I did it, not joyfully, not with expertise, but willingly.

This was, in my mind, a lousy setback, an unfortunate rut in the road. But it wasn't the end of the ride by any means. In fact, while I worked those jobs, all I could think about was getting back on track, finding that open door, that one break that would pan out.

In the midst of money arguments and increasing daily tension at home, all the while that I was painting houses, junking, and mowing lawns a semblance of a strategy emerged. The one remaining possibility that I had going was over at Dean Witter, where they hadn't said yes but hadn't said a final no. My challenge was overcoming the placement argument: what was my connection to the business, my experience? A bigger challenge was having to explain that I was currently unemployed, after having been dropped by my last sales job. My thought was that if I could get someone to vouch for me, someone like maybe Joe Dutton, an African American entrepreneur in the high-tech field I'd met at a business seminar, that could make a huge difference.

When I called Joe to ask him for the favor, he was happy to help a brother. With that, I was able to set up the interview at Dean Witter. If they told me no this time, I wasn't sure what I'd do after that, so the interview loomed as though my life depended on it.

在接下来的几个小时以及后来这几天里，我意识到，在男女之间，没有什么比男人失业更火上浇油的了。至少，在我生活的世界上，这就是真理。依照我所受的教育，男人没了工作，就不是男人。只要是男人就得承担起养家糊口的责任。甚至连那个酗酒的混蛋弗莱迪，基本上也会每天都去上班。所以，对我来说，早上一睁开双眼，何去何从，茫然无措，这简直无法让人接受，尤其是自己原以为已走上通往华尔街的成功之路，更是如此。而且，我清楚地知道，这一切都是我自食其果。只是，我无法想象杰姬能否接受这个事实。

我会把发生的一切归结为意外，所有这些都凑在了一起，就像是墨菲法则①的完美例证一般。但所有这些复杂的法则都会让我和杰姬之间的关系愈发僵化。当我回到家一五一十地告诉她事情的经过时，她一言不发。她还能说什么呢？"很遗憾，不过要坚持住，"但是她什么都没说。我们没有积蓄、没有收入，只有账单。没有任何值钱的东西，只有那些普普通通的账单：食物、房租、罚单、日常开销和帮宝适。

很快我兜里又有了进账。我又重操旧业——打零工，这是以前在退伍军人管理署医院工作时，为额外补贴家用我做过的活计。就在那天，为一个承包商朋友粉刷了一天的房屋后，我赚到了50美元。还不错，当天我们能好好吃一顿，还能支付燃气账单。第二天，我的朋友雇我修理房顶，接下来我清理了一个地下室，再后来，我做了些园艺活。无论让我干什么活，我都会接受，虽然干起来并不开心，也不需要专业技巧，但我很愿意做。

在我的内心深处，这是个令人生厌的倒退，就像是刹车后在路面上留下的难看的车痕。但事情不会就这么完了。事实上，我干活儿的时候，满脑子都在想怎么回到正轨，找到那扇开启的大门，找到成功的出路。

家里每天都为了钱而争吵不休，冲突日渐升级，一片紧张的气氛。当我粉刷房子，运送垃圾、修剪草坪的时候，突然萌生一个想法。还有一线希望，就是到添惠公司去，因为他们最后并未明确拒绝我。经过反复思量，我不服输的性格最终战胜了自卑心理，我与这个行业有什么关系以及我的经历是什么？还有就是我得解释清楚自己为什么会丢掉上一份销售工作，陷入失业困境，成了现在这幅模样。我的想法是如果我能找人给自己担保，比如乔·达顿这样的人，那么情况就会大不一样。乔是我在一个商业研讨会上遇见的非裔美国企业家，从事高科技领域方面的业务。

于是我打电话给乔请他帮这个忙，他欣然接受了。这样，我就能去添惠公司面试了。如果这次他们告诉我不行，那么我恐怕就真的死心塌地了，所以当面试临近，我只能孤注一掷，成败似乎就在此一搏了。

---

① 编者注：Murphy's Law，西方常用俚语，指事情如果有变坏的可能，不管这种可能性有多小，它总会发生。

The PURSUIT of HAPPYNESS

Later I would wonder how different things would have turned out if the first training program had gone forward or the guy who hired me hadn't been fired. Would that have changed the turbulent dynamic in my household? The lack of money made everything worse, but there were other problems. In Jackie's view, my smoking weed to take the edge off was intolerable, as were my sometimes loud and critical comments. In my view, she had no confidence in me, which was infuriating. And my gut instinct warned me that she was capable of using Christopher to retaliate against me.

The showdown came on a Thursday night after we heard the news that my friend Latrell's little boy Sebastian had been killed on the street when he was playing on his tricycle and a car hit him. It wasn't what we were arguing about, but the tragic news compounded our emotional state when we began to bare all our complaints in an epic verbal argument that was so exhausting, we finally both fell sleep without any resolution. On Friday midmorning, the minute our feet hit the floor, everything picks up where it left off.

When she starts getting dressed to leave, an indication to me that because I'm not going anywhere I need to get Christopher dressed and over to day care, where we have no money to pay for his care but need to keep him so we don't lose our place when we get the work, I panic. Moving quickly, Jackie heads out the front door, and I follow her out, demanding to know, "Where are you going? We gotta work this out, and you ain't going nowhere until we do!"

Refusing to acknowledge me, she starts down the steps and I run after her and attempt to take her by the hands and turn her toward me. As she pulls away, I grab her by both wrists and she pulls back again, trying to get away. Upset that I've stooped so low, I release my grip and let go, only to watch her fall back into the rosebushes.

I watch her stand up, brush herself off, looking slightly scratched, and as I start to swallow my damn pride to apologize, Jackie seethes, "You're getting the fuck out of here."

Now I'm back in the fight. "No, I ain't. I'm not going nowhere." Seething myself, I slam the door and go back into the house to get Christopher into his bath.

What follows is a series of events that spiral meteorically out of control, resulting in legal complications that to this day remain ambiguous—due to Jackie's ultimate decision not to press charges over the rosebush incident. Initially, however, it was apparent that was what she intended to do, when some ten minutes after she split, there was a knock at the front door and, with Christopher wrapped in a towel and in my arms, I open it to find two young Berkeley police officers, in uniform, on my doorstep. Behind them, on the sidewalk, is Jackie.

One of the officers asks, "Are you Chris Gardner?"

"Yes," I answer, with a shrug. Not following.

Chapter 9 Turned Out (advanced)

不久后我寻思，如果第一个培训项目如期施行，或雇佣我的那个人没被解雇，那么事情又会怎样发展呢。我的家庭矛盾会改变吗？由于缺钱，一切都变得很糟，但也有其他问题在火上浇油。我想靠吸大麻来缓解一下疲惫的心情，可是杰姬也觉得无法容忍，有时我会和她大声理论，她也接受不了。在我看来，她对我毫无信心，真是让人不可理喻。而且我的直觉警告我她会利用儿子对我进行报复。

在一个周四的晚上，我们听新闻里报道朋友拉垂尔的小儿子希巴斯汀在街上玩三轮车时，被车撞死了，我们俩也终于摊牌了。我们并没有为此争论不休，但这个悲剧让我们内心都受到深深的震撼，我们开始喋喋不休，彼此抱怨，唇枪舌战，最后疲惫不堪，最后所有问题都没解决，便倒头睡了过去。周五中午，我们俩一起床，争吵就又开始了。

当她穿好衣服准备离开时，因为我没有地方去，所以我明白，我得给儿子穿衣服，把他送到幼儿园，可我们没钱付他的日托费，可又需要把他寄托在那里，否则上班以后，幼儿园可能就没有空余的位子。这着实使我惊惶失措。杰姬箭步如飞地冲向大门，我跟着她一起出来，让她说清楚到底要去哪里，"你去哪？我们必须解决这个问题，否则你哪也不能去。"

她拒绝回答，并往楼下奔去，我在她后面跑着，想抓住她的手，让她转过身来。她不断把我的手搡开，我抓住了她两个手腕，她又往回拉，试图挣脱。我实在抓不住了，松开手，眼睁睁地看着她倒在了蔷薇丛中。

看着她站起来，拍掉身上的草棍，身上好像有些轻微的擦伤，于是我收起自己那该死的傲慢，向她赔礼道歉，杰姬怒气冲天地喊道："你给我滚开。"

我们又开始了争吵，"我不会离开的，我哪也不会去。"我怒气冲冲，猛地关上了门，回去给儿子洗澡。

后来又连续发生了一些事情，使情况不断急速恶化，最终局面失控，导致我们之间的法律关系错综复杂，直到今天也说不清楚，而杰姬最终决定不再对蔷薇丛事件提起控诉。然而，起初，很明显她是故意这么做的。杰姬离开十分钟左右，就有人敲响了房门，我用毛巾把儿子围裹起来，抱着他去开门，发现两个身穿制服的伯克利警官站在家门口。杰姬就在他们身后的过道上站着。

其中一个警官问道："你是克里斯·加德纳吗？"

"是的，"我回答说，耸了耸肩，没再接下去。

The PURSUIT of HAPPYNESS

The second cop explains, "We have a complaint from the woman who lives here. She said you beat her."

What? "No, I didn't beat her," I say, adamantly.

The first cop asks how she happened to have scratches on her body, so I point to the rosebushes, explaining how she fell. But the second cop says, "No, sir, she said you beat her, and the State of California treats domestic violence as a serious offense."

Just as I'm about to explode over the fact that I know domestic violence is a serious offense and that I know what a woman who's been beaten looks like and how I would turn myself in to the police before I committed that crime, I watch the first cop walk over to my car and write down my plate number.

After he verifies that it is my car, the two announce that they're taking me in to the police station.

When I object, saying, "No, I gotta get my baby ready and take him to day care," they announce that they will hand the baby over to his mother and she can take care of that. In shock, I helplessly watch as they hand my swaddled son to Jackie and watch her carry him inside the house, closing the door without a glance in my direction. In the meantime, I am handcuffed and put in the backseat of the police car.

In a state of total disbelief, I cuss under my breath at Jackie the whole way to the station. Whatever I'd done to deserve her resentment, I could accept responsibility, but the further we drive away from Christopher the more I start to lose it. Making matters worse, I learn next that besides the possibility of battery charges, I am definitely being charged with owing $1,200 of unpaid parking tickets. Now I go out of my mind, my anger giving way to fear and an overwhelming sense of powerlessness. Those two demons have lurked in the wings whenever circumstances have spun out of control and have suddenly emerged centerstage.

After they book and fingerprint me, I'm led to a holding cell where I'm informed that Jackie's complaint isn't the cause—since if it was just that I could sign myself out. But unless I can pay the parking tickets, I have to plead my case to a judge. This is where the screw gets turned, as I wait to be taken into court. But it's Friday. Soon it's Friday afternoon. After waiting and pacing in my holding cell, I see one of the desk guys heading back my way and listen as he explains, "Oh, about the parking tickets. The judge says it's too late today to do anything about this. He'll see you on Monday." He pauses, then adds, "You have to stay here. You can't leave until you see the judge."

"ARE YOU FUCKING TELLING ME I HAVE TO WAIT IN JAIL UNTIL MONDAY TO SEE THE JUDGE?"

第二个警察解释说："我们接到了住在这里的女士对你的控告，说你殴打她。"

什么？"不，我没有打她，"我肯定地说道。

第一个警察问她身上怎么会有划痕，我指着蔷薇丛，解释她是如何摔倒的。但第二个警察说："先生，她说是你打她了，在加州家庭暴力是严重侵犯人权的犯罪。"

我很清楚家庭暴力是犯罪，也知道挨打的女人会是什么样子，我想在犯罪之前向警察说明这点，但就在我要爆发时，看到第一个警察走到我的汽车旁记下了车牌号码。

在他确认那是我的车之后，两个警察宣布他们要把我带回警局。

我不同意，说道："我必须得帮孩子收拾停当，然后带他去幼儿园。"他们说会把孩子交给母亲照看。我惊诧万分，无助地看着他们把毛巾包裹着的孩子交给了杰姬，眼睁睁地看着她把孩子抱回了房里，头也不回地关上了房门。同时，我被戴上手铐，被押到了警车的后座上。

这完全出乎我的意料之外，在去警局的路上，我一直在低声诅咒杰姬。我到底做了什么值得她如此记仇。我是个愿意负责任的男人，但当警车离儿子越来越远的时候，我的失落感也就越加强烈。火上浇油的是，到了警局后，除了可能会被指控殴打以外，他们肯定还会强行要求我清还那1200美元的违章停车罚款。我简直要气得发疯，气愤演变成了恐惧以及难以名状的无奈。每当情况失控抑或愈演愈烈时，那怒火就会恶魔般蠢蠢欲动。

在登记入册并采集指纹之后，他们把我带到了关押室，在那里我才知道其实杰姬的指控并不是我进来的真正原因，因为如果仅仅是她的话，我自己完全可以保释。但我必须偿还那些违章停车罚款，否则就得向法官有个交待。所以问题就出在了这里。那天已经是周五了，很快就到了下午。我在关押室里踱着步子焦急地等着，这时值班警察朝我走过来说："关于违章停车罚单，法官说今天太晚了没时间办理这类案子，他周一早上再见你。"停顿了一下，他接着说，"但你只能呆在这里，见到法官后才能离开。"

"该死的，你是在说我得在监狱里一直待到周一才能见到法官吗？"

Like I've offended him personally, the desk guy says, "You owe the State of California money, and while we've got you here we're going to get this resolved."

The dictates of Murphy's Law demand that things get worse. And they do immediately as I'm escorted now to another cell and I see that they've put me in with three of the meanest, ugliest, freakiest motherfuckers I've ever seen in my life: a murderer, a rapist, and an arsonist. And now I'm in here on parking tickets? With heavy-duty flashbacks to the only other time I was put in jail, for stealing pants at the Discount Center, and was ridiculed for reading my books, I'm not saying a word as I listen to everybody taking turns telling their little jailhouse story and why they're in here. Of course, the first thing I learn, a lesson soon to be reinforced by other convicts, is that nobody did the crime for which they're serving time. It's all a case of mistaken identity or somebody who didn't tell the truth. Each of these bad asses says the same four words: "I didn't do it."

In unison they then turn their thick necks slowly toward me, leering my way, asking at the same time why I'm in here. Not about to admit that I'm in jail on parking tickets, I reach down to my lowest vocal register and squint up my eyes menacingly as I say, "I'm in here for attempted murder, and I will try it again, all right?" To establish my turf, I point to where I'm going to sleep and let them know, "And that's my bunk over there."

I'm jet black, mad as hell, and bigger than anybody there. My ruse works so well that I am able to obtain the most important coin of the realm for anyone incarcerated: cigarettes.

Ironically, I had started smoking back in the Navy while working on long night shifts in the hospital. By this point, I've quit because I can't afford it, but apparently a weekend in the slammer is going to get me back on the habit again. Smoking is far preferable to the stale bologna sandwiches and cold coffee we're served over the course of the longest, most excruciating weekend of my life.

Monday morning can't come fast enough. When it does and I'm standing before the judge, he barely looks up from his paperwork as he says, "Mr. Gardner, you owe the state of California $1,200. How do you want to settle this?"

He asks if I'm working, and I shake my head no. He asks if I can pay, and I again shake my head no.

For the first time in this ordeal, more than fear and anger, I feel unbelievably sad as I grapple with the reality of these circumstances. "I don't have the money," I mutter, at my wit's end.

"Well, Mr. Gardner, you give me no choice but to sentence you to ten days at Santa Rita." With a bang of his gavel, he calls out, "Next case!"

值班警察觉得我对他非常无礼,说:"你欠加州的钱,既然我们抓到你了,这事就得解决。"

在墨菲法则的作用下,事情一发不可收拾了。他们立即将我押送到另一间牢房,我这才发现这里还有三个人,他们是我这辈子所见过的最卑鄙、最丑恶、最变态的,有杀人犯、强奸犯,还有纵火犯。而仅仅为了区区几张罚单,就要把我关在这里受罪吗?我突然想起一件事情,那是我上次被关押的经历,就因为我在折扣中心偷了条裤子,警察因为我读书对我冷嘲热讽。可我在这里一言不发,只是静静地听人们轮着讲自己在监狱里的那些段子,还有各自来这的原因。当然,我在监狱学到的第一课,就是谁都没错,但大家都得坐牢,其他囚犯也在一遍遍地强调这一点。要么抓错了人,要么是有人说了谎,这些坏家伙个个都会说:"不是我干的。"

然后,他们一起探着脖子凑到我跟前,瞅着我,齐声问我为什么进来的。我没打算承认自己是因为几张罚单就被关到里面,于是把声音压低,眯起眼睛谎称:"我是因为要蓄意谋杀而被关进来的,但我决不会罢手,可以了吧?"这不过是为使自己有一席之地,能有个地方躺下睡觉,让他们知道:"那边的铺位是我的。"

我确实像个混世恶魔,皮肤黝黑,身材高大,目露凶光。我的谎言还真管用,有人给我递来了烟,我如获至宝,这对任何失去自由的人而言,它都是好东西。

可笑的是,我是在海军服役期间,在医院里值夜班时开始抽烟。也曾因付不起烟钱被迫戒烟,但在监狱里,一个周末我就重拾烟瘾,而且是在我生命中这个最为漫长、最折磨人的周末,比起那些不新鲜的腊肠三明治和冰咖啡,香烟简直就是个宝贝。

终于捱到了周一早上,我站在法官面前,他的视线几乎没有离开过桌上的文件,头也不抬地对我说:"克里斯·加德纳先生,你欠加州1200美元,你看该怎么办吧?"

他问我是否在工作,我摇摇头表示没有。他问是否我有能力偿还,我又摇摇头表示没有。

因为这是我第一次经受这样严酷的考验,内心充满恐惧和愤怒,但更多的是无法释怀的伤感,我尽力接受这些残酷的事实。"我没钱。"我黔驴技穷地咕哝说。

"好吧,克里斯·加德纳,没办法,我只能判你在圣塔瑞塔服刑十天。"随着手起锤落,他喊道:"下一个案子!"

The **PURSUIT** of **HAPP**_y_**NESS**

A guard appears instantly and chains me up, ushers me out of court, marches me to a bus that drives out to the boonies of the heat-trapped northern California Central Valley to the overcrowded, decrepit county prison, Santa Rita, where the current most famous convict is the crazy Mexican ax murderer Juan Corona. In shock, I look around at the pit bulls sitting next to me on the bus. My crime? Not the alleged battery, which was Jackie's initial complaint, and about which it was still unclear that she would go forward, requiring still more legal wrangling. But the parking tickets? There's no trial. They are a fact, proven documents of my disregard for the law because I was trying to get ahead in the world. If you can't pay, you've got to stay. Period. The end. *For ten days.*

Where is my attorney? Everybody else has a public defender, somebody. *That's it,* I think. My recourse, my way out. They didn't give me an attorney. So as they're letting me off the bus, I try to explain to the sympathetic-looking African American driver of the bus that he needs to take me back to court. Or maybe, I actually hope, he'll let me go. Well, the second I step out of line, prison guards start jerking the chain, dragging me right back in line.

If there was anything that helped me survive the dehumanizing effect of incarceration, it was my time in the military. It wasn't just the prison uniform of orange PJs and clear jelly sandals, it was the total control and regimentation, the diet consisting of more unpalatable bologna and nasty coffee, and the acclimation to ovenlike conditions. There were no Pacific Ocean breezes, no Santa Anas. Hot. Hot. Hot. It was a perfect recipe for me to get into an argument with one of the guards when I realized that my new contact lenses were hardening in my eyes like fish scales since there was no saline solution to be found. Convinced I was going to go blind, I demanded to see a doctor, and when the guard wouldn't respond, I muttered something brilliant like, "Fuck you."

That was rewarded with a fast trip to isolation, what turned out to be a brick hut without a roof, the size of a bathroom, not even large enough to lie down in, what they called "the hot box," where I was alone, suddenly missing the same prison conversations that had been driving me crazy earlier. Good thing I'd been talking to myself most of my life, as I began a two-way conversation by saying out loud, "Oh, man, this done gone from bad to worse, bro."

"No shit, man," I commiserated as best I could.

"So why they say they got to cool you off in the hot box? That's some kind of an oxymoron." With the sun baking down, it was demonically hot. Then again, it could rain, and there would be nothing to do but get wet.

When I ran out of small talk to make with myself, I started singing, then eventually just made noise, all in an effort to block out the fear: How did this happen? What was going to happen now?

护卫立即过来给我带上镣铐，带我走出法院，强行把我带到一辆大巴上面，车子将开往地热资源丰富的北部加州中央峡谷，关满犯人的古老监狱——圣塔瑞塔，在那里关押着臭名昭著的墨西哥斧头邦杀人犯约翰·考罗那。我诧异地环顾着坐在身边满脸麻子的彪形大汉。我的罪刑？并不是所谓的殴打，那不过是杰姬的片面之词，但我不确定她是否会得寸进尺，给我更多法律上的麻烦。可违章停车罚单呢？这不需要审讯，那只是个事实，证实自己无视法律的存在，因为我曾努力走在世界的前面。如果还不起，就得必须呆在这里，呆上整整十天。

我的律师哪去了？其他人都有公共辩护律师。我想自己只能求援，但他们就是不给我找律师。所以当他们把我带下巴士的时候，我想让那个黑人司机解释解释，让他把我送回到法院去，他看上去还是蛮有同情心的。或者也许，我真希望他能把我放了。可我一走出警戒线，狱警就开始猛扯镣铐，把我拖回警戒线这边来。

多亏我曾经的军旅生涯，我才得以在丧失人性的监禁中幸存下来。这里不仅有橘红色狱服以及洁净的胶质拖鞋，还有铜墙铁壁和严密的控制与组织，腊肠味道相当可怕，咖啡更是难以下咽，而且周围的环境热得仿佛跟火炉一样。没有来自太平洋的宜人和风，没有圣阿纳斯的美丽风光。这里除了热，还是热。当我发现自己的新款隐形眼镜在眼睛里彻底僵硬了，而且上哪儿都找不到盐溶液时，我只能和狱警大吵特吵了。为了让他相信我真得快瞎了，我要求看医生，但狱警却根本不予理睬，于是我就只能咕哝着"去死吧"之类，也别无他法。

结果很快我就得到了隔离奖励。隔离室是个没有房顶的砖房，只有浴室那么大，甚至连躺下身子的地方都不够，他们称之为"热箱"，在那里我孤零零一个人，突然间监狱里那些把我逼疯的声音都消失了。不过大部分时间我可以自言自语，我会大声地说："老兄，这里的情况变得更糟了。"

"没事，老兄，"我尽可能用同情的音调说。

"为什么要把你关在这么热的地方，让你好好冷静冷静呢？太自相矛盾了吧。"阳光炽烈地照射下来，像炼狱般炎热。有时也会下雨，但我就会成了落汤鸡。

我开始聊以自慰，或者唱歌，最后再弄些动静出来，其实完全是为了解闷，驱散内心的恐惧：这是怎么回事？现在又会出些什么事呢？

The hot box cooled me off only to the extent that I tried to reasonably request a hearing to get to the funeral for Sebastian, knowing what it would mean to Latrell. But after quietly and calmly making my requests, I was turned down.

After serving my ten days, in lieu of paying the parking tickets, they were no longer an issue. Now, as I wearily awaited transfer back to the Berkeley jailhouse where I could have my hearing to find out if there was a charge from Jackie's complaint, I faced what I considered the biggest problem of this whole ordeal. The interview at Dean Witter was scheduled for the next morning. All those months and months of effort had come down to my last shot with the fellow who could say yay or nay to my future as a stockbroker. But upon arriving at the Berkeley jailhouse, I learned that I couldn't see the judge until the next morning. What to do? How could I show up at Dean Witter when I was still in jail?

The answer came in the form of a guard, a Latino brother, who must have gotten up on the right side of the bed that morning and who agreed to let me make a phone call to try to reschedule my meeting. Perhaps it was my begging. Perhaps it was my explaining that I had a real chance at this job, and I really needed it.

Whatever the reason was, he dialed the number and handed me the receiver through the bars into the cell. There I was, behind bars, calling Mr. Albanese at Dean Witter. When he answered, I greeted him warmly, with a "Hello, Mr. Albanese? This is Chris Gardner, how're you doing?"

"Fine," he said.

I went for it: "I've got a meeting with you tomorrow, but something's come up. I need to know if I can reschedule for the following day?"

Heaven smiled on me as he replied, "Fine, no problem. Be here at six-thirty in the morning."

Thank you, Lord, I prayed right in front of the guard. Mr. Albanese had said he was looking forward to meeting me. I told him that I'd see him the day after next.

My legal ordeal with Jackie continued the next morning when we had to meet in court. It was my intention to take the high road, apologize, and find a fair way of sharing equal responsibility for taking care of Christopher. Obviously, our relationship was over. My plan was to head home, get my stuff, and find a place to stay. But Jackie came armed with a desire to punish me, apparently, which resulted in a subsequent court date that was set for several weeks later. When I watched her leave that day, despite what I perceived as an icy cold demeanor on her part, I still had the hope such a court meeting wouldn't be necessary.

困在这里是让我冷静了些，我想让狱方听我解释，让我参加希巴斯汀葬礼，因为我知道那对当母亲的拉垂尔意味着什么。但当我提出这样的请求时，却被拒绝了。

服刑十天已经期满，等于偿还了违章停车罚单，现在没事了。我小心地等待着被转送回伯克利监狱，在那里我将会听取杰姬的控诉是否成立，但此时我却要面对一个非常严重的问题。添惠公司的求职面试是在出狱后的第二天上午。我之前所有的努力都是为此一搏，那个家伙会决定我的未来是否能成为股票经纪人。然而当我到达伯克利监狱时，才知道第二天早上才能见到法官。我该怎么办？我又不会分身术，怎么可能在置身监狱的同时又出现在添惠公司呢？

看守是个拉丁裔的老兄，他让我有了办法，他那天一定睡得很好，起床后精神不错，竟然同意我打电话过去重新安排面试时间。也许是因为我的恳求，也许是因为我向他解释自己必须抓住这个机会通过面试，因为我真的很需要它。

无论是什么原因，他拨了号码并通过铁网把话筒递到隔间里。就在那儿，在铁网的后面，我给添惠公司的阿尔巴尼斯先生打了电话。他接起电话后，我热情地说道："阿尔巴尼斯先生吗？我是克里斯·加德纳，您好吗？"

"很好，"他说。

我继续说："本来我与您明天有个见面预约，但出了些事情，不知能否改在后天？"

他说："好的，没问题。后天早上 6:30 过来吧。"此时我感到天堂在对我微笑。

谢谢你，上帝，在看守的面前我做了祈祷。阿尔巴尼斯先生说过他希望见到我，时间改在后天。

第二天早上我与杰姬的官司继续，我们在法庭上又见面了。我希望自己摆出高姿态，向她道歉，并找个公平的途径，共同承担抚养儿子的责任。显然，我俩之间是没希望了。我计划先回家，收拾东西，找个地方休息。但杰姬却是一副不依不饶的架势，很明显那导致了几周后还要继续开庭审理我们的案子。那天当我看着她离开的时候，尽管察觉到她那冰冷的表情，可还是认为没必要在法庭上见面。

My other comfort was the prospect that lay ahead, the possibility that the interview would be the open door to my future. By the time I hit the train heading back to our house, where I planned on packing up fast, spending some time playing with Christopher and figuring out how I could have him come stay with me, wherever I landed next, I was cheered up enough that I was willing to dismiss a gut instinct about how Jackie behaved toward me that day—as if there was another shoe that was going to drop. But after what she'd already put me through, that didn't seem plausible, so I let it go.

Nothing was out of the ordinary as I walked down the path to the house and up the steps to the front door. It was only when I glanced at the window that it struck me as odd that there were no curtains there. Hmmm. What was wrong with this picture? The bombshell exploded when I peered inside the window and saw that the house was empty. Bare. No Jackie. No Christopher. No furniture, stereo, pots and pans, clothes. No car on the street. The locks had been changed.

In a frantic, anguished daze, I stumbled down the sidewalk, approaching anyone who'd talk to me. "Where's my son?" I asked neighbors and strangers alike. "Where's Jackie?"

One woman, her close friend and a semi-landlord, wouldn't tell me anything. "You shouldn't have beat her," she scolded. "Don't ask me, 'cause I don't know nothing."

Obviously she knew everything. In fact, I was doubly mortified that everyone seemed to know what had happened except for me. It was too late to defend myself against whatever Jackie had said about me. All that mattered was that Jackie and Christopher had seemingly fallen off the face of the earth and I had to find them.

And first I had to find somewhere to sleep that night, and I had to go to the job interview the next morning in bellbottom blue jeans, T-shirt, maroon Members Only jacket (which matched the sporty maroon car I used to have), and the paint-speckled Adidas sneakers that had become my work shoes for odd jobs—the same outfit I'd gone to jail in and spent most of the time wearing, other than the prison orange PJs and jellies.

Days after she had buried her son, a subdued Latrell Hammonds took my phone call and said it was no problem for me to come over, wash my clothes there, and stay on her couch that night. Falling to sleep was difficult, especially as it came over me that these days and nights ever since the police drove me to the station had marked the first time in his life that I had been physically separated from Christopher. When I did finally give in to sleep, I didn't dream at all as the conscious question rammed insistently all night long in my brain: *Where is my son?*

我的慰藉就是面前的光明前景，这次面试可能会为我开启未来之门。在踏上回家的地铁时，我就计划着到家后收拾行囊，与儿子一起玩一会儿，并无论去哪，都要想法子让他和我在一起。我努力调整情绪，振作起来，并尽力不去想杰姬那天还会做出些什么，我心中总是有些隐隐的疑虑。她已经这样折磨我了，还会怎样呢，随她去了。

当我回到屋外，顺着台阶走到门口的时候，一切似乎都很正常。就在我看了一眼窗户后，才觉得很奇怪，怎么窗帘不见了。照片是怎么回事？透过窗户，我看到房子里空空如也，我整个人都快要气炸了。屋里仿佛洗劫一空，家徒四壁。空荡荡的，杰姬不见了，儿子也没了踪影。家具、音响、锅碗、衣服裤子统统消失得无影无踪。门口的车子也没有了，连门锁都换了。

恍惚间，我狂乱起来，茫茫然地陷入极度痛苦之中，在人行道上跌跌撞撞，逢人就问："我儿子去哪了？"不管是邻居还是陌生人，我都会问："杰姬去哪了？"

有个女人是杰姬的密友，也算是我们的房东，她什么也不愿意透露，反而怪我："你不该打她，别问我，我什么都不知道。"

显然她什么都知道。事实上，我很痛苦，怀疑每个人好像都知道发生的一切，只有我自己蒙在鼓里。杰姬一定是在背后对他们说了我的坏话，现在为自己辩护为时已晚。重要的是杰姬和儿子似乎从地球上消失了一般，可我得找到他们。

首先我得找到当晚的住处，第二天我穿着蓝色牛仔喇叭裤、T 恤衫、褐紫红色的制服夹克（与我过去驾驶的褐紫红色运动车很相配），还有沾满油漆斑点的阿迪达斯运动鞋去面试。这是我打零工时穿的工作鞋，整套衣服就是我入狱那天穿的衣服，并且大部分时间都在穿着，还好我没穿着橘红色狱服与胶质拖鞋去面试。

在拉垂尔·哈蒙德将儿子埋葬的几天之后，精神抑郁的她接到了我的电话，同意我到她家借宿，还给我洗了衣服。那天晚上我静静地躺在她家的长沙发上难以入眠，尤其是想到自从我被带到警局之后的这些日日夜夜，儿子长这么大以来，这是我第一次与他分开。当我最后不知不觉睡着的时候，一夜无梦，只是满脑子想着一个问题：儿子去哪儿了？

Chapter 10
California Dreamin'

Delivery's in the rear," says Mr. Albanese of Dean Witter, glancing up at me from his cup of coffee and his *Wall Street Journal* as I approach his desk at 6:15 a.m. that next morning.

Fortunately, no one else in the firm is in yet in this part of the office, so I don't have to endure any more embarrassing reactions to my jailhouse attire. True, my jeans are washed, and my Members Only jacket isn't too wrinkled. But the paint-speckled sneakers make me look like exactly what Mr. Albanese apparently thinks I am—a delivery guy or some dude who's wandered in from the street.

"Mr. Albanese," I say as I step forward and introduce myself, "Chris Gardner. We've got an appointment this morning at six-thirty, and I'm sorry I'm early."

"That's all right," he says. "I'm an early riser."

"I am too." I nod, go-getter that I am. Now I see that he's taking a closer look at me, my cue to come up with a genius explanation for my lack of professional attire. After a beat, I begin: "Today might be the most important day of my career, and I must admit, I'm underdressed for the occasion."

第十章
加州的梦想

第二天早上6:15我就来到面试的办公桌前,添惠公司的阿尔巴尼斯正在边喝咖啡边翻看《华尔街日报》,"邮件在后面,"他抬头看了我一眼。

幸好此时此刻办公室里还没别人,所以我穿这么一身行头,没让我太过尴尬。牛仔裤是洗过了,而且夹克衫也没太多的褶皱。但这双运动鞋满是油漆点,导致阿尔巴尼斯觉得我是个送快递的,要么就是街上的小混混。

"阿尔巴尼斯先生,"我上前一步,自我介绍,"我是克里斯·加德纳,我们约的是早上六点半,抱歉我来早了。"

"没关系,"他说,"我起得很早。"

"我也是,"我点着头,表示自己其实也很能干。我发现此时此刻,他正在上下打量着我,我知道自己要为这身太不地道的职业装想出天才的解释。停顿片刻,我张口说:"今天也许是我职业生涯中最重要的一天,可我必须承认,自己的穿戴非常不合时宜。"

Apparently not amused by my attempt at irony, he agrees: "So I see," then adds, "What happened?"

None of the lies that I can conjure in this instant are either bizarre or plausible enough to answer him. So I tell the truth, minus the part about going to jail, but including pretty much everything that's happened recently: Jackie emptying the house, taking everything, including my car, and especially how she has my son and I don't know where either of them are.

Listening intently, Mr. Albanese interrupts me before I can get out my last sentence: "You think what you're going through is rough? Try having to put up with three different broads pulling the same stuff!" Turns out, he's been married and divorced three times, taken to the cleaners each time, and he launches into a series of stories about his ex-wives. For twenty minutes he rants and raves. Just when I think we can segue back to the main question of my future, he remembers something else: "And then this gal I was seeing, let me tell you what she did."

The truth is that I'm here to tell him why I'm going to be an asset to Dean Witter in the firm's training program, and I am not so much interested in commiserating. But obviously this is a very cool guy, so I listen and nod and say at appropriate times: "Oh my God!"

Finally, he spends his wad. Instead of hearing me out or asking me questions, he stands up from his desk, takes a slug of coffee, and says, "Be here on Monday morning, and I'll walk you into the training session personally."

Just like that. The heretofore-locked gates to Wall Street had opened. I was in! It wasn't a million dollars in my pocket or the keys to my own red Ferrari, but it was validation. The funny part was that after worrying about my clothes—and only later learning that Jackie had taught herself to drive a stick shift in order to get our car, which I never saw again, and take Christopher to the East Coast, along with the key to the storage locker where she put all my stuff—the story about why I was underdressed was how I bonded with Albanese. It just went to show that God does work in mysterious ways.

Of course, there were no guarantees. As a trainee, I would make a stipend of $1,000 a month, and between putting in the actual training hours, assisting the brokers around the office later in the day, and studying every other waking hour for the exam, there wouldn't be a moment left over to earn any additional income. That was going to mean some very lean living. It also meant that until that first stipend check came in at the end of the first month, I had some major issues to tackle.

他显然对我这种自我解嘲不感兴趣，点头称是："我也这么认为，"然后又说，"出什么事了？"

此刻我所能编出的理由平淡无奇，也不合常理，难以令人信服。所以索性我把事情的原委一五一十地告诉了他，除了没有提入狱的事情，但把最近这些事情基本都包括在内了：杰姬把房子扫荡一空，带走了家里所有的东西，连我的汽车都没留下，尤其是我不知道她是怎么把孩子带走的，也不知道他俩身在何方。

阿尔巴尼斯先生认真地听着，还没等我说完，他就打断我说："你觉得自己的经历很悲惨吗？想知道这种压力再扩大三倍是什么滋味！"原来他结过三次婚，也离过三次婚，每次他都很无辜，他大谈特谈他那些前妻的故事。大约有20分钟，他都义愤填膺，一直在大声叫嚷。正当我准备打断话题，回到关于我未来工作的正题上时，他好像又想起了什么："然后我遇到这个女的，你猜猜她干了什么。"

事实上我来面试是想说自己为什么参加公司的培训项目，以便为添惠公司做出贡献。其实我对同情怜悯并无多大兴趣。但这家伙很有意思，所以我耐心听着，点着头，不时插上一句："我的天啊！"

最后，他终于结束了自己的长篇大论。他起身取了杯咖啡，没有再听我说什么，也没再问我什么问题，便说："周一早上再过来，我亲自送你去做培训。"

就这样，通往华尔街的那扇紧闭的大门在此刻向我敞开。我终于进来了，并非是说我立刻有了百万美金，或是有了自己的红色法拉利，而是我得到业内的认可。我没有必要为自己的穿着担心。后来我才知道，为了能开走我们那辆车，杰姬居然学会了用手动档，但我再也没有见到那辆车，她把我的全部家当锁在后备箱，带着儿子和后备箱的钥匙去了东海岸。而正是由于我如此寒酸的穿戴，才让阿尔巴尼斯先生决定打抱不平。这就是上帝的安排，让人永远捉摸不透。

当然，培训项目并没有为我的生活提供保障。作为接受培训的新手，我每月只能拿到1000块津贴，而且把所有时间都要投入进来，除了要接受培训，每天晚些时候还要在办公室里帮经纪人做些事情，其他时间就要忙着为考试做准备，所有这些让我从早忙到晚，根本没时间再去挣点外快补贴家用。我的日子就要过得紧巴巴的，而且在月底第一笔津贴到位前，我连基本的生计都是问题。

The PURSUIT of HAPPYNESS

By that next Monday I'd been able to secure some nights on various friends' couches, line up some meals, borrow enough money to ride BART to work, and find a buddy willing to loan me a suit and a pair of shoes that would get me to that first check. The suit was two sizes too small, and the shoes were two sizes too big. Even so, I walked tall and proud into work that first day, surprised to see a face I'd first seen there several months earlier. A brother named Bob—or "Bow Tie Bob," as I had dubbed him on account of his ever-present bow tie and horn-rimmed glasses and milquetoast, country club demeanor—who was a Stanford graduate and the first African American ever put in the training program. After I'd met him back when I first started stopping by, I was just eager to talk to anybody and happy to see another brother in there. Introducing myself, I'd said, "Wow, you're in here? Wow! How did you get in? What do I need to do to get over? What did you do?"

At the time of those first conversations, Bow Tie Bob had only recently started the training program and seemed more interested in talking about how he had graduated from Stanford, where he played on the golf team, than about how he had broken the color barrier in the financial world. Since it was obvious that I had no credentials, hadn't even gone to college, belonged to no clubs, and didn't play golf. He didn't have much reason to talk to me at all, although the looks he threw at me were quite articulate, saying in essence: *Where did you come from?*

For all I knew, Bow Tie Bob could have grown up in Watts. But he had gone to Stanford—which I wasn't knocking in the least— where it appeared his whole life history had begun and ended, and he had molded himself into the whitest black boy I'd ever met. At least that was my take earlier on.

In an interesting twist, I discovered that Bob was still in the basement, in the same training program, because he had yet to pass his test—after three tries. In the process, he had been transformed from preppy Bow Tie Bob into a radical Bobby Seale. Instead of welcoming me into the program, he greeted me by conveying just what the challenges were and letting me know that the test was culturally biased.

"Really?" I said, wondering if that was true.

"That test will beat you down, oh man," he warned me. "It'll beat you down."

From day one, it was clear to me that I had to do well my first time out of the gate on the test. Business was business, and no matter how much a company wanted to promote equal opportunity, I was sure there was no way they were going to have two black people on the payroll who flunked the test. Circumstances being what they were, I would have one shot. That was why I avoided even associating with Bob, as if his problem, whatever it was, might be catching. After he launched into his culturally biased complaint one too many times, I eventually called him on it, quipping, "Bob, didn't you go to Stanford? Culturally biased? What the hell! You of all people should know that stuff because that's where they teach it." That pretty much was the most contact we had from then on.

在下周一正式培训之前，我只能四处蹭房子住，在朋友家的沙发上过夜，凑合一起吃点饭，借点钱能做公车去上班。还有朋友借给我西装和皮鞋，这样我就可以坚持到拿到第一个月的补贴。这套西装穿着感觉小两号，而皮鞋却大了两号。即便如此，第一天我仍兴高采烈地穿着这身行头去上班，这时我居然碰到几个月前的一个熟人，是鲍勃，我叫他"领结鲍勃"，因为他总喜欢戴着领结和一副角质边框眼镜，他胆子很小，举手投足都土里土气的。他其实毕业于斯坦福大学，而且是首批接受培训的非裔美国人。这次我们再次相见，我就过去和他攀谈起来，其实我很希望和大家都能聊一聊，也很高兴在这能碰到熟人。我上前主动介绍自己："你在这里工作吗？你怎么也到这来了？我需要注意什么呢？你都是怎么干的？"

我们在这头一次见面的时候，领结鲍勃其实也刚来不久，他不太愿意谈及如何打破金融界对肤色的限制，相反更乐意谈及自己是如何从斯坦福毕业的，在学校里还参加过高尔夫球队。这其中的意味很明显，我没有文凭，也没上过大学，没参加任何俱乐部，也不会打高尔夫球，他没必要和我谈这些。但他脸上的表情显然是在说，你是从哪里来的？

据我所知，鲍勃可能是在沃茨长大的，但他去了斯坦福，我丝毫没有贬损他的意思，斯坦福似乎是他生命历程的起点也即将是终点，而且他本来是黑人，但他一心要把自己塑造成白人。至少这是早些时候我对他的看法。

在命运的捉弄下，我发现鲍勃还是停留在起点，还在做着同样的培训，因为他还没有通过测试，这已经是第四次重头再来了。在这个过程里，他已经从单纯的毕业生变成了激进分子。他并没有欢迎我的加盟，反而说培训测试的内容完全就是种族偏见。

"真的吗？"我说，不知他说的是真是假。

"考试就是为了让你彻底放弃，"他警告我，"就是想让你心灰意冷。"

从第一天起，我就明白自己第一次考试就要过关。公司就是这样，无论它多想提供平等发展的机会，我敢肯定公司绝对不会让两个成绩不合格的黑人破格录用。事实就是如此，我只能孤注一掷，所以我尽量避免和鲍勃纠缠在一起，好像无论他本人存在怎样的问题，都可能会传染到他身边的人。听他一遍遍抱怨什么文化偏见，我终于受不了了，"鲍勃，你不是去过斯坦福吗？种族偏见？见鬼吧！你们所有人都该知道那是怎么回事，因为在那里他们就教你们怎么偏见的。"此后，我们基本就没再打过交道。

第十章 加州的梦想

The PURSUIT of HAPPYNESS

In my habit of seeking out individuals from whom I could learn, I hooked up with Andy Cooper, a corner-office guy, one of the top producers at the firm who was selling tax shelters—before the tax laws changed in this era. These deals—usually in real estate, oil, or natural gas—could yield huge write-offs, anywhere from two-to-one up to four-to-one. The basic way these tax shelters were sold was to call and invite prospective investors to a seminar. From the advice given to me by Bob Bridges, I established standards of discipline as to how many phone calls I made every day, with two hundred being my daily requirement, no matter how discouraging the responses. Since Cooper had seen that I was pretty disciplined on the phone, he gave me the job of calling the tax shelter leads and getting them there in person, where he made the pitch, closed the deals, and took all the commissions. As a trainee, I was doing the grunt work for free, something that I didn't quite grasp until later. But it actually didn't matter to me. All I cared about was succeeding in this business, learning everything I could, and getting as much experience as possible.

When I wasn't training, working, or studying, all I cared about was finding out where Christopher was and reuniting with him. But that worry raised the ongoing problem that I had nowhere to live other than at Latrell's, at her mother's back house, where I had a room to myself; at Leon Webb's crib, where I crashed on the floor; at the apartment of my childhood friend Garvin's briefly; or occasionally with a couple of different women who didn't mind sharing their beds and their cooking, though I didn't have much to offer in return other than my lasting appreciation.

Unbeknownst to me, I was fine-tuning the ability to move frequently, even constantly, unaware of how critical these skills were going to become. After that first stipend came in, I went out immediately to buy a better suit. With the suit I wore on my back, the other one on a hanger in a garment bag slung over my shoulder, a few toiletries, and my books, I was self-contained. Rather than leave my stuff at anyone's house, I got in the habit of keeping everything with me. One evening at work when I hadn't lined up a place to stay that night, it occurred to me that since I was usually one of the last to leave the office, no one would be the wiser if I slept under my desk. After all, I was usually the first one there in the morning too.

That first night was strange, like I was going to get found out—not for sleeping at work, but for not having anywhere else to stay. But the fact was that I wasn't like Bow Tie Bob, who kept getting more chances, and I wasn't like Donald Turner, who was in the training program with me and whose big brother was a top producer at the firm: True or not, the other guys had infrastructures in their lives that I did not. Donald was high-strung and intent on passing, but if he didn't, his brother had his back, no question. Not that I felt sorry for myself, because that wasn't going to help me. But I had to face facts: there was no backup plan, no safety net, nobody needing me to succeed to make themselves look good. This was all on me. If I needed to sleep under the desk, then that was what I would do.

我总喜欢找人给我指点迷津，于是乎发现了安迪·库珀，他坐在办公室的一角，是公司里顶尖的业务高手，负责销售避税投资产品。这是在20世纪税法改革之前的特殊产品。这些交易通常集中在房地产、石油或天然气领域，能产生巨额销账，可减免税款高达一半甚至四分之三。销售这些避税投资产品的基本方法是打电话邀请潜在投资者参加研讨会。根据鲍勃·布里斯奇的建议，我制订出自己每天拨打电话的标准，那就是每天要拨打两百个电话，无论对方作何反应，都坚持不懈。自从库珀发现我非常自律，严格按照规定拨打电话之后，他便交代我给那些避税产品负责人打电话的工作，并让他们亲自接听电话，然后再由库珀定价，达成协议，收取全部佣金。作为新手，我做这些单调乏味的工作是没有一分钱的，这点直到后来我才逐渐搞明白。但这对我来说并不重要，我真正关心的是为了能有所建树，必须利用一切机会多多学习，尽可能积累经验，为己所用。

在培训、工作或学习之余，我的全部精力都放在寻找儿子，想方设法让父子团聚。但我现在连住的地方都没有，只能在拉垂尔家里借宿，在她妈妈家后面的老屋勉强找个房间度日，在里昂·韦伯家的婴儿床上，我还摔到了地板上，在我儿时的好友加文的寓所，我也临时住过几天，再有就是还曾在几个女人那里过夜，她们不介意我分享床铺，还给我做饭吃。对于所有这一切，除了心存感激之外，这份感情我无力偿还。

不知不觉中，我来回搬家的本事也提高了不少，而且我根本没有意识到这些本事对我以后会是多么关键。在第一份津贴到位后，我立刻去买了套像样的外套。穿着一件，另一件装在服装袋里用衣撑挂起来，搭在肩上，还买了些保洁用品，还有几本书，这让我有了一丝满足感。我从不把东西留在别人的房里，而是养成了随身携带的习惯。一天晚上由于工作耽搁，我没能到收容所排队等位过夜。想到既然自己通常是最后一个离开办公室的人，那么干脆就在桌子下面睡上一宿也不会有人发现。而且，通常我也是早上第一个到办公室的。

第一次在办公室里过夜感觉有点奇怪，总觉得自己会被发现，倒不是因为在这里睡觉会怎样，而是担心别人发现自己无家可归。事实上，我并不喜欢鲍勃，他总是能得到更多的机会，我也不喜欢唐纳德·特纳，我们一起接受培训，但他的哥哥是公司高层。无论是真是假，其他人都有自己的后台和关系，而我没有。唐纳德十分高调，考试势在必得，但如果他没有通过，有哥哥给他撑腰，也不会有问题。我倒也没过分焦虑，因为那于事无补。但我必须面对现实，我没有什么后台可以为我撑腰，没有人会因为我的成功而脸上有光，一切都要靠自己。如果我需要睡在办公桌下面，那么我就只能如此。

The PURSUIT of HAPPYNESS

After a couple nights, I discovered that sleeping at work was not only convenient but cut down on train fare and there was no bed to make. I would just lie down, sleep, get up before anyone got there, wash my face, freshen up as best I could, brush my teeth and hair, splash water from the sink on my body, paper-towel off, and get some deodorant action going. Sometimes I had the same clothes on, and sometimes I changed my suit and shirt—which I had in my hanging bag. By the time others walked in, I was already on the phone, making sure I got a head start on those two hundred calls a day. I would finish up relatively early in the evening, making sure I didn't call too late. Then it was back to studying.

During the weeks that followed, whenever worries about what I couldn't control overcame me, my focus saved me. If I could just put my head mentally in the call—being positive and friendly but sticking to business, in a time-efficient, productive manner—and create that discipline to keep going, keep dialing, keep putting the phone down and picking it up, then I could survive until night, when I could hit the books, which were really mind-numbingly technical but which I convinced myself were as captivating as the greatest stories ever told. Years of hearing Momma tell me that the public library was the most dangerous place in the world because you could go in there and figure out how to do anything *if* you could read, I also convinced myself that all this information I was learning in preparation for my exam was going to give me that competitive edge so I could pass it that first time.

When my brain wanted to give up, my attitude was that I had to study like I was in prison—because knowledge was power and freedom. An image rode along with me of Malcolm X in prison, teaching himself by studying the dictionary, starting with "aardvark."

With all this moving around, though, I hadn't had any luck locating Jackie and my baby. In fact, she was the one who actually managed to track me down and begin a series of torturous phone calls. At Latrell's, when she first called and asked for me, I got on the phone and was met with sheer silence from Jackie and the sound of Christopher screaming in the background. So I replied with sheer silence, my stomach tied up in knots. It was the first time but not the last, and whether by coincidence or not, every time she called, wherever she found me, Christopher would be crying in the background. Every time, I was in full-blown anguish, but my training from the Navy, and from the stillness I saw in my mother when she was under assault, kept me from saying a word. Finally, unable to provoke me, she would hang up. The *click* echoed for a long time after I put the receiver down.

这么凑合了几个晚上之后，我发现在办公室过夜不仅方便而且还节省车费，也不用到处去寻找床位。我只要躺下来，和衣而眠。在大家到办公室之前起来，洗漱干净，收拾停当。有时我穿着同一件衣服，有时我换上挂在衣袋里的外套和衬衫。当其他人来上班时，我早已开始打电话了，确保自己每天两百个电话任务能够顺利完成。晚上我会尽量不在电话上耗得太晚，从而可以腾出学习的时间。

接下来的几周里，每当觉得自己无能为力的时候，我就只能集中精力，克服这些困扰。一心扑在电话上，积极向上，关注业务，提高效率，注重业绩，忠于职守。一个电话接着一个电话地拨，从不停歇。这样就可以坚持到晚上，而夜里我就可以拿起书本，虽然专业技术知识确实生涩，但我总会想法心无杂念，全神贯注。以前妈妈说图书馆是世上最了不得的地方，如果识文断字，你就会所向披靡，无人能挡。我同时还觉得准备考试而学习的全部知识都会派上用场，是在积极备战，从而确保首战告捷。

每当萌生就此放弃的念头，我的内心就会提醒自己要像当初在监狱里那样坚持学习，因为知识就是力量和自由。黑人领袖马尔科姆·艾克斯在狱中学习的景象历历在目，他就是从字典的第一页开始学起的。

虽然这一切都在逐渐步入正轨，但我仍然不知道杰姬和孩子的下落。实际上，是她在追着我，用电话来折磨我。在拉垂尔家里，她第一次打来电话，我接过电话她却一言不发，只从电话那端传来儿子的尖叫声。我也沉默不语，但是心如刀绞。这才仅仅是开始，无论是否出于偶然，每次她来电，无论她在哪里找到我，儿子都会在电话里哭喊。每次，我都会黯然神伤，郁郁寡欢，但是从海军受过的训练以及妈妈遭到毒打时她所表现的镇定，都让我能够默默不作声，一语不发。最后，如果不能激怒我，她就会挂掉电话。在我把听筒放下之后，电话挂断的声音总会久久在耳畔回响，撕心裂肺。

第十章　加州的梦想

Each time I went through the process of mentally changing the channel, dialing into the frequency that tuned me into what I was studying. Sometimes the thought of Bow Tie Bob helped me kick into overdrive, reminding me of the test's requirements. With a 60 percent or higher failure rate, it covered the Wall Street gamut—financial instruments, products, stocks, bonds, municipal bonds, corporate bonds, convertible stock, preferred stock and regulations—to a depth rarely covered in college business courses or even in some MBA programs. Containing 250 multiple-choice questions, the test had several sections, and I would have to pass 70 percent across the board—options, equities, debt, municipal finance, corporate finance, regulations, rules. Failing even one section was automatic failure of the whole test.

With enough money from the stipends, I found a low-cost rooming house in Oakland, not too far from downtown and Lake Merritt. For all intents and purposes, it was a flophouse, though decently kept up, that included three meals a day or whatever I could eat while I was there. This was a different world than any I'd lived in before, with people just barely scraping by, some with mental problems or addictions, one stumble away from falling through the cracks. Not that I was judging, but I couldn't relate. The rooming house was just a temporary, low-cost option where I could sleep, study, and eat on the occasions that I made it back in time for the evening meal.

For a while I was able to eat during the day whenever tasked with gofer work to set up the conference room for Andy Cooper. As trainees, Donald Turner and I were responsible not only for making the initial calls to leads and following with mailings and more phone calls but for putting out the sandwiches and other light refreshments before the seminars began. If people didn't show, the sandwiches definitely didn't go to waste. Constantly hungry, I didn't mind being asked to do that job at all.

At the same time, I had started to look beyond my exam, at climbing the Dean Witter ladder, and wasn't sure it was such a good idea to cast myself too much in Andy Cooper's crew. For Donald Turner—whose brother was already established and aligned with Cooper, there wasn't much choice. Part of the reason he was so high-strung was the very real pressure on him to live up to expectations based on his brother's star performance.

He had to produce, especially when he was already being spoon-fed business—not all the time, but often enough—from his brother's contacts. This seemed to only make Donald, already pale, go whiter. About my age, clean-shaven, with his red hair combed like a schoolboy's across the front, he had a small, thin voice and a way of finishing up his pitches and his phone calls by saying, "All right, bye-bye."

I wanted to lean over and say, *Who the hell are you saying* bye-bye *to?*

每次我一发现自己要走神，就尽快调整到学习上。有时一想到鲍勃，我就会加大马力，注意考试要求。考试失败率高达 60% 以上，内容覆盖华尔街的全部领域：金融工具、金融产品、证券、债券、市政债券、公司债券、可转换股、优先股、相关规章政策，等等，不一而足。大学里的经济课程或 MBA 项目中都不会涉及这种深度。考试包含 250 道多选题，分成几部分，至少要完成 70% 的内容：期货、股权、债权、政府金融、公司金融、相关法律法规，等等。如果在其中一个部分失利，那么就会导致整个考试的失败。

凭借那点津贴，我在奥克兰找到一间廉价的住房，离市区和美德湖不远。这里经营有方，虽然只是个小客栈，却也打理得井井有条，包括一日三餐，我回去时也总有吃的。这和我以前住的条件是天壤之别。外面很少有人经过，无非是精神不大正常的人或是瘾君子会偶尔路过。我并没有对此做任何评断，不过和我也没有任何干系。这里价位低廉，只是暂时栖身之处，以便我在里面睡觉、学习，有时回去早就做一点晚饭吃。

在白天，每当完成为安迪·库珀安排会议室之类的杂务后，我都会有时间吃些东西。作为新手，唐纳德·特纳和我不仅负责为上司打先行电话、跟踪邮件以及拨打电话，而且还要在研讨会开始前把三明治和茶点摆放好。如果有人没有出席，那么三明治当然不会浪费掉。因为生活拮据，通常吃不饱，所以我并不介意接受消灭这些食物的任务。

同时，我开始考虑考试以后的事情，希望以后在添惠公司中职位也能步步高升，但我不确定，将精力过多投入到安迪·库珀的小组是否妥当。对于唐纳德·特纳来说，他的哥哥和库珀相识相交，别无选择。他如此高度紧张，也部分是源自哥哥对他期望甚高，特别是哥哥在公司的表现就已经相当出色。

他必须有所作为，尤其是得到哥哥的言传身教，虽然并非总是如此，但在与哥哥的接触中耳濡目染，就已经足够了。

这似乎使唐纳德原本苍白的脸色更加难看。他和我年龄相仿，胡须剃得很干净，一头红发梳到额前，一幅学生模样，说话细声细气，每次打完电话都会说："好的，再见。"

我真想凑过去问："你到底在和谁说再见？"

第十章 加州的梦想

And he had the good leads. Me, I made the cold calls. I didn't know them, they didn't know me, but they knew the name of the company and took my call. OJT allowed me to develop three important skills. First, I had to make my call quota. Next, I had to learn how to quickly assess whether this was someone who was just chatty or really worth pursuing. Finally, I had to know when it was time to wrap up. This became a game for me—to know if the prospect was getting ready to say no or hang up on me. My internal mantra was: *I'm going to hang up on you before you hang up on me.*

This way, no matter the outcome, I could win. In order to not seem rude, I'd always say the same thing: "Thank you very much, have a nice day," as clearly and quickly as I could. Polite and businesslike, I didn't have to hear no or the angry sound of the phone being hung up, the call didn't reflect badly on me or the company, and I could be on to the next call—dialing the old-fashioned rotary phone, like cranking away at a lottery wheel.

Whenever I stopped, with nothing else to concentrate on, there was nowhere else to go in my head except for my powerlessness at finding and seeing Christopher.

The other trainees knew I was intense, obviously. But I saw no reason to confide in anyone where I was staying or what drama was playing out in my personal life. It helped me to reflect on something Momma had said to me way back when I had illusions of becoming an actor—the time I asked her for five dollars and instead of giving it to me, she made a point by suggesting that I act like I had five dollars. That had cooled me off being an actor real fast. But there was something else in her message that became relevant now. No matter what I had in my pocket, no matter what my suit cost, nobody could prevent me from acting *as if* I was a winner. Nobody could prevent me from acting *as if* my problems were all in the process of being solved. Pretty soon, my acting *as if* was so convincing that I started to believe it myself. I began to think futuristically, *as if* I had already passed the test as I weighed what would happen next.

This was what I puzzled over while riding BART over from Oakland and back every day, every night. The patronage system of favors done in return for favors owed had started to make me wary. I realized that, by sticking with Andy Cooper, I'd end up more or less working for him and catching his overflow. That was one route to go, the stepping-stone path, maybe safer, but ultimately less lucrative. The riskier approach was to carve out a niche of my own, to build my own base from scratch. For a new guy who hadn't even passed his test yet, deciding to take that approach would be a couple notches past cocky and just shy of foolhardy. Still, from what I was learning around the office, the major players were the few brokers who did their own thing—putting time into research and combining traditional and nontraditional ways of getting the biggest bang for their clients' bucks and themselves.

他有很好的客户基础。而我只能碰运气。我与他们素未谋面，不曾相识，但他们听说过公司的名声，所以会接听我的电话。上岗培训帮我强化了三种重要的技能。首先，需要制定电话数量限额。其次，要学会如何迅速判定对方是在搪塞还是值得争取。最后，要掌握火候，知道何时收关。这对我犹如一场游戏，需要预见到对方是准备拒绝还是挂断电话。我心里暗想："在你挂电话前我就挂你的电话。"

无论结果如何，我都能借助这个办法赢得优势。为了听上去不显得唐突无礼，我总会尽可能清晰快速地说出："非常感谢，祝您今天愉快。"显得彬彬有礼，非常职业，有条有理，我没必要听到对方否定的回答或生气地挂掉电话，不过电话里对我和公司的反应还都不错，于是我能继续拨打下一个电话。老式的拨号电话就像彩票转盘，对我充满无限诱惑。

每当有了一点闲暇，不用再去考虑其他事情时，我满脑子都是对自己无力寻找儿子的无奈。

其他培训生都很清楚我非常忙碌。但我没必要对每个人倾诉，说自己住在哪里，或经历着怎样的人生不幸。我想起妈妈以前对我说过的话，当时我曾幻想成为演员，向她要五美元，但她却建议让我先演好自己拿到五美元的样子。此后我的演员梦想很快就降温了，最后终于放弃。但她话语中的深刻含义却启示了我现在的生活。无论我口袋里还剩多少钱，无论我穿的衣服值多少钱，没人能阻止我进入角色，要表现得自己就是个赢家。没有人能阻止我进入角色，就像问题已经有了眉目。很快，我便能表演到位，开始相信自己真的能行。我开始设想未来，仿佛自己已经通过考试。

我每天都要坐公车从奥克兰来回穿梭，路上我都会尽力整理思路。俗话说要礼尚往来。我意识到，如果与安迪·库珀总在一起，那么我最终会成为他的跟班，或多或少为他做事，并赚取他利润的零头。这是一种办法，这种助他一臂之力的做法确实安全，但终归空间有限。更冒险的一招是为自己定方向，白手起家。对于一个尚未通过考试的新手来说，决定采用这种方式会显得过分招摇，或者有勇无谋。但从我在办公室里所见所闻来看，这个游戏中的高手就是那几个拥有自己业务的经纪人，他们把大量时间投入到客户研究之中，将传统与非传统的方式相结合，为客户同时也为自己获取最大利益。

Dave Terrace was one of the cats I kept an eye on. With one of the biggest offices at the firm, he traded back where all the heavy hitters sat, behind the floor where us newcomers were, and whenever I could, I turned around to watch him do his thing. Pure business —no flash, solid, consistent. He might not have been making more than Andy Cooper, but he was in solo flight. That appealed to me. My choice was made. As it later turned out, to have gone and hitched a ride on the tax shelter bonanza that Andy and his guys were enjoying would have sent me into the same crash they all faced when the tax laws changed.

The day of the exam arrived. Donald Turner, wound up tighter than ever, looked so stressed I thought he'd kill himself if he didn't pass. Bow Tie Bob wasn't taking the test again at this exam, possibly because he was busy filing complaints about its cultural bias. Maybe to Donald and some of the other trainees I appeared to be annoyingly relaxed. Not so. Inside I had the raised adrenaline and tension of a warrior going into battle, a gladiator ready to take on his most lethal opponent—if need be. But I was prepared. Nothing stumped me; there were no tricks. No cultural bias either. I knew the answers. The test was easy. In fact, I whipped through the first half with time to spare, took the break, and did the same when we came back for the second half of the test.

We had to wait three days to find out the results. That was just enough time for the delayed-reaction freak-out to take place. What if I only thought it was easy? What if I didn't spot the trick questions or the cultural bias? What if the test was about to beat me down after all? Scolding myself, I repeated my mantra that there was nothing on there I'd never seen before and just to leave it alone.

The phone call couldn't have come fast enough. One of the associate branch managers was on the other end when I picked up the phone in my room.

"The suspense is over," he began, waiting for my reaction.

I waited too, saying nothing.

"You passed, Gardner," he chuckled, probably aware of the monstrous sigh of relief and release that came from my lungs. "Overall you scored eighty-eight percent," he went on. "You did great."

Neither surprised nor elated, I was grateful. Sitting on the edge of my bed in the rooming house, I let my mind go blank and just let myself breathe. There was no one to go celebrate with, nobody who understood what this meant. Whether or not Donald Turner passed, I never knew. But I did know that my colleague Bow Tie Bob wasn't going to be thrilled.

大卫·特拉斯就是我一直关注的高手。在整个公司里有些超大面积的办公室，其中就有他的一间。当很多大户抛出的时候，他则选择买入。在那一层后面的区域就是我们这些新手呆的地方，每当闲暇时分我就会绕过去观察他做事的样子。那其实纯粹就是工作，没有波澜起伏，却坚定而连续。他可能没有安迪·库珀赚得多，但他却特例独行。这对我很有吸引力。我当下决心已定。正如日后的证明，安迪他们原本是笼罩在避税投资的幸运光环下，乐享其中，但当税法变更之后，他们的事业就面临崩溃，如果当时我和他们拴在一条船上，那么后果也不堪设想。

考试的日子到了。唐纳德·特纳异常紧张，看上去压力很大，我想如果他没通过考试肯定会去自杀。鲍勃又没有参加考试，可能因为他还在忙着关于种族偏见的抱怨。也许在唐纳德和其他一些培训生看来，我表现得如此轻松着实让他们感到不爽。其实不然。我极度兴奋，斗志昂扬，好像武士将要投入战斗一样，或像角斗士准备与他最致命的对手展开一场厮杀。不过我确实有备而来，没有什么能难得住我；什么偏题怪题甚至什么偏见都不在话下。考试并不是很难。实际上，我很快便做完了试卷第一部分的题目，而且还剩下些时间可以检查，休息片刻后回来接着做第二部分题目，感觉也很轻松。

我们得等三天后才能知道考试结果。三天的时间足以让人反应迟钝、失去理智。即使我认为试题简单那又怎么样？即使我没能发现考题中的陷阱或者种族偏见又会怎样呢？即使考试最终会让我输得很难看又有何干系？我暗自给自己打气，一遍遍祈祷着，还是听其自然吧。

电话铃终于响起，是分公司助理经理打来的。

"悬念揭晓了，"他开口说，仿佛在等待我的反应。

我默默地等待着，什么也没说。

"你通过了，克里斯·加德纳，"他咯咯笑着，可能意识到我会如释重负。"你的总分是88分，"他继续说，"成绩非常好。"

我既没有喜出望外，也没有兴高采烈，而是心存感激。在屋里，我只是坐在床边上，任思绪一片空白，让自己机械地呼吸。没有人和我一起庆祝，没有人理解这对我意味着什么。不管唐纳德·特纳是否通过考试，但我确信鲍勃是不会高兴的。

The PURSUIT of HAPPYNESS

What did it mean? That I passed the test, but only one test. Like I'd won a qualifying race for the Olympics. My training was over and I was ready to compete. Now I was going back to scratch, back to cold-calling out of the white pages. I was going in to build my own book, whatever it took, cranking out calls that I'd pitch and close, finding my niche. In some ways, the stakes had just gotten higher than before when the company had an investment in training me. That was done. Now I had to produce. But something had changed. No longer did I have to prove a damn thing. My confidence was as big as the Pacific Ocean. I had passed. Finally, I was legitimate. I had my papers.

* * *

Jackie sits across from me at the Berkeley coffee shop, a month or so later on a Friday afternoon, as I try hard not to be rattled, no matter what she throws at me.

It has been four months since she left with my son, and our car that I'll never see again, putting me out into the cold. That alone is bizarre, but we have also just come from court, where things have taken an additionally strange turn.

In the days leading up to the court date, she had placed a few calls to me and had actually spoken, refusing to let me talk to Christopher or to give me any information as to his whereabouts, but baiting me with some details—like the fact that she taught herself to drive a stick shift in order to drive across the country and that she had lots of lawyer power. The lawyer was a "brother," someone I'd come to refer to as a "poindexter"—a dry, bland, nonthreatening eunuch. Though I suspected that she meant her brother the lawyer, when I walked into the hearing with my lawyer— whose fee cost me most of my salary that first month as a broker— I saw that her representation power consisted of someone from the local DA's office, representing the state, and the arresting police officer.

The next surprise was that Jackie decided not to bring charges. Just like that. In my analysis, right or wrong, it seemed that all of this had been Jackie's way of having contact with me. That was supported by her suggestion that we go somewhere and talk.

Fine. Here we are. She seems to know where I live, like she's been keeping tabs on me, which indicates that she knows I passed the test. But she's got nothing to say about that. Sure, maybe she has some sour grapes. After all, she never believed I could do it without the college degree, or possibly she was projecting her own insecurities, or maybe she has other people telling her that she's missing her dream while I'm chasing mine. Whatever is the case, of course she doesn't congratulate me that I have the license and the job. But then again, she has something that I don't have—our son. Oh yeah, and she has my stuff. Not that there's much I could use at the moment, given my temporary lodging, which in the foreseeable future isn't about to change.

那意味着什么？我通过了考试，但这只是个考试而已。我赢得了奥运会的预选赛。培训结束了，我准备开始投身到竞赛中。现在我又恢复到从头开始的状态，面对那些陌生的名单逐个拨通电话。我要建立自己的客户名单，无论代价是什么，我会给他们拨打电话，找准自己的市场定位。在某种程度上，现在的赌注比当初公司投资培训我的时候更高了。我需要拿出真正的业绩来。虽然一些情况发生了变化，但我不再需要证明什么了。我的自信心就像太平洋一样辽阔。我通过了测试，有了自己的合法身份。

* * *

大约过了一个月左右，在一个周五的傍晚，杰姬和我在伯克利咖啡店里面对面地坐了下来，我极力控制着自己的情绪，无论她说什么都不发火。

自从她带着儿子开着我们的车离开后，距今已有四个月了，我再也没有见到他们，这让我心灰意冷。单单这一点就很不对劲了，我们刚从法院里出来，但是那里发生的事情更加不对劲。

在接近法院开庭审理的日子之前，她给我打了几次电话，终于开口说话了，但不许我和儿子说话，也闭口不提任何关于儿子去向的信息，只是告诉给我一些细枝末节，让我饱受煎熬，比如为了把车开到东海岸，她自己学会了手动挡，再有就是她还有律师的强大保护。那个律师其实是一个兄弟，可我宁愿称他为"书呆子"，是干巴巴的、不足挂齿的娘娘腔。虽然我不知道她指的是不是就是这家伙，当我和我的律师进入听证会现场的时候（为支付律师费，我花掉了作为经纪人的第一个月的大部分工资），我看到她那边有几个来自当地区检察官办公室的代表，他们代表州政府，旁边还有警察。

接下来让我吃惊的是杰姬决定不再提出诉讼。就这样定了。依我分析，无论对错与否，那似乎是她为了与我取得联系的方式。她建议我们找个地方坐下来好好交谈。

那就在这里谈吧。她似乎知道我住在哪里，仿佛我就没有出过她的手心，而且似乎也知道我通过了经纪人考试。但她什么都没说。当然，也许她此时此刻心情非常复杂。毕竟，她从未想过我连大学都没上过，居然会成功闯关，或者她可能遇到了些麻烦，或可能有人说我在追逐自己的梦想，而她却失去了梦想。无论是哪种情况，总之她没有祝贺我取得经纪人资格，并找到新工作。但孩子在她那里，而我却见不到。还有她把我的东西带走了。目前我倒是用不上，我还没有地方放这些东西。

The PURSUIT of HAPPYNESS

My decision not to be part of the Cooper Clan wasn't the most practical initially. In terms of commissions, I was at about $1,200 a month now, though I could have made more had I been willing to help set up bigger deals for Andy to commission for himself while taking over some of his smaller deals as they became available. Instead, I wanted to nab bigger and smaller deals for myself, even though there was no promise that I'd get either. That was my choice—I had a higher ceiling but less of a floor. I approached the numbers game with eyes open, knowing full well that X number of calls equals X number of prospects equals X number of sales equals X number of clients equals X number of gross commissions, or dollars in my pocket. Out of two hundred calls, a great batting average was ten first-time clients, with half that many turning into repeat customers—where money was made. Doing my own thing, I was the assembly line, cranking, dialing, and smiling. I was good, so good that several more senior brokers made overtures to me to collaborate with them, to help boost their numbers. Whenever they did, without being ungrateful, I typically responded, "No, I don't think I'll take you up on that. I just want to build my own book. But thanks for thinking of me."

This entitled me to be named, nearly continuously, the "Broker of the Day." At first, this sounded like an honor, a step up. Broker of the Day was the point man for any office walk-ins who didn't already have a broker or an account at the firm. Usually walk-ins wanted specific information or had an idea of something they might want to buy. In San Francisco, where peace and free love had ruled not many years earlier, there were nonetheless racial biases in 1982, and it was soon clear that these walk-ins weren't expecting to see a black man as a stockbroker. That added another layer of challenge, but I acted as if it wasn't an issue and offered my full assistance. "How do you do? I understand you want to buy a Ginnie Mae?" We'd go over the particulars. Or: "You want to put money away for your grandkids? Yes, I have some suggestions."

A few times, after I had laid all the groundwork and basically written up the ticket, I subsequently learned that I hadn't gotten the commission. Why? "Well," the branch manager said on those occasions, "they wanted someone with more experience."

The first time this happened I steamed. The second time I confronted my boss. "Let me see if I got this right? They're basically buying stock in Commonwealth Edison, correct? To get the dividend yield, the income, it's not going to change based on who gets the commission. Same stock, same company. But they wanted someone with a little more experience? He gets the commission that I set up?"

起初我决定不和库珀一起干，但这并不非常实际。就佣金而言，我现在的月薪是1200美元，如果我愿意帮助他做些大单获利，时机成熟时接他的一些小单子，那么我还能赚得更多。然而，我想为自己抓住下单的机会，即使不一定能成功，那是我的选择，我往上往下做的空间都很大。我睁大眼睛做数字游戏，心里很清楚多少电话等于多少希望等于多少销售量等于多少客户等于多少净利润，也就是我口袋中的收益。在两百个电话中，平均的成功率是搞定10个第一次打交道的客户，其中一半还会再次打交道，成为老客户，这才会是财源的所在。我工作起来一气呵成，酣畅淋漓，摇曲柄、拨号、微笑……我的表现非常出色，以至于一些资深经纪人提出来和我联手，帮助提高成交量。但我心怀感激的同时，却都逐一拒绝了，"不行，我觉得自己心有余力不足，我只想建立自己的客户群，但还是要谢谢您把我考虑进来。"

我几乎连续被选做"当日经纪人"，起先，这像是一种荣誉，又有进步。可当日经纪人其实就是公司指派的一个专人，负责接待散客，这些散客在公司里面没有经纪人或尚未开户，通常就是想打听一些具体信息，或者购买些产品。早些时候，旧金山是个和平之声与自由恋爱风靡的城市，然而1982年那里出现了种族歧视，而这些散客不希望证券经纪人会是个黑人。这又多了一层挑战，但是我泰然自若，冷静对待，反而提供更为周到的服务。"您好，是想买吉利美证券的么？"我们也会提出具体建议，"您是想为孙子孙女留点钱吗？我这里有些建议。"

有几次，在我做好前期准备，基本上搞定订单后，却得知自己并没得到佣金。这是为什么呢？有时候，分公司经理会这么解释："他们想让更有经验的人帮他们做。"

第一次发生这种情况时，我很愤怒。第二次又发生同样情况，我就直接去与老板面对面交涉。"您看看我这么认为对不对？他们基本上是买的爱迪生电力公司的股票，对吗？他获得的收益和谁拿到佣金是没有关系的。股票还是一样，公司也一样。但他们想让更有经验的人帮他们做？让这人拿本该是我的那份佣金吗？"

第十章 加州的梦想

The PURSUIT of HAPPYNESS

It wasn't rocket science. The reality was that people had never dealt with a black person before and didn't want to, even though I'd done a great job and made them some money. But I was learning that I could turn down being Broker of the Day. Back I went to smiling and dialing. The lesson here wouldn't necessarily apply to other guys, but for me it was apparent that I did better on the phone. If I could get someone excited about the opportunity to make some money, if we could make the connection, that was the way to go. Besides, though I could resort to the vernacular any time, any day, I was not audibly black on the phone. Maybe that stemmed from the knack of learning other languages—musical, medical, financial, Anglo-Saxon, whatever. And a name like Chris Gardner? No telltale ethnicity there. I could have been anybody from any background.

The phone became my color shield. I actually discouraged new clients from coming into the office in person, which was one of the ways other brokers liked to close their deals. "Okay, here's what we're going to do," I'd say once we established that we were going to do some business. "Let's open the account, send me in the check, and we'll get the company to send your confirmations out, and we'll just get going. Will you be mailing the check today or would you like to do a wire transfer?"

When folks wanted to come in, I had an easy way of saying, "No, that's not necessary, because it's so hectic and crazy in here. Let's do it over the telephone."

After the four months since Jackie had split with Christopher, the ball was definitely starting to roll, but it hadn't translated into much of a change in my income yet. I had no outward symbol of my success so far to wave like a flag in front of Jackie.

Instead, I give her as little insight into where I'm at as she's giving me about my kid. Finally, she slides a key in my direction and tells me where the storage locker is that contains my stuff. But what I want most, she refuses to offer—my child. With the least amount of reaction I can give, I pocket the key and leave, reeling inside.

Well, I think, before I truck back to Oakland, I don't have anywhere to put my stuff yet, but at least I can go dig out a couple items of clothing and my trusty briefcase that I purchased almost a year earlier when I first made my foray into the business world.

Later that night at the rooming house, as I'm airing out the suit and shining the shoes that I pulled from storage, I pause to admire my stylish, brown-leather Hartman briefcase—something I'd spent what seems like an exorbitant $100 on. Just then, I'm startled by the sound of firm knocking at the door. The rhythm of the three knocks—short, short, long—reminds me of Jackie's way of knocking. But then again, that's highly unlikely.

Sure enough, as I open the door, there she is. Not alone. In Jackie's arms is Christopher. My son, my baby! He's nineteen or twenty months now—looking more like three years old, more beautiful than I had remembered him in my every waking and sleeping recollection. Between my shock and my euphoria, I don't know what to say.

其实这其中的奥秘并不难懂，事实是他们之前从未与黑人打过交道，也不想打交道，即使我工作得很卖力，并让他们赚了些钱，也于事无补。不过我了解到我可以拒绝成为当日经纪人。回来后我继续微笑着打我的电话。这个教训不一定适用于其他人，但是对我而言，很明显我电话销售的业绩会更好。如果我能让别人对挣钱机会怦然心动，如果我能与他建立联系，那就一切水到渠成。另外，虽然我可以随时随地变化说话的方式和语调，但在当时我说话口音并不像黑人。也许是受到我学习音乐、医学、金融等多种专业的影响。而且克里斯·加德纳这样的名字也毫无种族特点，我可以是来自任何背景的任何人。

电话成了我肤色的保护屏。如果新客户亲自到办公室来，可能反而不利于我们的成交，而其他经纪人可能会喜欢面对面的方式。"好的，那我们就这么定了。"一旦建立起某种业务关系我就会说："开个账户，把支票寄给我，我们会让公司把凭据给您送去，就可以了。您是想今天把支票寄过来还是通过电汇？"

如果他们想到办公室来，我会轻松地说："没有必要，这里又吵又乱，我们就在电话里说吧。"

自从杰姬与儿子离开了四个月以后，事情显然又发生了变化，但我的收入水平却基本依然如故。目前我还没有胜券在握，没办法在杰姬面前挥动胜利的旗帜。

然而，我没有向杰姬透露自己的住处，就像她没告诉我孩子的去处一样。最后，她在桌子那头把钥匙向我这边推过来，并告诉我装着我东西的储物箱放在哪里。但我最想要的是我的儿子，她却拒绝给我。我几乎没有任何反应，揣上钥匙就离开了，但内心却一阵阵翻江倒海，很不是滋味。

我想，在我回奥克兰之前，也没有任何地方可以放那些东西，但至少可以找出几件衣服，还有我那心爱的公文包，那个包大概是一年前买的，当时我首次准备进军商界。

那天晚些时候，在我住的地方，我把衣服挂了出来，把从储物箱里翻出的皮鞋打上了鞋油，正停下来欣赏自己那棕褐色的哈特曼皮质公文包，那好像是我花了100多美元买的。就在这时，我吃惊地听到有人在重重地敲我的房门。三个有节奏的敲击声，两短一长，这让我想起杰姬的敲门方式，但又觉得不大可能。

有了足够的心理准备后，我打开了屋门，正是她。但不是一个人，她还抱着克里斯多夫，我的儿子，我的宝贝儿子！他现在已经19个月或20个月大了，看上去更像是三岁大的孩子，比我记忆中每天叫醒他和哄他睡觉时的样子更漂亮了。我又惊又喜，不知该说什么好。

第十章　加州的梦想

The PURSUIT of HAPPYNESS

There is more shock and more euphoria to come as Jackie hands him to me and as she does says, "Here." From behind her she produces a huge, overstuffed duffel bag and his little blue stroller. Again she says, "Here."

I'm holding Christopher, hugging him tight to me, still not following what's happening.

Slowly it dawns on me that this isn't a visit but that she's actually leaving him in my care. Though she says little, I know her well enough to realize that this is it and that she just can't do this anymore.

From our brief exchange, it's apparent that she is feeling the pressure of raising a child as a single mother at the same time that she is establishing herself professionally. I also sense that she regrets taking him out of state and not working out a joint arrangement earlier on. But none of that is spelled out exactly in words. She does tell me what's inside the duffel bag, including the monster package of Pampers, what he needs to eat and how often, what he shouldn't eat—"no candy"—and then she tells Christopher good-bye and leaves.

"Christopher," I tell him over and over, "I missed you! I missed you!"

"I missed you too, Poppa," he says, talking in a full sentence now and with one of his wise expressions, like he's already a veteran of change and knows we may be in for a rough ride.

Or maybe that's what I'm thinking. Whatever is going to happen, two things I know are true. First of all, I have my son back with me and nobody on this earth is going to take him away from me again. That's a principle of the universe now. Second—and I already know this to be a fact—we have just become instantly fucking homeless.

* * *

Time changes when you're homeless. Seasons turn out of order, all in the course of a day. Especially in San Francisco, which has all four seasons all year round. During the daylight hours of the working week, time feels sped up, passing way too quickly. Nights and weekends are another story. Everything slows to an ominous crawl.

Your memory changes when you're homeless. Always moving around, changing geography, having no address, no anchors to tie to when events take place. It becomes hard to recall whether something happened a week before or a month before, yesterday or three days ago.

How did I become instantly homeless, especially now that I was a stockbroker working for Dean Witter? Because children were not allowed at the rooming house. No exceptions. The days of crashing on the couch at my friends' homes were over too. I'd imposed enough when I was in the training program, but to ask to stay for a few nights and add, "Oh, by the way, and my baby too?"—that wasn't going to fly. The ladies I was seeing may have been fond of me in the sack but weren't going to be pleased about me showing up with an inquisitive, active toddler.

杰姬把他送到我怀里说"拿着",我几乎被冲昏了头脑,她又从身后拿出一个硕大鼓鼓囊囊的粗呢包,还有儿子的蓝色婴儿车,说道:"这个也给你。"

我把儿子紧紧抱入怀中,但还是没缓过神来。

慢慢的我才明白过来,她这并不是带着孩子回来,而是要把儿子留给我照顾。虽然她什么也没说,但我太了解她了,意识到她坚持不下去了,事情到此为止。

在我们短暂的交谈中,我可以明显察觉到,作为单身妈妈她所担负的压力,尤其是要在事业上开创局面的同时还要抚养孩子。我也觉察出她很后悔当初没有安排双方抚养协议就把孩子带走了,这让她苦不堪言,但这些她都没有直接告诉我。不过她告诉我包里的物品,有一大包加厚帮宝适、孩子需要吃的食品和次数,不能吃的东西,比如"不能吃糖"之类,然后她和儿子道了别,便离开了。

"克里斯多夫,"我一遍又一遍地对他说,"我想你!我想你!"

"我也想你,爸爸,"他很会说话,现在已经能用完整的句子交流了,好像他已经习惯应对这些变迁,而且知道我们将一起面对生活的困境。

或许这只是我个人的想法。无论发生什么,我知道两件事情是真实的。首先,儿子回到了身边,在这世上没有人能再把他从我这里夺走。现在这就是一条宇宙定律。其次,我知道这很快就会成为事实,那就是我们马上就要无家可归了。

* * *

当你无家可归时,季节就会完全错位,好像在一天之内就会历经四季更替。在旧金山更是如此,一天之内四季都会光顾。在工作日里,白天的时间转瞬即逝。夜晚和周末又会截然不同,一切都会慢得像蜗牛一样爬行。

记忆也会在你流浪的时候发生变化。一切似乎总是处于移动当中,不停地变换着地理方位,没有固定地址,有事情发生的时候也没有办法停下来。很难回忆起一件事的发生是在一周前或一个月前,还是昨天或者三天前。

我怎么总是无家可归,尤其现在我已经是添惠公司的证券经纪人了啊?因为我住的地方不接收小孩留宿,无一例外。在朋友家沙发上过夜的日子也结束了。当初我参加培训时还能有个借口,但当我请求留宿几晚并加了一句"顺便问一下,我的孩子也能住这儿吗?"就没有下文了。我见到的那些女人可能会欣然让我留宿,但当我带着个爱刨根问底、天生好动的小家伙出现的时候,她们就改主意了。

第十章 加州的梦想

The PURSUIT of HAPPYNESS

The one lucky break I caught in trying to figure out how to navigate a whole new terrain was the fact that it was a Friday when Jackie showed up with Christopher, giving me at least that night at the rooming house before being thrown out the next day. That also gave me the weekend to find us a place to stay and a day care situation starting on Monday.

We hit the streets Saturday with all of our gear, him in the stroller, as I practice the new balancing act that's going to get all too familiar, heading down toward the "HOstro" to check out the price of some of the HOtels—emphasis on first syllables no accident. I'm having a major internal debate over the questions: *What* am I gonna do? *How* am I gonna do this? One line of thinking says, *I've got my baby, I'm not giving him up, that's not an option.* Another voice reminds me, *Ain't no backup here, no cavalry coming in for reinforcement.*

The day care center in San Francisco at $400 a month is out of the question. With rent at least $600, that would take up what I'm earning after taxes, leaving nothing for food, transportation, and diapers. At a pay phone I call a few friends to see if they've got any inside scoop on day care facilities in the East Bay. One of the places looks wonderful. It too turns out to be over my budget; besides, they don't accept kids who aren't potty-trained.

"Okay, Christopher," I tell him as we start to leave, "we'll work on that, okay, baby?"

As I'm looking around, hoping that it won't be too long until I can afford having him here, I notice that the day care management has a sign on the wall declaring the center to be a place of "HAPPYNESS."

For a minute, I start to question in my mind how good a child care facility can be that can't even spell "happiness" correctly. Of all the things I have to worry about, that's not one of them. Even so, back out on the street, I feel the need to make sure my son knows that the word is spelled with an *I* and not a *Y*. H-A-P-P-I-N-E-S-S.

"Okay, Poppa," says Christopher, repeating the word. "Happiness."

"That's a big word," I say with approval, wishing that I could ensure Chris's and my own happiness in the immediate future.

The ability to spell is not my main concern when I call the numbers I've been given for Miss Luellen at one house and Miss Bessie at another and a third place on Thirty-fifth Street—babysitters who keep kids on a regular basis but not any kind of day care centers with licenses and registrations. The woman on Thirty-fifth says to bring Christopher early on Monday and says that I can pay her by the week. One hundred bucks. There's no real money savings except that I can pay as I go. Though this doesn't do a lot to reassure me that he's getting the best care possible, it's better than nothing.

幸运的是，我还有一点点时间让自己努力琢磨该怎么应付这全新的局面，好在杰姬带着儿子出现的那天是周五，至少当天晚上我还有地方过夜，虽然次日就被撵了出去，但我在周末还有时间找四处地方，并赶在周一早上把儿子送到幼儿园。

周六的时候，我们带着全部家当走上街头，他坐在婴儿车里，我想出一个万全之策，以后这个做法将会熟悉得不能再熟悉，那就是朝着一个方向前进，去看旅馆的价钱。我心里一直在问自己：我该做什么？我该怎么办？这时脑子里忽闪过一个念头：我和孩子在一起，我决不会放弃他，这别无选择。另一个声音又提醒我说：这里没有谁能帮得上忙，只有你自己。

旧金山的日托中心每月收费400块，再加上住宿要花600块，这就会让我一个月的税后收入所剩无几，根本没钱吃饭，解决交通和孩子的尿布问题。在一部付费电话旁，我给几个朋友去了电话，想问问他们知不知道东海岸有什么合适的日托中心。有个地方似乎还不错，但是超出了我的预算，而且不会自己去洗手间的孩子这里也不接受。

"好的，小克里斯多夫，我们得学点东西了，"我们边说边离开电话亭。

我四处张望，希望很快能帮儿子找个地方，而且费用我还能支付得起，我看到一家日托中心，门口挂了个牌子，上面写着"幸富①"。

我不由得产生了质疑，如果日托中心连"幸福"两个字都能写错，还指望它能把孩子照顾得有多好呢。不管怎样，这个地方我是不能考虑的。即便如此，走到街上，我还是觉得需要让儿子知道"幸福"两个字到底该怎么写，于是一笔一划地给他做示范——幸福。

"记住了，爸爸，"儿子念着这两个字，"幸福。"

这个词非常重要，希望我能尽早给我们爷俩带来幸福。我挨个拨着手里这些日托中心的电话号码，有什么陆伦小姐、贝席小姐之类的，还有一个是经常帮着看孩子，但是没有执照，这个女人大概35岁的样子，说可以周一把儿子带过来，还可以按周付费，每周100块，这倒是不比别处便宜，但我至少还能有点周转的时间。我不知道孩子在这里能得到多好的照顾，但至少比没人管要强吧。

---

① 编者注：原文为"HAPPYNESS"，此处为该日托中心牌子上的拼写错误，正确拼法为"HAPPINESS"。作者在原英文书名中也使用了这一错误拼法，为这一细节埋下伏笔。

For a place to stay that night, I get us a room over in West Oakland on West Street at The Palms, so named for the one palm tree in the courtyard and a second one on the corner two hundred feet away. From what I can tell, the only residents besides us are the hookers. Later, this doesn't bother me, but for the time being all I can do is get us into the room as fast as I can, double-lock the door, and turn the volume up on the TV to make sure we don't have to hear the sound effects of any tricks being turned.

It costs me $25 a day for the room, which comes with a color TV, one bed, a desk and a chair, and a bathroom. But okay, we're here. That's my new philosophy: wherever we are, we're here, this is where we're at, and we're going to make the best of it. For now.

When I managed to step out of the blur of space and time to look at the big picture, the reality was that I had the job and the opportunity that was going to change our circumstances and lives forever. Nothing was going to shake my conviction, not even the mental and actual calculations of what I'd have left over after the cost of The Palms and babysitting, and not even the screaming and sobbing that Christopher began the minute we walked into the babysitter's place.

That killed me. He could probably feel my reluctance to leave him with strangers, but I had no choice. All I could do was reassure him, "I'll be back. I'll be back." Backing out, practically in tears myself, I kept repeating, "I'll be back."

When I came to pick him up that evening, he ran up and almost jumped into my arms. "See, I told you," I reminded him.

But the next morning it was worse. Getting him out of the hotel and into his stroller was a struggle, and he started wailing the second we rolled around the corner onto Thirty-fifth, me chanting all the way in the door and out: "I'll be back. I'll be back. I'll be back."

The days and images begin to streak by as the nights get longer and the air becomes colder and wetter. After picking him up, I usually take him for something to eat, somewhere warm and cheap where I air my concerns with my little sidekick, telling him, "Naw, this ain't gonna work. The Palms is too expensive, man. Remember the house? Yeah, in Berkeley, our little house. It was ours. This transient thing's no good."

Christopher gives me one of his furrowed-brow expressions.

How can I explain to him or myself? It's not just the whores, the dopeheads and winos, and the street lowlifes, it's the feeling of not being settled, of having no home base or support group. It's about the noise and the lights constantly going from the outside because The Palms is right on the drag, the "ho" stroll, with car horns honking, music playing, and people hollering. The TV helps drown some of it out, enough for me to chew on any and all options, to focus on what to do and how.

当天晚上要找个地方过夜，我在西奥克兰西街的棕榈旅店找了个房间，这家旅店院子里正好有棵棕榈树，几十米开外的街角还有一棵，故此得名。看得出来住在这里的都是些不三不四的女人。这应该不是问题，我只要飞快地跑到自己的房间，把门反锁上，再把电视的音量调到最大，盖住那些乱七八糟的声音就可以了。

这一晚上花了我 25 块钱，屋子配备了彩电、床、桌椅，还有洗澡间。不管怎样，我们在这儿了。这就是我的新理念，不管我们身处何方，我们就活在当下，就活在此时此刻，充分享受自己。

我不去想目前居住的窘迫，而去努力考虑一下全局，我现在有了工作，这就从长远角度有可能让我们渐入佳境。我意已决，没人能让我动摇，即便我付过日托费和旅店的费用后兜里已经所剩无几，即便儿子一进了托儿所的门就开始又哭又闹，这些都不能让我有丝毫的改变。

我的心如刀割，儿子可能也意识到我不愿把他和陌生人放在一起，但我别无选择。我只能安慰他："爸爸会回来接你的。"我眼含着热泪，抽身出来，不断地重复着这句话："爸爸会回来接你的。"

晚上我来接他的时候，他一头扎进我的怀里，"看，爸爸不是回来接你了吗？"我提醒着儿子。

但第二天情况更糟，让他从旅店出来，进手推车都不容易。我刚把车子推上三十五街，儿子就开始大哭大叫，我安慰着他："爸爸会回来接你的。"一路上把他送到托儿所都是这句话。

随着天黑得越来越早，情况似乎越来越糟，天气也越来越阴冷潮湿。每天接上儿子，我都会带他去吃点便宜的热乎东西。我就和这个小家伙聊聊天，和他谈谈我心里的担心，"孩子，这可不行啊，棕榈旅店太贵了，还记得我们在伯克利的小房子吗？对，现在这地方太贵了。"

儿子皱了皱眉头。

我怎么和他说呢，倒不是因为那里那些不三不四的女人、吸毒的人和酒鬼，以及街头的流浪汉，是因为那种居无定所、无家可归、无依无靠的感觉。再有就是这里临街，外面车水马龙，汽车喇叭震天响，音乐叮叮咣咣，乱七八糟。我们只能靠电视的声音来压住这一切，我好想清楚到底该怎么办，集中精力处理好当下的问题。

Every now and then, kindness sprang up out of nowhere, and in the least likely places, as it did one evening when we came back to The Palms and one of the sisters working the street approached us. She and her colleagues had seen me with Christopher in the stroller every morning and night and probably figured out our deal. A black man with a little boy in a stroller, a single dad—it wasn't anything they'd seen before.

"Hey, little player, little pimp," she said as she came close, a candy bar in her hand to give to Christopher. "Here you go."

"No, no," I insisted, maintaining Jackie's rule against sugar, "he don't need any candy."

Christopher, unfortunately, was disappointed and started to cry. "Don't cry," she said and reached down into her magical cleavage and produced a $5 bill, handing that to him.

Did I object? No. Christopher was so happy, he looked like he preferred the money to candy. Smart boy.

"Well, thank you," I muttered, not knowing if she knew that her $5 bill was going to buy us dinner around the corner at Mosell's, a soul-food kitchen both my son and I loved.

The same sister and a couple of the other ladies of the night started giving Christopher $5 bills on a regular basis. In fact, there were some days when we wouldn't have eaten without their help. At my hungriest moments, when we were running on empty, I would roll the stroller by their stretch of the sidewalk, on purpose, moving real slow just in case none of the familiar faces were working the street yet. There was a purity in the help these women gave us, with nothing asked in return. Kindness, pure and simple. On uncertain days, I thought of us as wandering in the desert, knowing that we were being led to a promised land and that God was sending his manna to feed us in a most unique way.

From this point on, nobody could demean a whore in my presence. Of course I don't advocate prostitution, but that's their business and none of mine.

My business was Wall Street, nothing else.

Dialing and smiling, at work I am soon the Master of the Phone, the ultimate cold-call salesperson. It's my life force. My way out. With every single one of those two hundred calls, I'm digging us out of the hole, maybe with a teaspoon, but bit by bit. The urgency increases, driving me that much more when I look at my son and have to leave him every day, knowing I don't have the luxury to just be positive and persevere. No, I've got to get there *today*. It's not like I can cruise for a bit, then crank it up tomorrow. Hell, no. It's *now*. There's nobody handing me business, I'm not Donald Turner with a brother upstairs, and I'm not one of the veterans with existing books just servicing clients. This is all on me. Every phone call is a shot, an opportunity to get a little bit closer to our own place, to the better life I want to live, a life of happiness for me and my son.

即便如此，我们也经常能遇到一些善良的人，甚至在一些最不可思议的地方都是如此，一天晚上，我们回到棕榈旅店，一个街头妓女走了过来。她和另外的几个妓女每天都见到我推着儿子，进进出出，也就猜出了八九分。是个黑人单亲父亲带着个孩子，这种事以前她们可没遇到过。

"嗨，小家伙，"她走了过来，手里拿着个糖果递给了小克利斯多夫，"拿去吃吧。"

"不用了，不用了，"我想起杰姬说过不可以给孩子吃糖的，"现在他不能吃这东西。"

可怜的儿子失望透顶，眼泪汪汪，"别哭别哭，"她从怀里摸出了 5 块钱，递给了儿子。

我该不该拒绝呢？我没有。儿子也破涕为笑，似乎他也觉得钱比糖果要好，真是个聪明的孩子。

"真谢谢你啊。"不知道她是不是意识到这 5 块钱可以让我们在街角的莫塞尔小吃店美美地吃上一顿。

从这以后，这个女子和她旁边的几个女子就这样隔三差五地给我们一些钱，有时候，若没有她们的接济，我们当天晚上连饭都吃不上。在我最饥肠辘辘的时候，我们一路上空着肚子赶回来，我会在经过她们的街角时刻意放慢速度，生怕她们当时会不在那里。这些女子对我的帮助是非常纯粹的，没有任何企图，也不求什么回报，是人性本真的那种善良。有时候，我恍惚觉得自己仿佛是在沙漠中行走，但一定会遇到绿洲，因为上帝会用他自己的方式送来甘露，让我们渡过难关。

从此，我再也不许别人在我面前诋毁妓女，当然我不赞成从事这种职业，但这是她们的选择，与我无关。

我的选择就是要在华尔街干出点名堂来。

在工作上，我总是面带微笑，拨打电话，俨然一幅专业人士的样子，我就是电话销售的终极狂人。这是我生命的全部动力，我的唯一出路。每天的 200 个电话，就是迈出的一小步，可我的目标在千里之外。我每天都不得不把儿子送去托儿所，知道自己根本谈不上什么坚持不懈、乐观向上，这些对我太奢侈，我根本没有时间，我需要立竿见影，马上见效。我没有时间可以浪费，只能分秒必争，工作上没有谁可以帮我，我不像唐纳德·特纳那样有个哥哥做靠山，我手上也没有什么老客户的资源，我只有依靠自己。每个电话都是一个机会，都会让我离目标更近一步，都会让我们离好日子更近一步，也会让我们和幸福生活更近一步。

The PURSUIT of HAPPYNESS

Without offering an explanation, on various occasions I brought Christopher to work with me, another sign to my coworkers of my diligence. After everyone left, usually by 5:00 p.m. on the dot, 5:30 at the latest, I would stay on, continuing to call, and then we'd both stretch out and sleep under the desk. The rest of the office was used to my staying late and never seemed to suspect anything. Some were amused, and most of them cheered me on with their usual parting words of, "Go get 'em, go get 'em."

In the morning they reacted the same way when most of them arrived around 7:30 or 8:00 and I was already at my desk, making phone calls, Christopher occupied with a picture book or scribbling on paper. For not even being two, he had an uncanny knack for playing on his own and not distracting me from work.

The only person who seemed puzzled at all was the branch manager, who was typically the first person in the office every day. He never said a word, but I was sure he wondered how I managed to beat him there on those days, with my baby in tow no less.

To my knowledge, no one there knew that I slept under the desk with Christopher on those nights when I didn't have anywhere to go—whether I took him to the babysitter early in the morning, picked him up in the evening, and came back to the office that same night, or whether he stayed with me in the office that day. What they did know was that I was hungry for success. How literally hungry they didn't imagine.

Part of what was driving me were my circumstances. Because I'd made the decision to build my own book, it was going to take longer to see the dollars in my pocket. I was starting small, building trust, developing relationships; it was like planting seeds, watering them, letting them grow until it was harvest time. It was a process that had its own cycle, often a four-to six-month cycle, sometimes longer. That farming metaphor took me straight into winter, when I knew it was going to be extremely tight until spring. So I cut back on everything, making sure that I carried all our stuff with me every day, juggling the duffel bag, the briefcase, my hanging bag, the Pampers box, and an umbrella as I moved us downstream from The Palms, where a room and a color television cost $25 to a trucker motel that got us a room and black-and-white TV for $10 a day. The neighbors were now mainly truckers and the prostitutes catering to that clientele, right off the freeway. Heavy-duty turnover. After eating, we came home each night and locked up tight, refusing to go out even in nicer weather.

On weekends, when there's no rain, we take advantage of San Francisco's many public parks and opportunities for free entertainment. One of our favorite stops is the children's playground in Golden Gate Park, where Christopher can play in the sandbox or climb on the jungle gym while I sit in a swing, mulling over how to get from today to tomorrow. One day I only have enough money to either get us back to Oakland on BART and stay in the trucker motel or get us a drink and a snack from the refreshment stand.

我也不做过多解释，有时候就直接带着儿子来到工作地点，这在别人看来，又是我勤奋工作的一个标志。通常大家会在下午5点钟离开公司，最晚不过5:30，而我会一直打电话到很晚，然后我就会和儿子直接在办公桌下面睡觉，公司同事对于我的加班加点已经习以为常，从未怀疑过什么。有些人觉得有趣，有些人则给我鼓劲，临走的时候总对我说："加油干啊。"

同事们大多是在早上7:30到8:00的时候到公司，而我已然进入工作状态，打着电话，而小克利斯多夫则会在一旁乖乖地看画册，或是在纸上写写画画，不吵不闹。他还不到两岁，就知道自己玩自己的，不影响我工作。

只有部门经理有些奇怪，以往都是他第一个到办公室，他虽然嘴上没说什么，但是我肯定他有些疑惑，我是怎么赶到他前面去的，而且还带着个孩子。

据我所知，没人知道那些日子，我和儿子就睡在了公司，因为我们确实无家可归了，我只能是一大早把他放在托儿所，晚上接回来，再回到公司过夜，要么就让他和我一起呆在公司一整天。大家只是觉得我在拼命工作，但是具体怎么拼命，他们就不得而知了。

让我如此奋力向前的还有我工作定位方面的原因。我决心要建立自己的客户群，这就需要更长的时间才能真正见到回报。我从点滴入手，逐步建立信任，发展自己的客户关系。就像是播种、浇水、施肥，等到最后才能收获。这是需要时间的，一般需要4~6个月才能见效，有时还要更长。但我现在是身处寒冬，还需要时日才能等到春暖花开的时节。所以我节衣缩食，轻装上阵，每天手拿肩扛就能把所有的家当带在身上，儿子的粗呢大包、我的公文包、西装袋、帮宝适再加把雨伞，就是我的全部家当。在棕榈旅店我们一个房间配上彩电需要25块钱一晚，而在汽车旅店加上黑白电视，每晚只要10块钱。这里住着的大多是卡车司机还有来招揽生意的妓女，旁边就是高速公路。重型卡车就停在外面。吃过饭后，我们就回到屋里，把门紧锁上，不管外面的天气有多好，都不再出来。

周末的时候，当外面不下雨，我们就会跑到旧金山的公园，这里大多都不收费。我们最喜欢去金门公园的儿童乐园，儿子可以在沙箱里面玩耍，还可以去小型游乐场，我则会在一边的秋千上坐着，冥思苦想怎么才能熬过今天。有一天，我口袋里的钱只够我们坐公车回奥克兰，在汽车旅店住一宿，或者去点心铺买些饮料和吃的，就分文不剩了。

"No drink, Christopher." I try to calm him down as he starts to cry. "We'll have a drink and popcorn next time." This kills me.

The next time we have the same dilemma, I buy him what he wants, unable to say no this time. That's one of the nights that's balmy enough that we sleep, or try to sleep, on a grassy corner of Union Square, not far from the same spot where the guy who tried to pick me up once called San Francisco "the Paris of the Pacific."

We sleep close to the side of the park that's underneath the Hyatt Hotel on Union Square, not as luxurious as some of the other hotels in the neighborhood, but clean and modern, a beacon of security and comfort that somehow makes me feel better, even sleeping in its shadows. Diagonally across from our corner is the city's truly dangerous real estate, particularly at night, bordered by the Tenderloin, the part of town where I first lived, back when it was easy to rough it.

But roughing it takes on a whole new meaning in this period. After thinking that I really knew San Francisco, I now come to know the city on a far more intimate basis—not just where there are and aren't hills, but the degree of their angle and grade, the number of steps it takes to push the stroller up them, or how many blocks to walk the long way around to avoid a hill, and even where the cracks in the concrete sidewalks are. Cracks in the concrete. Becoming familiar with cracks in the concrete is not some obsessive-compulsive pursuit, it is a matter of survival for maneuvering a child in a fragile stroller with everything I own on my person—under time and weather constraints.

The rains come hard this winter of 1982 and early 1983, eliminating the options of outdoor free activities or sleeping in the park. Though I've avoided food lines, I can't anymore, not with a hungry little boy, and we soon start making our way over to Glide Memorial Church in the Tenderloin, where the Reverend Cecil Williams and activists in the community have been feeding the homeless and hungry down in the church basement, at Moe's Kitchen, three times a day, seven days a week, three hundred sixty-five days of the year.

The best part for me is that on Sundays after church services, instead of standing outside in the lines that go down the street and around the corner, we can take a different route through the building and down the steps to Moe's. But no matter how we get there, as I take a tray and start down the cafeteria line, I see only dignity —no matter how fragile—in all the faces lined up with me, all of them adults, none with children, some who look like they're working like me, others who are definitely unemployed.

You never felt like you were less after going there to eat. You were in line with men, women, blacks, whites, Latinos, Chinese, like the United Nations, many at different stages of some kind of issue: drugs, alcohol, violence, poverty, or borderline crazy, on medication, on hard times. But we were just there to eat.

"儿子，今天没有喝的。"克利斯多夫在抹眼泪，我只能在一旁安慰他，"咱们下次再买饮料和爆米花好吗？"这简直要了我的命。

后来，又出现了这样捉襟见肘的情况，但我实在不忍心再让他难过，就依了他，给他买了饮料。那天夜里天气不错，我们就在外面过夜了，想睡却睡不着，就在联合广场的草坪上，这里离上次有人和我说"旧金山就是太平洋上的巴黎"的地方不远。

我们就睡在公园的边上，旁边就是联合广场的凯悦酒店，这家酒店不及附近那些酒店那么豪华，但是非常整洁，设施现代，让我觉得就是睡在酒店外面都有种安全感。可是斜对角方向，却是城中最为危险的地方，那就是田德隆区，我刚来这里时曾住在那里，很容易就勾起很多回忆。

回首昨日，在此时又新添许多含义。我觉得自己真正了解了旧金山，我对这座城市的了解已近乎于精确，这些山不再仅仅是山，我还知道山的坡度有多大，推着手推车上去要走多少级台阶，若不想爬山，那么需要绕道多远才能到山那边去，我甚至知道人行道上有多少裂纹。对这些裂纹的关注倒不是我有什么怪癖，而是因为我要推着颤巍巍的手推车，带着孩子，还有所有的家当，在各种天气，在这些路上经过。

1982年冬到第二年春，这段时间雨水特别多，这让我们出去参加免费户外活动或是去公园睡觉的机会都没有了。我自己不吃东西倒无所谓，可儿子受不了啊，我们就朝着田德隆区的格莱德教堂走去，威廉姆斯教士和一些社区积极分子在教堂的地下室为无家可归的人们提供食物，地点就在莫尔厨房，提供一日三餐，一年365天都不间断。

每当周日到教堂礼拜之后，我最高兴的就是自己不用站到大街上去排那长长的队伍，而是从教堂里面另辟蹊径，去莫尔厨房。但不管我们是怎么过去的，我都要端个托盘，进入自助区域。但在我周围的人的脸上，我还可以依稀看到那种做人的尊严，他们都是成人，没有谁还带着孩子，有些好像和我一样有工作，其他人就是无业。

来到这里吃饭，你就会真的觉得自己其实还算不错的。周围的男男女女、白人、拉美人、华人，形形色色，就像是到了联合国一样。很多人都有着不同程度的问题：吸毒、酗酒、暴力倾向、贫困潦倒、精神错乱，还有人是在依靠药物来解决问题，生活举步维艰。但我们在那里仅仅是为了填饱肚子。

There were no questions, no interrogations or credentials required for being needy. It didn't feel like a handout. It was more like someone's mother wanting to feed you—*Boy, you sit down and get something to eat.* And when we got to the food, it was an ample serving, not skimpy, but hearty and tasty. American fare. More manna.

In later years I would have to tell everyone at Glide to warn folks what can happen to children when you start them off eating at Moe's Kitchen. In fact, Christopher later shot up to six-foot-eight, 260 pounds. He could really eat at Moe's, even as a toddler. When you left, you were never hungry, and it wasn't just that you weren't hungry, you felt better. You felt better because you couldn't wear out your welcome at Glide. You couldn't wear out your welcome at Moe's Kitchen.

The Reverend's sermons fed my soul too, reminding me of what I kept forgetting—that the baby steps counted, even if it wasn't happening as fast as I desired. After church service, without fail, the Reverend stood outside the sanctuary in the hallway or on the steps outside, hugging every single person as they left. Anybody who wanted a hug got a hug. First time I went to get a hug, it felt like Cecil Williams knew me even before he knew me. With what looked to be a smile permanently etched on his wise, round, ageless, handsome face, and with his larger-than-life stature that convinced me he was much taller than he really was, his arms were outstretched as he bear-hugged me and said: "Walk that walk."

I hugged him back, blessing him with my thanks, telling him I was going to walk that walk, not just talk the talk, that I was going forward.

Later, the Reverend admitted that I came to his attention because it was so unusual to see a man standing in a food line with a baby. There wasn't anything I had to explain about my situation. He seemed to know. Not just that he could see I was a single father, but that he could see who I was, my degree from God, as Moms would have said, my good, my soul, my potential. Maybe that was why, when I found out about the homeless hotel he had started down the street, he agreed that I could stay there.

Kindness personified. The first homeless hotel in the country, housed in the Concord Plaza at O'Farrell and Powell, started by Cecil with the ambitious idea of giving women and children without homes a place in which to transition, to start over, to be empowered. Many eventually went on to work at the hotel, at the restaurant, or in one of the many different expanding programs that Glide offered. Though rooms were free for the night, for reasons of safety, fairness, and efficiency, there were rules of conduct that had to be followed explicitly.

When I talked to the Reverend, I acknowledged that obviously I wasn't a woman, but I was homeless and I did have a child. Most importantly, I had a job. I just needed someplace to live until I could put together the money to get an apartment.

没人会盘问我们，对我们刨根问底，或是要求提供生活穷困的证明材料，这并不是在施舍，而是就像有位好心的妈妈想帮你，孩子，坐下来吃点什么吧。我们拿到的食物也非常丰盛，美味可口。这就是美国，这就是来自上帝的恩赐。

若干年后，我告诉人们，如果你们让孩子去莫尔厨房吃东西，那么小心后果。因为后来小克利斯多夫身高超过了两米，体重达到 118 公斤。在他还蹒跚学步的时候，就已经在莫尔厨房吃饭了。从这里出去，你肯定不会再受到饥饿的困扰，而且格莱德教堂的大门永远会向你敞开，莫尔厨房也永远不会拒绝你，这让人备感欣慰。

神父的布道同样让我为之一振，他让我想起很多即将淡忘的东西，不积跬步，怎至千里，信念永存，永不言弃。礼拜过后，神父就站在大厅外或是台阶上，人们出来时，他都会拥抱他们，个个如此。我第一次接受他的拥抱时，威廉姆斯神父似乎已经了解了我，虽然我们未曾相识。他那英俊的面孔、睿智圆润的面庞，还有似乎比他本人还要高大的形象，都让我信服，他伸开臂膀，拥抱了我，说道："继续你的脚步。"

我也拥抱了他，用我的满心感激祝福他，并说我会继续，而且不仅仅是说说而已，我会继续前行。

后来，神父说，他注意到我是因为很少有男人带着孩子排队领取食物。我没有必要再解释什么，似乎他什么都已经知道。他不仅意识到我是个单身父亲，还了解我本人，我与上帝的缘分，就像妈妈说过的那样，我所具备的善行、我的灵魂和我的潜能。也许就是因为这样，当我看到他还在路边开办了收容所，他同意让我也住在里面。

如此伟大的善举。这是美国首家为收容无家可归的人开办的旅馆，在奥化大街和鲍威尔大街的交叉口，就在协和广场的一栋房子里，威廉姆斯神父提出了这样的想法，为了给无家可归的妇女和儿童一个栖身之地，让他们能得到片刻喘息，以便重整旗鼓。其中的很多人后来就索性为这个旅店、餐厅以及格莱德教堂开办的相关项目提供服务了。虽然房间是不收费的，但是出于安全、公平和效率的考虑，这里有许多规定需要遵守。

和神父谈过之后，我承认自己显然性别不合乎要求，但我确实无家可归，而且还带着孩子，更重要的是，我有份工作，我只是需要找个住的地方，需要撑到自己能有钱付房租为止。

"Fine," he said, not thinking twice. He had been watching me with Christopher. He trusted me. "Go on down there," he reassured me, letting me know who to see and what to say.

When I stepped inside the first time, I was swept up in a sea of fading pea green—pea green carpet and peeling pea green wallpaper. Looking pretty much like any skid row Tenderloin hotel, it had been taken over by Glide and just needed work—just as all of us in many of the programs at Glide needed some work, some TLC, some time. But it was beautiful to me all the same. The deal was this. No one was admitted into the hotel before 6:00 p.m., and everyone had to be out by 8:00 a.m. No one received a key. No going out once you were in for the night, and no leaving your things in the room because they'd be gone when you returned. When you left the room, you took everything you owned with you. No one was assigned the same room two nights in a row.

It was catch-as-catch-can. And if you didn't get there early, before the hotel filled up, you were out of luck. There were no reservations, no one giving you special treatment and saying, "We knew you were coming so we held you a spot."

The rooms were all different, most of them with just the basics—a bed and a bathroom. Some rooms had televisions. Really, Christopher and I cared more about getting fed at Glide and checking in at night, knowing we were set until tomorrow, than about what was on television.

For the rest of my life, there will never be enough I can do for Cecil Williams and Glide. He was so beautiful to me, to my son, and to generations of San Franciscans from all corners of the community. Every Sunday morning in church, as I prayed to find my way out of the problems of this period, I just knew that if I could hold on, everything would be so fine I'd never have a care in the world after that.

Well, of course, as I later would learn, it doesn't work like that. Anyone who believes that money saves all has never had any money—like me back then. The late great rapper Notorious BIG put it best when he said, "Mo' Money Mo' Problems." What I would discover was that while money is better to have than not to have, it not only doesn't fix all problems but brings with it problems that Chris Gardner circa the early 1980s couldn't have imagined. The only glimmer of the future that I had that was correct was the idea that whatever success I was able to achieve, I was going to share some with Glide, to put it back into Cecil's hands, even if I didn't yet know how.

Did I ever in my wildest, most confident visions imagine that I would help bankroll a $50 million project that Cecil Williams and Glide would undertake twenty-five years later to purchase a square block of real estate in order to create affordable housing for lower-income families and a complex of businesses and retail shops to create employment opportunity—right there in the Tenderloin where I used to count the cracks in the sidewalk, a block away from Union Square and $500-a-night hotels, not to mention the most expensive stores in the city like Neiman Marcus and Gucci? Not for a minute.

他二话没说就答应了，他一直在注意着我们父子俩，他信任我。"沿着这儿走过去，"他嘱咐着我，还告诉我应该去找谁，该怎么说。

我走进了这家旅馆，就仿佛步入了绿色的海洋，地毯是绿的，壁纸也是绿的。里面的格局和田德隆区的小酒店基本相似，就是格莱德教堂接手改造的，教堂发起的很多其他项目也是如此，只是在原有的基础上稍加改造，投入些关爱和时间，就一切妥当。但我已相当满意。对我们这些借宿的人还有些具体要求，比如，下午6点以后才能入住，早上8点必须离开，不提供钥匙，晚上入住后就不得离开，不得在房间里寄存个人物品，因为离开之后，这些物品就无从查找，所以就要随身携带所有个人物品。而且人们每天住的房间都不会相同。

入住就是讲个先来先得的原则，如果来晚了，没有房间了，那也没有办法。没人会给你保留房间，也不会有谁能享受优待，肯定不会说什么："我们知道您要来，所以给您留了个位置。"

房间和房间都不大一样，大多都有些基本的配置，比如床和卫生间。有些房间有电视，不过，我和儿子更关心的是能在这里混饱肚子，可以排上房间，知道晚上有地方过夜，可以坚持到明天，这就不错了，至于有没有电视都无所谓的。

这辈子，我愿意为威廉姆斯神父，为格莱德教堂奉献一切。他对我和儿子能如此慷慨相救，对旧金山的百姓都如此厚爱，这让我们感激不尽。每个周日的早晨，我去教堂礼拜之后，希望能为自己找条出路，但我知道只要自己坚持下去，一切都会好起来的，我就不必再为这些烦恼劳神费心。

当然，正如我后来所了解到的，钱不是解决所有问题的关键。过分迷信金钱的力量则永远不会真的有钱。后来著名的说唱组合"匪帮说唱大哥"就曾在歌中唱到，"金钱越多，麻烦越多。"的确如此。后来我才发现钱这东西还真是越多越麻烦，不仅不解决问题，而且还又生出不少问题，但所有这些在20世纪80年代初，我是无法想见的。但对于未来，我暗下决心，无论我取得怎样的成功，我都会拿出一部分金钱，交给格莱德教堂，交到威廉姆斯神父的手中，但具体怎么实现这一梦想，我还一无所知。

我怎么都没料到自己居然会在25年后，会资助神父和教堂一个5000万美金的项目，买下一处地产，帮助解决低收入家庭的住房问题，同时建造零售店，创造商业机会，提供就业，而且项目的所在就是田德隆，在这里，我曾一次次数过人行道上的裂缝，这儿离联合广场500美元一晚的豪华酒店仅一个街区之隔，和内曼·马库斯奢侈品店、古琦这些名牌店更是咫尺之遥。

第十章 加州的梦想

The PURSUIT of HAPPYNESS

All I knew was that if the Reverend had not been there, my dreams might never have come to pass. Maybe something else would've happened or someone else would have stepped forward. It's hard, though, to conceive of having the same incredible good fortune of being able to walk alongside greatness like his. Later married to the renowned Japanese American poet Janice Murikatani, Cecil was already a prominent social leader, someone who seemed tuned in at a higher level than most human beings. The important thing is that he was there, and he would be there long after I was blessed to have had his help, not just talking the talk with brilliant oratory but walking the walk—feeding, teaching, helping, sparking miracles daily.

An instant miracle took place for me once Cecil took us in. Without having to spend $300 to $600 a month on somewhere to sleep, I was able to get Christopher back into the San Francisco day care center in Hayes Valley, now at a cost of $500, but it was a place where I knew he was getting great care. Every morning, long before 8:00 a.m., I had us packed up with all our gear as I performed my poor impression of a man pretending to have eight arms, somehow holding the umbrella over my head after setting up the tent over the stroller and Christopher from the sheets of dry-cleaner plastic as we took off.

To get on the bus wasn't even worth it because unbalancing my hanging bag, the umbrella, the briefcase, the duffel bag, and the box of Pampers and then trying to fold up the stroller was more trouble than just walking the extra fifteen minutes. Even in the rain. That was, as long as I could avoid the hills. The good news was that I could park our car (the stroller) at day care, stash our stuff in it, and then hop on the bus downtown to the office.

On the weekends we had to be out of Concord Plaza during the day. These rules were stringent. There was no just laying up. You either went to work or to look for work. Christopher and I already had a routine of pursuing every free bit of entertainment in the city. We went to the park, the museum, the park, the museum, park, museum, then maybe we'd go see friends, or if we had a couple of extra bucks, we'd ride the train over to Oakland, go visiting and get something to eat, and head back in time to make sure we got into a room.

As long as I could stay in the light, figuratively speaking, by keeping my focus on what I could control, worry and fear were kept at bay. That's why I pinned my concentration to tasks in front of me, not letting myself agonize about the grade of the hill I was pushing our unwieldy ride up, but studying every crack and crevice in the concrete sidewalk, studying the sounds of the stroller wheels, noticing that I could move to that syncopated beat. Sometimes the effort made me happy, it let me dance, when some might have said that I didn't have anything to dance about. It made me happy to put money away, in small $100 or $50 increments, to just deposit it and not touch it, to not even think about it but to know I was doing something to move us closer to the goal of having our own place.

我所知道的就是如果没有威廉姆斯神父，我的梦想不会成真。也许是另外一个故事会发生，或者另一个人会继续奋勇前行。很难想象，有谁能如此幸运，和伟大的威廉姆斯神父相识相知。他后来和著名的日裔美国诗人贾尼斯·美里木谷喜结良缘，而他自己已然是当时杰出的社会领袖，处于人生更高的一种境界。

但对我而言，重要的是他就在我最需要帮助的时候，伸出援助之手，提供食宿，为我指点迷津，不仅仅是说说而已，而是真正付诸行动，日复一日，天天如此。

接下来，我就遇到了一个奇迹，就在神父接纳我们不久之后，我们不必每个月花上三五百块钱找地方栖身，我可以把儿子放到旧金山的日托中心了，那地方在海斯谷，每个月的费用是500块，但我知道儿子在那里会得到很好的照顾。每天早上，还不到8点，我就已经收拾停当，把家当都背在身上，仿佛三头六臂一般，还要撑着雨伞，给手推车上加个塑料棚子挡雨，就出发了。

赶公车其实很不值当，因为我得把衣服袋、雨伞、公文包、粗呢袋还有帮宝适统统放下来，再把手推车折叠起来，非常麻烦，还不如多走15分钟简单许多。好在我可以把手推车放在日托中心，把家当堆在里面，我就可以冲上公车，赶到公司上班。

周末的时候，我们白天就得离协和广场远远的，因为那里规定很严格，不可以逗留，必须是去工作，要么就是去找工作。儿子和我早已约定俗成，要在城里找各种免费的娱乐项目。我们去公园、博物馆甚至还去看朋友，口袋里若还有几个闲钱，就做地铁去奥克兰，四处走走，买些吃的之类，然后就赶紧回来，确保能排上免费的房间。

只要我手头有事情可做，能专注于自己可以控制的事情上，我就不会过分担心或害怕。这就是为什么我喜欢转移自己的注意力，不去想面前的路是怎样陡陡弯弯，自己怎样要一步步费力前行，相反去研究路上的裂缝，研究手推车的轮子在路面上发出的声响，觉得可以和音乐节拍有所类似。有时候，这种研究会让我开心甚至想手舞足蹈，也许别人不知道我为什么这么开心，可我自己知道，因为我又攒了50或100块，我就会把它存起来，彻底不去碰它。虽然这点钱微不足道，但我知道自己离目标又近了一步。

In order not to touch my stash, there were occasions when I sold blood, each time swearing I'd never do it again. It wasn't the shame of having to go there that ate at me, although I wasn't proud that I was choosing between the lesser of two evils—whether to sell blood so as to be able to afford a room if we missed the cutoff at the shelter or sleep in the park. What haunted me were some of the down-and-outers I saw at the clinic; some had made some bad choices, and some had gotten there through no choices of their own.

One rainy evening after I tore out of the Dean Witter office fifteen minutes late, raced across town on the bus and sprinted up the several steps to Christopher's room at the day care center, packed us up and then hauled ass at top speed over to the Tenderloin, we missed check-in at Concord Plaza by ten minutes.

Pissed, tired, wet, I head toward Union Square, walking Christopher under the awnings of the hotels and stores. With payday a week away, I have enough money for us to eat dinner and ride the train, which I've done before, just riding through the night until we've both had a little sleep and the morning comes. Aw, man, I realize, five more bucks and I could get us over to the trucker hotel for the night. Tense and tired, I get this whiff of cigarette smoke that smells so good. Of all the things that I'm not going to spend money on, it's cigarettes. But a Kool menthol cigarette right about now would definitely take the edge off.

"Poppa," Christopher says as we pass by the entryway to the Hyatt Embarcadero, "I gotta go to the bathroom."

"You do?" I say excitedly, since we've been working to get him out of Pampers. "Okay, now, you hold on, we'll get a bathroom," and I roll us right into the Hyatt lobby and follow signs to the back and down the steps to the men's room. After he does his thing, most successfully, we exit the bathroom and I notice a hotel guest, suit-and-tie guy, at the cigarette machine, putting in his quarters—ten of them—but having no luck getting the machine to give him his pack of cigarettes. Not about to walk away, he starts pounding the machine, rocking and humping it so that the cigarettes will fall down, apparently.

"Sir," says a bellman who comes to see what the ruckus is about, "that's okay, it must be broken. Just go to the front desk and tell them you lost your money. They'll give you a refund."

The hotel patron heads upstairs, and I follow, watching him weave through the crowd in the lobby and approach the front desk, soon pocketing the refund.

Two bucks fifty cents just like that. It's so easy, I have to give it a try. But instead of jumping on it immediately, Christopher and I mill about, acting *as if* we're patrons. Then I approach the young lady at the front desk and tell her about losing my change in the cigarette machine.

"So sorry," she nods, opening up a cash drawer, "somebody else lost their money earlier. We've got to put a note on that machine."

为了不动自己微薄的存款，有时候我还不得不去卖血，每次我都发誓再也不干这种事了，但有时也没有办法。倒不是要去卖血本身让我难堪，因为我只能做出选择，当没有排到免费住处时，我就得要么去卖血，这样才能付得起一晚的房租，要么就去公园过夜。真正让我恐怖的是医院里那些无家可归的流浪汉，他们卖血是因为别无选择了。

一天晚上下起了雨，等我从添惠公司赶出来，已经迟了15分钟，飞身上了公车，几步跑到日托中心，抱起儿子收拾停当，一路跑到田德隆区后，我们最后还是晚了10分钟，没有排到房间。

我筋疲力尽，浑身湿透，和儿子走在商店和酒店的雨篷下面，向着联合广场走去。还有一周才能发工资，我身上还有些钱还够吃顿晚饭，还能去坐地铁。这种事我以前干过，整夜呆在地铁里，睡上一会儿，捱到天亮。再有5块钱，我就可以在汽车旅店住上一宿了。又困又乏，我点燃了一支香烟，深吸了一口，顿时感觉好多了。我轻易不会买香烟的，但此时此刻的一支烟，确实能让我舒服很多。

"爸爸，我要去嘘嘘。"当我们经过四季酒店时，儿子喊道。

"真的吗？"我又惊又喜，因为我正在教他摆脱帮宝适，学会自己上厕所。"好的，稍稍坚持一下，我们马上去找卫生间。"我推着小车进了酒店大堂，顺着指示牌直奔卫生间。儿子成功地解决了问题，我们走出来，看到一位西装革履的酒店客人，往自动售货机里投了10枚硬币，想买包香烟，可是钱却卡住了。他不想就这么走开，把机器拍得很响，显然是想把香烟震出来。

服务生应声过来，来看究竟是怎么回事，然后对这人说："没关系的，这机器有问题了，您直接去前台，说机器吞了您的钱，他们会给您退的。"

这位客人于是就上楼了，我跟在他身后，看着他穿过大堂的人群，走到前台，很快就拿到退款。

好像是两块五左右，这还不容易？我也可以试试。但我们没有立刻行动，而是磨蹭了一会儿，然后做出一副入住客人的样子，走到前台，说香烟机吞了我的币，可什么都没有掉出来。

"真不好意思，"她冲我点点头，打开现金抽屉，说，"刚才也有人这么说，我们马上给机器贴上故障条。"

"Good idea," I say, graciously accepting my "refund" of two dollars and fifty cents.

That little hustle worked so well, I gave it a shot at the St. Francis, at the Hyatt Union Square, and at a couple of other hotels that same evening. With twenty-five or so hotels in the vicinity, in the days that followed I scored at as many as ten hotels at a time, making twenty-five extra dollars a day. Being really slick about it, I made sure that I slid in after a shift change, just so that nobody would recognize me from a previous time.

After two weeks of this, I called it quits before my luck ran out. Later, when I did pick up my cigarette habit again and could afford it, I figured that I paid back the tobacco companies big-time. As for the hotels, in years to come I would repay my debts to many of them many times over, although in early 1983, not long after Christopher's second birthday, that was not a future I could see.

While that million dollars and that red Ferrari I was going to drive one day still existed in the abstract of the future, there came a point when it wasn't like I could reach out and almost grab on to them anymore. My feet hurt, my body ached. A darkness began to seep into the days, not just outside in the weather, but in my head. At the office, no, that was where the sun was shining, where the brightness of my potential buoyed my spirits, where the crops I'd been planting were starting to bud all over the place. But the second I left work, my spirits dipped—because always in the back of my mind I knew that if the bus ran late, or if Christopher wasn't zipped into his cold-weather clothes fast enough, or if we got to the shelter late, or if I didn't have time to pick something up to eat before we went up to the room and locked ourselves in, I had to come up with a plan B right away.

Having to compartmentalize and organize all our stuff to keep it contained, like in the military, was beating me down. Everything had to be rolled up and ready to go at a moment's notice, everything had to be able to be located at all times, what you needed when you needed it—a sock, a Pamper, a shirt, a toothbrush, Christopher's clothes, a hairbrush, a book that someone left on the train that I was reading, a favorite toy. It started getting heavy, all that shit I was carrying and the weight of the stress and fear.

Weekends, when I tried to do fun things for Christopher and give him a sense of normalcy, I still had to carry the stuff. At the parks, the museums. At church.

The worst of this period takes place in approximately March, right when I know things are really about to bloom at work, and this one night I roll in to the front desk at the shelter, where they all know me, and I hear, "Well, Chris, we're all full, sorry."

What can I do? Out on the street, I head to the BART station, asking Christopher, "You want to go look at the airplanes at the Oakland airport?"

"是个好办法，"我说着，优雅地接受了"退款"，一共两块五。

这个小把戏效果还不错，我接下来直奔国际俱乐部和凯悦饭店，当晚又去了另外几家饭店。附近几家饭店我一共挣了25块，接下来的几天，我最高纪录一口气拿下10家饭店，一天就挣到25块。我非常谨慎，每次都确保服务员换班之后，才会进去，以免被识破。

我这么干了两周后，决定就此洗手不干了。后来，我真的重新开始吸烟，而且也可以支付得起香烟的费用，主要是想让烟草公司挽回些损失。后来，我再去酒店，都愿意多付钱，甚至多付很多倍的钱，来偿还当年所欠的烟钱。可是在1983年初，儿子两岁生日不久，我还想不到这么远。

当时我远远没想到自己有朝一日能腰缠万贯，能真的开上红色法拉利，一次，我觉得自己可能要与一切美好无缘了。我的脚疼痛难忍，浑身酸痛，我眼前几乎没有了光明，并非是天气原因，是我的心头满是乌云。在办公室，一切都很顺利，阳光普照，前景一片光明，我播下的种子已经开始吐芽，但我一离开公司，我就完全换了个人似的。因为我知道，如果汽车晚点，如果没有给儿子及时置办冬衣，如果我们没有赶上免费房间，如果我们没能找点吃的，把自己锁在廉价旅店的房门里，那么我就必须马上想出办法来。

我所有的家当必须分门别类打理好，一切仿佛是军事化管理，这一切终于要把我压垮了。每件物品都必须随时可以打包带走，随时都要待命，需要什么东西，它都得马上就在手边，袜子、尿布、衬衫、牙刷、孩子的衣服、梳子、玩具，还有一本书，这是有人落在车上的，被我捡来读的。所有这些家当我每天都要背在身上，我的身体和思想终于不堪重负。

每到周末，我都要为儿子想办法找点乐子，让他尽量过上正常的生活，但是我自己还要满负荷，无论是在公园、博物馆还是教堂，都是如此。

大约是三月份前后，情况是最为糟糕，而我知道工作方面很快就要见到成果了。一天晚上，我跑到救济旅店的前台，那里的人都认识我了，结果我听到的是："克里斯，今天满员了，不好意思。"

我该怎么办呢，我走上街头，朝着捷运车站走去，我问儿子，"想去奥克兰飞机场看大飞机吗？"

第十章 加州的梦想

. We've done this drill before, taking public transportation out to one of the two airports and finding a waiting area with semicomfortable benches—where we look like we're travelers anyway. As we ride over to Oakland and approach the MacArthur BART station, Christopher tells me he has to go to the bathroom, and I roll us off the train and head to an individual bathroom I've used there before—where I recall it being possible to lock the door from inside. As soon as we're in there I realize that we don't have to leave immediately. We can rest, wash up, take our time, even sleep.

"We're gonna wait," I explain to Christopher, " 'cause it's rush hour right now. So we're gonna wait in here and be quiet, all right?" I make up a game called "Shhh"—I tell him that no matter how loud someone knocks on the door, the object is not to say a word. No matter what.

MacArthur, a major transfer point in Oakland, is probably the largest station in the BART system, with every subway train coming through. With so much activity, they keep the bathrooms pretty clean, but they're much in demand. In no time, the pounding on the door starts—people obviously don't want to wait. But eventually we can hear the train coming and that wave leaves as those travelers probably realize they can use the bathroom in their own home. As it gets later the knocking becomes much more sporadic.

With no windows, no ventilation, no natural light, the bathroom was tiled from floor to ceiling and wasn't more than ten-by-five, with one toilet and one small wash basin and a mirror made out of reflective stainless steel. By turning off the light, it was completely dark—dark enough that if I was really tired I could sleep. Christopher had a gift for sleeping everywhere and anywhere. I couldn't bring myself to stay in there for too long, only once or twice staying the night, but for a short period, maybe a little more than two weeks, the blessed mercy of BART's public facilities gave me needed shelter during the darkest part of homelessness.

Maybe the reason I was able to see it that way came from the dual life I was living. At night, on weekends, and after hours, it was the dark side of California dreamin': being kept out, sneaking into fancy hotel lobbies to get out of the rain, wishing to be anywhere else but in that BART-station bathroom. By day redemption came from the fact that I was living the great American dream, pursuing opportunity, pushing myself to the limits of my abilities and loving every minute of it. My intimate knowledge of BART became a blessing in other ways. Many years later my firm was selected to be the senior manager on hundreds of millions of dollars in bond issues for BART. I do believe that my honestly being able to say to the BART board of directors, "Look, I know this system better than any of these guys from Merrill Lynch or Solomon Brothers because I used to live on BART," made the difference.

这办法我以前用过，乘坐公交去机场，在候机大厅找个舒服的椅子坐下，反正我们每天都像旅行者的样子。当我们经过奥克兰，快到麦克阿瑟站的时候，儿子说他要嘘嘘，我赶紧带他下了车，直奔附近的一个卫生间而去，那地方我以前去过，记得门还能从里面锁上。我们一到这里，我就知道不用马上就走了，这里完全可以休息洗漱，还能在这睡上一觉。

"我们要在这里等一会，因为现在是高峰期，"我和儿子解释着，"我们就呆在这儿，不要出声。"我当时就编了个游戏，就是不许出声，我告诉他，无论外面的人怎么敲门都不要开，就是不出声，不管怎样都不出声。

麦克阿瑟站是奥克兰的一个大站，可能也是捷运系统最大的一站，很多地铁都会经过这一站。因为客流量很大，所以卫生设施也非常清洁，但使用的旅客人次也很多。没多久，就有人开始擂门了，人们显然不愿意等得太久。但最后，我们听到地铁列车进站的声音，外面就没了动静，估计人们觉得还是用家里的卫生间更舒服一些。等到天色更晚的时候，敲门声就更稀少了。

这里没有窗户，没有通风，没有自然光，卫生间里面都贴着瓷砖，也就是一人多高，刚够容身，里面有个马桶，还有个小小的洗手池，还有面不锈钢的镜子。关上灯后，里面就一片漆黑，我太累了，真想立刻就在黑暗中倒头睡去。儿子最大的本事就是不管在哪里他都可以睡觉。这种地方我不敢睡熟，夜里也就打上一两个盹，而每隔两周，捷运公交系统就能帮我们这两个没家的人解决一晚上的免费住宿。

我之所以能这么看问题，应该取决于我过的这种双重生活。夜里，周末，下班之后，这就是加州梦并不光鲜的一面，无处可去，躲进酒店的大堂去避雨，希望自己不要沦落到去捷运地铁洗手间过夜的地步。而天一亮，我则又回到瑰丽的美国梦之中，追逐机遇，挑战个人极限，享受生命的每一分钟。而我对捷运系统如此亲密的情感终于通过其他方式得到了回报。多年以后，我的公司被选为捷运公司上亿美金债券的高级管理公司，我相信这与我对捷运董事会的坦诚不无关系，"我比美林和所罗门兄弟那些人都更了解捷运，因为我当初就住在这里。"

Though Glide was my saving grace back then, I did set a time limit for myself in terms of how long I would let myself stay there, knowing that I had some savings built up and that the time for my commissions to start adding up was just around the corner. Nobody was standing over me with a stopwatch or a calendar, of course. Still, I believed that if I could grab a few hours of rest during rush hour or stop in at that BART bathroom after sleeping at the airport or on the train, at least in time to wash up for work, then someone else could have a room at Concord Plaza that night. Or so I rationalized.

The one advantage to the BART station bathroom was that nobody else apparently ever thought of it, so there was no line to get in, not to mention that I didn't have to rush insanely at the end of the day to make sure we got there on time and there were no rules to follow other than my own. If I made it to Glide and got a room at the hotel, great. If I could

get a locker at the San Francisco BART station and not have to haul gear for a night, even better.

A question now pulsed maniacally in my brain. Why was I putting myself and my kid through this? Why couldn't I slow down, take longer to get out of the rut, dig into my savings, and put us up back at The Palms? Why did I refuse to break the $20 bill that could have bought us a night at the trucker hotel? I followed my gut, which told me that breaking that $20 bill meant we might not eat. Twenty dollars was and is some real money, but when it's fifteen, twelve, seven, four, it goes fast. Having a pristine, unbroken twenty in my wallet gave me peace of mind, a sense of security.

But it wasn't just the internal struggle over each and every expenditure that was raging inside me. There was also a fight of a much bigger and different magnitude, a battle royal between me and the forces that would control my destiny. These were the same forces that robbed my mother of her dreams, everything from her father and stepmother not helping her go to college, to my own father for giving her a child to raise on her own, to Freddie for beating her physically and psychologically, to a justice system that locked her up when she tried to break out of her bondage. Over the six, seven, eight months that I'd been without a home, a taunting voice that had lurked in the back of my mind now seemed to suddenly gather strength—right at a time when I could see the finish line. The voice mocked me, sounding a hell of a lot like Freddie, just telling me, *You slick motherfucker, think you so smart 'cause you can read and pass that test, but that don't make you shit, you big-eared motherfucker, WHO DO YOU THINK YOU ARE?* Sometimes it sounded like a damn sociologist, quoting statistics, telling me, *Unfortunately, your socioeconomic upbringing has predetermined that breaking out of the cycle of poverty and single-parenting is highly unlikely given the fact that you are among the 12 to 15 percent of homeless people who are actually working yet still can't manage a living wage.*

虽然格莱德教堂对我相当慷慨，但我对自己住在那里的期限做了规定，因为我自己的储蓄在不断增加，我所拿的佣金很快也会增长，当然没有人拿着秒表或者日历催我搬走，但我自己一定要这么要求自己。而且，我相信如果自己能在高峰期睡上几小时，在机场或地铁上睡一会儿之后，再到捷运的洗手间熬到天亮，这样我就可以让别人去协和广场的救济旅店休息一晚了，这也让我感到心安。

捷运地铁洗手间还有一个好处就是没人想过要在这里过夜，所以不用排队，也不用一下班就没命地往这里赶，生怕轮不上自己，而且也没有什么规矩需要遵守，这里我做主。如果我能在格莱德教堂的旅店排上位子，自然不错，但要是我能在旧金山捷运车站有个储物箱，不用再这么背着家当满街跑，那就更好了。

我脑子里一直在琢磨这么一个问题，我干嘛要把自己和儿子逼成这样？我为什么不能慢下脚步，让我们在贫困中再多熬些时日？动一点我的存款，再回棕榈旅店过上几日呢？我为什么不愿意把身上的20美金花掉呢？本可以在汽车旅馆里过上一晚的。但我知道只要动了这20美金，我们可能就没东西可吃了。20元是笔不小的钱，但当它变成15元、10元、5元的时候，它很快就会不见踪影。钱包里放上20元崭新的钞票，让我有一种安全感，让我心里非常踏实。

但是，不仅仅是因为每笔花销让我内心如此纠结，还有更大的原因让我不愿轻易放弃，那是对亲人的忠诚和那些改变我宿命的所有外力间的对抗。正是因为后者，我的母亲被剥夺了自己的梦想，她的生父和继母不愿送她读大学，我的生父抛下母亲，任凭她一个人把我抚养成人，任凭弗莱迪对她身心进行摧残，任凭她徒劳地想挣脱牢笼，反被投入深牢大狱。在我无家可归的这七八个月里，在我几乎可以看到曙光的时候，在我内心深处潜藏了很久的一个声音突然响了起来，他在嘲笑我，彻头彻尾都是弗莱迪的口吻，他在挖苦我："你这狗娘养的，你以为你是什么东西，你能认识字，能考试，就以为自己了不起了，你这大耳贼，你以为你是谁啊！"有时，那又像是社会学家、统计学家在一板一眼地提醒我："很不幸，从你的社会经济学背景来看，你注定要过着贫困和单亲的生活，特别是你还属于那12%~15%的虽然工作但无法满足基本生活需求的无家可归人群。"

The voice made me angry and made me fight harder. Who did I think I was? I was Chris Gardner, father of a son who deserved better than what my daddy could do for me, son of Bettye Jean Gardner, who said that if I wanted to win, I could win. I had to win, however I was going to do it. Whatever more I had to do, whatever burden I had to carry, I was going to rise up and overcome. But the quicker my pace and the harder I pushed, the louder the self-doubting voice became. *Are you crazy? You're deluding yourself!* At my lowest point of wanting to finally give up, throw in the towel, call it quits, spend whatever money I'd accumulated, and hitchhike to somewhere else, I caught a second wind—a burst of confidence—as a feeling of grace found me. *Hold on,* that feeling said, *hold on.* And I do.

Early spring arrives, bringing more rains, but it's warmer outside, my paychecks are starting to grow, and my savings account balance tells me that I've got enough to afford a cheap rent. San Francisco apartments are way too expensive, so that leaves Oakland, where I start my hunt on weekends. There are hurdles of questions: "Well, how long you been on your job? You're not married? You've got a baby? What's going on? What's a man doing with a baby?"

Some of the questions are overt, some not. But the process does become somewhat discouraging as I keep stepping down, notch by notch, both in the neighborhoods where I'm looking and in my expectations. In fact, as a last resort, one Saturday when the weather's taking a break—no rain, even some patches of sunshine breaking through the fog—I decide to go check in the vicinity of The Palms, back in the "Ho"-stroll.

As I'm passing by a place on Twenty-third and West, my attention is grabbed by the sight of an old man sweeping down a front yard—or really, more a patch of what could be called a front yard, now covered in concrete, with blades of rebellious grass still poking up from the cracks. It's not the grass that amazes me but what I see just in front of the little house—a rosebush. Of all the times I might have walked by this spot, I never saw this house, and certainly not that rosebush. Come to think of it, I never saw a rosebush anywhere in a rough urban part of town like this. I'm fascinated. How do you get roses in the ghetto?

I strike up a conversation with the old man, whose name is Jackson. By the count of wrinkles on his brown leathery face, either he is really up there in years or he has seen some rough living. After some friendly chitchat about the weather and my good-looking son, just as I get ready to keep on rolling, I notice that the front windows of the house are papered over.

"Anybody living in here?" I ask Mr. Jackson, nodding at the house.

"No, ain't nobody living in there," he says, explaining that he and his family own the building but live in an upper unit. They've been using it for storage for almost three years.

这声音让我怒不可遏，让我更加奋力前行。我以为我是谁？我是克里斯·加德纳，我是一个孩子的父亲，我对他比我父亲对我好上一万倍。我是贝蒂·让·加德纳的儿子，母亲说过，只要我愿意，我就能行。我必须赢，不管怎样，我都志在一搏。不管要付出多少，无论要承担什么，我都会义无反顾，坚持下去。我前进的步伐越快，我付出的越多，自我否定、自我反对的声音也会越强烈，你是不是疯了，别再骗自己了。就在我几乎想就此放弃，彻底认输，把辛苦积攒的那点钱花光，随便找个地方选择逃避的时候，我突然间找到了自信和自我，我突然间有了力量。我要坚持，坚持下去，我能行。

初春时节，雨水更多了，但是外面春意融融，我的收入开始增加，存款也够租间便宜的房子了。旧金山的房价高得离谱，我只好利用周末去奥克兰找房子。于是要面对一系列的问题："你工作多久了？结婚了吗？还带着孩子？你能行吗？男人怎么带孩子？"

有些问题很无理，有些倒没什么。但是找房子的进展不是很理想。我挨家挨户地找，在我现在住的附近，也在我觉得有希望的地方，一点点推进。周日的时候，天公作美，天色放晴，甚至还有几缕阳光透过了浓雾，我决定去棕榈旅店附近碰碰运气，回"家"看看。

当我经过第23大道西街的时候，我突然注意到一位老者正在清扫院子，这地方勉强可以称得上是前院吧，上面铺着水泥，水泥裂缝里还钻出了几根倔强的杂草。倒不是这几根杂草吸引了我，是小房子门前的一丛玫瑰让我停住了脚步。这里我曾经多次路过，但我从未注意过这所房子，更没看到过这丛玫瑰，在城里这么个地方别指望会有这种植物。我不禁有些奇怪，贫民区居然会有玫瑰？

我停下来和老人搭讪，他叫杰克逊，从他棕色的脸庞那些皱纹判断，要么他在这里住了很多年，要么他生活一直比较清苦。我们随便聊了聊天气，说了说我那俊俏的儿子，我正准备推车子继续往前走的时候，发现房子的前窗用纸贴住了。

"这里没人住吗？"我指着房子问杰克逊先生。

"没人住，"他解释说，这房子是他家，但现在他家住另外一处房子的上半层，这里就是放点东西，都闲了三年了。

第十章 加州的梦想

"Is it for rent?"

"It could be," he shrugs, then offers to show me the unit and the work that would be involved.

The minute we walk in, right as I'm drowned in a funky, musty smell of a place that hasn't had any light or air in a long, long time, I see this whole downstairs space, covering the entire length of the building, and the smell is suddenly minimal. It's so beautiful, even in the dim lighting, I'm speechless. There's a front room, then a big-ass bedroom perfect for Christopher, a bathroom, over here a kitchen, next to it a dining area, and there's a little doorway to another room that could be my bedroom.

Now comes the test. "Can I rent it?" I say, right at the top, and before he can say no or start the qualifying questions, I let him know from the get-go, "Look, I'm fairly new on my job. I have my baby here, and there's no wife in the picture but—"

"Son," he says, "you can stop right there. You done told me everything I need to know. Y'all can move in here."

For a few moments I don't trust that it's over, that the long night of homelessness is over, that I've won. Mr. Jackson confirms it by saying that all I need to give him is the first month's rent and a $100 cleaning deposit.

"What if I clean it up myself and save the hundred?" I counter.

As he studies me for a beat or two, my heart races as I worry that he'll change his mind. Then he says, "Okay, son."

This was it. This was the most beautiful spot in the world to me, somewhere to call home for me and my son. There is no feeling in the entire emotional spectrum of happiness that can ever come close to the feeling I felt in those moments and on that fine spring day and in every day that followed whenever I returned in my mind to seeing that rosebush in the ghetto and having it lead me to our first home off the road of homelessness.

Appropriately, it was not long before Easter, a celebration of rebirth and resurrection, a time of new beginnings, new roads. To remember this time, from these days on I made it a point of trying to get back to Glide for Easter Sunday each and every year—no matter how far away or busy I was—not to relive the painful memories of where I'd been before but to celebrate the miracles that happened next.

"你会出租吗？"

"也许吧。"他耸了耸肩，说可以带我进去看看房间，还有需要整理的东西。

我们刚进去的时候，迎面扑来一股霉味，一看就是很久没人住，没有通风没有光照的原因。整个楼下空间都很通透，异味也突然小了很多。在微微的光亮下，这里显得非常漂亮，我一时无语。有前厅，还有卧室，正好给儿子用，还有洗手间，再有就是厨房、边上还有就餐区，有个不大的走廊，过去是另一间卧室，我应该可以用。

现在就要进入面试环节了。"我能租吗？"没等他拒绝，或是提出各种问题，我直接告诉了他我自己的经历，"您看，我现在刚刚有了工作，还带着个孩子，现在也没有个女人帮我，但……"

"孩子，你就留下吧，我需要了解的你都告诉我了，你们俩都搬进来吧。"

过了好一阵子，我都没反应过来，难道无家可归的日子就这么结束了？难道真的给我租这房子了？杰克逊先生确认了这一点，告诉我只要先交一个月房租，再交100块钱清洁费就好了。

"那我要是自己打扫房间，能不能不用交这100块呢？"我问道。

他看了我一眼，我的心突突直跳，真担心他就此改变主意，结果他说，"好吧，孩子。"

就这样搞定了。这是世界上最美好的地方，这是我和儿子的家了。在我整个生命历程中，从来没有像此时此刻这般，这么真真切切地感到如此幸福。在那个春意融融地日子里，以及在那之后的岁月，每当我看到贫民区的那一丛玫瑰，想到是它带我们走出了无家可归的窘境，我就无比幸福。

而几天之后就是复活节了，庆祝重生和复活的节日，代表着万物复苏，一切从新开始。为了纪念这个特别的时刻，从此后，我决定每年复活节的周日都要去格莱德教堂，无论我当时身处何方，无论自己有多忙，都不会错过。这不是为纪念我曾经的苦痛，而是为了庆祝所有后来发生的一个个奇迹。

Part three

第三部

Chapter 11
Roses in the Ghetto

Everyone wanted to help as we began life in our new home—in our Oakland, California, inner-city version of Kansas. The minute I called friends who hadn't heard from me in a while, the offers started pouring in. There was the card table one friend had in his basement that we could have, a real bed and a mattress that someone else offered, sets of towels and dishes that weren't being used. As long as I could find a way to go pick the stuff up, it was ours.

My good friend Latrell Hammond insisted that I come get the five pounds of neck bones she had just bought that day. What the hell, I'd never cooked neck bones, but I went and got them just the same, figuring that I'd have some OJT in the kitchen, and then I went out to buy a secondhand freezer. At the grocery store, where the butcher, Ms. Tookie, had the hots for me, I got some helpful hints on the basics. And when the prospect of having to take on another domestic chore got me overwhelmed, I was set straight by the sight of a single mom with bags of groceries and two kids, plus a briefcase. If she could do it, so could I.

第十一章
贫民区的玫瑰

我们在加州奥克兰的新家准备一切重头再来的时候，大家都想过来帮忙，这里和堪萨斯有很多相似之处。我刚给久未谋面的朋友去电话，对方就立刻慷慨解囊，伸出援助之手。朋友地下室的牌桌给我们搬来了，还有人提供了床和床垫，甚至还有整套整套的崭新毛巾和餐具。只要我去取，那些东西就是我们的了。

我的好友拉垂尔·哈蒙德还让我去她家取 5 磅肉骨头，那是她当天刚买的。见鬼，我从没做过这东西，不过我还是去她那里把骨头取了回来，决定在厨房现学现做。之后，我去买了个二手冰箱。杂货店的图奇卖给我一些熟肉，我从中悟出点炖肉的技巧。接下来，家里这些杂七杂八的事情几乎让我晕头转向，突然看到有个单亲妈妈拎着几袋食物，还带着两个孩子，夹着公文包在路上走着，我觉得既然她可以，那我也行。

Friends from the different neighborhoods and stations in my Bay Area journey came over to help me get rid of the junk in the house and to clean the place, which was immediately improved simply from air and sunlight, which eradicated most of the musty smell. The place looked cool. Hell, it was the Taj Mahal compared to where we'd been staying.

Christopher was my number-one helper, not only with the mammoth undertaking of cleaning the place but also in helping organize our tasks and reminding me of what we had to do. "Poppa," he asked me before we moved in, "can we fix the backyard?"

I went to check out the three years of jungle growth back there and told him, "Not yet, son. We have to have a machete back here, and I don't have that yet." Step by step, though, inside, the place came together quickly.

After our first night in the new place, as we prepared to leave early that next morning so that I could get Christopher to day care and then get myself back on the train in order to get to the office on time, he became very concerned that we didn't have all our gear with us.

"It's okay," I explained and pulled out the single house key to show him why we didn't have to take everything with us. "We got a key, Christopher, see."

He looked at the one unassuming key in my opened palm and didn't get it. "Pop," he said, pointing to the duffel bag with all our stuff and my hanging bag with my second suit, "we have to carry this."

"No, son," I told him, "you don't have to carry nothing. We got a key. Let's leave all of this here, all right, and we can just go."

With a puzzled smile, he made sure that he understood. "We can leave it here?"

Bending down, bringing my face close to his, smiling with my own sense of wonder and relief, I repeated what I'd said. "Yes, we can leave all this stuff here."

Together we used the key to lock up, almost giggling, and then turned to go to the BART station, practically skipping all the way there.

It was still bizarre to me that we had journeyed in a full circle from the time I first found us a room at The Palms. Why had I never seen this place? The world had changed for us since then, and yet our four-hour round-trip commute every day took us right by the working women around the corner who remembered us from before.

"Hey, little player," they still called to Christopher, even though he was no longer in the blue stroller, which he'd outgrown, but walking hand in hand with me or playing a little game that the two of us liked to play to pass the time as we went to the BART station and back—taking turns kicking an empty plastic orange juice bottle. "Hey, little pimp," they'd call and sometimes hand him a $5 bill, just like before.

街坊四邻还有湾区的朋友都过来帮忙，帮我打扫卫生，清理房间。很快屋里就敞亮了许多，发霉的味道也散去了。这地方收拾出来还不错，比起我们以前住的地方，这里就像皇宫一般了。

儿子是我的好帮手，不仅能帮我打扫房间，还帮我归整事情，提醒我还有什么事情需要打理。我们准备搬进来之前，他提醒我："爸爸，我们要不要把后院也整理整理啊？"

那里三年以来都没动过了，杂草丛生，我瞅了瞅，说道："儿子，这得等以后用机器来整理才行，现在我没有这东西。"但一步步，这些东西都可以理顺的。

我们在新家过了第一个晚上，第二天早上，我们决定早起，这样就可以把儿子送到托儿所，我再去赶地铁，这样就能准时上班。我们这次不用大包小包地扛在身上，儿子还非常不自在。我一边拿出房门钥匙一边和他解释："没问题的，我们有钥匙。"

他看着我手中的钥匙，没有碰。指着我们的装着所有家当的露营包和装我换洗西装的袋子说："我们得带上这个。"

"不必，儿子，什么都不用带。我们有钥匙了，就把东西放在这，我们直接走就好了，"我耐心地向他解释。

他纳闷地笑了笑，好像明白了："那我们把东西留在这儿就行了吗？"

我俯下身，用脸贴了贴他的小脸，笑着又对他讲了一遍："对啊，把东西留在这就好了。"

我们一起把门锁上，几乎咯咯地笑出声来，然后几乎是一路小跑着赶到捷运车站。

这实在是件诡异的事情，从开始在棕榈酒店附近找到房间到现在，我们兜了这么大一个圈子。我怎么以前没见过这个地方。世界也变化了很多，我们每天都要在路上花上 4 个小时，碰上街角的女工，才帮我们介绍了现在这个地方。

"嗨，小家伙，"她们还会和儿子打招呼，现在他已经不用再坐那辆蓝色小推车了，我们手牵手一路走着，一边做些我们俩的游戏，一路朝着捷运车站走去。我们俩轮流踢橙汁空瓶，"嗨，小家伙，"周围人叫他，有时还会像以前那样给他 5 元钱。

第十一章　贫民区的玫瑰

The PURSUIT of HAPPYNESS

That was still manna to us. For one thing, it was usually nine o'clock at night when we returned from the city, so cooking wasn't the first thing I was dying to do, not to mention it wasn't my expertise yet. For another thing, the money was still tight, even with the modest rent I was paying. So $5 was dinner around the corner at Mossell's where the jukebox played Christopher's favorite song, "Rocket Love" by Stevie Wonder. Every time we walked in, somehow it was always playing, cause for Christopher to alert me, "Pop, it's Stevie. Stevie!" He already had great taste in music and in food.

After I ordered, he got to dig in first, and then I'd eat what was left over. As he and his appetite grew, I made sure to order whatever they served that would stretch the furthest—like red beans and rice with cornbread. We became such regulars that after a while the owners let me go on a payment plan, running us a tab that I'd pay off every two weeks when I got paid. We stuck with ordering the one plate, even then. Survival habits were hard to break, and I continued to look for every opportunity to save money.

But when the rice and beans came, I had to splurge on the jukebox so Little Chris could hear "Rocket Love" again. What a joyful image—my son chowing down as he grooved to his song, singing along and nodding his head. The hunger pangs and the salivating weren't necessarily joyful, especially one night when I watched him really go to town on that one dinner. He saw me watching, put down his fork, and said, "Why aren't you eating?"

"Naw, you go ahead and eat, son," was what I said, but frankly, I was thinking, *Damn, you're going to eat all of the food?* At almost two and a half, he could already eat like a little horse. Apparently he had learned at his young age that you eat it when you can get it.

This was also the case during the pizza party seminars hosted by Dean Witter at the recommendation of a consultant named Bill Goode, whose expertise was qualifying individuals as prospective investors on the telephone. I'd gotten pretty good but was always open to learning from the big guys. The concept was that after work a group of six or so of us would stay late and all call every single person in our book and let them know, for example, that there was a new stock offering coming out from companies like Pacific Gas & Electric. Amid the smiling and dialing, we could enjoy pizza on Dean Witter. I was able to go to day care, get Little Chris, and bring him back. As long as he could have some pizza, I was sure that he would be nice and quiet.

"Here, son," I told him at the first pizza party as I got back to work just in time for pizza to arrive and the dialing to begin, "you sit right here with your pizza. Poppa's got to talk on the telephone, all right?"

"Poppa, you're going to talk on the telephone again?"

"Yeah, I'm gonna talk on the telephone again."

我们也有自己的精神食粮。通常，当我们夜里 9 点从城里回来，我不会先忙着做饭，当时我的厨艺还并不精良。再有就是即便房租很低廉，我们手头的钱也很紧张。所以花上 5 块钱可以到街边买点吃的，同时听着小店里音乐宝盒放着小克里斯多夫最喜欢的歌曲，黑人盲歌手史蒂夫·汪德的《火箭爱》。每次我们走进来的时候，若恰巧放的是这首歌，小克里斯多夫就会拽一拽我，"爸爸，是史蒂夫的歌！"那时的他对音乐和食物就相当有品位了。

每次点了菜，都是让他先吃，我来打扫残羹。随着他一天天长大，胃口也渐长，我就尽可能多要点，什么红豆、米饭和玉米面包之类。我们经常来，后来店主都让我们每两周结一次账就好。每次我们都只要一盘食物，雷打不动。除了保证养家糊口之外，我努力节省每一分钱。每当米饭和豆子上来的时候，我就给音乐宝盒塞点钱，儿子就可以听《火箭爱》了。看着他吃着东西，欣赏着音乐，还一边哼着歌，按着节拍点着头，确实是一件很惬意的事情。可在一旁饥肠辘辘的感觉却不好受，一天夜里，我们又来到这里，我正看着他吃饭，他看我只是在一旁看着，就放下刀叉，问我："你怎么不吃呢？"

"儿子，你先吃吧，"我嘴上这么说，心里却在打鼓，孩子，你不是要把所有的东西都要吃光吧？他才两岁半，可是饭量大的就像匹小马驹。显然，他这么大的时候，只是知道，有多少就吃多少。

添惠公司还会举办匹萨晚餐会，这是咨询师比尔·古迪推荐的做法，他就是擅长培养电话投资人。我自己这方面做得还可以，但是一直都愿意向周围的高手学习。其实就是我们五六个人分成一组，下班晚些回去，都按着小本子上的人名逐个打电话过去，向对方推荐新上市的股票，比如太平洋天然气与电力公司之类。大家脸上都带着微笑，拨着电话，添惠公司的匹萨味道还是不错的。然后我就可以去托儿所接孩子，把他带到公司。只要有匹萨吃，他一定会很乖。

第一次匹萨晚餐会上，我刚回去工作，正好匹萨到了，我正给客户拨电话，"你就和你的匹萨坐在一起，爸爸要去工作了，好吗？"

"爸爸，你还要去讲电话吗？"

"对，我还得去讲一会儿电话。"

"Pop, you're going to still talk?"

"Yeah, I'm still talking."

"Pop, you like to talk?"

"Yeah, son. I like to talk. Have some more of this pizza."

Pretty soon I was laughing and dialing, and so was the rest of the office.

Since Christopher was so eager to help, no matter what the undertaking was, it occurred to me that I should enlist his assistance in getting him admitted to the Oakland day care center where they had the misspelled "happyness" sign. If we could do that, our long days of leaving at five in the morning and not returning until nine at night would be so much more manageable. The only hitch was potty training. He occasionally told me when he had to go to the john but wouldn't bother most of the time.

On the train headed back after the pizza party, I made my proposal. "Son, look, you want to help Poppa?"

"Yes!"

"The way to help Poppa," I said, "is when you think you might want to go to the bathroom, just raise your hand one time. When you think you might want to boo-boo, just raise your hand twice, okay?"

"Okay," he said, beaming, as though he was happy to have a job that was just his.

We made it a game. Sure enough, he was potty-trained in two weeks and enrolled at the day care center right next to the BART station. Our new routine was about as close as I could imagine at that point to a vacation. In the morning at 7:00 a.m., I dropped him off at day care, grabbed my train, and arrived at work early. In the evening I was back in time to pick him up at 6:00 p.m. so we could get to our soul-food greasy spoon for dinner, and afterward we stopped in to visit TV Joe—who owned a store by the same name that sold and repaired televisions.

A friendly, smart guy, Joe didn't mind if we just stopped to chat or if we sat down to watch television for a while. Most likely he figured out that we didn't have a TV set, but he never mentioned it. In fact, when there was a major sporting event being televised, like a Muhammad Ali fight I watched there once, we timed it right so that we happened along to catch whatever broadcast it was.

After dinner, a little television, and a visit with TV Joe, our last stop before heading home was to cruise by The Palms as the ladies of the evening gathered at their posts, several calling to me and my son, "Hey, Chris! Hey, little pimp!"

"爸爸，你就是要不停地说，是吗？"

"对，我得不停地说。"

"爸爸，你喜欢说话是吗？"

"对，爸爸喜欢说话，多吃点匹萨吧。"

我不由得乐出了声，整个办公室的人都笑了起来。

儿子小克里斯多夫非常想帮我的忙，不管是什么事，都是如此。我也确实需要他的配合，这样他在奥克兰托儿所的日子就会好过很多，那里居然连"幸福"这两个字都能写错。要知道我们早上5点就出门，晚上9点才能回家，他的自理能力若能提高，就会好办很多。首先就是要教会他上厕所，有时候，他会说想去厕所，但并不是总能这么做。

我们坐地铁回公司参加匹萨晚餐会时，我提了个建议："儿子，你想帮爸爸一个忙吗？"

"好啊。"

"你这么来帮忙，等你准备解小手时，就举一次手，准备解大手时呢，就举两次手，好吗？"

"好啊，"他咧着嘴笑了，好像有了一份自己的工作，非常开心的样子。

我们就像做游戏一样开始了训练，也就是两周的光景，他就过关了，就可以放心送他去捷运车站旁的托儿所了。我们每天都要这样开始，早上7点，我把孩子放到托儿所，赶上地铁，早早到了公司。晚上6点，我要去托儿所把他接回来，然后随便弄点吃的，之后就去乔伊电视修理店，老板就叫乔伊，店里卖电视，也负责维修。

老板人很好，也很聪明。我们在店里坐一坐，聊聊天，甚至看会儿电视，他都很欢迎。很可能他猜出我们家里没有电视，但他从不提这一点。实际上，当有大型赛事转播的时候，比如拳王阿里的比赛，我还在这里看过一次，那次时间正好赶上，其他时候我们就碰上什么看一会儿什么。

晚饭后，看一会儿电视，和乔伊叔叔聊一会儿，接下来就要去棕榈酒店那边去了，那些女工晚上都聚在摊位附近，还会和我们打招呼："嗨，克利斯，小东西。"

To Christopher, they were like family now. "Hey!" he waved back, knowing that even if we already had dinner, he might be lucky enough to be given one of those $5 bills he was used to getting.

Then we'd roll on down the street and come up to our house. A block away I had my hand in my pocket, making sure that key was still there. It reminded me of how nervous I was when I flew cross-country with the diamond ring in my pocket for Sherry. But the key was worth ten times the Hope Diamond to me. What I loved about it so much, I don't know. It wasn't attached to a key chain or key ring. It was just this bare little key. But it was ours.

And the feeling of elation I got every time I saw the roses blooming in the ghetto in front of our place and when I put my foot on that step, that first step, never diminished. What it meant, every time, to put my foot on the step with the key in my hand and to unlock the door and finally step into the house, is impossible to explain. It was the opposite of powerlessness; it was the antidote to the fear of not knowing what was happening that night, where we would go, how we would manage. The key was like the key to the kingdom, a symbol of having made it this far, all the way from where I had been, at the absolute bottom of the hole, to where I was now—an incredible transition.

Were things still rough? Sure they were. But they were manageable. Now that I could cover us having this home base, day care, transportation, and food, I felt that I could air my head out, just like the house, and then really kick into a higher gear at work. It wasn't that our worries were all behind us, a reality I faced early on in the new place when I missed a couple of electric bills and the electricity was turned off.

I set up candles, telling Christopher, "C'mon, you get to take a bath by candlelight," trying not to let him see that I was upset or overly frustrated about what was really only a minor setback in the scheme of things.

Even so, as I scrubbed Little Chris in the tub, I couldn't help fretting about how I could really accomplish the big vision if I continued to be dragged down by so much daily minutiae. Yes, of course, I saw the progress, but where I wanted to be still seemed too far in the distance. My most distinct thought was, *I ain't superman!*

At that very moment, out of nowhere, my son stood up in the bathtub and said to me, with a very serious look on his face, which was illuminated by the light of the candle, "Poppa, you know what? You're a good poppa."

Aw, man, I melted, forgot the worries, the minutiae, and knew that I was going to be fine. Coming from that little boy, those words were all I needed. Christopher could always cheer me up or give me whatever spark was missing at the time.

对于小克里斯多夫而言，他们就像一家人一样，他也会向她们招手，"你们好啊！"他知道，即便我们都吃过饭了，幸运的话，这些阿姨可能还会给他5块钱。

我们沿着街往下走，回到家门口。快到家的时候，我把手放到口袋里，看看钥匙在不在。那种心情让我想起口袋里放着给雪莉钻戒时的心情，那是我满世界找回来的钻戒啊。但是这把钥匙对我而言比钻戒都要值钱。我自己也不清楚为什么这么喜欢这把钥匙。上面没有钥匙链，也没有什么钥匙环，可这就是我们的。

看到家门前，在贫民区盛开的玫瑰，我就不由得满心欢喜。当我踏上台阶，踏上第一级台阶，就有一种非常踏实的感觉。每次我手里拿着钥匙，踏上台阶，打开房门，那种感觉难以言喻。一切疲惫和无力都烟消云散，不再担心夜里会有什么事情，不用担心我们会去往何方，或是无处安身。这把钥匙仿佛是通往一个王国的钥匙，我一路走来，从生活的谷底，能发展到今日，这已经是很大的改观。

当然，生活依旧有它艰难的一面，但是我可以应付了。现在有了这么个家可以遮风挡雨，白天孩子送托儿所，坐车东奔西走，解决吃饭问题，这些问题现在都可以解决。就像我们最终找到这所房子一样，一切在走上正轨，我可以全力工作了。也不是万事无忧，比如刚来这里，我忘记交电费，结果就家里就停电了，一片漆黑。

我点着了蜡烛，和儿子说，"你得点着蜡烛洗澡了。"我还要尽可能不让他看出来我的不安，仿佛就出了一点点小差错一样。

即便如此，给儿子洗澡的时候，我还是有些郁闷，若是总被这些琐碎牵绊着，我什么时候才能实现自己的远大理想。我已经有进步了，但这还远远不够，我头脑中最清晰的念头就是："我怎么不是超人啊。"

正想着，儿子从澡盆里站起身来，在摇曳的烛光下，他非常严肃地看着我，"爸爸，你知道吗，你是非常出色的老爸。"

天哪，我顿时感动得说不出话来，所有的烦恼，所有的不快，一时间烟消云散，我知道一切都会好起来的。有小家伙说的这句话，就全都足够了。他总能让我重振旗鼓，给我的生活中增添色彩。

第十一章 贫民区的玫瑰

A photograph taken of the two of us not long after he made that comment summed up what this period was all about. I called it the "Picture of Two Lions." In it, Christopher and I are sitting side by side in front of our house, right on that top step, and I'm looking above the camera lens, as if off into the horizon, with a proud, determined Poppa Lion face and a king-of-the-pride expression that says, *Where's the next meal coming from?* And on the face of my son, the lion cub, is a look that says: *I'm hungry. I'm hungry.*

That framed everything, that Picture of Two Lions, erasing all doubt in my mind that I was doing the right thing. We weren't looking back. Never. My focus was on that horizon. What was next? How did I pursue it? What did I need to know to make it happen?

* * *

My learning curve became activated again when Dean Witter brought in one of the company's top producers, a super-smart, no-bullshit powerhouse by the name of Gary Abraham from Las Vegas, Nevada. Tasked with visiting different branch offices and helping the greener guys build their business, Gary clicked with me right away.

In person or on the phone, whenever I called up for advice or to touch base, he was down to earth and available, asking, "Hey, how you doing? What's happening?"

In spite of Gary's easygoing demeanor, he was razor-sharp, a wizard, chockful of insights about what he was doing and how he had built his business. One of the concepts he helped me begin to understand—something I wouldn't really master until later— was the idea that rather than telling someone what they should buy and why they should buy it, a much more strategic, productive approach was to find out what my customer wanted to buy. In my understanding of supply and demand, this approach made a lot of sense, although applying it practically was going to take time.

When Gary was starting out in Vegas, where there's always an influx of new money, always booming, instead of doing the phone thing, he went out to scout locations for new developments, where they were building million-dollar homes in various states of constru-ction.

"You called on them in person?" I asked, trying to see myself doing something like that.

Gary recalled, "You bet. I put on my best blue suit and went and rang the doorbell on each and every one of those houses, without an appointment, and introduced myself."

Man, I wanted his script, his formula. What he had done and how he had done it.

There was nothing brilliant about it, he insisted. "I just said, 'Hi, I'm Gary Abraham, I'm with Dean Witter here in Las Vegas, and I'd like to know if there is anything we can do to help you settle in here, and by the way are you involved in the stock market?' "

他说这句话不久，我们照了张照片，可以称得上是这一时期真实的写照。我称之为《双狮图》。小克里斯多夫和我并肩坐在屋子前面的台阶，就是最上面的那级台阶。我向远方眺望，一脸的尊严，仿佛狮王爸爸带着那种骄傲狮子般的表情在说："我们下一顿晚餐在哪儿呢？"在儿子的脸上，那个小狮子的表情就是在说，我饿了，好饿啦。

这幅《双狮图》就说明了一切，让我心头一切疑云都散了开去，我知道自己的选择没有错。我们不会回头，我只会盯着远方。我们下一个目标是什么？我该怎样实现目标？我就是要让梦想变为现实。

* * *

当添惠公司引入一位顶级高手杰瑞·亚巴拉罕的时候，我的学习欲望又被点燃了。他来自内华达州的拉斯维加斯，天资聪颖，他拜访不同的部门，帮助新手逐渐进入工作角色。杰瑞很快就找到了我。

无论是面对面的请教，还是电话咨询，只要我有求于他，他都很愿意帮我，而且平易近人，一点都没有架子，总是问我："怎么样啊？出什么事儿了？"

尽管杰瑞非常和蔼可亲，但他聪慧过人，可以说是业界奇才，对工作有着独到见解。他帮我认识到一个根本性的问题，这我在最近才真正领悟，与其告诉别人要购买什么，以及为什么购买，不如直接投其所好，看他需要什么。后者更具有战略眼光，而且事半功倍。从供需的理解而言，这一点不言而喻，但是把它真正落到实处，学以致用，还是需要时日。

当杰瑞从拉斯维加斯出道的时候，当时一片欣欣向荣的景象，各种投资竞相到位。杰瑞没有墨守成规，守着电话，而是直接到新开发区见客户，这些开发商正在各州斥资建造数百万美元的房屋。

"你事先做过电话沟通吗？"我问道，想看看自己是不是也可以如此照搬。

杰瑞想了想："没有，根本就没有任何预约，我当时就穿上自己最好的蓝色西装，敲开每家每户的门，直接自我介绍。"

天哪，我需要记下他的秘诀，他当时是怎么做的，具体是怎么做到的。

其实没什么，他讲："我就是说你好，我是杰瑞·亚巴拉罕，在拉斯维加斯的添惠公司做事。想知道我们能帮您做些什么，帮您在这里安顿下来，比如适当参与股市之类？"

That kind of maverick approach was exactly what had made me take the long road by building my own book rather than sticking to the company program like most of the guys working around me. I looked at Gary and knew that's what I wanted to do, how I wanted to play the game.

At the age of twenty-nine, I came to the realization that I was inordinately fortunate to have been mentored—either directly or indirectly—by extraordinary individuals, true role models. What a cast of individuals I had pulling me forward, whether it was the early inspiration of Miles Davis, who first made me want to reach for greatness, or the determination to be on the cutting edge of whatever I did that Dr. Robert Ellis instilled in me, or the ambition to hit the numbers like Bob Russell back when I got my feet wet in business, or the belief and passion for making it on Wall Street that Bob Bridges and his red Ferrari first ignited, or the different styles of Dean Witter stars like Andy Cooper, Dave Terrace, and now Gary Abraham.

There was never a sense in my gut that these role models helped me more or less because I was black or expected more or less because I was black. If they did, I didn't pick up on it. Later I read a quote from Berry Gordy about how he achieved the big crossover appeal of Motown, why he was certain his records would sell to white kids as well as black kids. His point—that his music business success wasn't a black thing or a white thing but rather a green thing—resonated with me. In the financial arena that I was in, my mentors and the examples that I was learning from could have come from any background. It happened that most of them were white, but they were Italians, Jews, foreigners, WASPS, from all up and down the socioeconomic ladder. Success in this field wasn't a white thing or a black thing, it was a green thing. That was the measure—how much green you were moving and how much you were making.

Maybe without trying consciously, Gary Abraham helped me identify which of my strengths were going to help take me to the next level. At the top of that list was probably the ability to handle volatility—experience plucked right out of my life. This fact about myself struck me one day at work when the Dow started going crazy and went over 1,000, sending thrilling shock waves through the market. But one of the older brokers was beside himself. "You see that, son?" he said to one of the new guys. "It's all over. Sell everything."

We had been watching it inch up, around 850, then 900, in that vicinity. And when it broke 1,000 that day, he really thought it was the end of the world—which to a stockbroker translates as "Sell everything."

这种独辟蹊径的做法让我也蠢蠢欲动，准备亲自出发，去建立自己的客户名单资料，而不是像别人那样，死守着公司的客户名单逐个拨打电话。我看着杰瑞，知道自己该怎么做了，而且跃跃欲试。

在我29岁的时候，我意识到自己相当的幸运，总是能直接或间接地受益于这些高人的点拨。最早是受到爵士大师迈尔·戴维斯的启发，我总是想尽善尽美。接下来，受到罗伯特·艾里斯医生的悉心指导，立志要把工作做到极致，涉足商界的时候，我又决心像雷·莫斯那样，成为业界的顶尖人物。还有那个红色法拉利的车主鲍勃·布里奇，以及添惠公司那些大腕明星级人物，比如安迪·库珀、大卫·特拉斯还有眼前的这位杰瑞·亚巴拉罕，他们都对我产生了积极的影响。

在我心目中，所有这些人对我的帮助，并非与我的肤色有关，也并非觉得或多或少有这方面的因素。如果他们有这方面的想法，我是根本不会买账的。最近，我读到音乐人贝里·戈迪的一段话，说他如何在摩城唱片取得巨大成功，为何他的唱片黑人白人都喜欢，其原因就在于他做音乐不是为白人或黑人而做，其实是为绿色和谐而做，这句话让我颇有共鸣。在金融领域，对我产生积极影响的这些人，有着各种各样的背景出身，他们很多的肤色是白色，但有意大利人、犹太人、外国人等，来自社会各个阶层。这个领域的成功与肤色无关，而是绿色和谐的产物，取决于你前进的路途是否一帆风顺，能实现怎样的和谐。

也许，不经意间，杰瑞已经帮我指出了自己的长处所在，这会让我在事业上更进一步。我最大的特点就是应付不确定性，针对这一点，生活已经给我太多的磨练了。

当道琼斯指数突然飙升，突破1000点，在股市掀起狂澜。但是有个年长的经纪人对新手说，"看到了吧，孩子，这就到头了，全部抛掉。"我们正看着股指节节攀升，850点、900点附近徘徊，终于冲破了1000点大关，结果他却觉得是世界末日一般，让全部抛出。

第十一章 贫民区的玫瑰

Volatility and change had been the watchwords of my life. If I had learned anything it was that it's never the end of the world, no matter how bleak things can be. What this also showed at that time was that hardly anybody around me truly knew anything. Shocking. They had the talk down, as if they knew everything, but ultimately nobody had a clue as to what the market was really going to do. As a matter of fact, very few in the brokerage business have that gift. That wasn't my gift either, although I was going to be damn sure I knew the best analysts and paid attention to what they were saying. But predicting the market's ups and downs and permutations wasn't what I cared about.

What I did know was that the market was going to open. Then it was going to do one of two things: it was going to go up or go down. You could bet money on that. That awareness allowed me to stay steady, to offer assurances to customers that weren't bogus. Of everything I took away with me from this initiation period in Wall Street, where it was all about writing tickets, the most important principle I adopted was the commitment that if I was going to write a ticket, it had to be an honest ticket.

Gary Abraham said it this way: "Write a ticket that's going to set up your next ticket. Don't put somebody into something just to get a piece of business. Because that'll be the last piece of business you get from them."

Gary was a phenomenal resource whose advice I not only tried to follow but also never forgot and who never seemed at a loss for information or wisdom when I sought him out. In time I'd look back and was able to see that it was in San Francisco that I learned to sell, while it was New York that would really teach me the business. Little did I know until later that knowing the business and selling are two very different things. Gary Abraham sold the way great singers seem to hit those notes effortlessly. People wanted to work with him, yet he never pushed, he let them sell themselves.

He introduced me to the effectiveness of not trying to sell you what I got but to find out what you want to buy, or what you will buy, what you already own. Boiled down, the question was: *What can I show you that is similar to what you already own, that's going to meet your current objectives?*

That was the direction I wanted to pursue, a departure from *I've got this product and this stuff that I have to move, and I don't care what you want or already own*. Unfortunately, Dean Witter was a wire house like other, similar wire houses—a huge corporation with an agenda that was not always the same as that of its clients.

Nonetheless, even as my paycheck improved somewhat and as Little Chris and I ventured out for more of a social life on weekends, I began to wonder if I should scope out some options.

不确定性和变化无常一度是我生活的主调，但我知道无论如何都不会是世界末日的到来。那次经历让我意识到，这种情况下，周围的人其实并非什么都了解，但大家都摆出一幅专家的样子，似乎自己什么都懂，而实际上，没人知道股市下一秒会怎样。而且从事证券业的人，没有几个有这样的天赋能把脉股市冷暖，我自己也做不到这一点。虽然我也知道业界最好的分析师有哪些，而且我也关注他们的评论，但是预知股市走向和变化的言论，我是不感兴趣的。

我只知道股市会开市，那么就会有两种情况发生，或者攀升，或者走低。可以赌上一把。这种观念让我能够非常冷静地面对一切，也让客户能够放心。我在华尔街的初期就是负责下单，我所固守的原则就是任何一单都是诚实的，童叟无欺。

杰瑞这么说这件事："这一单下了是为了以后的单子，别指望就和一个人做一笔生意，因为一旦如此，那么这将是你和他做的最后一笔生意。"

杰瑞说的绝对是至理名言，他所说的我不仅尽量去付诸实践，而且还铭刻在心。每当我去求教时，他都不吝赐教，毫无保留。回首昨日，在旧金山我学会了销售技巧，可是在纽约，我才知道什么是生意场。从开始的懵懵懂懂，一无所知，到后来了解到销售和生意相去甚远，根本是两回事。杰瑞说起这些轻描淡写，就像歌唱家可以轻松唱出任何音符一般。人们都喜欢和他共事，他也从不勉强，而是一切顺其自然，让对方主动提出来。

他告诉我不要刻意去销售自己有的东西，而是要发现对方需要买什么，准备买什么，已经拥有什么。总结下来就是：我能不能拿出来你已有的类似东西，并且还能满足你的需要呢？

这就是我要努力的方向，不再一味地推销我手上的东西，只在乎我准备出手的东西，而不管对方需要什么或是有了什么。可惜的是，添惠公司和其他经纪公司相差无几，都是按照自家规定做事的大公司，而不会考虑客户的具体需求。

即便当我的收入有所提高，甚至有时可以带着儿子周末去参加一些社交活动，我开始考虑是不是可以有更多的选择呢？

The thought was on my mind when we hung out in a blues club in our neighborhood where the band, led by Troyce Key, an itty-bitty white boy who went with the finest sister you ever saw, was hot. The food, cooked up for five bucks a plate by Shep, was hotter. Christopher lucked into a musical and culinary education as we sat there all night long, listening to the blues, eventually trying everything on the menu. Shep fried up catfish with rice, beans, greens, and sweet potatoes, did ribs on the barbecue, smothered pork chops and steaks, both drenched with gravy and served with piles of hot-water cornbread. Chicken came every way it could come: fried, smothered, stuffed, barbecued. And I had to break the ban against sugar so Little Chris and I could both have sweetened ice tea. The best.

Afterward, we made our now-familiar stroll past the whore stroll—or the " ho"-stroll—and we waved at the same girls, had our same exchange, and usually headed home.

During the weekend days, when summer came, I'd sit out on the front stoop and bring Little Chris out on our concrete patch of a front yard, letting him know it was fine to play with the other neighborhood kids who came around but to stay close to the house and especially to stay away from the street. With two lanes going each way, it was a very busy thoroughfare, with parking and lots of streets intersecting the main drag. Days passed quickly outside watching the comings and goings.

In one part of my brain I was figuring how could I do more of the Gary Abraham kind of selling, and in the other part of my brain I was here on a summer day in the ghetto, all kinds of music blaring from cars and stereos and boom boxes. Straight-up ghetto with a palm tree down on the corner and one rosebush that happened to be in my front yard.

One of my favorite things to do if we felt like an outing was to put Little Chris in the shopping cart that had come to replace his blue stroller. Since I was nowhere near being able to afford an actual automobile and never would retrieve the one that I shared with Jackie, the cart became our only wheels. Christopher referred to it fondly as our car, inquiring, if we went inside anywhere, "Poppa, where'd you park the car?"

On good weather days, we'd roll on through the neighborhood, straight down Telegraph all the way to Berkeley—one hell of a long walk. Walking along, I'd forget everything and relax into the Zen of it all, feeling the vibrations and the bumps coming up through the wheels of the cart and into my hands. Making totally different sounds from the stroller, the cart made its own ghetto music with a *cluclack, cluclack, cluclack* as it rolled along the sidewalk. In Berkeley we sometimes stopped by my girl Latrell's mother's house, grabbed a bite from off the barbecue, and turned around to walk the long way home.

We were returning from one such excursion in our "car" when the sunny day all of a sudden went cold and blustery, with rain that began to fall in heavy slats.

一天，当我们坐在家附近的一个布鲁斯俱乐部，看着特伊斯·奇的乐队在演出，他是个女权主义的白人男子，和他在一起的女孩美艳绝伦，演出非常火爆，吃得也不错，5元钱一碟的牛肉，味道极佳。儿子享用着美食，欣赏着布鲁斯，我们在这里呆了一夜，最后几乎把菜单上的食物都点了一遍。而我的脑子里就想着这个问题，我可以有更多的选择吗？有煎鲶鱼配米饭、豆子、蔬菜和红薯、烧烤的猪排、熏猪肉，都浇着浓浓的肉汁，还有玉米面包。鸡肉的做法就更多了，煎炸烹炒，还有火烤。我干脆不再顾及医生要我忌糖的命令，和儿子一起品着甜冰茶，尽情享受。

之后，我们经过熟悉的街道，给街头妓女留点钱，和她们招招手，便朝家走去。

夏日里，在周末的时候，我会坐在屋外的凳子上，让儿子从水泥地面的院子里出来，告诉他和周围的小朋友一起玩耍没问题，但不可以走远，特别是不可以跑到马路上去。前面的马路双向都有两个车道，与很多主要街道和停车场相连，整天都车水马龙。看着外面的车来车往，一天很快就过去了。

可是我一方面在考虑着杰瑞的问题，怎样才能像他那样把销售做得出神入化，另一方面，我在享用着贫民区夏日的阳光，听着来往车辆中传出的音乐，音箱开得震天响。贫民区走下去，路边有几株棕榈树，还有一丛玫瑰正好长在我家前院。

若是想外出，我最喜欢的莫过于把儿子放在购物车上，现在婴儿推车可放不下他了。因为现在我们还买不起真正的汽车，和杰姬公用的那辆其实也拿不回来，所以这辆购物车就是唯一的代步工具。小克里斯多夫就把这叫做我们的汽车，当我们进到店里的时候，他会问："爸爸，我们把车停到哪里啊？"

天气好的时候，我们就一直推着车走街串巷，从电报大街一直可以走到伯克利，这段路可不短呢。这么走着，我几乎什么都会忘却，全然放松，感觉到车轮在地面上的震动和颠簸，这声音和婴儿推车的声音完全不同，推车仿佛是在人行道上哼唱着自己简朴的歌。在伯克利，我们有时会在拉垂尔的母亲家停留一下，从烤肉架上抓点什么吃的，然后就慢慢地往家走。

我们就用这样的"车"出行，结果一天，回来的途中，天色突然变暗，骤然间下起瓢泼大雨。

"Poppa," Chris said, looking up at me and blinking through the raindrops, "when we gonna get a car with a top on it?"

I must have laughed as loud as thunder. Of all the things he could have asked to improve on our shopping cart, it wasn't doors, or an engine, or leather seats. No, he wanted a top.

On another summer day I'm pushing the car over to a park in West Oakland and spot an elderly black couple loading food and supplies into a little wagon to take to a family reunion picnic. With all the space in our shopping cart, it's only right that I offer to help.

Little Chris immediately starts to check out the contents of their bags and serving containers.

"Christopher," I try to stop him.

The elderly couple think this is so cute and funny, they don't mind at all. When we arrive at the reunion, I'm helping them take the stuff out of the cart when someone hollers, "That's Willie's boy!" I turn around slowly and notice everyone is looking at me.

What can I do? Explain to everyone that I'm not Willie's boy, or just go along with it and have a bite to eat with all my kin? The smell of the barbecue's awful good. Taking my best shot, I turn to the guy who's just hollered and say, "What's going on? What's up with you?"

Instantly, we are seated and food is heaped on our plates. Treated as if we're royalty, we eat like absolute kings as all the while I'm being deluged with questions.

"Well, how Willie doin'?" "He still in jail?" "When he supposed to get out?"

Of course, I don't know anything about Willie, what he's done or how long he's been gone, so all I say is, "Well, you know, Willie, he's doing all right."

"That's right, baby," says a matronly woman, "now you want some more of this?" as she serves us our third helpings, adding, "You get you some of that 'tato salad over there."

Please! This is no manna, it's milk and honey, overflowing. It gets better as the party comes to an end and they start divvying up the food, telling us, "Y'all take some of this, now, and some of this over here, and that cake, just take it." I'm biting my lip to keep from grinning. We have a week's worth of food packed up in our shopping cart. Glory be.

Just as we're starting to say our good-byes, with everybody telling us to give their best to Willie, I find myself standing face-to-face with a pretty young sister and it is on.

For much of the time that my son and I have been on our own, the last thing on my mind is the sexual and romantic void in my life. Not that I quite qualified for the monastery, or that there wasn't potential around the office or with friends of friends, but until recently, even if there had been a will, there was no way to put it together.

儿子仰头望着我，说："爸爸，什么时候我们的车可以有顶棚啊？"

我不禁笑出声来，他没有想着要车门、发动机，甚至皮椅，却想到了要个车顶。

还有一天，我推着车路过西奥克兰的一个停车场，看到一对黑人老夫妇正往一辆小车上装大包小包，看来是家庭野餐会用的东西。我们的车里正好有地方，所以我就上前去帮忙。

小克里斯立刻翻开袋子看里面有什么，还拆开要吃。

"小克里斯多夫，"我想阻止他，让他别这么干。

可这对老夫妇倒是无所谓，觉得孩子很可爱。等我们到了聚会的地方，还帮着他们往出拿东西，有人冲着我们喊："这是威力的孩子吗？"我慢慢地转过身去，看到所有的人都在朝这边看。

我该怎么办呢？是当着大家的面说自己不是威力的孩子，还是就这么将错就错地进去和大家一起就餐？烧烤的味道实在是诱人。我就壮起胆子，转过身去，冲着他说："是啊，你怎么样啊？需要帮忙吗？"

很快，我们就进去落座，盘子里装得满满的，仿佛受到了皇室的待遇一般，我们大吃特吃，好不痛快，不过人们也在不停地问着我各种问题。

"这个威力怎么样了呢？""他还在监狱吗？""什么时候才能放出来呢？"

当然，我对威力一无所知，究竟他做了些什么，离开了多久，所以我只能说："嗯，那个，他现在一切都好。"

"那就好，孩子，"一个主妇模样的女子和我说，"再加点什么吃的吗？"她又给我加了第三次食物，"上面再弄点沙拉吧。"

这简直就是天上掉下的馅饼，牛奶、蜂蜜，美味应有尽有。特别是当聚餐接近尾声，大家纷纷把剩下的食物打包带走，还对我们说："你们也带些回去吧，还有蛋糕，多拿点。"我差点没乐出声来，我们的推车里足足装了够吃一周的食物，满载而归。

我们和大家相互道别，而且他们还表示向威力问好，突然，我和一个漂亮姑娘不期而遇。

在很多情况下，都是我和儿子相依为命，我对自己的感情生活基本不抱什么希望。倒不是我清心寡欲，只是办公室恋情基本没什么希望，和朋友或者朋友介绍的朋友则无甚机缘，而且即便最近我有这心思，也没有这方面的可能了。

The PURSUIT of HAPPYNESS

There had been an awkward visit from Jackie once we settled into the new home, when she showed up to visit Christopher. Interestingly enough, even though Little Chris had asked about her on occasion, he didn't cling to her or react like I had during and after separations from my own momma. Maybe it was because he didn't know her that well anymore. Or maybe it was just how she related to her child. In any event, my feelings were much more complicated, in part because of the mixed signals she sent me, but mainly because of so much residual anger I'd never expressed to her. Well, she sho nuff got an earful from me this time around. And then we fucked. That's what it was, not even a sport fuck, for the release of it, but more, from my point of view, a literal fuck-you. If she had any intention of getting back together now that I was moving up—not there yet, but beyond the gates she had been so sure I couldn't enter—she saw that wasn't going to happen and split for Los Angeles as suddenly as she had arrived.

Little Chris asked where she'd gone, and I explained, "She's moving to Los Angeles. You'll see her again soon." That was all he needed to know.

Now the slate's clean, and here I am trying to hook up with this fine beauty at an Oakland park family reunion where I'm fronting that I'm related to someone named Willie.

Just as I'm getting ready to get her phone number, one of the older gentlemen steps over and says, "You know, that's your cousin."

I'm nearly busted. Thinking fast, I say, "Oh, wow, I haven't seen her for so long, I didn't recognize her."

His hand on my shoulder, kind of eying me, he nods, saying, "Yeah, I can understand. Plus she got real good-looking, so you probably hoped she wasn't no kin to you, didn't you?"

"You got that right, she sure did grow up to be fine!"

"Yeah," he echoes me and looks at the young sister, who rolls her eyes and turns to walk away. "She sho did grow up to be a pretty little thing."

A close call. It's too late to volunteer my true identity to prove that I'm not really related after all. Instead, I turn to him and say, "Thanks for telling me."

"Don't mention it," he says, waving good-bye to me and Little Chris as I hurry us on out of there.

While I was delighted to be pushing a cart heavy from all the leftovers, and amused by how well a case of mistaken identity had turned out, that day marked another turning point for me. We were through the storms, and we had found a place in the ghetto in which to lay anchor long enough for me to get my bearings. And I was inching up toward a couple thousand a month. My next move, whatever it was going to be, was to double that, at least. With that, I could afford to move us back to San Francisco, which was, without a doubt, the Paris of the Pacific.

杰姬曾经到我们的新家来过一次，来看小克里斯多夫。有意思的是，尽管儿子也曾问过妈妈一次，但他没有缠着杰姬不放，或是像我当年被迫和母亲分别那样，母子情深，难舍难分。也许是他对杰姬了解不是很多，或是这就是她为人母的风格。可我在当时的情感却非常复杂，这其中也有她的原因，她内心也相当纠结，再有就是我对她还余怒未消。但这次我不会再对她喋喋不休，我们就这么上了床，但那不是为爱而爱，而是为恨，纯粹的发泄，至少我是这么认为的。当初哪怕是有一点点希望能够重修旧好，我都不至于这样。但是隔着大门，当时她是那样的决绝，我们在洛杉矶就这么一拍两散，就像如今她的突然到来一样，没有任何征兆。

小克里斯多夫问她去哪里了，我说："她去洛杉矶了，很快就能再见到她的。"让儿子知道这些就足够了。

现在，一切都过去了，我可以一身轻松地和这个美人，在奥克兰家庭聚会上书写浪漫，这还要感谢这个威力才是。

我正准备要她的电话号码，一位年长绅士走上前来，介绍说："这就是你的堂妹。"

我差点就扛不住了，脑子转得飞快，"噢，好久没见了，我都认不出来她了。"

长者把手搭在我的肩上，盯着我，点点头，说道："可以理解，非常希望这不是自己的亲戚才好，是吗？"

"说得对，女大十八变啊。"

"是啊，是啊。"他也随声附和着，看着我的"堂妹"，姑娘低下头，转身走开了，"确实出落得一表人才了。"

失之交臂啊。现在再道出自己的真实身份，说明我们没有血缘关系，已经为时已晚。我只得向这位长者道谢了："多谢您告诉我这些。"

"客气了。"他挥挥手和我们道别，我带着儿子匆匆离开了这里。

我兴高采烈地推着一车食物往家走，心里觉得这件将错就错的事情实在有趣，那一天对我而言，其实意味着是一个转折点。我们已经经历的风雨，终于在贫民区找到一处容身之所，让我能得以喘息。每个月，我都可以稍稍有所进步。不管下一步该怎么走，至少要比现在好很多，相信有朝一日我可以搬到旧金山，那里毋庸置疑，就是太平洋上的巴黎。

For the first time in a long time, maybe ever, I didn't feel like it was all on me, slugging it, pushing against the odds. Still a dreamer, yet more of a realist than ever before, I knew this was my time to sail. On the horizon I saw the shining future, as before. The difference now was that I felt the wind at my back. I was ready.

在很长一段时间里,我第一次不再觉得自己是在受着命运的捉弄,不是在泥泞中艰难前行。我对生活仍然充满梦想,但是要比以往更现实。我知道自己应该扬帆远行。在遥远的地平线上,我一如既往,仍旧可以看得到耀眼的光芒。不过,不同以往的是,现在风在助我,我准备启航。

Chapter 12
Sphere of Influence

Every day as lunchtime approached, a skinny little middle-aged guy showed up and took a seat in the cubicle next to mine in the bullpen on the trading floor at Dean Witter. Just doing my thing on the phone in the midst of fifty other brokers talking and trading, I barely noticed him or took into account that the reason he was there probably was to see Suzy, the beautiful blond broker whose cubicle it was.

When I did pick up on him, I figured he was a devoted client, stopping in to see his broker. In her late twenties or early thirties, Suzy was bright, energetic, and appealing in her miniskirts and high heels, with a bustline she either bought or was just very proud to have. Good at what she did, she was always going to do well in the game.

Whether or not he was a client wasn't any of my business anyway, so I had no idea that he'd been sitting there listening to me. It came as quite a shock then when he spoke to me out of the blue one day, saying, "What are you doing here? You don't belong here. Here's my card. Call me and come over. Let's have coffee."

第十二章
圈 子

每天临近中午，就会有一个瘦瘦的小个子中年人出现，他会在添惠公司的交易大厅的大屋子里，在我旁边找个位子坐下。我还是忙乎着自己的事情，和周围的经纪人一起谈论问题，忙着下单，几乎没怎么注意他。也许他来这里就是为了看到金发美女苏吉经纪人，这个位子就是她的。

后来，我和他闲聊，才知道他是个非常投入的客户，是来这里看经纪人工作的。苏吉也就二三十岁的样子，聪慧过人，精力充沛，穿着短裙和高跟鞋，身材惹火，非常引人注目。她不仅面容姣好，干起活来，也不逊色。

不管这个中年人是不是客户，他与我也无甚关系。所以我根本没有意识到他会在一旁听我讲话。所以，一天他突然张口，说道："你在这里干什么呢，你就不属于这儿，拿着我的名片，给我打电话，我们一起喝点咖啡。"

Turned out this was not some guy coming to see his broker, but rather she was his girlfriend. It also turned out that this wiry Jewish guy who looked and talked like a white Sammy Davis Jr. was Gary Shemano, the managing general partner for Bear Stearns in San Francisco.

What was Bear Stearns? That was exactly what I wanted to know when I looked at his card. I asked around. The answer came back that Bear Stearns was, at this time, one of the most profitable private partnerships in the history of Wall Street. I knew the big wire houses like Dean Witter, Merrill Lynch, E. F. Hutton, and Paine Webber. These wire houses might have ten, twelve, fifteen thousand brokers, with all transactions and communications done on the wire. Bear Stearns had only six to seven hundred brokers, and instead of being mass-market—the mom-and-pop investors, folks wanting IRAs and utilities, meat-and-potatoes—this smaller partnership was going after bigger fish in the institutional investment business: banks, pension funds, insurance companies, money managers, bigger businesses.

Selling directly to individual investors, you can tell clients about a new product that might be a great idea and let them know about a new stock offering. You'll move some shares. That's because, at least back in the day, they weren't savvy about the markets and what was out there to buy. They were relying on you, the broker, to tell them. But the large institutions really know the markets, and that's not what they need a broker for. They're investing humongous sums and don't want a little this or a little that; they want a broker to put together a lot of this and a lot of that, in the most profitable way possible. Down in the basement of mass-market selling, it's that numbers game of hitting X amount of calls that eventually become X amount of accounts and X amount of growth. You don't play that with big business. Instead of making two hundred calls to two hundred prospects, you might make one hundred calls to one prospect before you ever meet.

Up there it was then—and is now—about building relationships. Up there, in the Bear Stearns way of doing business, it's about the sphere of influence, something I would come to understand infinitely better in the months and years ahead.

Still not that hip about this company, I stop in to see my branch manager about getting more money, not long after Gary Shemano gives me his card. It's basically a no-brainer as far as I'm concerned. The attitude in the past whenever I've asked for more money than the smaller commissions I'm eking out has been: "Don't worry about the gross commission dollars. They'll come after you open the accounts."

原来这人不是来看他的经纪人的,也不是来看什么女朋友的。这个瘦瘦的像犹太人的家伙长相和谈吐都有几分像小山米·戴维斯,实际上叫做盖瑞·许曼诺,是旧金山贝尔斯登商业银行的管理合伙人。

贝尔斯登商业银行是干什么的呢?我看到他的名片最想知道的就是这个问题。我向周围人打听了一下。这才知道原来这是华尔街历史上最赚钱的私营合作机构。像添惠公司、美林集团、赫顿公司、潘恩韦伯公司这些都是大型的证券经纪公司,下设数万家经纪分公司,所有的交易和沟通都是在线上完成的。贝尔斯登只有六七百家经纪公司,不做散户市场,因为这些地方都是老头老太太在做,都是指望着个人退休账户、水电费、柴米油盐这些来过日子的。贝尔斯登关注的是真正的大鱼,是那些机构,比如银行、退休基金、保险公司、资金经理、大企业客户,等等。

针对个人投资者,你可以和他讲,这是新推出的产品,是新股上市,很有投资潜力之类。这还能做成一些单子,因为他们也许就不懂股市,就是指望经纪人的推荐,来买些股票回去。但是大型机构对市场了如指掌,根本没有经纪人什么机会。机构投资动辄就是斥巨资,根本不会在乎在这里抓一点,那里买一点。需要经纪人帮他们搜集足够多的筹码,而且要实现最赢利的模式。在散户市场,需要打无数的电话,然后拿到无数多的户头,接着再帮着挣到无数的小钱。大笔交易不是这么运作的。散户市场需要为200单买入和200种预期做准备,在机构市场,只需要做100单,考虑一种预期就好了。

在机构市场,重要的是构建联系。在贝尔斯登,重要的是用影响力说话,这在未来的几个月乃至几年中,我才渐渐领悟其中的奥妙。

在盖瑞·许曼诺给我名片不久,我去见部门经理,看是否能加薪,其实我还不了解我所在的公司。这种举动基本是不会有什么成效的。以前我不满足于小小的一点佣金,去提加薪的时候,得到的回答总是:"别担心佣金的事情,只要你开了足够多的户头,我们都会给你提成的。"

Now I go in to ask for more money because I've earned it—I'm opening new accounts and doing the Dean Witter program, meaning I'm selling what the company wants me to be selling and producing all the way, and feeling confident about it. While I'm there, I casually run the question by him because I'm planning on meeting with Gary Shemano. "Who is Bear Stearns?"

Eyes narrowing, my branch manager says, "Why are you asking me that?"

"This guy named Gary Shemano just gave me his card. Can we do some business over there?" I'm naive perhaps, thinking it's a new business contact I've scored, because I don't see this as a conflict.

The branch manager does. He also knows a lot more about Bear Stearns than I do. Apparently, he knows that Bear Stearns has no training program for brokers and because they're building up their retail operation, Bear Stearns is making a practice of scouting talent at other firms, pulling out brokers who've already been trained and licensed by other firms, and luring them to their side of the street. That's what my branch manager knows.

But I don't. All I'm doing is asking for more money.

"No," he answers, without any room for discussion. "You haven't done enough to deserve more money."

That was a shove out the door. I resented his attitude as much as I did when I was constantly being made Broker of the Day only to set up business that was promptly given to a white broker because the client wanted "someone with more experience."

But the deal was really sealed the instant I walked into the offices of Bear Stearns to have coffee with Gary Shemano. It was the same jolt of juice that hit me the first time I stepped inside a brokerage house, only harder, and my instinctual reaction, just like before, was: *Oh yeah, this is where I'm supposed to be.*

At Dean Witter, I was the only guy topping the charts with two hundred calls a day. Here everybody was on my wavelength, making those many calls in pursuit of a couple of high-echelon prospects. Major VIPs on the institutional level or individuals with significant net worth, portfolio managers, investment advisers, corporations, bankers, insurance-company executives, the chief investment officer for the State of California, the City of San Francisco, or the City of Los Angeles. They didn't have to take calls from anybody. So to get them to call you back, you had to have it going on.

我现在去提加薪，因为是我自己挣的，我不断地开新户头，而且照着添惠公司的项目做事，公司让我卖什么，我就卖什么，不断给公司赢利，我觉得信心十足。我见到经理时，顺便问了些问题，因为我准备去见这位盖瑞·许曼诺。"贝尔斯登是谁啊？"

我的经理眼睛眯了起来："你问这个干什么呢？"

"这位盖瑞·许曼诺先生给了我一张名片，我们能去那里找点生意做吗？"我可能想法太简单了，觉得这又是一次建立客户关系的时机，没觉得有什么不妥。

可经理却不这么认为。他了解更多的背景。显然，他知道贝尔斯登没有经纪人培训计划，而且现在正在开拓零售业务，所以正在广泛招兵买马，从其他公司雇佣熟练经纪人入手，诱使其改换门庭。我的经理清楚地知道这一点。

可我不知道，我只是想得到加薪。

"不行，"他断然拒绝，"你的表现不足以得到加薪。"

我用力地关上门出来了。他的态度让我怒火中烧，让我想起当初刚干上这一行，客户见了我就走，要求找个更有经验的，这也让我同样恼火。

但是当我走进贝尔斯登的大门，和盖瑞·许曼诺一起喝咖啡的时候，我知道自己已经打定了主意。刚进来时的那种感觉就像我刚走进证券公司时的那般，只是更为强烈，这里就是我该来的地方。

在添惠公司，只有我一天可以做两百张单子，而这里几乎人人都是如此，实现更高的赢利预期。机构大客户或者个人大客户掌握着大量的资产，投资组合经理、投资顾问、企业、银行、保险公司的高管、加州政府、旧金山市、洛杉矶的掌管投资的官员，不必和所有这些人打电话，他们会来找你的，只是需要让一切转起来就好。

第十二章 圈子

These Bear Stearns guys did. That first time I was stunned by the intensity of what they were doing. I thought I was the only guy who could focus like that. Once again, I felt like I was coming home to a place where I belonged, at the same time that I was moving into a whole mind-boggling new dimension. You could feel the energy, like these guys at Bear Stearns were on steroids or something. At Dean Witter, the environment seemed composed, very officious, almost formal. Guys sat at their desks, often with their coats on, especially if a client was coming in. At Bear Stearns, the guys had their sleeves rolled up, their ties loosened, some of them with a cigar in their mouth or between their fingers, everyone connected, on the phone, hammering out a deal, trying to get a better price for their client, hunting down information about a security that nobody else had. The adrenaline was flowing. You could feel it, taste it, and touch it. You couldn't miss it. Even Stevie Wonder could've seen this shit!

The timing could not have been more perfect. As it so happened, Bear Stearns wanted to build on the growth the company had already achieved in the institutional business by doing more business with high-net-worth individuals who were now starting to show up as Silicon Valley was set to explode. Even though the mega-boom of the nineties was still to come, there were some rocket-scientist types already striking oil in the high-tech world, and Bear Stearns was gunning for a big piece of the action. This was the start of the halcyon days of restricted stock sales, promising IPOs, and new clients who yesterday were engineers making fifty grand a year but today had a couple million all of a sudden.

Bear Stearns wanted to be out in front to ask these new millionaires relevant questions: "Do you want to put your money in one thing or spread it out? Do you want to think about putting some away for your kid's college? Do you want to buy some tax-free bonds?"

Gary Shemano, not a shy, easygoing type of dude by any stretch, invites me for coffee and tells me that he thinks I'm the perfect guy to help Bear Stearns get a foothold in this end of the business—based on observing me at Dean Witter.

A descendant of many generations of San Francisco Shemanos, Gary is hooked up every which way all over town, besides being a scratch golfer. Passionate and excitable, he's a table pounder too, and that's what he's doing as he tells me, "You're wasting your time over there, you know? You need to be over here. Here's where you need to be. Here!"

Pounding the table myself, I say, "Yeah! I want to be over here."

"Okay," Gary says without batting an eye, "what do you need to get going? How much draw?"

Going for the honest truth, I ask for what I need for me and Christopher to get a nice place in San Francisco: "Five thousand." That's five times the draw I've been getting at Dean Witter.

这些贝尔斯登的员工干的就是这些。我一开始就被他们工作的强度打动了。本以为只有自己才能一心不二地完成这种工作，却发现这里个个都如此。我又一次感到一种归属感，一种找到家的感觉，我即将进入的是一个全新的领域。这里的人们身上仿佛有使不完的劲，就像是注射了兴奋剂。但在惠添公司则是另外一番景象，一切都是规规矩矩的，有板有眼的。人人都做在办公桌的后面，西装革履，接待客户。在这里，大家干得热火朝天，袖子都卷起来，领带松了也顾不及，有些人手里夹着雪茄，但每个人都不闲着，永远都在电话上，下单子，尽量为客户拿到好价格，搞定绝密的信息。这里人人都热血沸腾，这完全可以感觉得到、看得到甚至摸得着。这一切太明显了，就是盲人都能感觉出来。

现在的机会绝佳。贝尔斯登准备在蒸蒸日上的机构业务基础上，继续发展高资产的个人业务，这些个人在硅谷颇有作为，而且前途不可估量。20世纪90年代的大发展即将到来，但已经有一些科技人才在高科技领域有所作为，贝尔斯登就准备在这方面大有动作。股市将一反往日的平庸，即将走入全胜时期，新股纷纷上市，曾几何时，还是一名不闻的工程师，如今就可能一夜之间身价数百万。

贝尔斯登就准备针对这群新贵开展攻势，会问他们这么几个问题："你希望自己的鸡蛋放在一个篮子里，还是多个篮子里？希望给自己的孩子留些钱，支付以后的教育吗？想不想买一些免税的债券呢？"

盖瑞·许曼诺做事直截了当，他请我喝了杯咖啡，告诉我，通过在对我在添惠公司表现的观察，觉得在现在的新业务点上，我是贝尔斯登的不二之选。

许曼诺家族在旧金山已经有很多世代，盖瑞在这里的人脉盘根错节，同时还是高尔夫高手。他激情满怀，容易兴奋，喜欢支持新事物新项目。看到我在公司的所作所为，他就说："你在浪费时间，明白吗？你应该在这里工作，你就该在这里！"

我当下就拍了桌子："对，我就该在这里。"

盖瑞眼睛都没眨："那怎么过来呢，你开个价钱吧。"

我坦言自己和儿子需要在旧金山住得舒服一点，"5000美金吧。"这是添惠给我的薪水的5倍之多。

"Fine," he says, no eye batted yet again. "And I'll throw in a fifty percent payout. Be over here in two weeks, let's go to work."

Whoa! For a second I wonder if I should have asked for more. But what I am offered is the ideal structure—guaranteed six months of drawing five grand per month, with a requirement for the next six months to make twice that for the company, in order to maintain it, with a 50 percent commission on every dollar earned over and above that. It's security, pressure, and incentive. Oh baby.

Leaving Dean Witter wasn't hard on either side. If I felt like I owed them anything for giving me my shot, my debt was repaid when I was informed that they were taking over all my accounts. All my detailed notes about what stocks my clients owned, where they worked, what their family histories were, names of pets and secretaries. All those accounts and the priceless information that I'd cultivated for months and months, handed out willy-nilly to the yokels who'd never called anybody.

My first day on the job at Bear, I have to work up the guts to admit that I've arrived without any of my former accounts. When I do, Gary sneers, "Don't worry about that. We don't want any of those people anyway."

The Bear philosophy is, "No trade is too big. No trade is too small. We want a shot at all of them." But I come to find out that they really want the former rather than the latter. This is good news to me. I'm in.

The first day I also get a chance to meet some of the guys who'll be working with me in the new retail room that Bear is starting up. One's a fellow named Jerry Donnelly who has his own cold-call specialist named John Asher, affectionately known as "Asher the Basher." Then there's Bob Edgar, a poker player who's not calling anybody, but his phone is ringing all the time. In a group of eight guys to spearhead this new business, I'm coming in at a top tier. Again, I'm the only black broker at the firm, which is no big deal for me or my new colleagues, from what I can tell.

With a combination of nerves and excitement, I'm arranging my new desk, trying to put away my pencils, when I hear a receptionist calling from the next room, "Chris, you've got a phone call, pick up."

Clueless as to who it is, since nobody knows I'm here, I pick up and ask, "Who is it?"

The receptionist tells me, "It's Ace Greenberg."

To myself I say, *Ace Greenberg?* Out loud to her, I say, "Ace Greenberg?" I don't know any Ace Greenberg, but in unison everybody in the room with me says, "Take the call, take the call!"

"没问题，"他一口答应，"我先付你50%，两周后来上班，一起干吧。"

天啊，我有点后悔自己怎么没有多要一点。但我的薪酬组合非常理想，头6个月保底5000块，但后6个月，需要至少给公司挣回两倍的效益，才能保证5000块，超过部分可以提成50%。这是将稳健、压力和动力集于一身，让人兴奋。

离开添惠公司对双方而言都没有什么，即便我有一点愧疚，但当我被告知自己的所有账目全部由公司收走之后，我也就不觉得有什么了。对于客户所持有的每只股票我都有详细的记录，甚至包括客户的工作信息、家族史、所养的宠物、秘书的信息都包括在内。所有这些都是我多年的心血，都是无价之宝，结果就被那群傻瓜拿走了。

我在贝尔斯登工作的第一天确实难熬，因为我是两手空空而来。不过盖瑞却无所谓，他说："没关系，我们不用你和那些人再打交道的。"

贝尔斯登的宗旨是："大单小单，照单全收。"但我来了之后发现它们其实更喜欢大单，不过，好消息是我来了。

第一天，我就有机会见了同在贝尔斯登新建的零售部工作的几个人，一个叫杰瑞·唐纳利，还有一个冷面专家约翰·阿什尔，还有鲍勃·埃德加，他从不主动给别人打电话，可是他的电话总是响个不停。一共有8名才俊在这新部门挑大梁，我直接步入了塔顶。而且，我还是这里唯一的黑人经纪人，不过这对我对别人都无所谓，这可以看得出来。

有几分紧张，也有几分兴奋，我有了自己的新办公桌，刚想把铅笔收起来，前台就在隔壁喊我："克里斯，有电话，接听一下。"

我一头雾水，因为没人知道我在这，我接起电话，问道："是哪位啊？"

前台告诉我："是埃斯·格林伯格。"

我不认识叫这么个名字的人啊，但屋里的人都冲我喊："快接电话，接电话。"

第十二章 圈子

The **PURSUIT** of **HAPP**y**NESS**

The call is put through. "Hello?" I say, oblivious to the fact that Ace Greenberg is the senior partner and CEO of Bear Stearns, responsible for building the firm up to where it is at this point in time.

His call is to welcome me to Bear Stearns, to which he adds, "We want you to know something, Chris Gardner. Bear Stearns was not built by people who have MBAs. Bear Stearns was built by people with PSDs!"

PSDs? I'm stumped.

But before I can ask, Ace Greenberg explains, "PSDs are people who are Poor, Smart, with a deep Desire to become wealthy. We call them PSDs. Welcome to the firm, Chris."

Then the phone goes click. I have died and gone to heaven! Poor, Smart, with a deep Desire to become wealthy.

That's me, to a tee, a PSD.

That phone call kicked it all off. It was *on*.

* * *

Over the next year, as my star rose at Bear Stearns, I found myself making another full circle when I moved myself and Christopher back into the city, to a beautiful second-floor apartment in a large corner Victorian building on Mason and Hays in Hays Valley. We were back in the 'hood, within walking distance of our regular day care center, living the San Francisco life, not lavishly, but with security and stability.

Filled with rented furniture, the apartment had hard-wood floors, two bedrooms, a big living room, and a fireplace. One of its most quirky assets was the bus stop right outside the front door: if our windows or blinds were open, whenever the bus stopped and people stepped off, it was as though they were going to walk into our living room for a visit.

This was the American dream, 1980s San Francisco style. We could make choices. If we needed something, we could buy it. We could stay home and I'd cook, make a sandwich or warm up some soup, or we'd go out to eat. The difference in not having that commute anymore was staggering. My biggest indulgence was taking a cab to work every day. Now, that was a luxury. It was six dollars, plus a buck and a half for tip, and I'd sit in the back and appreciate every second, like sitting in the back of a limousine in a slightly later era.

Having noticed that every time he saw me I was wearing the same suits—either the blue one or the gray one, with my white shirt and one of two ties—Gary Shemano had even given me an advance so I could get a new suit.

电话转接过来了。"您好",显然,这位埃斯·格林伯格是贝尔斯登的高级合伙人、CEO,负责公司的全部业务。

他来电是为了对我表示欢迎,他又加了一句:"我们希望告诉你的是,克里斯·加德纳,贝尔斯登不是靠MBA发展起来的,它的发展依靠的是PSD。"

"PSD?"我一时没有反应过来。

没等我发问,埃斯·格林伯格就进一步解释道:"PSD就是出身贫寒(poor)、天资聪颖(smart)、愿意用勤奋改变自己的命运(desire),我们需要具备这些特点的人,欢迎你。"

电话挂断了。我几乎直上九霄!出身贫寒、天资聪颖、愿意用勤奋改变自己的命运的人。

这就是我啊。我就是PSD。

这个电话就为我的新生活拉开了序幕。一切从此开始了。

* * *

第二年,我在贝尔斯登的业绩蒸蒸日上,我和儿子在城里的生活也发生了新的变化。在海兹谷的维多利亚建筑群中,我们有一栋二层公寓。住的地方离托儿所只有步行距离,过着旧金山式的生活,不奢华,但是稳定安宁。

屋里的家具都是租来的,有硬木地板、两间卧室、一个大起居室、一个壁炉。有点诡异的是门口就有个公交站,若前门的窗户或百叶打开的话,车一停,人们下车,就像是直接要来家里做客一样。

这就是20世纪80年代旧金山版的美国梦。我们可以选择自己想要的生活。需要什么,就去买什么,应有尽有。我们可以呆在家里,我来下厨,可以做个三明治,或是煲一点汤,或是出去吃饭。不用再每天去赶班车,日子和从前简直天壤之别。我最大的幸福莫过于每天打车去上班。这种幸福太过于奢侈,只需要6块钱,再加1块5的小费就足矣。我做在后座上,享受着每一分每一秒。那种感觉和后来我做在豪华轿车上不相上下。

注意到我每次不是穿着蓝西装就是灰西装,总是配着那件白衬衫,永远都是那两条领带,盖瑞还给我加了点薪,让我能买套新西装。

Gary was always sharp. He was partial to Brioni suits, alligator shoes, loafers, cuff links, beautiful ties, and an ever-present pocket square. Money didn't change me on the inside, but it definitely allowed me to give in to my clothes habit. As the months went on and my buying power rose, I had the resources not only to wear the kind of sharp suits I'd always loved but to add subtle touches of color and style that other guys might not be able to pull off. One of the senior guys at Bear Stearns, Dave "Socks" Cranston, with his distinctive accessorizing, was extremely impressed later on when I took to wearing fire red socks with whatever I was wearing. A sharp blue suit with a crisp white shirt and fire red socks. Subtle but strong. My first real splurge was one I could barely believe I'd gone and done: buying my first anaconda belt at Neiman Marcus. Four hundred bucks for a belt? It took me many months to feel okay about indulging like that.

But there was no splurge big enough for Little Chris as far as I was concerned. At two and a half, three, three and a half, even he understood what it meant to have new things. A new bed, new clothes, new toys. He was excited. What was more, he and I were so connected emotionally, he could feel my peace of mind. We could go do fun things in San Francisco, not because we had nowhere to live, but because we wanted to go to Golden Gate Park and fly a kite or try to ride a skateboard together that I'd made instead of buying—because I could. Now, unlike the days when he and I had to find shelter where we could sleep or escape from the rain, we spent rainy weekends going to the movies, sometimes seeing as many as three or four in a day, sometimes the same movie.

We went to see *Ghostbusters,* during which Christopher freaked out at the sight of the monster Pillsbury Doughboy thundering down the street. "Poppa," he whispered to me, "I want my seat belt on."

During one of our many trips to see Prince's *Purple Rain,* Christopher had an accident and peed himself, probably because we had stayed inside the movie house too long, but I snapped and said, "All you have to do is say, 'I gotta pee'!"

We marched up to the bathroom so I could wash him off, and he saw that I was still annoyed, just wanting things to always be easier, and he said very seriously, "Poppa, I don't want to make you mad. I want to make you happy."

There weren't enough times that I could tell him after that, "You make me happy, Little Chris, you make me the happiest!"

If I had learned anything about being a parent, that right there was the most important lesson, just as my son said it—kids don't want to make us mad, they want to make us happy.

It was unbelievable how many times we went to see *Purple Rain*—not just because it was entertaining but because it kept us out of the damn rain. We saw it so often that it was inevitable that we'd run into someone we knew, and indeed, not long after I'd started at Bear Stearns, I found myself sitting next to another new guy at one of the showings.

盖瑞则每天一尘不染。意大利布莱奥尼的西装、鳄鱼皮鞋，或是乐福便鞋，袖扣、领带都非常讲究，甚至衣服口袋都是平平整整，一丝不苟。金钱不会对我的内在产生任何影响，但是它却让我着实改变了着装习惯。几个月后，我的腰包逐渐鼓了起来，终于可以去购买那些中意的西装，但是款式和颜色的搭配，我总是搞糟。公司的一个高管，戴维·克兰斯顿一次就分外诧异，他看到我喜欢穿一双火红色的袜子，而且无论配什么衣服，都用这双袜子。深蓝色的西服、笔挺的白衬衫、配火红的袜子。怎么看，怎么别扭。我第一次大手大脚，想起来连自己都不敢相信。我在内曼·马库斯奢侈品店买了有生以来第一条蟒皮腰带。花了整整 400 块。我一连过了好几个月才想明白这事。

但这些都不及儿子所经历的变化之大。从他两岁半、三岁到三岁半，连他自己都明白了新东西的含义。新床、新衣服、新玩具，一切都是新的，他兴奋异常。而且我们都是那么心心相惜。我们可以在旧金山尽情享受快乐，不是因为我们没地方可去，而是因为我们就想去金门桥公园放放风筝，去试一试我亲手做的滑板，因为我有这本事。当年我们为了躲雨，无处藏身，而现在在雨季的时候，我们就喜欢在电影院泡着。有的时候，一天要看三四部片子，有的时候，就是重复看一部片子。

我们一起去看《捉鬼特工队》，看到怪物满街跑，儿子吓得偷偷和我讲："爸爸，我想把安全带系上。"

我们一起看音乐鬼才王子自传片《紫雨》的时候，小克里斯多夫不小心尿了裤子，可能是我们在电影院坐得太久的缘故，我厉声说："你想撒尿就说一声不行吗？"

我们一起去了洗手间，我把他洗干净，儿子看我余怒未消，就想缓和一下，但是他的语气非常严肃："爸爸，我不想让你生气，我就想让你快乐。"

我后来一直没有机会告诉他："儿子，你让我非常快乐，因为你，我是世界上最快乐的老爸。"

关于为人父母，其实这才是我上的最重要的一课。因为儿子告诉我，孩子不想让我们生气，就想让我们快乐。

我们记不清已经看了多少次《紫雨》了，不只是因为这片子好看，还因为我们可以不必在外面淋雨。因为我们常去，所以难免会碰上一些熟人。一次，也是我刚去贝尔斯登不久，我旁边刚巧坐了一个也是刚来公司的同事。

His name was Mike Connors, one of the smartest guys at the firm, and he was destined to be one of my best friends, and someone with whom I could launch a business one day. In Wall Street terms, even though he was white and I was black and we came from very different backgrounds, we were homies.

The atmosphere at Bear Stearns, leading up to the era of the avalanche of the eighties' mega-mergers, was conducive to everyone finding their own niche—that product or segment of the market you really know inside and out, your own little special group of institutions to pursue. One guy covered nothing but thrifts. Someone else handled bank trust departments. Another guy only talked to insurance companies. As I searched for what my specialty might be, just as I had been a complete sponge in the medical field, learning from Rip Jackson and Gary Campagna, I wanted to learn everything I could from the very best and master it, but right away.

Pretty soon that's what I was doing, learning not just how to get my calls returned but how to cultivate those relationships based on my command of information that my competitors might not have. So if Bill Anderson called, I could easily say, "I understand you've got a broker. Now, we're not interested in interfering with that relationship. However, we would like to be able to complement that relationship by showing you one or two special situations here."

A smart investor was almost always open to that.

"Great. The next time the partners at Bear Stearns are doing something, we'd like to just give you a call. Is that fair enough?"

The answer was almost always yes, because who would want to miss out on the chance at least to hear what the special offering might be? Another yes almost always followed that one in response to the question of whether I could send some materials out, along with my card. Thus, a relationship was established, so that when I followed up, it was not to waste his time but to build a rapport and a dialogue, to find out what Bill Anderson wanted to buy, what he had been buying, whether he liked or understood technology stock. Was he looking for some opportunities for capital appreciation? If he was older, was he looking for ways to supplement his income when he retired? What about his pension-fund assets if he was close to retirement?

Borrowing perhaps from my background in medicine and health care, I approached these conversations exactly in the same way we might have discussed something as vital and personal as his personal health—his personal financial health. In my own way, I was becoming Dr. Chris Gardner after all.

他叫迈克·康纳斯，注定要成为我最好的朋友，他也是公司最聪明的员工。直到后来，我们合伙做了一家公司。在华尔街，即便我们俩肤色不同，来自不同的背景，但是我们相濡以沫。

正是受到贝尔斯登的这种氛围的影响，20 世纪 80 年代的大并购狂潮时代终于到来了，这其实对每个人找到自己的利基都不无益处，是你所了解的企业细分出的产品市场，市场不大，但是值得特定的群体去寻求发展。有人专做节约成本和开支，有人专做银行信托，还有人专攻保险公司，我考虑自己的优势只能是在医药领域。利普·杰克逊和盖里·坎帕尼亚医生都让我收获颇丰，我希望自己即刻就能把所有最好的东西全部掌握，而且就是现在。

很快，我就开始不仅要让人给我回电话，而且还要基于自己对信息和知识的掌握来培育人脉，这些都是我的竞争对手所或缺的。比如比尔·安德森来电，我就会说："我知道你有经纪人，我们不希望影响这种关系，但是我们可以在某些情况下，与您的经纪人互为补充。"

聪明的投资人大多会愿意听我们讲下去。

"很好，下次贝尔斯登的合伙人若再有什么动作，我们一定告诉您，您觉得怎么样呢？"

对方的答复多数是肯定的，因为谁都不想错过了解特殊优惠的机会。接下来，对方就会顺理成章的接受我送去的资料，我还会一同附上我的名片。这样，就可以和客户建立联系，在我们后来的交往中，就会顺畅很多，不必再花时间寒暄或找话题，我可以了解这位比尔究竟想买什么，买过什么证券产品，他是否了解科技股，对资本增值基金是否感兴趣？若对方年纪较大，他是否考虑退休后能增加收益？若他马上到了退休的年龄，那么他的退休基金资产的状况如何？

从我以往的医药行业和健康护理方面的经验，我可以和他们从个人健康角度引出个人财务健康的话题，我又成了那个克里斯·加德纳医生，这次是财务医生。

Thankfully, from the start the Bear Stearns brass liked what they were seeing me accomplish. Gary was a fan right out of the gate, but Marshall Geller was *the* guy, and the jury stayed out for a while with him. Gary ran the office, Marshall ran Gary. In fact, Marshall simultaneously ran offices for Bear Stearns in San Francisco, Los Angeles, and Hong Kong. Marshall—or "the Screaming Skull," as he was popularly known behind his back—was six feet tall, wore glasses, had thinning white hair that he managed to maintain in what I called the Jewish Afro style, and had a small overbite on his front two teeth that made him look almost cute. Indeed, much of the time he was the most charming, nicest, sweetest guy. But just like that, in a blink of an eye, he would lash out, "Do you ever fucking think? Do you people ever fucking think?!"

If Marshall was on your case, you could be in his office with the door closed and everybody on the floor knew he was chewing your ass out. I definitely tried to stay on his best side or avoid him altogether.

Eventually, however, when he saw me going over my call list one day and arranging the contact cards for the two hundred calls I had to make, Marshall decided it was time for a lecture.

"Hey, Gardnerberg," he said, using the nickname that made me part of the almost-all-Jewish club at the firm, "come here." I followed him into the conference room, where he pointed at the stack of contact cards still in my hand. "That's not how the big guys do it," he said, letting me know that the numbers volume game that I'd been trained to work didn't impress him.

I thought—*Well what do the big guys do?* But I said nothing.

"Let me show you how we do it here at Bear Stearns. Big guys do it through a sphere of influence." Seeing that I had no idea what he meant, he beckoned to me once more. "Come with me."

Down the hall we stopped in to observe Phil Schaeffer, a guy who supposedly could not tie his shoes, so he wore loafers. His sphere of influence included Walter Mondale, the soon-to-be Democratic presidential candidate. Phil's top client was the State of Minnesota's pension fund. Oh, simple, right? Great, but how could I get there?

"Sphere of influence," Marshall repeated, pointing me back to my desk, without one practical suggestion as to how I could develop that. The implication was that I would know it when I found it.

谢天谢地，公司对我的所作所为表示认可。盖瑞为公司的事情经常抛头露面，但马歇尔·盖勒在幕后操控着一切。盖瑞掌管公司，马歇尔管着盖瑞。实际上，马歇尔同时要负责旧金山、洛杉矶、中国香港等地的公司业务。马歇尔早已谢顶，我们背后都叫他"亮脑壳"，他身高有1米80以上，带着眼镜，头发花白，且十分稀疏，发型有点像犹太和非洲式的结合，两颗门牙有点重叠，让人觉得他有些可爱。的确，这人大多时候都极富个人魅力，人也不错，待人接物非常和善。可当他眼睛一眯，就会厉声断喝："你就不能动动脑子吗？你们这些人的脑子是干什么用的？"

若马歇尔找到谁头上，那么就要在他办公室，把门紧闭，那整层楼的人都知道马歇尔是在训斥手下，我和他相处一直都小心谨慎，或者避免和他正面接触。

可最后，当他看到我把所有的电话单都过了一遍，又在准备另外两百份联系卡片，马歇尔决定该是时候给我上一课了。

"你好啊，大块头，你过来一下，"他叫着我的绰号，让我觉得和办公室的犹太人都没有距离。我跟着他进了会议室，他指着我手里的联络卡，说道："高手都不用这些的。"让我觉得自己受过的那么多数字训练都让他无动于衷。

我心想，那高手都是怎么做的呢？但我嘴上什么都没说。

"我来告诉你贝尔斯登的人是怎么做事的，高手是通过圈子来做事的。"

来到大厅，我们在菲尔·薛华的身边停下来，看他怎么工作，他不喜欢系鞋带，所以穿乐福便鞋，他的圈子包括即将成为民主党总统候选人的沃特·蒙代尔，菲尔最大的客户是明尼苏达州退休基金，就这么简单，可我怎么能做到呢？

"圈子，"马歇尔又重复了一遍，带我回到座位上，但没有给我任何的建议来实现这个目标。这就是说，我需要自己去领悟。

第十二章　圈子

The PURSUIT of HAPPYNESS

That would take me another twenty years, but in the interim, in order to build relationships, I still had to hit the numbers. I still had to work my magic to get past the gatekeepers, the secretaries who liked my Barry White crooning voice, and the proverbial alligators who would bite my head off if they even suspected I was calling their boss about an investment opportunity. Every now and then, I struck gold and the prospect actually picked up the phone. That was exactly what happened one day after I decided to pursue some Texas oil millionaires by cold-calling.

"J.R.," I begin, "this is Chris Gardner out at Bear Stearns, San Francisco."

"Yeah, I know y'all, what you want?"

"Well, I just wanted to tell you about . . ."

"Well, look here, before you tell me anything, let me tell you something." Then he proceeds to tell me every nigger joke, every Jew joke, every spic joke in the world. Not knowing whether I should hang up or get on a plane to kick his racist ass, I get real still and just listen. Then, taking a breath, I return to right where I was before, pitching him on me and the firm.

That's all he needs to hear. "Okay, now," he says, "buy me fifty thousand shares of whatever you called me about and let's see how that works."

Fifty thousand shares at 50¢ a share was a commission of $25,000! For that much money, hell, yeah, I can put up with a nigger joke. And I do. I start calling him, and he throws me bigger business every time, always telling me all the most racist, demeaning jokes he's accumulated since the last time we talked, without repeating himself. To further my sphere of influence, I go on, laughing myself silly—"Hilarious!"—sometimes even finding a joke or two funny. Every now and then I do stop to think, *If only he knew that I was black.* Obviously, he has no clue.

Much to my chagrin, he calls me to say, "Hey, this is J.R. My wife is going to China. I'm going to bring my girlfriend up to Lake Tahoe, and we're going to stop in San Francisco so I can see this broker named Chris Gardner who has been making me all this money."

Oh boy, here we go. In a panic, flashbacking to the Broker of the Day era when all the clients had an issue with the "more experienced" thing, I'm seeing all his business go away when he realizes he's been telling all those nigger jokes to a "nigger." Trying to stay calm, I remind myself that only one of two things is going to happen. In scenario A, he'll close his account with me, and that'll be the end of our relationship. In scenario B, if I play it right, he'll close the accounts he has at all those other places and let me handle all of his business. What can I do to play it right?

我还得修炼20年才能达到这种境界，但是这期间，我为了建立关系，还是需要数量的积累。我还得一点一点来，通过看门人还有秘书的层层关卡，用自己甜美的嗓音打动他们，因为他们若知道我是找他们的老板谈投资机会的，一定会把我的脑袋咬下来。但时不时，我也会交上好运，拿起电话就碰巧能找对人。一天，我正准备联系一位得州的石油大亨，干脆就给他直接去电话。

"J.R.，"我开门见山，直入正题，"我是旧金山贝尔斯登的克里斯·加德纳。"

"嗯，知道，有什么事情？"

"我想告诉您的是……"

"你先别说，还是先来听我说吧。"然后他就开始给我讲黑人的段子、犹太段子、西班牙段子，等等，我一时不知所措，不知道该把电话挂了，还是直接坐飞机过去，为他的种族主义踢他的屁股，但我一声不吭，静静地听着。最后，我深呼一口气，把话题引回到公司上来。

最后，他说："好吧，给我买5万股你说的那东西，我们看看效果怎样。"

5万股，每股50美分，那就相当于25000美金的佣金。看在这么一大笔钱的份儿上，给我说点黑人的段子，我可以忍了。我后来再找他，他每次都会给我一些大单子，但也要给我讲上一通种族歧视的各色段子，而且每次都不会重样，为了巩固这个圈子，我会应声附和，还会哈哈大笑，有时自己也会回敬一两个段子。有几次，我自己还琢磨，他要是知道我是黑人会怎样呢？显然，他并不知道这一点。

不过，有一次，他的电话让我异常恐惧："你好，我是J.R，我老婆去中国了，我要带女朋友去太浩湖，准备在旧金山停一下，想见见这位克里斯·加德纳，你可让我赚了不少钱啊。"

天哪，这可如何是好。我回想起当年的"当日经纪人"活动，当时就谈到有关经验的问题。我仿佛看到他发现自己一直和黑人在聊有关黑人的段子，一怒之下把所有的单子都撤走。我努力让自己平静下来，无外乎会有两种情况，一种就是他愤然撤单，我们两个就此完蛋。另一种就是，若我处理得当，他会把委托别人做的单子全部撤回，全部交给我来做。我怎么做才能处理得当呢？

As it so happens, Marshall "the Screaming Skull" Geller is out of the office on the day J.R. and his girlfriend are coming. There's no one to say that I can't temporarily move into Marshall's huge executive office. Nor is there any harm in replacing his name with mine on the door. Thinking fast, I also take all those pictures of his cute white family off his desk and put them in his drawer.

My secretary and colleagues agree to go along with this temporary setup, saying nothing. When J.R. and his woman companion arrive, they are welcomed by my secretary, and she leads them back to come see me. When J.R. walks in, I'm sitting in Marshall's big chair, looking out his window at the spectacular view of San Francisco, and pretending like I'm talking on the telephone, just reaming somebody's ass out in unedited, colorful vernacular. As if just noticing my Texas visitors, I hang up, whip around in my chair, and say, "Hey, J.R., how you doing? Have a seat. How about a cup of coffee?"

Literally, I can see blood draining away from J.R.'s face. He is in fucking shock. It's not just the nigger jokes and the color of my skin, although that's enough to give him a coronary. It's also that he's a short, little, wide cowboy— clean-shaven, in his midsixties, with a crew cut, gleaming aviator glasses, jeans, some kind of boots made out of the hide of an endangered species, and a big-ass buckle, like he's just won some rodeo—who has to look up to me to shake my hand. His girlfriend—not a spring chicken, though younger than J.R., also taller than him, with the big blond hair and the big chest—just looks on, not sure what's happening but apparently happy to be anywhere other than where she's usually tucked away.

So here I go, spreading out paperwork on the close to half a million he has invested with Bear Stearns, in a full report: every position, every recommendation, every stock we ever put in his portfolio, where we bought it, where we sold it, and the percentage gained. Showing him how much money I've made him so far, the numbers look good: between a 34 and 35 percent return. This is my shot to go for double or nothing. Straight out I say, "Based on these numbers and what you've let me know about the other accounts you've got, we need to be doing more of your business here, J.R. What do you think?"

What he thought, it turned out, was that I was right. It seemed that he had undergone an epiphany and seen the light: it wasn't a white thing or a black thing, it was a green thing. He closed his accounts at Goldman, Lehman and Morgan and at wherever else he had his money invested so that I and Bear Stearns could oversee all his business. From then on, with his account alone, I probably made $200,000 a year. Interestingly enough, after that visit he stopped the nigger jokes. In all our contact that followed, he never uttered the "n" word again. He still told me a couple Jewish jokes and a couple spic jokes, but by all indications he was henceforth down with his black brethren.

当 J.R 和他的女友来找我的时候："亮脑壳"马歇尔碰巧不在办公室，没人说过，我不能临时用用马歇尔的大办公室，我临时把他的名字换成了我的，也无伤大雅。我顺便把他所有家人的照片从桌上撤下来，全都收进了抽屉。

我的秘书和同事都非常配合，没有提出异议。当 J.R 和他的女友到了的时候，秘书领着他们来到了这间办公室，我端坐在马歇尔的大椅子上，正眺望旧金山的街景，做出一副打电话的样子，瞟见他从外面进来。装作刚刚注意到我这位得州客户的样子，我挂起电话，从椅子上站起来："你好啊，J.R，最近怎么样啊？坐吧，来点咖啡吗？"

我眼睁睁地看着他变得面无血色，他确实吃惊不小。不仅是我的肤色和他的黑人段子让他几乎心脏病发作，再有就是他短小身材，五大三粗，胡子刮得干干净净，年近六旬，带着一副亮闪闪的眼镜，靴子的质地一看就是珍稀的兽皮制成，腰上系着宽宽的腰带，仿佛刚参加了斗牛比赛的样子，他抬头望着我，上前来和我握手。他的女友年纪也不轻，不过比 J.R 还是年轻很多，但是个头也比他高不少。这女子金色长发，身材也不错，傻傻地看着，不知是出了什么事情，但看来去哪里她都觉得比呆在家里强。

接下来就看我的了。我把一叠文件铺开，上面有他在贝尔斯登投的 50 万美金的详细情况，每只推荐的股票，在他投资组合里的每一只股票，在什么点位买进的，什么价位抛出的，收益情况，还给他看了我们迄今为止一共帮他赚了多少钱，还不错，都是 34%～35%的收益率。我知道自己这是最后一搏，或者赚个盆满钵满，要么就干脆颗粒无收："看看这些数据，再有就是根据您说过您在其他地方投资的情况，我们觉得您该考虑把投资更多向这边倾斜了，您觉得呢。"

他知道我说得是正确的，仿佛他终于找到了方向，这不是和肤色有关的问题，这是对大家都有益的问题。他把在高盛、雷曼、摩根的账户都统统停掉，把所有的钱都转到贝尔斯登。从此，就从他一个人身上，我每年就可以拿到 20 万美金，有趣的是，那次见面后，他就闭口不谈黑人的段子，我们交往的时候，他也不拿黑人开玩笑了，但还是会讲一些犹太或西班牙的段子，但所有迹象表明，他不敢再把黑人兄弟不当回事了。

第十二章 圈子

Because I did *all* his business and he was my biggest account, he was the first phone call I made every day, financially more than compensating for all those nigger jokes I had endured at the start.

Every day our morning pow-wow began with my report on what the market looked like for that day and my recommendations on whether we should sit tight or trade. Because of the vast amounts of money I was making for him, his answer was always, "Whatever you think, Chris."

This went on for over two years, starting there in San Francisco and continuing after I made the inevitable move to New York City—to work at the Bear Stearns office there on the real Wall Street, the mother ship.

While not all brokers have to go to New York to hit the big time, from the moment I had fantasized about being in this business, that was always part of the dream. It was embedded in my DNA, part of being a PSD, just as it was inevitable that I had to buy that Ferrari one day—which I did, by the way, after I moved to Chicago in the late 1980s to establish my own company. Then again, dreams do change. While my first Ferrari was red, the second one I bought was black. In fact, I bought Michael Jordan's black Ferrari, and as a symbolic gesture that only Moms and I could truly appreciate, my personalized license plate read not mj.

When I was seventeen, my mother had set me on the path, letting me know, in effect, that I didn't have to be a basketball player to make a million dollars. Seventeen years later, I proved her right when I made my first million for that year alone. To get to that point, once I started to make a living as a stockbroker in San Francisco, it was always in my mind that I had to go live in New York. That was to be the ultimate proving ground: like the song said, if you could make it there, you could make it anywhere.

Lots of folks in the San Francisco office weren't happy with my decision. My buddy Dave "Socks" Cranston warned me the minute he heard that I was leaving the West Coast: "Are you fucking crazy? Do you know to live like a fucking dog in New York you're going to have to make three hundred thousand fucking dollars your first year?"

"Yeah, I know," I lied.

I didn't know, and damn if he wasn't right. Plus, what he didn't know was that besides having to support myself like a dog, my income now had to cover not one but two kids.

因为我在帮他打理所有的业务，而且他也成了我最大的客户，我每天第一件事就是给他打电话，他给我带来的财务上的收益，已经远远大于当初让我忍受那些黑人段子的侮辱了。

每天早上，我都先要介绍市场情况，进而再建议他该如何操作，是按兵不动，还是出手交易。因为我已经帮他挣到了大笔的钱，他总是说："克里斯，都听你的。"

这种情况持续了两年多，从旧金山开始，到我后来调动到纽约市，这是贝尔斯登总部的所在，也是真正的华尔街的所在。

并非所有的证券经纪人必须到华尔街才能有所作为，但从我当初想干这行开始，我就一直梦想着能有朝一日来到华尔街。这些都是我的基因所决定的，也是作为一个 PSD 所决定的，就像有朝一日我必须要买一辆法拉利一样，这些都是命中注定的。20 世纪 80 年代后期，我去了芝加哥，开办了自己的公司，我真的买了一辆法拉利。我又开始希望能有所改变。我第一辆法拉利是红色的，那第二辆就是黑色的。实际上，我买的是迈克尔·乔丹的黑色法拉利，这其中的意味只有我和妈妈才能真正体会。

当我 17 岁时，妈妈帮我设定发展的道路，让我知道，不必成为篮球明星，我也能挣到 100 万。17 年后，当我挣到第一个 100 万，我证实了妈妈当年的判断。为实现这个夙愿，我成为了旧金山的证券经纪人，但我一直梦想着去纽约生活，这是成就自己的最终证明，就像歌中唱的那样，只要你能在这里成功，那么成功就不在乎是这里，还是远方。

旧金山的很多朋友对我的决定都不是很理解，我的好兄弟戴维·克兰斯顿听到我要离开西海岸，就说："你有没有搞错啊，在纽约生活得要不少银子啊，头一年你至少得挣 30 万才行啊。"

"嗯，我知道。"可其实我并不知道。

我也不知道他说得是否正确，此外，他还不知道的是我不但要养活自己，还要抚养两个孩子，而不再是一个儿子了。

Yep, surprising as that might sound, by 1985 I was the proud father of a gorgeous, brilliant, amazing baby girl named Jacintha Gardner. Her mother was Christopher's mother, Jackie, my ex. Conceived during a visit that Jackie made to see Little Chris, Jacintha, like her brother, was always going to have me in her life, and I was always going to be there for her. This was despite whatever issues I had with her mother. For twelve hours that one night when I gave in yet again to the sexual temptation that Jackie had always been for me, I actually convinced myself that we were supposed to get back together. Even with everything that had happened before, there was a part of me that thought, *Well, for Christopher's sake.* Maybe now that the money wasn't so tight and I had established myself in the business, she'd have the chance to pursue her goals. God knows what I was thinking. Sometimes, it seemed, I had to just put myself in the fire in order to find out that's how you get burned. It took me less than twenty-four hours to come to my senses.

When I decided to move to New York, Jackie, now pregnant, was busy campaigning to get back together. While I was adamant that the possibility was out of the question, I did propose that, with my financial help, she should have Christopher come live with her and our new daughter in Los Angeles. This was a practical choice, considering that I would most likely be working even longer hours and making Little Chris adjust to a whole new day care system. She eventually agreed, and ultimately getting to spend some time with his mother was the best thing for him, even though I went through horrible separation pains those first few weeks apart.

Going in, New York was as daunting as everyone had told me it would be. Fortunately, I had just scored a new account that helped set the stage for me to make a splash in the New York office. Again, just like with J.R., this was the result of a cold call.

The guy I contact while dialing numbers in Las Vegas is a fellow named Ed Doumani, who says in response to my introduction, "No, I don't buy too much stock, but I might want to sell some stock."

Not sure where this is headed, I'm polite and say, "Well, what stock is that?"

Ed casually notes, "I own a piece of a little company down here in Las Vegas, and I'm thinking about selling some shares."

"Oh, yeah? What company is that, Mr. Doumani?"

"The Golden Nugget," he says.

"Great," I say, then ask, "how much of it do you own?"

"About six million shares."

这确实令人意外，1985年，我又喜得千金杰西塔·加德纳，她非常漂亮，聪慧过人，她的母亲就是克里斯多夫的生母，我的前妻杰姬。一次，杰姬来看儿子，杰西塔喜欢和哥哥在一起，也一直希望我能不离她左右，而我也何尝不是如此。不管我和他们的母亲之间有怎样的纠结，亲情是无法隔断的。那一夜，我没有抵挡住杰姬对我的诱惑，终于决定我们应该重新生活在一起。无论曾经发生过什么，至少我觉得为了儿子，我们也应该重修旧好。也许是因为经济比较宽裕，我在工作上也开始有了起色，她也有机会去追求她的目标，天知道，我当时是怎么想的。有时候，我似乎就是愿意把自己放到烈焰之上，来看自己烤熟后，是什么样子。我花了不到一天的时间，来恢复自己的理智。

当我决定去纽约的时候，杰姬已经身怀六甲，希望能跟着我一起走。但我非常坚定，这绝对不可行，我觉得应该由她来带儿子和即将诞生的女儿生活在洛杉矶，钱由我来出。这是更切实际的选择，因为我需要工作更长的时间，而儿子也要适应新的日托环境。杰姬终于同意了，儿子能和母亲待在一起最为理想，但我前几周也饱受了分离之苦。

我终于来到纽约，这里确实和我听到的一样繁华。幸运的是，我搞定了一个新客户，让我在纽约办公室也能崭露头角，这次和J.R那次类似，也是我未经预约，直接打电话过去拿下的。

这次这位是拉斯维加斯的艾德·杜曼尼，我电话里一番介绍后，他说："我不想买股票，倒是想卖些股票。"

不知道他葫芦里是什么药，我只有礼貌性地问道："那您准备卖什么股票？"

艾德随意地说："我手上有拉斯维加斯一家小公司的股票，准备出手一部分。"

"那这家公司的名称是什么呢？"

"是金箔公司。"

"太好了，那您手上有多少股份呢？"

"大概有600万股吧。"

Not skipping a beat, I let Ed know that Bear Stearns specializes in restricted stock sales. "So let us know if there's a way we can help, and if there's a way we can help you to minimize the tax bite."

"Yeah, I'd be interested in that."

After I hang up the phone, somewhat in a daze, I have to figure out how I'm going to play this out. It takes me a while to put the pieces together that Ed and his brother Fred are the producers of the scandal-ridden movie *The Cotton Club*, along with Bob Evans and some other cats, not to mention that the Doumani brothers are having some issues with the New Jersey gaming commission.

Rather than trying to pull off the trade for six million shares of stock myself, I put Ed and Fred together with the right people at Bear Stearns—which turned me into an overnight star by the time I arrived in New York. Bringing in six million shares, or about 6 percent of the ownership of the Golden Nugget, gave me instantaneous credibility with the heavyweights at the New York Bear Stearns office. The buzz was: "Who is this fucking guy in San Francisco? How did he get this? Who does he know?"

It wasn't only that I was handing their office what was potentially a ten-million-share trade, it was also that Ed Doumani would only talk to me and he wouldn't talk to nobody out of New York without me on the telephone with him.

So even though I had a lot to learn to hold my own with these guys, I came in with a few arrows in my quiver. What I came to see right away was that Bear Stearns, east or west, was kind of like the Oakland Raiders of Wall Street. Everybody there on both coasts was tough and talented, many were PSDs, and many didn't necessarily go to Harvard. There were plenty of colorful characters, but the bottom line was that in spite of the competition, everybody cared about each other, and everybody at some point and time was there for the other. The difference between the Bear offices in San Francisco and New York was a lot like the difference between those two cities. Bear Stearns in San Francisco had energy, drive, creativity, opportunity, and super-bright people. The New York office of Bear Stearns was all that, but on steroids! Everything was done to the nth degree. The added intensity suited me and I suited it. Plus, there was a whole new level of challenge. Where I was coming from, we were writing tickets, taking commissions on every trade we made. In New York a lot of the cats were talking about establishing a fee-based business that would eliminate the need for writing tickets—setting up a revenue stream of, say, $3 million a year.

That was the business I wanted to be in. But how? Same as I always had done, by asking questions: "How do you do that?" The answer was to get into the asset management business for clients. One of the guys broke it down for me, and I was frankly flabbergasted.

我想都没想，立刻就告知了对方贝尔斯登在限制性股票的销售方面独具特长。"那么，我们来看看怎么才能帮到您？或者怎么帮您才能让税务方面的损失最小，您觉得怎样呢？"

"嗯，我对这事感兴趣。"

我挂上电话，眼前有点眩晕，我必须找出办法来。我花了些时间才搞清楚，这位艾德和他的兄弟福来德以及鲍勃·埃文斯等是一部电影《棉花俱乐部》的制片人，这部片子丑闻缠身，而且这兄弟俩和新泽西赌博业委员会也有些问题。

我自己一个人可对付不了这600万股票的事情，我在贝尔斯登找到了专业人士，和兄弟俩一同探讨这笔大单交易，这让我来到纽约办公室后，一夜成名。拿下这600万的股份后，这相当于金箔公司6%的股权，我就此名声大振，纽约贝尔斯登的人们都在打听，那个旧金山的家伙是谁啊？他怎么搞定的？他认识些什么人啊？

这并非仅仅是因为我给公司带来了一笔上千万美元的大单，而且还因为在整个纽约城这位艾德只愿意在电话上和我一个人聊这事情。

虽然，让我和这些家伙能谈在一起，我还有很多工作要做，但我还是自己有一套的。在我看来，无论是东海岸还是西海岸，贝尔斯登多少有些美国橄榄球的克兰突袭者队的风格，两边的员工都很聪明能干，很多都是没有背景自学成才，不一定个个都是哈佛毕业，大家各有所长，但是不管怎样彼此竞争，大家还是相互关照，每个人都可以帮助别人。两地公司的区别很大程度上就像两个城市间的区别。旧金山的贝尔斯登，大家都精力充沛，创意十足，捕捉机会，精明强干。可在纽约，人们干起活来都不要命，每件事都要尽善尽美，这种风格和强度适合我的胃口。而且，挑战也上升了一个档次。在旧金山，我们要下单，每单做提成，可在这里，大家都把下单的环节省去，直接把费用做到每一单里，这一项就可以带来300万美元的收益。

我就是希望在这样的环境里和大家打拼。但是具体怎么做呢？我又是故伎重演，开始提问"你是怎么做到的呢？"有人告诉我，要接触到客户的资产管理业务中去，听得我目瞪口呆。

第十二章 圈子

The PURSUIT of HAPPYNESS

"Let me see if I got this right. So somebody gives you one hundred million dollars a year to manage. They pay you fifty basis points, so you make five million dollars a year?"

That was the sphere of influence Marshall Geller had been talking about. In the meantime, between the Doumani brothers, a couple of other meaty accounts, and J.R., I didn't start my New York Bear Stearns adventure empty-handed. But then, early in 1986, J.R.'s secretary called me to say, "Chris, I've got bad news. J.R. died in his sleep last night at home."

It was really bad news. My biggest account was gone! This wasn't going to kick in down the road, this was immediate pain. That was because, when an account dies, trading is halted by the estate, which then comes in and divvies everything up between a whole host of vultures and beneficiaries. Ironically, over the last few days J.R. had been worried about the market and telling me that we should sell everything and just go to cash. So to honor his last order, I picked up the phone and sold every last share in his portfolio, taking my $60,000 commission as a repayment for all the nigger jokes. The estate had nothing to say about it, not after all the money I'd made for him and his heirs.

But with good old J.R. gone, I wasn't looking to replace him with a similar type of account. My idea was to give the fee-based asset management business a shot. On a cold call, yet again, I connected with Bob, an executive who was in charged of a fixed-income portfolio for an Ohio company called the Great American Insurance Company. We hit it off, and he was interested in working with me, but there was a problem, as it turned out, in that the company was supposed to already be covered by Bear Stearns. To be on the safe side, I called Ace Greenberg, the CEO and senior partner who had first introduced me to the meaning of PSDs. Asking for his okay on my covering Great American Insurance, I was fine when Ace checked out the situation and told me, "Here's the story, Chris. You can cover the account, but I want to hear from you once a week. I want to hear how you're doing." Click.

Two weeks go by, and I'm working with Bob, showing him ideas, bonds, all kinds of things, and he likes what he's seeing and gives me my first order for starters. And it's a $25,000 ticket. Not bad, and I'm in the institutional arena. Thrilled, I call Ace and tell him, "We just made $25,000."

Dead silence. After a pause, he says, "Gardner, you're fired." On the spot, this is it. His reasoning? "You've been talking to this guy for two weeks and all you got out of him was twenty-five grand?"

For about the second time in my life I know what it means to have a sphincter muscle engage that prevents me from shitting myself. Being fired by Ace Greenberg is the end of my career. There is no higher appeal, no higher court.

"那是不是这个意思,有人给你一年管理1个亿,支付你5个基点,每年是不是就可以挣到500万呢?"

这就是马歇尔曾经提过的圈子的概念,还有杜曼尼兄弟那笔大单,以及J.R的单子,所有这些都是如此,在纽约,我并非空手而来。可是,1986年初,J.R的秘书打来电话:"克里斯,有个坏消息告诉你,昨晚J.R在家睡着后,就没再醒来。"

这的确是个坏消息,我最大的客户就这么消失了。这种痛是立竿见影的,因为一旦客户故去,他名下的所有交易就会中止,然后诸多受益人就会瓜分他的财产。有讽刺意味的是,前几天,J.R还认为股市情况不妙,让我把股票统统抛掉变现。遵循他最后的遗愿,我卖掉他名下的所有股票,拿到6万美金佣金,作为他讲的所有那些黑人段子的补偿。负责遗产分配的人对我无可厚非,毕竟我为他和继承人赚到了大笔的金钱。

但随着J.R的离世,我却不准备继续找类似的客户作为替代,因为我看中了收费资产管理业务,又是通过电话销售,我结识了鲍勃,他负责俄亥俄大美国保险公司固定收入的资产组合,我俩一拍即合,他愿意和我共事,但是有个问题,这家公司已经是贝尔斯登的客户了。出于保险起见,我给公司CEO兼高级合伙人埃斯·格林伯格去了电话,也是他给我介绍了PSD的概念,埃斯问清了情况,告诉我:"这个事值得一做,你可以负责这个客户,但是你每周要和我汇报一次。我希望了解事情的进展。"

两周过去了,我和鲍勃一起合作,沟通各种想法、介绍债券,等等,他非常满意,给了我第一笔单子,佣金就有25000块,这在机构客户里还不错,我兴高采烈地给埃斯去了电话,告诉他:"我们挣了25000块。"

他一言不发。过了一会,他说:"克里斯,你被解雇了。"我当下愣在那里,他是认真的吗?"你和那家伙费了两周的时间,就从他那挣了25000块?"

我愣挺了两秒钟,咬牙没让自己骂出声来。被埃斯开除,就等于我的事业的终结了,欲哭无泪,欲告无门。

Before I can think of what to say, the biggest belly laugh you ever heard comes booming over the phone line. Ace says, "Nice going, Chris. Have a good day."

That was a definite rite of passage into the world of institutional investment, and an example of Ace Greenberg's perverse sense of humor. The experience also opened my eyes to the intense competition for the institutional market. To have that cutting edge, to be able to offer something unique, I developed an innovative strategy in the months that followed for going after that asset management and fee-based business the other New York guys were talking about. But my approach was strictly my own. It was a multi-step process that involved first contacting the number-two person in the management hierarchy and offering some special investment opportunities and then, when there wasn't interest right away, tracking in real dollars what they had turned down. Three months later I would place a call to the number-one person at the company and note that I had called before, saying, "I would have been calling you to send you a check for one hundred thousand dollars, but you didn't feel that it was of interest at the time. Here's what I'm calling you about now. . . ." Almost across the board immediate interest and some subsequent trading followed.

As I was mastering this strategy, it finally dawned on me what business I really wanted to be in, the market that was being grossly ignored by Wall Street, the niche that I would be allowed to develop in New York and that would soon become a key part of my own business when I opened up shop in Chicago.

My idea was to go after this untouched market and offer prospects the scope of the products and services provided by Bear Stearns—one of the most profitable firms in the history of Wall Street. What was this untouched market? Well, I wanted to start calling on African Americans. I wanted to manage money for individuals in the sphere of influence shared by Quincy Jones, Stevie Wonder, Oprah, Michael Jordan. I wanted to invest not only for famous entertainers and athletes but on behalf of black institutions, black banks, black insurance companies, black entrepreneurs and executives, black foundations. That's what I wanted to do. Besides the fact that nobody else was pursuing this market, I liked the idea of promoting minority ownership and prosperity.

With the support of Ace Greenberg and my other bosses at Bear, I went to town, sometimes hitting, sometimes missing. But at the end of the day, which took place in early 1987 when things really started to roll, I was doing so much business that no one questioned my decision to take the next leap and set up shop under my own auspices.

我还没想好该怎么答复,电话那边就传来了爽朗的笑声,埃斯对我说:"好样的,克里斯,干得不错。"

这终于标志着我走入机构投资的大门,而埃斯的冷幽默更加深了我的记忆。在机构市场的激烈竞争中,我睁大双眼,渴求着更多的知识和经验。为了扩大优势,为了使提供的服务与众不同,在接下来的几个月中,我制定了自己战略,以应对资产管理,还有人们谈及的收费资产管理。但我的方法是自己摸索出来的,具体分几步走,首先要接触管理层的二号人物,提供投资机会建议,若对方不感兴趣,我就把他因此而产生的损失记录下来。三个月后,我会再次来电,给公司的一把手,称:"我本想给你寄送一张 10 万美元的支票,但是当初你们不感兴趣,一口回绝了。这次,我来电话是想……"对方顿时就来了兴趣,接下来就可以谈成一笔笔单子。

当我对这一套驾轻就熟之际,我终于意识到自己应该在哪一行发展,应该在华尔街忽视的市场有所作为,这就是可以在纽约发展的利基市场,这也很快成为我在芝加哥自立门户后,我自己的主营业务。

我的想法就是开垦这片处女地,并且提供贝尔斯登的产品和服务,因为它是华尔街有史以来最挣钱的公司。那么这片处女地在哪里呢?我想到了非裔美国人,我希望为这个圈子的成功人士管理个人资产,他们包括美国天王音乐制作人昆西·琼斯、黑人歌手史提夫·汪达、脱口秀女王奥普拉、篮球明星迈克尔·乔丹,等等。我希望不仅投资这些王牌演艺体育明星,还希望能涉足黑人机构、黑人银行、黑人保险公司、黑人企业家、黑人高管、黑人基金会,等等。这些就是我想做的事情,而且是别人从未做过的事情,我喜欢能为少数族裔的财富而努力。

在埃斯·格林伯格以及其他贝尔斯登老板的支持下,我开始跌跌撞撞起步了,终于在 1987 年初,事情开始有了眉目,我意已决,要自立门户,这时没有人对我再产生质疑。

I was going forward. The vision kept expanding. In addition to the minority business, I wanted to honor my hardworking uncles and manage money for the labor market. I wanted to invest for educators and proponents of public education and literacy. To create the rainbow coalition of expertise that I envisioned, I wanted to hire PSDs, maybe not exactly like me, but with similar abilities to dream big; I wanted to take the same kind of chance on cultivating potential that Dean Witter and Bear Stearns had taken with me. To grow my business, I wanted to explore some ideas I had about what I eventually began to call "conscious capitalism"—both as a personal philanthropic interest in returning a percentage of my business profits back into public sectors in the areas where I made the money and as a way for investment to encourage potential and opportunity on a global level. Some of these ideas had been shaped by the Reverend Cecil Williams and Glide Memorial Church, and others had come from some reading I had been doing in advanced economics; I'd stopped by public libraries whenever I could, just to reassure Moms that I hadn't forgotten all of her advice.

By picking Chicago as the town in which to plant Gardner Rich & Company, as I dubbed my enterprise, I had once again made a round trip, returning to a spot not far from Milwaukee and Moms, as well as a town where I had plenty of relatives. This move made sense because Chicago was a city where six-year-old Christopher and two-year-old Jacintha—both of whom moved from Los Angeles to Chicago—could grow up and have a place to call home. So in a sense, I had circled back around. But I was breaking new ground as well, by raising my kids, I had broken the cycle of fatherless children that my own father had started.

As my company grew and my dreams materialized, giving me the opportunity to work for institutional pension funds and assets to the tune of several billion dollars and to nurture the growth and financial health of organizations like my top client, the National Education Association, with its millions of members, I lived out that other dream of getting to travel and see the world. The women were everything Uncle Henry had described and more.

All that travel is inevitably exhausting, but it never gets old. Arriving in the next city for the next opportunity is always a thrill. As busy as I am, wherever I am, I try to get out and walk the streets, to check out the sidewalks for cracks, to remember how far I've come and appreciate every baby step of the way, to stand in amazement and joy that the pursuit never ends.

我的想法不断在扩大，除了要做少数族裔的业务之外，我还想致力于劳动市场的资产管理，帮助那些像我舅舅那样辛苦工作的人群。我还想投资教育，支持公众教育。为了让自己的特长得到充分发挥，我还希望雇佣那些贫苦出身但不弃不馁的 PSD，他们不一定完全是我的翻版，但应该同样精明强干，敢于梦想。我还希望自己有同样的机会，让人才能得到添惠公司和贝尔斯登对我这样的培养。为了发展我的业务，我还希望能探索一些理念，其中包括我后来称之为的"意识资本主义"，这包括在个人方面，愿意拿出部分企业所得投入公共事业，在这其中我也会有所回报，同时作为一种投资形式，在全球范围内，鼓励各种人才捕捉机遇，发展自己。上述观点部分是受到塞西尔·威廉姆斯牧师和格莱德教堂的启发，还有一些是我在学习高级经济学时广泛涉猎的结果。每当路过公共图书馆，我都会尽可能多做停留，积极阅读。这都是为了告慰母亲，我从未忘记过她的教诲。

以芝加哥作为我开办的个人公司加德纳·里奇公司的选址，我又一次回到了起点，因为故乡威斯康星密尔沃基和母亲就离此不远，那里还有我很多的亲朋好友。这次搬家非常必要，因为儿子已经 6 岁，女儿也已两岁，他们都从洛杉矶移居这里，继续成长，他们需要一个可以称之为家的地方。

随着我的公司业务不断扩大，我的梦想也在逐一实现，我终于有机会接手机构退休资金，可以触及数亿美金的资产，使得我的大客户能从中受益并得以发展，这其中就包括美国国家教育协会及其数百万的成员机构。我终于有机会去各地旅游，看大千世界。亲眼看到亨利舅舅所描述的那些异国风情和各国女子，不一而足。

所有这些旅程确实很劳累，但它能让我永葆青春，每到一个城市，都让我感到生机勃勃，充满机遇。不管我有多么忙碌，我都会上街走走，在人行道上体验一下。回想这些年来，我到底走过了多远的旅程，感激着每一步的前行，满心欢喜和愉悦，并且永远不会停歇。

Epilogue
Blessea Beyona the Dreams of a Thousand Men

April 2004

Nothing can prepare you for the stark beauty that is Johannesburg, South Africa, as you descend through the clouds and behold the southern outline of Africa spreading out below you. It is indeed a living map.

No matter how many times I've visited South Africa, each time I return I experience an emotional intensity unlike anything else I've known. Those feelings are made even more intense as my plane touches down for this visit, in April 2004, after I received an invitation from the leadership of COSATU (Congress of South African Trade Unions) to be one of two hundred observers from around the world to observe the 2004 elections—a monumental event that will coincide with the celebration of the tenth year of democracy and freedom for the people of South Africa.

While I had accepted this invitation—this honor—with great pride, I threw in a caveat, saying, "I will not leave South Africa without having a one-on-one meeting with Nelson Mandela." Fine, I was told; if I could be patient, they would make it happen.

尾声
祝福永存

2004 年 4 月

南非约翰内斯堡的魅力无处能敌，乘机从云端降落，南部非洲的美景在脚下展开，就像一幅鲜活灵动的画卷。

无论我曾多少次来到南非，每次再回到这片土地，都会经历一种情感的震撼，这是我在其他地方所不曾有过的经历。2004 年 4 月，应南非总工会之邀，作为 200 多名世界观察员中的一名，见证 2004 年的南非大选，这是一次意义非凡的盛会，因为这年恰逢南非人民获得自由和解放的十周年。所以这次来的时候，当飞机逐渐下降，那种情感的震撼则显得愈发强烈。

能接受这个邀请，更多是一种殊荣，而且我还表示："如果不能和纳尔逊·曼德拉单独会面，我就不会离开南非。"结果，我被告知，只要我耐心等待，就一定能梦想成真。

Excited about the total experience, upon my arrival I do something that I've never done in my life—I go out and buy a camera, intent on capturing the reality of what I am about to witness, the culmination of ten years of democracy and freedom. I, like so many millions of South Africans and people all around the world, am in a state of awe. Who knew this would ever come to pass?

During my first visit to South Africa, I was accompanied by a man I've come to regard as a father, Bill Lucy of AFSCME (American Federation of State County and Municipal Employees) and CBTU (Coalition of Black Trade Unionists), and he introduced me to Mr. Mandela. Mr. Mandela shook my hand firmly and said words to me that I'd never heard from a man in my life. "Welcome home, son," Mr. Mandela said to me.

I broke down and cried like a baby. At that time, to be forty-six years old and have Nelson Mandela be the first man to ever say these words to me was worth every day of the no-daddy blues.

Now, four years later, I am back. On April 14, election day, all international observers have been placed in small groups after receiving credentials and instructions the previous day. I am placed with two black South African women, both of whom are experienced observers and veterans of the struggle against apartheid that has been going on their entire lives. My camera at the ready, we begin our rounds in East Rand, then journey on to Alexandra, Orlando, and finally Soweto. Seeing the unbelievably long queues— or lines, as we call them in the USA—of black South Africans, all standing with such grace, dignity, humility, and patience, I do not take the camera out of my pocket one time. To do so would have been as disrespectful as taking pictures in church.

The faces strike old and familiar chords in me, as if they might be folks I know from back in Chicago, New York, Oakland, Milwaukee, or down home in Louisiana. These folks, however, seem to know that I'm not from South Africa. I later mention this and ask Jan Mahlangu of COSATU how everyone knows that I'm not South African. With a smile, Jan says, "It's the way that you walk. You walk in like you own the space. Must be all the time on Wall Street."

I can't help but laugh.

Election night finds me in a polling place converted into a fortress. Our tent is in a parking lot in downtown Johannesburg, not far from the Nelson Mandela Bridge. Our instructions are simple: among others, "no one in and no one out" until we've all agreed on a final count. My first thought is, *No more coffee or fluids.* There is no restroom in our tent. Finally, after some very long, tense, and sometimes anxious hours, we are done. As expected, the ANC has captured 86 percent of the vote in our count alone.

此行使我兴奋异常，我到了目的地后，做了件有生以来从未有过的事情，我去买了架相机，准备把见到的一切都拍摄下来，以见证这十年所取得的民主和自由。数百万南非人民和世界各地的民众都和我一样，为此时此刻，肃然起敬。谁会料到这一切有朝一日会发生改变呢？

在我首次来南非的时候，美国联邦工会和黑人工会联盟的比尔·鲁西和我在一起，是他把我引见给曼德拉。曼德拉紧紧地握着我的手，说了一句使我今生今世都难以忘怀的话，"欢迎回家来，孩子。"

我当下就撑不住了，泣不成声。我当时已经46岁，有生以来，是纳尔逊·曼德拉第一个对我说了这么一番话，让我这么多年来没有父亲的忧郁瞬间得以化解和补偿。

4年后，我再次回来。2004年4月14日是大选之日，所有国际观察员头一天都收到委任状和具体指示，按照要求分成小组。我坐在两名南非黑人女子中间，两人都是经验丰富的观察员，而且一生都致力于对种族隔离的坚决斗争。我的相机已然就绪，依次经过东兰德、亚历山德拉、奥兰多，最后是索维托的队伍。大家都排着长长的队伍，这些在美国会被称之为"黑鬼"的人们，各个神采飞扬，神情坚毅，不乏尊严和庄重。我没有拿出相机，因为感觉会亵渎他们，就像在教堂里拿相机拍照别无两样。

这一副副面孔陌生而熟悉，仿佛他们就是我在芝加哥、纽约、奥克兰、密尔沃基或路易斯安那老家所见到的父老乡亲，但他们却似乎可以看出我并非来自南非。后来我和南非总工会的简·马兰问起这一点，他们怎么会知道我不是南非的呢？她笑了笑答道："是你走路的模样，你走路的速度和别人不一样，可能你在华尔街都是这么走的吧。"

我忍不住哈哈大笑。

竞选当夜，投票站严阵以待。我们的帐篷就在约翰内斯堡的城中，离纳尔逊曼德拉大桥不远。对我们的要求很简单，最后准确票数出来之前，"谁都不可进出这里"。我首先想到的是不可以再喝咖啡和饮料了，因为帐篷里没有洗手间。经过几小时漫长紧张焦急的等待，我们终于大功告成。不出所料，非洲国民议会在我们这片就拿下86%的选票。

尾声

For me it is very interesting to observe not just the count but also the interaction between the blacks, coloreds, and Indians. The chains of apartheid, while physically broken, are evidently still psychically functional.

Continuing to digest much of what has transpired during my visit so far, on April 15, 2004, my wait for my appointment with Mr. Mandela officially begins. As I was made aware, the anniversary of South Africa's democracy and freedom is being celebrated around the world with seemingly every country on the planet sending representatives, ambassadors, and heads of state. My place in line, while secure, seems to be very fluid. No problem, I'll wait.

During my waiting period, the inauguration of Thabo Mbeki to his second five-year term is another unprecedented experience in my life. Black folks have never looked so good, so beautiful, so royal. It is almost life imitating art—in a scene right out of Eddie Murphy's film *Coming to America,* a procession and ceremony take place at the Union Building, the South African White House, and on its enclosed lawn, equivalent to our Rose Garden. Cheers erupt while leader after leader makes an entrance. The Jumbotron monitors show the crowd across from us, numbering over 100,000 folks awaiting the inauguration and subsequent party. Finally, there is a roar like nothing I've ever heard. It can only mean one thing: Mandela has arrived!

At this stage in my life, I have had the pleasure of sitting courtside at NBA playoff games, ringside at boxing matches, and in front-row seats at concerts, but I have never in my life experienced a sound like 100,000 souls crying out, "Mandela!" Again I cry, and others around me ask why. They can't understand, but as I approach nearly fifty years of life, this is the first time that I've ever seen a black president!

My sobs are drowned out only by the sounds of three 747s from South African Airlines that fly over our heads in a salute to the president.

In the days that follow I use my time awaiting my meeting with Mr. Mandela to prepare. Nelson Mandela was trained as the first black attorney in South Africa and went on to found the firm of Tambo and Mandela with ANC leader Oliver Tambo, his dear friend. I keep this in mind in preparing to make a case—a clear, concise, compelling case.

I also find the company that manufactures the beautiful silk shirts that Nelson Mandela always wears. "I have a meeting with Mr. Mandela," I announce as I enter their main offices. "You must make me a shirt. I want to be appropriately attired."

对我而言，能亲临现场，看到大家唱票，并能看到所有黑人、有色人种、印第安人在此时此刻的表现都是非常有趣的事情。种族隔离虽然形式上已经废除，但是对人们心理的影响还依然存在。

我还在为自己此行百感交集，2004年4月15日，我一直期盼的和曼德拉的正式会面终于到来了。我获悉，为庆祝南非获得自由民主十周年，几乎各国都纷纷派来代表、使节乃至国家元首以示祝贺。所以我的会面安排肯定能够实现，只是时间比较机动。没关系，我有足够的耐心。

在我等待的时候，塔博·姆贝基蝉联总统宣誓就职，更让我深受触动。我从未见过黑人可以如此英俊潇洒、气派尊贵。仿佛是生命铸就的精彩，那种场面可以与艾迪·墨菲主演的电影《美国之旅》相提并论，仪式是在联合大楼门前的草坪上举行的，联合大楼就相当于南非的白宫，而那草坪就相当于白宫的玫瑰园。当各个政要依次进入时，人们掌声欢呼声雷动。超大的电子屏幕显示着面前经过的人群，共有近10万人在等待着就职宣誓仪式以及后面的欢庆活动。最后，人群仿佛沸腾一般，我从未经历过这般场面，这只能说明一件事，曼德拉亲临现场！

此时此刻，我兴奋异常，我曾经现场观看NBA的总决赛，也曾在现场欣赏拳击比赛，甚至是在最前排倾听音乐会，但我从未经历过十几万人高呼曼德拉的激动场面。我又一次热泪盈眶，周围的人不解，问我何故。他们不会理解，我活了半辈子，这是我有生以来第一次见到黑人总统。

突然我的抽泣声被三架波音747的声音所淹没，这是南非航空派出的飞机向总统表示致敬。

在随后的几天内，我一直在等着曼德拉的接见。曼德拉是南非第一个黑人律师，并与非洲国民议会的领袖也是他的好友奥利佛·坦博建立了坦博律师行。我记下了这一点，决定要以此做些文章。

我还找到一家衬衫厂，曼德拉经常穿着的衬衫就是出自这里，我一进他们的大楼就讲，"我将和曼德拉见面，你们得给我也做一件衬衫，我的衣着必须得体。"

尾声

While continuing to wait, I explore Johannesburg, Soweto, and Cape Town, and my eyes are opened in ways they have not been before. I used to think that I knew something about poverty. You have not seen poverty until you've seen it in Africa. My heart aches as I see and learn more about the conditions that human beings are forced to live in. Yet in spite of this abject poverty, there is a sense of hope everywhere I go. The sense among South Africans is that, yes, things are difficult, yes, we need jobs, yes, we need housing, yes, we must address HIV/AIDS, but yes, also for the first time in all of our lives we can dream. The impossible is now simply possible.

The waiting is not stressful at all. The sense of what is possible eases the passing days. I also find the exact place where I will one day live. The property is not for sale, but, yes, it is possible.

Again preparation consumes me. I have two pages of notes to discuss, which I condense to two envelopes front and back, then to one envelope front and back, and finally the phone rings. "Mr. Mandela will see you tomorrow at 11:00 a.m.," I am told.

I'm ready. I've waited twenty-seven days, but I figure Mr. Mandela waited twenty-seven years in prison, and I stayed in a much nicer place than he was in. When the morning arrives, the only decision that remains is which of the fabulous silk shirts I will wear to the meeting. Hazel, my favorite employee at the Park Hyatt, looks at them all and selects the most regal shirt of all, explaining, "That's the one—you look like Madiba!" She is using Mandela's clan name to describe the shirt and why I must wear it.

I'm accompanied to the meeting by one of the leading businessmen in South Africa, Eric Molobi, who at one point was also imprisoned on Robben Island with Mr. Mandela.

I have never been so positively tense in my life. I've been in a few big meetings with what I'm sure are very important people, but this is mythical, beyond the realm of anything that has happened to me before or since. Only a few true heroes have mattered to me—my mother, Miles Davis, Muhammad Ali. The fact that I'm about to meet Nelson Mandela, a hero personified, makes me realize what it is to have an out-of-body experience.

Finally, Mr. Mandela's personal assistant, Zelda, comes to escort me in, informing me that I've been scheduled for fifteen minutes with Madiba.

I walk through the door, and there he stands, ramrod straight, looking nothing less than royal wearing a fabulous "Madiba" shirt. Sensing the tension in me, he proclaims in a most majestic voice, "Chris, why are you wearing my shirt?"

在我接下来等待的时间里，我参观了约翰内斯堡、索维托、好望角，这番经历让我眼界大开。我本以为自己对贫穷并不陌生，但是只有到了非洲，才会知道什么是真正的贫穷。当我看到他们窘迫的生存状态，我的心如刀绞。尽管生计艰难如是，但我每到一处，都会感到那里的希望犹存。在南非，生活条件的确艰苦，的确需要更多工作机会，的确需要住房，的确需要和艾滋病作斗争，但是生命的第一要义是要心存梦想。一切的不可能因为梦想而变得可能。

所以等待并非十分难熬，那种一切都有可能的心态伴我度过每一天。我还发现一处住所，我希望有朝一日能住在这里。那里并不出售，但我并非没有希望。

我继续为这次会见做着准备，整整写了两页纸，但我又继续精简，把文字缩成信封的前后两面，这时，电话铃响了，我被告知："曼德拉先生明天上午 11 点想见您。"

一切就绪，我等了整整 27 天，而我相信曼德拉为今天等了 27 年，而且我所在的地方要比他当初待的地方条件好上一万倍。当清晨到来，我需要做的最后一个决定是到底该穿哪件衬衫去见他合适呢？我在柏悦酒店最喜欢的员工海瑟仔仔细细地帮我看了所有的衬衫，挑了一件最气派的，说道："就这件吧，你穿上这件最像马迪巴！"她用曼德拉的族名来形容这件衬衫，以说明为什么选这件的原因。

陪我一同前往的是南非的一位顶级商界人物埃里克·莫罗比，他也曾同曼德拉一起被关押在罗本岛。

我以前从未如此紧张过，我也曾出席过一些重要会议，也曾和一些重量级人物打过交道，但这次完全不同，完全超乎了我以往的经历，而且可能以后也不会再有。我生命中，真正在乎的无外乎就是母亲、迈尔·戴维斯、拳王阿里。这次可是要见纳尔逊·曼德拉，一个神一样的人物，这种感受让我无法用语言形容。

最后，曼德拉的私人助理萨尔达出来迎我进去，告诉我可以和曼德拉谈 15 分钟。

我推门进去，曼德拉站起身来，身材笔挺，穿着非常得体的马迪巴衬衫，尊贵威严。看出我的紧张，他大声说道："克里斯，你怎么穿着我的衬衫啊？"

尾声

The PURSUIT of HAPPYNESS

I totally relax and sit across from him as directed. Eighty-six years old, he moves purposefully but gingerly. The eyes, however, are scanning me. These are the eyes of an eighty-six-year-old freedom fighter who for most of those years had to look at someone and make an instant decision: *Can I trust this person? Is this information correct? Is this worth my time?*

I begin to make my case. U.S. public funds have increased their allocations to emerging markets around the world but have not returned to South Africa. A very significant number of the "young Turks" in the U.S. labor movement who led the movement to divest American companies of South African investments are now presidents, secretary-treasurers, and trustees of their pension funds. As such, they are in a position to influence, control, or direct billions of dollars of capital. On a comparative basis, South Africa has outperformed all other emerging markets. South Africa has recently celebrated ten years of democracy and freedom. Just as capital was once used as a tool to help create change in South Africa, capital can again be used as a tool to help sustain the growth and development of South Africa.

Zelda comes in and gives the international hand signal for "time's up" and says, "Mr. Mandela, the ambassador is here for his appointment."

Mr. Mandela speaks again in his rich, majestic voice. "Tell the ambassador he can wait."

Now I'm really pumped. I conclude my pitch with a comment that I clearly see touches a nerve. "Sometimes the stars just line up," I remark. "This is our time. This is my time. This is my opportunity to use everything that I've learned in twenty-five years of working Wall Street and capital markets to help make a difference in the world for people that look like me." It's an opportunity, I tell him, to make economic freedom as available as political freedom. Mr. Mandela asks a few questions after I'm done and finally says, "How can I help you?" I mention specifics, and we agree to see where my idea takes us.

At long last I am able to use the camera I purchased for the election, asking Zelda to take a shot of Madiba and me, sitting side by side. It remains my most valued possession to this day.

We shake hands, and I lean down to kiss his forehead. He smiles. He knows what our time has meant to me. I am prepared to go forward, prepared to pursue.

Ironically, as I leave the meeting and pass by the ambassador who has been kept waiting for forty-five minutes, he and his entourage look at me, all appearing to wonder, *Who the hell is this guy?*

我一下子就放松下来，按着他的指引，在他对面坐了下来。他已经86岁高龄，但是头脑敏捷，行事谨慎。他用眼睛上下打量着我，这是一双86岁的为自由而战的斗士的眼睛，他只用片刻就可以判断出此人是否值得信任、我所获信息是否准确、他值不值得我为他花费时间？

我开始说明来意，美国公共基金在向世界新兴市场增加拨款，但尚未开拓南非市场。美国工运中的一些利己分子，他们曾倡导美国公司在南非撤资，现在这些人已经成为政界要人、财长、退休基金的保管人。因此他们可以对数十亿的美元资本的支配产生影响和控制。而相对于其他新兴市场，南非的表现可圈可点，加之，南非正逢获得民主自由的十年庆典，以往资本就曾作为产生变革的工具，如今南非仍旧需要这样的资本工具来帮助南非实现持续发展和繁荣。

这时私人助理萨尔达进来了，做了个国际惯用的手势，表示时间到了，并说："曼德拉先生，大使在外面等您。"

曼德拉又一次用他浑厚的声音说道："告诉大使，让他再等等。"

现在的我已经彻底进入了状态。我可以看出我的话对他产生了触动，"有些时候，我们需要通力合作，现在就是我们的机会，也是我的机会，我希望能用我25年以来在华尔街和资本市场所积累的全部经验，来帮助这个世界上和我一样的人们，让他们的生活能有所改观。"我对他讲这是一次机遇，实现经济的自由，同时也是政治的自由。我说完之后，曼德拉又问了几个问题，最后他说道："我能帮上什么忙呢？"我提了具体的几点要求，我们同意观察事态会有怎样的进展。

最后，为大选专门购置的相机终于可以派上用场了，我请萨尔达帮我和曼德拉拍了合影，照片中我和他肩并肩坐在一起。这张照片时至今日都是我最珍贵的礼物。

我们握了握手，我还亲吻了他的前额。他笑了。他知道这次会见对我而言意味着什么。我已经整装待发，准备扬帆启航了。

可笑的是，当我经过大使身旁，他和随从望着我，似乎都在奇怪，这家伙是谁啊，因为他们在外面已经等了整整45分钟。

尾声

The PURSUIT of HAPPYNESS

In this same time frame, continuing with the pursuit of my concept of conscious capitalism, I flew from South Africa to San Francisco where I met with Rev. Cecil Williams in order to discuss his vision for the economic development of the Tenderloin (my old 'hood). Cecil's basic idea was to purchase an entire square block in the 'Loin to be developed into a complex large enough to include a small convention center, retail stores, and restaurants, even parking, but most importantly affordable housing for working people in downtown San Francisco. The meeting concluded with the decision that our original plan be scaled down from purchasing the entire square block for approximately $250 million to select sites and properties at a cost of close to $50 million. It was never the size of this undertaking that motivated me. It was truly about coming full circle. It's not business, it's personal.

What is the American dream if it isn't about the possibility that someone, anyone, can go from walking the streets of the Tenderloin and wondering how to take the next step to being able to help provide safe affordable housing in that same neighborhood for working folks? After all, studies have shown that approximately 12 percent of all the homeless people in America have jobs and go to work everyday. More and more Americans are seeing the dream slip away from them and that's wrong. And, by the way, the attainment of wealth that we all want to strive for shouldn't be about the attainment of money. In fact, I've often been asked how much money equates to real wealth. My answer is always the same. By my definition, money is the least significant part of wealth. My net worth is not among the Forbes 400, nor is it my ambition to be so listed, but I am healthy, have raised two children as a single parent (blessed with a village of support) that have become outstanding young people, and I'm in a position to do work that reflects my values. That's my definition of wealth.

Wealth can also be that attitude of gratitude with which we remind ourselves everyday to count our blessings. It has been a blessing for me to have been able to break the cycle that prevented me from having a relationship with my father—one of the reasons I was so intent to be there for my kids. And they have been there for me. My son, Christopher, and my daughter, Jacintha, are two remarkable young adults, and really some of my favorite people in the world—so much so that I hired them to work for my company, not just because I love them but also because they're hard working and capable. They have always made me proud to be their father and have always given me true happiness.

在这次会见后不久，我继续实践着我那意识资本主义的理念。从南非飞回旧金山，见到塞西尔·威廉姆斯神父，以求探讨田德隆区（我曾住在这里）的经济发展问题。神父的基本想法是购买这里的整个街区，修建一座大型建筑群，以容纳小型会议中心、零售店、餐厅，甚至停车场，更重要的是为旧金山市中心的工作族提供住房。会后，我们决定把当初的宏伟目标进行精简，原计划购买价值 2.5 亿美元的整个街区，现在改为购置 5000 万美金的地产。这件事并非是因其规模让我备感兴趣，我更在乎的是这其中所代表的价值回归。

所谓美国梦不就是在田德隆的街头来往的行人，有朝一日也可以帮助邻里购置经济、安全、舒适的住房？毕竟有研究资料显示，在美国 12% 的无家可归的人其实是有工作的，而且每天还要上下班。越来越多的美国人在眼睁睁地看着梦想一天天从身边溜走，而这是非常令人痛心的。此外，所谓我们为之奋斗的财富并不等于单纯金钱的积累。实际上，我被问及拥有多少金钱才算是拥有财富。我的答案总是一成不变。在我看来，金钱是财富的重要组成部分。我的净资产在福布斯 400 富豪榜还榜上无名，但我也并不希望自己能荣登富豪榜。但我很健康，作为一个单亲父亲，还抚养了两个孩子长大成人（这要感谢周围这么多人的热心帮助），我还可以做些真正体现个人价值的工作，这便是我所理解的财富。

财富还可以是自己每天要心存感激，感激人们对我们的帮助和祝福。对我而言，我要庆幸自己重复父亲的老路，我也刻意用他为人父的方式来对待我的孩子，从孩子的身上，我已经看到了回报。儿子克里斯多夫和女儿杰西塔是我在世上最亲爱的人，而且让他们到我的公司工作，这并非仅仅是出于我对他们的欣赏和喜爱，而是因为他们确实出色且勤奋。作为他们的父亲，我感到由衷的自豪，而且总是让我心怀喜悦。

The PURSUIT of HAPP*y*NESS

Being happy, for a workaholic like me, can also mean taking some time off from the pursuit of this, that, and the other to have some fun. June 26, 2005, presented me with such an opportunity. Our firm hosted a party for the National Education Association in Los Angeles. My partner, Ndaba Nstele, flew in all the way from South Africa. Sydney Kai Inis, our special-events coordinator, once again outdid herself by producing Grammy-award-winning artists such as Dave Koz, Jonathan Butler, and Waymon Tisdale for the event. To raise funds for the NEA Black Caucus, we arranged a raffle. First prize was two round-trip business-class tickets to South Africa, including a ground tour package. The total value of the trip was over $30,000 while the price of a raffle ticket was only $10 and we sold a lot of them.

The celebratory atmosphere and coming together of wonderful friends and clients was unforgettable while the true highlight of the evening for me personally was an opportunity to pay thanks to so many who have been part of my journey—all of our NEA family, and a special acknowledgment of my old boss, Marshall Geller.

It was Marshall Gellar who gave the final nod to my being hired at Bear Stearns and who taught me the value of the sphere of influence. To this day, Marshall never knew how I used his office as a prop when J.R., my racist joke-telling client, decided to visit me in person that first time. But Marshall did know my heart. He saw me, day in and day out, attempt to make a quota of two hundred phone calls a day, often while he stood over my desk, and ultimately commented, "That's not how big guys do it, big guys do it through a sphere of influence." It took me the next twenty years to develop that sphere. Recently, I think that I've gotten the hang of it. I've got to tell you that it is amazing who you can get on the phone when you can honestly say that Mr. Mandela suggested I call.

In addition to fund-raising for the NEA's Black Caucus, our party in Los Angeles was to honor dear friends and educational powerhouses, Anne Davis of the Illinois Education Association and Linda Poindexter-Chesterfield of the Arkansas Education Association—both of whom were retiring after decades of representing public school teachers and school support personnel. The event, which attracted close to eight hundred representatives of the NEA, was a perfect venue to publicly say thank you to Marshall. My mom always taught me that the most important words in the English language are *please* and *thank you*.

For many kids growing up, I reminded the crowd, sometimes there is only one person in their life, often a teacher or employer, who is willing to give them that chance, that vote of confidence, that needed break. Marshall Geller, I explained, was someone who'd given a break to a young stockbroker named Chris Gardner.

作为我这样的工作狂，我也喜欢拿出些时间来，找寻各种各样的快乐。2005年6月26日，我就有了这样一次机会。公司为美国国家教育协会在洛杉矶举办了一次晚会，我的合伙人纳达巴·斯泰勒特意从南非赶来，我们的特别活动协调人西尼·凯·英尼斯又做了精彩的安排，把格莱美奖的得主都请到现场来助兴，比如著名音乐人戴夫·考兹、乔纳森·巴特勒、威曼·迪斯戴尔都到了现场。为资助美国教育协会的黑人联盟，我们特意准备了一次抽奖，头奖是去南非的往返机票，其中还包括当地游玩的费用。整个旅程的费用价值3万美金，可是抽奖的奖券却只卖10块钱，而且我们还卖出去不少。

整个晚会高潮迭起，众多嘉宾和客户都印象深刻，而对我个人而言，这是我对大家表示感谢的绝好机会，他们都是我人生道路上的财富，这其中包括所有美国国家教育协会的成员，还有我的老上级马歇尔·盖勒。

是马歇尔最后拍板让我能真正就职贝尔斯登，是他教会我圈子的作用。直至今日，马歇尔都不知道我曾用过他的办公室作为道具，应付那个爱讲种族段子的客户J.R，在他办公室安排了我们头一次见面。但马歇尔真正了解我的所思所想。看到我每天都要打上200个电话，最后他来到我的办公桌前，告诉我："高手不是这么干的，高手是通过圈子做事的。"我花了20年的时间才建起了自己的圈子。时至今日，我才真正领悟到这句话的真谛，而且，当我拿起电话，和对方真诚地讲，是曼德拉先生建议我和您打这个电话，这种感觉实在是太美妙了。

除了为美国国家教育协会的黑人联盟筹款，我们在洛杉矶的聚会还为两位教育界的泰斗颁奖，他们分别是伊利诺伊教育协会的安妮·戴维斯和阿肯色切斯特菲尔德教育协会的灵科·波因德克斯特，两人都已退休多年，是代表公立学校的教师和学校工作人员领这个奖项的。这次晚会吸引了美国国家教育协会近800名代表参加，是我向马歇尔公开致谢的理想所在。妈妈常常教导我，英语中最重要的两个词，一个是"请"，一个就是"谢谢"。

我对大家讲到，在很多孩子成长的过程中，有时其实就是一个人对他们起到了决定性的作用，通常这个人是师长或者老板，是他愿意给孩子这样的机会，让他们树立自信，实现自我。而马歇尔·盖勒就是这样一个人，是他成就了一个年轻的证券经纪人克里斯·加纳。

Marshall followed up my comments by telling the crowd he was in the business of making lots of decisions, some good ones and some bad. "Chris Gardner turned out to be a good decision we made," he said with feigned modesty, even though he couldn't hide his almost paternal pride.

The one person who was missing from this unforgettable night was Moms. Had I never been able to share my success with my mother, it would have broken my heart. Thankfully, before she passed away ten years ago, she had a chance not only to see me prosper but also to share in it. For some time, Moms didn't under stand what the hell it was that I did for a living. After numerous explanations and attempted analogies, I finally put it this way: "Let's say all these companies that I represent are at the casino and I'm the house." That clicked for her.

Toward the end of her days Bettye Jean wasn't at all well. What her body and her psyche had been put through over the years had taken their toll. If money could have given her back her health, I would have spent every dime I had to give that to her. But that wasn't possible, and when I got the news that we had lost her, I and my sisters were fairly certain that Moms, that pretty lady who first came to make candy for me so very long ago, had hastened her own death by drinking when her doctors had forbidden it.

Losing Moms did break my heart, creating a void in the world where once her smile had been—the sight of which I will miss until the day I die. There was so much more to come that I still wanted to share with her, to make her happy.

That was what I told my Aunt Dicey Bell when I got caught up with her back in Chicago to let her know about all of the exciting happenings, not only the NEA party but the unfolding projects with Glide and my partnership with Pamodzi Investment Holdings in South Africa. I had grown up right and had graduated to become a citizen of the world, credit due to many who took those chances on me, but no one more so than Moms. It was so important to me that she know how far I had been able to come, thanks to her.

Aunt Dicey Bell assured me that my mother was exulting in every single glorious second of all my adventures. "Chris," she said to me, and it was all I needed to know, "right now your momma is in heaven dancing with her wings on."

That was so perfect; just the way she said it, I had to believe that it was true. She was dancing with her wings on and making sure that I continued to be blessed beyond the dreams of a thousand men. Absolutely.

马歇尔接着我的话讲，在这么多年从业生涯中，他做过很多决定，其中有正确的也有错误的。"但是选择克里斯·加纳是我们的明智之举，"他说话时非常谦虚，但是谁都可以看出他脸上那种子贵父荣的骄傲神情。

这次难忘晚会上却没能看到一个人的身影。那就是妈妈，我终究没能让她分享到我成功的喜悦，这让我心痛欲裂。妈妈十年前就过世了，所幸她生前看到我事业有成。只是，有时妈妈搞不懂我到底是靠什么挣钱的。我做了无数的解释之后，还是没说清楚，最后只好说："就当这些公司都是赌徒，我就是那个赌场。"妈妈终于明白了。

在她临终之前，妈妈的状况非常差。她的身心备受摧残，多年前噩梦般的回忆让她痛苦万分，如果金钱能够买回她的健康，我愿意倾囊相救，但我们还是没能留住她，我和姐妹们都十分确信，那个很久以前拿着糖果来看我们的漂亮女子，我们的母亲是故意违背了医生的禁酒指令，让自己尽早结束了生命。

丧母之痛让我悲痛欲绝，我再也无法见到她的笑脸，我这一生都会永远怀念她那迷人的微笑。我还有那么多的话想对他讲，希望她能快乐幸福。

这就是我在芝加哥见到姨妈戴希·贝尔之后，和她所说的一切，告诉了她所有的一切，不仅包括美国国家教育协会的晚会，还有和格莱德教堂以及南非所做的项目正在积极筹备。我已经真正的长大成人，成为世界的公民，这要感激所有给我机会的人，但所有这些都不及妈妈对我的付出。她知道自己的儿子可以成就些什么，这一点非常重要，我必须感谢她。

戴希姨妈安慰我，妈妈在为我取得的每个辉煌而欢欣雀跃，她说，我只需要知道一点就足够了，那就是："此时此刻，妈妈正舞动着翅膀在天堂跳舞。"

这就太完美了，正如她所说的那样，我必须相信这一点。她正舞动着翅膀在天堂跳舞，而且深信还有无数人在继续为我祝福，这一点我深信不疑。

尾声